Adobe Premiere

2026 Release

Classroom in a Book®

The official training workbook from Adobe

Maxim Jago

Adobe Premiere Classroom in a Book® 2026 Release

Adobe Press is an imprint of Pearson Education, Inc. For the latest on Adobe Press books, go to *peachpit.com/adobepress*. To report errors, please send a note to errata@peachpit.com. For information regarding permissions, request forms, and the appropriate contacts within the Pearson Education Global Rights & Permissions department, please visit *pearson.com/global-permission-granting.html*.

Writer: Maxim Jago
Adobe Press Executive Editor: Laura Norman
Sponsoring Editor: Anshul Sharma
Development Editor: Victor Gavenda
Adobe Press Production Editor: Tracey Croom
Technical Reviewer: Jarle Leirpoll
Keystroke Reviewer: Megan Ahearn
Copyeditor: Linda Laflamme
Proofreader: Kim Wimpsett
Compositor: Kim Scott, Bumpy Design
Indexer: James Minkin
Cover Illustration: May Xiong
Interior Designer: Mimi Heft

ISBN-13: 978-0-13-556127-0
ISBN-10: 0-13-556127-2

1 2026

WHERE ARE THE LESSON FILES?

Purchase of this Classroom in a Book in any format gives you access to the lesson files you'll need to complete the exercises in the book.

1. Go to *peachpit.com/register* and sign in or create a new account.
2. On the Register a Product page, enter ISBN **9780135561270** and click Submit.
3. Answer the proof-of-purchase challenge question by looking in your book for the answer.
4. Navigate to the Registered Products tab on your Account page to access the lesson files.
5. Click the Access Bonus Content link below the title of your product to proceed to the download page. Click the lesson file links to download them to your computer.
6. The Web Edition can be accessed from the Digital Purchases tab on your Account page. Click the Launch link to access the product.

Note: If you encounter problems registering your product or accessing the lesson files or web edition, go to *peachpit.com/support* for assistance.

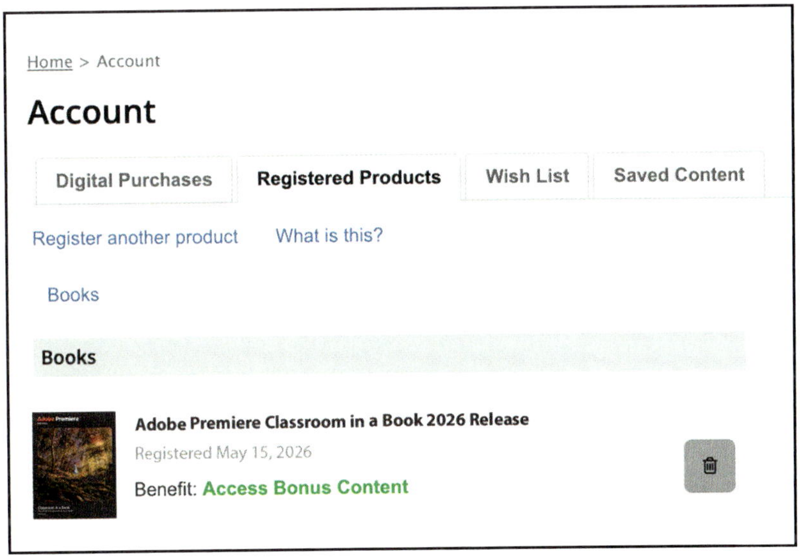

Note: If you purchased a digital product directly from *peachpit.com*, your product will already be registered. Look for the Access Bonus Content link on the Registered Products tab in your account.

Important!

The video clips and other media files provided with this book are practice files, provided for your personal, educational use in these lessons only. You are not authorized to use these files commercially or to publish, share, or distribute them in any form without written permission from Adobe Inc., and the individual copyright holders of the various items. Do not share videos created with these lesson files publicly. This includes, but is not limited to, distribution via social media or online video services including YouTube and Vimeo. You will find a complete copyright statement on the copyright page at the beginning of this book.

ACKNOWLEDGMENTS

Producing effective learning materials for such an advanced technology is a team effort. Friends, colleagues, fellow filmmakers, and technology experts have all contributed to this book. There are too many names to mention, but let's say this: I have often joked that in Britain we don't say "awesome." Instead, we say "perfectly acceptable." On this occasion, "perfectly acceptable" simply isn't enough. Rather, I will have to say our British equivalent of "super awesome." Those people who make this world better by sharing, nurturing, caring, showing, telling, demonstrating, making, and helping are all definitely "much more than acceptable."

Everything on these pages was inspected by a team of experienced editors who checked and corrected typos, spelling errors, naming errors, false attributions, suspect grammar, unhelpful phrasing, and inconsistent descriptions. This wonderful team didn't just highlight text that needed correcting. They offered positive alternatives that I could simply agree to, and so, in a literal sense, this book is the product of many people's contributions. I'd like to thank the teams at Peachpit and Adobe Press, who made it possible to produce such a beautifully finessed work.

As each draft lesson was completed, the most amazing and highly experienced Victor Gavenda checked over the text to make sure it was ideally accessible for learners, and all references to the technology were reviewed by the remarkable media technology expert Jarle Leirpoll, who has an incredible depth of knowledge of Premiere. I tip my hat to Linda Laflamme for reviewing the copy and spotting things we would otherwise have completely missed. Laura Norman, Tracey Croom, and Anshul Sharma kept us all on track, Kim Scott takes the credit for the beautiful layout you see before you, Kim Wimpsett brought exceptional proofreading skills, and Megan Ahearn has the enviable title of Keystroker—checking each and every step in the exercises presented here to make sure everything happens just as expected.

Some of the content of this book is derived from material originally written by the world-renowned media trainer Richard Harrington. The original table of contents was worked out by the two of us, and a substantial amount of the content remains unchanged or is informed by his original work.

Finally, let's not forget Adobe. The passion and enthusiasm demonstrated by those wonderful individuals, who are so committed to creatives like you and me, qualifies as "the most acceptable of all." They are, indeed, extraordinarily awesome!

—Maxim Jago

CONTENTS

16 EXPORTING FRAMES, CLIPS, AND SEQUENCES 478

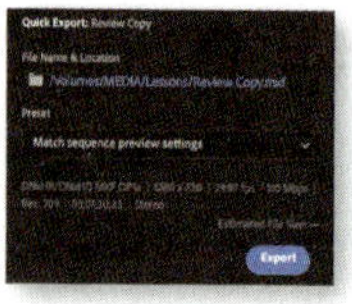

GETTING STARTED

Adobe Premiere, the essential video-editing application for professionals and video enthusiasts, is an incredibly scalable, efficient, and flexible video-editing system. It supports a broad range of video, audio, and image formats. Premiere lets you work faster and more creatively without converting your media. The complete set of powerful and exclusive tools lets you overcome any editorial, production, and workflow challenges to deliver the high-quality work you demand.

Adobe has developed a user experience that is intuitive, flexible, and efficient, with unified design elements that match across multiple applications, making it easier to explore and discover new workflows.

About Classroom in a Book

Adobe Premiere Classroom in a Book 2026 Release is part of the official training series for Adobe. The lessons are designed so that you can learn at your own pace. If you're new to Premiere, you'll learn the fundamental concepts and features you'll use to create projects. This book also teaches many advanced features, including tips and techniques for using the latest version of this software.

The lessons in this edition include opportunities for hands-on practice using features such as chroma keying, dynamic trimming, color correction, media management, audio and video effects, audio mixing, and captioning. You'll also learn how to create files for the web and social media with Adobe Media Encoder. Premiere is available for both macOS and Windows and uses the same project files on both platforms.

Note: Adobe Premiere on mobile includes comprehensive editing tools on mobile devices, including multi-track editing for video and audio, generative AI, effects and a media asset library. Projects created using Premiere on mobile can be transferred to Premiere on your desktop for advanced finishing.

Prerequisites

Before following the exercises in the *Adobe Premiere Classroom in a Book 2026 Release,* make sure your system is set up correctly and that you've installed the required software and hardware. You can view updated system requirements here:

helpx.adobe.com/premiere-pro/system-requirements.html

You should have a working knowledge of your computer and operating system. For example, you should know how to use the mouse or trackpad and standard menus and commands and also how to open, save, and close files. You should also feel comfortable navigating folders and copying files between folders. If you need to review these techniques, see the support pages for your macOS or Windows system.

It's not necessary to have a working knowledge of video concepts and terminology. If you come across a term you're not familiar with, consult the glossary at the end of the book.

Installing Premiere

You must purchase an Adobe Creative Cloud subscription, or obtain a trial version, separately from this book. For system requirements and complete instructions on installing the software, visit the Adobe Help Center at *helpx.adobe.com/support*. You can purchase Adobe Creative Cloud by visiting *adobe.com/creativecloud*. Follow the on-screen instructions. In addition to Premiere, you may want to install Photoshop, After Effects, and Audition. Adobe Media Encoder is installed automatically when you install Premiere. These are all included with the full Adobe Creative Cloud license.

Selecting audio hardware

Premiere has preferences to choose the audio hardware to use for playback and recording. This is useful because you may want the audio for your editing projects to come through professional studio monitors while other system sounds come through smaller or built-in computer monitors.

When you open Premiere for the first time, you may need to select the audio hardware to use before playback will work. Access the Audio Hardware preferences in Premiere > Settings > Audio Hardware (macOS) or Edit > Preferences > Audio Hardware (Windows).

There are advanced options for configuring audio hardware, but you'll generally just need to choose the System Default Input and System Default Output. With the System Default options selected, Premiere can automatically switch to your system audio selection if you change it—for example, if you plug headphones in.

Optimizing performance

Editing video places high demands on your computer processor and memory. A more powerful computer will make your editing experience faster and more efficient, which translates to a more fluid and enjoyable creative experience—that is, more creative flow.

Premiere takes advantage of multicore processors (CPUs) and multiprocessor systems. Modern processors handle video decoding and AI calculations much better than ones only a few years old, so the more recent your computer, the better the performance you'll experience.

The minimum system memory is 8 GB, and 16 GB or more is recommended for High-Definition (HD) media; 32 GB or higher is recommended for Ultra-High-Definition (UHD, or 4K) media.

The speed of the storage drives you use for video playback is also a factor. A dedicated fast storage drive is recommended for your media. A RAID disk array or fast solid-state drive for your media files is strongly recommended, particularly if you're working with high-resolution or high data-rate RAW media. Storing your media files and program files on the same hard drive can affect performance. Keep your media files on a separate disk, if possible, for speed and easier media file management.

Premiere can use the power of your computer's graphics hardware, or *graphics processing unit* (GPU), to improve playback performance. GPU acceleration provides a significant performance improvement, and most video cards with at least 2 GB of dedicated video memory (VRAM) will work—4 GB VRAM or more is recommended. You will find information about hardware and software requirements on the Adobe website at *helpx.adobe.com/premiere-pro/system-requirements.html*.

Online content

Your purchase of this Classroom in a Book includes online materials provided by way of your Account page on *peachpit.com*.

Lesson files

To work through the projects in this book, you will need to download the lesson files by following the instructions.

◆ **Warning:** For access to the lesson files, please register and download your files by December 31, 2030.

Web Edition

The Web Edition is an online interactive version of the book providing an enhanced learning experience. Your Web Edition can be accessed from any device with a connection to the internet, and it contains the following:

- The complete text of the book
- Hours of instructional video keyed to the text
- Interactive quizzes

Accessing the lesson files and Web Edition

You must register your purchase on *peachpit.com* to access the online content.

1 Go to *peachpit.com/register*, and sign in or create a new account.

2 On the Register A Product page, enter ISBN **9780135561270** and click Submit.

3 Answer the proof-of-purchase challenge question by looking in your book for the answer.

4 Navigate to the Registered Products tab on your Account page to access the lesson files.

5 Click the Access Bonus Content link below the title of your product to proceed to the download page. Click the lesson file links to download them to your computer.

6 The Web Edition can be accessed from the Digital Purchases tab on your Account page. Click the Launch link to access the product.

Note: If you encounter problems registering your product or accessing the lesson files or web edition, go to *peachpit.com/support* for assistance.

Note: If you purchased a digital product directly from *peachpit.com*, your product will already be registered. Look for the Access Bonus Content link on the Registered Products tab in your account.

Bonus material

This book has so much great material that we couldn't fit it all in the printed pages, so we placed these items on *peachpit.com*:

- Lesson 17, "Managing Your Projects"

You will find this bonus material on your Account page (Lessons & Update Files tab) once you register your book, as described in "Accessing the lesson files and Web Edition."

Using the lesson files

The lessons in this book use the downloadable lesson files, including video clips, audio files, photos, and image files created in Photoshop and Illustrator. Some lessons use files from other lessons, so you'll need to keep the entire collection of lesson assets on your storage drive as you work through the book. You will need about 7 GB of storage space for the lesson files.

Tip: If you don't have a dedicated storage location for your video files, placing the lesson files on your computer's desktop will make them easy to find and work with.

Relinking the lesson files

The Premiere projects included with the lesson files have links to specific media files. Because you are copying the files to a new location, you may need to update those links when you open projects for the first time.

If you open a project and Premiere is unable to find a linked media file, the Link Media dialog box should open automatically, inviting you to relink offline files. If this happens, select an offline clip on the list and click the Locate button. A file browser panel will appear.

Locate your copy of the Lessons folder using the navigator on the left, and click Search. Premiere will locate the media file inside the Lessons folder. To hide all other files, making it easy to select the correct one, select the option to display only exact name matches.

Premiere displays the last known file path and filename and the currently selected file path and filename at the top of the panel for reference. Select the file, and click OK.

The option to automatically relink other files is enabled by default, so once you've located one file, the rest should reconnect automatically. For more information about relinking offline media files, see Lesson 17 (if you have the print version of this book, see "Bonus material" earlier in this section).

How to use these lessons

The lessons in this book include step-by-step instructions. Each lesson stands alone, but many build on previous lessons. For this reason, the best way to learn from this book is to proceed through the lessons one after another.

The lessons teach you new skills in the order you might normally use them. The lessons begin with acquiring media files such as video, audio, and graphics; and they go on to creating a rough-cut sequence, adding effects, sweetening the audio, and ultimately exporting the project.

Many pages contain additional sidebars, information boxes that explain a particular technology or offer alternative workflows. It's not necessary to read these additional boxes, or follow the alternative workflows, to learn Premiere, but you may find them interesting and helpful, as they will deepen your understanding and often provide additional context.

By the end of these lessons, you'll have a good understanding of the complete end-to-end video post-production workflow, with the specific skills you need to edit on your own.

As you explore the skills described in this book, you may find it helpful to review earlier lessons you have already completed and to practice the fundamental editing techniques regularly. The later advanced workflows build on fundamental principles introduced early on, and if you take a few moments to recap earlier lessons, it makes it easier to discover the common principles that apply. The more you practice, the faster you will build your confidence as an editor.

The focus of this book is on the technical skills editors use every day to produce film, television, and social media videos. Taking time to try different ways of achieving results can help to expand your artistic skills. As you learn new technical skills, watch videos created by experienced editors with a critical eye and see if you can recognize the technical workflow they employed. More often than not, the most impactful techniques are the simplest, once you know the workflow.

Practice makes perfect!

Additional resources

Adobe Premiere Classroom in a Book 2026 Release is not meant to replace documentation that comes with the program or to be a comprehensive reference for every feature. Only the commands and options used in the lessons are explained in this book. For comprehensive information about program features and tutorials, refer to the following resources, which you can reach by choosing commands from the Premiere Help menu.

Adobe Premiere Learn and Support: *helpx.adobe.com/premiere.html* is where you can find and browse Help and Support content on Adobe.com. You can also reach that page by choosing Help > Premiere Help or by pressing F1. On the Learn & Support page, click a topic for documentation on individual features.

Premiere tutorials: For a wide range of interactive tutorials on Adobe Premiere features that you can follow in the app, choose Help > Premiere In-App Tutorials. For online tutorials, choose Help > Premiere Online Tutorials or visit *adobe.com/learn/premiere*.

Adobe video blog: *blog.adobe.com/en/disciplines/video* brings you tutorials, product news, and inspirational articles about using Premiere as well as other video products from Adobe.

Learn Adobe Apps: For inspiration, key techniques, cross-application workflows, and updates on new features, go to the Adobe Learn page, *www.adobe.com/learn*.

Adobe Community: Tap into peer-to-peer discussions, questions, and answers on Adobe products at the Adobe Support Community page at *community.adobe.com*. Click the Premiere link to visit the Premiere community.

Resources for educators: *adobe.com/education* and *edex.adobe.com* offer a treasure trove of information for instructors who teach classes on Adobe software. Find solutions for education at all levels, including free curricula that use an integrated approach to teaching Adobe software. These curricula can be used to prepare for the Adobe Certified Professional exams. To learn more about the exams, visit *edex.adobe.com/adobe-certified-professional/exams*.

Adobe Premiere product home page: *adobe.com/products/premiere* has more information about the features and functionality of the application.

1 TOURING ADOBE PREMIERE

Lesson overview

In this lesson, you'll learn how to do the following:

- Perform nonlinear editing.
- Understand the standard digital video workflow.
- Enhance the workflow with high-level features.
- Explore workspaces.
- Customize workspaces.
- Set keyboard shortcuts.

This lesson will take about 75 minutes to complete. To get the files used in this lesson, refer to the instructions in "Accessing the lesson files and Web Edition" in the "Getting Started" section at the beginning of this book. Store the files locally on your computer in a convenient location.

Adobe Premiere is a video-editing system that supports the latest technology and cameras with powerful tools that are intuitive to use and that integrate perfectly with almost every video acquisition source and delivery standard.

Starting the lesson

There is always great demand for high-quality video media. Today's video producers, editors, and content creators work in a fast-changing landscape of old and new technologies. Despite rapid change in camera systems and the video creation and distribution landscape—particularly with the expansion of social media platforms, generative artificial intelligence (usually shortened to "generative AI" or "genAI") technologies like Adobe Firefly, and ever-higher media production values—the goal of great video editing remains unchanged: You want to take your source media and shape it, guided by your original vision, so that you can effectively communicate with your audience.

In Adobe Premiere, you'll find a powerful and intuitive video-editing system that supports the latest technology, cameras, and formats with flexible tools that are easy to use. These tools integrate perfectly with almost every type of media and support a wide range of third-party plug-ins and other post-production tools.

Many of the tools and workflows available in Premiere serve one particular purpose. For example, Remix allows you to extend or shorten music clips while maintaining the musicality of the content (see Lesson 10, "Editing and Mixing Audio"). You don't need to learn about all of the available tools to edit video.

In this lesson, you'll begin by reviewing the essential post-production workflow that most editors follow, and then you'll learn about the main components of the Premiere interface and how to create custom workspaces—that is, arrangements of panels.

Performing nonlinear editing in Premiere

Premiere is a nonlinear editor (NLE). Like a word processing application, Premiere lets you place, replace, and move video, audio, and images anywhere you want in your final edited work. You don't need to make adjustments in a particular order; you can change any part of your project at any time—that's the nonlinear part of an NLE.

You'll combine multiple pieces of media, called *clips*, to create a *sequence*. You can edit any part of the sequence in any order and then change the contents or move clips so that they play earlier or later. You can blend layers of video together, change the image size, adjust the colors, add special effects, adjust the audio mix, and more.

In Premiere, organizing the clips you're working with is like organizing files on your computer.

Premiere supports many media file formats, including both compressed and RAW video from professional cameras, DSLR cameras, phone cameras, and animation applications—for a full list, visit *helpx.adobe.com/premiere/desktop/organize-media/import-files/supported-file-formats.html*.

Premiere features native support for RAW media from RED cameras, with settings to control the way the media is interpreted.

Following the standard digital video workflow

As you gain editing experience, you'll develop your own preferences for the order in which to work on the different aspects of your project. You'll find that each stage of post-production requires a particular kind of attention and different tools. Also, some projects call for more time spent on one stage than another.

Whether you skip through some stages with a quick mental check or spend hours (even days!) dedicated to perfecting an aspect of your project, you'll almost certainly go through the following steps:

1. **Acquire your media:** This can mean recording original footage, creating new animated content, selecting stock media, using generative AI to create new original media, or gathering a variety of assets for a project.
2. **Copy the media files to your editing storage:** Premiere can read media files (like video files from a camera) directly, usually with no need for conversion. Be sure to back up your files to a second location because storage drives sometimes fail unexpectedly. For video editing, use fast storage for smooth playback.
3. **Organize your clips:** You may have a lot of video content to choose from. Invest the time to organize clips into special folders in your project called *bins*—a term taken from the days of editing celluloid film, when organized strips of film would be stored in large cloth-lined bins to allow quick access for the editor. You can add color labels and other reference information as metadata (metadata is additional information about the clips or media files, like tags) to help keep things organized.

4 **Create a sequence:** Selectively combine the parts of the clips that you want into a sequence. A *sequence* is the edited video you will create.

5 **Add transitions:** Place transition effects between sequence clips like dissolves for video or crossfades for audio, add video effects, and create composite visuals by placing clips on multiple layers (called *tracks*).

6 **Create or import titles, graphics, and captions:** Add them to your sequence to help tell the story.

7 **Adjust the audio mix:** Adjust the volume of your audio clips to get the relative levels just right, and use transitions and effects on your audio clips to improve the sound.

8 **Output:** Export your finished project to a file or directly to social media.

Premiere supports each of these steps with industry-leading tools. A large community of creative and technical professionals is waiting to share their experience and support your development as an editor. To join the community, visit *community.adobe.com/p/premiere*.

Enhancing the workflow with Premiere

Premiere has easy-to-use tools for video-editing beginners. It also has advanced tools for manipulating, adjusting, and fine-tuning your videos.

You may not make use of all the following features in your first few video projects. However, as your experience and understanding of nonlinear editing grows, you'll want to expand your skillset.

It's beyond the scope of one book to cover all of the expansive creative tools and capabilities of Premiere. Still, this book will enable you to fully post-produce professional projects and get you ready to take your skills to the next level.

The following topics will be covered:

- **Advanced audio editing:** Learn to use the advanced audio effects and editing tools in Premiere. As well as producing a soundtrack mix, you can clean up noisy audio, reduce reverb, make sample-level edits, apply multiple audio effects to audio clips or whole tracks, change the duration of music, and use state-of-the-art Virtual Studio Technology (VST) plug-ins.
- **Color correction and grading:** Correct and enhance the look of your footage with advanced color-correction controls, accessed via the dedicated Lumetri Color panel, and video effects. You can make secondary color-correction selections that allow you to adjust isolated colors, adjust selected areas of an image to improve the composition, and automatically match the colors in two images.
- **Keyframe controls:** Premiere gives you precise control over the timing of visual and motion effects without using a separate compositing or motion graphics application. Keyframes use a standard interface design; if you learn to use

them in Premiere, you'll know how to use them in other Adobe Creative Cloud applications.

- **Broad hardware support:** Choose from a wide range of compatible input and output hardware. Premiere system specifications range from low-cost desktop computers and laptops for video editing up to high-performance workstations that can easily edit high-resolution 8K, 3D stereoscopic, and 360° video.
- **GPU acceleration:** The Mercury Playback Engine uses the graphics processing unit (GPU) in your system to dramatically enhance playback performance. GPU acceleration mode requires graphics hardware that meets minimum specifications in your workstation. For a list of recommended graphics cards, visit *helpx.adobe.com* and search for **Premiere specifications**. Most modern cards with a minimum of 4 GB of dedicated video memory will work (8 GB unified memory for Apple Silicon).
- **Multicamera editing:** You can quickly and easily edit productions shot with multiple cameras. Multiple camera sources are displayed in a split view, and you can choose a camera view by clicking the appropriate screen or using a shortcut key. You can automatically sync multiple camera angles based on clip audio or timecode.
- **Project management:** View, delete, move, search for, and reorganize clips and bins. Consolidate your projects by copying just the media used in sequences to a single location, and then reclaim storage space by deleting unused media files.
- **Metadata:** Premiere supports Adobe XMP, which stores additional information about media as metadata that multiple applications can access. You can use this metadata to locate clips or communicate important information, such as preferred takes or copyright notices.
- **Creating titles:** Select an editable pre-built template graphic in the Graphics Templates panel or create original graphics and titles from scratch. You can also use graphics created in almost any suitable software. For instance, you can import Adobe Photoshop files as flattened images or as separate layers that you can combine or animate selectively.
- **Advanced trimming:** Make precise adjustments to the start and end timing of clips in sequences using dedicated trimming tools. Premiere provides quick, simple trimming keyboard shortcuts, as well as advanced on-screen trimming tools to make complex timing adjustments to multiple clips.
- **Reframing visual elements:** Perhaps you are delivering widescreen, vertical, and square video versions of your content. You can adjust and perfect the composition for every type of output manually or automatically.
- **Media encoding:** Export your sequence to create a media file that is perfect for your needs using simplified Quick Export presets or detailed settings. Use the advanced features of Adobe Media Encoder to create copies of your finished

sequence in multiple formats, based on presets or your own detailed specifications. You can apply color adjustments, timing changes, and information overlays during export, as well as upload media to social media platforms in a single step.

Expanding the workflow

Although you can work with Premiere as a stand-alone application, it is also a team player. In addition to creating projects that are stored in a single project file, you can create Team projects, which support collaborative editing with shared timelines, and Productions, which allow you to divide large complex projects into more manageable connected but separate project files.

Premiere is part of Adobe Creative Cloud, which means you have access to several other specialized tools.

Understanding the way these software components work together will improve your efficiency and give you more creative freedom.

Including other applications in the editing workflow

Premiere is a versatile video and audio post-production tool, but it's just one component of Adobe Creative Cloud—a complete print, web, and video environment that includes video-focused software for the following:

- High-end 3D motion effects creation
- Complex text animation generation
- Layered graphics production
- Vector artwork creation
- Audio production
- Generative AI content creation

To incorporate one or more of these features into a production, you can use other components of Adobe Creative Cloud. The software set has everything you need to produce advanced, professionally finished videos.

Here's a brief description of the other components:

- **Adobe Express:** All-in-one design, photo, video, and generative AI tool to make content creation easy.
- **Adobe Premiere Mobile:** Intuitive mobile video-editing tool that can produce projects compatible with Premiere (for advanced finishing).
- **After Effects:** The popular tool of choice for motion graphics, animation, and visual effects artists.

- **Adobe Character Animator:** A tool for creating advanced animation with natural movement for 2D puppets using your webcam for face and body movement tracking.
- **Adobe Photoshop:** The industry-standard image-editing and graphics-creation product. You can work with photos and video to prepare them for your project.
- **Adobe Audition:** The powerful and intuitive system for audio editing, audio cleanup and sweetening, music creation and adjustment, and multitrack mix creation.
- **Adobe Illustrator:** Professional vector graphics-creation software for print, video, and the web.
- **Adobe Media Encoder:** A tool that allows you to process files to produce content for any screen directly from Premiere, After Effects, and Audition.
- **Adobe Dynamic Link:** A cross-product technology that enables you to work in real time with media, compositions, and sequences shared between After Effects, Audition, and Premiere.
- **Adobe Firefly:** Generative AI content-creation technology that is embedded in Creative Cloud applications as Generative Fill and Generative Extend features, as well as accessible for free using Adobe's web-based Text to Image feature.

Exploring the Adobe Creative Cloud video workflow

Your Premiere and Creative Cloud workflow will vary depending on the needs of each project. Here are a few scenarios:

- Use Photoshop to touch up and apply effects to still images and layered image compositions from a digital camera, a scanner, or a video clip. Then use them as source media in Premiere. Changes made in Photoshop update in Premiere.
- Send clips directly from the Premiere timeline to Adobe Audition for professional audio cleanup and sweetening. Changes made in Audition update in Premiere.
- Send an entire Premiere sequence to Adobe Audition to complete a professional audio mix, including compatible effects and level adjustments; the session can contain video so you can compose and adjust levels in Audition based on the action.
- Using Dynamic Link, include video compositions from After Effects in Premiere projects. Apply special effects, add animation, and add visual elements in After Effects. Adjustments made in After Effects appear in Premiere immediately.
- Use After Effects to create Motion Graphics templates for Adobe Stock that are directly editable in Premiere. Dedicated controls allow editors to adjust any settings they wish; or changes can be limited to specific options, locking in options like company colors, fonts, or animation styles.

- Use Adobe Media Encoder to export video projects in multiple resolutions and codecs for display on websites, display via social media, or archiving. You can use the built-in presets, effects, and social media support to upload directly from Premiere to social media platforms.

Naturally, most of this book focuses on workflows involving only Premiere. However, sidebars will explain ways to include Adobe Creative Cloud components in your workflows for additional effects work and finishing.

Touring the Premiere interface

Note: To ensure that the tools function and the defaults are set exactly as described in this lesson, reset the Premiere preferences by holding any modifier key (such as Shift) while launching the application, selecting Reset App Preferences, and then clicking Continue in the Reset Options dialog box.

It's helpful to begin by getting familiar with the editing interface so you can recognize the tools, menus, and panels as you work with them in the following lessons. To make it easier for you to customize the user interface, Premiere includes workspaces. Workspaces quickly position the various panels and tools on-screen in ways that are helpful for particular activities, such as editing, special effects work, or audio mixing.

You'll begin by taking a brief tour of the Editing workspace. For most of the exercises in these lessons, you'll use a Premiere project from this book's lesson files. Before you continue, make sure you've downloaded and extracted all the lesson folder ZIP files to your computer storage. Follow the instructions carefully to ensure the folders are correctly arranged because Premiere uses the folder structure to locate media.

Next, launch Premiere. The Home screen appears. If you have opened projects previously, a list will appear in the middle of the Home screen.

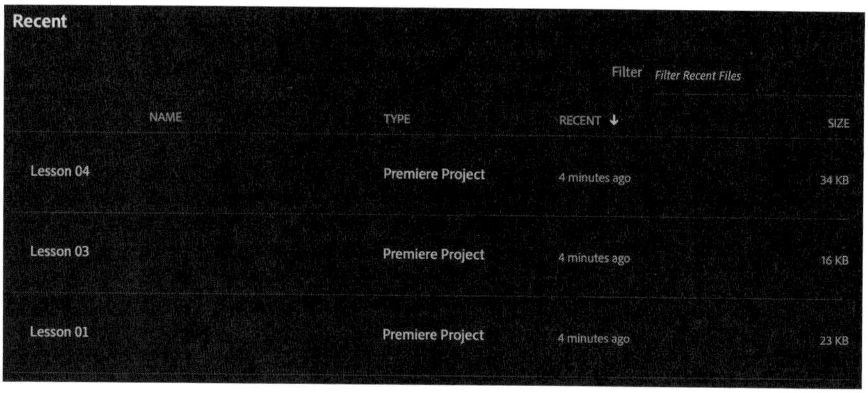

You can hover the pointer over a recent item to see the project file location in a pop-up window.

A Premiere project file contains all your creative decisions for a project, links (referred to as *clips*) to your selected media files, sequences made by combining those clips, special effects settings, and more. Premiere project files have the filename extension *.prproj*.

Lesson 01.prproj

Whenever you work in Premiere, you will be making adjustments to a project file. You need to create a new project file or open an existing one to use Premiere.

Project index files

Once you have imported media into a project or if you open a project that already has media imported, a new file will be created automatically with the same name as the project but the extension *.prin*.

PRIN files contain media intelligence information to make it easier to search for content in your project. You can safely delete these files as they will be generated whenever needed.

There are a few important buttons on the Home screen, some of which look like text but can actually be clicked (look out for text that works as a button in the Premiere interface):

- **New Project:** Creates a new project file. It's a good idea to choose a name that will be easy to identify later (in other words, avoid using the name New Project).
- **Open Project:** Click this to open an existing project by browsing for the project file. You can also double-click an existing project file in the macOS Finder or Windows Explorer to open it in Premiere.
- **Home:** Takes you back to this screen.
- **Templates**: Displays previews of prebuilt template project files that will open in Adobe Express, the online content creation app. You can edit the template there or send it back to Premiere for more advanced editing workflows (Adobe Express is beyond the scope of this book).
- **New Team Project:** Creates a new collaborative project using the Adobe Team Project service. Team Projects are beyond the scope of this book but use the same tools and editing techniques that you will learn here—just collaboratively.
- **Open Team Project:** Opens the Manage Team Projects dialog box to allow you to select an existing Team Project to work on.
- **Open Premiere Rush Project:** Opens an existing Premiere Rush project in Premiere. Any projects you created with Premiere Rush will be available here, as long as you used the same Adobe ID as for Premiere on both devices.

Note: If you are using a version of Premiere later than the one used in making this book, when you open the Lesson 01.prproj file, an alert may ask you to save it in a new format. Updating the format of the file won't interfere with working through the exercises, so click OK.

Try opening an existing Premiere project:

1 Click Open Project.

2 In the file navigation dialog box that appears, navigate to the Lessons folder; then double-click the Lesson 01.prproj project file to open the first lesson. Leave the file open for the next exercise.

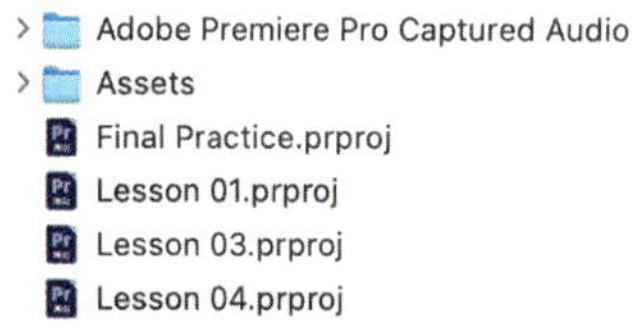

Linking media

After you open an existing project file, the Link Media dialog box may open, asking where a particular media file is. This will occasionally happen when the original media files are saved on a storage device (or drive letter) different from the one you're using. You'll need to tell Premiere where the file is.

In the Link Media dialog box that prompts you to link the media file, you'll see a list of missing items, with the first already highlighted. Click Locate, at the bottom right.

At the top of the Locate File dialog box you'll see Last Path (that's the last known location for the file) and Path (that's the current location you have browsed to).

Using the folders on the left, navigate to the Lessons/Assets folder, and click Search at the bottom right. Premiere will locate the missing file and highlight it on the right side of the window. Select the file, and click OK. Premiere will remember this location for other missing files and relink them automatically without your needing to link each one individually.

Choose File > Save to save the updated file locations in the project file.

To learn more about managing media, see the online bonus lesson, "Managing Your Projects."

Hands-on: Editing your first video

Note: It's best to keep all the lesson assets in your computer storage and leave them there until you complete this book; some lessons reuse assets from previous lessons.

The first series of exercises walks you through editing a simple video. You'll get hands-on experience using the principal features of Premiere.

Because you are going to make changes to the project file, you'll start by saving a new version. Then, to ensure the steps described here match your screen, you'll reset the Premiere user interface to its default layout. After that, you'll learn about the main editing tools and user interface features in Premiere.

1 With Lesson 01.prproj open in Premiere, choose File > Save As. Save a separate copy of the project with the name **Lesson 01 Working.prproj**.

2 By default, Premiere opens in the Learning workspace. We're going to dive right in to editing using the Editing workspace: Choose Window > Workspaces > Editing to make sure the Editing workspace is selected (see "Exploring workspaces" for more information on workspaces).

3 Choose Window > Workspaces > Reset To Saved Layout to reset the workspace to the default settings.

This project contains a number of video clips. Some have already been edited into a sequence in the Timeline panel (for more information about panels, see "Exploring workspaces").

Note: Unlike most other panels, the Timeline panel does not include its own name in its heading. Instead, the name of the current sequence is shown. In this case, it's Desert Montage.

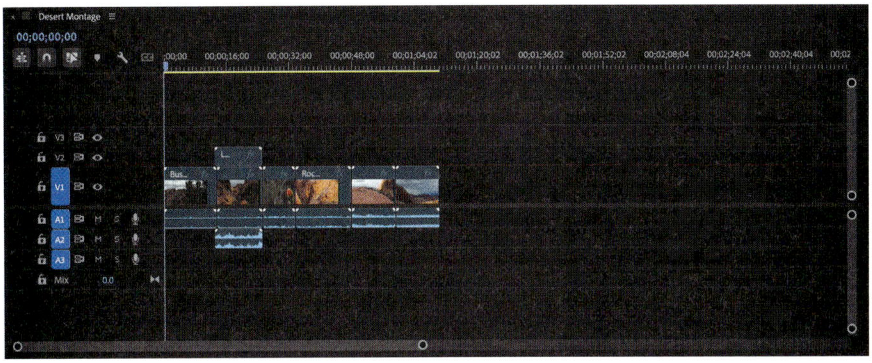

4 Along the top edge of the Timeline panel, named Desert Montage in this project, notice the horizontal bar with a series of numbers—the time ruler. The blue playhead control connected to the time ruler works the same way as the playhead when viewing video files in a player. Try clicking a location on the time ruler—the playhead jumps to the time you click.

5 Place the playhead to the far left of the Timeline panel time ruler.

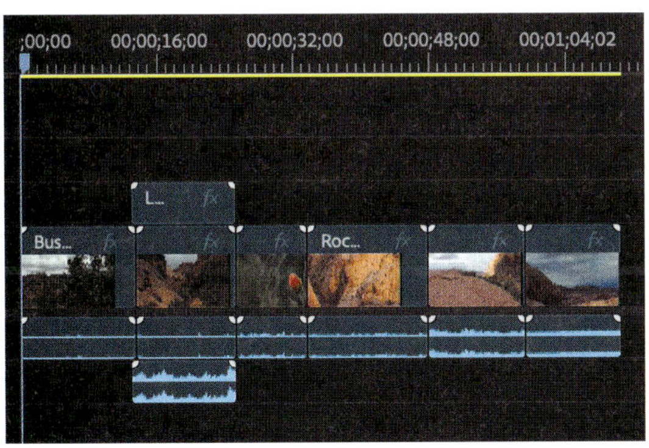

6 Press the spacebar to play the current sequence. The Program Monitor (upper middle-right of the Premiere interface) displays the contents of the sequence.

In the lower-left corner of the Premiere interface, you will find the Project panel, which contains clips and other assets associated with the current project. The panel name includes the current project name, Project: Lesson 01 Working.

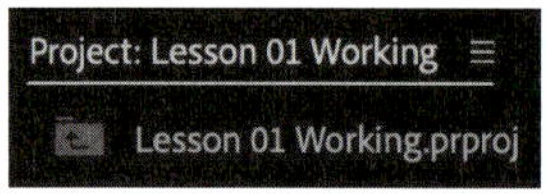

The lower-left corner of the Project panel holds a series of buttons that you use to select different ways of viewing the contents of the panel.

Let's add some more clips to the sequence.

7 Click the Icon View button if it's not already selected.

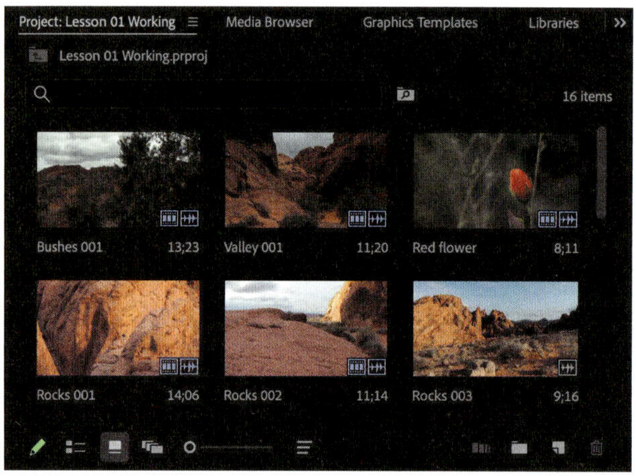

Icon view makes it easier to identify clips based on their contents.

8 Drag the clip named Bushes 001 from the Project panel to the end of the existing series of clips already in the Timeline panel. Be sure to drag it by the thumbnail image and not the clip name.

If you line up the new clip with an existing clip, you'll notice the new clip jumps into position, exactly aligning with the end of the existing clip. If this does not happen, snapping is turned off in the Timeline panel. Click the Snap In Timeline button at the upper-left corner of the Timeline panel to turn it on.

9 Scroll down in the Project panel and find several more clips of your choice to add to the sequence. Drag each one into the sequence.

At any time, you can review your sequence by positioning the Timeline playhead at the beginning of the sequence (at its left end) and using the spacebar to start and stop playback.

10 When you have finished adding several clips to the sequence, play through it to see the result.

You can place the Timeline playhead anywhere and play from that moment.

There is one item you will not be able to drag from the Project panel into the sequence: the sequence itself, called Desert Montage.

The Project panel displays both clips and sequences. You can have as many sequences as you like in a project, and they are identifiable by the icon in the lower-right corner of the clip thumbnail (in Icon view or in Freeform view) or the item icon in List view.

Congratulations! You edited a sequence!

Exploring workspaces

The Premiere interface is divided into *panels*. Each panel has a particular purpose. For example, the Effects panel lists all the effects available for you to apply to clips, while the Effect Controls panel gives you access to the settings for those effects.

Tip: The Reset To Saved Layout command displays a keyboard shortcut in the menu. Many tasks can be performed using keyboard shortcuts, including choosing workspaces. If you're using a computer with a non-U.S. keyboard, the shortcuts available to you might use different keys from the ones shown here. See "Using and setting keyboard shortcuts" later in this lesson for more information.

A *workspace* is a preset arrangement of panels, organized to make particular tasks easier. For example, there's one for editing, another for working on audio, and another for making color adjustments.

Every panel is accessible from the Window menu, but workspaces are a quicker way to access several panels at once and have them laid out exactly as you need them.

Before you begin, make sure you're using the default Editing workspace by choosing Window > Workspaces > Editing. Then, to reset the Editing workspace, choose Window > Workspaces > Reset To Saved Layout.

The name of your current project is displayed at the top of the Premiere interface.

At the top left of the interface, the Home button opens the Home screen, allowing you to quickly open a recent project or create a new one.

Next to the Home button, the words *Import*, *Edit*, and *Export* are all buttons you can click; these floating words are examples of an elegant design feature you'll discover in a number of areas in Premiere. The buttons switch the interface between these three important modes.

For now, stay in the Edit mode—you will learn about the other modes in later lessons.

At the top right of the interface, the Workspaces menu gives quick access to several workspaces for particular tasks. You'll use some of these workspaces as you progress through these lessons. For now, make sure Editing is the active workspace.

Tip: In the Workspaces menu, choose Show Workspace Label to display the name of the current workspace next to the menu.

If you're new to nonlinear editing, the default Editing workspace might look like a lot of new buttons and menus to learn. Don't panic. Things become simpler when you know what the buttons are for, and you can often ignore the ones you don't recognize. The interface is designed to make video editing easy, so commonly used controls are immediately accessible.

Workspaces consist of particular panels positioned and sized helpfully. You can save space by gathering several panels into a *panel group*. The names of all the panels in the group are displayed across the top. Click a panel name to bring that panel to the "front" of the group.

When many panels are combined, there may not be enough space to display all their names. If this is the case, a list of all the panels in the group becomes available. Click the double chevrons in the upper-right corner of the panel group to display a menu of hidden panels.

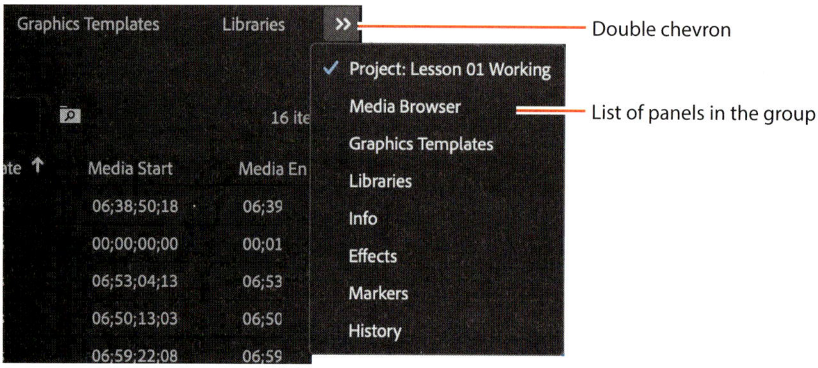

You can display any panel by choosing it from the Window menu, so if you can't locate a panel, just look there. After exploring the interface, return to the Editing workspace and reset the workspace.

Some of the important interface elements in the Editing workspace include:

- **Project panel:** This is where you organize your clips (these are the links to your media files), sequences, and graphics in *bins*. Bins are similar to folders—you can place one bin inside another for more advanced organization of your project.
- **Timeline panel:** This is where you'll do most of your creative work. You view and work on *sequences* (the term for video clips edited together) in the Timeline panel.

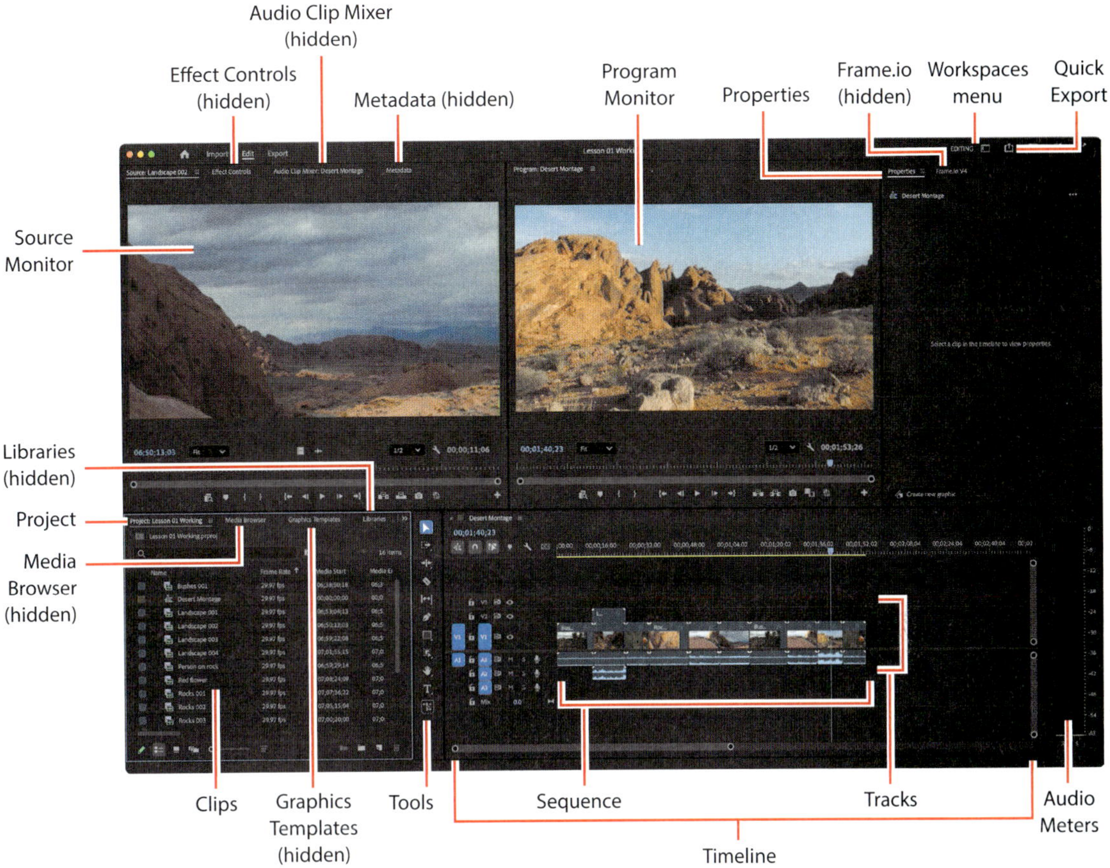

- **Tracks:** You can layer—or *composite*—video clips, images, graphics, and titles on an unlimited number of tracks. Video and graphic clips on upper video tracks cover whatever is directly below them on the timeline. Therefore, you need to give clips on higher tracks some form of transparency or reduce their size if you want clips on lower tracks to show.
- **Monitors:** Use the Source Monitor (on the left) to view and select parts of clips (your original footage). To view a clip in the Source Monitor, double-click its icon in the Project panel or drag it into the Source Monitor. The Program Monitor (on the right) shows the contents of your current sequence, displayed in the Timeline panel.
- **Media Browser:** This panel allows you to browse your storage to choose media to import into your project. Like Import mode, the Media Browser is especially useful for camera media and RAW files because it allows you to preview the files before importing. You can use Import mode to import, too, but the Media Browser has additional options to help you stay organized.

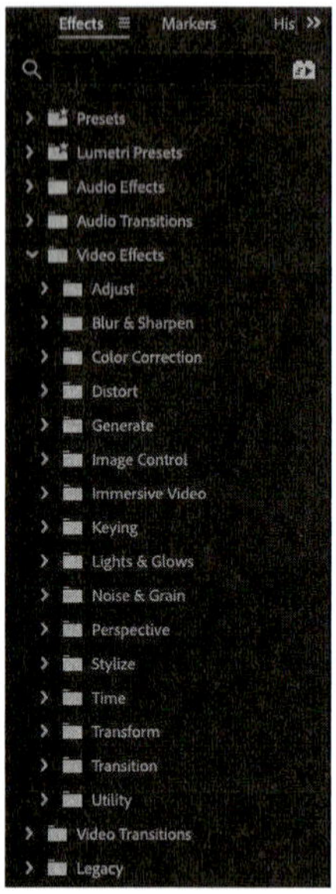

- **Libraries:** This panel gives access to assets that you can share between projects, such as custom Lumetri color Looks, Motion Graphics templates, graphics, and shared libraries.
- **Effects panel:** This panel contains most of the effects you will use in your sequences, including video and audio effects and transitions. Effects are grouped by type to make them easier to find, and there's a search box at the top of the panel. Once applied, the controls for these effects are displayed in the Effect Controls panel.
- **Effect Controls panel:** This panel displays the controls for any effects applied to a clip you select in a sequence or open in the Source Monitor. If you select a visual clip in the Timeline panel, Motion, Opacity, and Time Remapping adjustment controls are automatically available. Most effect settings can be adjusted over time. The Effect Controls panel allows you to change settings for one selected clip at a time.
- **Properties panel:** When one or more clips are selected in a sequence, you'll use this panel to adjust settings like their Position, Scale, and Rotation. You'll notice there is some repetition in the settings available in the Effect Controls panel and the Properties panel. Think of the Properties panel as a way to quickly access commonly used controls. One major difference is that you can make changes to multiple selected clips in the Properties panel, while the Effect Controls panel is for working on one clip at a time. You'll also use the Properties panel to adjust the contents of graphics and titles.

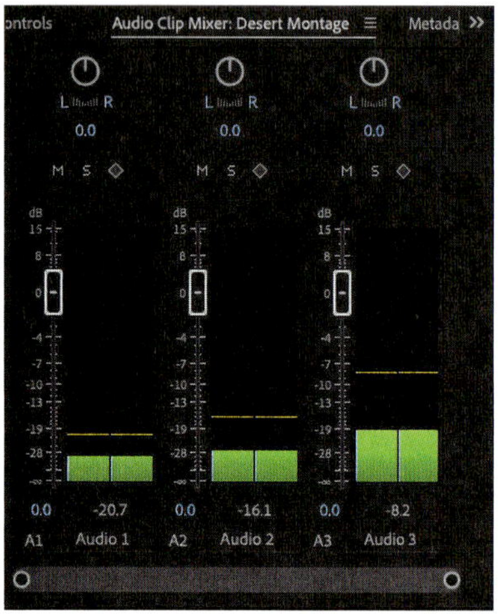

- **Audio Clip Mixer:** This panel is based on audio production studio hardware, with volume sliders and pan controls. There is one set of controls for each audio track on the timeline. The adjustments you make are applied to audio clips. There's also an Audio Track Mixer for applying audio adjustments to tracks rather than to clips.

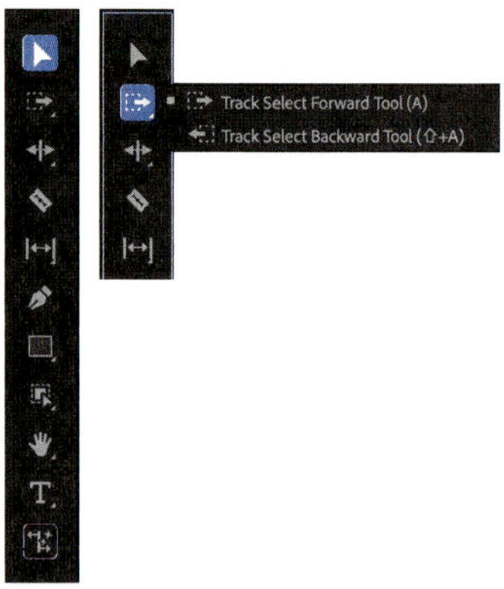

- **Tools panel:** Each icon in this panel gives access to a tool that performs a specific function in the Timeline panel or the Program Monitor. You'll use and learn more about many of these tools in upcoming lessons. The Selection tool is contextsensitive, which means it changes function depending on where you click. If your pointer doesn't work as you expect, check to see you have the right tool selected.

  Several tools have a small triangle icon, indicating a menu of additional tools. Click and hold one of these tools to see the menu of options.

- **Info panel:** The Info panel displays information about any item you select in the Project panel or any clip or transition you select in a sequence.
- **History panel:** This panel tracks the steps you take and lets you easily undo a series of changes. When you select a previous step, all steps that followed it are also undone.
- **Quick Export:** This button in the upper-right corner gives fast access to popular media file export options for sharing your work.

Most panels display their name at the top. When a panel is grouped with other panels, the name is underlined when you select it. The currently active panel is outlined in blue. Most panels have a menu next to their name with options particular to that panel; this important menu is simply called the *panel menu*. For example, the Project panel menu provides options for the Project panel.

Using the Learning workspace

Although other workspaces are intended to facilitate a particular creative activity, the Learning workspace is an exception. This workspace includes the Learn panel, which offers tutorials to help you build familiarity with the Premiere interface and learn important skills.

These tutorials complement the exercises in this book well, and you may find it helpful to practice first with this book and then explore the panel's relevant tutorials to reinforce the lessons you have learned.

Customizing a workspace

In addition to choosing between the default workspaces, you can adjust the position and location of panels to create a workspace that works best for you. You can create multiple custom workspaces for different tasks.

- As you change the size of a panel or panel group, other panels change size to compensate.
- Every panel within a panel group is accessible by clicking its name.
- All panels are movable—you can drag a panel from one group to another.
- You can drag a panel out of a group to become a separate floating panel.
- You can double-click the name of any panel to toggle it between full screen and its original size.

In this exercise, you'll adjust some panels and save a customized workspace.

1 In the Project panel, double-click the icon for the clip Valley 001 to open it in the Source Monitor.

2 Position your pointer on the vertical divider between the Source Monitor and the Program Monitor. The pointer will change to a double-headed arrow  when it's in the right position. Drag left and right to change the sizes of those panels. You can choose to have different sizes for your video displays, which is useful at different stages of post-production.

3 Now place the pointer on the horizontal divider between the Program Monitor and the Timeline panel. The pointer will change when it's in the right position. Drag up and down to change the sizes of these panels.

4 Click the name of the Media Browser (at its top), and drag it to the middle of the Source Monitor until a blue rectangle appears (the *drop zone*—displayed as a center highlight). Release the Media Browser to dock it in that panel group.

5 Drag the Effects panel (which is grouped with the Project panel by default) by its name to a point just inside the right edge of its current panel group until a blue trapezoid-shaped area (the drop zone) is highlighted. Remember, if you can't see the Effects panel, you can choose it from the Window menu.

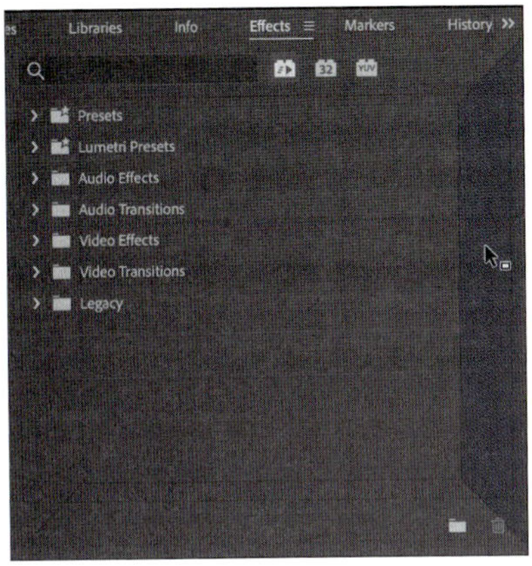

6 Release the Effects panel; it is now alone in its own panel group.

When you drag a panel by its name, a drop zone is displayed. If the highlighted drop zone is a rectangle, the panel will go into the selected panel group as an additional tab when it's dropped. If the drop zone is a trapezoid, it will create a new panel group. If the drop zone is green, you'll create a new panel group that is the full height or width of the Premiere interface.

You can also pull panels into their own floating windows.

7 Command-drag (macOS)/Ctrl-drag (Windows) the Source Monitor out of its panel group.

8 Drop the Source Monitor anywhere, creating a floating panel. You can resize the panel by dragging a corner or a side.

Tip: You may need to resize some panels to see all of their controls.

> **Note:** You can save changes to new workspaces you have created. When you do, resetting to default will restore the most recently saved version of the workspace.

As you gain experience, you might want to create and save the layout of your panels as a customized workspace. To do so at any time, choose Window > Workspaces > Save As New Workspace. Type a name, and click OK.

9 Now, to return to a recognizable starting point, choose Window > Workspaces > Editing. Then, to reset the Editing workspace, choose Window > Workspaces > Reset To Saved Layout.

Introducing preferences

The more you edit video, the more you'll want to customize Premiere to match your specific needs. Premiere has several types of settings. For example, panel menus, which are accessible by clicking the menu button next to a panel name, have options that relate to each panel, while individual clips in a sequence have settings you can access by right-clicking them.

The panel name, displayed at the top of each panel, is often referred to as the *panel tab*. This is the area of a panel you use to move the panel, almost like a handle you can grab the panel by.

There are also application-wide user preferences, which are grouped into a single dialog box for easy access. These don't change from project to project. Preferences (called "Settings" in macOS) will be covered in depth as they relate to the individual lessons in this book. Let's look at an example.

> **Note:** When you open the Preferences dialog box, it's not too important which category you choose from the menu first, as you can always quickly switch to another.

1 Choose Premiere > Settings > Appearance (macOS) or Edit > Preferences > Appearance (Windows).

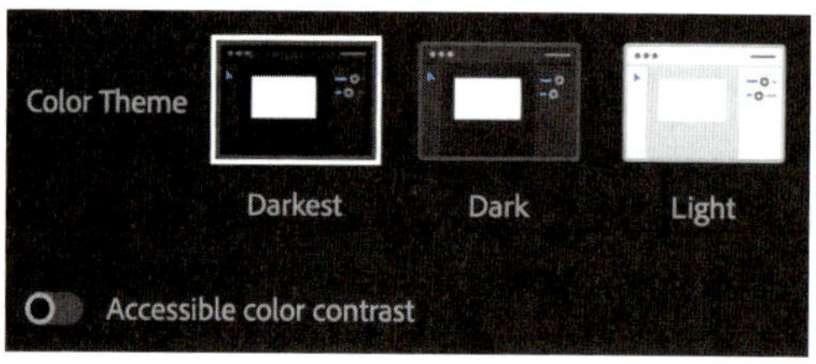

> **Note:** You can change the font size for List view in the Project panel by choosing Font Size from the panel menu and then choosing Small, Medium (Default), Large, or Extra Large from the submenu.

2 Click each of the Color Theme options to see the immediate impact on the interface.

The default color theme is the darkest. The Premiere interface is always gray to help you see colors correctly (human perception of color is influenced by surrounding colors).

3 Click to enable Accessible Color Contrast. This increases contrast in the Premiere interface to make it easier to read text and distinguish smaller interface elements.

4 For now, turn off Accessible Color Contrast and set the Color Theme to Darkest to make it easier to follow along with the screenshots in this book.

5 Switch to the Auto Save preferences by clicking Auto Save on the left.

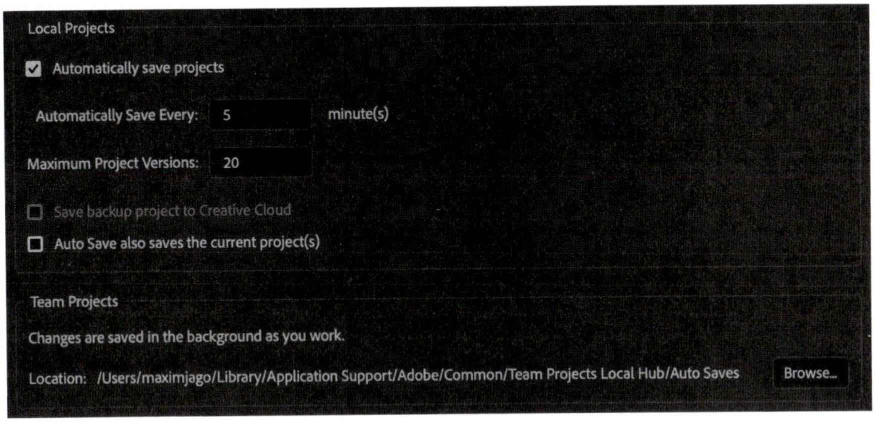

Imagine if you had worked for hours and then there was a power outage for your desktop or the battery failed on your laptop. If you hadn't saved recently, you'd have lost a lot of work. With the Auto Save options, you can decide how often you would like Premiere to automatically save a backup of your project file and how many versions you would like to keep. Auto Save backups have the date and time they were created added to the filename.

Project files are small relative to media files, so you can usually increase the number of project versions without impacting system performance.

6 Click Cancel to close the Preferences dialog box without applying any changes.

Note: Premiere allows you to open multiple projects at the same time. For this reason, you'll see options for "project(s)" rather than just "project."

Using and setting keyboard shortcuts

Premiere makes extensive use of keyboard shortcuts. Once you know them, these are usually faster and easier than clicking an item in a menu or hunting down an item in a panel. Several keyboard shortcuts are shared universally by nonlinear editing systems. The spacebar, for example, starts and stops playback—this even works on many websites.

Some standard keyboard shortcuts come from celluloid film-editing traditions. The I and O keys, for example, are used to set In and Out points for footage and sequences: These special marks indicate the start and end of a selected section and were originally drawn on celluloid directly.

Many shortcuts are available, but not all are assigned a key by default.

1 Choose Premiere > Keyboard Shortcuts (macOS) or Edit > Keyboard Shortcuts (Windows).

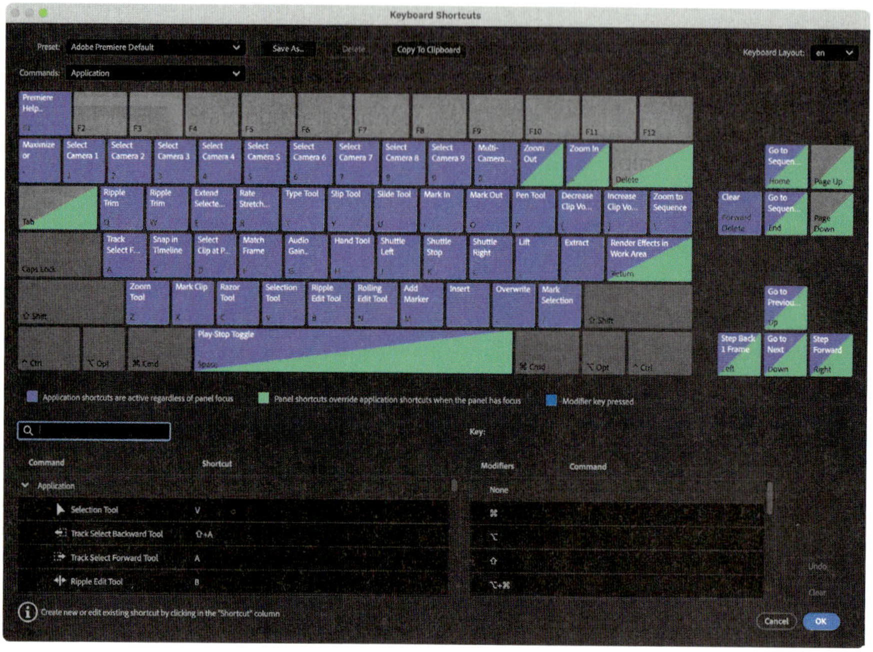

It can be a little daunting to see the number of keyboard shortcuts available, but by the end of this book you will recognize many of the options displayed here. Note that some keyboard shortcuts are specific to individual panels and will work only when the right panel is active.

2 You can use the Commands menu at the top of the dialog box to choose the name of a panel to create or edit shortcuts for that panel. By default, the dialog box shows application-wide shortcuts.

   Specialized keyboards are available with color-coded keys that have shortcuts printed on them. These make it easier to remember commonly used shortcuts.

3 When you open the Keyboard Shortcuts settings, the search box is automatically active to help you find a particular shortcut. Click outside of the search box (to deselect it), and try pressing Command (macOS) or Ctrl (Windows).

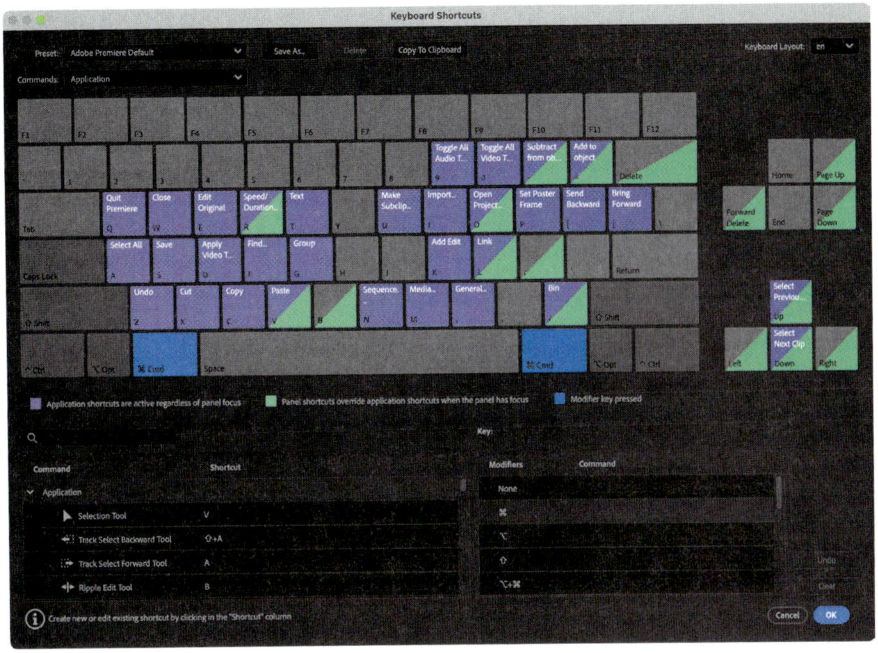

The keyboard shortcut display updates to show the results of combining the modifier key with the character keys. Notice there are many keys without shortcuts assigned when you use a modifier key. These are available for you to assign your own shortcuts.

4 Now try combinations of modifier keys including Shift+Option (macOS) or Shift+Alt (Windows). You can set keyboard shortcuts with any combination of modifier keys.

   If you press a character key, or character and modifier key combination, information about that particular shortcut is displayed.

   The list at the bottom left of the Keyboard Shortcuts dialog box includes every option you can assign to a key—it's a long list, so use the search box at the top to help you find the option you want.

5 To change a keyboard shortcut:

   - Having found an option you would like to assign to a key, drag it from the list onto the key you would like to use in the upper part of the dialog box. If you hold modifier keys while performing this operation, they'll be included in the shortcut. You can also drag a key from the virtual keyboard onto an option.
   - To remove a shortcut, click the key, and choose Clear at the lower-right corner.

6 For now, click Cancel.

Review questions

1 Why is Premiere considered a nonlinear editor?

2 Describe the basic video-editing workflow.

3 What is the Media Browser used for?

4 Can you save a customized workspace?

5 What is the purpose of the Source Monitor and the Program Monitor?

6 How can you open a panel as a separate, floating panel, separated from other panels?

Review answers

1. Premiere lets you place video clips, audio clips, and graphics anywhere in a sequence; rearrange items already in a sequence; add transitions; apply effects; and do any number of other video-editing steps in any order that suits you. You're not tied to a particular line of action.
2. Transfer media to your computer; create a sequence by combining video, audio, and still-image clips in the Timeline panel; make color correction adjustments; add effects and transitions; add text and graphics; mix your audio; and export the finished product as a video file.
3. The Media Browser allows you to browse and import media files without having to open an external file browser. It's particularly useful when you're working with video camera footage because it allows you to easily preview footage.
4. Yes. You can save any customized workspace by choosing Window > Workspaces > Save As New Workspace.
5. You can view and select part of your original footage in the Source Monitor and use the Program Monitor to view the contents of the current sequence displayed in the Timeline panel.
6. Drag the name of the panel while holding down Command (macOS) or Ctrl (Windows).

2 SETTING UP A PROJECT

Lesson overview

In this lesson, you'll learn how to do the following:

- Create a new project.
- Choose project settings.
- Choose video rendering and playback settings.
- Choose video and audio display settings.
- Set scratch disks.
- Use sequence presets.
- Customize sequence settings.

This lesson will take about 60 minutes to complete. To get the files used in this lesson, refer to the instructions in "Accessing the lesson files and Web Edition" in the "Getting Started" section at the beginning of this book. Store the files locally on your computer in a convenient location.

Before you begin editing, you'll learn how to create a new project and choose sequence settings that tell Premiere how to play your video and audio clips.

Starting the lesson

If you're not yet familiar with video and audio technology, you might find all the options available a little overwhelming. Luckily, Adobe Premiere gives you easy shortcuts to get started. Plus, the principles of video and sound reproduction are the same no matter what kind of project you're creating.

Note: Premiere project files are identical on macOS and Windows. Apart from a small number of differences in menu layouts and keyboard shortcuts, the user experience is the same on both operating systems too.

It's just a question of knowing what you want to do. To help you plan and manage your projects, this lesson contains information about formats and video technology. You may decide to revisit this lesson later, as your familiarity with Premiere and nonlinear video editing develops. You don't need to understand all of these concepts to edit videos.

In practice, you're unlikely to make changes to the default settings when creating a new project, but it's helpful to know what the options mean.

Lesson 01.prproj

A Premiere project file stores links to all the video, graphic, and sound files you have imported.

Each item is displayed in the Project panel as a clip. The term *clip* originally described a section of celluloid film (lengths of film were literally clipped to separate them from a roll), but these days it refers to any item in the project, regardless of the type of media. You could have an audio clip or an image sequence clip, for example.

Clips displayed in the Project panel appear to be media files, but they are actually only links to those files. It's helpful to understand that a clip displayed in the Project panel and the media file it links to are two separate things. For example, you can delete one without affecting the other (more on this later).

When working on a project, you will create at least one *sequence*—that is, a series of clips that play, one after another, sometimes overlapping, with special effects, titles, and sound, to form your completed creative work. While editing, you will choose which parts of your clips to use and in which order they'll play.

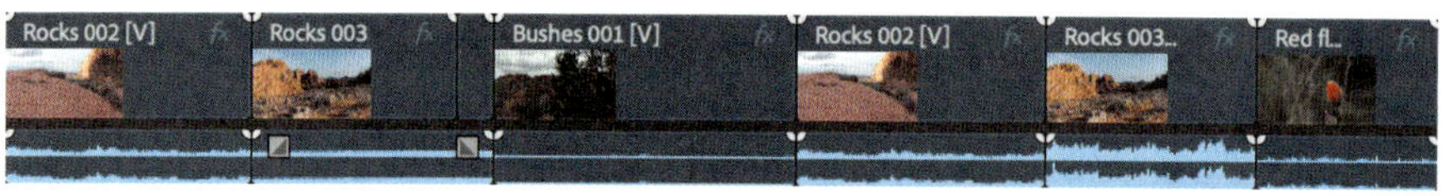

The beauty of nonlinear editing with Premiere is that you can change your mind about almost anything, at any time.

Premiere project files have the file extension *.prproj*.

Starting a new project is straightforward. You create a new project file, import media, choose sequence settings, and start editing. The first three of these steps can be completed all at once!

When you create a new project, you can choose to automatically create a sequence with settings that match your media. You can also create one or more sequences later. Whichever method you choose, your sequence(s) will have playback settings (such as frame rate and frame size).

It's important to understand how the sequence settings change the way Premiere plays your video and audio clips (all clips can be automatically adjusted, if necessary, to match the sequence settings). If you decide to configure sequence settings manually, you can speed up the process by using a preset to choose the settings and then make adjustments, if necessary, for your particular project.

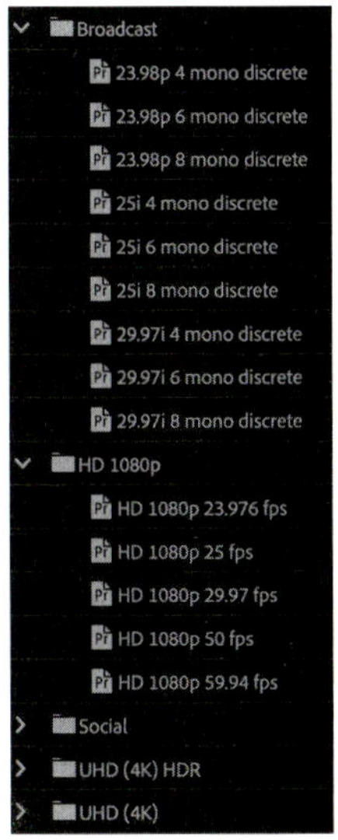

Even if you create a sequence automatically based on your media, it's helpful to understand all of the settings because you may discover you need to adjust one or more options for a particular project.

It's helpful to know the kind of video and audio your camera records because your sequence settings will usually be based on your source footage to minimize conversion during playback. Sequence settings presets are named after delivery standards like Broadcast, HD, Social, and UHD. Still, you'll usually want to choose an option that is as close as possible to your original media, leaving any conversion to the final output stage.

In this lesson, you'll learn how to create a new Premiere project and choose sequence settings. You'll also learn about different kinds of audio tracks and what preview files are.

About seconds and frames

When a camera records video, it captures a series of still images of the action. It captures enough images each second for the result to look like moving video during playback. Each picture is called a *frame*, and the number of frames each second is usually called the *frames per second* (fps) or the recording or playback *frame rate*.

The fps will vary depending on your camera/video format and settings. It could be any number, including 23.976, 24, 25, 29.97, 30, 50, or 59.94. Most cameras allow you to choose between more than one frame rate and more than one frame size. It's important to know the recording settings for your media so you can be sure you have selected the correct playback options in Premiere.

Note: To ensure that the tools function and the defaults are set exactly as described in this lesson, reset the Premiere preferences by holding any modifier key (such as Shift) while launching the application, selecting Reset App Preferences, and then clicking Continue in the Reset Options dialog box.

Creating a project

Let's begin by creating a new project.

1 Launch Premiere. The Home screen appears. Click the magnifying glass at the top right of the Home screen to open a multipurpose Search screen. If you enter text into the text box at the top of the screen and press Return (macOS) or Enter (Windows), Premiere will list previously opened project files whose names

contain the typed text, as well as suggest tutorials from Adobe Premiere Learn & Support that relate to the text. You must be connected to the internet to access the tutorials. Click Exit Search to return to the Home screen.

Notice that next to the magnifying glass icon, and a "gift box" icon you can click to learn about new features, is a thumbnail of your Adobe ID profile picture. If you just signed up, this may be a generic thumbnail. Click the button to manage your Creative Cloud account online.

2 Click New Project.

The New Project dialog box appears.

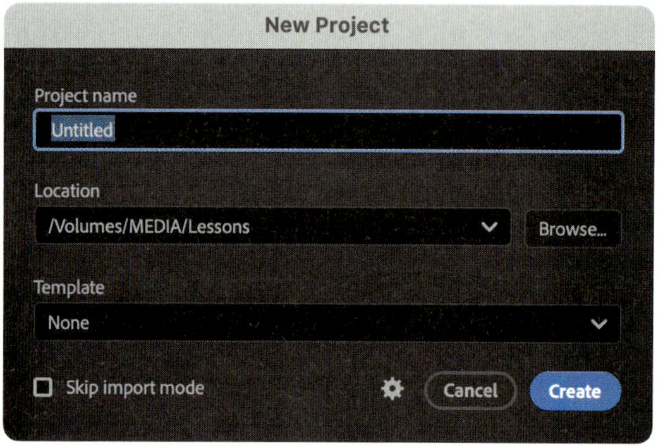

3 Enter the Project Name, **First Project**. In the Location menu, choose the Lessons folder. If this location is not listed, click Choose Location, browse to the Lessons folder, and click Select (macOS) or Save (Windows).

The Template menu offers several predefined custom project types to speed up getting ready to edit. You can add your own templates, which is useful if you expect to work on lots of similar projects. For this exercise, you'll set up the new project manually.

The New Project dialog box has an option to skip import mode. Keep this unselected so you can explore Import mode in the next step.

There's also a settings icon  you can click to open the Project Settings dialog box. You'll explore those settings later.

4 Click Create to open Premiere in Import mode, with project creation options displayed.

Premiere opens in Import mode, which serves two purposes.

While creating a new project or working on an existing project, this is the screen you'll use to browse and import media. You can also automate creating a new sequence.

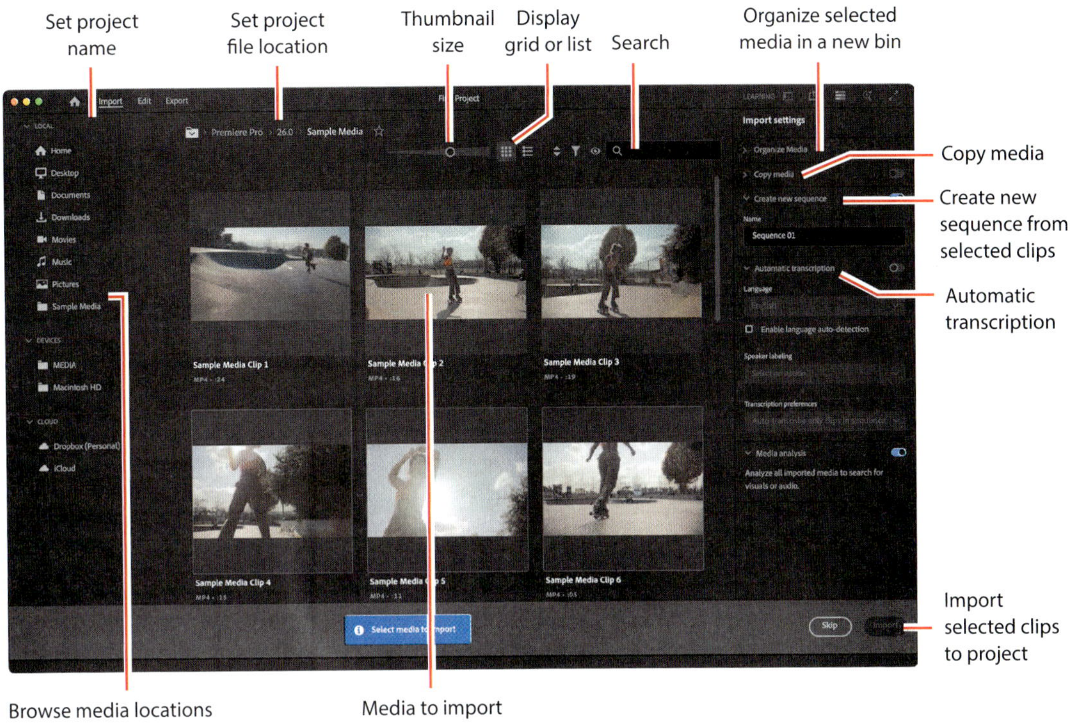

On the left side, you can browse the various storage locations on your system. When you select a location, media files stored there will appear in the middle section of the screen. By default, sample media is displayed.

You can change the size of thumbnails and switch between displaying thumbnails in a grid or a list of items using the controls at the top.

Tip: The Sample Media folder is one of the storage locations available on the left in Import mode. You can use this media to try out editing and finishing in Premiere.

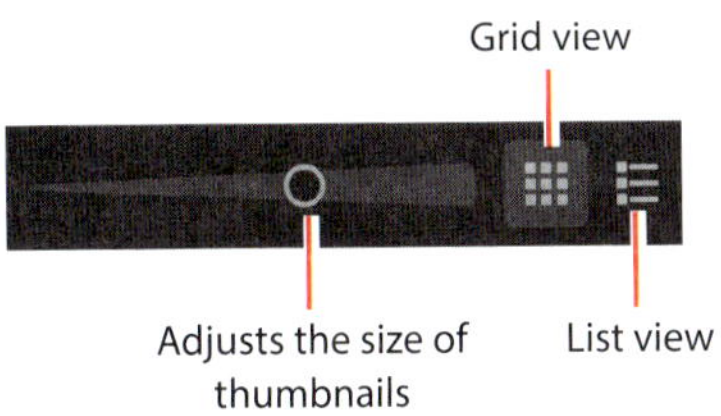

On the right side, there are five options you can select to speed up project creation. You can expand and collapse the options for each by clicking the chevrons:

- **Organize Media:** In a project, clips can be organized in containers that work a lot like folders, called *bins*. With the Add To New Bin option selected, a bin will be added to the project automatically with selected clips placed inside it.

- **Copy Media:** Copies of the media files you have selected will be placed in the location of your choice. Premiere will then use these copies in your project, not the original files. This can be useful if you are adding media from external drives or camera storage that you might disconnect later.
- **Create New Sequence:** Automatically create a sequence with settings that match the first clip you select (for more information on sequence settings, see "Setting up a sequence" later in the lesson).
- **Automatic Transcription:** Automatically transcribe clips to allow Text-Based Editing techniques and fast caption creation.
- **Media Analysis:** Perform detailed analysis of your media to make searching for content easier. Information from the analysis is stored in the separate PRIN file mentioned earlier, with the same name as your project file.

For now, you'll create a new project and sequence with just three clips so you can explore the important settings relating to project sequence setup.

Tip: Be careful not to single-click a folder when you want to browse inside it. If you do, you will select the entire contents of the folder. You can reverse this by single-clicking the folder again or by clicking to select and then right-clicking the folder where it appears at the bottom of the window and choosing Clear All.

5 From the list of storage locations on the left side of the interface, select the location for the Lessons folder.

When browsing and selecting clips in the middle of the window, clicking and double-clicking have very different effects:

- A single-click selects a clip or entire folder and its contents.
- A double-click selects a clip or browse inside a folder.

In the middle of the window, browse to the folder Lessons/Assets/Video And Audio Files/Theft Unexpected. Make sure the display is set to Grid View so you can view the clip thumbnails.

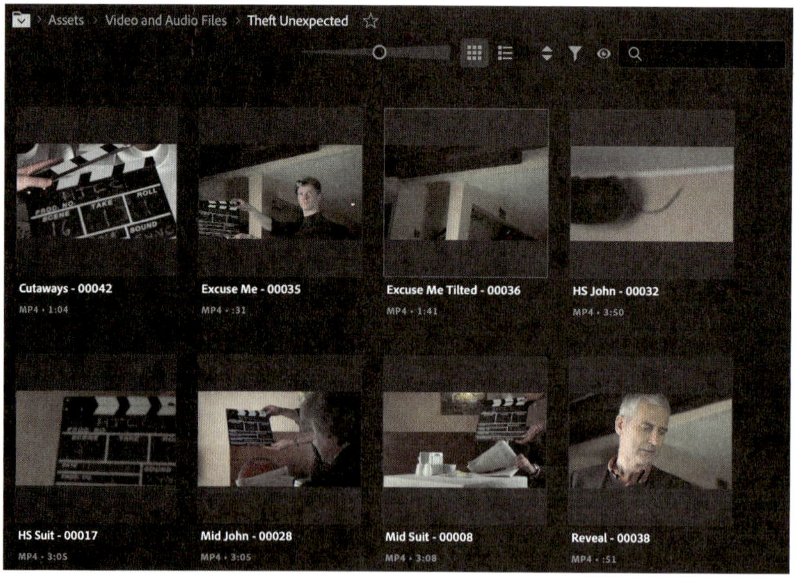

6 Click the Excuse Me – 00035 clip once to select it. Notice you can hover over thumbnails in the grid view to see a preview of their contents.

When you select the clip, Premiere highlights it in blue and adds it to a collection at the bottom of the window.

7 Single-click the clip HS John - 00032 and the clip Mid Suit - 00008. Notice all three clips are highlighted in blue and displayed in the collection at the bottom of the window.

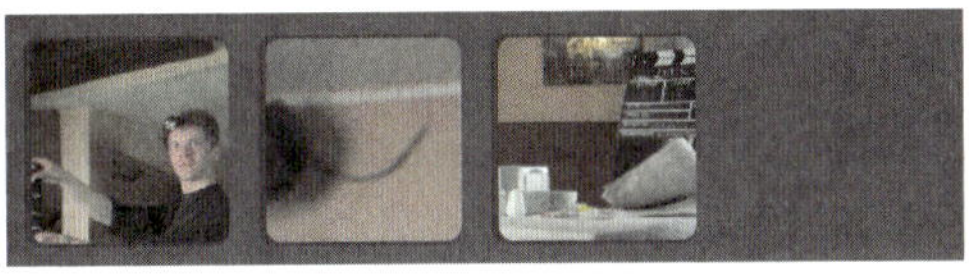

You have now selected three clips to include in your new project. It's not necessary to select media while creating a project, but it can speed up the process, particularly if you are working on a simple project with few clips.

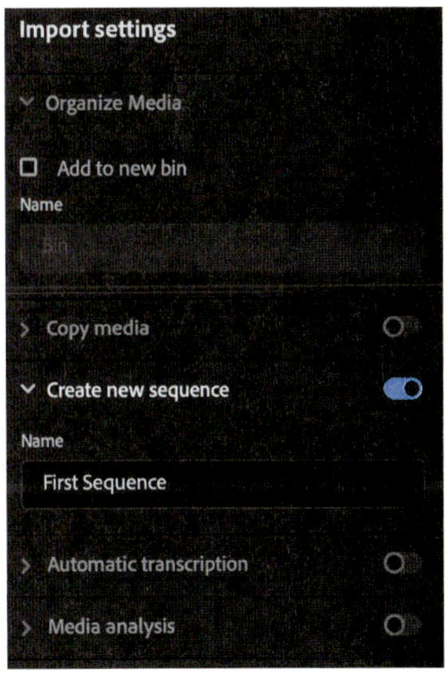

8 On the right side of the window, in the Import Settings area, make sure Add To New Bin, Copy Media, Automatic Transcription, and Media Analysis are all not selected. You may need to click the chevron for a settings heading to reveal its options.

Make sure Create New Sequence is selected.

Then, expand the Create New Sequence options and enter the name **First Sequence**.

9 Click Import to open your new project and import the selected clips.

You just created a project with three clips already added along with a sequence, ready and waiting for you to begin editing.

10 Until now, you have been selecting and resetting workspaces using the Window menu, but there's a handy shortcut: In the upper-right corner, click the Workspaces menu and choose Editing.

11 To ensure you are viewing the default version of the Editing workspace, open the Workspaces menu again, and choose Reset To Saved Layout.

12 This is probably a good time to save your work. Choose File > Save.

Setting up a sequence

In your Premiere project, you will create a sequence (or several sequences) into which you'll place video clips, audio clips, and graphics. A *sequence* is an item that appears in your project, a little like an empty bucket that you will fill with clips. Just like media files, sequences have a frame rate (frames per second) and frame size (image resolution). If a clip has a frame rate or frame size that doesn't match the sequence settings, it's converted during playback. This automatic process of adapting all clips in a sequence to match the sequence settings (if necessary) is called *conforming*.

Each sequence in your project can have different settings. Unless you plan to distribute with a different aspect ratio (to deliver vertical video made from horizontal video clips, for example), you'll generally want to choose settings that match your original media as precisely as possible. This minimizes conforming during playback. Matching the settings reduces the work your system must do to play your clips, improving playback performance and maximizing image quality.

If you're editing a project with mixed-format media, you may have to choose which media to match with your sequence settings. You can mix formats easily, but because playback performance improves when the clips match the sequence settings, you'll often choose settings that match the majority of your media files.

If the first clip you add to a sequence does not match the settings of your sequence, Premiere checks if you would like to change the sequence settings automatically to match it.

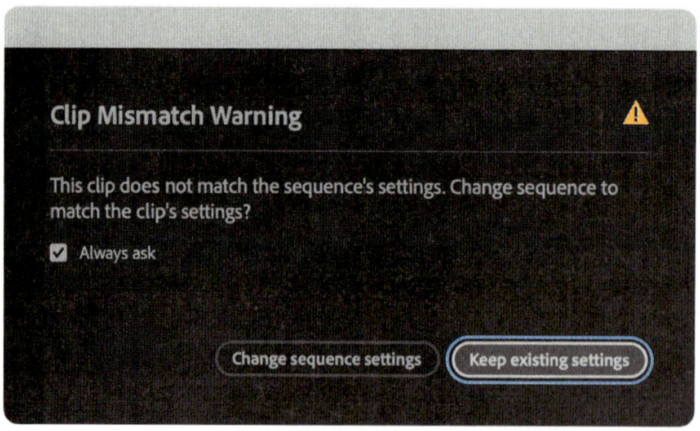

There are a lot of available file types, codecs, and formats used in video production and post-production. Premiere can work natively with a wide range of video and audio formats and codecs and will often play mismatched formats smoothly.

However, when Premiere has to adjust video for playback because of mismatched sequence settings, your editing system must work harder to play the video, and this will impact real-time performance (you might experience more dropped frames—frames that aren't played—that make the playback appear to freeze occasionally). It's worth taking the time before you start editing to make sure the sequence settings closely match your original media files.

The essential factors for video formats are always the same: the number of frames per second, the frame size (the number of pixels in the picture horizontally and vertically), and the audio format (Stereo, Mono, or 5.1 Surround Sound). If you were to turn your sequence into a media file with matching settings, then the frame rate, audio format, frame size, and so on for the new file would all match whichever settings you chose when you created the sequence.

When you output your sequence to a file, you can choose any format you like and Premiere will apply a conversion as necessary (for more on exporting, see Lesson 16, "Exporting Frames, Clips, and Sequences").

Creating a sequence that automatically matches your source

If you're not sure what sequence settings you should choose, don't worry. Premiere can create a sequence based on your clip. In fact, you already made a sequence this way, while creating your first project.

You can also automatically create a new sequence with matching settings in the Project panel. At the bottom of the Project panel, you'll find the New Item menu. You may need to resize the panel to see the icon. Use this menu to create new items for your project, including sequences, bars and tone, and color mattes (usually full-screen color graphics useful for backgrounds).

To automatically create a sequence with format settings that match your media, drag any clip (or multiple clips, or even a whole bin) in the Project panel onto the New Item menu. A new sequence will be created with the same name as the first clip selected (or the bin you dragged), as well as a matching frame size and frame rate.

You can also select one or more clips, right-click your selection, and choose New Sequence From Clip.

Using this method, you can be confident your sequence settings will work with your media. If the Timeline panel is empty, you can also drag a clip (or multiple clips) into it to create a sequence with matching settings.

Choosing the correct preset

If you know exactly the settings you need for a new sequence, you can manually adjust the sequence settings after choosing a preset.

> **Tip:** You can also press the keyboard shortcut Command+N (macOS) or Ctrl+N (Windows) to open the New Sequence dialog box.

1 Click the New Item menu at the lower-right corner of the Project panel now and choose Sequence.

The New Sequence dialog box that opens has five tabs: Sequence Presets, Settings, Color Management, Tracks, and VR Video.

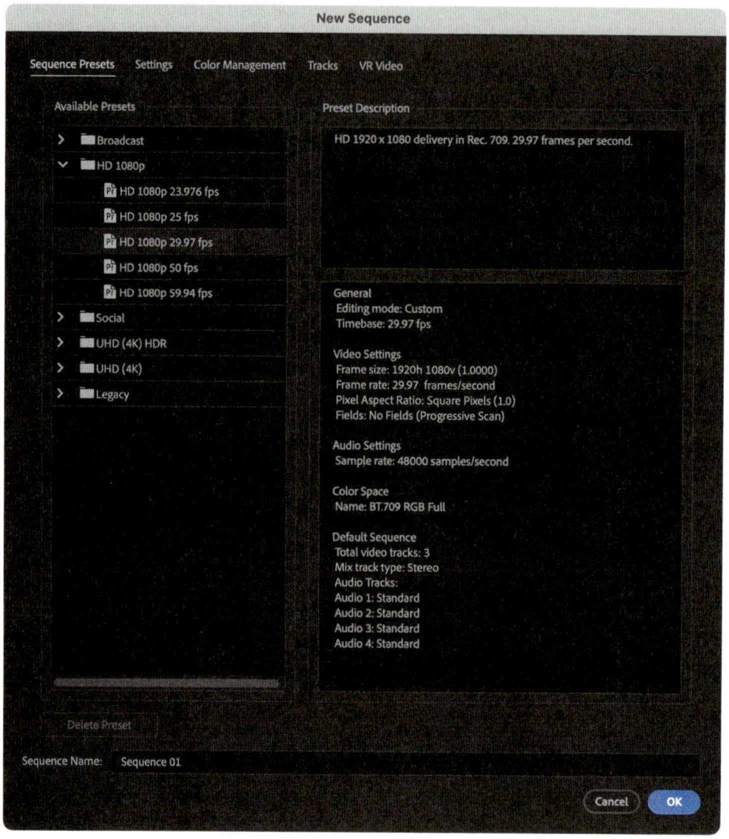

When you choose a preset, Premiere applies several settings that control the way video clips will be displayed when added to the sequence. After choosing a preset, you can re-configure it on the Settings tab if necessary.

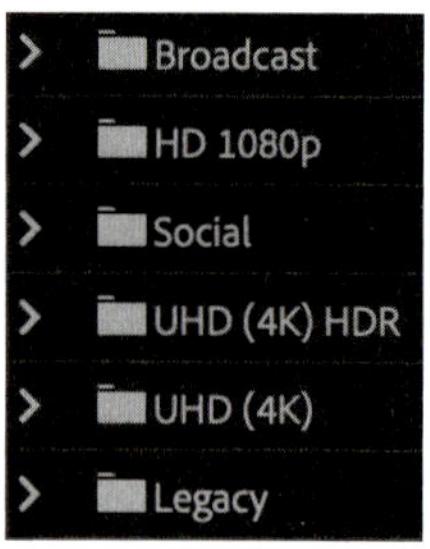

> **Note:** Although it's best to choose sequence settings that match your source media, the Preset Description area on the right side of the Sequence Presets tab describes the intended delivery format.

You'll find a wide range of preset configuration options for the most commonly used media formats, grouped based on delivery formats. There are also several legacy presets used by previous versions of Premiere.

You can click the chevron to see specific formats in a group. These are typically designed around frame rates and frame sizes. Let's look at an example.

2 Click the chevron next to the group HD 1080p.

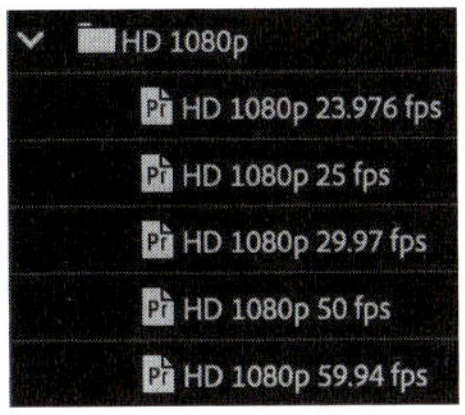

There are five options based on frame rates, all with the same frame size. Remember that video cameras can often shoot video using multiple frame rates.

3 Select the HD 1080p 29.97 fps preset by clicking its name.

For this sequence, use the default settings. Take a moment to familiarize yourself with the description displayed on the right.

4 Notice the entry in the Sequence Name box: Sequence 01. You can change this to help stay organized, but for now click OK to create the sequence.

You now have two sequences in the Project panel, First Sequence and Sequence 01, and they have confusingly similar names! Even with a simple project of this kind, it's clear that staying organized is important.

5 Choose File > Save.

Congratulations! You have made a new project with Premiere.

Codecs and formats

Codec is a shortening of the words *coder* and *decoder*. It's the way video and audio information is stored and replayed.

A file used to store video and/or audio, such as QuickTime MOV, MP4, or MXF, is a *container* that can contain one of many different video and audio codec configurations.

The media file is referred to as the *wrapper*, and the video and audio inside the file, stored using a codec, are sometimes referred to as the *essence* inside the wrapper.

When you output your finished sequence to a file, you'll choose a format, a file type, and a codec.

The word *format* has multiple meanings depending on the context.

A format is a frame rate, frame size, audio sample rate, and so on. The word is also used to describe a type of media file or a collection of settings that incorporate both the visual and sound settings and the type of codec used, as well as its configuration.

For clarity, in this book we will generally use the word *format* to describe the frame rate, frame size, audio sample rate, and so on.

Customizing sequence settings

Once you've selected the sequence preset that most closely matches your source video, you may want to adjust the settings to meet a particular delivery requirement or in-house workflow. Let's take a look at those settings.

▶ **Tip:** You created a new sequence using the File menu this time. There are often several ways to achieve the same goal in Premiere.

1 Choose File > New > Sequence.

2 Choose the HD 1080p 29.97 fps preset again by clicking its name.

Premiere will automatically conform footage you add to your timeline so that it matches your sequence settings, giving you a standard frame rate and frame size, regardless of the original clip format. This makes the sequence settings a critical part of your project configuration.

3 Click Settings at the top of the dialog box.

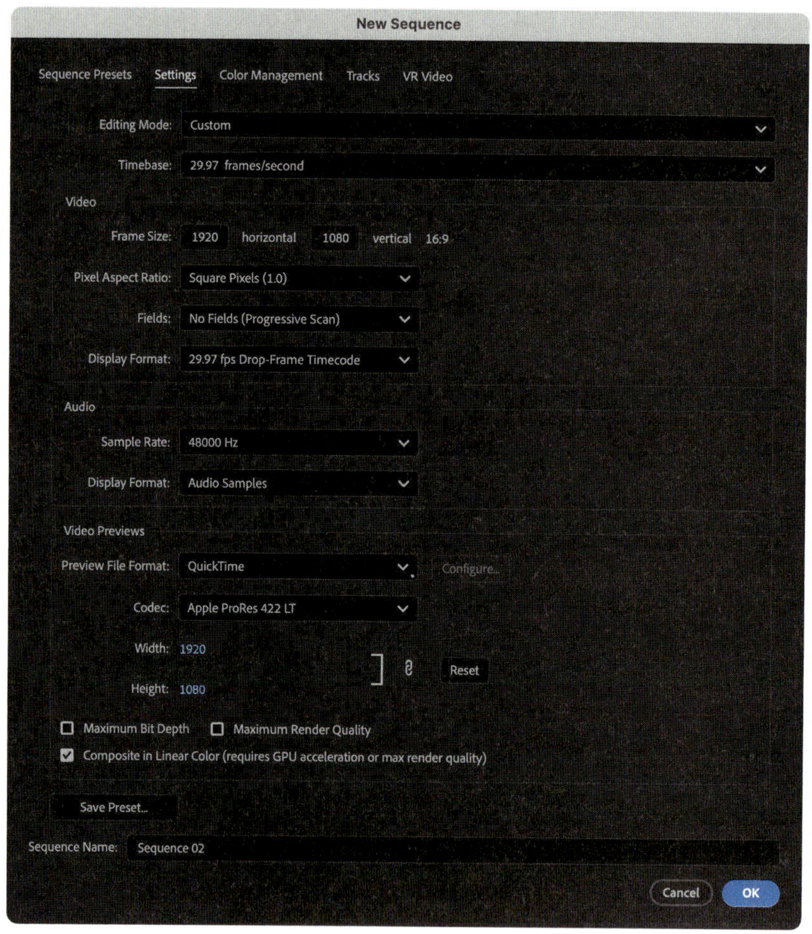

You chose a 29.97 fps (frames per second) preset, which is used when broadcasting NTSC video on traditional TV networks.

Creating a sequence preset

Although the standard presets usually work, you may sometimes need to create a custom preset. To do so quickly, first choose a sequence preset that matches your media closely, and then make custom selections in the Settings and Tracks areas of the New Sequence dialog box. Having adjusted the settings, you can save your custom preset for future use by clicking the Save Preset button.

When you save a preset, give it a name in the Save Sequence Preset dialog box, add notes if you want, and click OK. The preset will appear in a Custom folder along with the other sequence presets.

4 If your media matches the selected preset, it probably won't be necessary to change the settings. Take a moment to look at each setting in the New Sequence dialog box to build familiarity with the choices required to configure a sequence.

 The new sequence you are creating is intended for online distribution only, so change the Timebase to **30 frames/second** to accurately measure playback duration.

Tip: If you wanted to produce a square video for social media, you could change the frame size to 1080x1080 (or any other square resolution). You could also begin with the Social Media Square 1x1.

Maximum Bit Depth and Maximum Render Quality sequence settings

When you're editing with GPU acceleration (that's when dedicated computer graphics hardware performs some of the visual effects rendering and playback), advanced algorithms are used, and effects that support it always render in 32-bit color—which is very high quality.

When working without GPU acceleration, you can enable Maximum Bit Depth in the sequence settings, and Premiere will render effects at the maximum quality possible. For many effects, this means 32-bit floating-point color, which allows for trillions of color combinations. This is the best possible quality for your effects but is more work for your computer, so you may get lower performance in real-time playback (unwanted video freezing during playback).

If you enable the Maximum Render Quality option or if you have GPU acceleration enabled in the project's settings, Premiere uses a more advanced system for visual adjustments such as scaling, rotation, and repositioning. Without this option, you might see minor artifacts or video noise in the picture when you perform these kinds of transforms.

Both of these options can be turned off or on at any time, so you can edit without them to maximize performance and then enable them when you output your finished work. Even with both options enabled you can use real-time effects and expect reasonable performance from Premiere.

For a more detailed explanation of these settings, see *blog.frame.io/2021/06/07/premiere-pro-max-render-quality-max-bit-depth*.

The Editing Mode menu can be used to limit the options available to settings that best match specific types of camera media. Some options will make several menus unavailable to help avoid choosing incompatible options. For complete flexibility, keep the menu set to Custom.

5 Click the Color Management tab to view those settings.

6 Keep the Color Setup menu set to Direct Rec. 709 (SDR). See the sidebar "Color management" for more information about these options.

Click the Tracks tab to view those settings.

7 See "Understanding audio track types" for more information about audio tracks.

Color management

Premiere offers advanced tools for managing the way color is interpreted and presented. For most projects, you will choose Rec. 709 (SDR) color. If you are not familiar with the various color modes, gamuts, dynamic range options, and delivery standards, it's a pretty safe bet that choosing Rec. 709 will work for you.

Provided your Color Setup and Output Color Space settings are configured for the Rec. 709 standard, you can be confident that the automated color conversion technologies built into Premiere will correctly interpret your media and display it correctly in your sequence.

If you are familiar with these advanced color management options, you can configure them in the New Sequence dialog box and in the Lumetri Color panel Settings tab, which you will learn about in Lesson 13, "Applying Color Correction and Grading."

Understanding audio track types

When you add a video or audio clip to a sequence, you'll always put it on a *track* in the Timeline panel. Tracks are horizontal areas in the Timeline panel that hold clips in a particular position in time.

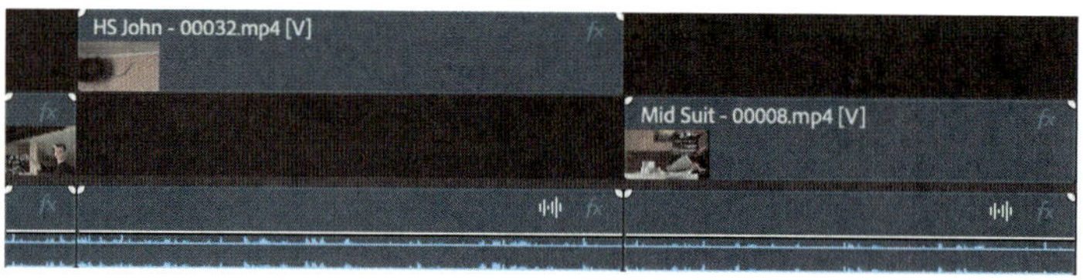

There is more than one video track, and video clips placed on an upper track will appear in front of clips on a lower track. For example, if you have a graphic on your second video track and a video clip on your first video track (below it), you'll see the graphic in front of the video.

The Tracks tab in the New Sequence dialog box allows you to preselect the track types for the new sequence. You can add or remove tracks at any time while editing, so these options are perhaps most useful when creating a custom sequence preset with names already assigned to audio tracks.

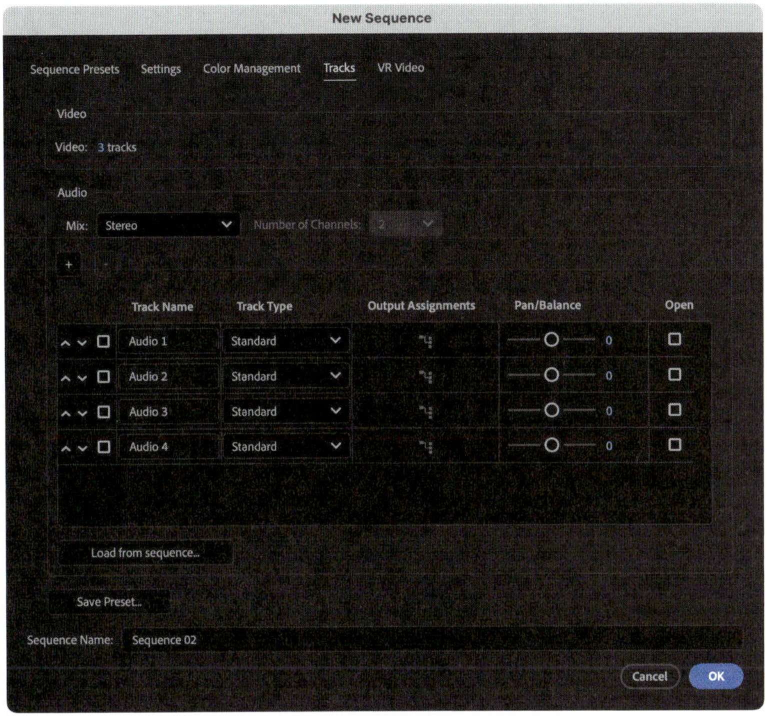

All audio tracks are played at the same time to create a combined audio mix. To create a mix, simply position your audio clips on different tracks, lined up in time. Narration, sound bites, sound effects, and music can be organized by putting them on different tracks. You can also rename tracks, making it easier to find your way around more complex sequences.

Premiere lets you specify how many video and audio tracks will be included when the new sequence is created. The setting you choose from the Mix menu configures the type of audio mix output your sequence will produce. This can be Stereo, 5.1, Multichannel, or Mono. You can't change this setting later, so choose carefully when creating a new sequence. For now, leave this set to Stereo (the default).

An individual audio track can be one of several types. Each track type is designed for a specific type of audio clip. When you choose a particular track type from the menu in the Track Type column, Premiere shows appropriate controls to make adjustments to the sound, based on the number of audio channels in the track. For example, stereo clips need different controls than 5.1 surround-sound clips.

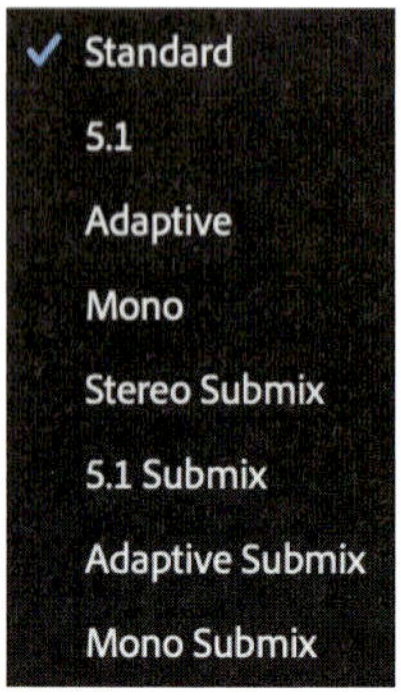

The types of audio tracks are:

- **Standard:** These tracks are for both mono and stereo audio clips.
- **5.1:** These tracks are for audio clips with 5.1 audio (the kind used for surround-sound mixes).
- **Adaptive:** Adaptive tracks are for mono, stereo, or multichannel audio and give you precise control over the output routing for each audio channel. For example, you could decide the track audio channel 3 should be output to your mix in channel 5. This workflow is used for multilingual TV, where precise control of audio channels is used at the point of transmission.
- **Mono:** This track type will accept only mono audio clips.

The Submix options available in the Track Type menu, which allow you to combine outputs from tracks, are used in advanced audio mixing workflows that are beyond the scope of this book.

You can't accidentally put an audio clip on the wrong kind of track. In fact, when you add a clip to a sequence, Premiere will automatically create the right kind of track if one doesn't exist already. You'll explore audio more in Lesson 10, "Editing and Mixing Audio."

For now, click Cancel to close the New Sequence dialog so you can explore more of the Premiere interface.

Exploring the Project Settings dialog box

Now that you have created a new project and added sequences and clips, let's explore the important options available in the Project Settings dialog box.

Tip: While creating a new project, you can click the Settings icon in the New Project dialog box to access the Project Settings.

Choose File > Project Settings > General to open the Project Settings dialog box for your current project. You can modify any of these settings at any time, so don't worry about getting things wrong.

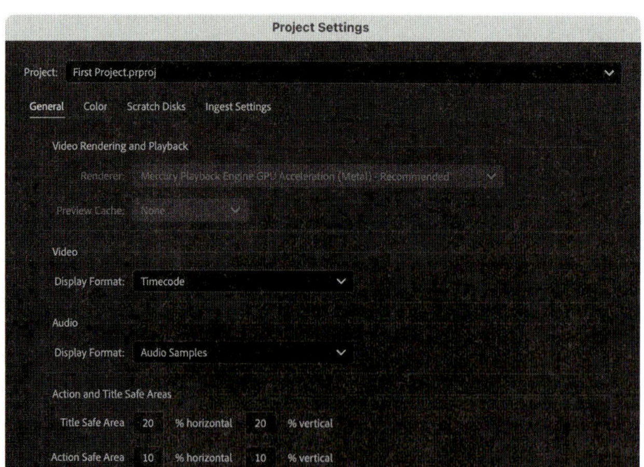

Choosing video rendering and playback settings

While you're working creatively with video clips in your sequences, it's likely you will apply some visual effects to adjust the appearance of your footage. Some special effects can be played immediately, combining your original video with the effect and displaying the results as soon as you click Play. When this happens, it's called *real-time playback*.

Real-time playback is desirable because it means you can watch the results of your creative choices right away, staying in your creative flow without waiting.

If you use lots of effects on a clip or if you use effects that are not designed for real-time playback, your computer may not be able to display the results at the full frame rate. Premiere will attempt to display your video clips, combined with the special effects, but it may not show every single frame each second. When this happens, it's described as *dropping* frames.

Premiere displays colored lines along the top of the Timeline panel, where you build sequences, to tell you when extra work is required to play back your video. No line, a green line, or a yellow line means Premiere expects to be able to play without dropping frames. A red line means Premiere expects to drop frames when playing that section of the sequence.

Note: A red line at the top of the Timeline panel doesn't mean frames definitely will be dropped. It just means visual adjustments aren't accelerated, so on a less powerful machine dropped frames are more likely.

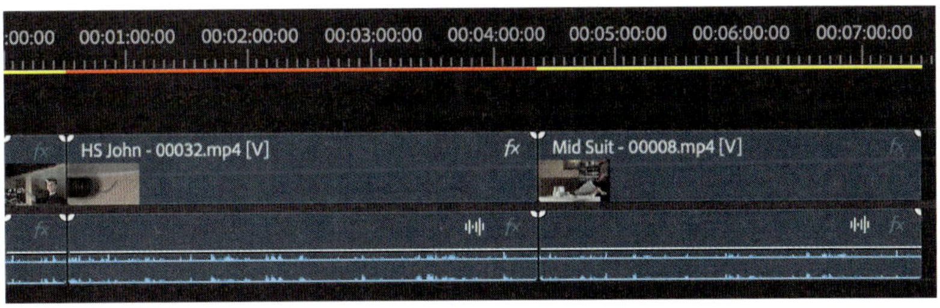

If you can't see every frame when you play your sequence, it's okay! It won't affect the final results. When you're done editing and you output your finished sequence, it'll be full quality, with all the frames intact (more on this in Lesson 16).

Real-time playback can make a difference to your editing experience and your ability to preview the effects you apply with confidence. If frames are being dropped, there is a simple solution: preview rendering.

Tip: Many menu items display a keyboard shortcut on the right. In this case, the shortcut for Render Effects In To Out is Return (macOS) or Enter (Windows).

When Premiere renders, it creates new media files that already have the effects applied and then plays back those files in place of the original footage. The rendered preview is a regular video file, so playback is at reasonable quality and full frame rate, without your computer having the extra work of applying the effects to clips while they play.

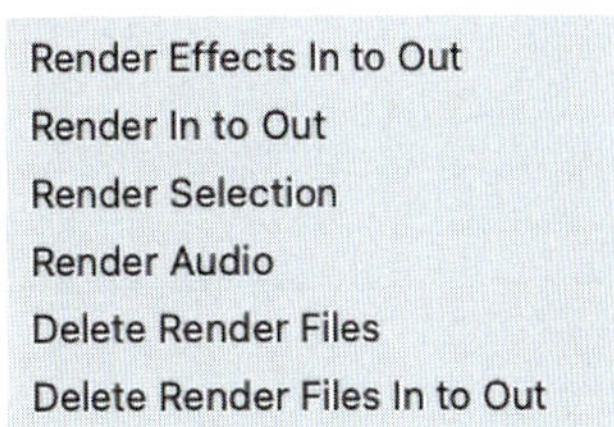

You render effects in a sequence by choosing a render command from the Sequence menu.

What do *rendering* and *real time* mean?

Rendering visual effects is a little like producing an artist's rendering with a pencil. Drawing an image takes up paper and time—both of which are limited resources.

When you render a section of a sequence, it takes time and the newly created media file takes up media storage space.

For example, imagine adding a complex third-party effect that does not support GPU acceleration to a video clip. The video-editing system you are using may not be able to both play the original video and display the results of the effect at the same time. In this situation, you'd have your system render the effect, creating a new temporary video file that looks like the original video combined with the visual effect that makes it brighter.

When your edited sequence plays, sections that are rendered display the newly rendered video file instead of the original clip (or clips). The process is invisible and seamless. In this example, the rendered file would look like the original video file but brighter.

When the part of your sequence with the brightened clip has finished playing, your system invisibly and seamlessly switches back from playing the preview file to playing the other original video files in the sequence.

Once a section of your sequence is rendered, you will be able to preview the results of your effect smoothly with the Playback Resolution set to Full.

Real-time playback, by contrast, is immediate! When using a real-time effect, your system plays the original video clip combined with the effect right away, without waiting for the effect to render. The only limitation with real-time performance is that the amount you can do without rendering depends on how powerful your system is. More effects require more work to play back, for example. You can dramatically improve real-time performance by using the right kind of graphics card.

Back in the Project Settings dialog box, in the Video Rendering And Playback settings on the General tab, if the Renderer menu is available, it means you have more than one graphics card to choose between.

Using the Mercury Playback Engine for GPU Acceleration, Premiere will send many rendering tasks to the graphics hardware on your computer, giving you lots of real-time effects and smooth preview playback of mixed formats in your sequences. If you have more than one graphics card available, you may see more than one option to use CUDA, OpenCL, or Metal (depending on your graphics hardware and your operating system).

Performance can vary, and some graphics hardware configurations allow multiple types of acceleration, so you may need to experiment to find the best option for your system. On macOS, you will only be able to use Metal. Some advanced system GPU configurations also allow you to choose a persistent Preview Cache in Premiere to improve playback. You'll want to experiment with this option for optimum playback performance.

Choose a GPU option now, if the menu is available.

Choosing the video and audio display formats

The next two areas of the General tab in the Project Settings dialog box allow you to choose how Premiere should display time for your video and audio clips.

You can choose to measure time for video clips using timecode, feet, and frames (for celluloid film), or you can just count the frames.

For audio clips, you can choose to measure time in samples per second or in milliseconds.

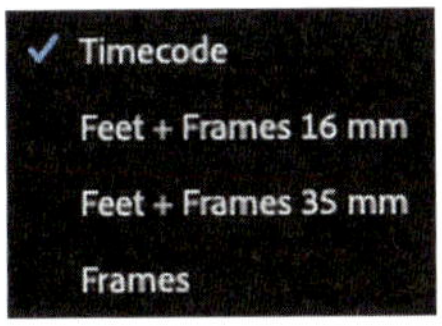

What is timecode?

Timecode is a universal system for counting hours, minutes, seconds, and individual frames of video. The same system is used by cameras, professional video recorders, and nonlinear editing systems around the world.

What is audio sampling?

When digital audio is recorded, the sound level (technically, the air pressure level) captured by the microphone is sampled thousands of times a second. During playback, each sample is replayed accurately to reproduce the sound.

In the case of most professional video cameras, audio sampling happens 48,000 times per second.

For now, choose the default options: From the Video Display Format menu, choose Timecode, and from the Audio Display Format menu, choose Audio Samples. For most projects, these are the options you'll use.

These settings don't change the way Premiere plays video or audio clips, only the way time measurement is displayed—and you can change the settings at any time.

Action- and title-safe areas

When creating projects intended for home TVs, you'll probably need to compensate for the way TVs crop the edge of the picture.

Traditionally, there are two areas to be concerned with:

- **Action-safe:** The area that most TVs might crop the image to; keep important image content inside this area.
- **Title-safe:** The area that really badly calibrated TVs might crop the image to; keep titles inside this area so they will always be readable and not cropped by the edge of the screen.

Premiere can display on-screen overlay guides to indicate the title-safe and action-safe areas. Before using these guides, however, carefully consider the type of screen you are delivering for. Modern screens, for example, have smaller margins than older displays, showing more of the image. See Lesson 4, "Organizing Media," to learn more about configuring on-screen overlays.

Color settings

Premiere offers support for High-Dynamic Range (HDR) video, which allows you to capture and produce video content with much more dynamic range between the dark and light areas of the frame as well as more saturated colors. Full end-to-end HDR workflows are beyond the scope of this book but is well worth exploring, as it is quickly becoming an industry standard for broadcast and online video delivery.

Producing HDR content requires a camera capable of capturing the content, an editing system that supports it (Premiere), and a screen capable of displaying it.

The Color tab provides advanced options for handling the interpretation and display of color and brightness information in clips and sequences. There are shortcuts for these settings in the Lumetri Color panel, which you will explore in Lesson 13, "Applying Color Correction and Grading."

If you are working with mixed media files, recorded using different color spaces (including log), consider enabling the Color Manage Auto Detected Log and Raw Media option. This allows Premiere to automatically identify clip color spaces and adjust them for playback according to your color settings.

If you choose the Enable Color Space Aware Effects option, effects will process colors correctly no matter what the working color space is set to. Without this option selected, all effects assume the color space to be Rec. 709.

For now, click the Scratch Disks tab to view the options.

Setting up the scratch disks

Whenever Premiere renders special effects, saves backup copies of the project file, downloads content from Adobe Stock, or imports animated Motion Graphics templates, or whenever you record a voiceover, it creates new files.

The various *scratch disks* are the storage locations where Premiere stores these files. The name comes from scratch *paper*, used to temporarily capture notes. Although they are described as disks, they are actually folders. Some of the files that are stored will be temporary, and some will be new media created in Premiere or imported.

Scratch disks can be stored in any subfolder in your system. Scratch disks can be located all in the same place or in separate locations, depending on your hardware and workflow requirements. If you're working with really large media files, you may get a performance boost by putting each scratch disk on a physically separate hard drive.

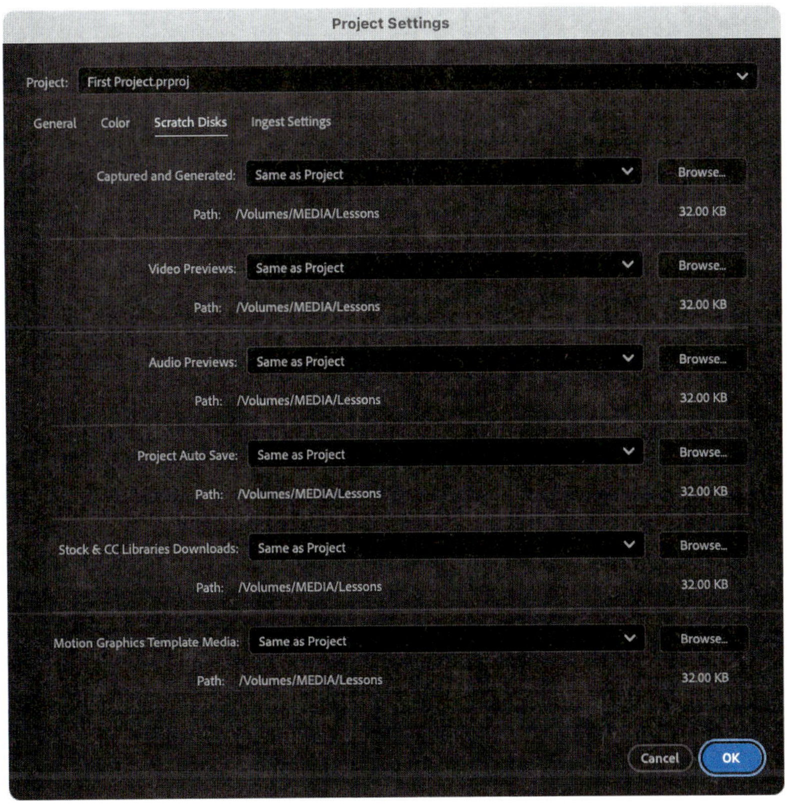

There are generally two approaches to storage for video editing:

- **Project-based setup:** All associated media files are stored with the project file in the same folder. This is the default option in the Scratch Disks menus and the simplest to manage.

- **System-based setup:** Media files associated with multiple projects are saved to one central location (often high-speed network-based storage), and the project file is saved to another location. This might include storing different kinds of media files in different locations.

To change the location of the scratch disk for a particular type of data, choose a location from the menu next to the data type. The choices are:

- **Documents:** Stores the scratch disk in the Documents folder in your system user account, using a subfolder for Premiere.
- **Same As Project:** Stores the scratch disk with the project file. This is the default option.
- **[Custom]:** Enables you to specify any location. This option is automatically chosen if you click Browse and choose a specific location for the scratch disk.

Below each Scratch Disk location menu, a file path shows the current setting and the space available at that location.

Your scratch disks might be stored on local hard drives inside your computer or on a network-based remote storage system; any storage location your computer has access to will work. However, the speed and responsiveness of your scratch disks can have a big impact on both playback and rendering performance—choose fast storage if possible.

Using a project-based setup

By default, Premiere keeps newly created media together with the associated project file (this is the Same As Project option in the Scratch Disk menus). Keeping everything together this way makes finding relevant files simple.

It also makes staying organized easier if you move media files into the same folder before you import them into the project. When you're finished with your project, you can remove everything from your system by deleting the single folder your project file is stored in.

You can use subfolders to keep your project media, notes, scripts, and associated assets organized.

There's a downside: Storing your media files on the same drive as your project file means the drive has to work a little harder while you edit, and this can impact playback performance on slower drives.

Using a system-based setup

Some editors prefer to have all their media stored in a single location, for all projects. Others choose to store their capture folders and preview folders in a different location from their project. This is a common choice in editing facilities where multiple editors share several editing systems, all connected to the same network-based storage.

There's a downside with this setup too: Once you finish editing, it's likely you'll want to gather everything together for archiving. This is slower and more complex when your media files are distributed across multiple storage locations. See the online bonus lesson, "Managing Your Projects," for more information.

Typical drive setup and network-based storage

Although all file types can coexist on a single storage drive, a typical editing system will have two storage drives: Drive 1, dedicated to the operating system and programs, and Drive 2 dedicated to media, including captured video and audio, video and audio preview files, still images, and exported media. For even better performance, a third storage drive, preferably a solid-state drive (SSD), can be dedicated to temporary Media Cache files.

Modern storage drives can be so fast that you may never notice any impact on playback performance when storing everything on one drive. Nonetheless, it can make project organization simpler to use a separate drive for media, and you are likely to see an impact when working with particularly large media files, like 8K RAW.

Some storage systems use local computer networks to share storage between multiple systems. If this is the case for you, check with your system administrators to make sure you have the right settings and then check the performance.

Setting up a Project Auto Save location

In addition to choosing where new media files are created, you can set the location to store automatically saved project backup files. These additional copies of your project file are created in the background while you work. Choose a location from the Project Auto Save menu on the Scratch Disks tab.

Storage drives occasionally fail, and you may lose files stored on them without warning. In fact, any computer engineer will tell you that if you have only one copy of a file, you can't count on having the file at all! For this reason, it's a great idea to set the Project Auto Save location to a physically separate storage location.

If you use a synchronized file sharing service like Dropbox, OneDrive, iCloud, or Google Drive, storing your auto-save files using that service will mean you always have access to all your automatically saved project files.

Note: For this project, leave all your scratch disks set to the default option: Same As Project.

Creative Cloud Libraries downloads

The Libraries panel provides access to media assets that can be shared between projects and with other users. Assets can be dragged from the Libraries panel into the Project panel or Timeline panel to add them to your current project.

Motion Graphics template media

Premiere can import and display prebuilt animated Motion Graphics templates and titles that have been created with After Effects or Premiere. When you import a Motion Graphics template into the current project, a copy will be stored in the location you choose.

Choosing ingest settings

Professional editors describe adding media to a project as *importing* or *ingesting*. The two words are often used interchangeably but actually have different meanings.

When you *import* a media file into a Premiere project, a clip is created in the project that is linked to the original file. The media file stays in its current location, and you're ready to include the clip in a sequence.

If you select one of the options in the Action menu on the Ingest Settings tab or select Copy Media while in Import mode, things are a little bit different. The original media file may also be copied to a different location (which is useful for keeping your media files organized) and/or converted to a new format and codec before it's imported into your Premiere project.

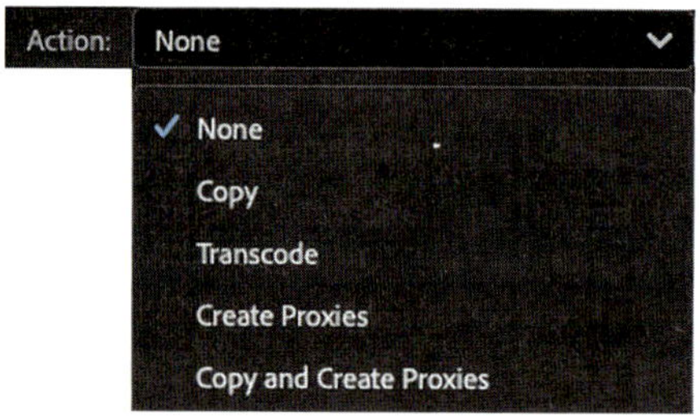

From the Ingest menu you can choose to:

- **Copy** the media files to a new storage location. This option is useful if you want to be sure all your media is in one folder.
- **Transcode** the media files to a new codec and/or format. This option is useful if you choose to standardize your media as part of a larger-scale organization-wide workflow.
- **Create Proxies** of the media file. This option creates lower-resolution copies of media files that are easier for a lower-powered computer to play and that take up less storage space. The original media is always available too, and you can switch between the full-quality and proxy-quality files whenever you like.

- **Copy And Create Proxies** to copy the media files to a new location and create proxies for them in a single step.

You'll be exploring these settings in Lesson 3, "Importing Media." They can be changed at any time; for now, leave the Action menu set to None.

Now that you have checked that the settings are correct for this project, click OK to apply any changes. Save, and close the project by choosing File > Close Project.

Note: There are several ways to import clips into a project. Once you enable the ingest options, Premiere applies them regardless of the import method you use. Note that existing clips that have already been imported into your project will not have new ingest options applied automatically.

VR video

Premiere offers exceptional support for 360° video and 180° video. Both are often described as *VR video* or *immersive video*, where multiple cameras or an extremely wide lens is used to capture a video image that can be viewed with a VR headset to create an immersive experience.

On the VR Video tab in the New Sequence dialog box, you can specify the angle of view captured so Premiere can accurately display the image.

VR video is beyond the scope of this book, but it is well worth exploring when you have mastered the basics of video editing.

Review questions

1 What is the purpose of the Settings tab in the New Sequence dialog box?

2 How should you choose a sequence preset?

3 What is timecode?

4 How do you create a custom sequence preset?

5 How can you choose where to store temporary files created automatically while editing?

Review answers

1 The Settings tab is used to customize an existing sequence preset or to create a new custom preset.

2 You will generally get better playback performance by choosing a preset that matches your original footage to minimize conversion during playback. If you are working with multiple source media formats or you know your delivery format already, you may prefer to choose a preset that is ready for delivery. Premiere makes this easy by describing the presets in terms of delivery standards.

3 Timecode is the universal system for measuring time in hours, minutes, seconds, and frames. The number of frames per second varies depending on the recording format.

4 When you've chosen the settings you want for your custom preset on the Settings tab in the New Sequence dialog box, click the Save Preset button, give the preset a name and a description, and click OK.

5 Use the settings on the Scratch Disks tab of the Project Settings dialog box to specify locations for newly created files.

3 IMPORTING MEDIA

Lesson overview

In this lesson, you'll learn how to do the following:

- Use the Media Browser and Import mode to add video files.
- Use the Import command to load graphic files, including files from Photoshop and Illustrator.
- Work with proxy media.
- Record a voice-over.
- Choose where to store cache files.

This lesson will take about 75 minutes to complete. To get the files used in this lesson, refer to the instructions in "Accessing the lesson files and Web Edition" in the "Getting Started" section at the beginning of this book. Store the files on your computer in a convenient location.

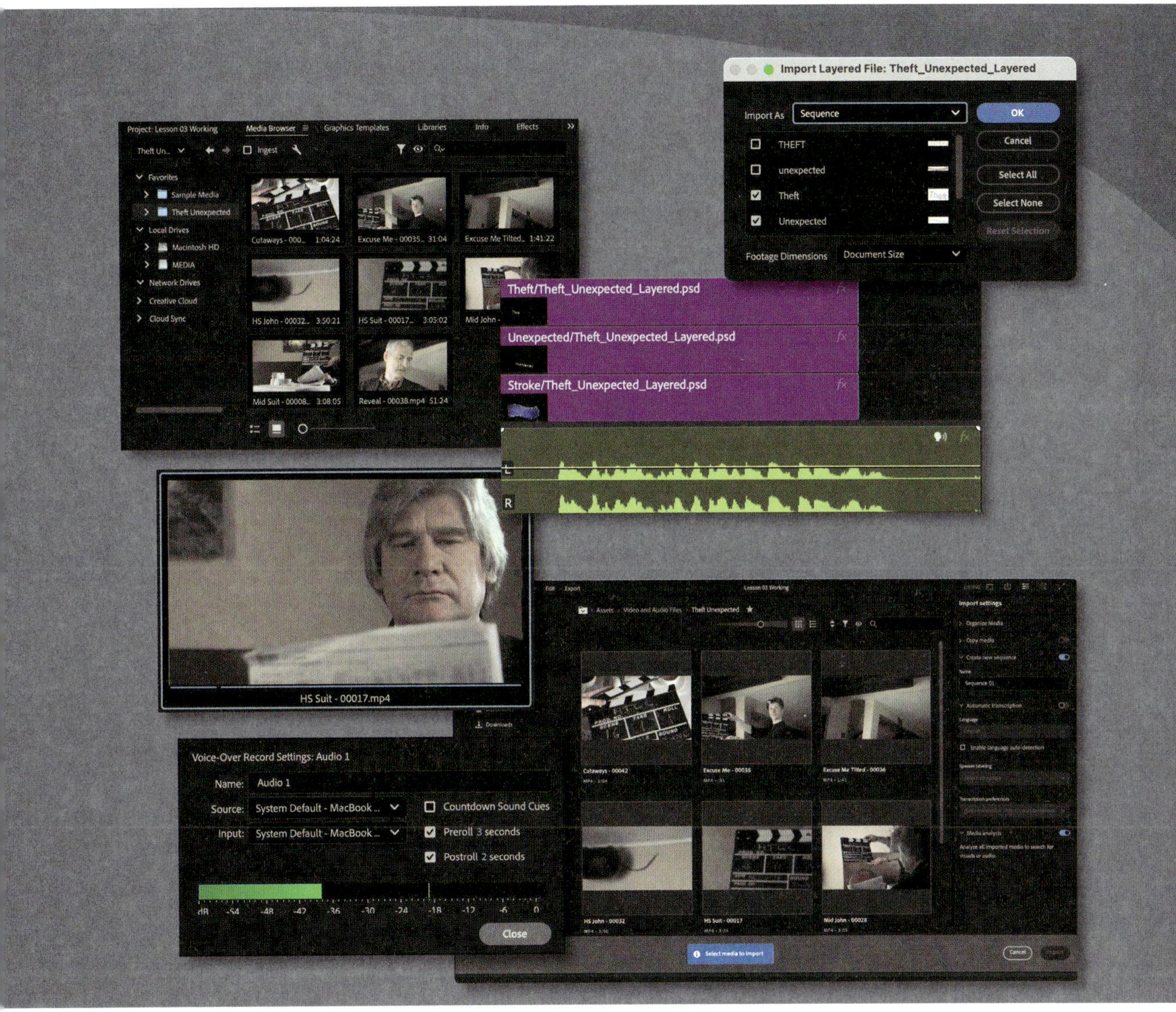

However you approach editing sequences, importing clips to the Project panel and getting them organized are the first steps. In this lesson, you'll learn multiple methods for browsing and importing media.

Starting the lesson

Note: To ensure that the tools function and the defaults are set exactly as described in this lesson, reset the Premiere preferences by holding any modifier key (such as Shift) while launching the application, selecting Reset App Preferences, and then clicking Continue in the Reset Options dialog box.

Before creating a sequence, you'll usually import media files into your project. This might include video footage, animation files, narration, music, atmospheric sound, graphics, or photos. In brief, anything that you might incorporate into a sequence will be imported into your project first.

With the exception of the graphics, titles, and captions that you create in Premiere, items in sequences always also appear in the Project panel. For example, if you import a video clip directly to a sequence, it will also automatically appear in the Project panel. If you delete that clip in the Project panel, it will also be removed from sequences that it appears in (you'll be given a warning and the option to cancel the action before this happens).

In this lesson, you'll learn to import media assets into Adobe Premiere. For most media, you'll import using Import mode or the Media Browser, a robust asset browser that works with many media types you'll import into Premiere. You'll also learn about special cases, such as importing single and multilayer graphics.

Note: When you open a project created on another computer, you may see a message warning you about a missing renderer. It's fine to click OK in this message. It indicates that the project was last saved with project settings configured for a different (or missing) GPU.

For this lesson, you can continue to use the project file you created in Lesson 2, "Setting Up a Project," called First Project. If you do not have the previous lesson file, you can open the file Lesson 03.prproj from the Lessons folder.

1 Continue to work with your project file from the previous lesson, or open it from your hard drive.

2 Click the Workspaces menu, choose Editing, and then click the Workspaces menu again and choose Reset To Saved Layout.

3 Choose File > Save As.

4 Browse to Lessons, and save the project with the name **Lesson 03 Working.prproj**.

Importing media files

When you import items into a Premiere project, you are not actually copying the file into the project. Instead, importing creates a link to the media file with a pointer that lives inside your project.

The pointer is called a *clip*. Think of a clip as a special kind of alias (macOS) or shortcut (Windows).

When you work with a clip in Premiere, you are not making a copy of the original file or modifying it; instead, you're selectively playing a part of, or all of, that file from its current location, nondestructively.

For example, if you choose to include only part of a clip in your sequence, you're not throwing away the unused media. A copy of the clip is added to the sequence with built-in instructions to play only the part you selected. This changes the apparent duration in the sequence, even though the full original duration in the media file is unchanged and still available.

Also, if you add an effect to a clip to brighten the image, the effect is applied to the clip, not the media file it links to. In a sense, the original media file is played "through" the clip, with interpretation settings and effects applied.

You can import media in four principal ways:

- Choose File > Import.
- Drag media files directly from Finder (macOS) or Explorer (Windows) into the Project panel or Timeline panel in Premiere.
- Use Import mode.
- Use the Media Browser.

Let's explore the benefits of each.

When to use Import mode or the Media Browser

If in doubt, use Import mode. It has a robust, user-friendly interface that automatically manages reviewing your media assets and makes it simple to import them into Premiere. If your camera has produced footage made up of multiple fragmented files, they will automatically be presented as whole clips; you'll see each recording as a single item, with the video and audio combined, regardless of the original recording format.

This means you can avoid dealing with complex camera folder structures and instead work with easy-to-browse thumbnails.

For more advanced media browsing tools, use the Media Browser while in Edit mode. This panel offers similar media previewing and navigation options to Import mode, with the additional option to preview clips in the Source Monitor before importing them, and full access to clip metadata. Being able to see this metadata (which contains important information, such as clip duration, recording date, and file type) makes it easier to select the correct clip in a long list. The Media Browser also supports Illustrator files and image sequences, which are not supported by Import mode.

Accessing Import mode is straightforward. Click to select the mode at the top-left corner.

To browse for files in Import mode, select a location from the list on the left and double-click folders displayed in the middle of the window to access their contents. As you navigate into subfolders, you'll see the folder path displayed at the top—click a folder name inside the path to navigate to that folder.

If you have a cloud-based storage location on your computer, you'll find it listed under the Cloud heading at the end of the locations list.

If there is a folder you expect to visit often, click the star to the right of the folder path to add the location to the Favorites list, which you'll find on the left side of the screen above the available locations.

Switching back to Edit mode, in the default layout of the Editing workspace, you'll find the Media Browser in the lower-left corner of your Premiere Editing workspace. It's docked in the same panel group as the Project panel.

Tip: You can also quickly access the Media Browser by pressing Shift+8 (be sure to use the 8 key at the top of the keyboard, not the one in the numerical keypad, if you have one).

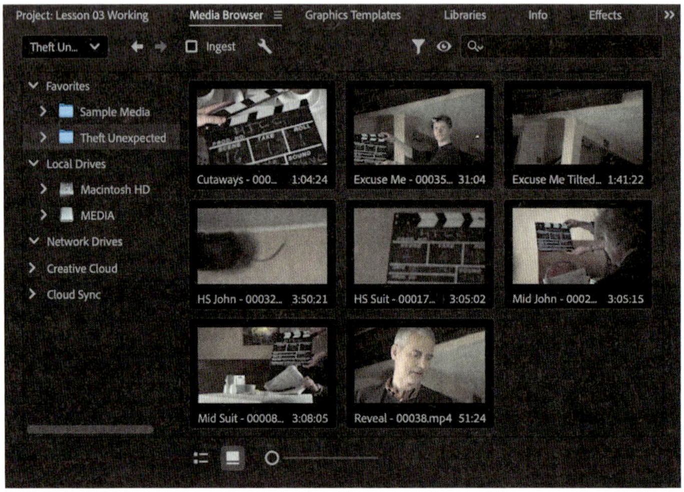

As you can any other panel, you can position the Media Browser in another panel group by dragging its panel tab (identified by the panel name).

You can also undock it to make it a floating panel by clicking the panel menu next to the panel name and choosing Undock Panel.

Browsing for files in the Media Browser is similar to browsing with Finder (macOS) or Explorer (Windows). The contents of your storage are displayed as navigation folders on the left, with buttons to navigate forward and backward at the top.

After you select a folder or media file in the Media Browser, you can use the arrow keys to select items.

You can use Import mode and the Media Browser interchangeably at any time. As your familiarity with Premiere grows, you'll quickly discover the occasions you prefer one option over the other.

Both Import mode and the Media Browser offer several benefits over the regular Import option:

- Filtering the display while browsing a folder. In fact, while Import mode allows you to filter video, audio, or image files, the Media Browser's File Types Displayed menu enables you to narrow the clips displayed to a specific file type, such as JPEG, PSD, XML, or ARRIRAW files.
- Autosensing camera data—in formats like XAVC, Canon XF, RED, Cinema DNG, Sony XAVC or X-OCN, Canon RAW, ARRI RAW, Nikon N-RAW, and ProRes RAW—to correctly display and import the clips.
- Correctly displaying and importing media files that span multiple camera media cards. Premiere will automatically import the files as a single clip even if a longer video file filled a storage card and continued onto another.
- In the Media Browser, viewing and customizing the kinds of metadata to display.
- In Import mode, automatically creating a bin or sequence when importing new clips.

Opening or browsing projects

Premiere allows you to open multiple project files at the same time. This makes it simple to copy clips and sequences from one project to another.

All open projects are editable, which means you'll need to be careful not to make unwanted changes to a project you have opened just to copy a clip from it.

You can switch between projects by choosing Window > Projects, followed by the project you would like to work on. Alternatively, make the Project panel or Timeline panel for the project you want active by clicking it.

You can also browse inside another project file using the Media Browser. Use the Media Browser to locate the project file, and double-click it to view its contents. You can then select and import clips and sequences to your current Project panel.

Projects you browse inside using the Media Browser are locked, meaning you cannot make unwanted changes.

Remember, when copying clips or sequences from one project to another, you are not copying media files—only clips that link to the media files.

When to use the Import command

Using the Import command is straightforward (and may match your experience in other applications). To import a file, just choose File > Import.

Tip: Another way to open the Import dialog box is to double-click an empty area of the Project panel.

You can also use the keyboard shortcut Command+I (macOS) or Ctrl+I (Windows) to open the Import dialog box.

This method works best for self-contained assets such as graphics and audio files or video files like MOV (QuickTime) or MP4 (H.264), especially if you know exactly where those assets are on your drive and can quickly navigate to them.

This import method is not ideal for RAW media files or when camera media has separate folders for audio, video, and important additional data describing the footage (metadata). For most camera-originated media, you'll want to use Import mode or the Media Browser.

Showing source clip names and label colors in the Timeline panel

In the Project panel, it's possible you will change a clip name or label color to help keep everything organized. If you then add it to a sequence, the new name and label color will be displayed in the Timeline panel. However, by default, instances of that clip *already* in the Timeline panel will still show their original name and label color.

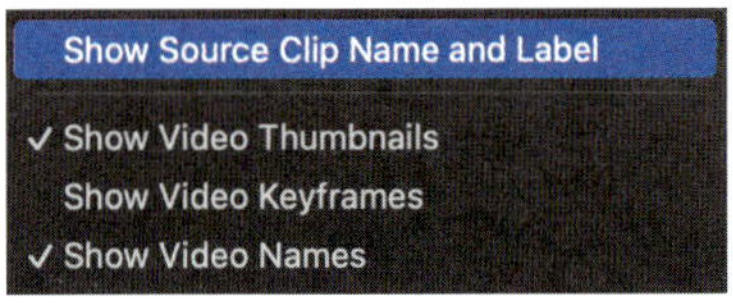

You can choose to display the original clip names and label colors or the updated names and label colors in the Timeline panel. Make sure that a sequence is open in the Timeline panel to enable access to the Timeline Display Settings menu. Click the menu, and choose Show Source Clip Name And Label.

Both options can be useful, depending on your chosen workflow for a particular project, and you can switch between them at any time.

For more information about clip labels, see Lesson 4, "Organizing Media."

Working with ingest options and proxy media

Premiere offers advanced automated options for managing your media files like copying your files to your local storage from camera memory cards or creating proxy media associated with your clips that is easier for your system to preview.

You can configure the ingest options in the Project settings by choosing File > Project Settings > Ingest Settings and making a choice from the Action menu.

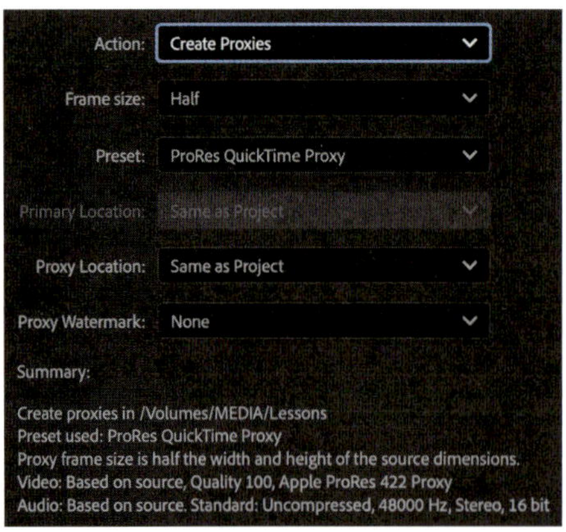

Depending on your workflow, you might choose to create low-quality proxies or transcode all media to a high-quality standard format and codec that has been selected by your organization.

For more information, see the online bonus lesson, "Managing Your Projects," and for a complete overview, see the Adobe Premiere Help. For a deep dive, visit *blog.frame.io/2024/07/29/updated-guide-premiere-pro-proxies-and-proxy-workflows.*

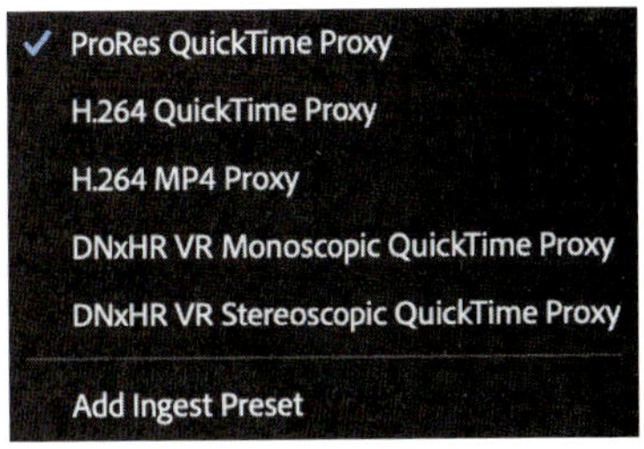

Working with Import mode and the Media Browser

You can switch to Import mode at any time to browse your available media files and add clips to your current project. Alternatively, you can open the Media Browser while in Edit mode. This panel can stay open as part of your editing workspace, allowing you to quickly access and compare available media with clips already in your project.

Note: To complete this lesson, you will import files from your computer. Be sure you have copied all the lesson files included with this book to your computer. For more details, see "Getting Started" at the beginning of the book.

Working with media files

Premiere can use footage from file-based cameras without conversion, including compressed native media from camera systems such as GoPro; Insta360; all popular smartphones (including pro camera app media); RAW media from Canon, Sony, RED, and ARRI; and post-production-friendly codecs such as Avid DNxHD and Apple ProRes.

For best results, follow these guidelines (no need to follow along for now):

- Create a separate media folder for each project. This will make it easier to differentiate between projects when cleaning up your storage or archiving.
- Copy camera media to your editing storage with the existing folder structure intact. For example, transfer the complete data folder directly from the root directory of the memory card. For best results, consider using the transfer application that is often included by the camera manufacturer to move your video files. Check that all media files have been copied and that the original card and the copied folder sizes match.
- Clearly name the copied folder of the media with the camera information, including card number and the date of the shoot.
- Create a second copy of the media on a physically separate drive, in case of hardware failure. Many editors use cloud-based storage to create ongoing backups for both media and project files.
- Really do actually create that second copy of your media on a physically separate drive, and consider making a third copy! Storage fails without warning.

- Ideally, create a long-term archive copy of your media using another backup method, such as Linear Tape-Open (LTO—a popular long-term storage system), an external storage drive, or cloud-based file storage.

Understanding supported video file types

It's not unusual to work on a project with video clips from multiple cameras using different file types, media formats, and codecs. This is no problem for Premiere because you can mix different types of media in the same sequence. Also, Import mode and the Media Browser can display and import almost any media file type.

Premiere supports media from many camera manufacturers, including:

- Most smartphones
- Most DSLR cameras and mirrorless system cameras
- Panasonic
- RED
- ARRI
- Canon
- Sony
- Nikon
- Blackmagic Design

Many standard media types are also supported, including QuickTime, MXF, DPX, and OMF. For a full list of supported camera and delivered media types, see *helpx.adobe.com/premiere/desktop/organize-media/import-files/supported-file-formats.html.*

Adding clips using Import mode

Import mode offers a simplified, easy-access approach to locating and importing media. Storage locations and favorites are listed on the left, with their contents displayed in the middle and additional import options available on the right.

Note: When importing media, be sure to copy the files to your local storage, or use the project ingest options to create copies before removing your memory cards or external drives.

Add some clips to your current project using Import mode, and then try using the Media Browser to compare the experience.

1 Switch to Import mode by clicking Import at the top-left corner.

2 By using the locations listed on the left and double-clicking subfolders in the middle, browse to the folder Lessons/Assets/Video And Audio Files/Theft Unexpected. Be careful to always double-click folders you want to open, not to single-click them (which will select them). To deselect an item, single-click it again.

You can also select and then right-click unwanted items at the bottom of the window and choose Clear. If you have chosen many clips to import, you may need to scroll to find items you want to remove.

3 If it is not already selected, click the Grid View button at the top, and drag the Resize slider next to it to enlarge the thumbnails of the clips. Choose any size you like.

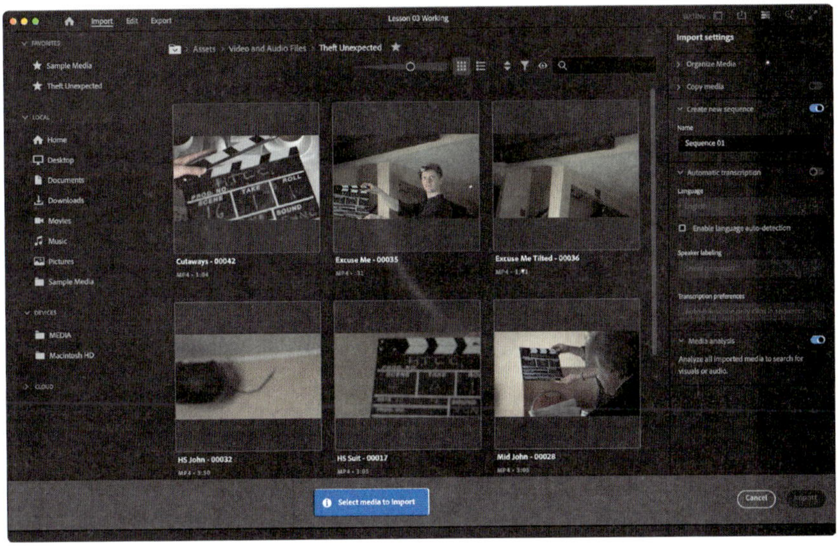

You can hover your pointer over any clip thumbnail to see a preview of the clip contents. Hovering over the left edge shows the start of the clip; hovering over the right edge shows the end of the clip.

4 Select the following clips by single-clicking them:

Excuse Me Tilted – 00036

HS Suit – 00017

Mid John – 00028

5 Under the Import Settings heading, click the Organize Media chevron and make sure that Add To New Bin is not selected. Likewise, make sure that Copy Media and Create New Sequence are also not selected, and click Import. It's not important if Media Analysis is turned on or not as you can perform this analysis later.

You have now imported some clips! Edit mode is restored, your newly imported clips have been added to the Project panel, and they are highlighted.

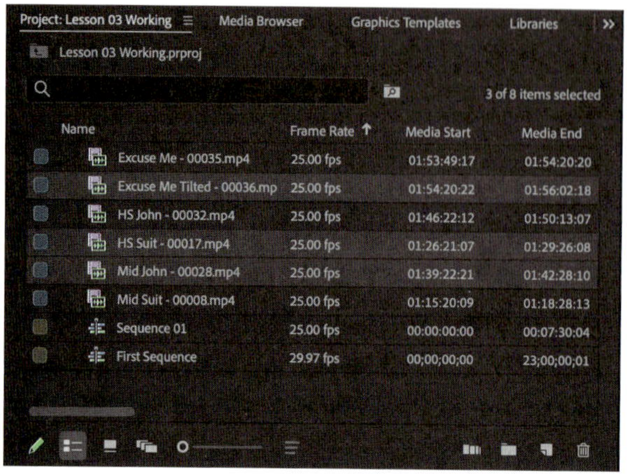

You can easily switch between Import and Edit modes at any time while working on a project, so it's quick and easy to add new content to your project as it becomes available. Now let's compare this import method with importing using the Media Browser.

Adding clips using the Media Browser

The Media Browser controls are similar to those in Finder (macOS) or Explorer (Windows). It has Forward and Back buttons to go through your recent navigation. If you select a storage location in the left area, its contents are displayed on the right.

1 Begin by resetting the workspace to the default: From the Workspaces menu, choose Editing. Then, open the menu again and choose Reset To Saved Layout.

2 Click the Media Browser's name to bring the panel to the front of the panel group (it should be docked with the Project panel by default).

Note: The Media Browser filters out non-media and unsupported files, making it easier to browse for video or audio assets.

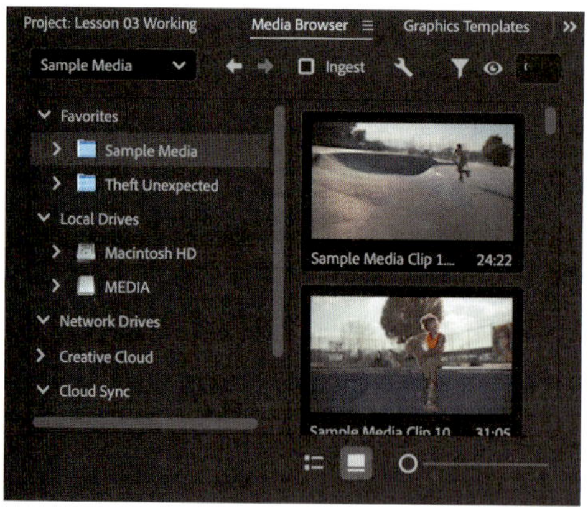

3 To make the Media Browser easier to see, position your pointer over the panel, and then press the ` (accent grave) key (it is often in the upper-left corner of a keyboard; non-English keyboards may use a different key) or double-click the panel name.

The Media Browser should now fill the screen.

4 In the navigation area, browse to and select the folder Lessons/Assets/Video And Audio Files/Theft Unexpected.

5 If it is not already selected, click the Thumbnail View button at the lower left of the Media Browser, and drag the Resize slider next to it to enlarge the thumbnails of the clips. Choose any size you like.

Just as in Import mode, you can hover your pointer over any clip thumbnail that is *not* selected, without clicking, to see a preview of the clip contents. Hovering over the left edge shows the start of the clip; hovering over the right edge shows the end of the clip.

6 Click any clip once to select it.

You can now preview the clip using keyboard shortcuts. When a clip is selected while in Thumbnail view, a small preview navigator appears under the clip.

Tip: Finding the ` (accent grave) key can be difficult in some keyboard layouts. If you can't locate the correct key, you can double-click the name of a panel to enlarge it to fill the screen.

Tip: It can take quite a lot of clicks to navigate to the subfolder you want when browsing for media—you can see the time saving that creating favorites provides!

Tip: As you browse a folder system, the navigation area on the left of the Media Browser can fill up with folders. Drag the vertical divider to resize the navigation area or scroll within the navigation area to display the folders you are interested in.

7 Press the L key or the spacebar to play a clip.

8 To stop playback, press the K key or press the spacebar again.

9 To play backward, press the J key.

Note: If you can't hear audio, check the Audio Hardware preferences to make sure the correct output device is selected.

10 Experiment with playing other clips. You should be able to hear the clip audio during playback.

You can press the J or L key multiple times to increase the playback rate for fast previews. Use the K key or the spacebar to pause playback.

11 Now you'll import the two remaining clips into your project. Click the clip Cutaways – 00042 once to select it. Next, hold Command (macOS) or Ctrl (Windows) and click the clip Reveal - 00038. This selects both clips.

Tip: You can also drag selected clips onto the Project panel's tab and then down into the empty area to import the clips.

12 Right-click one of the selected clips and choose Import.

The Project panel opens automatically and displays the clips.

13 Position your pointer over the Project panel and press the ` (accent grave) key or double-click the Project panel name to restore the panel group to its original size.

Making the most of Import mode and the Media Browser

Both Import mode and the Media Browser have a number of features that make it easy to navigate your storage.

- If you expect to import files from a location often, you can add the folder to a list of favorites at the top of the navigation area. To create a favorite in the Media Browser, right-click the folder and choose Add To Favorites. In Import mode, click the Favorite Location button. Whichever way you add a favorite location, it will appear in both views.
- To ignore regular media file types and just display media from a particular camera system, open the Directory Viewers menu and choose a camera system.
- The Media Browser Forward and Back buttons work like those in a web browser, allowing you to navigate to locations you have viewed previously.
- You can limit the types of files displayed to make it easier to browse large folders by opening the File Types Displayed menu.
- In the Media Browser, just above the navigation area on the left, there's a menu with recent storage locations. Choose an option to jump straight to that location.
- You can open multiple Media Browsers and access the contents of several folders at once. To open a new Media Browser, open the panel menu and choose New Media Browser Panel.
- By default, when in List view, the Media Browser displays limited information about clips (unlike the Project panel, which displays lots of information by default). To display more information while in List view, you can add multiple columns of metadata by clicking the Media Browser panel menu and choosing Edit Columns. In the Edit Columns dialog box, select each type of metadata you would like to display.

As in Import mode and the Media Browser, you can view clips in the Project panel as icons or as a list, with information about each clip displayed. There is an additional, more flexible viewing mode for working with icons, called Freeform view. You can switch between these three viewing modes by clicking the List View button, Icon View button, or Freeform View button at the bottom left of the Project panel.

Importing still image files

Graphics are an integral part of post-production. People expect graphics to both convey information and to add to the visual style of a project. Premiere can import almost any image file type. Support is especially excellent when you use Adobe Photoshop PSD files.

Anyone who works with print graphics or performs photo retouching has probably used Adobe Photoshop. Photoshop is a powerful tool with great depth and versatility, and it's an important part of the video production world. Let's explore how to properly import files from Photoshop.

First, you'll import a basic graphic.

Importing single-layer image files

Most graphics and photos you will work with will have a single layer—one flat grid of pixels that you can work with as a simple media file. Let's import one.

1 Choose File > Import, or press Command+I (macOS) or Ctrl+I (Windows).

2 Navigate to Lessons/Assets/Graphics.

3 Select the file Theft_Unexpected.png, and click Import.

   This PNG graphic is a simple logo file, and it appears in the Premiere Project panel. If the Project panel is in Icon view, it will display the contents of the graphic as a thumbnail.

   Note: If your system is configured for NTSC drop-frame frame rates, clips will import with a duration of 00:00:04:29. If you're using PAL non-drop frame timecode, they'll import with a duration of 00:00:05:00. You can change this setting by choosing Premiere > Settings > Media (macOS) or Edit > Preferences > Media (Windows) and making a choice from the Indeterminate Media Timebase menu.

Importing layered Adobe Photoshop files

Adobe Photoshop can create graphics with multiple layers, which are saved as files in PSD or TIFF format. Layers are similar to tracks in a Premiere sequence and allow for separation between visual elements. Although TIFF files with layers are imported as flattened images, you can import Photoshop document layers into Premiere individually to make separate adjustments and apply more complex animation.

As with any other media you import, changes made to the PSD file in Photoshop will update automatically in Premiere when the file is saved. This means a designer can continue to work on an image in Photoshop that you have already incorporated into a sequence.

If you import a layered Photoshop file, the Import Layered File dialog box appears automatically, allowing you to choose options for handling the layers.

- **Merge All Layers:** Merges all layers into one, importing the file into Premiere as a single, flattened clip.
- **Merged Layers:** Merges only the specific layers you select in this dialog box into a single, flattened clip.
- **Individual Layers:** Imports only the specific layers you select in this dialog box, with each layer becoming a separate clip in a bin in the Project panel.
- **Sequence:** Imports only the layers you select in this dialog box, each as a single clip. Premiere then automatically creates a new sequence (with its frame size based on the imported PSD dimensions) containing each clip on a separate track (matching the original stacking order).

If you choose Sequence or Individual Layers, you can choose one of the following from the Footage Dimensions menu:

- **Document Size:** Brings all the selected layers into Premiere at the frame size of the original Photoshop document.
- **Layer Size:** Matches the frame size of the new Premiere clips to the frame size of their individual layers in the original Photoshop file. Layers that do not fill the entire canvas will be cropped tightly, as transparent areas outside of the rectangle containing the layer's pixels are automatically removed. Layers are also then centered in the frame, losing their original relative positioning.

Tip: There are good reasons to import individual PSD layers with different layer sizes. For example, some graphic designers create multiple images for editors to incorporate into video edits, with each image occupying a different layer in the PSD. The PSD itself is a kind of one-stop image store when used this way.

Let's import a layered Photoshop file into our project.

1. Double-click an empty area of the Project panel to open the Import dialog box, or choose File > Import.
2. Navigate to Lessons/Assets/Graphics.
3. Select the file Theft_Unexpected_Layered.psd, and click Import (macOS) or Open (Windows).

   The Import Layered File dialog box appears.

   Note: There are some unselected layers in this PSD. These are layers with layer visibility turned off in Photoshop but not deleted. Premiere honors this layer selection automatically on import.

4 For this exercise, choose Sequence from the Import As menu, and make sure Document Size is chosen from the Footage Dimensions menu. Click OK.

5 Look in the Project panel for the newly created bin  called Theft_ Unexpected_Layered (named after the file). Double-click the bin icon to open it.

6 Inside the bin, double-click the sequence Theft_Unexpected_Layered to open it in the Timeline panel.

Sequences have a particular icon in List view . A similar icon is displayed as an overlay on their thumbnail in Icon view .

If you're unsure which item is which, hover your pointer over an item name (not the icon) to display a detailed tool tip, which will tell you if it's a clip or a sequence.

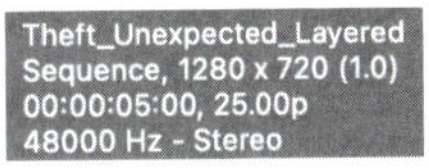

The sequence opens in the Timeline panel and is displayed in the Program Monitor.

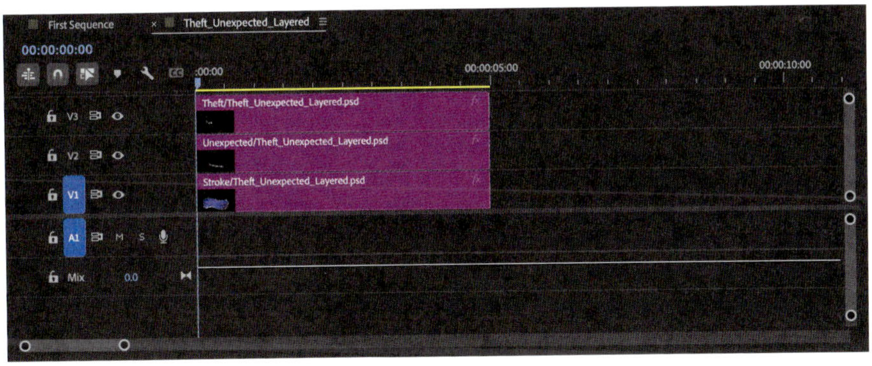

7 There's a navigator along the bottom of the Timeline panel.

Drag one end of the navigator to shorten it. This will zoom in to the position of the playhead so you can see the clips in the sequence more clearly.

Note: In the Project panel, when you double-clicked the Theft_Unexpected_ Layered bin, it opened in the same panel group as the Project panel. You can also open a bin in a new panel by holding Command (macOS) or Ctrl (Windows) when you double-click. Bins have the same options as the Project panel, and opening multiple bins to browse their contents is a common way to navigate the available media in a project.

Note: Bins in the Project panel look and behave a lot like folders in your computer file system, but they exist only inside the project file. They are a great way to stay organized.

Note: Premiere uses your system keyboard language to set the default frame rate for clips that don't have one (like graphics). You can change this setting in the Media Preferences by changing the Indeterminate Media Timebase.

8 Look at the sequence in the Timeline panel. The contents of the sequence are displayed in the Program Monitor. Try clicking the Toggle Track Output button at the left of the timeline for each track to reveal and hide the content on each layer.

9 Click the Navigate Up button in the Theft_Unexpected_Layered bin to return to the Project panel.

Working with Adobe Photoshop files

Here are a few tips for working with images from Adobe Photoshop:

- Importing a layered Photoshop document as a sequence with Footage Dimensions set to Document Size produces a clip in Premiere with the same frame size as the pixel dimensions of the whole Photoshop document.
- Even if you don't plan to zoom in or pan around the image, try to use full-frame image files with a frame size at least as large as the frame size of the project. Otherwise, you'll have to scale up the image, and it may appear to lose some of its sharpness.
- If you do plan to zoom or pan, create images so that the resulting zoomed or panned area of the image has a frame size at least as large as the frame size of the sequence. For example, if you were working in full HD, which is 1920×1080 pixels, and you wanted to perform a 2X zoom, you'd need 3840×2160 pixels in the image to keep it perfectly sharp without scaling up the pixels.
- Importing large image files uses more memory and can slow down your system. If you are working with original photos (which can be massive), consider processing them to make them smaller before using them.
- If possible, use 16-bit RGB color. The CMYK color mode is for print workflows (and is not supported by Premiere). For video editing, use RGB or YUV color modes.
- If you add a layer to a PSD file in Photoshop after importing it, the new layer will not appear in Premiere. To access the new layer in Premiere, re-import the PSD file.

Importing Adobe Illustrator files

Another important graphics component of Adobe Creative Cloud is Adobe Illustrator. Unlike Photoshop, which is primarily designed to work with pixel-based (or raster) graphics, Adobe Illustrator is a vector-based application. *Vector graphics* are mathematical descriptions of shapes rather than drawn pixels. This means you can scale them to any size in Adobe Illustrator and they always look sharp—useful for titles and graphics.

Vector graphics are typically used for technical illustrations, line art, or complex graphics.

Let's import a vector graphic.

1 If it's not already, make the Project panel active (you'll see a blue outline) by clicking the panel name.

2 In the Project panel, make sure the Theft_Unexpected_Layered bin is unselected (otherwise, the item you are about to import will be imported into that bin).

3 Double-click an empty area of the Project panel to open the Import dialog box, or press Command+I (macOS) or Ctrl+I (Windows).

4 Navigate to Lessons/Assets/Graphics.

5 Select the file Brightlove_film_logo.ai and click Import, or double-click its icon.

6 A clip linked to the Illustrator file you imported appears in the Project panel. Double-click the clip icon to view the logo in the Source Monitor.

   There's black text in the logo that disappears into the black background of the Source Monitor. That's because the logo has transparent areas, and the background of the Source Monitor is black.

7 The Source Monitor has a Settings menu with options that change the way clips are displayed. Use this menu to choose Transparency Grid.

Note: If you right-click Brightlove_film_logo.ai in the Project panel, you have the option to choose Edit Original. If you have Adobe Illustrator installed on your computer, choosing Edit Original will open the graphic in Illustrator, ready to be edited. This means, even though the layers are merged in Premiere, you can return to Adobe Illustrator, edit the original layered file, and save it; the changes will update automatically in Premiere.

   Now you can see the text more clearly because the background of the Source Monitor has been replaced with a grid.

8 Use the Source Monitor Settings menu to select Transparency Grid again to disable it. You'll learn more about working with layers and transparency in Lesson 14, "Exploring Compositing Techniques."

How Premiere deals with Adobe Illustrator files

- Like the Photoshop file you imported earlier, Illustrator files can be layered. However, Premiere doesn't give you the option to import Adobe Illustrator files in separate layers. It always merges them into a single-layer clip.
- Premiere uses a process called *rasterization* to convert the vector-based Adobe Illustrator art into the pixel-based image format used by Premiere. This conversion happens during import automatically, so be sure your graphics are configured in Illustrator to be high enough resolution before importing them into Premiere.
- Premiere automatically anti-aliases (smooths the edges of) Adobe Illustrator art.
- Premiere sets all empty areas of Illustrator files as transparent so that clips on lower tracks in your sequence will show through.
- Illustrator files (which end in .ai) cannot be imported using Import mode. Instead, use the File > Import command, double-click the background of the Project panel to browse to the file, or use the Media Browser.

Importing subfolders

Note: If you import an entire folder, it's possible some of the files will not be media supported by Premiere. If so, a message will inform you that some files could not be imported.

Note: You can import folders and subfolders using the Media Browser, too. Select a folder on the right side of the Media Browser, and import it to achieve the same result. Importing folders this way while in Import mode will always merge the contents of the subfolders into a single collection in the Project panel.

When you bring media into Premiere, you don't have to select individual files. You can select a whole folder. If your files are organized into folders and subfolders on your storage drive, when you import them, Premiere will re-create the folders as bins.

This method is not suitable for importing fragmented camera media, with video and audio files stored in different folders. You'll want to use Import mode or the Media Browser for those file types.

For self-contained media file types like QuickTime movies or MP4 files, regular importing works perfectly.

Try this now.

1 Choose File > Import, or press Command+I (macOS) or Ctrl+I (Windows).

2 Navigate to Lessons/Assets, and select the Stills folder. Don't browse inside the folder; just select it.

3 Click the Import (macOS) or Import Folder (Windows) button. Premiere imports the folder and its contents, including two subfolders containing photos. In the Project panel, you'll find bins were created to match the folders. In List view, you can click the triangle next to any bin to toggle the display of its contents.

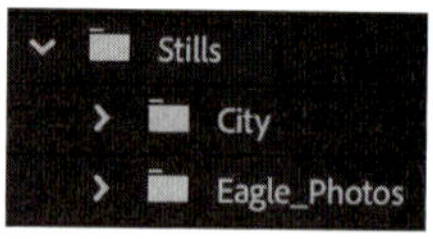

Recording a voice-over

You may be working on a video project that includes a narration track. It's likely you will have the narration recorded by professionals (or at least recorded in a location quieter than your desk), but with the right hardware, you can record high-quality audio right into Premiere.

This can be helpful because it will give you a sense of timing for your edits.

Try recording a scratch audio track.

1 If you're not using a built-in microphone, make sure your external microphone or audio mixer is properly connected to your computer. You may need to consult the documentation for your computer or audio hardware.

2 In the Timeline panel, make sure the Theft_Unexpected_Layered sequence is displayed by clicking its name in the Timeline panel. If you have closed the sequence, re-open it by double-clicking the sequence icon in the Project panel.

3 Every audio track has a set of buttons and options on the far left. This area is called the *track header*. There's a Voice-Over Record button for each audio track.

   Right-click the microphone Voice-Over Record button, and choose Voice-Over Record Settings to choose your microphone. Use the Source menu to choose the audio hardware you will use, and use the Input menu to choose the particular input for that hardware.

   Tip: The Voice-Over Record Settings dialog box also allows you to name the new audio file.

   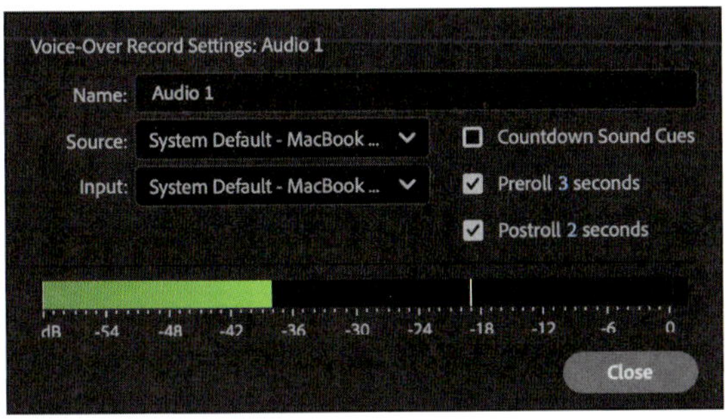

   Then click the Close button.

4 Turn down your computer speakers, or use headphones to prevent feedback or echo.

5 To see the result more clearly, increase the height of the A1 track in one of the following ways:

   - Double-click an empty space on the right side of the track header (next to the Voice-Over Record button).
   - Drag down on the horizontal dividing line between two audio track headers.
   - Hover the pointer over the track header while holding Option (macOS) or Alt (Windows), and scroll.

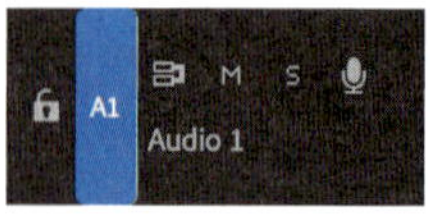

6 In the Timeline panel, time moves from left to right, just as it does with any online video. At the top of the Timeline panel, where the time ruler is displayed, a playhead indicates the current frame displayed in the Program Monitor. You can click any point in the time ruler, and the playhead will move to show that frame. You can also drag the time ruler itself to view the contents of the current sequence. This is called *scrubbing* (like scrubbing a floor).

   Position the Timeline playhead at the beginning of the sequence, as far left as it will go, and click the Voice-Over Record button for track A1 to begin recording.

7 After a brief countdown in the Program Monitor, recording will begin. Say a few words, and press the spacebar to stop recording.

   Premiere creates a new audio clip and adds it to the Project panel and the current sequence.

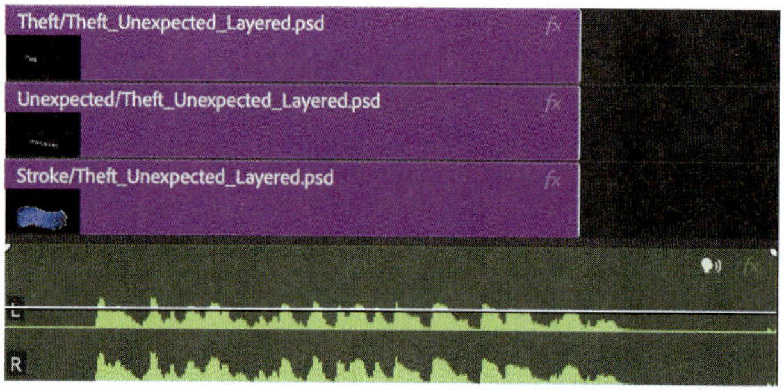

   The newly recorded audio file is added to the Captured And Generated file location specified in the project Scratch Disks settings. By default, this is a subfolder in the same location as the project file.

8 Choose File > Save to save the project. You can close the project or keep it open, ready for the next lesson.

Importing from Adobe Stock

Adobe Stock offers a wide range of images, videos, templates, illustrations, and audio files that you can incorporate into your projects.

The dedicated Adobe Stock panel (accessible in the Window menu) provides access to the Adobe Stock service, and adding an asset to your project is as easy as clicking a download button.

Many assets are free, while others require a subscription to the Adobe Stock service.

Adobe Stock is also available in the Essential Sound panel, allowing you to try out stock music and sound effects before adding them to your sequence.

For more information about Adobe Stock, check out *stock.adobe.com*.

Customizing the media cache

When you import files in certain video and audio formats, Premiere may need to process and cache (temporarily store) a version of the file or additional files to make clip playback or waveform display smoother. This is particularly true for highly compressed formats, and the process is called *conforming*.

Note: The word *conform* is used to describe both the way clip playback is adjusted to match sequence settings and the way certain formats are processed when imported to Premiere. That's because the principle is the same: The original material is adapted to improve performance.

If necessary, imported audio files are automatically conformed to a new CFA file (conformed audio file). Most MPEG files are *indexed*, resulting in an extra MPGINDEX file that makes it easier to read the file (it's a little like creating a map of the file to make playback easier).

You'll know that the cache is being built if you see a small progress indicator in the upper-right corner of the screen when importing media.

The media cache improves preview playback performance by making it easier for your editing system to decode and play media. You can customize the cache to further improve performance. A media cache database helps Premiere manage these cache files, which are shared between multiple Creative Cloud applications.

Let's take a look at the options. Choose Premiere > Settings > Media Cache (macOS) or Edit > Preferences > Media Cache (Windows).

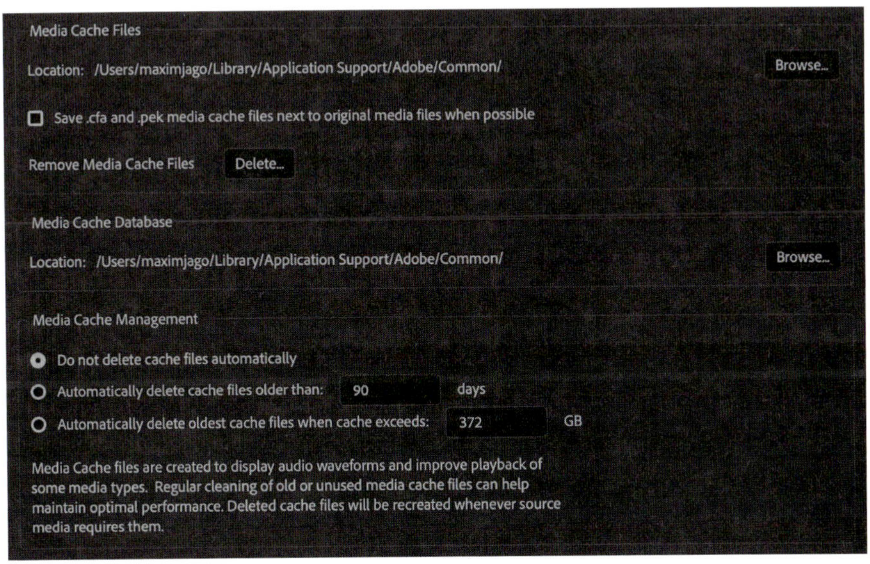

Here are the options:

- To move the media cache files or the media cache database to a new location, click the appropriate Browse button, select the desired location, and click Choose (macOS) or Choose Folder (Windows).
- To keep media cache files stored on the same drive as the media, select Save .cfa And .pek Media Cache Files Next To Original Media Files When Possible. This can be useful if your audio is stored on an external drive that you intend to move between editing systems, as it saves you waiting for them to be automatically re-created after changing systems. If you want to keep everything in one central folder, leave this option unselected. Remember, the faster the drive for the media cache, the better the playback performance you're likely to experience in Premiere.
- You should clean the media cache database on a regular basis to remove old conform and index files that are no longer required. To do so, click the Delete button. In the Delete Media Cache Files dialog box, click OK.

  It's a good idea to do this after you wrap up projects because it removes unnecessary preview render files too, saving space.
- The Media Cache Management options allow you to configure a degree of automation in the management of cache files. Premiere will automatically re-create these files if they are needed, so it's safe to enable these options to save space.
- To remove *all* media cache files, including those that are in use, restart Premiere while holding Option, Command, or Shift (macOS) or Alt, Ctrl, or Shift (Windows) and select Clear Media Cache Files. It's a good idea to do this after updating to a new version of Premiere to maintain a well-organized cache.

For now, click Cancel to close the Preferences dialog box without saving any changes.

Review questions

1 What are some of the most common camera media formats?

2 What is an advantage of using Import mode or the Media Browser rather than the File > Import method to import multiple media files that are part of one clip?

3 When you're importing a layered Photoshop file, what are the four ways the file can be handled?

4 Where can media cache files be stored?

Review answers

1 R3D, ARRIRAW, Canon RAW, RED RAW, MXF, AVCHD, MP4, and MOV are all popular formats—and there are more!

2 Import mode and the Media Browser automatically honor the complex folder structures created by some cameras, automatically stitching multiple media files together into a single clip where it's needed.

3 You can merge all the visible layers in the Photoshop file into a single clip by choosing Merge All Layers from the Import As menu in the Import Layered File dialog box; or select the specific layers you want by choosing Merged Layers. If you want layers as separate clips, choose Individual Layers and select the layers to import, or choose Sequence to import the selected layers and create a new sequence from them.

4 You can store media cache files in any location you specify or automatically on the same drive as the original files (when possible). The faster the storage for your cache files, the better the playback performance.

4 ORGANIZING MEDIA

Lesson overview

In this lesson, you'll learn how to do the following:

- Navigate the Project panel.
- Organize your project with bins.
- Add clip metadata.
- Search for clips in your project
- Review your footage using essential playback controls.
- Configure footage interpretation.
- Make changes to your clips.

This lesson will take about 90 minutes to complete. To get the files used in this lesson, refer to the instructions in "Accessing the lesson files and Web Edition" in the "Getting Started" section at the beginning of this book. Store the files on your computer in a convenient location.

Once you have some video and audio assets in your project, you'll begin looking through your footage and adding clips to a sequence. Before you do, it's well worth spending a little time organizing the assets you have—this can save you from spending hours hunting for things later.

Starting the lesson

Note: To ensure that the tools function and the defaults are set exactly as described in this lesson, reset the Premiere preferences by holding any modifier key (such as Shift) while launching the application, selecting Reset App Preferences, and then clicking Continue in the Reset Options dialog box.

When you have lots of clips in your project, especially many imported from several different media types, it can be a challenge to stay on top of everything, let alone find that magic shot when you need it.

In this lesson, you'll learn how to organize your clips using the Project panel. You'll create special containers, called *bins*, to divide your clips into categories. You'll also learn about adding important metadata and labels to your clips, and ways to search for content.

You'll begin by getting to know the important Project panel and organizing your clips.

1 For this lesson, open the project file Lesson 04.prproj from the Lessons folder.

2 To begin, choose Window > Workspaces > Editing. Then choose Window > Workspaces > Reset To Saved Layout to reset the workspace to the default.

3 Choose File > Save As.

4 Rename the file **Lesson 04 Working.prproj**.

5 Browse to the Lessons folder, and click Save to save the project.

   By saving a new version of the project file you can always go back to the previous version—it's an electronic paper trail.

   Tip: You can choose Save As or Save A Copy from the File menu. Save As saves the current project file with a new name, leaving the previous version untouched. Save A Copy creates a new separate project file while you continue to work on your existing project file.

Using the Project panel

Everything you import into your Adobe Premiere project will appear in the Project panel. The Project panel has folder-like bins that you can use to stay organized and tools for browsing your clips and working with their metadata.

In addition to acting as the repository for all your clips, the Project panel gives access to important options for interpreting media. All your footage will have a frame rate (frames per second, or fps), a pixel aspect ratio (pixel shape), and a color space, usually set by the camera. You may want to change these interpretation settings for creative or technical reasons.

For example, if a video file is tagged with the wrong playback frame rate, you could change the clip interpretation to correct it. You might also receive a video file that has the wrong pixel aspect ratio setting and want to correct it.

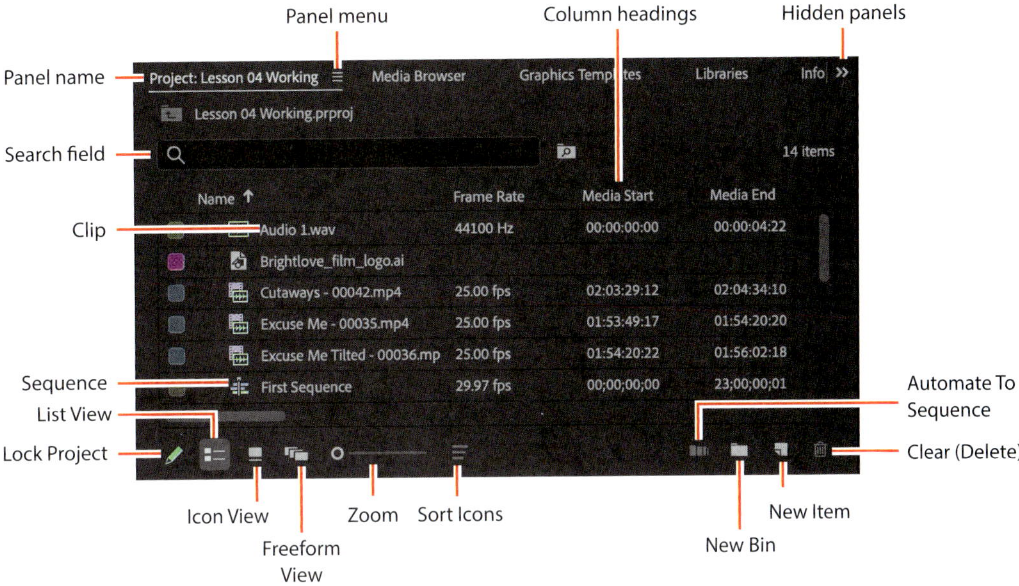

Premiere uses metadata associated with footage to know how to play it back and can display and edit additional metadata (such as location log notes) in the Project panel or the dedicated Metadata panel. If you want to change the clip metadata, you can do so in both the Project panel and the Metadata panel.

Customizing the Project panel

It's likely that you'll want to resize the Project panel from time to time. You'll also alternate between looking at your clips as a list or as thumbnail icons. Sometimes it's quicker to resize the panel than to scroll to see more information.

Tip: You can access a lot of clip information by scrolling List view horizontally or by hovering your pointer over a clip name.

Tip: You can scroll the Project panel view up and down using the scroll wheel on your mouse or a gesture on your touchpad.

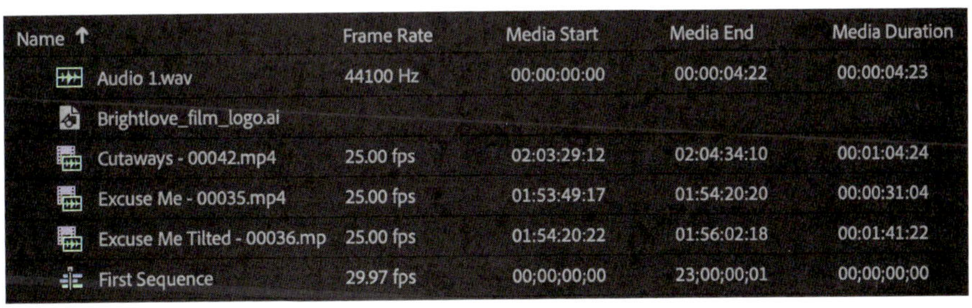

Tip: There's a quick way to toggle between seeing the Project panel in a frame and seeing it full-screen: Hover your pointer over the panel, and press the ` (accent grave) key. You can do this with any panel. If your keyboard does not have a ` (accent grave) key, you can double-click the panel name.

There is also the Freeform view  in the Project panel, which can be used to organize clips or even begin to build sequences.

Finding assets in the Project panel

Note: You may need to drag a heading divider to expand the width of a column before you can see its sort order indicator or all of the information available in the column.

Note: When you scroll to the right in the Project panel, Premiere always maintains the clip names and labels on the left so you know which clips you're seeing information about.

Working with clips is a little like working with pieces of paper at your desk. If you have just one or two clips, it's easy. But when you have 100 to 200, you need an organizational system.

One way you can help make things smoother throughout the edit is to invest a little time in organizing your clips right at the beginning. If you rename your clips after importing them, you can more easily locate content later (see "Changing names" in this lesson). It also helps to know how to sort items in the Project panel.

1 Click the Name column heading at the top of the Project panel. Each time you click the Name heading, items in the Project panel are displayed in alphabetical order or reverse alphabetical order. A direction indicator next to the heading shows the current sort order.

If you're searching for several clips with particular features—such as a duration or a frame size—it can be helpful to change the order in which the headings are displayed, from left to right.

Tip: The Project panel display configuration is saved with workspaces, so if you want to always have access to a particular setup, save it as part of a custom workspace. You can also click the Project panel menu and choose Save As New View Preset. The preset will be available to select in the panel menu.

2 Scroll to the right until you can see the Media Duration heading in the Project panel. This shows the total duration of each clip's media file. You may find it helpful to resize the Project panel to see more columns.

3 Click the Media Duration heading. Premiere now displays the clips in order of media duration. Notice the direction arrow is now on the Media Duration heading.

Each time you click the heading, the direction arrow toggles between showing clips in order of increasing duration and decreasing duration.

4 Drag the Media Duration heading to the left until you see a blue divider between the Frame Rate heading and the Name heading. When you release the heading, it will be repositioned right next to the Name heading.

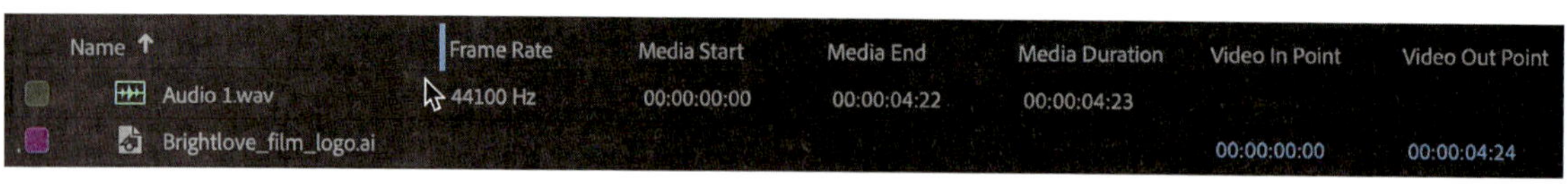

Note: Graphic and photo files such as Adobe Photoshop PSD, JPEG, and Adobe Illustrator AI files import with a default frame rate (timebase) and duration. You can choose a new default frame rate in the Media Preferences, using the Indeterminate Media Timebase menu. You can choose a new default duration in the Timeline Preferences, using the Still Image Default Duration menu.

Filtering bin content

Premiere has search tools to help you find your media. Even if you're using the non-descriptive original clip names assigned in-camera, you can search for clips based on a number of factors, such as frame size or file type.

At the top of the Project panel, you can type in the Search (or Filter Bin Content) box to display only clips with names or metadata matching the text you enter. This is a quick way to locate a clip if you remember its name (or even part of its name). Clips that don't match the text you enter are hidden, and clips that do match are revealed, even if they are inside a closed bin.

Try this now.

1 Click in the Filter Bin Content box, and type **jo**.

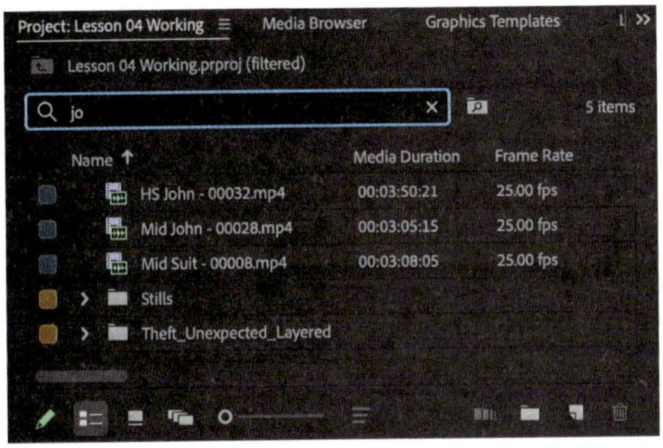

Premiere displays only the clips with the letter combination *jo* in the name or in the metadata, expanding bins if necessary. Notice that the name of the project is displayed above the text-entry box, along with *(filtered)*. This, along with the letters you typed, is the only indication that some of the clips in the Project panel may be hidden.

2 Click the X on the right of the Filter Bin Content box to clear your search.

3 Type **psd** in the box.

Premiere displays only clips that have the letter combination *psd* in their name or metadata, along with all project bins.

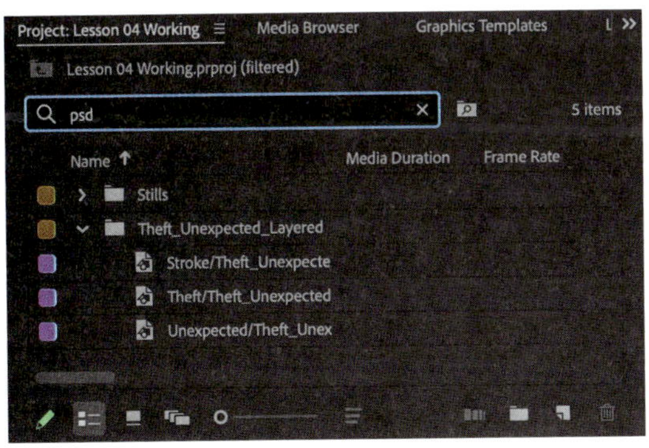

Note: The name *bin* comes from old-school film editing. The Project panel is also effectively a bin; it can contain clips and functions like any other bin.

Tip: Look out for *(filtered)* just above the search box. It's easy to press the spacebar while the Filter Bin Content box is active, which adds an otherwise invisible filter—the space you typed!

Note: When filtering bin contents, all bins remain visible, even if they don't contain the letters you are filtering with.

Using the Filter Bin Content box in this way, you can search for particular types of files. Notice that these clips are inside a closed bin, which opens automatically to display clips that meet your search criteria.

Note: Notice there's a Search box at the top of the Metadata Display dialog box. Enter the name of an item here to locate it if you're not sure which category to browse in.

Note: Several useful bin columns are displayed by default, including the Good checkbox. Select this box for clips you prefer, and then click the column heading to sort selected shots from unwanted content.

Customizing bins

When set to List view, the Project panel displays a number of columns of information about each clip. Depending on the clips you have and the types of metadata you are working with, you might want to change the columns that are displayed.

To accomplish this, open the Project panel menu and choose Metadata Display.

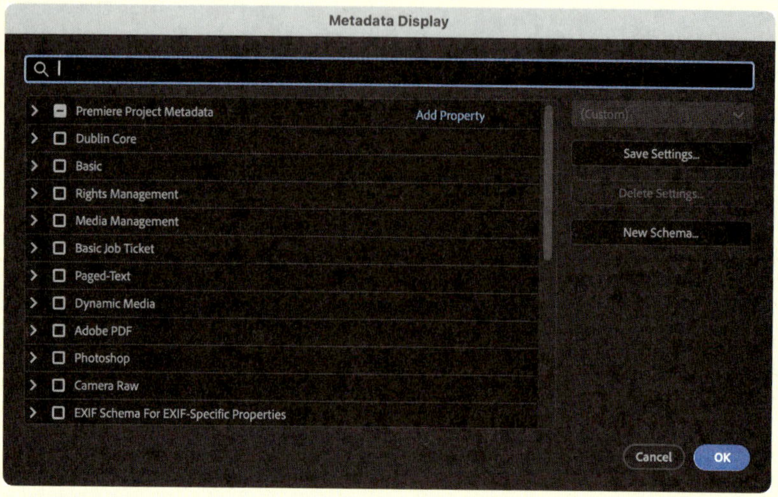

The Metadata Display dialog box allows you to select the kinds of metadata to display in the List view of the Project panel (and any bins). The dialog box lists the types of data in groups; click the chevron for a group to display the properties in that group.

Select a single property to add it as a column heading in the Project panel or bin. Select a group to add all the properties in that group.

Keep in mind that, although in most ways bins work the same way as the Project panel, metadata display settings for individual bins are saved in the project file, while metadata display settings for the Project panel are saved with the workspace.

Any bins that you have not yet opened will inherit the settings from the Project panel, so make changes in that panel if you want them to be applied to every bin.

When you have finished selecting the properties to display, click OK to apply the change or Cancel to undo your selection.

Some types of metadata can be edited directly in the Project panel. For example, you can add notes to the Description field, and these notes will immediately be searchable.

Note: In this context, *field* means a box or space into which you can enter text or numerical information. For clips in the Project panel, many fields are already filled, but there are several you can use freely to help organize your project.

Be sure to click the X on the right of the Filter Bin Content box to clear your filter when you have found the clips you want. Do this now to reveal all the clips in the project.

Creating Search Bins

When using the Filter Bin Content box to display specific clips, you have the option to create a special kind of virtual bin, called a Search Bin.

After typing in the Filter Bin Content box, click the Create New Search Bin From Query button.

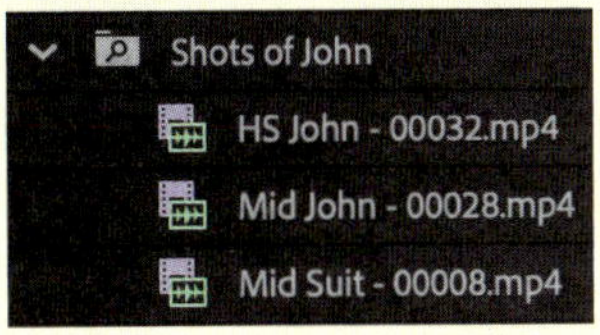

A new Search Bin appears in the Project panel. Search Bins display the results of a search performed when using the Filter Bin Content box. You can rename Search Bins, edit their settings, add more search criteria, and place them in other bins.

The contents of Search Bins update dynamically, so if you add new clips to a project that meet the search criteria, they'll appear in matching Search Bins automatically. This can be a fantastic time-saver when working with documentary material that might change over time as you obtain new footage.

Using advanced Find

Premiere also has an advanced Find feature. To learn about it, let's import some more clips.

Using any of the methods described in Lesson 3, "Importing Media," import these items:

- Seattle_Skyline.mov from the Assets/Video and Audio Files/General Views folder.
- Under Basket.mov from the Assets/Video and Audio Files/Basketball folder.

Open the Edit menu and choose Find, or press Command+F (macOS) or Ctrl+F (Windows).

Premiere displays the Find dialog box, which has more advanced options for locating your clip.

You can perform two searches at once with the advanced Find dialog box. You can choose to display clips that match all search criteria or any search criteria. For example, depending on the setting you choose from the Match menu, you could do either of the following:

- Search for a clip with the words *john* **and** *excuse* in its name.
- Search for a clip with the word *john* **or** *excuse* in its name.

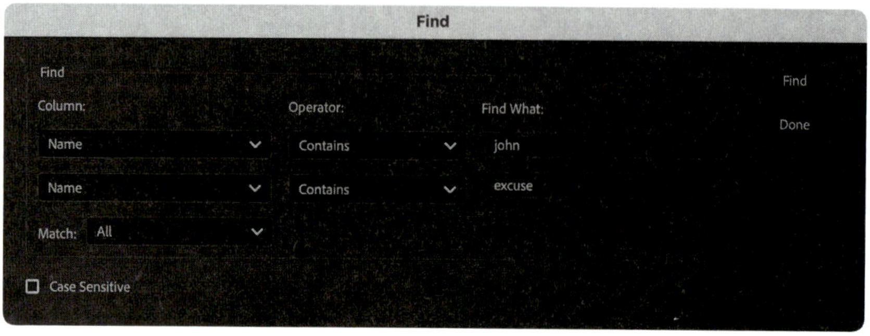

You can refine your search by choosing items from the following menus:

- **Column:** This menu lists the columns in the Project panel. When you click Find, Premiere will search only within the column you choose.
- **Operator:** This menu contains a set of standard search options. You can choose to have the search return clips that contain your search term, match it exactly, begin with it, end with it, or lack it entirely.
- **Match:** Choose All to find a clip with both your first and your second search text. Choose Any to find a clip with either your first or your second search term.
- **Case Sensitive:** Select this option to return only results that exactly match the uppercase and lowercase letters you enter.
- **Find What:** Type your search text here.

Tip: You can find clips in sequences too. With a sequence open and the Timeline panel active, choose Edit > Find.

When you click Find, Premiere highlights a clip that matches your search criteria. Click Find again, and Premiere highlights the next clip that matches your search criteria.

Click Done now to exit the Find dialog box.

Searching with Media Intelligence

If you select the Media Analysis option when using Import mode to add clips to your project, Premiere will analyze media so that you can search for visuals or audio using the dedicated Search panel.

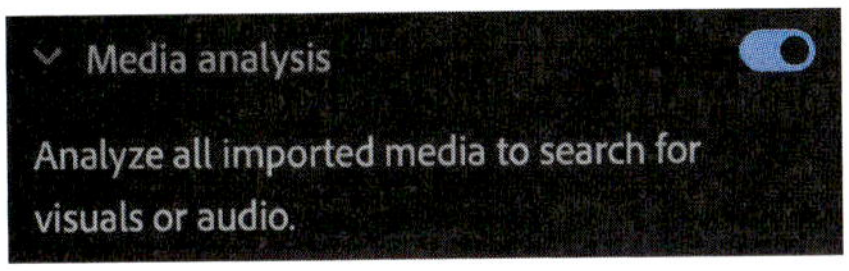

▶ **Tip:** Selecting (or deselecting) this option updates the Media Analysis option for all imported media, even if it is already imported and in your project. In fact, the option you set in Import mode is a shortcut to the Media Analysis preference, which you can find in the Media Analysis & Transcription preferences.

Media Analysis is processed in the background. Once the analysis is complete, you will be able to search based on the contents of your media, not just the associated metadata.

Try the Search panel now.

1 Enter Import mode by clicking Import at the top-left corner of the Premiere interface, and check that Media Analysis is selected.

2 Return to Edit mode by clicking Edit at the top-left corner of the Premiere interface, and open the Search panel by choosing Window > Search.

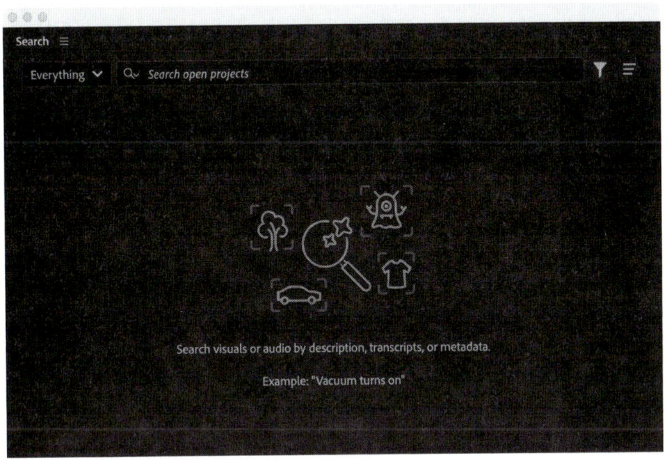

By default, the Search panel appears in a floating window. You can group it with other panels just as you would with any other panel, if you choose to.

3 In the search box at the top of the Search window, type the word **cup**.

Multiple clips that match your search are displayed, starting with visual matches, followed by audio matches. If you scroll down, you'll see text and metadata headings, although there are no such matches for this search.

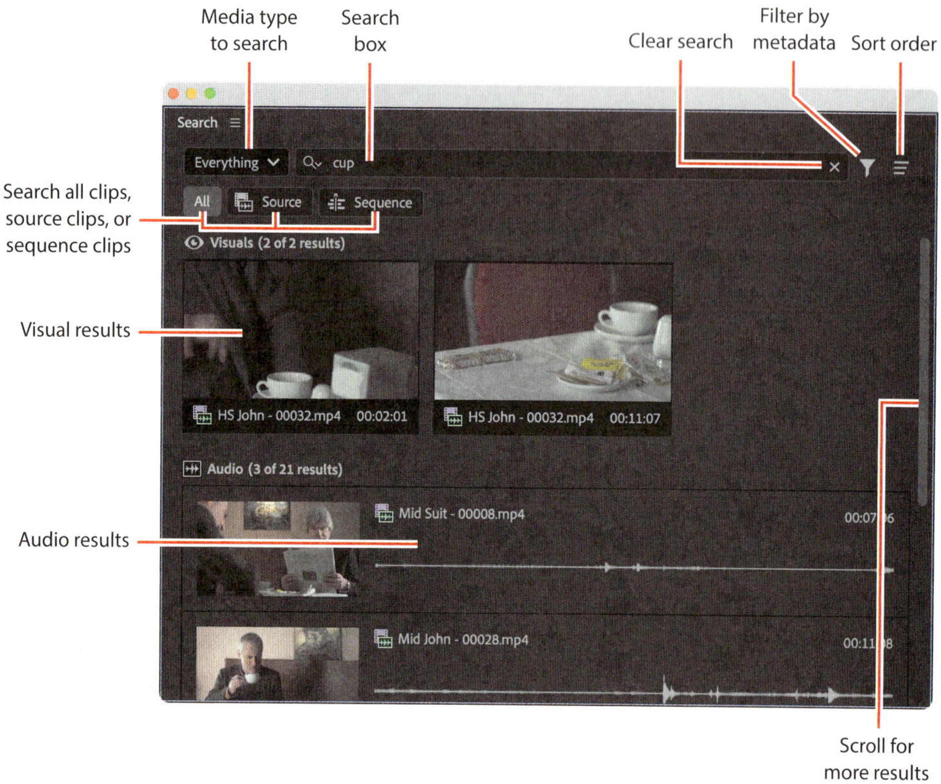

The Search panel shows results based on the contents of your media—a powerful way to find that elusive clip that you remember but can't find.

Notice that the visual clips have short durations, displayed in the lower-right corner below each thumbnail.

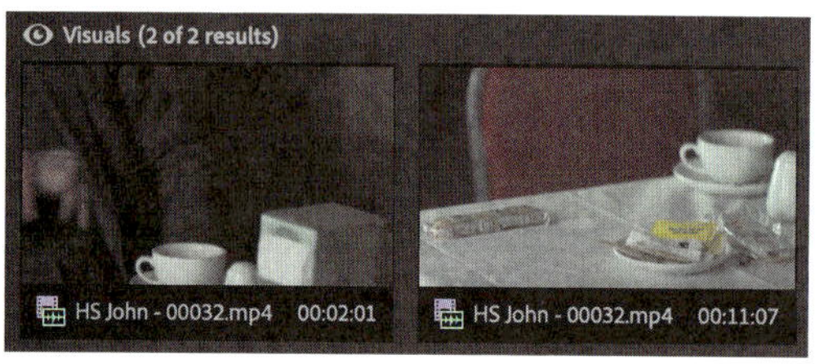

This is because only the parts of the clips that match your search are included. You can hover your pointer over a thumbnail to see a preview of the contents in the thumbnail.

The audio results are based on the sound the china cup makes. You can preview the audio results by clicking the Play button that appears on the thumbnail when you hover your pointer over it.

If you get too many results, you can refine your search by choosing a media type at the top left of the panel; by choosing between all clips, source clips only, or sequence clips; and by using the Filters menu. You can use the Sort By menu to set the order in which results will be shown.

You can add clips from the Search panel directly to a sequence by dragging them. You can also review clips by double-clicking them or dragging them from the Search panel into the Source Monitor.

If you do, you will notice that the results are full length clips with In and Out points automatically applied to select the part of the clip with the search result. You will learn about In and Out points in Navigating With Timecode in this lesson.

It's possible a search will produce multiple results from the same full-length Source clip, which makes the Search panel a fantastic way to locate similar kinds of contents that appear at different times in the same original clip.

Try a few searches, working with the clips in this project. When you have finished experimenting, close the Search panel by clicking the panel menu and choosing Close Panel.

Later in this lesson you will learn how to review clips in the Source Monitor. Both the Source Monitor and the Program Monitor have a Search Similar Frames button. When you click Search Similar Frames, the Search panel opens and displays similar moments from the current clip and others in your project.

Working with bins

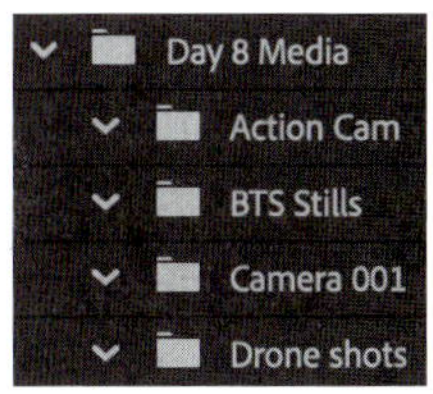

Bins allow you to organize clips, sequences, graphics, and so on, by dividing them into named groups.

Just as with folders on your hard drive, you can have multiple bins inside other bins, creating an organizational system as complex as your project requires.

There's an important difference between bins and the folders on your storage drive, however: Bins exist only in your Premiere project file. You won't find individual folders representing project bins on your storage drive.

Creating bins

Let's create a bin.

1 Click the New Bin button at the bottom of the Project panel.

Premiere creates a new bin and automatically highlights the name, ready for you to rename it. It's a good habit to name bins as soon as you create them.

Tip: If you accidentally create a new bin inside an existing bin, drag the new bin out of the selected bin or choose Edit > Undo to remove the new bin and create it again after deselecting.

2 You have already imported some clips from a short film, so let's give them a bin. Name the new bin **Theft Unexpected**, and press Return or Enter. But wait—what happened?

▶ **Tip:** If your keyboard has a Function (fn) key, you may find that you can hold the key to switch the way the Return/Enter key works. Try this now to apply the next new bin name.

If your new bin is at the end of the list of items in the Project panel, pressing Return/Enter applies the new name and highlights the first item on the list. However, if the new bin is anywhere else on the list, pressing this key applies the new name and then automatically highlights the next item name on the list, so you can easily rename it too.

This useful shortcut allows you to quickly rename several items in your project. If you want to apply a new name without highlighting the next item, just click elsewhere to apply the new name. If you have a numerical keyboard, you can also press that Enter key to apply a new entry without highlighting the next item.

3 You can also create a bin using the File menu. Let's do this now: Make sure the Project panel is active, and deselect the bin you just created. (If a bin is selected when you create a new bin, Premiere places the new bin inside the selected bin.) Choose File > New > Bin.

● **Note:** It can be difficult to find a blank part of the Project panel to click when it's full of clips. Try clicking just to the left of the icons, inside the panel, or choose Edit > Deselect All.

4 Name the new bin **Graphics**.

5 You can also make a new bin by right-clicking a blank area in the Project panel and choosing New Bin. Try this now.

6 Name the new bin **Illustrator Files**.

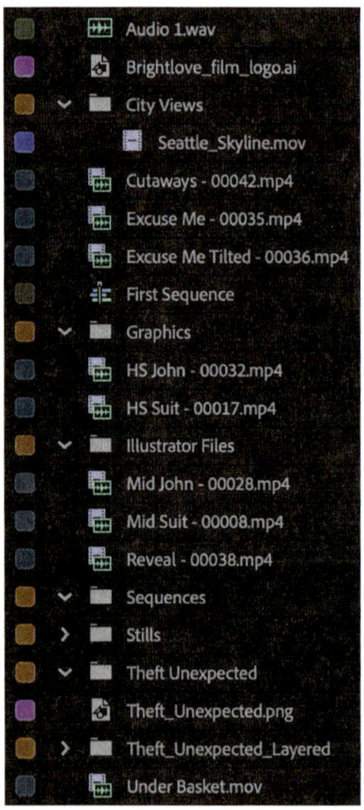

7 Drag the clip Seattle_Skyline.mov onto the New Bin button at the bottom of the Project panel and release it.

The clip is moved into a new bin. This is one of the quickest and easiest ways to create a new bin for selected clips you have already imported into your project.

8 Name the newly created bin **City Views**.

9 Make sure the Project panel is active but no existing bins are selected. Press the keyboard shortcut Command+B (macOS) or Ctrl+B (Windows) to make another bin.

10 Name the bin **Sequences**.

If your Project panel is set to List view, with the Name heading selected for sorting at the top of the panel, bins appear in alphabetical order among the clips. Newly created bins in List view are automatically expanded, with their triangles set open. You may need to click the Name heading to reset the sorting order after creating the new bins. Click the heading twice to sort in ascending order again.

● **Note:** To rename a bin, you can right-click it and choose Rename. Type the new name, and click away from the text to apply it.

Managing media in bins

Even for this small example project, the Project panel already contains quite a lot of items, including bins. Suppose you were working on a larger project with 200 or even 2,000 clips—it's not hard to imagine how useful bins would be!

Now that you have some bins, let's put them to use. As you move clips into bins, use the triangles to hide their contents and tidy up the view.

1 Drag the clip Brightlove_film_logo.ai onto the Illustrator Files bin icon. This will move the clip into the bin.

2 Drag Theft_Unexpected.png into the Graphics bin.

3 Drag the whole bin called Theft_Unexpected_Layered (created automatically when you imported the layered PSD file as individual layers) into the Graphics bin.

Note: When you import a Photoshop file with multiple layers and choose to import it as a sequence, Premiere automatically creates a bin for the layers and their sequence. For more information on this workflow, see "Importing layered Adobe Photoshop files" in Lesson 3.

4 Drag the clip Under Basket.mov into the City Views bin. You may need to resize the panel or switch it to full-screen to see both the clip and the bin.

5 Drag the sequence called First Sequence into the Sequences bin.

6 Drag all the remaining clips into the Theft Unexpected bin.

Tip: You can Shift-click, as well as Command-click (macOS) or Ctrl-click (Windows), to make selections in the Project panel, just like you can with files on your hard drive.

You should now have a nicely organized Project panel, with each kind of clip in its own bin.

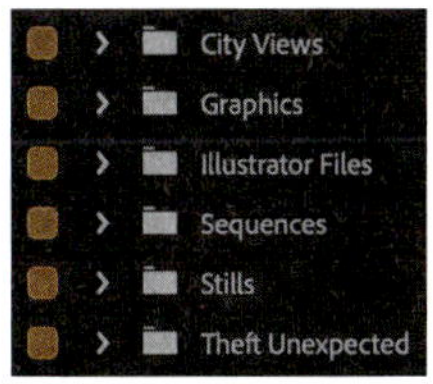

Tip: To expand or collapse all chevrons, hold Option (macOS) or Alt (Windows) while you click any chevron.

7 Click the chevron for the Graphics bin to display the contents.

You can copy and paste clips to make extra copies if this helps you stay organized. In the Graphics bin, you have a PNG file that might be useful for the Theft Unexpected content. Let's make an extra copy.

8 Right-click the Theft_Unexpected.png clip and choose Copy.

9 Click the chevron for the Theft Unexpected bin to display the contents.

10 Right-click the Theft Unexpected bin and choose Paste to add a copy of the clip to the Theft Unexpected bin.

When you make copies of clips, you are not making duplicate copies of the media files they are linked to. You can make as many copies as you like of a clip in your Premiere project. Those copies will all link to the same original media file.

Finding your media files

If you would like to know where a media file is on your hard drive, you can right-click the clip in the Project panel and choose Reveal In Finder (macOS) or Reveal In Explorer (Windows).

The folder in your storage drive that contains the media file will open. This can be useful if you are working with media files stored on multiple hard drives or if you renamed your clips in Premiere.

If you moved all the remaining clips into the Theft Unexpected bin, you should have an Audio 1.wav clip in that bin now, which is the voice-over you recorded in an earlier exercise (in this instance, it's a version provided with the project files). If you tried recording that voice-over multiple times, you may have more than one audio clip, each with a different number. Let's remove the clip but keep the audio file:

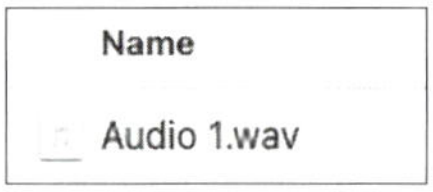

1 Right-click that voice-over clip and choose Reveal In Finder (macOS) or Reveal In Explorer (Windows).

2 Switch back to Premiere. Click the icon for the Audio 1.wav clip to select it, and press Delete (macOS) or Backspace (Windows) to remove it.

   Premiere displays a warning message to remind you that the clip is currently used in a sequence.

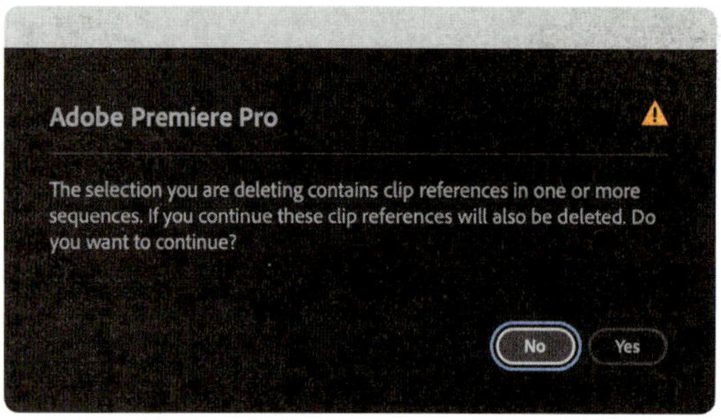

   Clicking Yes will remove the clip from the Project panel and any sequence that contains the clip.

   Tip: Notice that the No option in this dialog box is highlighted in blue. If you press Return/Enter, this is the option that you are selecting.

   Click Yes to remove the clip.

3 Switch back to the folder containing the file in your storage. The audio file is still there!

   Removing a clip in Premiere does not remove the linked media file from your storage. Also, making changes to a clip in Premiere does not make changes to the linked media file.

Changing bin views

Although there is a distinction between the Project panel and the bins inside it, they have the same controls and viewing options. For all intents and purposes, you can treat the Project panel as a bin; many Premiere editors use the terms *bin* and *Project panel* interchangeably.

Bins have three views. You choose between them by clicking the buttons at the lower left of the Project panel.

- **List view**: By default, this view displays your clips and bins as a list, with a significant amount of metadata displayed. You can scroll through the metadata and use it to sort clips by clicking column headers.
- **Icon view**: This view displays your clips and bins as thumbnails you can rearrange and use to preview clip contents.
- **Freeform view**: This view displays clips and bins as thumbnails that you can assign different sizes, group together, and place freely in a large area.

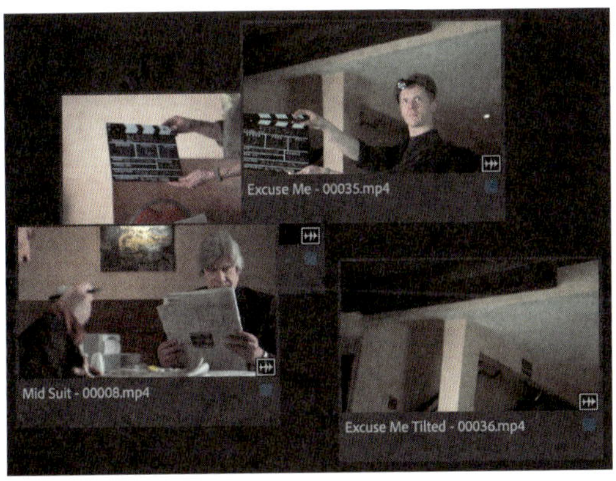

The Project panel has a Zoom control, next to the List View, Icon View, and Freeform View buttons, which changes the size of the clip icons or thumbnails.

Note: You can change the List view font size in the Project panel or a bin by clicking the panel menu and choosing Font Size. This is particularly useful if you are working on a high-resolution screen.

If you double-click a bin in the Project panel, that bin will open in place of the Project panel. You can navigate back up to the Project panel by clicking the Navigate Up button at the top of the panel.

This button appears whenever you are viewing the contents of a bin. Just as Finder (macOS) and Explorer (Windows) have navigation buttons, you can use this button to browse "up" to the container of the current bin. In this case, it's the Project panel, but it could just as easily be another bin.

You can also open a bin in a separate panel by double-clicking while holding a modifier key. Try this now.

Tip: The option to open bins in a new panel when double-clicking by default, rather than the same panel, can be changed in the General preferences.

1 Hold Command (macOS) or Ctrl (Windows) while you double-click the Theft Unexpected bin. The bin opens in a new panel in the same group as the Project panel. You can keep as many bin panels open as you like and place them anywhere in the interface to help you stay organized.

2 Click the Icon View button on the Theft Unexpected bin to display thumbnails for the clips. You may want to resize the Project panel to view more thumbnails.

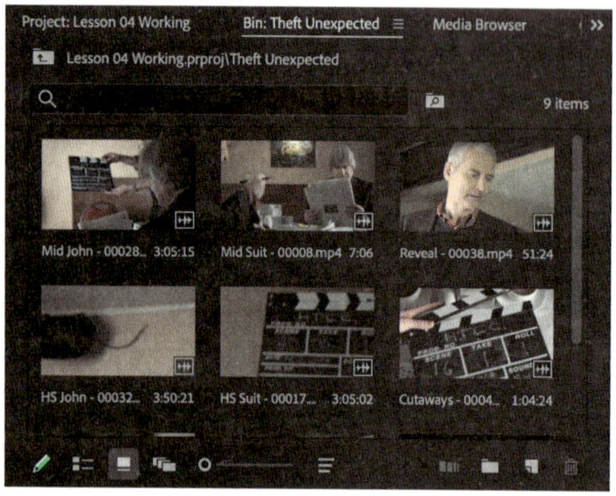

3 Try adjusting the Zoom control.

Premiere can display large thumbnails to make browsing and selecting your clips easier.

You can also apply various kinds of sorting to clip thumbnails in Icon view by clicking the Sort Icons menu.

4 Switch to List view.

When you're in List view, it doesn't help that much to zoom, unless you turn on the display of thumbnails in this view.

5 Open the panel menu next to the Theft Unexpected bin name at the top of the panel, and choose Thumbnails.

Premiere now displays thumbnails in List view, as well as in Icon view.

6 Drag the Zoom control to the right to increase the size of thumbnails.

Notice the numbers in the clip names. These are the original media filenames that were retained when descriptive names were added. For these lessons, we'll refer to the descriptive clip names only and omit the numbers taken from the original media.

By default, the clip thumbnails show the first frame of the media. In some clips, the first frame will not be particularly useful. Look at the clip Cutaways, for example. The thumbnail shows the clapperboard, but it would be useful to see the content.

7 Switch to Icon view .

In this view, you can hover your pointer over clip thumbnails to preview clips.

8 Hover your pointer over the Cutaways clip. Without clicking to select the clip, move the pointer until you find a frame that better represents the shot.

Tip: You can also change the poster frame by pressing the I key, which is the keyboard shortcut for Mark In, a command that sets the beginning of a selection when choosing part of a clip that you intend to add to a sequence. This shortcut will update the poster frame only if you haven't already set one.

9 While the frame you have chosen is displayed, press Command+P (macOS) or Shift+P (Windows).

This keyboard shortcut sets the poster frame for the clip.

Note: While in Icon view or Freeform view, selecting a clip by clicking its thumbnail reveals a small timeline control under it. Drag this timeline to view the contents of the clip.

10 Switch back to List view.

Premiere shows your newly selected frame as the thumbnail for this clip.

11 Choose Thumbnails from the Project panel menu to turn off thumbnails in List view.

12 Drag the Zoom control to the left to restore the default size for the clip icons.

Assigning labels

Every item in the Project panel has a label color. In List view, the Label column shows the label color for every clip. When you add clips to a sequence, they are displayed in the Timeline panel with this label color.

▶ **Tip:** Once your clips have the right label colors, you can right-click a clip at any time and choose Label > Select Label Group to select and highlight all visible items with the same label.

Let's change the label color for a title clip.

1 In the Theft Unexpected bin, right-click Theft_Unexpected.png and choose Label > Forest.

You can change label colors for multiple clips in a single step by selecting them and then right-clicking them to choose another label color.

2 Press Command+Z (macOS) or Ctrl+Z (Windows) to change the Theft_Unexpected.png label color back to Lavender.

When you add a clip to a sequence, Premiere creates a new instance, or copy, of that clip—you'll have one copy in the Project panel and one copy in the sequence. Both link to the same media file.

When you change the label color for a clip in the Project panel or rename a clip, it may or may not update copies of the clip in sequences.

You can toggle this setting by opening the Timeline Display Settings menu and choosing Show Source Clip Name And Label.

Changing names

Because clips in your project are separate from the media files they link to, you can rename items in Premiere without affecting the names of your original media files on the hard drive. This makes it safe to rename clips, which can be helpful when organizing a complex project.

When you opened the Theft Unexpected bin by holding Command (macOS) or Ctrl (Windows) while double-clicking it, it opened as a new panel in the same group as the Project panel. Let's begin by navigating between these bins.

1 At the top left of the Theft Unexpected bin, click the Navigate Up button to return to the Project panel.

The Project panel comes to the front and becomes the active panel, with an underline for the panel name. The Theft Unexpected bin is still open.

Whenever you navigate between bins that are already open, Premiere brings the existing open instance to the front. This way, you won't have multiple instances of the same bin taking up screen space.

2 Open the Graphics bin by double-clicking it.

3 Right-click the clip Theft_Unexpected.png and choose Rename.

4 Change the name to **TU Title BW** (that is, Theft Unexpected Title Black and White). After typing the new name, click the background of the Project panel to apply it.

5 Right-click the newly renamed clip, TU Title BW, and choose Reveal In Finder (macOS) or Reveal In Explorer (Windows).

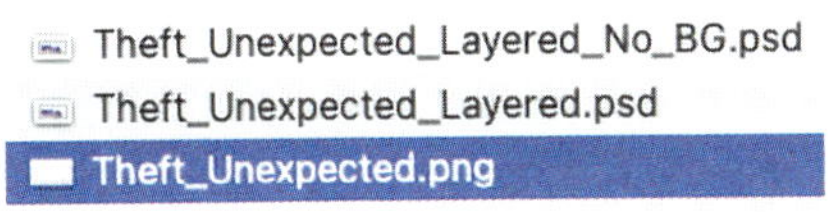

The original media file is displayed in its current location. Notice that the original filename has not changed.

Earlier you deleted a clip in this project and the original media file remained untouched—in a sense this is similar to renaming a clip in a project. Changing the clip in Premiere does not change the media file.

It's helpful to be clear about the relationship between your original media files and the clips inside the Premiere project because it explains much of the way the application works.

Tip: To rename an item in the Project panel, you can also click the item name, wait a moment, and click again, or you can select the item and press Return or Enter. Be sure to use the Return or Enter key on the right edge of the main alphanumeric keyboard rather than the Enter key on the numeric keyboard, if you have one.

Note: When you change the name of a clip in Premiere, the new name is stored in the project file. Different Premiere project files may use different names for the same clip. In fact, you could have two copies of a clip in the same project with different names.

Reviewing footage

The greater part of video editing is spent reviewing clips and making creative choices about them.

In Premiere, you can perform common tasks, such as playing video clips, in multiple ways. You can use the keyboard, click buttons with your pointer, or use an external device such as a jog/shuttle controller.

1 Navigate to the Theft Unexpected bin.

2 Click the Icon View button at the lower-left corner of the bin, and use the Zoom control to set the thumbnails to a size you are happy with.

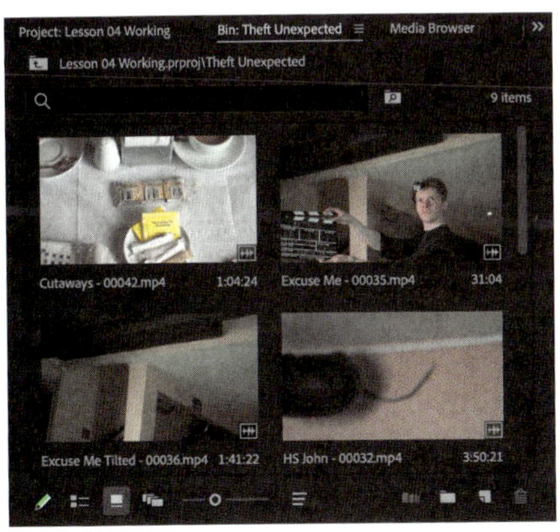

3 Hover your pointer over any of the thumbnails in the bin.

Premiere displays the contents of the clip as you move your pointer. This is called *hover scrubbing*. The left edge of the thumbnail represents the beginning of the clip, and the right edge represents the end. In this way, the width of the thumbnail represents the whole clip. While you're hover scrubbing, a tiny navigator appears at the bottom of the thumbnail.

4 Select a clip by clicking it once (be careful not to double-click, which will open the clip in the Source Monitor).

When you select the clip and hover your pointer over it, the navigator at the bottom of the thumbnail grows larger, and a small gray playhead appears. Try dragging through the clip using this playhead. When you do so, the clip audio will also play.

When a clip is selected, you also can use the J, K, and L keys on your keyboard to perform playback.

- **J:** Play backward
- **K:** Pause
- **L:** Play forward

Tip: If you press the J or L key multiple times, the video will play at multiple speeds. Pressing Shift+J or Shift+L reduces or increases playback speed in 10% increments.

5 Select a clip, and use the J, K, and L keys to play the video in the thumbnail. You can also use the spacebar to play and stop.

When you double-click a clip, Premiere displays the clip in the Source Monitor and also adds it to a list of recent clips.

6 Double-click five or six clips from the Theft Unexpected bin to open them in the Source Monitor.

Touchscreen editing

If you are working on a touchscreen computer, you may see additional controls on thumbnails in the Project panel.

These allow you to perform editing tasks without a mouse or trackpad. To see these controls on a non-touchscreen computer, click the panel menu and choose Thumbnail Controls For All Pointing Devices.

7 Open the Source Monitor panel menu to browse your recent clips.

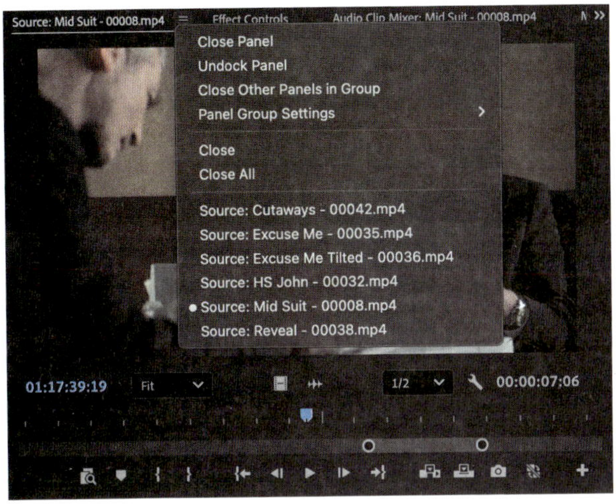

▶ **Tip:** Notice that you have the option to close a single clip or close all clips, clearing the menu and the monitor. Some editors like to clear the menu and then open several clips that are part of a scene by selecting them in the bin and dragging them into the Source Monitor together. You can then use the Source Monitor panel menu to browse only the clips from that selection. You can also quickly cycle through clips on this recent list by pressing Shift+2 with the Source Monitor active.

8 Open the Zoom Level menu at the bottom left of the Source Monitor.

By default, this is set to Fit, which means Premiere will display the whole frame, regardless of the original size. The resolution of your clips will often be higher than that of your Source Monitor. Change the setting to 100%.

Set to 100%, it's possible the image will be too large to fit the Source Monitor. If you are working on a very high-resolution screen, it's possible the image got smaller.

▶ **Tip:** Premiere has multiple tools for different purposes. You can use the Hand tool (with the keyboard shortcut H) to drag the view around in the Source Monitor and Program Monitor. Be sure to switch back to the Selection tool when you are finished.

The benefit of viewing with Zoom set to 100% is that you see every pixel of the original video, which is useful for checking the quality.

9 Now choose Fit from the Zoom Level menu.

Using essential playback controls

Let's look at the Source Monitor playback controls.

1. Double-click the shot Excuse Me (not Excuse Me Tilted) in the Theft Unexpected bin to open it in the Source Monitor.

> **Tip:** Hover your pointer over each button to see the name and keyboard shortcut (in parentheses).

2. At the bottom of the Source Monitor, you'll find a blue playhead marker. Drag it along the bottom of the panel to view various parts of the clip. You can also click wherever you want the playhead to go, and it will jump to that spot.

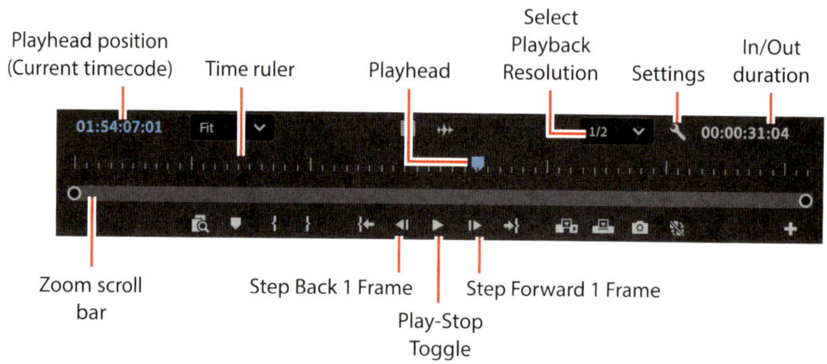

3. Below the time ruler and its playhead, there's a scroll bar that doubles as a Zoom control. Drag one end of this scroll bar toward the other to zoom in on the time ruler. This will make it easier to navigate longer clips precisely.

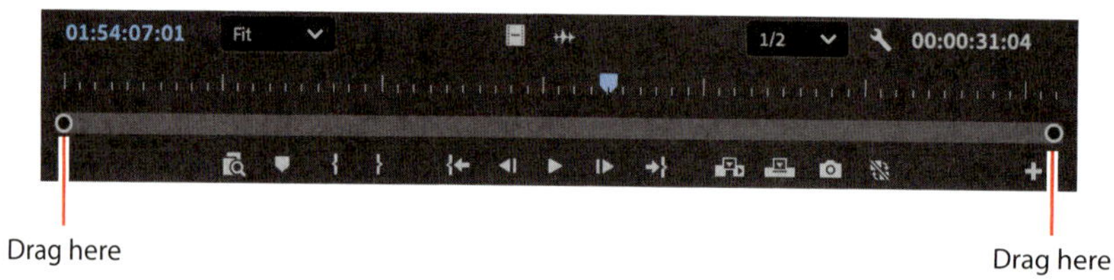

4. Click the Play-Stop Toggle to play the clip. Click it again to stop playback. You can also use the spacebar to start and stop playback.
5. Click the Step Back 1 Frame and Step Forward 1 Frame buttons to move through the clip one frame at a time. You can also use the Left Arrow and Right Arrow keys on your keyboard.
6. Try using the J, K, and L keys to play your clip.
7. Try holding K while you press and release the J or L key. The playhead will move one frame and play the associated audio, making it useful when seeking a precise moment in dialogue.

> **Note:** Panel selection is important when using keyboard shortcuts (and menus). If you find the J, K, and L keys don't work, double-check that the Source Monitor is selected (outlined in blue).

Lowering the playback resolution

If you have an older or slower computer processor or are working with large frame sizes, such as Ultra High-Definition (UHD, 4K, 8K, or above), your computer may struggle to play all the frames of your video clips. Clips will play with the correct timing (10 seconds of video will still take 10 seconds), but some frames may not be displayed.

Tip: If you are working with a particularly powerful computer, you may want to choose High Quality Playback from the monitor Settings menu. This maximizes preview playback quality, particularly for compressed media like H.264 video, graphics, and stills (potentially at the expense of playback performance).

To work with a wide variety of computer hardware configurations, from powerful desktop workstations to lightweight portable laptops, Premiere can lower the playback resolution to help make playback smoother.

There are separate menus in the Source Monitor and Program Monitor to set the playback resolution. The default resolution is 1/2.

You can change the playback resolution using the Select Playback Resolution menu on the Source Monitor or Program Monitor.

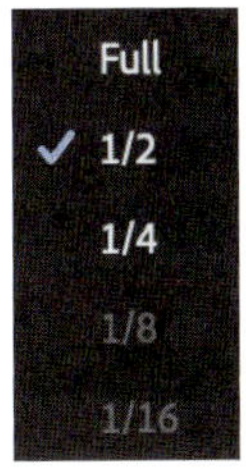

Some lower resolutions are not available when working with particular media types. For these media types, the work of converting the image to a lower resolution might be more than the work saved by not playing full resolution (not all codecs can be played back at a lower resolution efficiently). In these cases, some resolutions will automatically be dimmed and unavailable.

Navigating with timecode

At the bottom left of the Source Monitor, a timecode display in blue shows the current position of the playhead in hours, minutes, seconds, and frames (00:00:00:00), according to the clip's timecode. For example, 01:54:07:01 is 1 hour, 54 minutes, 7 seconds, and 01 frame.

Clip timecode may not begin at 00:00:00:00, so you should not count on this number to assess the duration of a clip.

At the bottom right of the Source Monitor, a timecode display in light gray shows the duration of your current clip selection.

By default, this shows the whole clip duration, but later you'll add special In point and Out point marks to make a partial selection. When you do, the duration shown will update.

In and Out points are simple to use: Click the Mark In button to set the beginning of the part of a clip you want to use, and click the Mark Out button to set the end of the part of a clip you want. You'll learn more about this in Lesson 5, "Editing Video—the Essentials."

Displaying safe margins

Television monitors often crop the edges of the picture to achieve a clean edge. Open the Settings menu at the bottom of the Source Monitor, and choose Safe Margins to display useful outlines over the image.

The outer box is the action-safe zone. Aim to keep important action inside this box so that when the picture is displayed, edge cropping does not hide what's going on.

The inner box is the title-safe zone. Keep titles and graphics inside this box so that even on a badly adjusted display, your audience will be able to read the words.

Modern televisions crop the frame very little, and online videos are not cropped at all, though you may be delivering content with planned graphic overlays that cover the edges of your video. You'll probably want to adjust the size of the safe zones according to your intended delivery medium.

Premiere has advanced overlay options that you can configure to display useful information in the Source Monitor and Program Monitor. To enable or disable overlays, open the monitor's Settings menu and choose Overlays.

You can access the specific settings for overlays and safe margins by clicking the monitor's Settings menu and choosing Overlay Settings > Settings.

You can disable Safe Margins or Overlays by choosing them from the Source Monitor or Program Monitor's Settings menu again. Do so now so you can see the image clearly.

Customizing the monitors

To customize the way a monitor displays video, open each monitor's Settings menu .

The Source Monitor and Program Monitor have similar options. In the Source Monitor, you can view the waveform of the audio in the clip, which shows amplitude over time (useful if you are searching for a particular sound or the start of a word).

For now, make sure Composite Video is chosen from the Source Monitor Settings menu.

You can quickly switch between viewing the clip audio waveform and the video by clicking Drag Video Only or Drag Audio Only, just under the middle of the video display.

These icons are mainly used to drag only the video or only the audio part of a clip into a sequence, but they also provide this useful shortcut to view the audio waveform or composite video.

You can add, move, or remove buttons at the bottom of the Source Monitor and Program Monitor. Note that any customizations you make to the buttons on one of the monitor panels are applied only to that panel.

1 Click the Button Editor at the lower right of the Source Monitor.

  The complete set of available buttons appears on a floating panel.

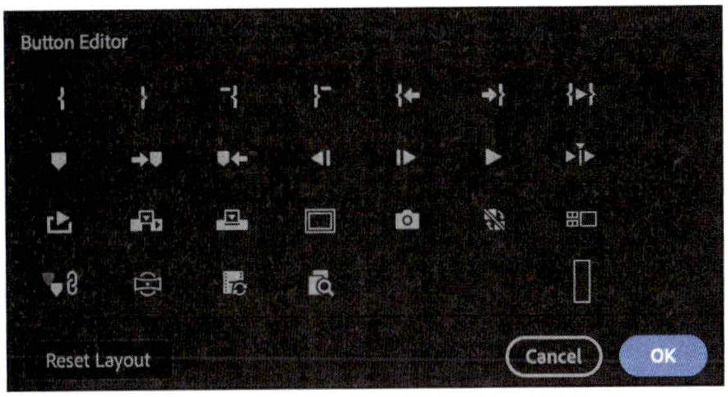

2 Drag the Loop Playback button from the floating panel to a spot to the right of the Play button on the Source Monitor (the other buttons will automatically make space for it), and click OK to close the Button Editor.

3 Make sure that the Excuse Me clip is still open in the Source Monitor.

4 Click the Loop Playback button you added to activate it. The button has a gray highlight when it's activated.

5 Click the Play button to play the clip. Play the video using the spacebar or the Play button on the Source Monitor. Stop the playback when you see the video start again.

  With Loop turned on, Premiere continuously repeats playback of a clip or sequence. If there are In and Out points set, playback loops between them. This is a great way to review a section of a clip.

Tip: If you are comfortable using keyboard shortcuts only, you can hide all of the buttons along the lower edge of the Source Monitor or Program Monitor. To do so, deselect Show Transport Controls in the Source Monitor or Program Monitor Settings menu. Choose this item again to restore the buttons.

Modifying clips

▶ **Tip:** If you are not familiar with terms like *metadata*, check out the glossary at the back of the book. It offers explanations for many of the specialized terms used when describing post-production.

Premiere uses metadata associated with media files to know how to play linked clips. For example, information about the playback frame rate is stored in the media file as metadata. This metadata is normally added when the media is created (by the camera, for example), but occasionally it might be missing or set wrong. Sometimes, you'll need to tell Premiere how to interpret clips.

You can change the interpretation for one clip or multiple clips in a single step. All instances of selected clips (including copies already edited into a sequence) are affected by changes you make to interpretation.

Choosing audio channels

Premiere has advanced audio management features. You can create complex sound mixes and selectively target output audio channels with original clip audio. You can work with mono, stereo, 5.1, Ambisonics, and even 32-channel sequences and clips with precise control over the routing of audio channels.

If you're just starting out, you'll probably want to produce sequences mastered in stereo using mono or stereo source clips. In this case, the default settings are most likely all you will need.

When recording audio with a professional camera, it's common to have one microphone record onto one audio channel and a second microphone record onto another audio channel. These are the same audio channels that would be used for regular stereo audio, but they now contain completely separate sound.

What is an audio channel?

When an audio recording is created, it's always captured and stored as one or more audio channels. Think of a channel as a single signal—something you could hear with one ear.

Because we have two ears, we are able to hear in stereo—sensing where a sound comes from by comparing differences in the way the sound arrives at each ear. The process happens automatically and precognitively (your conscious mind doesn't do any analysis to sense where a sound comes from).

To capture stereo (the sound two ears can detect), you need two signals, so two channels are recorded using microphones.

One signal (let's say the sound a microphone captures) is captured as one channel in an audio recording. For output, one channel will play through one speaker or headphone ear. The more channels you have for recording, the more sources you can capture independently (think of capturing an entire orchestra with many channels to be able to adjust the volume of each instrument separately in post-production).

To play audio with different volume levels on multiple speakers (for surround sound, for example), you need multiple playback channels. You'll learn more about working with audio in Lesson 10, "Editing and Mixing Audio."

Your camera adds metadata to the audio to tell Premiere whether the sound is meant to be mono (separate audio channels) or stereo (channel 1 audio and channel 2 audio combined to produce the complete stereo mix).

You can tell Premiere how to interpret audio channels when new media files are imported by choosing Premiere > Settings > Timeline > Default Audio Tracks (macOS) or Edit > Preferences > Timeline > Default Audio Tracks (Windows).

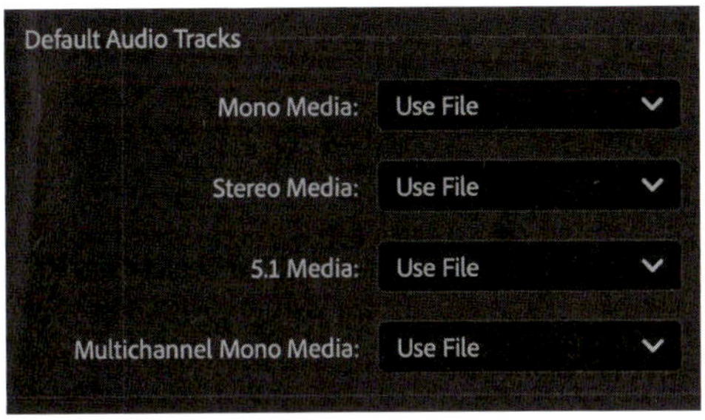

The Use File option means Premiere will use the audio channel settings applied to the clip when it was created. You can override that option for each media type using the appropriate menu.

If the setting was wrong when you imported your clips, it's easy to set a different way to interpret the audio channels in the Project panel.

1 Click the name of the Theft Unexpected bin to bring it to the front. If the bin is not open, double-click it to open it in the Project panel.

2 Right-click the Reveal clip in the Theft Unexpected bin and choose Modify > Audio Channels (or press Shift+G).

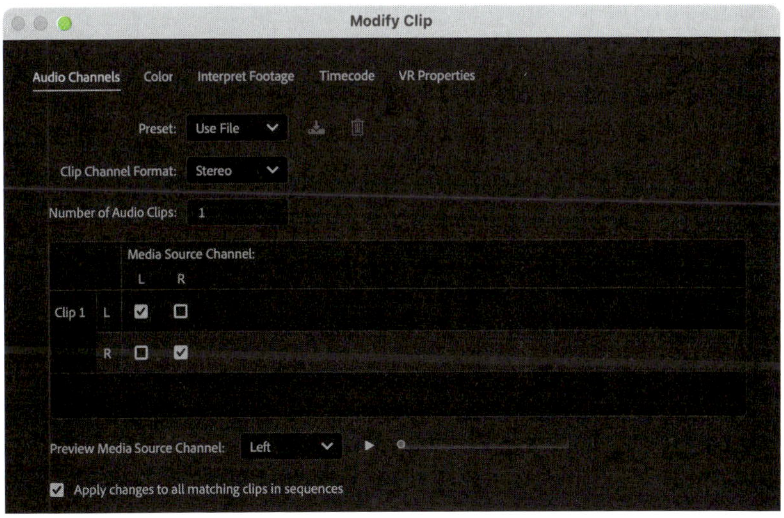

When the Preset menu is set to Use File, as it is here, Premiere will use the file's metadata to set the channel format for the audio.

Note: Changes made to clip interpretation are applied to the clip, not the media file it is linked to. This means you could have two copies of a clip, both linked to the same media file but with different interpretation settings. The media file is not changed.

In this case, Clip Channel Format is set to Stereo, and Number Of Audio Clips is set to 1—that's the number of audio clips that will be added to a sequence if you edit this clip into it.

Now look at the channel matrix below those options. The Left and Right audio channels of the source clip (described as Media Source Channel) are both assigned to a single clip (described as Clip 1).

When you add this clip to a sequence, it will appear as one video clip and one audio clip, with both audio channels in the same audio clip.

3 Open the Preset menu, and choose Mono. Be sure to use the Preset menu and not the Clip Channel Format menu.

Premiere switches the Clip Channel Format menu to Mono, so the Left and Right source channels are now linked to two separate clips.

This means that when you add the clip to a sequence, each audio channel will go on a separate track, as separate clips, allowing you to work on them independently.

4 Click OK.

A few tips on audio clip channel interpretation

Here are some things to keep in mind when working with audio clip channel interpretation:

- In the Modify Clip dialog box, every available audio channel will be listed. If your source audio has channels you don't need, you can deselect them, and those empty channels won't take up space in your sequence as clips.
- If you override the original file audio channel interpretation (mono, stereo, etc.), you may need a different type of audio track when the clip is added to a sequence. If one isn't available, a new track of the correct type will be added automatically to accommodate the clip.
- The list of clips on the left (which may be as short as one clip) shows how many audio clips will be added to a sequence when edited in.
- Use the checkboxes to choose which source audio channels are included when the clip is edited into a sequence. This means you can combine multiple source audio channels into a single sequence clip or separate them into different clips in any way that works for your project.
- Changes made to audio clip channel interpretation will not update clip instances that are already edited into a sequence. The next time you edit a modified clip into a sequence, the new interpretation will apply. This means you could have two instances of the same clip in a sequence with different audio channel configurations.

Merging clips

It's common for professional video to be recorded on a camera with relatively low-quality audio, while high-quality sound is recorded on a separate device. When working this way, you'll want to combine the high-quality audio with the video by merging them in the Project panel.

The most important factor when merging video and audio files in this way is synchronization for the audio. You will either manually define a sync point—like a clapperboard mark—or allow Premiere to sync your clips automatically based on their original timecode information or by matching up their audio.

If you choose to sync clips using audio, Premiere will analyze both the in-camera audio and the separately captured sound and match them up. The option to sync automatically using the audio in both clips makes it worthwhile attaching a microphone to your camera, even if you know you won't use the audio in post-production. The following steps are described for your information only—no need to follow along.

1 If you don't have matching audio in the clips you are merging, you can manually add a marker to each clip you want to merge on a clear sync point like a clapperboard or a visible and audible hand clap. The keyboard shortcut to add a marker is M.

2 Select the camera clip and the separate audio clip, right-click either item, and choose Merge Clips.

   There's an option to use audio timecode (sometimes useful for older, archived tape-based media).

   There's also an option to automatically remove the unwanted audio included with the audio-video clip. You may want to keep that audio, though, just in case there's a momentary issue with the external microphone audio, like something bumping the microphone.

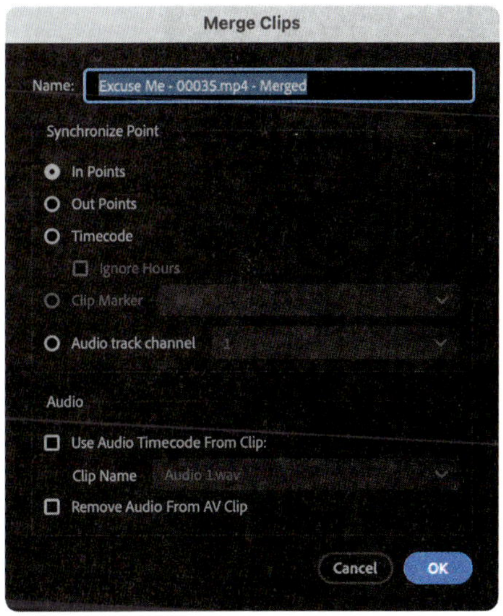

3 Under Synchronize Point, select your sync method, and click OK to create a new clip that combines the video and the "good" audio in a single item.

   A new clip is created that contains the selected video and audio.

Note: You can also sync multiple video and audio clips in a single step using the more advanced Multicamera Source Sequence workflow. For more information on this workflow, check out the Best Practices and Workflow Guide for Long Form and Episodic Post Production, available at *helpx.adobe.com*.

Interpreting video footage

For Premiere to play a clip correctly, it needs to know the frame rate for the video, the pixel aspect ratio (the shape of the pixels), the color space, and, if your clip is interlaced, the order in which to display the fields. Premiere can usually find out this information from the file's metadata, but you can override the interpretation easily. Let's try this now:

1. Use the Media Browser panel to import RED Video.R3D from the Assets/Video and Audio Files/RED folder. Then double-click the clip to open it in the Source Monitor. It's full anamorphic widescreen, which is wider than regular 16×9 footage. This wider aspect ratio is achieved by using pixels that are wider.
2. Right-click the clip in the Project panel and choose Modify > Interpret Footage.

   The option to modify audio channels is unavailable because this clip has no audio.

   Right now, the clip is set to use the pixel aspect ratio setting from the file: Anamorphic 2:1. This means the pixels are twice as wide as they are tall.
3. In the Pixel Aspect Ratio section, select Conform To, choose Square Pixels (1.0), and click OK.

   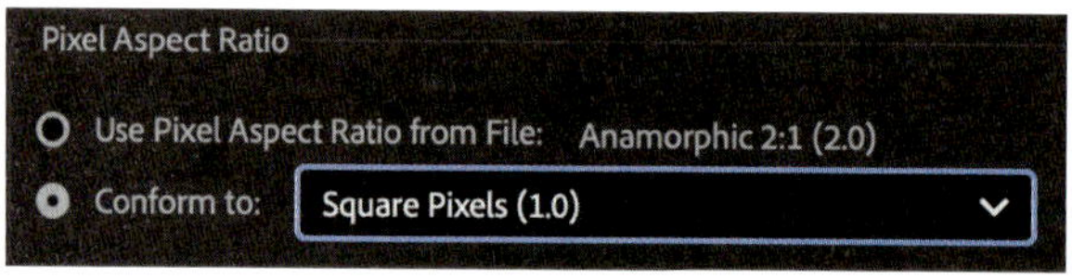

   Take a look at the clip in the Source Monitor. The clip looks almost square!
4. Try another aspect ratio. Right-click the clip in the Project panel and choose Modify > Interpret Footage. Choose DVCPRO HD (1.5) from the Conform To menu. Click OK, and take a look at the clip again in the Source Monitor.

From now on, Premiere will interpret the clip as having pixels that are 1.5 times wider than they are tall. This reshapes the picture to make it standard 16:9 widescreen.

Changing the pixel aspect ratio is rarely a good solution because it widens or compresses horizontal space in the picture—all circles will become ovals, for example. However, if all circles already appear to be ovals and all squares appear to be rectangles, it may be that you need to correct the pixel aspect ratio interpretation for technical reasons.

Review questions

1 How do you change the List view column headings displayed in the Project panel?

2 How can you quickly filter the display of clips in the Project panel to make finding a clip easier?

3 How do you create a new bin?

4 If you change the name of a clip in the Project panel, does it change the name of the media file it links to on your hard drive?

5 What keyboard shortcuts can you use to play video and sound clips?

6 How can you change the way clip audio channels are interpreted?

Review answers

1 Open the Project panel menu, and choose Metadata Display. Select the checkbox for any column heading you want to appear. You can also right-click a heading and choose Metadata Display to access these settings.

2 Click the Search field, and start typing the name of the clip you are looking for. Premiere hides clips that don't match what you typed and reveals those that do, even if they are in a closed bin. Any clips with the characters you type in their metadata will be displayed.

3 There are several ways to create a new bin: by clicking the New Bin button at the bottom of the Project panel, by choosing File > New > Bin, by right-clicking a blank area in the Project panel and choosing New Bin, or by pressing Command+B (macOS) or Ctrl+B (Windows). You can also drag clips onto the New Bin button on the Project panel. Premiere can even automatically create a new bin when importing media.

4 No. You can duplicate, rename, or delete clips in your Project panel, and nothing will happen to your original media files.

5 The spacebar starts and stops playback. You can use the J, K, and L keys like a shuttle controller to play backward and forward, and you can move one frame backward or one frame forward with the arrow keys. If you are using a trackpad, you may be able to position your pointer over the video in a monitor or over the Timeline panel and use gestures to scrub through the content.

6 In the Project panel, right-click the clip you want to change and choose Modify > Audio Channels or press Shift+G. Choose the correct option (usually by selecting a preset), and click OK.

5 EDITING VIDEO—THE ESSENTIALS

Lesson overview

In this lesson, you'll learn how to do the following:

- Work with clips in the Source Monitor.
- Create sequences.
- Use essential editing commands.
- View timecode.
- Understand tracks.

This lesson will take about 75 minutes to complete. To get the files used in this lesson, refer to the instructions in "Accessing the lesson files and Web Edition" in the "Getting Started" section at the beginning of this book. Store the files on your computer in a convenient location.

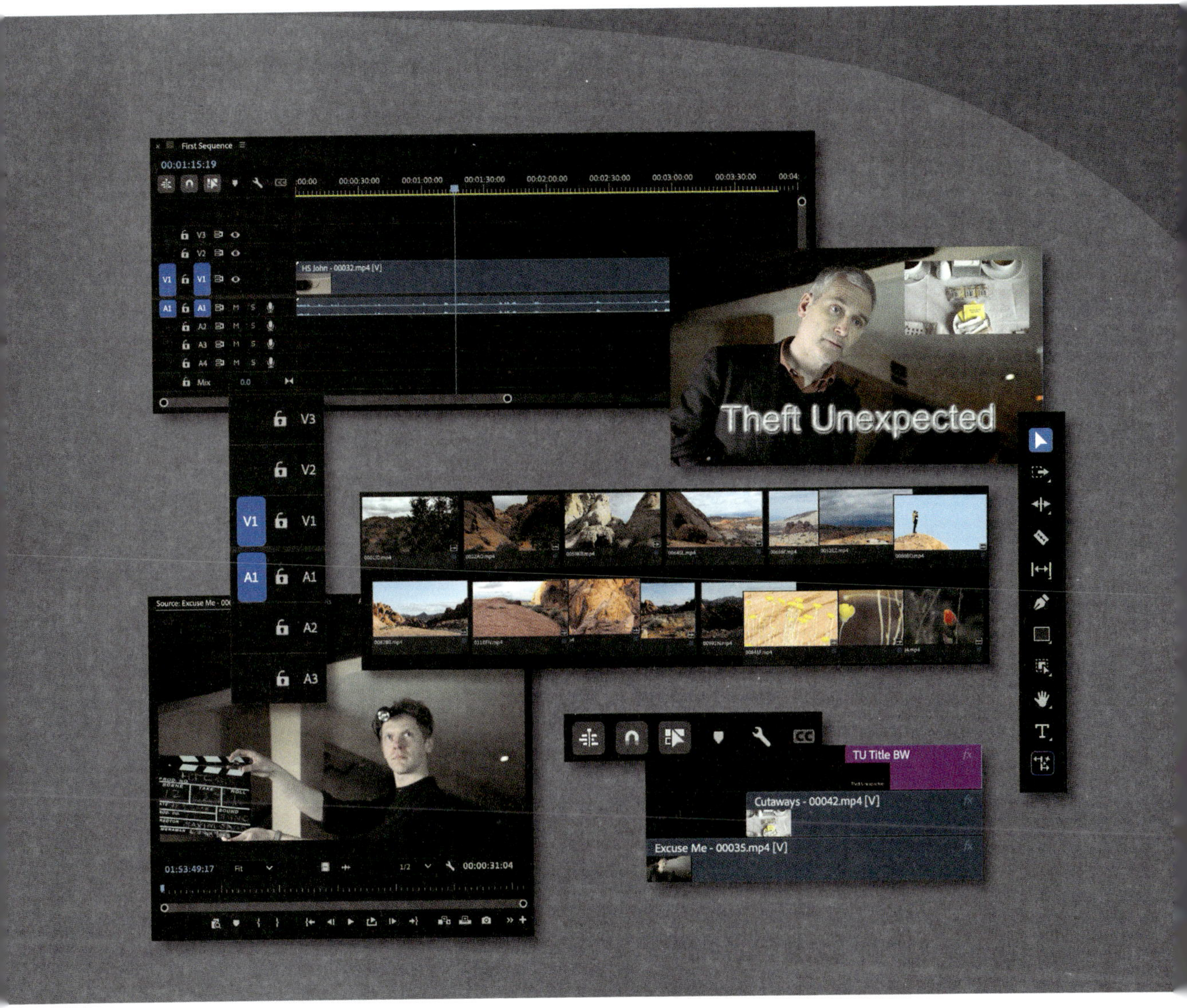

This lesson will teach you the core editing skills you will use again and again in Adobe Premiere. Editing is much more than choosing shots. You'll choose your edits precisely, place clips in sequences at exactly the right point in time and on the tracks you want (to create layered visual effects), add new clips to existing sequences, and remove unwanted content (that you can restore later if you want—this is *nonlinear* editing, after all).

Starting the lesson

● **Note:** To ensure that the tools function and the defaults are set exactly as described in this lesson, reset the Premiere preferences by holding any modifier key (such as Shift) while launching the application, selecting Reset App Preferences, and then clicking Continue in the Reset Options dialog box.

There is much more to video editing than cutting and pasting footage into sequences—it's the art and craft of visual storytelling. Many of the exercises in this book will walk you through the steps of crafting a short video, making creative decisions for you, so you can focus on learning the tools and techniques.

For the following examples, you'll use footage of a chance encounter between two strangers in a London café. The footage was shot from a variety of angles to allow the editor to choose the way the story will be told, from the points of view of either a participant or a nonparticipating, hypothetical observer.

Editing helps to propel the story and maintain the viewer's interest by switching between the viewpoints of the participants and by revealing events to the audience that neither participant is aware of.

The start of the process is to review all the available footage and to choose the best shots. To save time, the sifting has already been done for you, and you will be guided to the shots to use and given the precise timing for the edits.

Working with clip names

Clip names are important. Having well-organized and clearly named clips can save hours of post-production time.

The clip names in this project incorporate new regular names (to help identify the contents) as well as the original media file numbers to help track the footage.

There are no fixed rules about naming and organizing clips, and throughout these lessons you will encounter various naming conventions. In the later sidebar "Shot types and clip names," you'll learn about common abbreviations.

Throughout these exercises, the additional numbers in the clip names will be ignored for brevity.

No matter how you approach video editing, you'll use a few simple techniques time and again. Most of the practice of video editing is carefully reviewing and making partial selections of your clips and placing them in your sequence. There are several ways to do this in Premiere.

Before you begin, you'll make sure you're using the Editing workspace.

1. Open the Lesson 05.prproj project file from the Lessons folder.
2. Open the Workspaces menu in the upper-right corner of the Premiere interface and make sure Editing is selected. Then use the same menu to choose Reset To Saved Layout.
3. Choose File > Save As.

4 Rename the file **Lesson 05 Working.prproj**.

5 Browse to the Lessons folder, and click Save to save the project.

You'll begin by learning more about the Source Monitor and how to add In and Out points to your clips to select the parts that will be added to a sequence. Then you'll learn about the Timeline panel, where you'll work on your sequence.

Using the Source Monitor

The Source Monitor is the main place you'll go when you want to review your assets before including them in a sequence.

> **Tip:** Change clip interpretation by right-clicking the clip in the Project panel and choosing Modify > Interpret Footage.

When you view a video clip in the Source Monitor, you watch it in its original format. That is, it will play back with its frame rate, frame size, field order, audio sample rate, and audio bit depth exactly as when recorded, unless you changed the way the clip is interpreted. For more on how to do this, see Lesson 4, "Organizing Media."

When you add a clip to a sequence, however, Premiere conforms it to the sequence settings. For example, if the clip and the sequence don't match, the clip frame rate and audio sample rate will be adjusted so that all the clips in the sequence play back the same way.

As well as being a viewer for multiple types of media, the Source Monitor provides important additional functions. You can add comments to a clip in the form of markers that you can refer to later or use to remind yourself about important facts relating to a clip. For example, you might include a note about part of a shot you don't have permission to use. You can also use two special kinds of markers, called the *In point* and *Out point*, to select part of a clip for inclusion in a sequence.

Opening a clip in the Source Monitor

Opening clips in the Source Monitor is a little like opening files in the Finder (macOS) or Explorer (Windows). First, you'll try navigating the Project panel.

> **Tip:** Notice that the currently active panel has a blue outline. It's important to know which panel is active because menus and keyboard shortcuts sometimes give different results depending on your current selection.

1. In the Project panel, presuming your preferences have default settings, double-click the Theft Unexpected bin to open it.

   In the same way that you would double-click a folder in the Finder (macOS) or Explorer (Windows), you have navigated into the bin.

2. Return to the Project panel contents by clicking the Navigate Up button at the top left of the bin panel.

3. Double-click the RED Video.R3D video clip, or drag it into the Source Monitor. You may need to scroll down in the Project panel to find the clip.

   Premiere displays the clip in the Source Monitor, ready for you to review and add In and Out points.

4. Position your pointer so that it is over the Source Monitor, and press the ` (accent grave) key. The panel fills the Premiere application frame, giving you a larger view of your video clip. Press the key again to restore the Source Monitor to its original size. If your keyboard does not have a ` (accent grave) key, you can double-click the panel name to toggle the full-screen view.

Viewing video on a second monitor

If you have a second monitor connected to your computer, Premiere can use it to display full-screen video.

Choose Premiere > Settings > Playback (macOS) or Edit > Preferences > Playback (Windows), and make sure Enable Mercury Transmit is selected. Under the Device Name heading, you'll see all connected monitors. Select the Video Stream checkbox for the monitor you want to use for full-screen playback.

The Adobe SRT (Secure Reliable Transport) option on the Primary Audio Device menu allows you to monitor video via Wi-Fi or a wired network.

You also have the option of playing video via third-party hardware, if it is installed. It's common to use third-party hardware to make different physical connections available for monitoring purposes. Check your third-party hardware user guide for installation and setup.

> **Tip:** For more information about Adobe SRT, check out *blog.frame.io/2024/08/25/complete-2024-premiere-pro-color-correction-guide/#Remote_viewing_with_SRT_Secure_Reliable_Transport*.

Using Source Monitor controls

As well as playback controls, there are some important additional buttons in the Source Monitor.

- **Add Marker:** Adds a marker to the clip at the location of the playhead. Markers can provide a simple visual reference, can be various colors, and can store comments.
- **Mark In:** Sets the In point at the current playhead location. The In point is the beginning of the part of the clip you intend to use in a sequence. You can have only one In point per clip or sequence, so a new In point will automatically replace an existing one.
- **Mark Out:** Sets the Out point at the current playhead location. The Out point is the end of the part of the clip you intend to use in a sequence. You can have only one Out point, so the new Out point will automatically replace an existing one.
- **Go To In:** Moves the playhead to the clip In point.
- **Go To Out:** Moves the playhead to the clip Out point.
- **Insert:** Adds the clip to the active sequence displayed in the Timeline panel using the *insert edit* method (see "Using essential editing commands" later in this lesson).
- **Overwrite:** Adds the clip to the active sequence displayed in the Timeline panel using the *overwrite* edit method (see "Using essential editing commands" later in this lesson).
- **Export Frame:** Allows you to create a still image file from whatever is displayed in the monitor. See Lesson 16, "Exporting Frames, Clips, and Sequences," for more on this.
- **Toggle Proxies:** If your media has proxies attached, click to toggle between viewing the proxy media and original media.

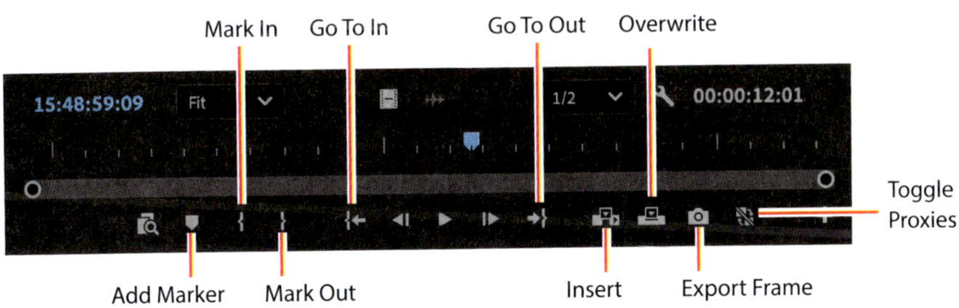

Selecting a range in a clip

You will often want to include only a specific part of a clip in a sequence. Much of an editor's time is spent watching video clips and choosing not only which ones to use but also which *parts* to use, including only the best performances and excluding technical mistakes or fluffed lines. Let's make some partial selections:

Note: In and Out points added to clips are persistent. That is, they will still be present if you close and reopen the clip—or even the project.

1. In the Theft Unexpected bin, double-click the clip Excuse Me (not Excuse Me Tilted) to open it in the Source Monitor. It's a shot of John nervously asking whether he can sit down.

2. Play the clip to get an idea of the action.

   John walks on-screen about halfway through the shot but takes a moment to speak.

Tip: If you hover your pointer over a button, a tool tip appears displaying the name of the button followed by its keyboard shortcut in parentheses (if it has one).

3. Position the playhead around 01:54:06:00, just as John pauses briefly and speaks. Note that the timecode for this clip does not start at 00:00:00:00.

4. Click the Mark In button {. You can also press the I key on your keyboard.

   Premiere highlights the section of the clip that you selected. You have excluded the first part of the clip, but you can easily reclaim this part later if you need to do so—that's the freedom of nonlinear editing!

Tip: Most cameras will record timecode in such a way that repetition is avoided, which can result in large numbers. If you want the timecode for all clips to be displayed as starting at 00:00:00:00, you can choose this option in the Media preferences, using the Timecode menu.

5. Position the playhead just as John begins to sit down. Around 01:54:14:00 is perfect.

Using a numeric keypad

If your keyboard has a separate numeric keypad, you can use it to enter timecode numbers directly. For example, if you type 700 and press the Enter key when the Source Monitor is active, Premiere will position the playhead at 00:00:07:00. There's no need to enter the leading zeros or number separators. Be sure to use the numeric keypad, on the right on your keyboard, and not the numbers along the top of your keyboard (these have a different use). This works in the Program Monitor and Timeline panel too.

Tip: If you have added the Loop Playback button to the Source Monitor (see Lesson 4) and the option is activated (the button has a gray highlight), clips will loop between In and Out points when you play them.

6. Click the Mark Out button } or press the O key on your keyboard to add an Out point.

Some editors prefer to go through all the available clips, adding In and Out points as required, before building a sequence. Some editors prefer to add In and Out points only as they use each clip. Your preference may depend on the kind of project you are working on.

Now you'll add In and Out points for two more clips. Double-click the icon for each clip in the Project panel to open it in the Source Monitor.

Our goal is to produce an edited sequence with natural-looking movement from one shot to the next and nuanced timing for dialogue.

As an editor, you would normally carefully review content to find the ideal moments to cut between shots. To save time, the precise timing has already been worked out and included in these steps.

First, we'll get a couple of seconds of the man in the suit giving John permission to share his table; then, we'll get another clip from the opposite angle showing John taking his seat.

Tip: To help you find your way around your footage, Premiere can display timecode on the Source Monitor and Program Monitor time rulers. Toggle this option on and off by clicking either monitor's Settings menu and choosing Time Ruler Numbers.

Editing from the Project panel

In points and Out points applied to clips remain active in your project until you change them, so you can add clips to a sequence directly from the Project panel, as well as from the Source Monitor. If you have already looked at all your clips and selected the parts you want, this can be a quick way to create a rough version of a sequence.

You can add In and Out points directly in the Project panel too: While in Icon view, hover over a clip to see a preview of the contents and press the I and O keys to add In and Out points. You can even use the J, K, and L keys to play selected clip thumbnails.

Premiere applies the same editing controls when you're working from the Project panel as it does when you're using the Source Monitor, so the experience is similar—and a few clicks quicker.

Of course, although it's faster to work this way, there's also value in having one last look at your clips in the Source Monitor before you add them to a sequence.

7 For the HS Suit clip, add an In point just after John's line of dialogue, about a quarter of the way into the shot at 01:27:00:16.

8 Add an Out point when John passes in front of the camera, blocking our view at 01:27:02:14.

9 For the Mid John clip, add an In point just as John begins to sit down at 01:39:52:00.

Tip: If the Source Monitor is active, you can press Tab to make the Playhead Position timecode active and selected, ready to type in new timecode. You can copy and paste new timecode in or type new numbers.

10 Add an Out point after he has a sip of tea at 01:40:04:00.

Shot types and clip names

Filmmakers use common names for types of shot framing, and these are often abbreviated when naming clips to make identifying footage quicker and easier.

For example, the HS Suit clip is a *head and shoulder shot* of the Suit character, while the Mid John clip is a *mid shot* of the John character.

Here are some common shot types and their abbreviations. These descriptions vary, and there are subtle differences from one cinematographer to another, but this brief list shows the broad differences in coverage between the types:

- **Extreme Close-Up (ECU):** A very close shot of a character's face—close enough to crop out their hair and/or chin.
- **Close-Up (CU):** A close shot of a character's face that usually incorporates just the character's head.
- **Head and Shoulder (HS):** A close shot that incorporates the character's head and shoulders.
- **Mid/Medium (Mid or MS):** A shot that includes the character's head to their waist.
- **Mid-Wide or Medium Wide (MWS):** A shot that includes the character's head to their knees.
- **Wide (WS or Wide):** A shot that includes the whole body of the character from their head to their toes.
- **Extreme Wide (EWS):** A shot that includes the whole body of the character and a substantial amount of space around them.
- **Two Shot (2S):** A shot that includes two characters.
- **Group Shot (GS):** A shot that includes several characters.
- **General Views (GV):** Views of the environment or exteriors, often used for story exposition to introduce the location.
- **Cutaways/B-Roll (Alt or B-Roll):** Shots that the editor can cut to during a scene, allowing cuts between takes to be disguised. Cutaways also add to the scene by offering additional visual cues to inform the audience. For example, as a character describes an object they are looking at, we might cut away to a shot of that object.

Creating subclips

If you are working with a long clip, you might want to use more than one part in your sequence. It can be useful to separate the parts so they can be organized in the Project panel prior to building your sequence.

This is exactly what subclips let you do. *Subclips* are partial copies of clips. They are commonly used when working with long clips, such as interview footage, where there are several parts of the same original clip that might be used in a sequence.

Subclips have a few notable characteristics.

- They can be organized in bins and renamed, just like regular clips, although they have a different icon in the Project panel.
- They have a limited duration based on the In and Out points used to create them, which makes viewing their contents easier when compared with viewing potentially much longer original clips.
- They share the same media as the original clip they are based on, so if an original media file is deleted or moved to a different folder, both the original clip and any subclips will go "offline"—with no media displayed.
- They can be edited to change their contents and even converted into a copy of the original full-length clip.

The short film *Theft Unexpected* depicts a comic moment between two characters at a railway café. Our protagonist, John, believes a stranger at his table is shamelessly stealing his cookies. At the last moment, it's revealed that John's cookies were safe under his newspaper the whole time; John has been stealing the other man's cookies accidentally.

Let's make a subclip to make it easier to find a critical moment with the packet of cookies.

1. In the Theft Unexpected bin, double-click the Cutaways clip to view it in the Source Monitor.
2. Click the Project panel to make it active, while displaying the contents of the Theft Unexpected bin. Click the New Bin button at the bottom of the panel to create a new bin. The new bin will appear inside the Theft Unexpected bin.
3. Name the bin **Subclips**, and double-click it to open it.
4. Choose a section of the clip to turn into a subclip by marking the clip with an In point and an Out point. Around 02:04:05:00, before the second time the packet is removed, would make a good In point. Around 02:04:15:00, after the packet is placed back on the table, would make a good Out point.

As with many workflows in Premiere, there are several ways to create subclips, and the outcome is always the same.

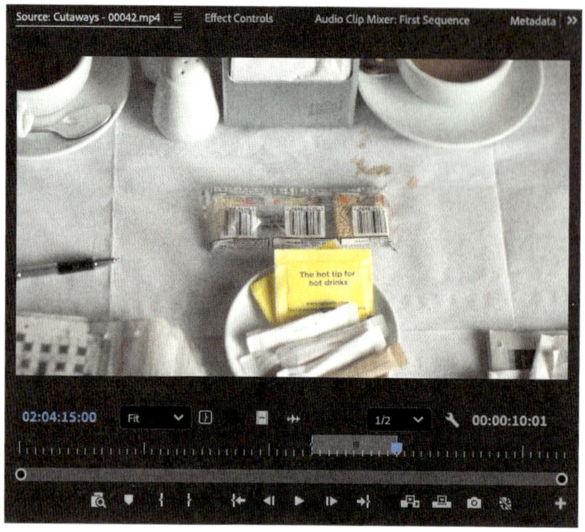

5 Try one of the following:

- Right-click in the picture display of the Source Monitor and choose Make Subclip.
- With the Source Monitor active, choose Clip > Make Subclip.
- With the Source Monitor active, press Command+U (macOS) or Ctrl+U (Windows).
- While holding Command (macOS) or Ctrl (Windows), drag the picture from the middle of the Source Monitor into the Project panel bin.

The Make Subclip dialog box opens.

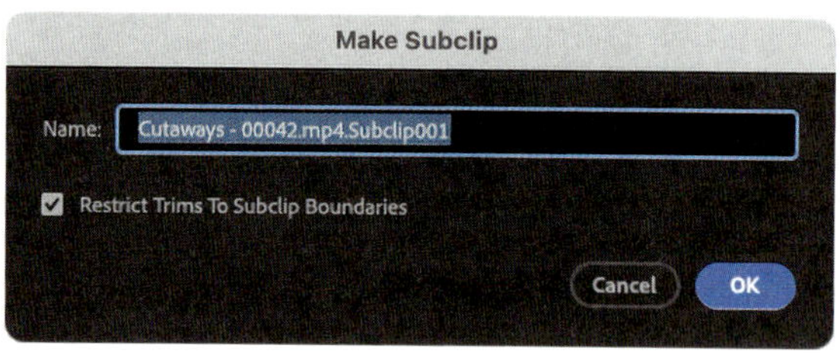

6 In the dialog box, name the new subclip **Packet Moved**, and leave Restrict Trims To Subclip Boundaries selected. Click OK.

With Restrict Trims To Subclip Boundaries selected, you won't be able to access the parts of your clip that are outside your selection when viewing the subclip. This might be exactly what you want to help you stay organized (and you can change this setting by right-clicking the subclip in the bin and choosing Edit Subclip).

Premiere adds the new subclip to the Subclips bin, with the duration you specified with your In and Out points.

Scene Edit Detection

If your original footage contains multiple different shots as part of a continuous clip, you may find it helpful to separate the parts. This is common when working with archive footage, for example. Each time a new shot begins, it's considered to be a scene change.

In the Timeline panel, Premiere can detect scene changes in a clip and separate the clip into multiple clips automatically.

To do so, select a clip in a sequence and choose Clip > Scene Edit Detection.

Choose the result you would like (adding cuts, subclips, or markers), and click Analyze.

Editing in the Timeline panel

The Timeline panel is your creative canvas. In this panel, you'll add clips to your sequences, make editorial changes to them, add visual and audio special effects, mix soundtracks, and add titles and graphics.

To see a very simple sequence, if it is not open already, open the Sequences bin and double-click the sequence First Sequence to display it in the Timeline panel.

Here are a few facts about the Timeline panel. Refer to this list as you make progress through these lessons to make sure you are comfortable with all the features of the Timeline panel.

- You view and edit clips in sequences in the Timeline panel.
- The Program Monitor shows the contents of the currently displayed sequence, at the position of the playhead.
- You can open multiple sequences at the same time, with each displayed in its own Timeline panel.
- The terms *sequence* and *timeline* are often used interchangeably by editors, as in "the clip is in the sequence" or "the clip is on the timeline." Sometimes *timeline* (lowercase) is used when speaking of a sequence of clips in the abstract, without reference to a specific panel.
- If you add clips to a completely empty Timeline panel, a new sequence is created automatically with settings that match the clip you selected first.
- You can add any number of video tracks. Preview playback is limited only by your system's hardware resources.

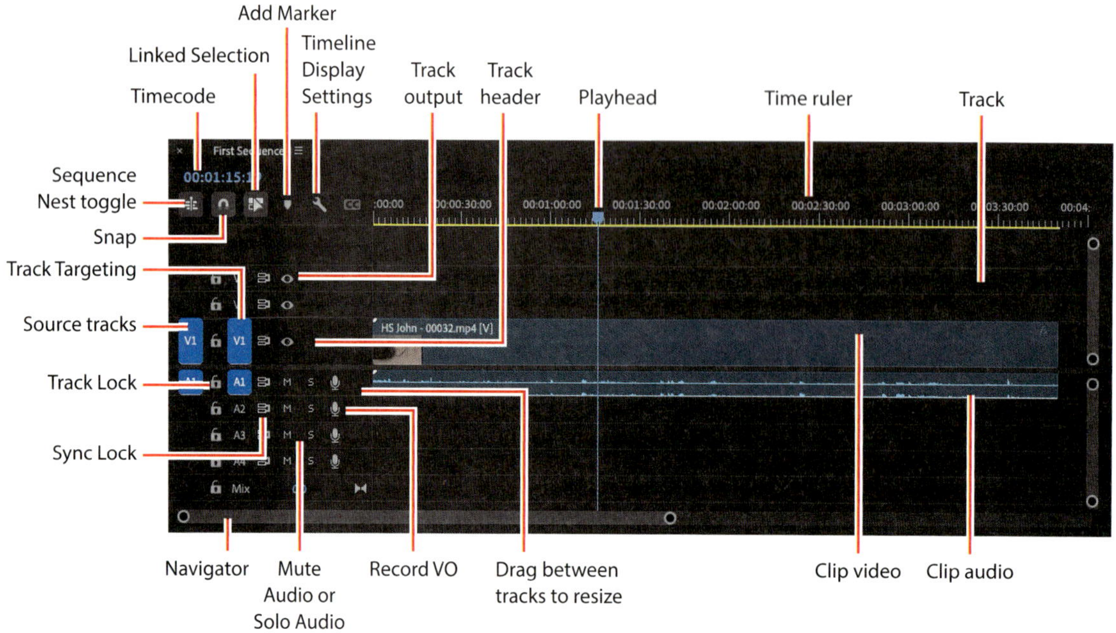

- Upper video tracks appear "in front" of lower ones, so foreground graphic clips should be placed on tracks above background video clips.
- You can add any number of audio tracks, and they all play at the same time to create an audio mix. Audio tracks can support mono clips (1 channel), stereo clips (2 channels), 5.1 clips (6 channels), or adaptive audio—with up to 32 channels.
- You can change the height of tracks in the Timeline panel to gain access to additional controls and thumbnails on your video clips.
- Each track has a set of controls, shown on a track header on the far left, to change the way it functions.
- Time moves from left to right in the Timeline panel, so when you play a sequence, the playhead will move in that direction.
- You can zoom in and out of the sequence using the = (equals) and – (minus) keys (at the top of your keyboard). Use the \ (backslash) key, if your keyboard has one, to toggle the zoom level between your current setting and to show your whole sequence. You can also double-click the navigator at the bottom of the Timeline panel to view the whole sequence.

  If your keyboard doesn't have dedicated = (equals) and – (minus) keys, it's straightforward to assign alternative keyboard shortcuts. See Lesson 1, "Touring Adobe Premiere," for more information about setting keyboard shortcuts.

- The series of buttons at the top left of the Timeline panel gives you access to alternative modes, markers, and settings. You will learn about most of these buttons later. For now, unless described otherwise, if the Timeline panel seems to be acting strangely, check to make sure these modes are set as shown here.

Note: The modes, markers, and settings buttons at the top left of the Timeline panel are available only when a sequence is open.

Selecting a tool

Premiere makes use of tools that change the way the pointer works. In this way, it's similar to Adobe Photoshop.

For most operations in the Timeline panel and some operations in the Program Monitor, you will use the standard Selection tool, which you will find at the top of the Tools panel. Make a tool active by clicking its icon in the Tools panel; an active tool has a blue icon.

There are several other tools that serve different purposes, and each tool has a keyboard shortcut. If in doubt, press the V key—the keyboard shortcut for the Selection tool.

What is a sequence?

A *sequence* is a series of clips that play one after another—sometimes with multiple blended layers and often with special effects, titles, and audio—making a complete film.

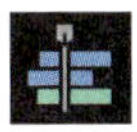

You can have as many sequences as you like in a project. Sequences are stored in the Project panel, just like clips, and have their own icon.

Let's make a new sequence for the Theft Unexpected project.

1. In the Project panel, if you are still browsing inside the Subclips bin you created, click the Navigate Up button in the upper-left corner to view the contents of the Theft Unexpected bin.
2. In the Theft Unexpected bin, drag the clip Excuse Me (not Excuse Me Tilted) onto the New Item menu icon at the bottom of the panel and release the drag. You may need to resize the Project panel to see the icon.

   This is a shortcut to make a sequence with playback settings that perfectly match your media.

Tip: As with clips (and just as easily), you can edit sequences into other sequences, in a process called *nesting*. This creates a dynamically connected set of sequences for advanced editing workflows.

The newly created sequence has the same name as the clip you used to create it. If you already have a sequence open when you create a new sequence, the new sequence opens in a new panel in the same Timeline panel group.

▶ **Tip:** You can use the Timeline Display Settings menu 🔧 to choose Minimize All Tracks or Expand All Tracks to change the height of all tracks in a single step.

3 The sequence is highlighted in the bin, and it would be a good idea to rename it right away. Right-click the sequence in the bin and choose Rename. Name the sequence **Theft Unexpected**. Notice that the icon used for sequences in List view (shown here) and in Icon view is different from that used for clips.

The sequence contains the clip you used to create it. This works for our purposes, but if you had used a random clip to perform this shortcut (just to make sure you had the right sequence settings), you could select that clip in the sequence now and delete it by pressing Delete (macOS) or Backspace (Windows).

● **Note:** The other sequence in this project, called First Sequence, is still open in its own tab in the same group as your new Theft Unexpected sequence. You can switch between sequences by clicking their tabs in the panel group. You can close sequences to tidy your workspace by hovering over the sequence tab and clicking the small X that appears.

You can zoom in to the sequence, with its single clip, using the navigator at the bottom of the Timeline panel. If you can't see a thumbnail on the clip, increase the height of the V1 track by dragging the dividing line between the V1 and V2 tracks in the track header area (where the track controls are located).

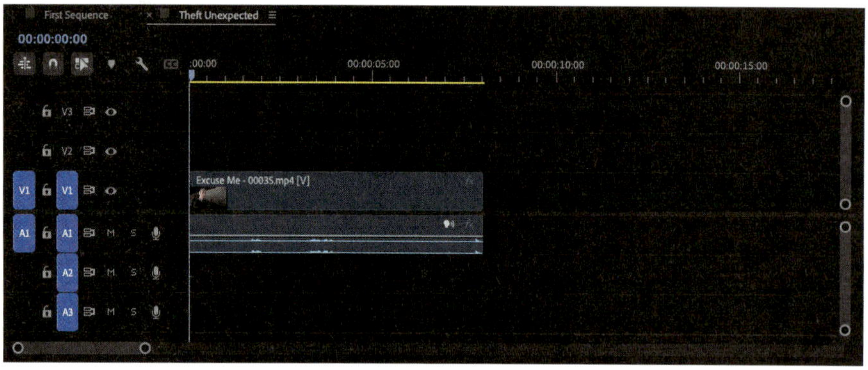

Opening a sequence in the Timeline panel

To open an existing sequence in the Timeline panel, do one of the following:

- Double-click the icon for the sequence in a bin.
- Right-click the sequence in a bin and choose Open In Timeline.

You can also drag a sequence into the Source Monitor to use it as if it were a clip. Be careful not to drag a sequence into the Timeline panel to open it because this will add it to your current sequence or create a new sequence from it instead.

Conforming

Sequences have a frame rate, a frame size, and an audio mastering format (mono or stereo, for example). They *conform*, or adjust, any clips you add to match these settings.

You can choose whether clips should be scaled to match your sequence frame size automatically by selecting a Default Media Scaling option in Settings > Media.

For example, for a sequence with a frame size of 1920x1080 (high-definition HD) and a video clip that is 3840x2160 (ultra-high-definition UHD), you might decide to automatically scale the high-resolution clip down to match your sequence resolution or leave it as it is, viewing only part of the picture through the reduced "window" of the sequence.

When clips are scaled, the vertical and horizontal sizes are scaled equally to keep the original aspect ratio. If a clip has a different aspect ratio from your sequence, it may not completely fill the frame of your sequence when it is scaled. For example, if your clip has a 4:3 aspect ratio and you add it, scaled, to a 16:9 sequence, you'll see gaps at the sides.

Using the Motion controls in the Effect Controls panel or Transform controls in the Properties panel (see Lesson 9, "Putting Clips in Motion"), you can adjust which part of the picture you see or even create a dynamic pan-and-scan effect inside the picture.

Understanding tracks

Much as railway tracks keep trains in line, sequences have video and audio tracks that constrain the positions of the clips you add to them. The simplest form of sequence would have just one video track and perhaps one audio track. You add clips to tracks, one after another, from left to right, and they play in the order you place them.

Sequences can have multiple video and audio tracks. They become layers of video and additional audio sources in the complete sound mix. Higher video tracks appear in front of lower ones, so you can place clips on different tracks to produce layered compositions.

For example, you might use an upper video track to add titles to a sequence or to blend multiple layers of video using visual effects to create a complex composition.

You might use multiple audio tracks to create a complete audio composition for your sequence, with original source dialogue, music, spot audio effects such as gunshots or fireworks, atmospheric sound, and voice-over.

You can scroll through clips and sequences in multiple ways, depending on the location of your pointer.

- If you hover your pointer over the Source Monitor or Program Monitor Time Ruler, you can navigate earlier or later using the scroll wheel; trackpad gestures work too.
- You can navigate sequences in the Timeline panel this way if you choose Horizontal from the Timeline Mouse Scrolling menu in the Timeline preferences.
- If you hold Option (macOS) or Alt (Windows) while scrolling with your pointer, the Timeline view will zoom in or out horizontally.
- If you hover your pointer over a track header and scroll while holding Option (macOS) or Alt (Windows), you'll increase or decrease the height of the track.
- If you double-click a blank space in a track header, you'll toggle the header between being tall or shortened.
- If you hover your pointer over a video or audio track header and scroll while holding the Shift key, you'll increase or decrease the height of all tracks of that type (video or audio tracks).

Tip: If you're scrolling to change track height while holding Option/Alt or while holding Shift, you can also hold Command or Ctrl for finer control.

Targeting tracks

Source tracks

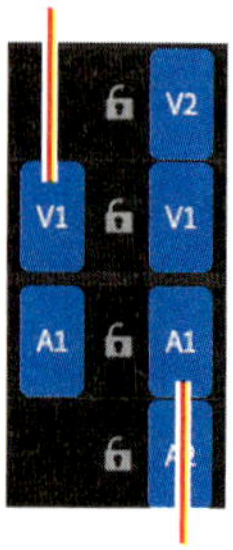

Timeline tracks

When you edit a clip (which usually has one video and one audio track) into a sequence (which may have multiple video and audio tracks), how do you know which sequence tracks your clip tracks will land in?

The *Source Track* and *Timeline Track* targeting buttons at the far-left end of the track headers will determine this for you.

The *source track indicators* represent the tracks available in the clip currently displayed in the Source Monitor or selected in the Project panel. They are numbered just like the Timeline tracks.

The position of a source track indicator relative to a Timeline track header sets the track to which the new clip will be added. A source track indicator also needs to be selected, in blue, for the contents of that track to be added to the sequence.

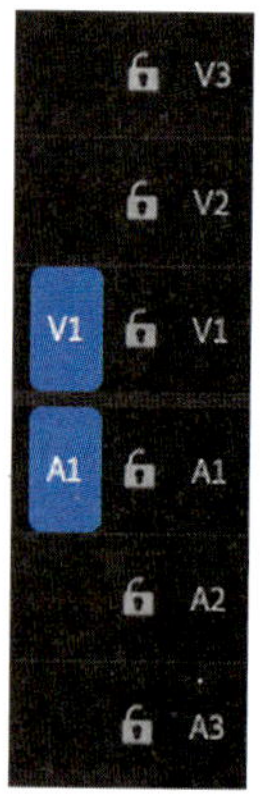

To change the position of a source track indicator, drag it up or down to a new location. If a source clip has just one video track or audio track, you can also click next to a Timeline Track targeting button to resposition the source track indicators.

In the example shown, the position of the source track indicators means a clip with one video track and one audio track would be added to the Video 1 (V1) and Audio 1 (A1) tracks in the Timeline panel when using buttons or a keyboard shortcut to add a clip to the current sequence.

Note: Remember, the Source Track enabling buttons (the left column) allow you to enable or disable the contents of your source. The Track Targeting buttons (the right column) are for making selections in a sequence. Disabling Timeline Track targeting buttons will not impact the video or audio added to a sequence when you apply an edit; only the source track indicators do.

In the next example, the source track indicators have been moved to new positions relative to the Timeline panel track headers. In this example, the clip would be added to the Video 2 (V2) and Audio 2 (A2) tracks on the Timeline when using buttons or a keyboard shortcut to add a clip to the current sequence.

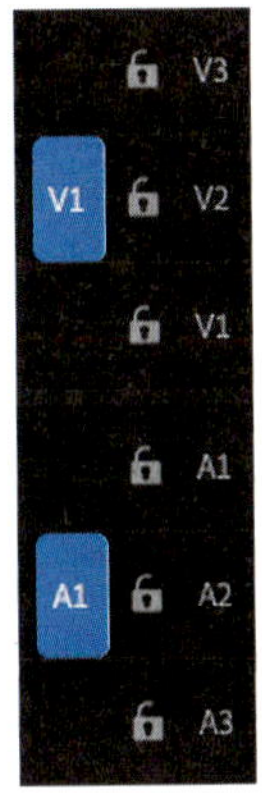

With a clip selected in the Project panel or open in the Source Monitor, click a source track indicator to enable it or disable it. A blue highlight indicates a track is enabled.

When performing edits in this way, enabling or disabling timeline tracks won't affect results. The source track indicator and sequence track selection controls look very similar, but they have different functions.

If you drag a clip into a sequence, Premiere adds content from enabled (highlighted in blue) source tracks but ignores the position of the source track indicators, adding the content to the tracks you drag them to.

Note: If you accidentally click a source track indicator while holding Option (macOS) or Alt (Windows), it will have a black border. This indicates that blank space will be added to the sequence when you perform the edit—an option that is sometimes used to maintain sync or leave space for alternative content. To remove the black border, click the source track indicator while holding Option/Alt again.

Using In and Out points in the Timeline panel

The In and Out points set in the Source Monitor define the part of a clip you will add to a sequence.

The In and Out points you use in the Timeline panel have two primary purposes.

- To tell Premiere where, in time, a new clip should be positioned when it is added to a sequence.
- To select parts of a sequence you want to remove. You can make precise selections to remove whole clips, or parts of clips, from specific tracks by using In and Out points in combination with the track selection buttons.

Selected parts of a sequence, defined by In and Out points, are highlighted in the Timeline panel. The track highlighting (and selection) includes only tracks that are targeted.

In the following example, all the timeline tracks are targeted except V2, so there's a gap in the highlight where In and Out points define a selection. Notice the source track V1 is enabled, but this does not impact sequence track selection.

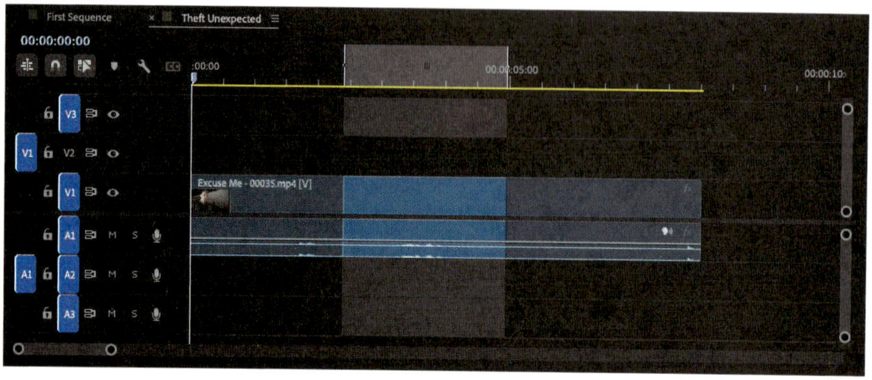

Setting In and Out points

Adding In and Out points in the Timeline panel or in the Program Monitor is almost the same as adding them in the Source Monitor.

One key difference is that unlike the controls in the Source Monitor, the Mark In and Mark Out buttons on the Program Monitor also apply changes to the currently displayed sequence.

To add an In point to a sequence at the current position of the playhead, make sure either the Timeline panel or the Program Monitor is active and then press the I key or click the Mark In button on the Program Monitor.

To add an Out point to a sequence at the current position of the playhead, make sure either the Timeline panel or the Program Monitor is active and then press the O key or click the Mark Out button on the Program Monitor.

Clearing In and Out points

If you open a clip that already has In and Out points, you can change them by adding new ones; your new In and Out points will replace the existing ones.

You can also simply remove existing In and Out points from a clip or from a sequence. It's the same technique to remove In and Out points on the Timeline, in the Program Monitor, and in the Source Monitor.

1 In the Timeline panel, position the playhead over the Excuse Me clip.

2 Press the X key. This adds an In point to the Timeline at the start of the clip (on the left) and an Out point at the end of the clip (on the right). Both appear on the time ruler at the top of the Timeline panel.

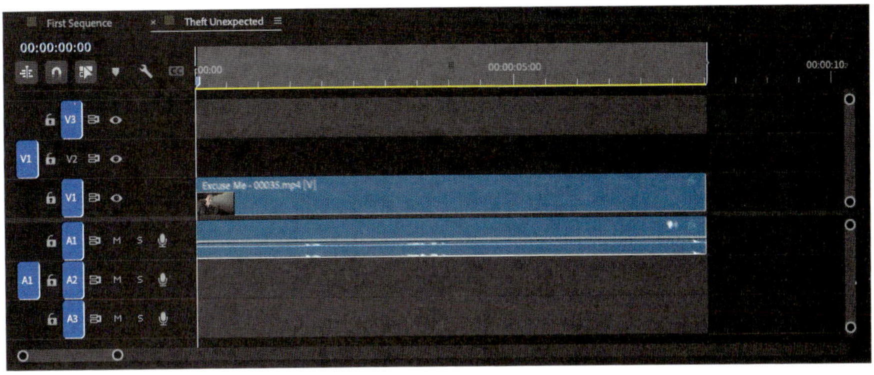

3 Right-click the time ruler at the top of the Timeline panel, and take a look at the menu commands.

Choose the command you need from this menu, or use one of the following keyboard shortcuts:

- **Clear In:** Removes the In point (Option+I, macOS; Ctrl+Shift+I, Windows)
- **Clear Out:** Removes the Out point (Option+O, macOS; Ctrl+Shift+O, Windows)
- **Clear In And Out:** Removes both the In point and Out point (Option+X, macOS; Ctrl+Shift+X, Windows)

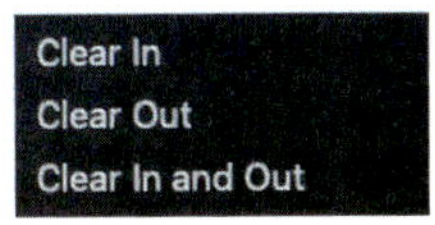

4 That last option is particularly useful. It's easy to remember and quickly removes both In and Out points. Try it now to remove the In point and Out point you just added.

Using time rulers

The time rulers at the bottom of the Source Monitor and Program Monitor, and at the top of the Timeline panel, all serve the same purpose: They help you navigate through your clips or sequences in time.

Time goes from left to right in Premiere, and the location of the playhead gives you a visual reference in relation to your clips.

- Drag left and right in the Timeline panel time ruler now. The playhead moves to follow your pointer. As you drag across the Excuse Me clip, you see the contents of the clip in the Program Monitor. Dragging through your content in this way is called *scrubbing*.

  Notice that the Source Monitor, Program Monitor, and Timeline panel all have navigation bars at the bottom.

- You can zoom the time ruler by hovering over it and using your mouse wheel to scroll while holding Option (macOS) or Alt (Windows) (trackpad gestures work too).
- Once you have zoomed in, move through the time ruler by dragging the middle of the navigator.
- Adjust the zoom level of the time ruler by dragging one end of the navigator to resize it or using your mouse wheel to scroll.

Using the Timecode panel

There is a dedicated Timecode panel that, like other panels, can float in its own window or be added to a panel group. To open it, choose Window > Timecode.

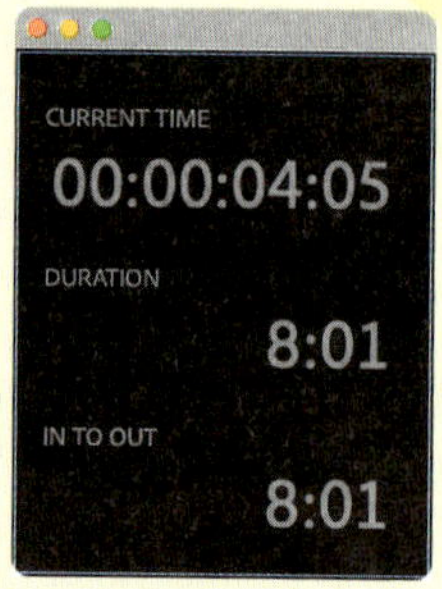

The Timecode panel offers multiple lines of timecode information. Each line can be configured to show a particular type of time information. Because the panel can be set to a large size, it's particularly useful when you want to sit back and review your footage—and read the numbers from a distance.

The default configuration shows the current time, the total duration, and the duration set by In and Out points for the active panel—Source Monitor, Program Monitor, or Timeline panel.

The current time matches the timecode displayed at the bottom left of the Source Monitor or the Program Monitor and the top left of the Timeline panel.

Close the Timecode panel now.

Customizing track headers

Just as you can customize the Source Monitor and Program Monitor controls, you can change several options on the Timeline track headers.

1 To access the options, right-click a video or audio track header and choose Customize, or click the Timeline Display Settings menu and choose Customize Video Header or Customize Audio Header from the menu.

  There are no additional video track header buttons, but opening the editor allows you to move, remove, and restore buttons by clicking Reset Layout. Additional audio track header buttons allow you to extend the functionality of the track headers.

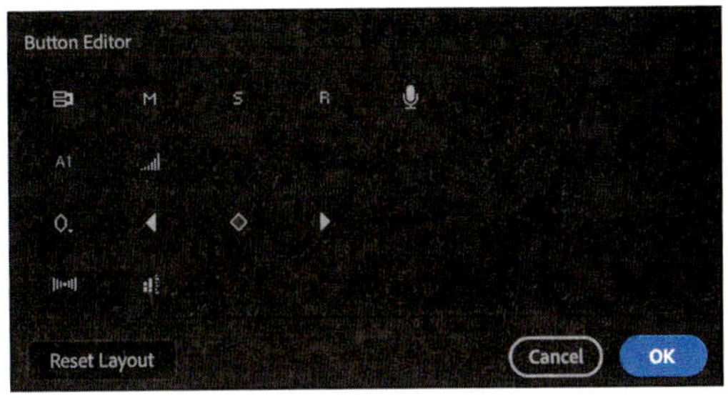

2 Hover your pointer over buttons in the Button Editor to see the tool tip. Some of these will be familiar to you already; others will be explained in later lessons.

3 Add a button to a track header by dragging it from the Button Editor onto a track header. You can remove a button from a track header by dragging it away while the Button Editor is open.

   Note that all audio or video track headers update to match the one you adjust.

4 Experiment with this feature a little more. You can always click the Reset Layout button on the Button Editor to return the track header to the default options.

5 When you have finished, click Cancel to leave the Button Editor.

Using essential editing commands

No matter how you add a clip to a sequence—by dragging, clicking a button on the Source Monitor, or using a keyboard shortcut—you'll choose one of two kinds of edits: an insert edit or an overwrite edit.

When a sequence has existing clips at the location where you want to add a new clip, these two choices—insert and overwrite—will produce different results.

Performing one or other of these two types of edit is at the absolute heart of nonlinear editing. Of all the skills you will learn in this book, this is the one you will perform most often. Fundamentally, this *is* nonlinear editing, so take a little extra time to be sure you are comfortable with this workflow before you continue.

Performing an overwrite edit

Continue working on the Theft Unexpected sequence. So far, you have just one clip, in which John asks if a seat is free.

> **Tip:** Professional editors use the terms *shot* and *clip* interchangeably.

First, let's use an overwrite edit to add a reaction shot to John's request for a chair.

1 Open the shot HS Suit in the Source Monitor. You have already added In and Out points to this clip.

You'll next need to set up the Timeline panel carefully. This may seem like a slow process at first, but after practice, you'll find editing is fast and easy. Also, it's common to perform several edits with the same settings before you need to change them.

Tip: You can copy and paste timecode into the current time indicator at the bottom left of the Source Monitor or Program Monitor. Click to select the timecode, paste the new timecode, and press Return (macOS) or Enter (Windows) to move the playhead to that time. This is a useful feature when working with camera logs that allow you to quickly locate a particular part of a clip.

2 Position the Timeline playhead (rather than the Source Monitor playhead) just after John makes his request. Around 00:00:04:00 is perfect.

Unless an In point or Out point has been added to the Timeline, the playhead is used to position new clips when editing with the keyboard or on-screen buttons, which you will do in a moment. When you drag a clip into a sequence, the location of the playhead and existing In or Out points are ignored.

3 Though the new clip has an audio track, you don't need it. You'll keep the audio that is already in the timeline. Click the source track selection indicator A1 to turn it off. The button should be gray rather than blue.

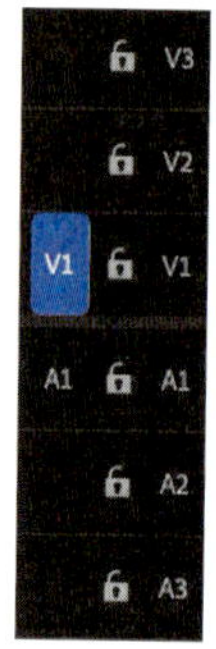

4 Check that your track headers look like the example shown, with only the Source Track Indicator for V1 enabled, and positioned next to the sequence track V1.

5 Click the Overwrite button in the Source Monitor or press . (period).

Premiere adds the clip to the sequence on the Video 1 track, replacing part of the existing clip. When you perform an overwrite edit, existing sequence clips do not move to make room for the incoming clip.

Note: When editing clips into a sequence, the track targeting buttons have no effect.

Note: Editors often use the words *sequence* and *edit* interchangeably. In this case, the word *edit* means any change made to one or more clips in a sequence.

Congratulations! You have completed an overwrite edit.

By default, when you drag a clip into a sequence, rather than using an on-screen button or keyboard shortcut, you'll perform an overwrite edit. You can perform an insert edit instead by holding down Command (macOS) or Ctrl (Windows) while you drag.

6 Now position the playhead at the beginning (far-left end) of either the Timeline panel or the Program Monitor, and click the Play button on the Program Monitor (or press the spacebar) to play the result of your edit.

The timing might not be perfect, but you're now editing!

Performing an insert edit

Now try an insert edit.

1 In the Timeline panel, position the playhead over the Excuse Me clip, just after John says, "Excuse me," at around 00:00:02:16. Make sure there is no In point or Out point in the sequence.

2 From the Theft Unexpected bin, open the clip Mid Suit in the Source Monitor, add an In point at 01:15:46:00, and add an Out point at 01:15:48:00. This is actually from a different part of the action, but the audience won't know, and it works well enough as a reaction shot—we'll adjust the timing later.

3 In the Timeline panel, adjust the Source Track Indicators as necessary to match the example.

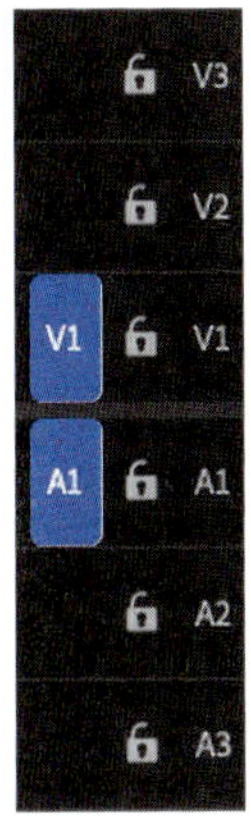

4 Click the Insert button in the Source Monitor or press , (comma).

Tip: As your sequence gets longer, you may find yourself often zooming in and out to get a better view of your clips. It can speed things up to use the keyboard shortcuts. At the top of the keyboard (not on the numeric keypad), the = (equals) key zooms in, while the – (minus) key zooms out.

The clip Excuse Me, already in the sequence, splits, with the part after the playhead moved later to make space for the new clip. This is the major difference between insert edits and overwrite edits: When you apply an insert edit, it makes your sequence longer. The clips already on the selected tracks, located to the right of the new clip, will move later (to the right) in the sequence to make room for the new clip.

5 Position the playhead at the beginning of the sequence and play through your edit again. If your keyboard has a Home key, you can use it to jump to the beginning, you can drag the playhead with your pointer to move forward or back, or you can press the Up Arrow key to jump the playhead to earlier edits (the Down Arrow key jumps to later edits).

Tip: If your keyboard does not have a Home key, try holding the Fn key and pressing the Left Arrow.

There is more work to be done, and there's a continuity issue near the start as John moves his jacket from one arm to the other, but this is beginning to look like a story unfolding.

6 Now open the Mid John (not the Mid Suit) clip in the Source Monitor. You've already added In and Out points to this clip.

> ▶ **Tip:** If your keyboard does not have an End key, try holding the Fn key and pressing the Right Arrow key.

7 Position the Timeline playhead at the end of the sequence—on the frame after the Excuse Me clip. When dragging the playhead, you can hold the Shift key to have the playhead snap to the ends of clips. You can also press the End key to move the playhead to the end of the sequence.

8 Click either the Insert or Overwrite button in the Source Monitor. Because the Timeline playhead is at the end of the sequence, there are no clips in the way, and it makes no difference which kind of edit you perform.

Now you'll insert one more clip.

9 Position the Timeline playhead just before John takes a sip of tea, around 00:00:14:00 in the sequence.

10 Return to the Mid Suit clip in the Source Monitor, and use In and Out points to choose a part you think would go well between John sitting down and his first sip of tea. An In point around 01:15:55:00 and an Out point around 01:16:00:00 might work well.

Notice that the existing In and Out points are replaced when you add new ones.

> ● **Note:** You can also edit clips into a sequence by dragging them from the Project panel or Source Monitor into the Program Monitor.

11 Edit the clip into the sequence using an insert edit.

The timing of the edit may not be perfect, but that's okay; you can change your mind about the timing later—that's the beauty of nonlinear editing. The important thing, to begin with, is to get the clips in the right order.

Performing a three-point edit

When adding clips to a sequence by dragging, the duration of the part of the clip that will be added is set by In and Out points on the clip. The timing in the sequence is set by the location you drop the clip in the sequence.

When adding a clip to a sequence using a keyboard shortcut or button, Premiere needs to know both where and when and it should be placed.

This means there should be two In points and two Out points:

- An In point for the clip
- An Out point for the clip
- An In point for the sequence, setting the beginning of the clip once it has been added
- An Out point for the sequence, setting the end of the clip once it has been added

In fact, you need to specify only three of these points; Premiere calculates the fourth automatically based on the selected duration.

Here's an example: If you choose four seconds of a clip in the Source Monitor, Premiere automatically knows it will take four seconds of time in your sequence. Once you have set the location for the clip to be placed, you're ready to perform the edit.

Using just three points to perform edits in this way is called *three-point editing.*

When you performed your last edit, Premiere aligned the In point from the clip (the start of the clip) with the In point in the sequence (the playhead is used as the In point if no In point has been added).

Even though you didn't manually add an In point to the sequence, you're still performing a three-point edit, with the duration calculated from the selection you made in the Source Monitor.

You can achieve a similar result by adding an Out point to the sequence instead of an In point. In this case, Premiere will align the Out point of the clip in the Source Monitor with the Out point in the sequence when you perform the edit.

You might choose to do this, for example, if you have a piece of timed action, like a door closing at the end of a clip in the sequence, and your new clip needs to line up in time with it—this is called *back-timing* the edit.

What happens if you use four points?

You *can* use four points to make an edit: both In and Out points in the Source Monitor and In and Out points on the Timeline. If the clip duration you select matches the sequence duration, the edit will take place as usual. If they're different, the Fit Clip dialog box will appear and Premiere will invite you to choose what you want to happen.

You can selectively ignore one of your In or Out points or stretch or compress the playback speed of the new clip to fit the selected duration on the Timeline.

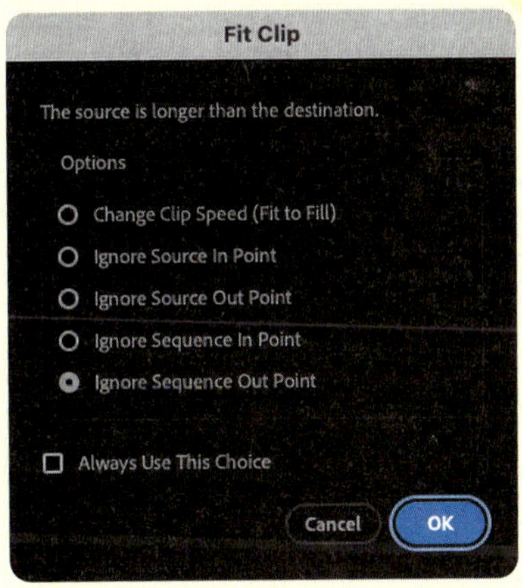

Performing storyboard-style editing

The term *storyboard* usually describes a series of drawings showing the intended camera angles and action for a film. Storyboards are often quite similar to comic strips, although they usually include additional technical information, such as intended camera moves, lines of dialogue, and sound effects.

You can use clip thumbnails in Icon view and Freeform view in a bin as storyboard images.

Drag the thumbnails to arrange them in the order you want the clips to appear in your sequence, from left to right and from top to bottom; select them; and then drag them all into your sequence. The order the clips are selected is the order they will be added to the sequence.

Using a storyboard to build an assembly edit

An *assembly edit* is a sequence in which the order of the clips is correct but the timing of the edits has yet to be worked out. It's common to build sequences as an assembly edit first, just to make sure the structure works, and then adjust the timing later.

You can use storyboard editing to quickly get your clips in the right order.

1 Save your current project. This is good practice when you reach any major milestone in the development of your project.

2 Without closing your current project, open Lesson 05 Desert Sequence.prproj in the Lessons folder.

Note: You now have two project files open at the same time, each with its own Project panel. You can switch between them by choosing one of them from Window > Projects, and you can close all projects by choosing File > Close All Projects.

3 Make sure the Project panel is the active panel, and choose File > Save As. Save the project as **Lesson 05 Desert Sequence Working.prproj**.

Tip: Project filenames can become quite long. It's fine to include useful information to help you identify a project, but avoid making the name so long it's hard to manage the file.

4 In the Project panel, double-click the Desert Montage sequence to open it in the Timeline panel.

This sequence has music but no visuals. You'll add some shots using a storyboard edit.

The audio track A1 has been locked (click the track padlock to lock and unlock a track). This means you can make adjustments to the sequence without risking making changes to the music track.

Arranging your storyboard

It's not necessary to pre-arrange clips in the Project panel prior to adding them to a sequence. However, it's a helpful step to quickly give you a sense of the sequence structure.

1 Double-click the Desert Footage bin to open it.

2 Click the Freeform View button at the lower-left corner of the bin to see thumbnails for the clips.

   You can set the Project panel to Icon view to arrange clips as a storyboard, but Freeform view gives you more…freedom! It's a more flexible way to display clip thumbnails.

> **Tip:** You can use the Zoom control at the bottom of the bin window to resize the clip thumbnails.

3 Double-click the Desert Footage bin name to toggle it to full screen. Then, right-click the background of the bin and choose Reset To Grid > Name.

   This neatly arranges the clips, sorted by name.

4 Drag the thumbnails in the bin to position them in the order in which you want them to appear in the sequence, from left to right and from top to bottom—just like a comic strip or storyboard. This will make it easier to select them in the correct order in the next step. In Freeform view, thumbnails can overlap and be arranged loosely. The order in which clips will be selected in the next step is the order that Premiere will add them to a sequence.

5 Drag around all the clips to select them in the order you'd like them to appear in the sequence, or select them in the correct order while holding Command (macOS) or Ctrl (Windows).

6 Double-click the Desert Footage bin name to toggle it back to its original position. Drag the clips into the sequence, positioning them on the Video 1 track right at the beginning of the timeline, above the music clip. Because all the clips are selected, they will drag into the Timeline panel together.

   The clips are added to the sequence in the order you selected them in the Project panel.

Freeform view gives great flexibility when reviewing and arranging clips, ready to add them to a sequence, but Icon view offers an even faster workflow:

1 Press Command+Z (macOS) or Ctrl+Z (Windows) to undo the last step.

2 Double-click the Desert Footage bin name to toggle it to full screen, and click the Icon View button to switch to that view.

3 Drag the clip thumbnails into the order you'd like them to appear in the sequence. In this view, the thumbnails always stay in an ordered grid.

4 Double-click the Desert Footage bin name to toggle it back to its original position.

> **Tip:** You may need to scroll to see the clips after toggling the bin panel back to its original size.

5 Make sure the Desert Footage bin is selected (with a blue outline), but click the background of the bin to deselect any clips. Now press Command+A (macOS) or Ctrl+A (Windows) to select all the clips in the bin.

6 Drag the clips into the sequence, positioning them on the Video 1 track right at the beginning of the Timeline, above the music clip.

   Premiere adds the clips to the sequence in the order you originally selected them in the Project panel. Because you selected the clips in one step by selecting them all using a keyboard shortcut, the selection order is based on the thumbnail placement in the bin.

7 Position the Timeline panel playhead at the beginning of the sequence. Play your sequence to see the result.

   Although you chose an order for the clips to play in the bin, remember that you are always free to change the order or the timing of the clips in the sequence.

Now that you have two projects open at the same time, it may not be clear which project you are working on. If in doubt, look at the project filename, displayed in the middle at the top of the Premiere interface. The word *Edited* after a project name indicates changes have been made to that project since it was last saved.

Close each project by choosing File > Close Project twice or by choosing File > Close All Projects. If you are asked if you would like to save, do so.

Setting the duration for still images

These video clips already had In and Out points, which were used automatically when you added them to the sequence.

Graphics and photos can have any duration in a sequence. However, they have default In and Out points that are applied as you import them.

To change the default duration, choose Premiere > Settings > Timeline (macOS) or Edit > Preferences > Timeline (Windows) and enter a new number in the Still Image Default Duration field. This setting applies to clips when you import them, so it won't affect clips that have already been imported.

Still images and still image sequences (a series of images intended to play one after another, as animation) have no timebase—that is, the number of frames that should play per second (fps or frame rate). You can set the default timebase for still images by choosing Media in the Preferences dialog box and choosing an option from the Indeterminate Media Timebase.

Review questions

1 What do In and Out points do?

2 Is the Video 2 track in front of the Video 1 track or behind it?

3 How do subclips help you stay organized?

4 How would you select a time range in a sequence to work with in the Timeline panel?

5 What is the difference between an overwrite edit and an insert edit?

6 How much of your source clip will be added to a sequence if the source clip has no In or Out points and there are no In or Out points in the sequence?

Review answers

1. In the Source Monitor and in the Project panel, In and Out points define the part of a clip you would like to use in a sequence. On the Timeline, In and Out points are used to define parts of your sequence you want to remove, edit, render effects, or export as a file.
2. Upper video tracks are always in front of lower ones, so the Video 2 track is in front of the Video 1 track.
3. Although subclips make no difference to the way Premiere plays back video and sound, they make it easier for you to divide your footage into different bins. For larger projects with lots of longer clips, it can make a big difference to be able to organize content this way.
4. You'll use In and Out points to define parts of your sequence you want to work with. For example, you might render when working with effects, export parts of your sequence as a file, or remove parts.
5. Clips added to a sequence using an overwrite edit replace any content already in the sequence where they are placed. Clips added to a sequence using an insert edit displace existing clips, pushing them later (to the right) and making the sequence longer.
6. If you don't add In or Out points to your source clip, the entire clip will be added to the sequence. Setting an In point, an Out point, or both will limit the portion of the source clip used in the edit.

6 WORKING WITH CLIPS AND MARKERS

Lesson overview

In this lesson, you'll learn how to do the following:

- Understand the differences between the Program Monitor and the Source Monitor.
- Use markers.
- Search for clips with similar frames.
- Apply sync locks and track locks.
- Select items in a sequence.
- Move clips in a sequence.
- Remove clips from a sequence.

This lesson will take about 90 minutes to complete. To get the files used in this lesson, refer to the instructions in "Accessing the lesson files and Web Edition" in the "Getting Started" section at the beginning of this book. Store the files on your computer in a convenient location.

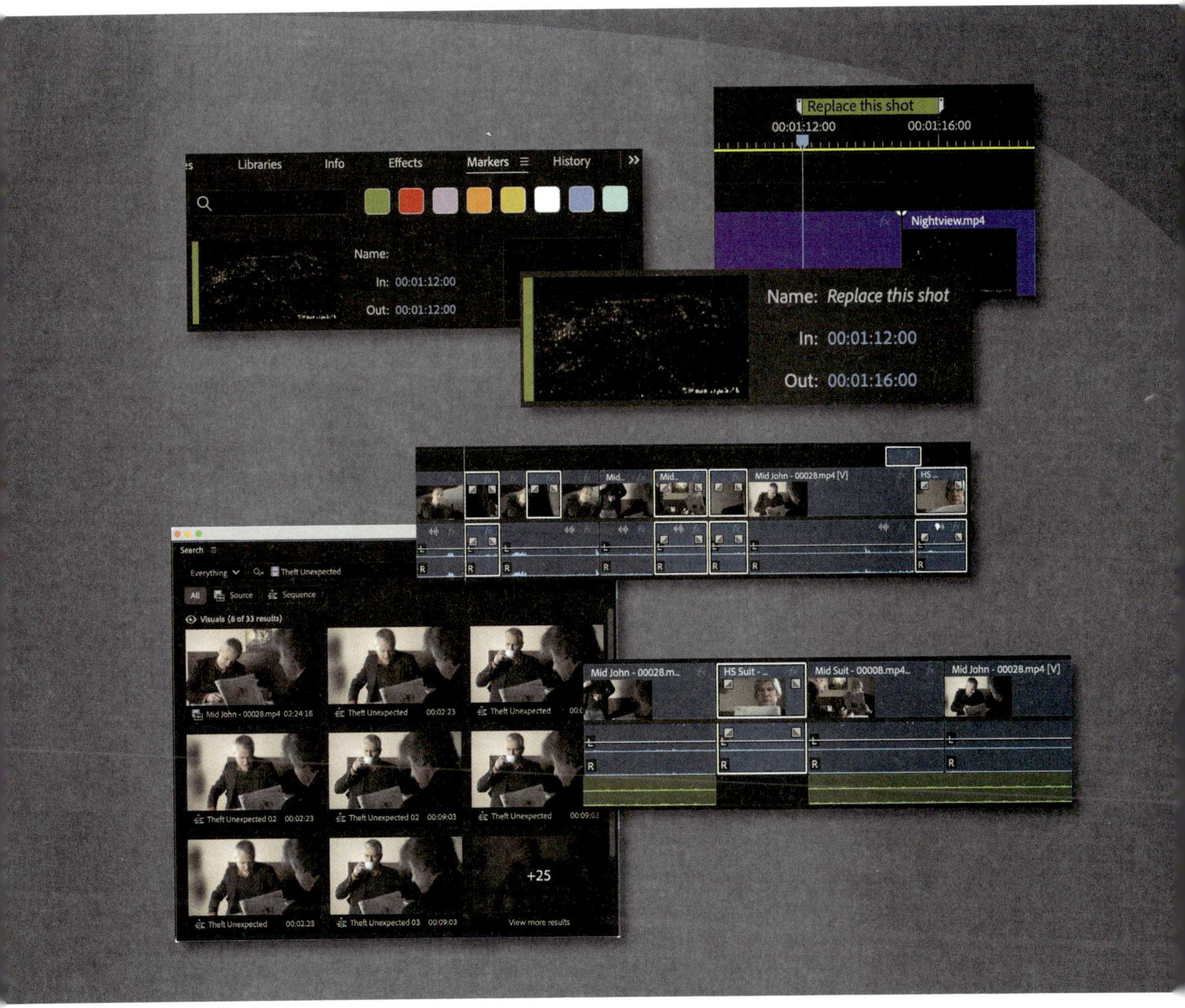

Adobe Premiere makes it easy to fine-tune your edits with markers and advanced tools for syncing and locking tracks when you're editing clips in your video sequence.

Starting the lesson

Note: To ensure that the tools function and the defaults are set exactly as described in this lesson, reset the Premiere preferences by holding Option (macOS) or Alt (Windows) while launching the application, selecting Reset App Preferences in the Reset Options dialog box, and then clicking Continue.

The art and craft of video editing is perhaps best demonstrated during the fine-tuning phase after the first version of your sequence is completed. Once you've chosen your shots and put them in approximately the right order, the process of carefully adjusting the timing of your edits begins.

You'll move clips around in your sequence and remove the parts you don't want. You can also add markers with comments to store information about clips and sequences, which can be useful during your edit or when you send your sequence to other Adobe Creative Cloud applications.

In this lesson, you'll learn about additional controls in the Program Monitor and discover how markers help you stay organized.

You'll also learn about making changes to clips that are already on the timeline—the "nonlinear" part of nonlinear editing with Adobe Premiere.

Before you begin, make sure you are using the Editing workspace.

1 Open the file Lesson 06.prproj from the Lessons folder.
2 To begin, reset the workspace to the default. Choose Window > Workspaces Editing. Then choose Window > Workspaces > Reset To Saved Layout.
3 Choose File > Save As.
4 Rename the file **Lesson 06 Working.prproj**.
5 Browse to the Lessons folder on your hard drive, and click Save to save the project.

Using the Program Monitor controls

The Program Monitor is almost identical to the Source Monitor, but there are a small number of important differences.

What is the Program Monitor?

The Program Monitor displays the frame your sequence playhead is sitting on or playing. In the Timeline panel, the sequence is presented as clip segments and tracks, while the Program Monitor shows the resulting video output. The Program Monitor time ruler is like the one in the Timeline panel, and the two are linked.

In the early stages of editing, you're likely to spend a lot of time working with the Source Monitor, reviewing and marking your clips. Once your sequence is roughly edited together, you will spend most of your time using the Program Monitor and the Timeline panel.

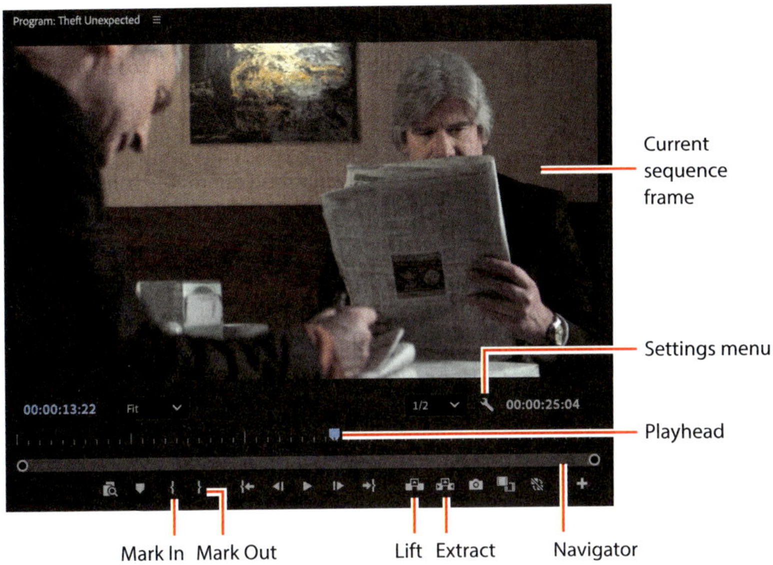

Comparing the Program Monitor and the Source Monitor

Key differences between the Program Monitor and the Source Monitor include the following:

- The Source Monitor is usually used to show the contents of a clip; the Program Monitor shows the contents of whichever sequence is currently displayed in the Timeline panel. In particular, it shows whatever is under the playhead in the Timeline panel.
- The Source Monitor has Insert and Overwrite buttons for adding clips (or parts of clips) to sequences. By contrast, the Program Monitor has Extract and Lift buttons for removing clips (or parts of clips) from sequences (more on extract and lift edits is coming up).
- Both monitors have a time ruler. The playhead on the Program Monitor matches the playhead in the sequence you're currently viewing in the Timeline panel (the name of the current sequence is displayed at the top left of the Program Monitor). As one playhead moves, the other moves as well, so you can use either panel to change the currently displayed frame.
- When you work with special effects in Premiere, you'll see the results in the Program Monitor. There's one exception to this rule: Source clip effects are viewed in both the Source Monitor and the Program Monitor (for more information about effects, see Lesson 12, "Adding Video Effects").
- The Mark In and Mark Out buttons in the Program Monitor work in the same way as the ones in the Source Monitor. In and Out points are added to the currently displayed sequence when you add them in the Program Monitor, and they are persistent in sequences in the same way that they are persistent in clips.

Adding clips to a sequence with the Program Monitor

You've already learned how to make a partial clip selection with the Source Monitor and then add the clip to a sequence by pressing a key, clicking a button, or dragging.

You can also drag a clip from the Source Monitor or Project panel into the Program Monitor to add it to a sequence.

When you do so, several overlay images appear in the Program Monitor, each highlighting a drop zone that gives different options for the edit you're about to perform.

Take a look at the options now (you'll put them to work in this section's second exercise):

1 If it's not open already, in the Sequences bin, open the Theft Unexpected sequence (not Theft Unexpected 02).

2 From the Theft Unexpected bin, drag the clip HS Suit over the viewing area of the Program Monitor, but don't release it yet (remember to always drag the icon rather than the clip name). Take note of the drop zones that appear in the Program Monitor.

> **Tip:** It's usually safe to experiment in Premiere. Use the Undo command to reverse one or more changes you have made by choosing Edit > Undo or pressing Command+Z (macOS) or Ctrl+Z (Windows).

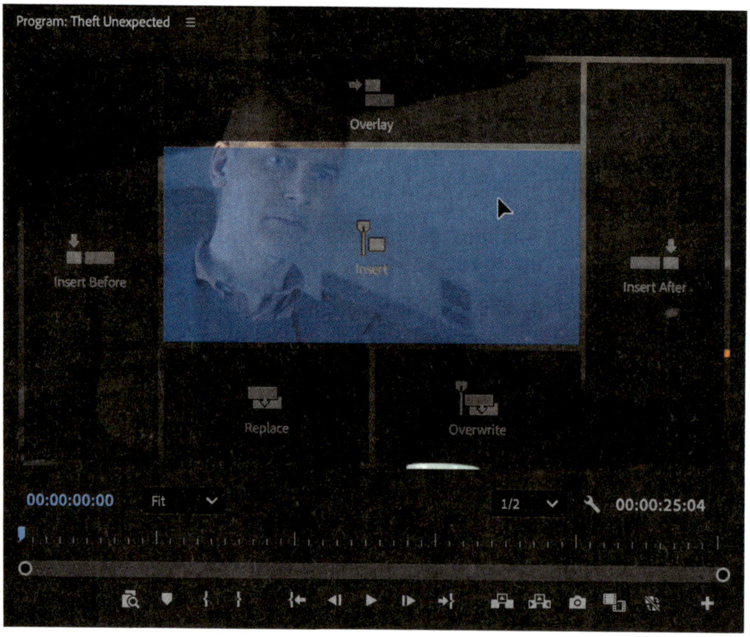

3 Move the pointer over each drop zone. As you do, Premiere highlights the drop zone to indicate the type of edit you will apply if you release the clip (don't, though).

4 Continue to drag the clip into the Source Monitor and release it. Most of the time you will double-click to open clips in the Source Monitor, but intuitive steps like dragging work too.

You can drag clips into the Program Monitor from the Project panel or Source Monitor. Here's the list of overlay options:

- **Insert:** This performs an insert edit, using the source track selection indicators to choose the track (or tracks) the clip will be added to.
- **Overwrite:** This performs an overwrite edit, using the source track selection indicators to select the track (or tracks) the clip will be added to.
- **Overlay:** If there is already a clip under the Timeline panel's playhead in the current sequence, this adds the new clip to the next available track above it. If there's already a clip on the next track, the one above that is used, and so on.
- **Replace:** This replaces the clip currently under the Timeline playhead with the new clip (more on replace edits in Lesson 8, "Editing Video—Advanced Techniques"). Replace edits cannot be used to replace graphics and titles created in the Timeline panel but will work when replacing imported photos and graphics.
- **Insert After:** This inserts the new clip immediately after the clip currently under the Timeline playhead.
- **Insert Before:** This inserts the new clip immediately before the clip currently under the Timeline playhead.

Note: The Overlay, Insert Before, and Insert After edits are available only when dragging a clip onto the appropriate drop zone in the Program Monitor. There are no buttons or single-key shortcuts that achieve the same results.

Note: Even if you drag a clip directly into a sequence, Premiere still uses the Timeline panel's source track indicators to control which components of the clip (video and audio channels) are used.

The Program Monitor overlays give maximum flexibility when editing by touch, with a computer screen that allows touch interaction. You can use the mouse or trackpad to drag clips in, as well as drag clips by touch.

Now that you are familiar with the options, let's add that HS Suit clip to the sequence. Continue working on the Theft Unexpected sequence.

1. Position the Timeline panel's playhead anywhere over the last clip in the sequence, Mid John. Somewhere around 00:00:20:00 would work.
2. If it's not already open, open the clip HS Suit from the Theft Unexpected bin in the Source Monitor. This is a clip that has already been used in the sequence, but you'll choose a different part.

   Tip: When the Project panel is set to List view, you can use the Left Arrow and Right Arrow keys to expand and collapse bins that are selected in the Project panel or to navigate up and down a list of items.

3. Set an In point for the clip around 01:26:49:00. There's not much going on in the shot, so it works well as a cutaway. Add an Out point around 01:26:52:00 so you have a little time with the man in the suit.
4. Click in the middle of the picture in the Source Monitor and drag the clip into the Program Monitor, but don't release it yet.

Tip: You can press the End key to move the playhead to the end of the sequence, and pressing the Home key moves the playhead to the start of the sequence. If your macOS keyboard lacks these keys, you can use Fn+Right Arrow in place of the End key and Fn+Left Arrow in place of Home.

For this edit, release the clip in the Insert After drop zone. Though the Timeline panel playhead was in the middle of the Mid John clip, the new clip is edited into the sequence immediately after it.

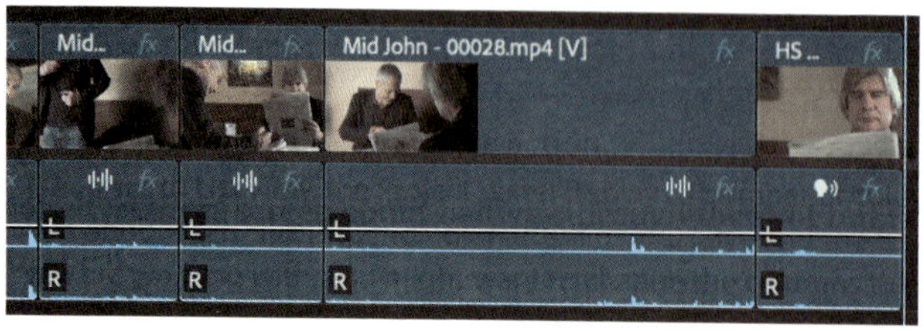

The Insert After and Insert Before drop zones can make it easier to place new clips precisely in sequences without replacing or splitting existing clips.

Typing timecode

You can click a timecode display, type the timecode you want the playhead to move to *without punctuation*, and then press Return (macOS) or Enter (Windows).

For example, if you want the playhead to move to 00:00:27:15, you can type **2715**. There's no need to enter leading zeros.

When typing timecode, you can use a period (full stop) as a replacement for two zeros or to skip to the next number type.

For example, if you want the playhead to move to 01:29:00:15, you can type **1.29..15**.

You can also type incremental amounts. For example, typing **+200** will move the playhead 2 seconds later (because the punctuation will be added automatically, making this 00:00:02:00).

Insert editing with the Program Monitor

Let's try an insert edit into the middle of the current sequence using the same technique.

1 Position the Timeline panel playhead around 00:00:13:00, at the beginning of the Mid Suit shot. Play through the next edit, between this shot and the following shot, Mid John.

   The continuity of movement isn't perfect on this cut, so let's add another part of that HS Suit clip.

2 Position the timeline playhead anywhere over the Mid John shot toward the end of the sequence. Somewhere around 00:00:20:00 would work, just to try this technique.

3 Add a new In point and Out point to the HS Suit clip in the Source Monitor. Choose any part you like that has no dialogue, selecting about two seconds in total. You can see the selected duration at the lower-right corner of the Source Monitor.

4 Drag the HS Suit clip from the Source Monitor onto the Insert Before drop zone in the Program Monitor viewing area. When you release it, the clip is inserted into your sequence before the Mid John clip.

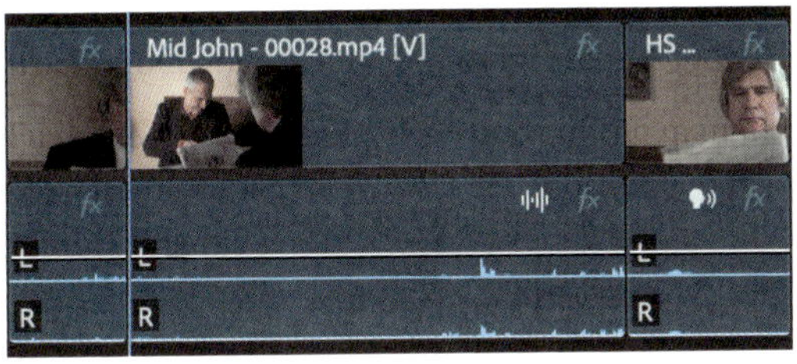

Dragging only video or audio into a sequence

If you prefer to drag clips into the Timeline panel, there's a way to bring in just the video or audio part of a clip.

Now try an Overlay edit.

1 Position the Timeline panel playhead at 00:00:25:20, just before John takes out his pen.

2 Open the Mid Suit clip in the Source Monitor. At 01:15:54:00, John is wielding his pen. Add an In point there. If the clip already has an In point, it will be replaced with the one you add.

3 Add an Out point at 01:15:56:00. You just need a quick alternative angle for now, to give the audience a better perspective on the action.

4 At the bottom of the Source Monitor, you'll see the Drag Video Only and Drag Audio Only icons.

These icons serve three purposes:

- They tell you whether your clip has video, audio, or both. If there is no video, for example, the filmstrip icon is dimmed. If there is no audio, the waveform is dimmed.
- You can click one or the other icon to switch between viewing the clip audio waveform or video.
- You can drag them to selectively edit video or audio into your sequence.

Note: Remember, only the source track selection indicators on the left matter when editing clips into a sequence, not the track targeting controls to the right of them in the Timeline panel.

Drag the filmstrip icon from the bottom of the Source Monitor into the Program Monitor, and release it on the Overlay drop zone. When you release, just the video part of the clip is added to the Video 2 track in the sequence (the next available empty track).

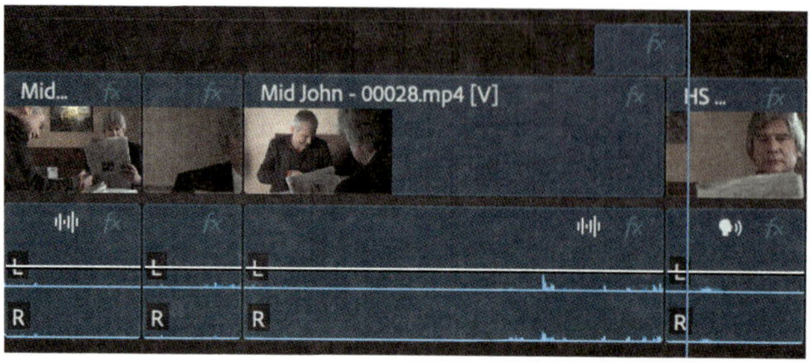

This works even if both the Source Video and Source Audio selection buttons in the Timeline panel are enabled, so it's a quick, intuitive way to select the part of a clip you want. You could achieve the same effect by selectively disabling source track selection buttons in the Timeline panel, but it would require more clicks.

5 Play your sequence from the beginning.

The timing may not be perfect, but this edit is off to a good start. The clip you just added plays in front of the end of the Mid John clip and the start of the HS Suit clip, changing the timing. Because Premiere is a nonlinear editing system, you can adjust the timing later. You'll learn how to do this in Lesson 8.

Why are there so many ways to edit clips into a sequence?

As you continue to develop your editing skills and build experience, you'll find that some ways of adding clips to sequences work better than others, depending on the particular situation. Perhaps you need to be absolutely sure you've got the timing right, so you carefully select options in the Source Monitor and Timeline panel. Perhaps you are in a hurry to throw something together, so you drag clips from the Project panel into the Timeline panel and worry about timing later.

In addition, you'll find you naturally tend toward one editing style or another. To ensure editors can work flexibly according to their own styles, Premiere includes multiple workflows for the same outcome.

Setting the playback resolution

Premiere uses the power of your computer hardware to boost performance. This means the speed (and number of cores and type) of your CPU, the amount of RAM (memory) you have, the power of your GPU (video card), and the speed of your storage drives are all factors that impact playback performance.

If your system has difficulty playing back every frame of video in your sequence (in the Program Monitor) or in your clips (in the Source Monitor), you can lower the playback resolution to make playback smoother. If you see your video playback stuttering, stopping, and starting, it usually indicates that your system is unable to play the file because of a hardware limitation.

It's worth remembering that playing high-resolution video files is *hard!* A single frame of uncompressed full HD video is roughly equivalent to more than 8 million letters of text. And, of course, there are usually at least 24 frames per second, adding up to 192 million letters of text a second for HD video playback. UHD video (often described as 4K video) is four times that!

Reducing the playback resolution means you won't see every pixel in your pictures, but for some media formats it can dramatically improve performance, making creative work much easier. It's common for video to have a higher resolution than can be displayed, because your Source Monitor and Program Monitor are often smaller than the original media size. For this reason, you may not always see a difference in the display in any case.

Choosing playback resolution

Let's try adjusting playback resolution.

1 Open the clip Snow_3 from the Boston Snow bin in the Source Monitor, and double-click the Source Monitor tab to view it full screen.

   At the bottom right of the Source Monitor (and the Program Monitor when it's visible), you'll see the Select Playback Resolution menu.

   By default, playback is set to half-resolution. If it isn't, choose that option now. In fact, it's half-horizontal resolution and half-vertical resolution, so it's really quarter-resolution.

2 Play the clip to get a sense of the quality when it's set to half-resolution.

3 Change the resolution to Full, and play it again to compare. It probably looks similar. With some media formats, changing the playback resolution can make a big difference to the visual quality.

4 Try reducing the resolution to 1/8 and play the clip—a dramatic difference! Notice that the picture is sharp when you pause playback. This is because the pause resolution is an independent setting from the playback resolution (see the next section).

You'll notice the biggest differences in images with lots of detail, like text. Compare the detail in the tree branches, for example.

5 Try dropping the playback resolution to 1/16. Premiere makes an assessment of each kind of media you work with, and if the benefits of reducing resolution are less than the effort it takes to drop the resolution, the option is unavailable. In this case, the media is full 4K (4096×2160 pixels), and the 1/16 option is available.

You certainly wouldn't want to work at 1/16 resolution all of the time, but it can make an enormous difference when working with very high-resolution media on a low-powered computer.

6 Return the setting to 1/2, ready for the other clips in this project, and double-click the Source Monitor tab to restore the panel to its original position.

Note: The choices on the Playback Resolution menu are the same on the Source Monitor and the Program Monitor, but the option you choose on one of the menus is independent of the other.

If you're working on a powerful computer, you may want to maximize the playback quality when previewing at full resolution. There's an extra option to do this. You can choose High Quality Playback from the Settings menu for the Source Monitor or Program Monitor.

With High Quality Playback selected, playback is performed at the same quality as file export. Without this option enabled, a small amount of quality loss is allowed in exchange for better playback performance.

Choosing resolution when playback is paused

The playback resolution control is also available in the Settings menu on the Source and Program Monitors.

If you look in the Settings menu on either monitor, you'll find a second set of options related to display resolution: Paused Resolution.

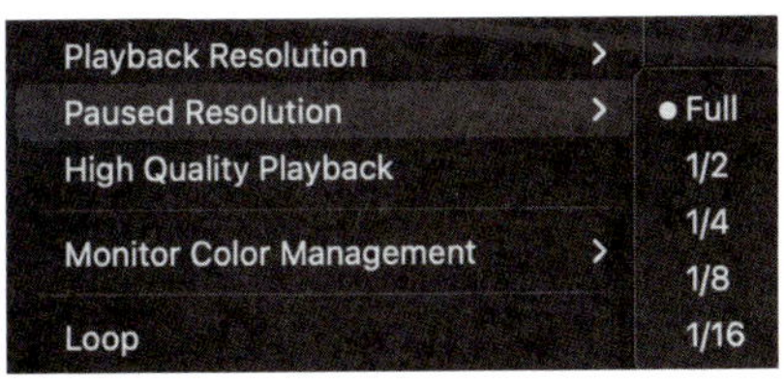

This menu works in the same way as the menu for playback resolution, but as you might have guessed, it changes the resolution only when the video is paused.

Most editors choose to leave Paused Resolution set to Full. That way, during playback you may see lower-resolution video to get the timing right, but when you pause playback, Premiere reverts to showing you a full-resolution image. When adjusting effects, you'll see the video at the playback resolution. As soon as you stop adjusting settings, the pause resolution is applied.

Some third-party special effects may not make use of your system hardware as efficiently as Premiere does. As a consequence, it might take a long time to update the picture when you adjust the effect settings. You can speed things up by lowering the paused resolution.

The playback resolution and paused resolution settings have no impact on output quality when exporting to a file.

Playing back VR video

Premiere has built-in support for 360° video and 180° video for VR headset display, with clip interpretation options, dedicated immersive video visual effects, desktop playback controls, and Ambisonics Audio support.

For more information about VR Video support in Premiere, check out the Adobe Help at *helpx.adobe.com* and search for "VR Video."

What's the difference between 360° video and virtual reality?

360° video is captured a little like a panoramic photo. Video is recorded in multiple directions, and the different camera angles are merged (a process called *stitching*) into a complete sphere that surrounds the viewer. The sphere is flattened into 2D video footage that's described as *equirectangular*. This is the same term used to describe a globe of the Earth that has been flattened into an atlas you can view in a book.

Equirectangular video looks distorted, which makes it hard to view. However, although the appearance is strange for human eyes, it's still a regular video file like any other, and Premiere can work with it.

To view 360° video properly, it's usually necessary to wear a virtual reality headset. In the headset you can turn your head to see different parts of the image. Because a VR headset is required to see 360° video properly, it's often referred to as *VR video*.

True VR isn't actually video. It's a complete 3D environment you can move around in, viewing things from different directions, like 360° video, but also viewing things from different locations in the virtual reality space. In a sense, VR is a little like a 3D gaming experience.

The key difference is this: In 360° video, you can view in different angles, but in true VR you can move around within the scenario.

Using markers

Sometimes it can be difficult to remember where you saw that useful part of a shot or what you intended to do with it. Wouldn't it be useful if you could mark clips with comments and flag areas of interest for later?

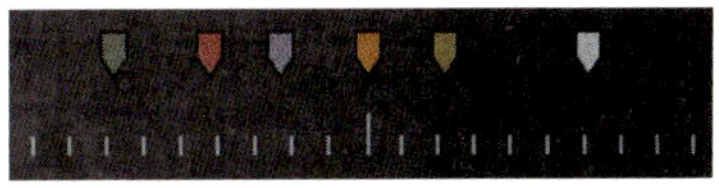

What you need are markers.

What are markers?

Markers allow you to identify specific times in both clips and sequences and add comments to them. These temporal (time-based) markers are a fantastic aid to help you stay organized and communicate with co-editors.

You can use markers for personal reference or for collaboration. You can add markers to clips or sequences.

Exploring the types of markers

More than one type of marker is available, and, like clips, markers can be assigned a color. You can change a marker type and color by double-clicking it.

- **Comment Marker:** This is a general marker; you can assign it a name, duration, and comments.
- **Chapter Marker:** Originally intended for DVDs, this kind of marker can be included in QuickTime movie exports, allowing viewers to skip to different sections.
- **Segmentation Marker:** This marker makes it possible for video distribution servers to divide content into parts.
- **Web Link:** Certain video formats can use this marker to automatically open a web page while the video plays. When you export your sequence to create a supported format, web link markers are included in the file.
- **Flash Cue Point:** This is a marker used by other Adobe animation tools. By adding these cue points to the timeline in Premiere, you can begin to prepare your Animate project while still editing your sequence.

Note: If a clip is selected in a sequence in the Timeline panel when you add a marker, the marker will be added to the selected clip rather than the sequence. See "Selecting clips" later in this lesson for more information about selecting clips in sequences.

Sequence markers

Let's add some markers to a sequence.

1 Open the City Views sequence from the Sequences bin.

This is a simple assembly edit with a few shots from a travelogue program.

2 Set the Timeline panel playhead to around 00:01:12:00, and make sure no clips are selected (you can click the background of the timeline or press the Escape key to deselect clips).

3 Add a marker in one of the following ways:

- Click the Add Marker button at the top left of the Timeline panel or the left end of the Program Monitor transport controls.
- Right-click the Timeline panel's time ruler and choose Add Marker.
- Press M.

Premiere adds a green marker to the timeline, just above the playhead.

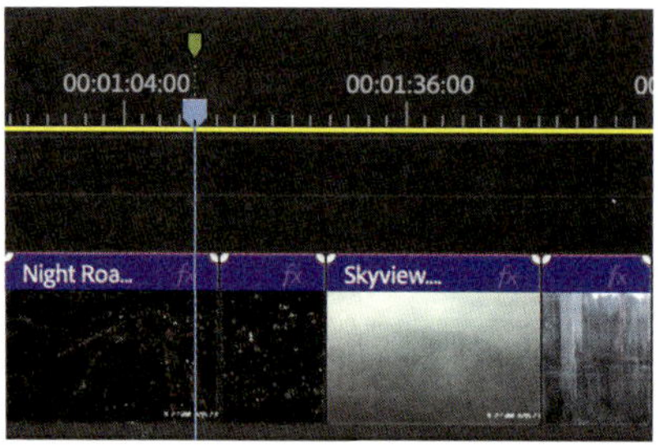

The same marker appears at the bottom of the Program Monitor.

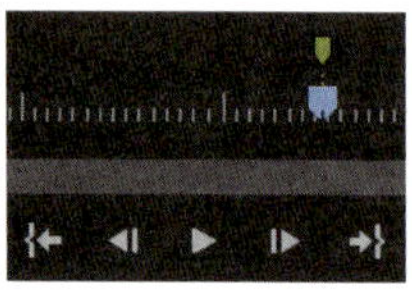

You can use this as a visual reminder of an important moment in time or change it into a different kind of marker. You'll do that shortly, but first let's look at this marker in the Markers panel.

Note: The Markers panel will display markers associated with the currently active sequence or a clip you open in the Source Monitor. If the panel is blank, try clicking in the Timeline panel or Source Monitor to make it active.

4 Open the Markers panel. By default, the Markers panel is grouped with the Project panel. If you don't see it there, choose Window > Markers.

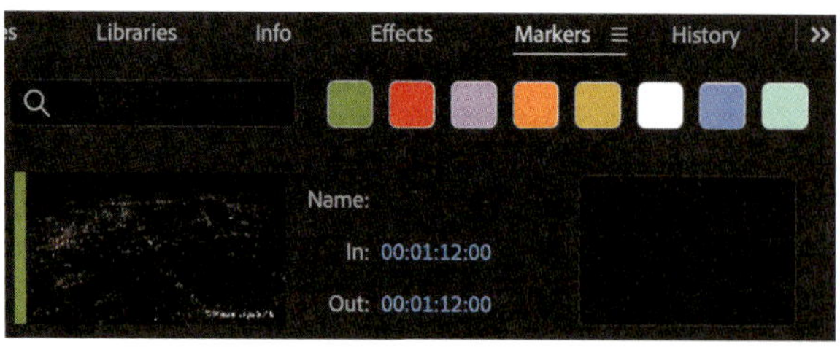

The Markers panel shows you a list of markers, displayed in time order. The same panel shows you markers for a sequence or for a clip, depending on whether the Timeline panel, a sequence clip, or the Source Monitor is active (selected).

Tip: The Markers panel has a Search box at the top that works the same way as the Search box in the Project panel. Next to the Search box are marker color filters. Click one (or several) of these to see only markers with matching colors in the Markers panel.

5 Double-click the thumbnail for the marker in the Markers panel. This displays the Marker dialog box.

> **Tip:** You can open the Marker dialog box by double-clicking a marker in the Markers panel or by double-clicking the marker icon in the Timeline panel or a monitor.

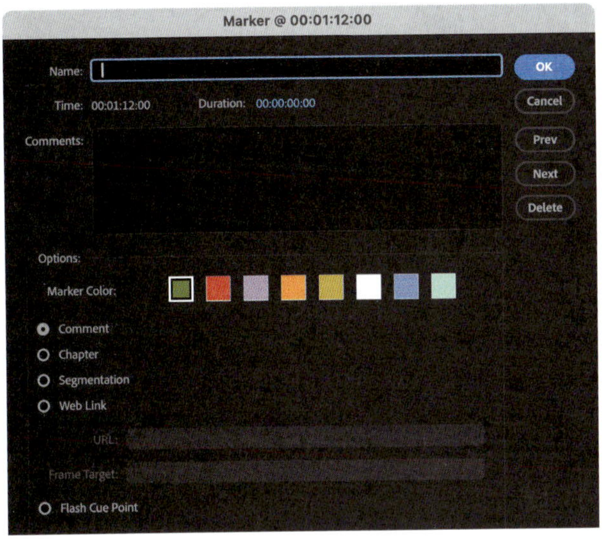

6 Notice the insertion point is already flashing in the Name box. Type a production note, such as **Replace this shot**.

7 Click the Duration field (the blue numbers), and type **400**. Avoid the temptation to press Return or Enter for now, as this will close the panel. Premiere automatically adds punctuation, turning this into 00:00:04:00 (four seconds) as soon as you click away or press the Tab key to move to the next field.

Press the Tab key now so you can review the new setting.

> **Tip:** You can quickly add a marker and immediately display the Marker dialog box by pressing M twice.

> **Tip:** You can press Return or Enter after setting a name or duration for a marker and the dialog box will close, applying your chosen settings.

8 Click OK, or press Return/Enter.

The marker now has a visible duration in the Timeline panel and Program Monitor. Zoom in to the timeline a little, and you'll see the text you typed into the Name field.

> **Tip:** You can assign a keyboard shortcut to each type of marker, as well as for each marker color. Working with markers using the keyboard is generally faster than using the mouse or trackpad.

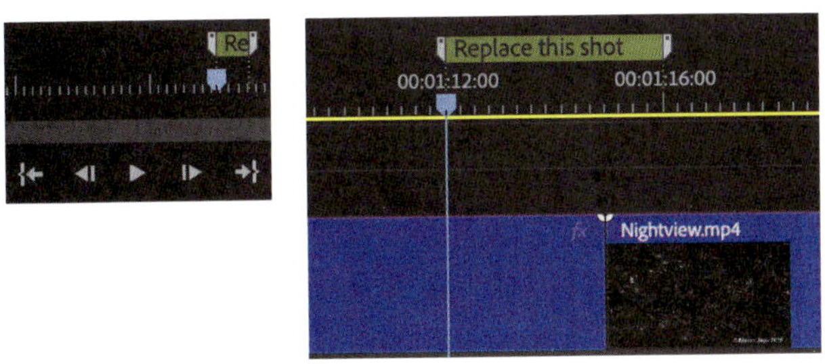

The name of the marker is also displayed in the Markers panel.

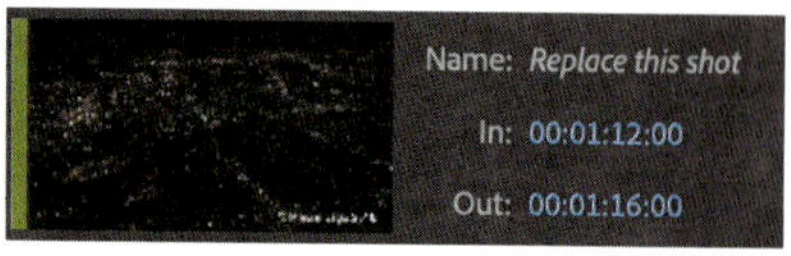

9 Take a moment to open the Markers menu on the main menu bar, to see the available commands.

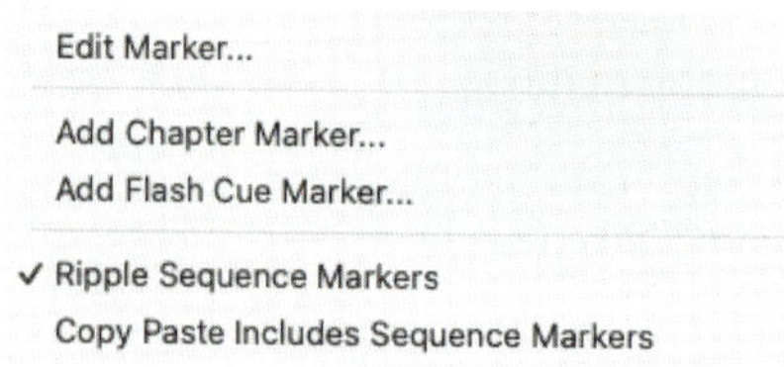

At the bottom of the Markers menu is the Ripple Sequence Markers command. With this chosen, sequence markers will move in sync with clips when you insert and extract clips—these are editing operations that change the sequence duration and timing. With this option disabled, markers stay where they are when your clips move.

At the very bottom of the same menu, you'll find a command with the "snappy" name Copy Paste Includes Sequence Markers.

With this option enabled, when you copy a section of a sequence that you've selected using In and Out points and then paste that content somewhere else, any sequence markers in the selection are included.

Clip markers

Let's add markers to a clip.

1 Open the clip Seattle_Skyline.mov from the Further Media bin in the Source Monitor.

2 Play the clip, and while it plays, press the M key several times to add markers.

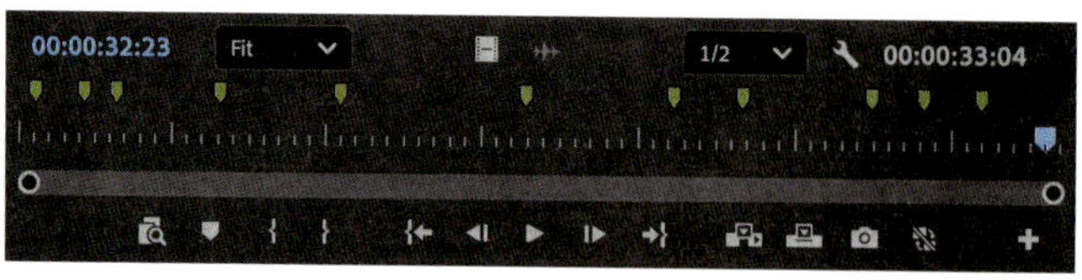

Tip: You can add markers using a button or a keyboard shortcut. If you use the keyboard shortcut, M, it's easy to add markers that match the beat of your music because you can add them during playback.

3 Look in the Markers panel. If the Source Monitor is active, every marker you added will be listed. You may need to scroll down to see all the markers.

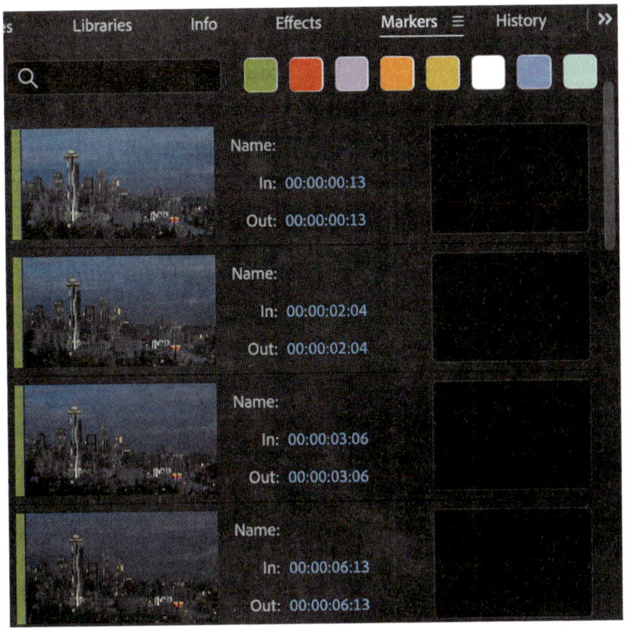

When clips with markers are added to a sequence, they retain their markers.

Tip: To clear markers—or the current marker—right-click in the Source Monitor, in the Program Monitor, or on the Timeline panel time ruler and choose Clear Markers or Clear Selected Marker.

4 Make sure the Source Monitor is active by clicking it. Choose Markers > Clear Markers to remove all the markers from the clip.

Tip: You can use markers to quickly navigate your clips and sequences. If you single-click a marker icon or select a marker in the Markers panel, the playhead will move to the location of the marker—a fast way to find your way around. If you double-click a marker, Premiere will display the Marker dialog box.

Exporting markers

You can export markers associated with a clip or sequence as a text file, as an HTML page with thumbnails, or as a CSV (comma-separated value) file readable by spreadsheet-editing applications. This is great for collaboration and as a reference.

To export markers, select a sequence or clip with markers and choose File > Export > Markers.

Finding clips in the Timeline panel

As well as searching for clips in the Project panel, you can search for them in a sequence. Depending on whether you have the Project panel active or the Timeline panel active, choosing Edit > Find or pressing Command+F (macOS) or Ctrl+F (Windows) will display search options for that panel.

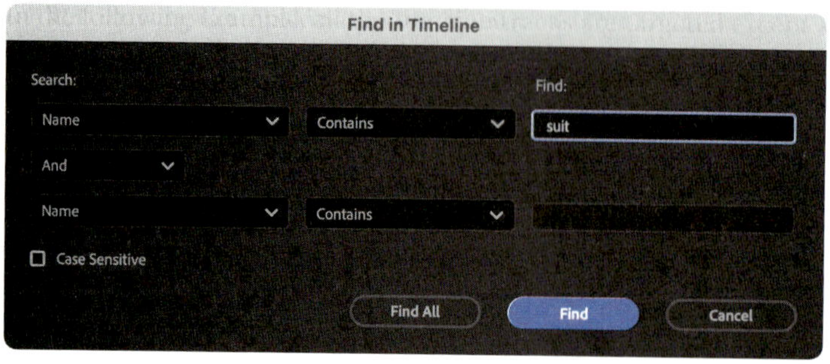

When clips in a sequence are found that match your search criteria, Premiere highlights them. If you choose Find All, Premiere will highlight all clips that meet the search criteria.

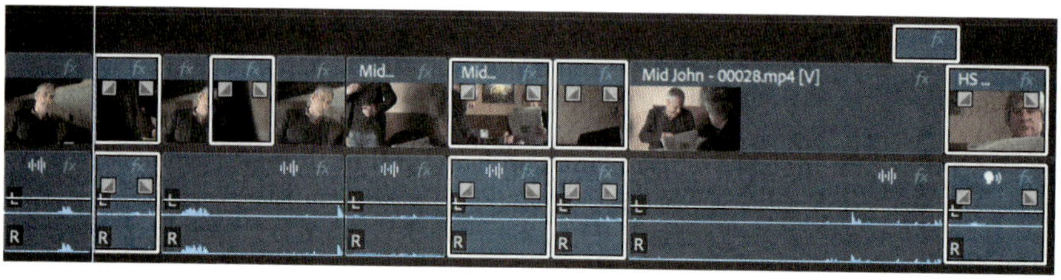

Searching similar frames

When viewing a clip in the Source Monitor, you may wonder if you have other similar shots available in the Project panel. Also, when viewing the contents of a sequence, you may wonder if you have similar shots elsewhere already in the Timeline panel.

At the lower-left corner of the Source Monitor and the Program Monitor, you'll find the Search Similar Frames button. Click this while a reference shot is displayed, and the Search panel will open, displaying similar content, thanks to Premiere's media analysis.

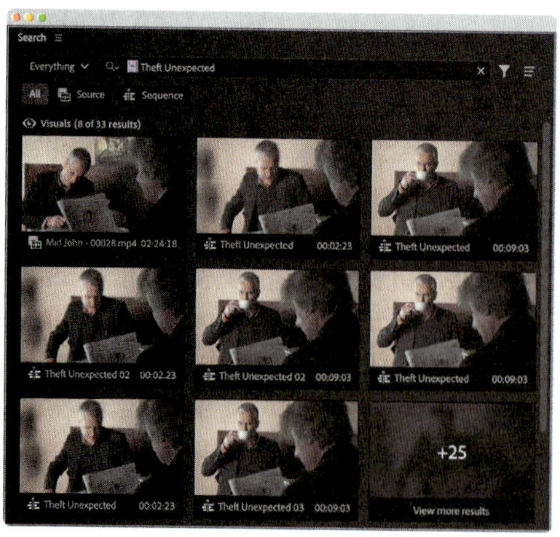

If you don't see results immediately, you may need to wait for analysis to be complete.

Clicking the button in the Program Monitor will display similar shots in the current sequence, while clicking the button in the Source Monitor will display source clips in the Project panel.

Within the Search panel, you can limit results to source clips or sequence clips by clicking at the top of the panel. You can also limit the search visuals, audio, text, or metadata using the menu at the top-left corner.

Using Sync Locks and Track Locks

There are two distinct ways to lock clips on tracks in the Timeline panel.

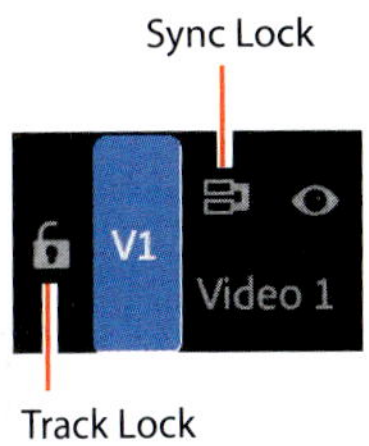

- Sync locks keep clips in sync, so when you apply an insert edit or extract edit, clips on other tracks stay synchronized.
- Track locks enable you to lock a track so that absolutely no changes can be made to it.

Using sync locks

If an actor's lips move out of time with the audio of the person's voice, it's considered bad lip-sync. It's obvious when this kind of synchronization (*sync*) goes wrong, but other types of sync issues may be harder to detect.

It's helpful to think of syncing as coordinating any two things that are meant to happen at the same time. It might be a musical event that happens at the same time as a climactic visual or something as simple as a lower-third title that identifies a speaker. If it happens at the same time, it's synchronized.

1 Open the Theft Unexpected 02 sequence from the Sequences bin. Make sure there are no In or Out points on the timeline.

   This sequence contains two takes of John arriving and saying, "Excuse me." We'll fix that later.

   When John arrives, at the beginning of the sequence, the audience won't know what he's looking at. Let's add a new opening shot of the other actor to set the scene.

2 Open the Mid Suit clip, from the Theft Unexpected bin, in the Source Monitor. Add an In point at 01:15:35:18, and add an Out point at 01:15:39:00.

3 Click the Sync Lock button for the Video 2 track to turn it off.

4 Check that your Timeline panel is configured as in the next example, with the Source V1 track patched to the timeline V1 track (drag it into position or click to select a new position if necessary). The timeline track targeting indicators are not important for the edit you are about to perform, but having the right source track selection buttons enabled is.

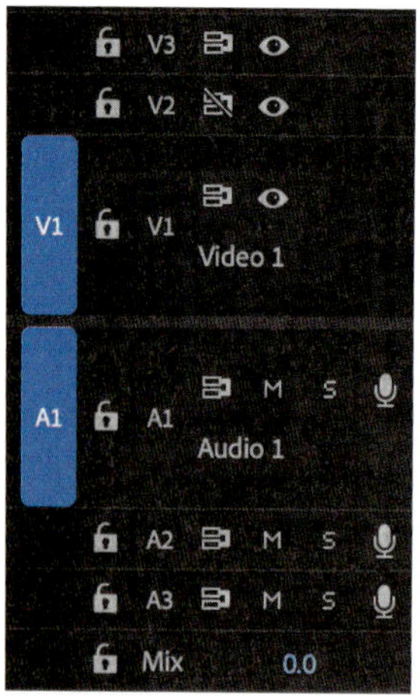

● **Note:** You may need to zoom out to see the other clips in the sequence.

Take a quick look at the position of the Mid Suit cutaway clip on the Video 2 track, toward the end of the sequence.

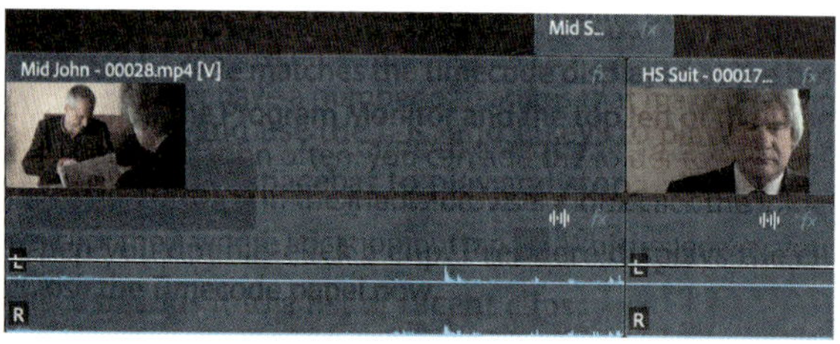

It's just over the cut (the edit) between the clips Mid John and HS Suit on Video 1, covering that edit for the viewer.

5 Position the Timeline panel playhead at the beginning of the sequence.

6 Insert edit the Mid Suit source clip into the beginning of the sequence (you can click the Source Monitor Insert Edit button).

Take another look at the location of the Mid Suit cutaway clip.

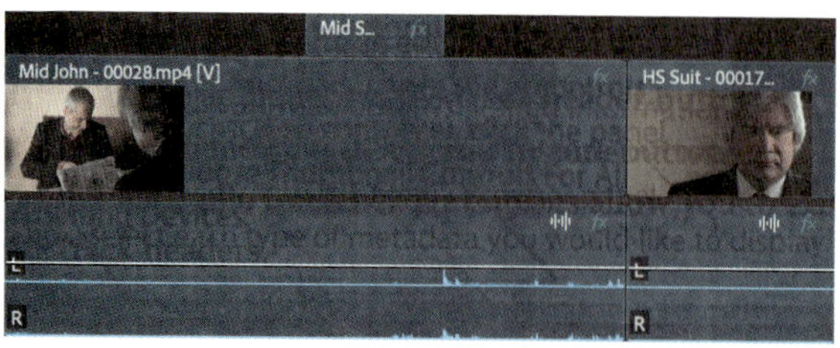

The Mid Suit cutaway clip on the Video 2 track did *not* move when you inserted the new clip because the sync lock was turned off for that track. The other clips, on the Video 1 track, have moved to the right to accommodate the new clip.

This is a problem! The cutaway is now out of position with the clips to which it relates—it no longer covers up the cut!

7 Undo by pressing Command+Z (macOS) or Ctrl+Z (Windows).

8 Click the Video 2 track's Sync Lock button again to turn it on, and perform the insert edit again.

This time, the cutaway clip moves with the other clips on the timeline, even though nothing is being edited onto the Video 2 track. This is the power of sync locks: They keep things in sync!

Sometimes you will choose to turn off sync locks, as, for example, when you have music clips that you don't want to move while you add visuals.

Note: Sync locks only impact insert edits or extract edits, which change the timing of sequence clips. Overwrite edits do not change the duration of your sequence, so they are not affected.

Using track locks

Track locks (which are separate from sync locks) prevent any changes being made to a track. They are an excellent way to avoid making accidental changes to your sequence and to fix clips on specific tracks in place while you work.

For example, you could lock your music track while you insert different video clips. By locking the music track, you can simply forget about it while editing because no changes can be made to it.

The content of a locked track is still included in the sequence; you just can't make changes to that content.

Lock and unlock a track by clicking the Track Lock button. Clips on a locked track are highlighted with diagonal lines.

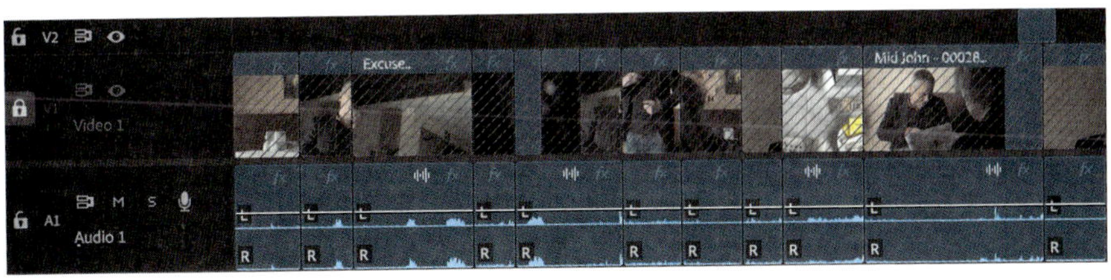

Track locks override sync locks, so even though the sync locks are enabled in this example, you'd break sync with the video clips if you were to change the position of the audio clips.

Working with gaps in the sequence

Until now, you've been exclusively *adding* clips to a sequence (not removing them). Part of the power of nonlinear editing is in having the freedom to move clips around in a sequence and remove the parts you don't want.

When removing clips or parts of clips, you'll either leave a gap by performing a *lift edit* or not leave a gap by performing an *extract edit*. You will learn more about these two types of edit later in this lesson.

An extract edit is a little like an insert edit but in reverse. Rather than other clips in a sequence moving out of the way to make space for a new clip, the other clips move in to fill the gap left behind by a clip you are removing.

When you zoom out of a long complex sequence, it can be difficult to see smaller gaps between clips. To automatically locate the next gap, choose Sequence > Go To Gap > Next In Sequence.

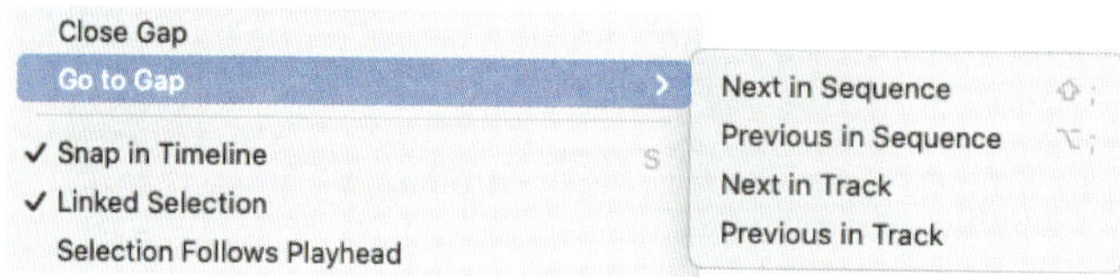

Once you've found a gap between clips, you can remove it by selecting it (click the gap) and pressing Delete (macOS) or Backspace (Windows). Clips after the gap will move to close the gap.

Let's explore working with clips in a sequence a little more. Continue working with the Theft Unexpected 02 sequence in the next section.

Selecting clips

Selection is an important part of working with Premiere. For example, depending on the panel you have selected to be active (with a blue outline), different menu options will be available. Select clips in your sequences carefully before applying adjustments.

When working with clips in sequences that have both video and audio, you'll have two or more segments for each clip: one video segment and one or more audio segments.

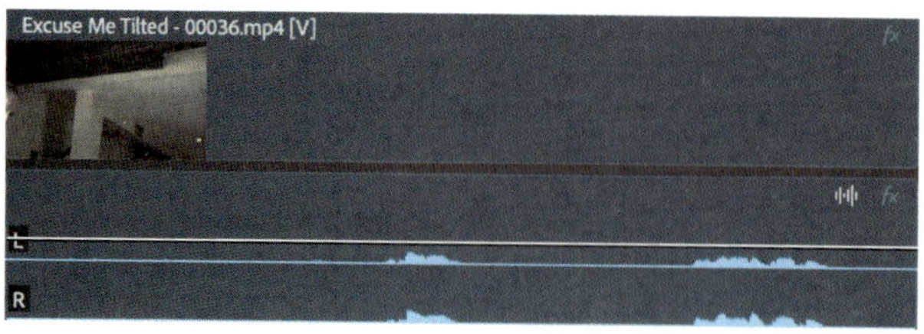

When the video and audio clip segments come from the same original media file, they are automatically linked together when added to a sequence. If you select one, the other is automatically selected too.

By default, the Linked Selection button is on with a gray highlight. To ignore links between clips, toggle Linked Selection off, at the top left of the Timeline panel. All clip linking will be ignored. For example, if there are linked video and audio segments, you'll select just the one you click.

> **Tip:** Because video and audio track locks are separate, you can easily move video and audio clips apart that are linked without unlinking them first by locking one or other track first. Be warned, though, that this can lead to unwanted sync issues!

There's a quick way to ignore linked selections without clicking the Linked Selection button: Hold Option (macOS) or Alt (Windows) while selecting clip segments in a sequence.

Leave the Linked Selection option on for now.

Selecting a clip or range of clips

When selecting clips in a sequence, there are two approaches.

- Make time selections by using In and Out points.
- Make clip segment selections.

The simplest way to select a clip in a sequence is to click it using the Selection tool. Be careful not to double-click, which will open the sequence clip instance in the Source Monitor, ready for you to adjust the In or Out points (these will update, live, in the sequence).

When making selections, you'll generally use the Selection tool, which is selected in the Tools panel by default. This tool has the keyboard shortcut V.

If you hold the Shift key while selecting sequence clip segments, you'll add or remove clips from the selection. Selected clips do not have to be contiguous.

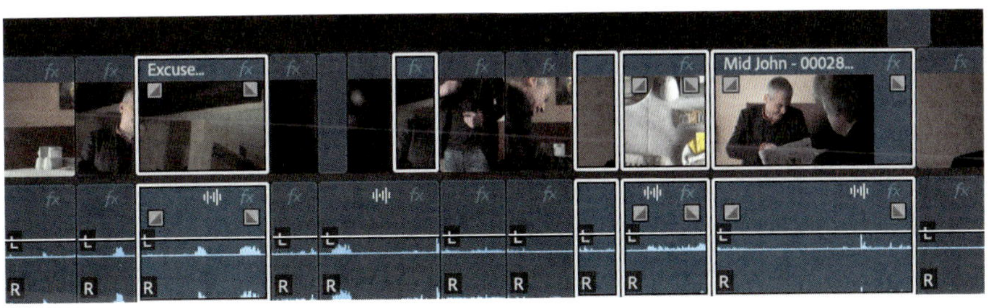

You can also drag the Selection tool over multiple clips to select them. Begin by placing the pointer over an empty part of the Timeline panel and then dragging to create a selection box. Any clip you drag over (even partially) with the selection box will be selected.

There is also an option to automatically select whichever clip the Timeline panel's playhead passes over, on the highest targeted track. This is particularly useful for keyboard-based editing workflows and effects setup. You can enable the option by choosing Sequence > Selection Follows Playhead.

You can also press the keyboard shortcut D to select the clips under the timeline playhead. Clips on targeted tracks (whose track targeting indicator is highlighted in blue) will be selected.

Note: If no tracks are targeted, pressing D will select all clips under the Timeline panel's playhead.

Selecting multiple clips on a track

If you want to select every clip in a sequence, on every track, make sure the Timeline panel is active and press Command+A (macOS) or Ctrl+A (Windows).

There are also two handy tools to select all clips in a particular direction in a sequence: the Track Select Forward tool, which has the keyboard shortcut A, and the Track Select Backward tool, which has the keyboard shortcut Shift+A. You can click and hold the Track Select Forward tool to access the Track Select Backward tool.

Tip: The V key is a useful shortcut. If the Timeline panel seems to be acting strangely, try pressing V to return to the Selection tool.

Try this now. Select the Track Select Forward tool and click any clip on the Video 1 track.

Every clip on every track, from the one you select until the end of the sequence, is selected. This is useful if you want to add a gap to your sequence to make space for more clips; you can drag all the selected clips to the right.

When you click a clip with the Track Select Backward tool, every clip up to and including the one you clicked is selected.

If you hold the Shift key while using either of the tools, you'll select clips on only one track. You may need to deselect Linked Selection to see a difference.

When you have finished, switch to the Selection tool by clicking it in the Tools panel or by pressing the V key.

Splitting a clip

It's common to add a clip to a sequence and then realize you need it in two parts. Perhaps you want to take just a section of a clip and use it as a cutaway, or maybe you want to separate the beginning and the end to make space for new clips.

You can split clips in several ways:

- Using the Razor tool, click a clip to add an edit where you click. If you hold the Shift key while clicking with the Razor tool, you'll split the clips on every track.
- Make sure the Timeline panel is selected, and choose Sequence > Add Edit. Premiere adds an edit at the location of your playhead to clips on any tracks that are targeted (with the track targeting indicators on). If you have selected one or more clips in the sequence, Premiere adds the edit only to the selected clips, ignoring track selections.
- Choose Sequence > Add Edit To All Tracks to add an edit to clips on all tracks, regardless of whether they are targeted.
- Use the Add Edit keyboard shortcuts. Press Command+K (macOS) or Ctrl+K (Windows) to add an edit to targeted tracks or selected clips, or press Shift+Command+K (macOS) or Shift+Ctrl+K (Windows) to add an edit to all tracks.

Tip: The keyboard shortcut for the Razor tool is C.

Clips that were originally continuous will still play back seamlessly unless you move them apart or make separate adjustments to different segments.

If you click the Timeline Display Settings menu, you can choose Show Through Edits to see a special icon on edits of this kind, between two clips that were originally continuous.

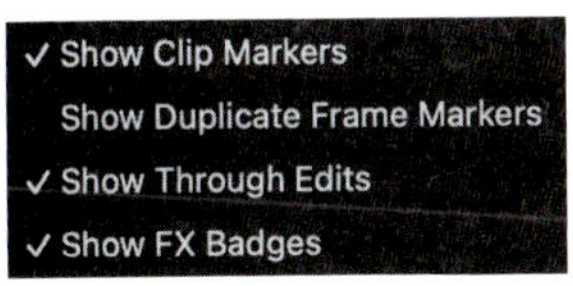

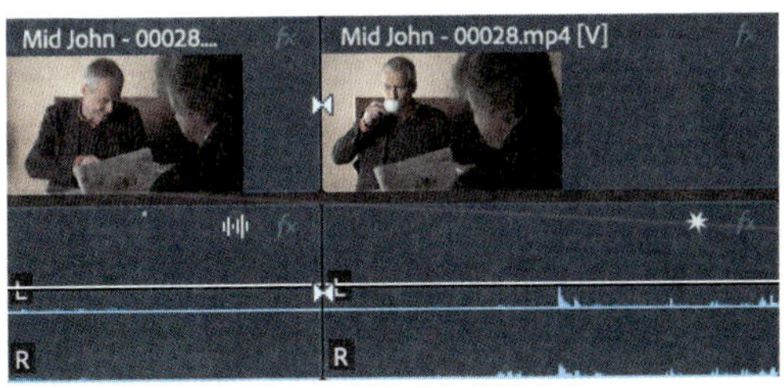

Using the Selection tool, click a Through Edit icon, and press Delete/Backspace to rejoin the two parts of the clip. When you hover over an edit, the cursor will change to a trimming tool that you'll learn about later. Ignore the change to the cursor and click any Through Edit icon.

You don't need the Through Edit icons to be displayed for this to work, but they are a handy visual indicator.

Try splitting some clips in your current sequence using these techniques. Then try rejoining them. When you're done, be sure to use the Undo command repeatedly until you've removed all of the new cuts you added.

Grouping clips

If there are several clips in a sequence that you would like to select, move, and apply effects to in a single step, you can group them.

> **Tip:** Even when clips are grouped, you can select them separately by holding Option (macOS) or Alt (Windows) when you click.

Select the clips, right-click the selection, and choose Group. From now on, selecting any of the clips in the group selects them all.

To separate the clips from the group, right-click any of the clips and choose Ungroup.

Linking and unlinking clips

The link between specific connected video and audio segments can be switched off and on easily. Just select the clip or clips you want to change, right-click the selected clips, and choose Unlink.

You'll find the command in the Clip menu too. You can link the clip segments again by selecting both segments, right-clicking one of them, and choosing Link. There's no harm in linking or unlinking clips—it won't change the way Premiere plays your sequence. It just gives you flexibility when selecting clips.

Even if video and audio clip segments are linked, you'll need to make sure the Timeline Linked Selection option is enabled to select linked clips together.

Moving clips

Insert edits and overwrite edits add new clips to sequences in dramatically different ways. Insert edits push existing clips out of the way, whereas overwrite edits simply replace them. This theme of having two ways of working with clips extends to the techniques you'll employ to move clips around a sequence and to remove clips.

When moving clips using Insert mode, you may want to ensure the sync locks are switched on for all tracks to avoid losing sync.

Let's try a few examples.

Dragging clips

At the top left of the Timeline panel, you'll find the Snap button, which is on by default. When snapping is enabled, clip segments snap automatically to each other's edges. This simple but useful feature will help you position clip segments frame-accurately.

The keyboard shortcut to toggle snapping on or off is S. Even if you have already begun dragging an item to perform an edit, you can still press S to enable or disable snapping—while dragging. It's common to forget if snapping is off or on, so this can be a useful shortcut to learn.

1 Return to the Theft Unexpected 02 sequence in the Timeline panel. Select the last clip on the timeline, HS Suit, and drag it a little to the right.

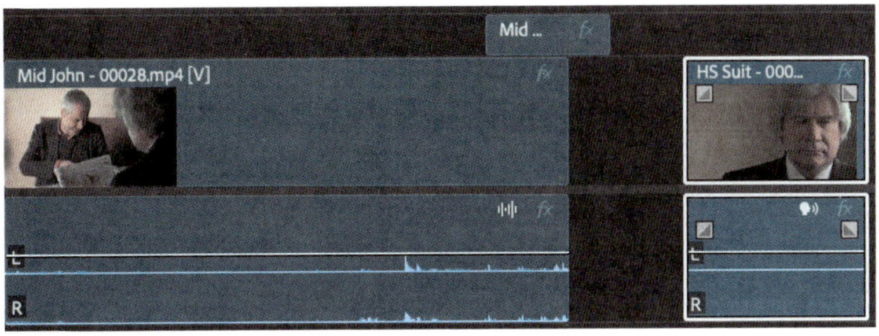

Because there are no clips after this one in the sequence, you simply introduce a gap before the clip. No other clips are affected.

2 Make sure the Snap option is enabled (highlighted in gray), and drag the clip back to its original position. If you move slowly, you'll notice that the clip segment jumps into position at the last moment. When this happens, you can be confident it's perfectly positioned. Notice that the clip also snaps to the end of the cutaway shot on the Video 2 track, and the playhead.

3 Drag the clip left until the right edge of the clip snaps to the right edge of the previous clip so they are overlapping. When you release it, the new clip replaces the end of the previous clip.

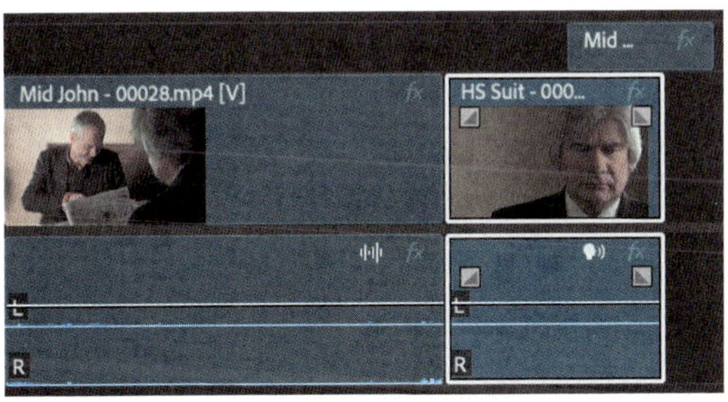

When you drag clips, the default editing mode is Overwrite.

4 Undo enough times to return the clip to its original position.

Nudging clips

Note: When you nudge clips, an overwrite edit is performed, removing clips or parts of clips overlapped by the clip you are moving. If you nudge a clip back into its original position, you will leave a gap.

Many editors prefer to use the keyboard as much as possible, minimizing the use of the mouse or trackpad because working with the keyboard is usually faster.

You can reposition clip segments in a sequence using the arrow keys in combination with a modifier key, nudging the selected items left and right (earlier or later in time) or up and down between tracks.

Because of the separator between the video and audio tracks in the Timeline panel, when you nudge linked video and audio clips up or down, one of the clips may be left in its original position. This introduces a vertical gap between the linked clips which won't impact playback but can make it a little harder to see which clips are linked together.

Default clip-nudging shortcuts

Premiere has many keyboard shortcut options, some of which are available but not yet assigned to keys. You can configure these in the Keyboard Shortcuts preferences, prioritizing the use of available keys to suit your workflow.

Here are the default shortcuts for nudging clips (macOS versions listed first, followed by Windows):

- Nudge Clip Selection Left 1 Frame (add Shift for 5 frames): Command+Left Arrow or Alt+Left Arrow
- Nudge Clip Selection Right 1 Frame (add Shift for 5 frames): Command+Right Arrow or Alt+Right Arrow
- Nudge Clip Selection Up: Option+Up Arrow or Alt+Up Arrow
- Nudge Clip Selection Down: Option+Down Arrow or Alt+Down Arrow

Rearranging clips in a sequence

If you hold the Command (macOS) or Ctrl (Windows) key while you drag clip segments in the Timeline panel, Premiere uses Insert mode (rather than Overwrite mode) to place the clip when you release it.

To try this out, open the Theft Unexpected 03 sequence from the Sequences bin. This sequence has a music clip that plays from beginning to end.

Tip: You may need to zoom in to the timeline to see the clips clearly and move them easily.

The HS Suit shot that begins around 00:00:16:00 might work better if it appeared before the previous shot—and it might help to hide the poor continuity between the two shots of John.

1 Make sure Snapping is turned on (with a gray highlight) at the top left of the Timeline panel.

2 Start dragging the HS Suit clip to the left of the clip before it. After you have begun dragging but *before* you release the clip, hold the Command (macOS) or Ctrl (Windows) key.

3 Drag until the left edge of the HS Suit clip snaps to the left edge of the Mid Suit clip. Release the drag to drop the clip, and then release the modifier key.

You just performed a lift edit, leaving a gap, followed by an insert edit. Notice that because of the Sync Locks, the music clip also now has a gap.

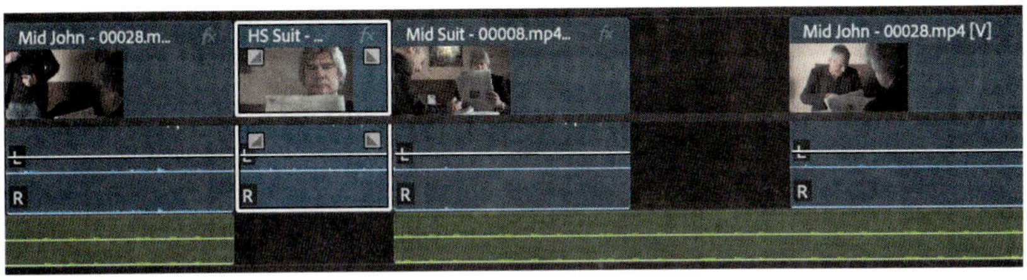

Let's try that again with a different use of the modifier key to avoid leaving that gap.

4 Undo to restore the clips to their original positions.

5 First hold Command (macOS) or Ctrl (Windows) and *after* you have begun holding the key, drag the HS Suit clip to the beginning of the previous clip again.

This time, you have performed an extract edit, leaving no gap, followed by an insert edit in a single step. This leaves the video and audio clips without any unwanted gaps but, once again, the sync locks have added a gap to the music clip.

Play through the edit to see the result.

There's a third way to move clips that makes most sense if there are clips on other tracks.

6 Undo to restore the clips to their original positions.

7 Start dragging the HS Suit clip to the left of the clip before it. After you have begun dragging, but before you release the clip, hold Command+Option (macOS) or Ctrl+Alt (Windows) keys.

Tip: Be careful when dropping the clip into position. The ends of clips snap into position just like the beginnings do.

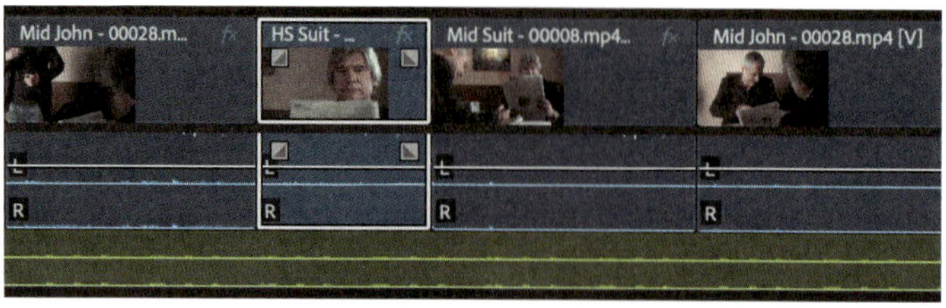

This switches the location of the clip without inserting and so no gap is added to the music clip.

It can take some getting used to the various combinations of modifier keys to change the way the Selection tool works. Don't worry about memorizing, just know what you want to achieve and try different combinations until it works. You'll learn which is which automatically through practice.

Using the clipboard

You can copy and paste clip segments on the Timeline panel just as you might copy and paste text in a word processor.

1 In a sequence, select any clip segment (or segments) you want to copy, and then press Command+C (macOS) or Ctrl+C (Windows) to add them to the clipboard.

2 Position your playhead where you would like to paste the clips you copied, and press Command+V (macOS) or Ctrl+V (Windows).

Premiere adds copies of the clips to your sequence based on their original track location. For example, if a clip that you copied was originally on the V1 track, when you paste it will be added to the V1 track at the location of the sequence playhead.

Pressing Command+V (macOS) or Ctrl+V (Windows) adds the copied clips using an overwrite edit. To insert the copied clips instead, use Shift+Command+V (macOS) or Shift+Ctrl+V (Windows).

You can use In points and Out points combined with track selection buttons to select the parts of clips that you'll copy.

Tip: Using the Keyboard Shortcuts dialog box, you can add a shortcut to the Paste To Target Track option. This will paste to targeted tracks rather than the track the original clips came from.

Extracting and deleting segments

Now that you know how to add clips to a sequence and how to move them around, all that remains is to learn how to remove them. Once again, you'll be operating in either a kind of Insert or Overwrite mode.

Premiere offers two ways to select the parts of a sequence you want to remove. You can use In and Out points combined with track selections, or you can select clip segments.

Performing a lift edit

A lift edit will remove the selected part of a sequence, leaving blank space. It's similar to an overwrite edit but in reverse.

1 For this exercise, if you have turned on the Selection Follows Playhead option, turn it off now by choosing Sequence > Selection Follows Playhead.

2 Click the name of the Theft Unexpected 02 sequence in the Timeline panel to bring it into view. This sequence has two unwanted clips.

Next, you'll set In and Out points on the timeline to select the part that will be removed. You could do this by positioning the playhead and pressing I or O, but the next step will show you a handy shortcut.

3 Position the playhead so that it's somewhere over the Excuse Me Tilted clip (the third clip in the sequence).

4 Make sure the Video 1 and Audio 1 tracks are targeted (with the buttons to the right of the Track Lock icons, highlighted in blue), and then press X. There's no need to select the clip first.

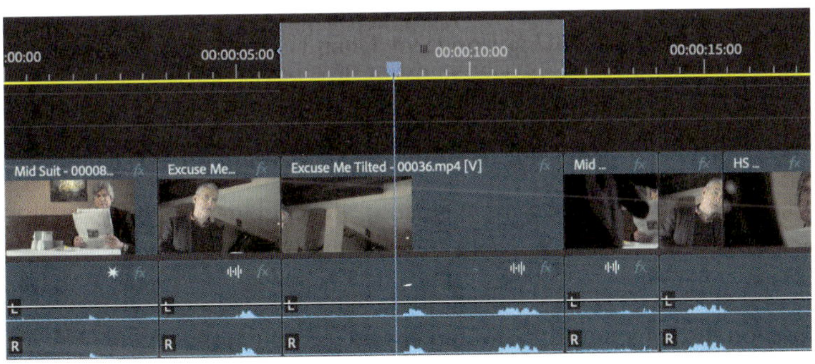

This adds an In point and an Out point that match the beginning and end of the clip. You'll see a highlight that shows the selected part of the sequence.

5 Click the Lift button at the bottom of the Program Monitor. If your keyboard has a ; (semicolon) key, you can press that instead.

Tip: When you perform a lift or extract edit, the content you remove is added to the clipboard just as if you had copied it, allowing you to paste the content somewhere else in your sequence.

Note: When adding In and Out points to select part of a sequence, use the Track Targeting buttons to specify which tracks will be affected.

Premiere removes the part of the sequence you selected, leaving a gap. This might be fine on another occasion, but on this occasion, we don't want the gap. You could remove the gap now, but for the next exercise you'll try performing an extract edit so no gap is left.

Different shortcuts for In and Out points

You can set In and Out points at the beginning and end of a selected clip (or multiple selected clips) by pressing the / (forward slash) key. This is the keyboard shortcut for the Mark Selection command. This shortcut is a little different from using the X key after positioning the playhead over the clip (without selecting it) with the correct tracks selected.

The difference is subtle, but X is perhaps even faster than using the selection-based / key, provided your track selections are already set up and you only want to select one clip.

Performing an extract edit

An extract edit removes the selected part of your sequence and does not leave a gap. It's similar to an insert edit but in reverse.

1 Undo the last edit.

2 Click the Extract button at the bottom of the Program Monitor. If your keyboard has an ' (apostrophe) key, you can press it.

Note: Non-English keyboards may not include an ' (apostrophe) key. If your keyboard lacks that key, set up a new keyboard shortcut in the Keyboard Shortcuts preferences.

This time, Premiere removes the selected part of the sequence, and the other clips in the sequence move to close the gap.

Performing delete and ripple delete edits

Just as there are two ways to remove part of a sequence based on In and Out points, there are also two similar ways to remove clips by selecting clip segments: delete and ripple delete.

Click once to select the Cutaways clip in the sequence, and try these two options:

- Press the Delete/Backspace key to remove the selected clip (or clips), leaving a gap behind. This is similar to a lift edit but the contents are not copied to the Clipboard.
- Press Shift+Forward Delete (macOS) or Shift+Delete (Windows) to perform a ripple delete. This removes the selected clip (or clips) without leaving a gap behind. This is similar to an extract edit.

If you're using a Mac keyboard without a dedicated Forward Delete key, you can achieve the same result by pressing Option+Delete.

The result is similar to that achieved when performing a lift or extract edit. You can even use a delete or ripple delete selectively on parts of clips by combining In and Out points with track targeting selections.

However, when you perform an extract or a lift edit to remove content, the content is added to the clipboard and can be pasted somewhere else in your sequence. When you delete content, it is simply removed.

Disabling a clip

You can turn a whole track's output off or on, or you can turn the output of individual clips off or on. Clips that you disable are still in your sequence, but they cannot be seen or heard.

This is a useful feature for selectively hiding parts of a complex, multilayered sequence when you want to see background layers or compare different versions or different performance takes that you have placed on different tracks.

Try this on the cutaway shot on the Video 2 track, toward the end of the sequence.

1 Right-click the Mid Suit clip on the Video 2 track and choose Enable to deselect the option.

   Play through that part of the sequence, and you'll notice that the clip is present, but you can no longer see it. The clip segment has also changed to a darker shade.

2 Right-click the clip again and choose Enable to make the clip visible once more.

3 Choose File > Close to close the current project. Choose to save the file if you are prompted.

Note: When right-clicking clips in a sequence, be careful not to right-click the small clip FX badge, as this will give you options relating to effects instead of the general clip options.

Review questions

1 When dragging clips directly into the Timeline panel, what modifier key (Command/Ctrl, Shift, or Option/Alt) should you use to make an insert edit rather than an overwrite edit?

2 How do you drag just the video or audio part of a clip from the Source Monitor into a sequence?

3 How do you reduce the playback resolution in the Source Monitor or Program Monitor?

4 How do you add a marker to a clip or sequence?

5 What is the difference between an extract edit and a lift edit?

6 What is the difference between delete and ripple delete?

Review answers

1 Hold the Command (macOS) or Ctrl (Windows) key when dragging a clip into the Timeline panel to make an insert edit rather than an overwrite edit.

2 Rather than dragging the picture from the Source Monitor, which will bring both the video and the audio if they are available, drag the filmstrip icon or the audio waveform icon at the bottom of the monitor to take only the video or audio part of the clip, respectively. You can also use the source patching buttons in the Timeline panel to deselect the parts you want to exclude when dragging the picture from the Source Monitor or dragging a clip from the Project panel or a bin.

3 Use the Select Playback Resolution menu at the bottom of the monitor to change the playback resolution.

4 There are several ways add a marker:

- Click the Add Marker button at the bottom of a monitor or on the Timeline panel.
- Press the M key.
- Choose Add Marker from the Markers menu.

5 When you extract a section of your sequence using In and Out points, no gap is left behind. When you lift, a gap remains.

6 When you delete one or more clip segments in a sequence, a gap is left behind. When you ripple delete, no gap is left.

7 ADDING TRANSITIONS

Lesson overview

In this lesson, you'll learn how to do the following:

- Understand edit points and handles.
- Understand transitions.
- Add video transitions.
- Modify transitions.
- Fine-tune transitions.
- Apply transitions to multiple clips.
- Add content with Generative Extend.
- Work with audio transitions.

This lesson will take about 75 minutes to complete. To get the files used in this lesson, refer to the instructions in "Accessing the lesson files and Web Edition" in the "Getting Started" section at the beginning of this book. Store the files on your computer in a convenient location.

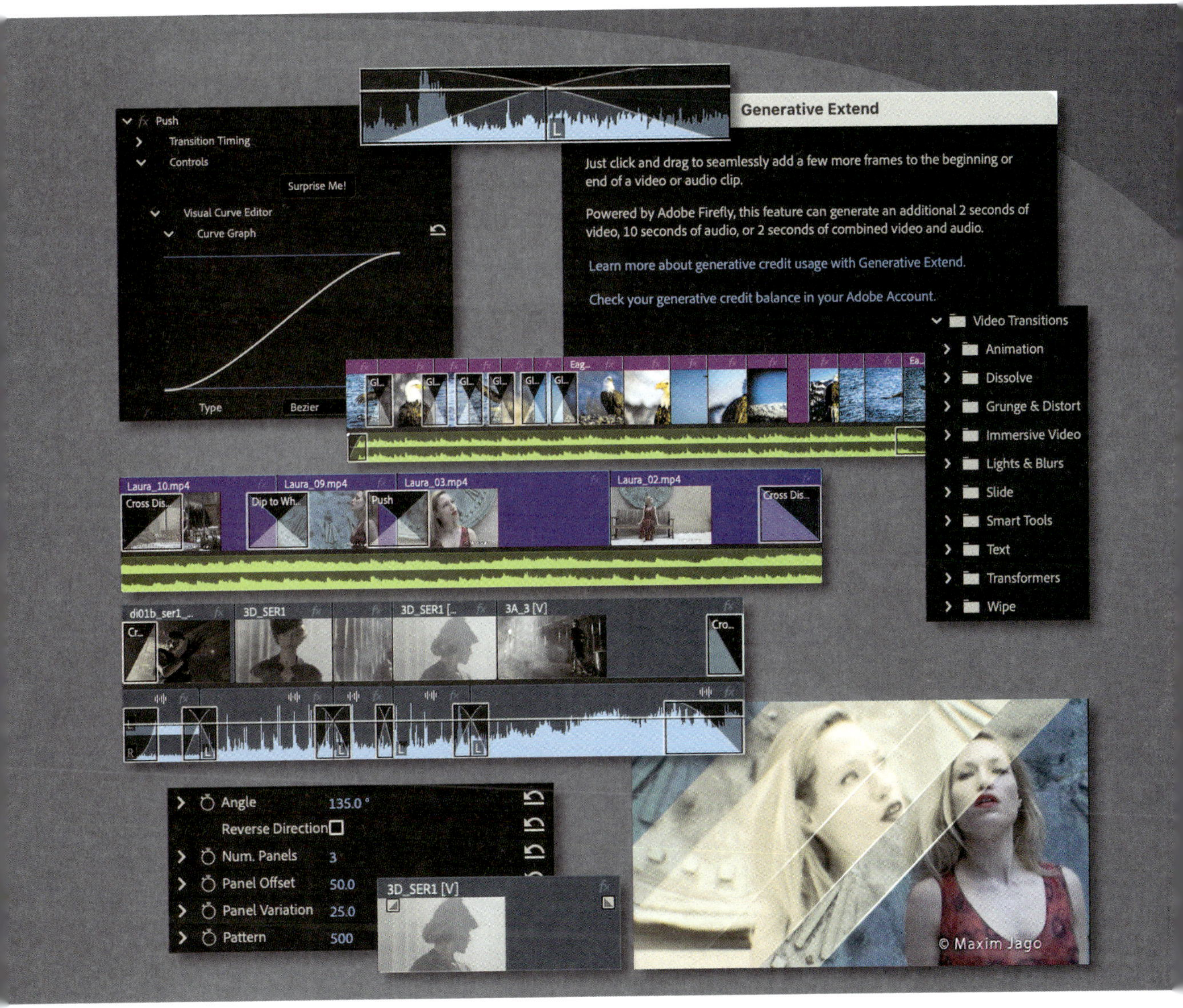

Transitions can help create a seamless flow between two video or audio clips or inform the viewer that a change of scene has begun. Video transitions are often used to signify a change in time or location. Audio transitions provide a useful way to avoid abrupt edits that jar the listener or to blend the significance of two scenes.

Starting the lesson

● **Note:** To ensure that the tools function and the defaults are set exactly as described in this lesson, reset the Premiere preferences by holding any modifier key (such as Shift) while launching the application, selecting Reset App Preferences, and then clicking Continue in the Reset Options dialog box.

Although the most common transition is a *cut*—where one clip abruptly ends and another begins—there are great opportunities for creativity using transition effects you can animate.

In this lesson, you'll learn to use transitions between video and audio clips to help your edits flow more smoothly. You'll also learn best practices for choosing the most appropriate transitions.

For this lesson, you'll use a new project file.

1 Start Adobe Premiere, and open the project Lesson 07.prproj from the Lessons folder.

2 Use the Workspaces menu to choose Effects. Reset the workspace to the saved layout.

   This changes the workspace to a preset optimized for working with transitions and effects. In particular, the Effects panel is now in the upper-right corner with the Properties panel beneath it.

   In the Effects panel, you can click any effect category's chevron to display its contents.

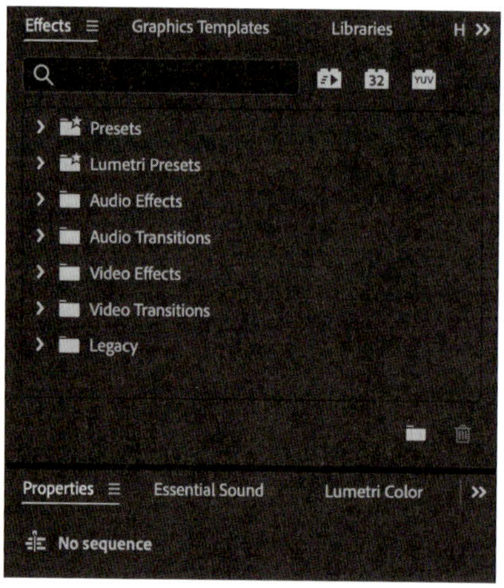

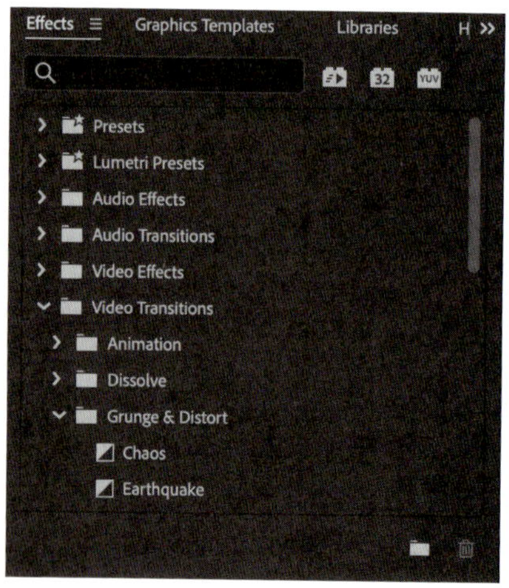

3 Save the project as **Lesson 07 Working.prproj** in the same folder.

Because most effects are applied to clips in sequences, the Source Monitor is now hidden in its panel group, and the Effect Controls panel has been brought to the front.

What are transition effects?

Adobe Premiere offers several special effects and preset animations to help you bridge neighboring clips in a sequence. These transitions—such as dissolves, wipes, dips to color, and so on—provide a way to ease viewers from one scene to the next. As well as smoothing the join between two clips, transitions can be used to focus attention on a major jump in the story.

Choosing and configuring transitions is an art. Applying them is simple enough: Drag the transition you want from the Effects panel onto the edit point between two clips in a sequence. The skill comes in their placement, length, and settings, such as direction, motion, and start/end positions.

You can adjust some transition settings directly in the Timeline panel, but it's usually easier to make precise adjustments in the Effect Controls panel. To view the settings for a transition effect in the Effect Controls panel, select it in a sequence.

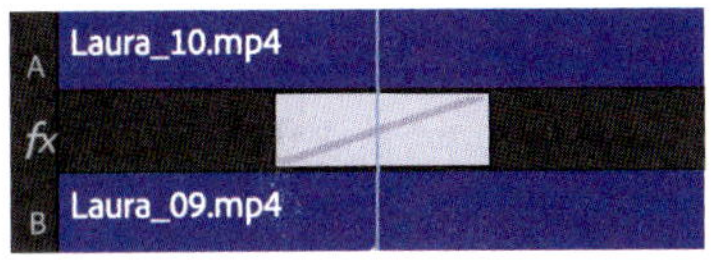

In addition to the unique options for each transition, the Effect Controls panel features a helpful *A/B timeline display* (more on this later).

This display makes it easy to change the timing of transitions relative to an edit point, change the transition duration, and apply transitions to clips that don't have enough head or tail frames—that is, additional content to provide an overlap at the beginning (head) or end (tail) of a clip.

Knowing when to use transitions

Transitions are a standard storytelling tool in video editing, and the rules for their use are similar to the rules of screenwriting. They're effective when they help the viewer understand the story.

For example, you may switch from indoors to outdoors in a video, or you may jump forward in time. An animated transition, a fade to black, or a dissolve can help the viewer understand that the location has changed, that time has passed, or that a character's perspective has changed.

A fade to black at the end of a scene is a clear indication that the scene has finished. The trick with transitions is to be intentional—and this often means using restraint—unless, of course, a total lack of restraint is the creative result you want!

As long as it looks like you intended to include a particular effect, your audience will tend to trust your decision (whether or not they agree with your creative choice). It takes practice and experience to develop sensitivity for the right time, and the wrong time, to use effects such as transitions. If in doubt, less is usually best.

There is an established visual language that modern audiences recognize and respond to. For example, if a character falls asleep and the picture goes soft-focus, with everything in the frame glowing and bright, your audience will immediately know that we are witnessing that character's dream. Studying this kind of visual language can help you make creative choices.

Following best practices with transitions

You may be tempted to use a transition effect on every cut. Don't! Or at least get them out of your system with your first project.

Most TV shows and feature films use cuts-only edits. You'll rarely see any transition visual effects. Why is this? An effect should be used only if it gives an additional benefit; transition effects can sometimes be a distraction from the video, reminding viewers they are watching a story and preventing them from connecting with it emotionally.

Premiere has many visually engaging video transition effects to choose between—the challenge is in finding a way to make them look like part of your intentional design.

If a news editor uses a transition effect, it's for a purpose. The most frequent use in newsroom editing is to transform what would have been a jarring or abrupt edit into a more comfortable experience.

A jump cut is a good example of a scenario where a transition effect can help. A *jump cut* is a cut between two similar shots. Rather than looking like a continuation of the story, they look a little like a piece of the video is unintentionally missing. By adding a transition effect between the two shots, you can make a jump cut look intentional and less distracting.

Dramatic transition effects do have their place in storytelling. Consider the *Star Wars* movies with their highly stylized transition effects, such as obvious, slow wipes. Each of those transitions has a purpose. In this case, it's to create a look reminiscent of old serialized movies and TV shows. The transition effects send a clear message: "Pay attention now. We're transitioning across space and time."

Understanding the importance of clip handles

To understand transition effects, you'll need to understand edit points and handles. An *edit point* is the point in your sequence where one clip ends and the next begins. This is often called a *cut* and sometimes simply called an *edit*. These are easy to see because Premiere displays vertical lines to show where one clip segment ends and another begins (much like two bricks next to each other). By default, a thumbnail shows the first frame of each clip.

Before you first edit a clip into a sequence, you set an In point and an Out point to select the part you want to use. When you edit that selected part of the clip into a sequence, the unused sections at the beginning and end are still available but hidden in the Timeline panel. Those unused sections are referred to as *clip handles* or simply *handles*.

There's a handle between a clip's original beginning and the In point you set. There's also a handle between a clip's original end and the Out point you set. The time ruler in the Source Monitor shows you how much footage is available in your handles.

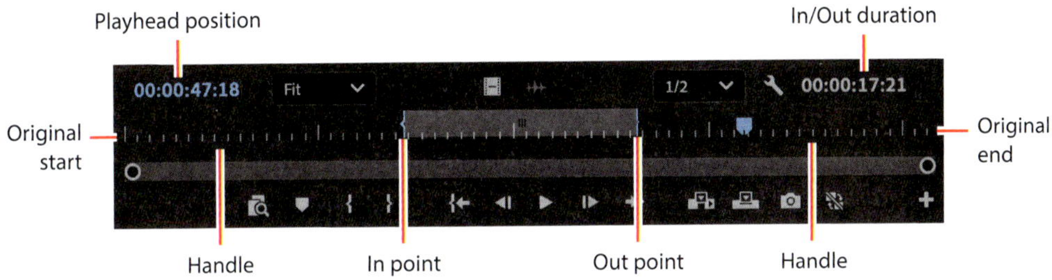

Of course, you may not have used In or Out points, or you may have set just an In point or an Out point at the very beginning or end of the clip. In this case, you would have either no unused media or unused media at only one end of the clip.

In the Timeline panel, if you see a tiny triangle in the upper-right or upper-left corner of a clip, it means you've reached the end of the source clip and there are no additional frames available.

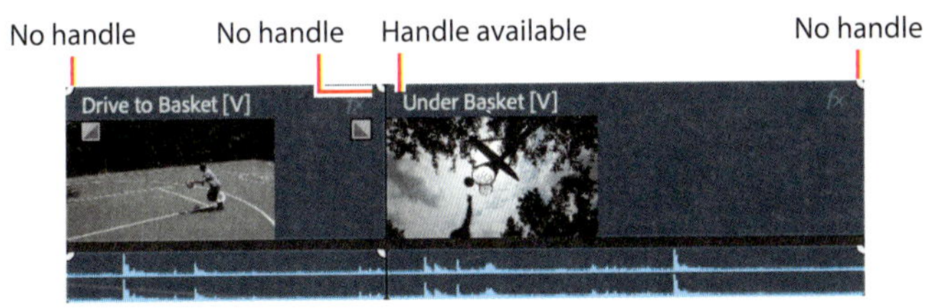

For transition effects to work, you need handles because the effect creates an overlap between the outgoing clip and the incoming clip.

For example, if you want to add a two-second Cross Dissolve transition centered between two video clips, you need at least a one-second handle available on both clips (one additional second each that would not normally be visible in the sequence). In the Timeline panel, the transition effect icon gives a visual indication of the duration of the effect and, therefore, the clip overlap.

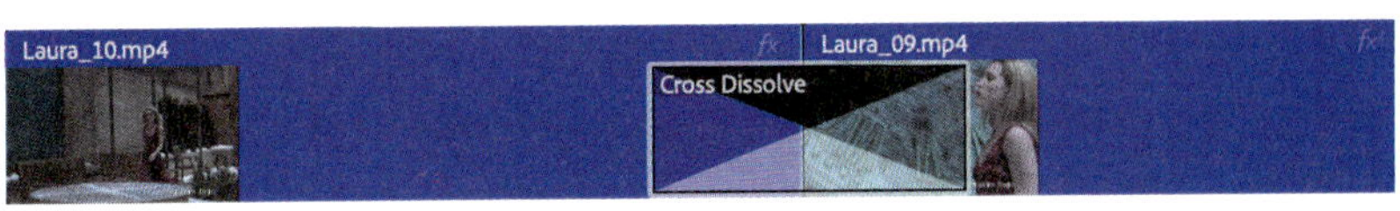

Adding video transition effects

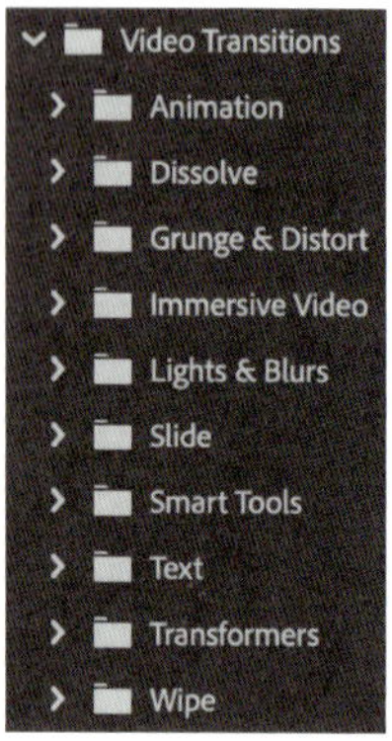

Premiere gives you many video transition effects to choose from. Some, like the classic Cross Dissolve, produce a simple effect, while others like VHS Damage might introduce complex additional visual elements. Most options are available in the Video Transitions group in the Effects panel.

Video transitions are organized into 10 subcategories.

Applying a single-sided transition

The easiest transition to understand is one that affects just one end of a single clip. This could be a fade from black on the first clip in a sequence or a dissolve into an animated graphic. Let's give it a try.

1 If it's not already open, open the sequence called Transitions.

This sequence has four video clips and background music. The clips have handles, so transition effects can be applied between them (no tiny triangles are visible at the ends of the clips, which would indicate the first or last frames are already visible).

Note: You can use the Search field, at the top of the Effects panel, to locate an effect by name or keyword, or you can browse the folders of effects.

2 In the Effects panel, open the Video Transitions > Dissolve group. Find the Cross Dissolve effect.

3 Drag the effect onto the start of the first video clip. A highlight shows you where the transition effect will be added. When the transition is in the right position, release it.

4 Drag another Cross Dissolve effect onto the end of the last video clip.

The Cross Dissolve icon shows the timing of the effect. For example, the effect you just applied to the last clip in the sequence will start before the end of the clip and complete by the time it reaches the clip's end.

Transitions of this kind don't extend the clip (using a handle) because the transition doesn't reach past the end of the clip.

Because you're applying the Cross Dissolve transition effect at the end of the last clip, where there is no connected clip, the picture dissolves into the background of the Timeline, which is black. The result is that this looks like a Dip To Black effect.

In reality you are causing the clip to become gradually transparent in front of a black background. The difference is clearer when you work with multiple layers of clips, with different-colored background layers.

5 Play the sequence to see the result.

You should see a fade from black at the start of the sequence and a fade to black at the end.

Applying a transition between two clips

Let's apply transitions between a few clips. For the purposes of exploration, you'll break the less-is-best rule and try several options in one sequence. As you go through these steps, play the sequence regularly to view the results.

1 Continue working with the previous sequence, called Transitions.

2 Move the Timeline playhead to the edit point between clip 1 and clip 2 and then press the equal sign (=) key two or three times to zoom in fairly close. If your keyboard does not have the = key, use the navigator at the bottom of the Timeline panel to zoom. You can also create a custom keyboard shortcut for this purpose (see Lesson 1, "Touring Adobe Premiere").

Tip: On an English-language keyboard, it's easy to remember that pressing the = key (if your keyboard has one) zooms in because there is usually a + symbol on the same key.

3 Drag the Dip To White transition effect from the Dissolve group in the Effects panel onto the edit point between the first clip and the second clip. The effect will snap to one of three positions, and the pointer will change to indicate which position the transition will occupy.

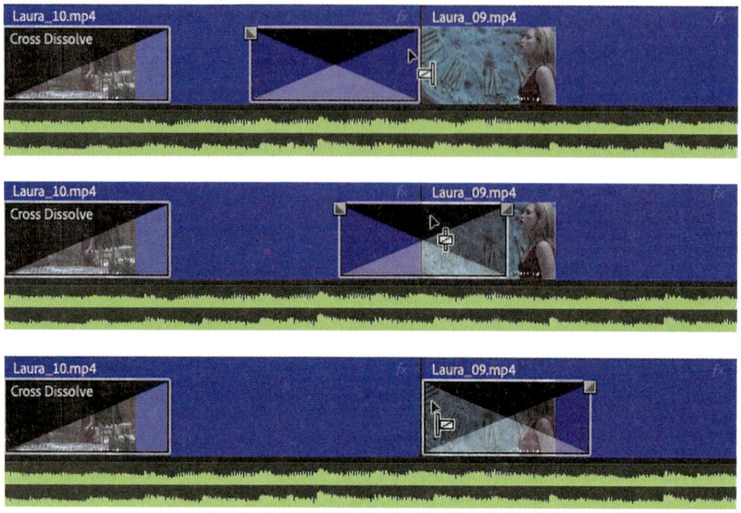

Be sure to line up the effect with the middle of the edit, not the end of the first clip or beginning of the second clip.

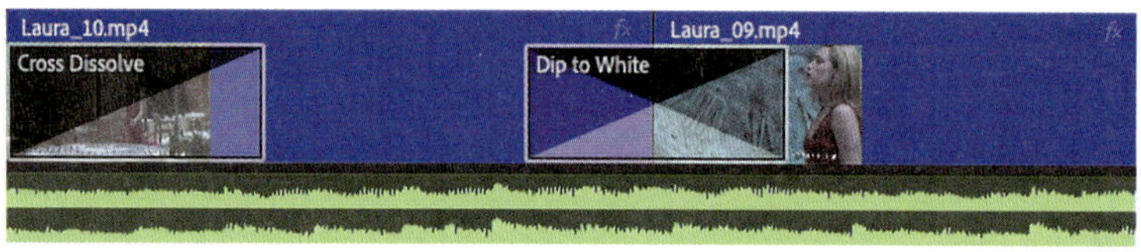

The Dip To White transition effect gradually builds to a completely white screen, which obscures the cut between the first clip and the next.

4 In the Effects panel, click the chevron for the Slide group of video transitions to display its contents. Drag the Push transition onto the edit point between the second clip and the third clip in the sequence, centered on the cut.

▶ **Tip:** Keyboard shortcuts are usually panel-specific. If the arrow keys don't move the playhead, check that the Timeline panel is active, with a blue outline.

5 Play through the transition to see the result, and then position the playhead on the edit between clip 2 and clip 3 by pressing the Up Arrow key. The Up and Down Arrow keys are shortcuts to move the Timeline playhead to the previous or next edit on targeted tracks.

6 Click the Push transition effect icon in the Timeline panel once to select it, and open the Effect Controls panel.

The Effect Controls panel provides controls for any single clip or effect that you select in the Timeline panel, or source clip that you select.

In this instance, the panel shows detailed controls for the Push transition effect you selected. You may need to scroll down to see all the controls.

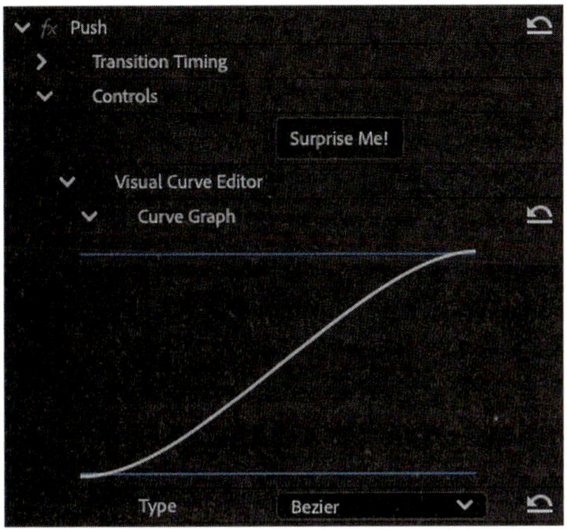

7 Any adjustment made using the controls in the Effect Controls panel will update the effect in the Program Monitor. Click the Surprise Me! button.

This button intelligently randomizes the settings for the effect. You will often get interesting results that demonstrate imaginative ways to use an effect, though there are so few controls available for the Push effect that the result may not be dramatic.

In the Timeline panel, play through the transition to see the result.

8 In the Effects panel, expand the Transformers group in the Video Transitions category. Drag the Page Peel transition effect onto the edit point between the third clip and the fourth clip, centered on the cut.

If you select the Page Peel effect in the Timeline panel and then look in the Effect Controls panel, you'll see that there are Randomize buttons for different groups of controls. These are a little like the Surprise Me! button but limit randomization to specific related controls.

9 Review the sequence by playing it from beginning to end.

Having watched this sequence, you can probably see why it's a good idea to use transitions with restraint!

Let's try replacing an existing transition effect.

10 Drag the Panel Wipe transition from the Wipe group onto the existing Push transition effect icon, between the second clip and the third clip. The new transition effect replaces the old one, taking the duration and timing of the existing effect.

Tip: If the Effect Controls panel is empty when you open it, click once on the Push transition effect again to re-select it.

Note: When you drag a new video or audio transition effect from the Effects panel on top of an existing transition, it replaces the existing effect. It also preserves the alignment and duration of the transition it replaces. This is a quick way to experiment with alternative transition effects.

● **Note:** You may need to scroll down in the Effect Controls panel to access further controls.

11 Select the Panel Wipe transition effect icon on the timeline so its settings are displayed in the Effect Controls panel. Using the controls in that panel, set Num. Panels (number of panels) to 3 to add more layering to the divide between the two clips.

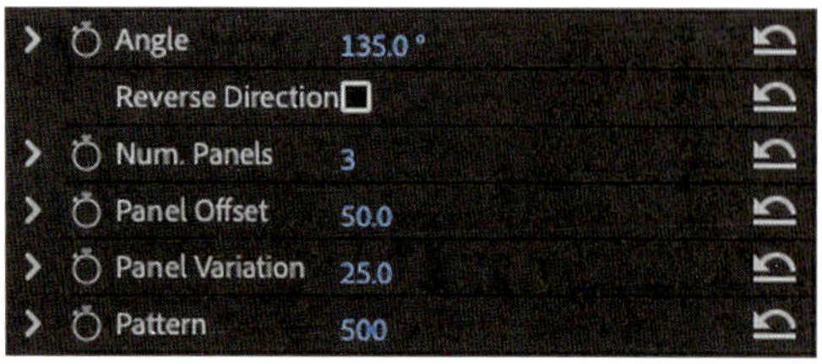

12 Play through the transition to view the result. The best way to do this is probably to click a little earlier in the sequence to watch the video leading up to the transition.

Video transitions have a default duration, which can be set in seconds or frames (it's frames by default). If the default duration is set in frames, the effective playback duration of a transition effect will change depending on the sequence frame rate. The default transition duration can be changed in the Timeline section of the Preferences panel.

13 Choose Premiere > Settings > Timeline (macOS) or Edit > Preferences > Timeline (Windows). Depending on your geographic region, you may see a Video Transition Default Duration setting of 30 Frames or 25 Frames.

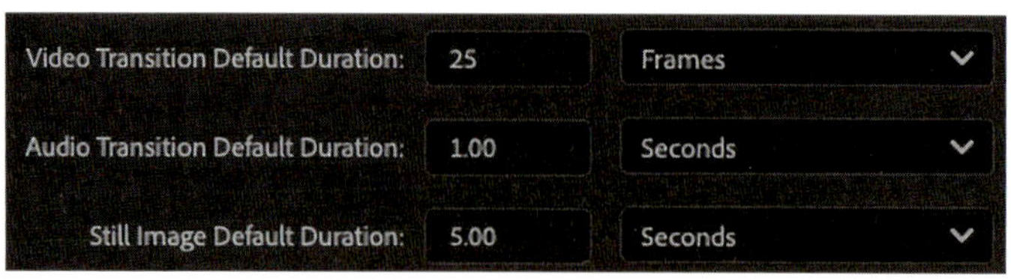

14 This is a 24-frames-per-second sequence, but this doesn't matter if you change the Video Transition Default Duration option to 1 second. Do so now, and click OK.

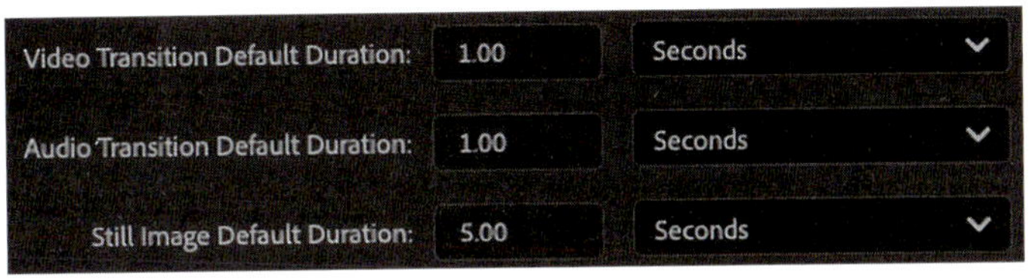

Existing transition effects keep their existing settings when you change the preference, but any future transitions you add will have the new default duration.

The duration of an effect can dramatically change its impact, and later in this lesson, you'll learn about adjusting the timing of transitions.

Applying the default transition effect to multiple clips

So far, you've been applying transitions to video clips. You can also apply transitions to still images, graphics, color mattes, and even audio, as you'll see shortly.

It's common for editors to create a photomontage, which might look good with transitions between the multiple photos. Applying transitions between two or three photos is quick and easy, but if you have 100 images, it will take a long time!

Premiere makes it straightforward to automate this process by allowing you to set a default transition effect.

1 In the Project panel, find and open the sequence Slideshow.

This sequence consists of several images placed in a particular order. Notice that a Constant Power audio crossfade has already been applied to the beginning and end of the music clip to create a fade in and out.

2 Play the sequence by making sure the Timeline panel is active and pressing the spacebar.

There's a cut between each clip.

3 Press the backslash (\) key to zoom out the Timeline panel so the whole sequence is visible. If your keyboard does not have a \ key, drag the right end of the Timeline panel navigator to adjust the zoom.

4 If necessary, increase the height of the V1 track to see thumbnails on the clips (you can drag the dividing line between V1 and V2 in the track header).

Tip: If you discover a useful keyboard shortcut that uses a key not included on your keyboard, you can use the Keyboard Shortcuts dialog box to assign a different key.

> **Tip:** If you're working with clips that have linked video and audio and Linked Selection is enabled in the Timeline panel, you can select just the video or audio portions by Option-dragging (macOS) or Alt-dragging (Windows) with the Selection tool. Then choose Sequence > Apply Default Transitions To Selection.

5 Using the Selection tool, draw a marquee around all the clips (video and audio) to select them. Begin dragging in an empty area, away from the clips, or you'll move the first clip you click instead.

6 Choose Sequence > Apply Default Transitions To Selection.

> **Tip:** You'll find the option to apply audio-only or video-only transition effects in the Sequence menu too.

This applies the default transition between all the currently selected clips. Notice that the Constant Power audio crossfades at the beginning and end of the music clip are now shorter because the default audio transition duration has been applied.

The default video transition effect is a 30-frame or 25-frame Cross Dissolve (though you changed this earlier to 1 second), and the default audio transition effect is a 1-second Constant Power crossfade. The shortcut you used replaced the existing audio crossfades with new, shorter ones.

You can set the default transition by right-clicking any transition effect in the Effects panel and choosing Set Selected As Default Transition. The icon for the selected default transition effect has a blue outline.

7 Play the sequence to see the difference the new Cross Dissolves make to the montage.

Copying a transition effect to multiple edits

You can copy an existing transition effect to multiple edits using the keyboard. Let's try it.

1 Press Command+Z (macOS) or Ctrl+Z (Windows) to undo the last step, and press Esc to deselect the clips.

2 Select any transition effect in the Effects panel, and drag it onto the cut between the first two video clips in the Slideshow sequence.

3 You can change the length of any transition by dragging its edge in the Timeline. Drag one end of the transition you just applied to make it longer.

Notice that dragging one end of the transition also adjusts the other end. To make asymmetrical changes, hold the Shift key while you drag.

4 Select the transition by clicking its effect icon once in the sequence.

5 Press Command+C (macOS) or Ctrl+C (Windows) to copy the effect. Then hold Command (macOS) or Ctrl (Windows) while you use the Selection tool to drag a marquee around multiple other edits to select them, rather than clips.

6 With the edits selected, press Command+V (macOS) or Ctrl+V (Windows) to paste the transition effect onto all the selected edits.

This is a great way to add transition effects with matching settings to multiple edits, especially if you have taken the time to customize the effect.

Red, yellow, and green render bars

When you add a transition to a sequence, a red or yellow horizontal line (or *render bar*) may appear above it in the Timeline panel. A yellow bar indicates that Premiere expects to be able to play the effect smoothly. A red bar means that this section of the sequence may need to be rendered before you can play a preview without dropped frames.

You can choose to render at any time to make these sections preview more smoothly on a less powerful computer.

The easiest way to render is to press the Return/Enter key. If you add In and Out points to select a part of your sequence and then render, only the selected section of the sequence will render. This is useful if you have many effects that need to render but you're concerned with only one part for now.

Red or yellow bars will turn to green when those sections of a sequence are rendered. Premiere creates a video file for each section where the bar has turned green. The new video files are stored in the Preview Files folder (as set in the project's Scratch Disk settings). As long as the render bar is green, playback should be smooth.

Using A/B mode to fine-tune a transition

When you review transition effect settings in the Effect Controls panel, you have access to an *A/B editing mode* that splits a single video track into two. What would normally be displayed as two consecutive and contiguous clips on a single timeline track are now displayed as individual clips on separate tracks, with a transition between them. Separating the elements of the transition in this way allows you to manipulate the head and tail frames (or handles) and to change other transition options.

Changing parameters in the Effect Controls panel

You can customize all transitions in Premiere. A major benefit of the Effect Controls panel is that, in addition to it giving you access to the settings for transition effects, you can see the outgoing and incoming clip handles (unused media in the original clip). This makes it easier to adjust the timing of an effect.

Let's modify a transition.

1 In the Timeline panel, switch back to the Transitions sequence.

2 Position the Timeline playhead over the Panel Wipe transition you added between clips 2 and 3, and click the transition to select it.

Tip: It's possible to shorten a transition to a duration of one frame. This can make it hard to grab and position the transition effect icon, so try using the Duration and Alignment controls. If you want to remove a transition, select it in the sequence in the Timeline panel and press Delete (macOS) or Backspace (Windows).

3 In the Effect Controls panel, open the Alignment menu, and choose Start At Cut.

The transition in the Effect Controls panel timeline, and in the sequence, switches to show the new position.

4 Now change the transition duration. In the Effect Controls panel, click the blue numbers for the Duration, type **300**, and click away from the numbers or press the Tab key to apply the new setting. Premiere will add the correct punctuation automatically, changing 300 into 00:00:03:00—that is, 3 seconds.

The Alignment menu changes to Custom Start because the effect now reaches beyond the beginning of the next transition effect. To make the new transition duration fit, Premiere automatically moves its start two frames earlier.

Tip: You can position the start time of a transition effect asymmetrically by dragging it to a new position. This means you don't have to settle for the Centered, Start At Cut, and End At Cut options. You can drag the position of a transition effect directly on the Timeline too.

Examine the A/B timeline display in the Effect Controls panel timeline, at the right side of the panel. There is a zoom navigator at the bottom of the Effect Controls panel timeline that works just like the one in the Monitors and Timeline panel. Zoom out by dragging one of the circles on the navigator to make it longer, so you can see the ends of the clips.

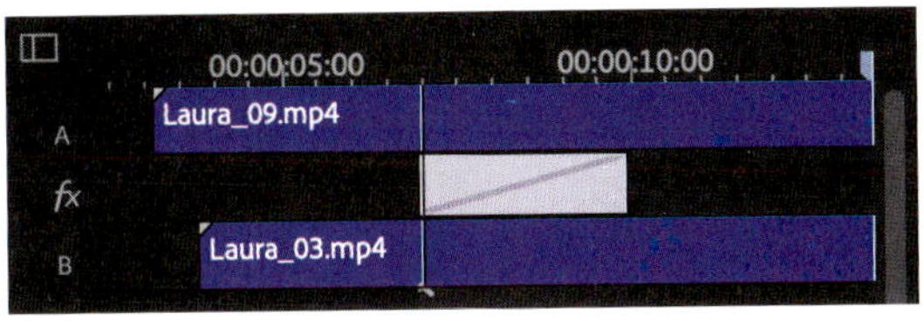

In this example, the Effect Controls panel timeline shows the cut between the two clips, and you can see the way the effect timing has been adjusted automatically.

Tip: If the Effect Controls panel timeline is not visible, click Show/Hide Timeline View at the upper-right corner of the panel. You may need to resize the panel to make the button visible.

5 In the Timeline panel, play through the transition to see the change.

These automated adjustments can be subtle (in this example, it's just two frames), so always double-check the results of new settings by playing through the effect. That way, you can be sure you're happy with the newly revealed media taken from the clip handles—the media that was hidden from view until you added the transition effect.

Although it's useful that Premiere automatically modifies the timing of effects when necessary, it makes it even more important to check the transition before you move on.

Now let's customize the transition.

6 In the Effect Controls panel timeline, hover the pointer over the middle part of the vertical black line that crosses all three layers (the two video clips and the transition effect between them). The line is the edit point between the two clips. If your pointer is correctly positioned, it will change to the red Rolling Edit tool.

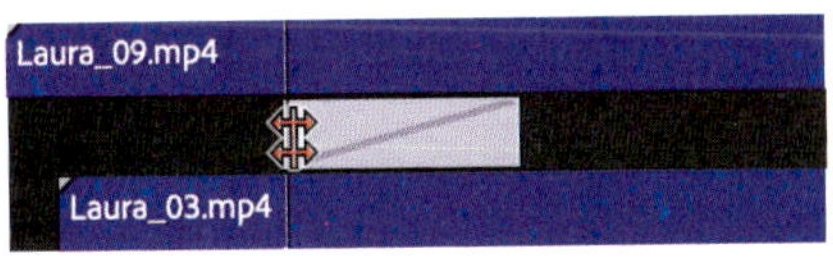

Tip: You may need to move the playhead out of the way—earlier or later—to see the edit point between two clips in the Effect Controls panel timeline.

This edit line is close to the left edge of the effect, so you might want to zoom in to the Effect Controls panel timeline using the navigator at the bottom to conveniently make adjustments.

In the Effect Controls panel, the Rolling Edit tool lets you reposition the timing of an edit between two clips by dragging the edit line.

7 Still in the Effect Controls panel, drag left and right with the Rolling Edit tool. As you do, you're changing the timing of the cut. The Out point of the clip on the left of the edit and the In point of the clip on the right of the edit update in the Timeline panel when you release the drag. This is a form of *trimming*.

   You'll explore trimming and rolling edits in more detail in Lesson 8, "Editing Video—Advanced Techniques."

8 Move the pointer over the transition to the left or right of the edit line in the Effect Controls panel, and the pointer changes to the Slide tool. If there is a blue line, it's the time ruler playhead.

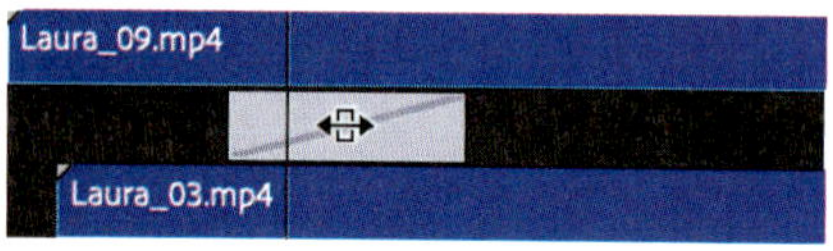

   Using the Slide tool changes the start and end points of the transition without changing its overall duration. Unlike using the Rolling Edit tool, moving the transition rectangle with the Slide tool does not change the edit point between the two sequence clips. Instead, it changes the timing of the transition effect.

9 Use the Slide tool to drag the transition rectangle left and right and compare the results.

Using a Morph Cut effect

Morph Cut is a special transition effect that aims to be invisible. It's designed to help with "talking head" video interviews, where a single speaker looks in the direction of the camera. If your subject pauses a lot or there is inappropriate content in the footage, you may want to remove a section of the interview.

This would normally produce a jump cut (when the image seems to jump suddenly from one piece of content to another), but with media that changes very little over time, and a little experimentation, the Morph Cut effect might yield an invisible transition that seamlessly hides what you have removed. Let's try it.

1 Open the sequence Morph Cut. Play the beginning of the sequence.

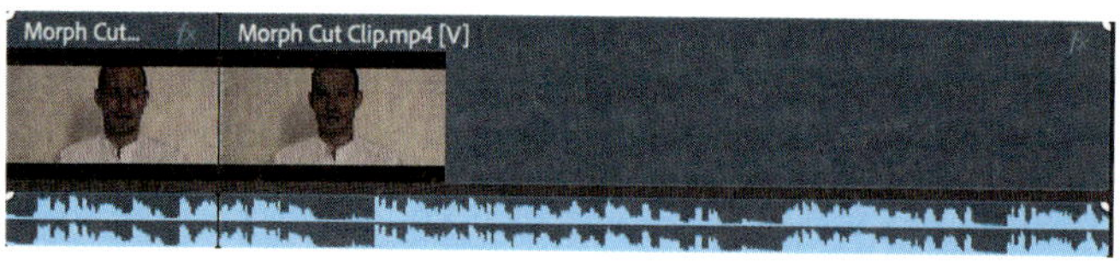

   This sequence has one clip, with a jump cut near the start. It's a small jump cut but enough to jar the audience.

2 In the Effects panel, look in the Video Transitions > Dissolve group for the Morph Cut effect. Drag this effect to the join between the two clips.

The Morph Cut transition effect begins by analyzing the two clips. If the playhead is over the transition effect, you'll see a banner across the screen while the analysis takes place, but you can continue to work on your sequence without waiting.

Depending on your media, you may achieve improved results with the Morph Cut transition effect by experimenting with different durations.

3 In the Timeline panel, double-click the Morph Cut transition effect to display the Set Transition Duration dialog box. Change the duration to **16** frames (you can double-click any transition effect to access this setting).

4 When the analysis is complete, press Return/Enter to render the effect (if your system requires it) and play a preview.

The result is not perfect, but it's close, and it's unlikely an audience will notice the join between the clips.

Tip: The Morph Cut transition effect usually produces the best results with shorter durations.

Dealing with inadequate head or tail handles

If you try to extend a transition for a clip that doesn't have enough frames in the handle for the new duration of the effect, the transition still appears but has diagonal warning bars through it. This means Premiere is using a freeze frame to extend the duration of the clip. The last available frame is held onscreen to complete the transition effect.

You can adjust the duration and position of the transition to resolve the issue.

1 Open the sequence called Handles.

2 Locate the edit between the two clips.

These two sequence clips have no heads or tails. You can tell this immediately because of the little triangles in the corners of the clips; a triangle indicates the first or last frame of the original clip.

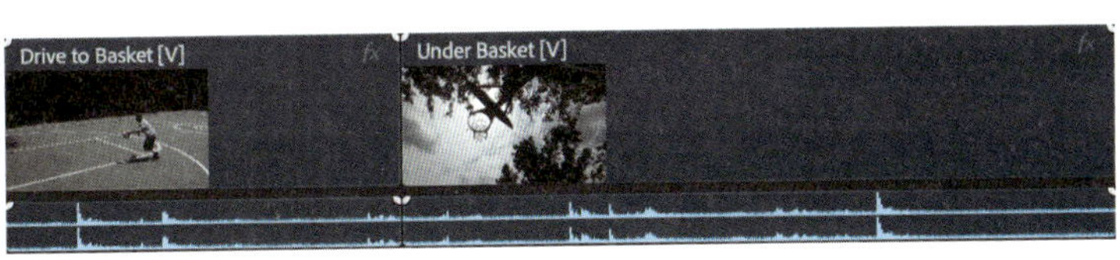

3 Select the Ripple Edit tool in the Tools panel, and use it to drag the right edge of the first clip to the left (begin dragging just to the left of the cut between the two clips). Drag to shorten the duration of the first clip to about 1:10, and then release. A tool tip appears while you trim to show the new clip duration.

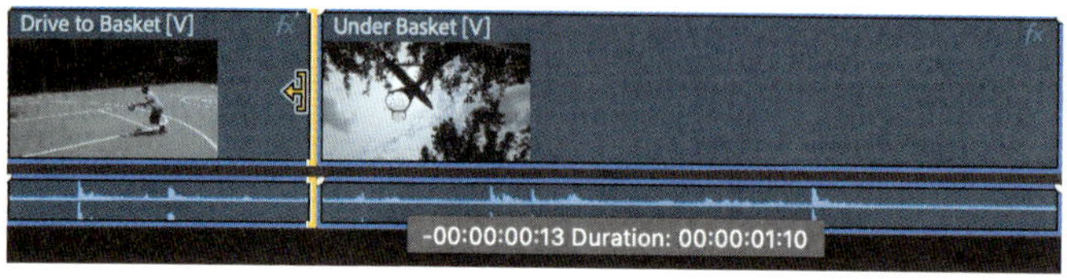

The clip to the right of the edit point ripples (moves) left to close the gap. Notice that the little triangles at the end (the right edge) of the clip you just trimmed are no longer present.

4 Drag the Cross Dissolve transition effect from the Effects panel onto the edit point between the two clips.

You'll discover that you can drag the transition onto the right side of the edit but not the left. That's because there's no handle available at the beginning of the second clip to create a dissolve that overlaps the end of the first clip without using freeze frames.

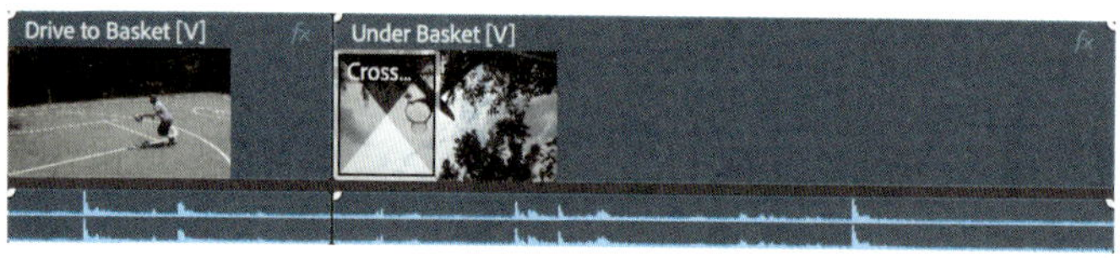

5 Press the V key to select the Selection tool, or click to select the tool in the Tools panel. In the Timeline panel, click the Cross Dissolve transition once to select it. You may need to zoom in to make it easier to select the transition.

▶ **Tip:** If you can't see the full handles in the Effect Controls panel timeline, use the navigator at the bottom to zoom out.

6 In the Effect Controls panel, set the duration of the effect to **1:12**.

The clip handle is not long enough to create this effect; the diagonal lines on the transition, both in the Effect Controls panel and in the Timeline panel, indicate Premiere automatically added a freeze frame to fill the duration you set.

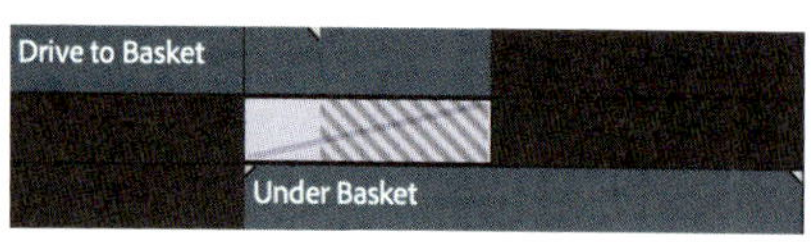

7 Play the transition to see the result.

8 In the Effect Controls panel, change the alignment of the transition to Center At Cut.

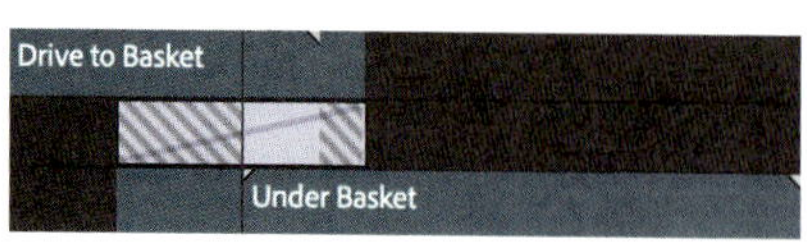

9 Drag the Timeline panel playhead slowly through the transition and watch the result.

- For the first half of the transition (up to the edit point), the B clip is a freeze frame, while the A clip continues to play.
- At the edit point, the A clip and the B clip start to play.
- After the edit, a short freeze frame is used.

There are several ways to fix this kind of issue.

- You can change the duration or timing of the transition effect.
- You can drag the edit in the Timeline panel using the Rolling Edit tool (click and hold the Ripple Edit tool in the Tools panel to access it) to change the timing of the transition in the Timeline panel. Be sure to drag the edit between the clips and not the transition effect. This won't necessarily remove all the freeze frames, but it may improve the overall result.

Note: The Rolling Edit tool lets you move the transition earlier or later but does not change the overall length of the sequence because it extends one clip while shortening another.

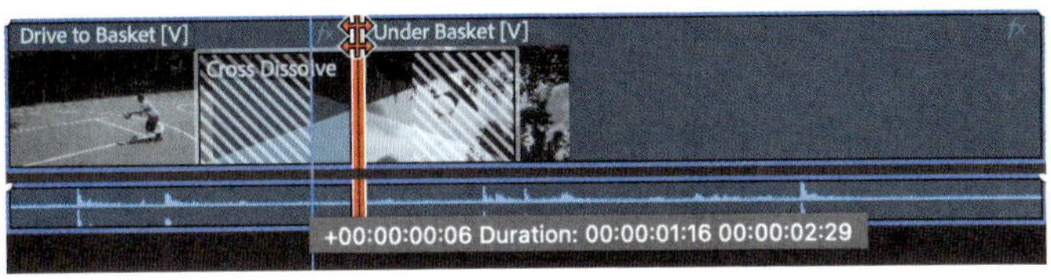

- You can drag one side of the edit in the Timeline panel using the Ripple Edit tool to shorten a clip, increasing the length of the handle. Again, be sure to click the edit between the clips and not the effect icon.

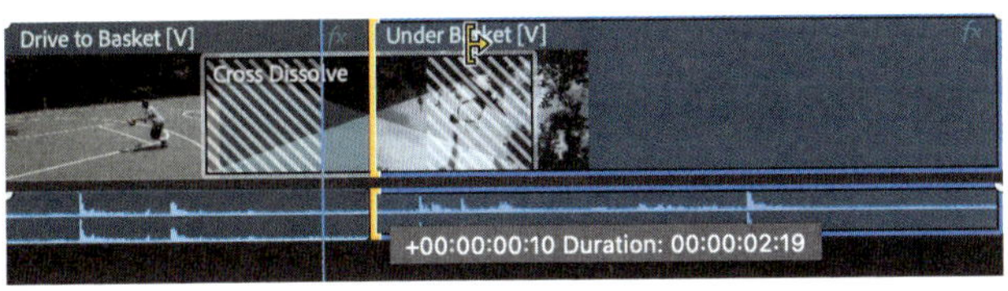

- You can add content to your clips using the Generative Extend tool.

You'll learn more about the Rolling Edit and Ripple Edit tools in Lesson 8. For now, make sure you have the Selection tool selected. You'll learn how to use the Generative Extend tool in the next section.

Adding content with the Generative Extend tool

When your media is just a little too short, you can use the Generative Extend tool to add content. Powered by the Adobe Firefly AI model, this amazing tool will generate additional frames that match the appearance, movement, and audio of your original media.

You can add up to two seconds of video or 10 seconds of audio.

Use the tool in the same way that you would use the Ripple Edit tool or Selection tool to extend the In point or Out point for a clip by trimming (for more information about trimming, see Lesson 8).

Try this with the Handles sequence. The Generative Extend tool needs room to work, so if you want to add content between two clips, you'll need to move them apart first. For this exercise, we'll use the end of the sequence.

The second clip in this sequence has white triangles to indicate the end of the source clip—there is no more media available.

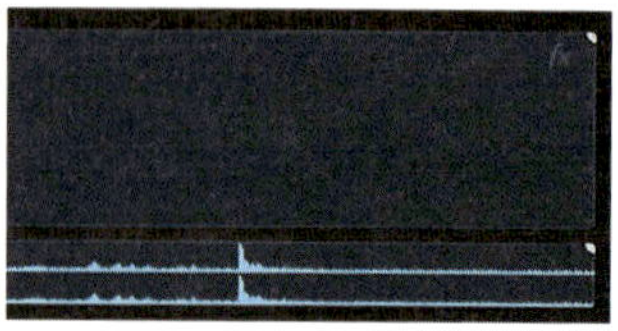

1 Select the Generative Extend tool. The first time you select the tool, you may see an information dialog box with links to further information. You can click Get Started on that dialog. When you first click with the tool, you may see a dialog box with a link to check if your media is compatible. You can click through that dialog box, too.

Note: The Generative Extend tool has some media requirements. For example, there is a minimum and maximum supported resolution and media must be 16:9 aspect ratio. For a full description of the requirements, visit *helpx.adobe.com* and search for Generative Extend.

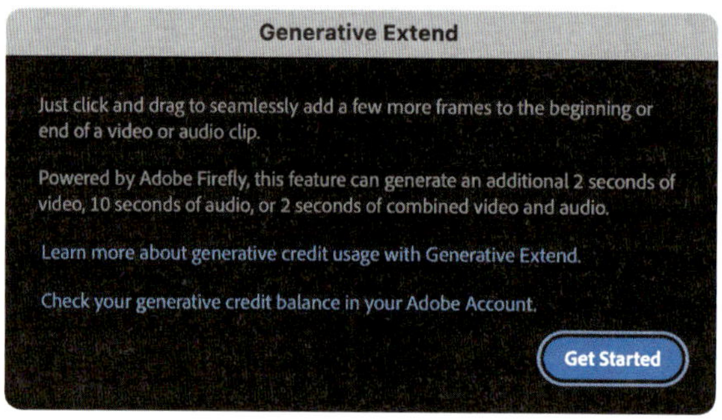

2 Using the Generative Extend tool, click the end of the second clip, and drag right to extend the clip by up to two seconds.

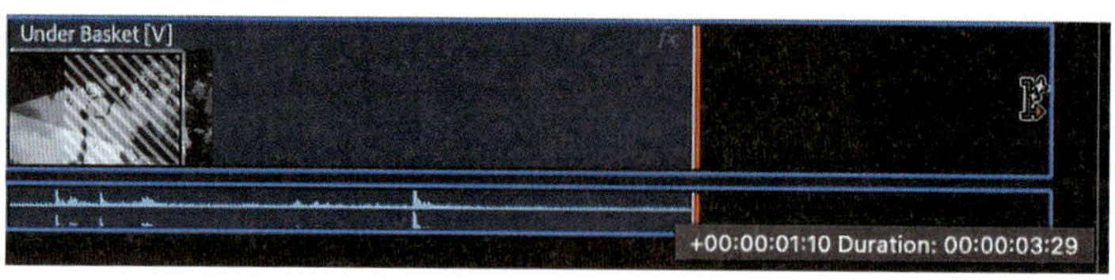

After a little processing time, a highlight will appear on the clip indicating the part that is AI generated.

3 Play through the clip and see if you can detect the join between the original content and AI-generated content. Results from generative AI content creation can vary, and you may find you need to experiment with different sections of media to get the result you want.

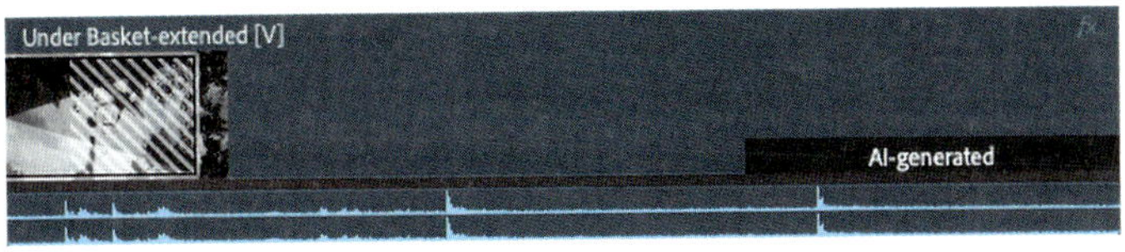

Note that generating content in this way uses generative AI credits. Some are included with your Creative Cloud subscription and more can be purchased.

Now that you have extended the clip, you can add more clips to the sequence and apply transition effects where the new AI-generated content is used in the transition overlap.

As with all generative AI tools, results may vary. For further information about Generative Extend, visit *helpx.adobe.com* and search for Generative Extend.

Adding audio transition effects

Audio transitions can dramatically improve a sequence's soundtrack by removing unwanted audio pops or abrupt edits. Audiences are usually much more aware of inconsistency in the soundtrack than they are of the overall quality of the soundtrack, and crossfade transitions can have a big impact in smoothing variation between clips.

Creating a crossfade

When you apply a fade or crossfade, the audio level adjustment over time is illustrated by a curve on the effect icon on the sequence clip.

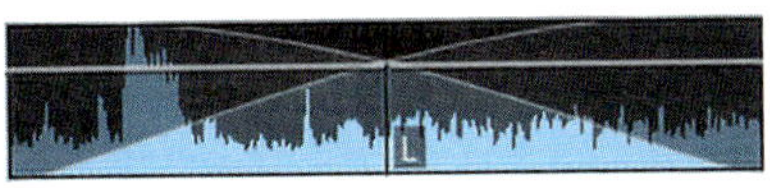

There are three styles of crossfade.

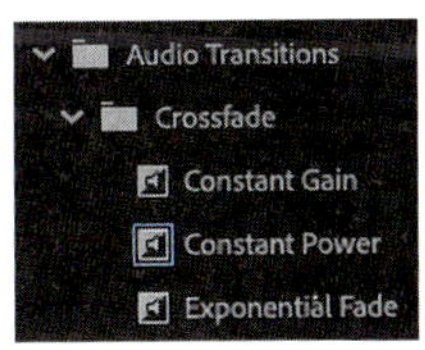

- **Constant Gain:** The Constant Gain crossfade (as its name implies) transitions audio by using a constant audio gain (volume) adjustment between the clips. Although this transition can lead to a slight perceived dip in the audio level for the listener, some editors find it useful. It's most useful in situations where you do not want much blending between two clips but rather more of a dip out and in between the clips—it's perfect for music edits.

- **Constant Power:** This is the default audio transition. It creates a smooth, gradual transition between two audio clips. The Constant Power crossfade works in a similar way to a video dissolve. The outgoing clip fades out slowly at first and then faster toward the end of the clip. For the incoming clip, the opposite occurs—the audio level increases quickly at the start of the incoming clip and more slowly toward the end of the transition. This crossfade is useful in situations where you want to blend the audio between two clips, without a noticeable drop in level in the middle.
- **Exponential Fade:** The Exponential Fade transition creates a fade between clips. It uses a logarithmic curve to fade out and fade up audio. Some editors prefer the Exponential Fade transition when performing a single-sided transition (such as fading in a music clip from silence at the start or end of a program).

Applying audio transitions

There are several ways to apply an audio crossfade to a sequence. You can, of course, drag an audio transition effect just as you would a video transition effect, but there are also useful shortcuts to speed up the process.

Audio transitions have a default duration, measured in seconds or frames. You can change the default duration by choosing Premiere > Settings > Timeline (macOS) or Edit > Preferences > Timeline (Windows).

Let's take a look at the three methods for applying audio transitions.

1 Open the sequence called Audio, and switch to the Selection tool.

The sequence has several clips with audio.

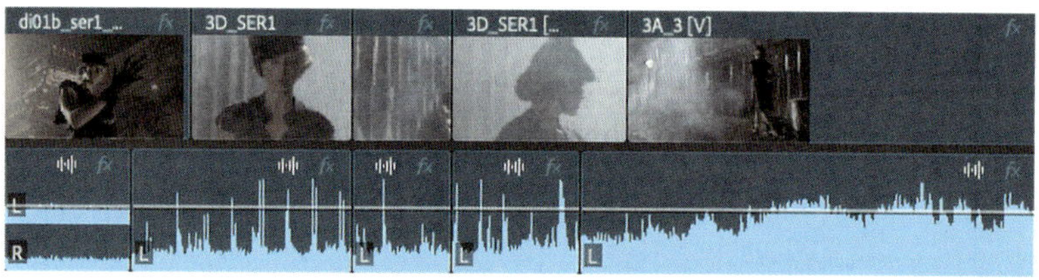

2 Play the sequence to review the contents.

3 Open the Audio Transitions > Crossfade group in the Effects panel.

4 Drag the Exponential Fade transition to the start of the first audio clip.

> **Tip:** To add only an audio transition, hold Option (macOS) or Alt (Windows) when right-clicking to select only the edge of the audio clip.

5 Right-click the right edge of the last clip in the sequence and choose Apply Default Transitions.

A default video transition and default audio transition are added to the end of the clip. Because the video and audio are linked, selecting one selects them both.

6 Drag the left end of the audio transition you just created to extend the duration, and then listen to the result.

To polish the project, next you'll add an opening Cross Dissolve transition effect to the video clip at the beginning of the sequence. Press Esc to deselect the transition effect you just adjusted.

7 Move the playhead near the beginning of the sequence, and press Command+D (macOS) or Ctrl+D (Windows) to add the default video transition. The default video transition is a Cross Dissolve.

You now have a fade from black at the beginning and a fade to black at the end. Now let's add a series of short audio dissolves to smooth out the sound mix.

Note: When you use keyboard shortcuts to apply transition effects, Premiere uses track targeting or clip selection to work out where exactly the effects should be applied.

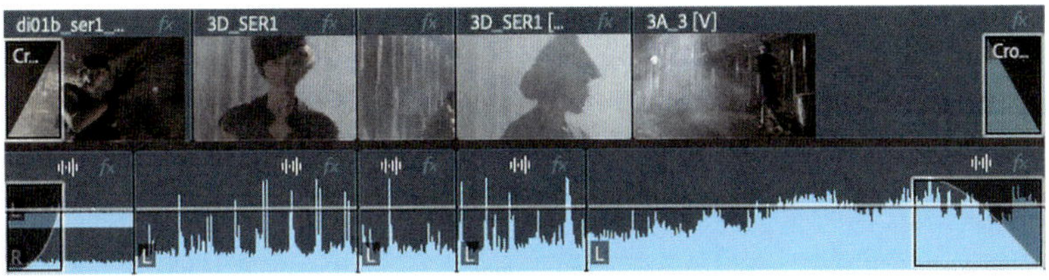

8 Ordinarily, making a marquee selection in the Timeline panel would select clips, but you can override this by holding a modifier key and select edits instead.

Using the Selection tool, while holding Command+Option (macOS) or Ctrl+Alt (Windows), drag a marquee selection over all of the audio edits between the clips on track Audio 1, being careful not to select any video clips—drag from below the audio clips to avoid accidentally selecting items on the video track.

Holding Command/Ctrl allows you to select edits rather than clips. Holding Option/Alt temporarily unlinks the audio clips from the video clips to isolate those edits while making a selection.

Note: The selection of clips does not have to be contiguous in the Timeline panel. You can Shift-click clips to select individual clips in a sequence.

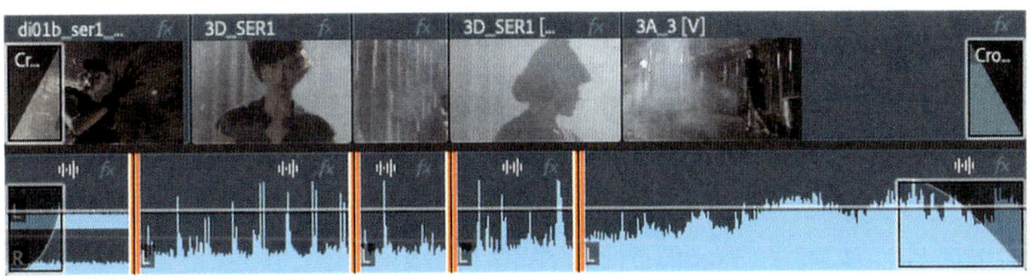

9 Press Shift+D to apply the default transition effect to all selected clips. You exclusively selected audio clips, so Premiere knows to add only audio transition effects.

You could have pressed Shift+Command+D (macOS) or Shift+Ctrl+D (Windows), which is the shortcut to add an audio-only transition. This is useful if you have selected both video and audio clips and want to apply audio transition effects only.

Command+D (macOS) or Ctrl+D (Windows) applies the default video-only transition.

Tip: You could choose Apply Audio Transition from the Sequence menu to add transitions exclusively to audio clips, but if you have already selected audio-only clips, there's no need, as the default transition option will have the same effect.

Tip: You can also right-click any of the selected edits and choose apply default transitions.

10 Deselect the transitions by clicking an empty area of the Timeline panel or by pressing Escape. Play the sequence to see and hear the changes you made.

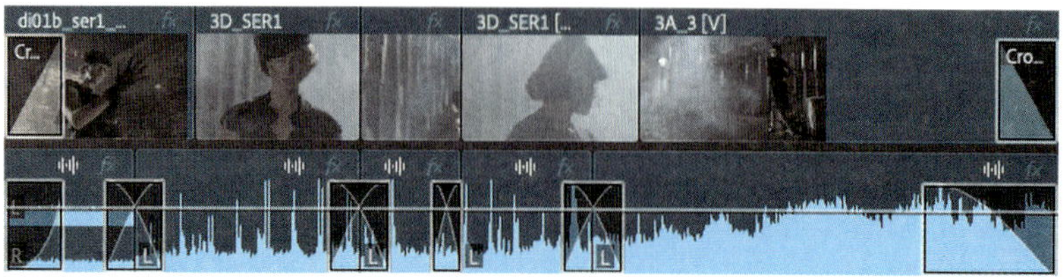

It's common for audio editors to add one-frame or two-frame audio transitions to every cut in a sequence to avoid jarring pops when an audio clip begins or ends. If you set the default duration for audio transitions to two frames, you can select multiple clips and then choose Sequence > Apply Audio Transition to quickly smooth your audio mix.

Working with fade handles

Throughout this lesson you have used transition effects to create dissolve, fade, and crossfade effects. There's another way to achieve these effects that is quick to apply and adjust right in the Timeline panel: fade handles. These handles appear on clips in the Timeline panel when you hover over them.

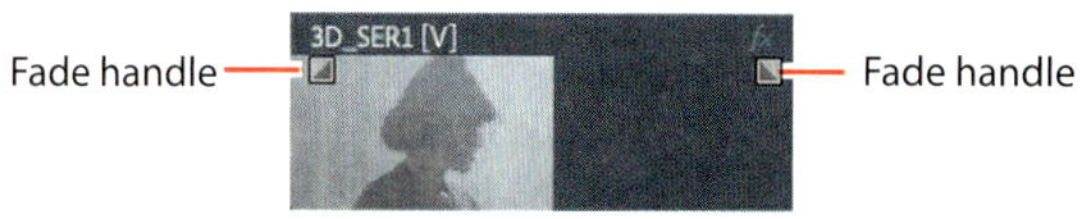

To set the duration of a transition effect, drag a fade handle. If you drag across an edit between two clips, you'll create a video cross dissolve or audio crossfade.

When applying or adjusting an audio fade or crossfades, you can also drag up or down to precisely adjust the curve, which sets a gradual or accelerated transition over time.

Fade handles provide a quick way to add precisely timed fades to clips, and effects that are applied have the same kinds of controls available as those created by dragging an effect from the Effects panel.

Now choose File > Close Project to close the current project. Click Yes to save the file if you are prompted.

Review questions

1 How can you apply the default transition to multiple clips in a sequence?

2 In the Effects panel, how can you locate a transition effect by name?

3 How do you replace one transition with another?

4 What are three ways to change the duration of a video transition effect?

5 What is an easy way to gradually increase the audio level at the beginning of a clip?

Review answers

1 Select the clips, and choose Sequence > Apply Default Transitions To Selection or press Shift+D.

2 Start typing the transition name in the search box in the Effects panel. As you type, Premiere displays all effects and transitions (audio and video) that have that letter combination anywhere in their names. Type more letters to narrow your search.

3 Drag the replacement transition on top of the transition you're rejecting. The new transition inherits the timing of the effect it replaces (but not other settings, like border colors).

4 Use the Selection tool to drag the edge of the transition icon in the Timeline, do the same thing in the A/B timeline display in the Effect Controls panel, or change the Duration value in the Effect Controls panel. You can also double-click the transition icon in the Timeline panel and change the Duration value in the dialog box that appears.

5 Apply an audio crossfade transition to the beginning of the clip or drag the clip fade handle to apply a fade.

8 EDITING VIDEO—ADVANCED TECHNIQUES

Lesson overview

In this lesson, you'll learn how to do the following:

- Perform a four-point edit.
- Change the speed or duration of clips in your sequence.
- Replace a clip in a sequence.
- Replace footage in a project.
- Use Text-Based Editing.
- Perform basic trimming on media to refine edits.
- Apply slip and slide edits to refine your edit.
- Trim clips dynamically.

This lesson will take about 120 minutes to complete. To get the files used in this lesson, refer to the instructions in "Accessing the lesson files and Web Edition" in the "Getting Started" section at the beginning of this book. Store the files on your computer in a convenient location.

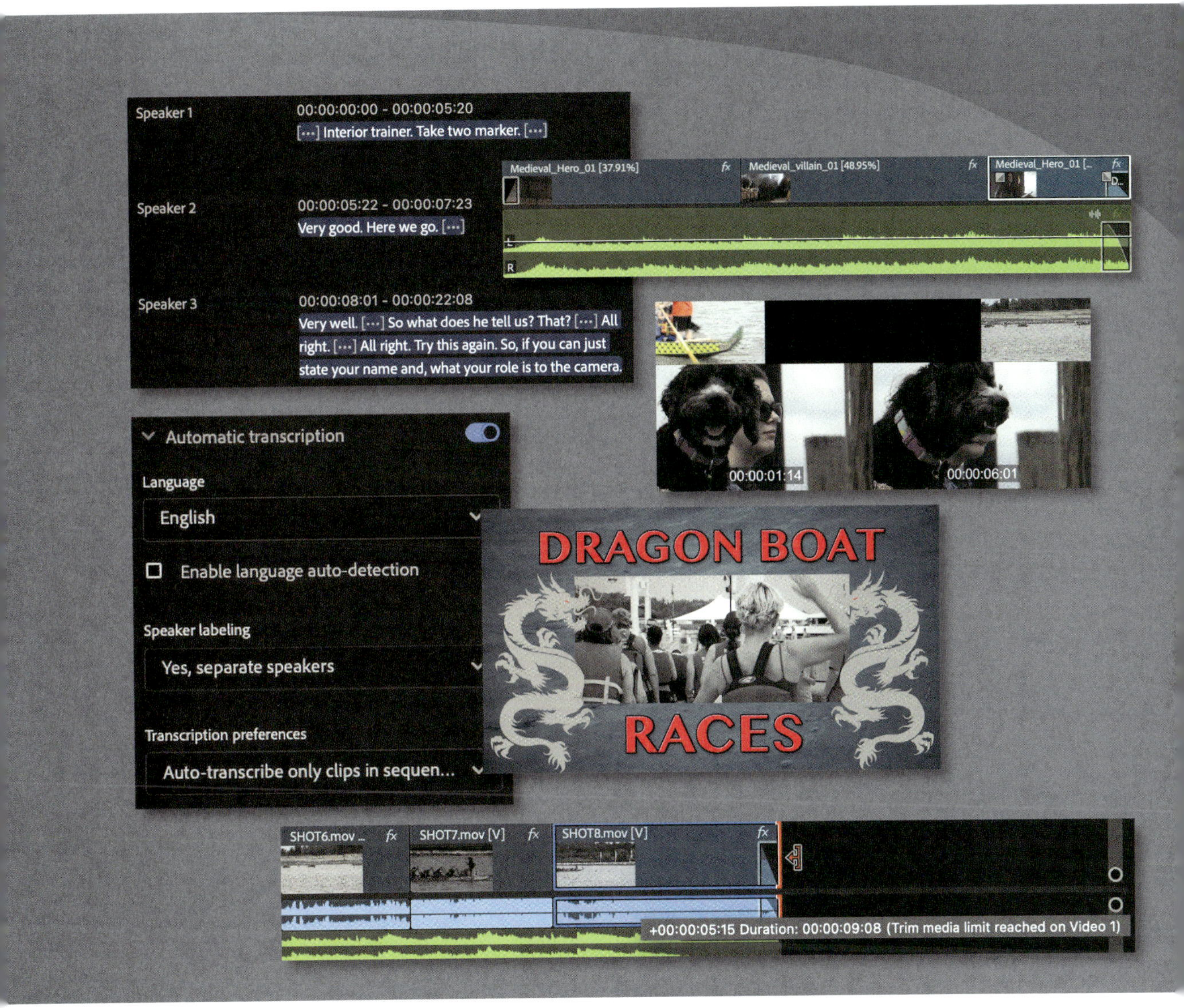

In Adobe Premiere, the main editing commands are straightforward to learn. More advanced techniques take a little time to learn, but they're worth it! They'll accelerate your editing and provide the understanding you'll need to produce the highest-level professional results.

Starting the lesson

● **Note:** To ensure that the tools function and the defaults are set exactly as described in this lesson, reset the Premiere preferences by holding any modifier key (such as Shift) while launching the application, selecting Reset App Preferences, and then clicking Continue in the Reset Options dialog box.

In this lesson, you'll use several short sequences as you explore advanced editing concepts in Adobe Premiere. The goal is to get hands-on with the techniques you'll need for advanced editing.

1 Open the project Lesson 08.prproj in the Lessons folder.

2 Click Editing in the Workspaces menu, or choose Window > Workspaces > Editing.

3 Reset the workspace to the saved version by clicking the Workspaces menu and choosing Reset To Saved Layout, or by choosing Window > Workspaces > Reset To Saved Layout.

4 Save the project as **Lesson 08 Working.prproj** in the Lessons folder.

Performing a four-point edit

In previous lessons, you used the standard technique of three-point editing. You used a combination of three In and Out points (split between the Source Monitor as well as the Program Monitor or Timeline panel) to set the source, duration, and location of an edit.

But what happens if you set four points?

The short answer is that you have to make a choice. It's likely that the duration you've marked in the Source Monitor differs from the duration you've marked in the Program Monitor or in the Timeline panel.

In this case, when you attempt to perform the edit using a keyboard shortcut or on-screen button, a dialog box warns you the durations don't match and asks you to make a decision about what to change. Most often, you'll discard one of the points.

Setting editing options for four-point edits

If you perform a four-point edit with mismatched selected durations in the clip and the sequence, the Fit Clip dialog box appears with options to resolve the issue. You can ignore one of the four points or automatically change the speed of the clip to fit the new duration in the sequence.

- **Change Clip Speed (Fit To Fill):** The first choice assumes that you set four points with different durations deliberately. Premiere preserves the source clip's In and Out points but adjusts its playback speed to match the duration you set in the Timeline panel or in the Program Monitor. This is a good choice if you want to precisely adjust clip playback speed to fill a gap.

- **Ignore Source In Point:** The source clip's In point is ignored, converting your edit back to a three-point edit. When you have an Out point and no In point in the Source Monitor, Premiere works out the In point automatically based on the duration set in the Timeline panel or Program Monitor (or the end of the clip). This option is available only if the source clip is longer than the duration set in the sequence.
- **Ignore Source Out Point:** The source clip's Out point is ignored, converting your edit back to a three-point edit. When you have an In point and no Out point in the Source Monitor, Premiere determines the Out point based on the duration set in the Timeline panel or Program Monitor (or the end of the clip). This option is available only if the source clip is longer than the targeted duration.

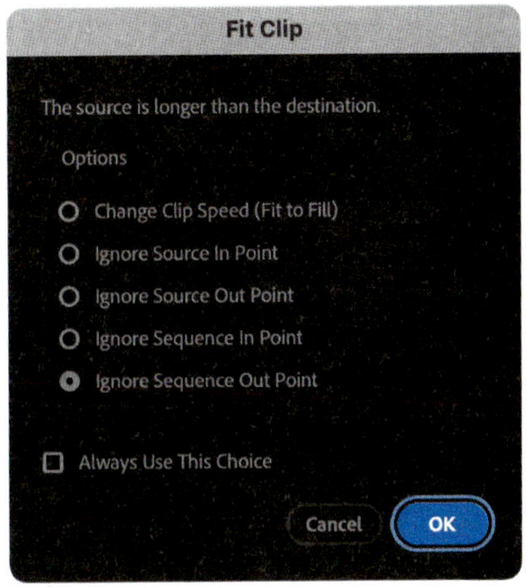

- **Ignore Sequence In Point:** The sequence In point is ignored, making this a three-point edit. The duration is taken from the clip In and Out points.
- **Ignore Sequence Out Point:** The sequence Out point is ignored, making this a three-point edit. The duration is taken from the clip In and Out points.

You can set a default option to apply automatically when performing a four-point edit by selecting an option and selecting Always Use This Choice in the Fit Clip dialog box. If you change your mind, open the Premiere Preferences, select Timeline, and select Reset Fit Clip Dialog. The Fit Clip dialog box will then open when an edit duration mismatch occurs.

Making a four-point edit

Let's perform a four-point edit. You'll change the playback speed of a clip to fit a duration set in the sequence.

1 If it's not already open in the Timeline panel, open the sequence 01 Four Point. Play through the sequence to review the content.

2 Locate the section with In and Out points already set. You should see a highlighted range in the Timeline panel.

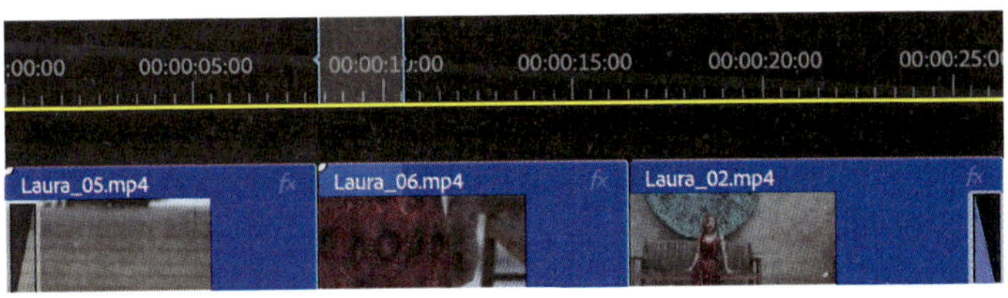

3 Browse inside the bin called Clips To Load, and open the clip called Laura_04 in the Source Monitor.

In and Out points are already set on this clip.

4 Take a look at the selected duration at the lower-right corner of the Source Monitor—8 seconds and 4 frames of this clip have been selected. Next, take a look at the selected duration at the lower-right corner of the Program Monitor—only 2 seconds and 5 frames of this sequence have been selected.

   This duration difference is important when performing a four-point edit because the way you decide to resolve the difference will impact the result.

5 In the Timeline panel, check that the source track indicators are patched correctly, with Source V1 positioned next to Timeline Video 1. There's no audio in this source clip, so you just need to check the Source V1 (also, note that the track targeting buttons have no effect on editing clips into a sequence).

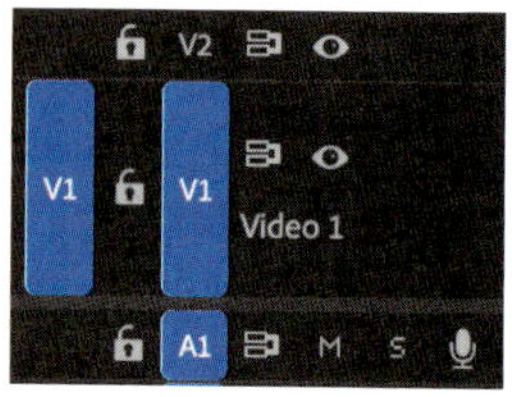

6 In the Source Monitor, click the Overwrite button to perform the edit.

7 In the Fit Clip dialog box, select Change Clip Speed (Fit To Fill), and click OK.

   Premiere applies the edit, replacing the selected part of the clip in the sequence with the selected part of the source clip and adjusting the clip playback speed to fit the new duration.

Note: Changing the playback speed of a clip counts as a visual effect. Notice the small FX badge on the clip turns white to indicate an effect has been applied.

8 Zoom in to the Timeline panel by dragging one end of the Navigator at the bottom of the panel until you can see the name and speed information on the Laura_04 clip you just edited into the sequence.

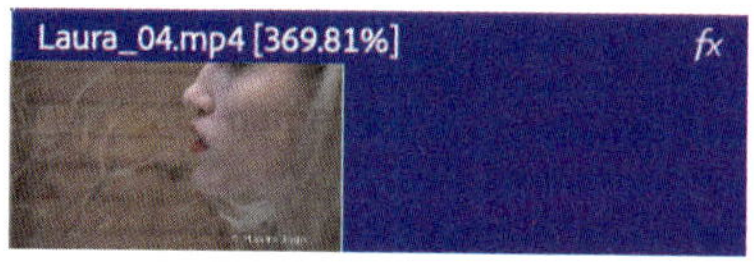

   The percentage between square brackets shows the new playback speed. The speed has been adjusted perfectly to fit the new duration.

9 Play the sequence to see the result of your edit and the speed change. The playback may not be super smooth, but you'll learn ways to improve the results when applying speed adjustments next.

Changing clip playback speed

Slow motion is one of the most commonly used effects in video post-production. It can be an effective way to add drama or to give the audience more time to experience a moment. You might change the speed of a clip for technical reasons or for artistic impact.

The fit-to-fill edit you just learned about is one way to change clip playback speed, and its results can vary. If the media originally had clear, smooth motion, you'll probably get better results.

When changing the speed of a clip, you will usually achieve smoother playback if the new speed is an even multiple or a fraction of the original clip playback speed. For example, changing a 24-fps clip to play back at 25% speed will result in 6 fps, and this will usually look smoother than if the clip is set to an unequally divided playback speed, like 27.45%. Frame rates that are not whole numbers can produce inconsistent, stuttered playback.

Sometimes you'll get the best results by changing clip speed to an even-numbered frame rate and then trimming to get a precise duration.

You can achieve high-quality slow motion by recording at a higher frame rate than your sequence playback frame rate. If you play the video at a slower frame rate than it was recorded at, you'll see slow motion—provided the new frame rate is still at least as high as your sequence frame rate.

For example, imagine a 10-second video clip was recorded at 48 frames per second but your sequence is set to 24 frames per second. You can set your footage to play at 24 frames per second, matching the sequence. Playback will be smooth, with no frame rate conversion when the clip is added to the sequence. However, the clip will be playing at half its recording frame rate, resulting in 50% slow motion. It will take twice as long to play back, so the clip will now have a 20-second duration.

Overcranking

Recording video footage at a higher frame rate than you intend to play it back at is a technique called *overcranking* because early film cameras were driven by turning a crank handle.

The faster the handle was turned, the more frames per second were captured. Slower turning would capture fewer frames per second. When the film was played back at a regular speed, filmmakers would achieve slow motion or fast motion.

Modern cameras often allow recording at faster frame rates to provide excellent-quality slow motion in post-production. The camera assigns a playback frame rate to the clip metadata that might differ from the recorded rate (the camera's system frame rate is used for playback).

This means clips may play in slow motion automatically when you import them into Premiere. Use the Interpret Footage dialog box to tell Premiere how to play clips.

Let's try this.

1 Open the sequence 02 Laura In The Snow. Play the sequence.

   The clip plays in slow motion for two reasons:

   - The clip was recorded at 96 frames per second but…
   - The clip is set to 24-fps playback (this was set by the camera and stored in the metadata for the media file).

This is a common way for cameras to record video. It results in slow motion playback in any player without the need to change playback speed.

The sequence is also configured for 24-fps playback, so it matches the clip playback setting and no conforming is necessary.

2 In the Timeline panel, right-click the clip and choose Reveal In Project to highlight the clip in the Project panel.

3 Right-click the clip in the Project panel and choose Modify > Interpret Footage. You'll use the Interpret Footage tab in the Modify Clip dialog box to tell Premiere how to play back this clip.

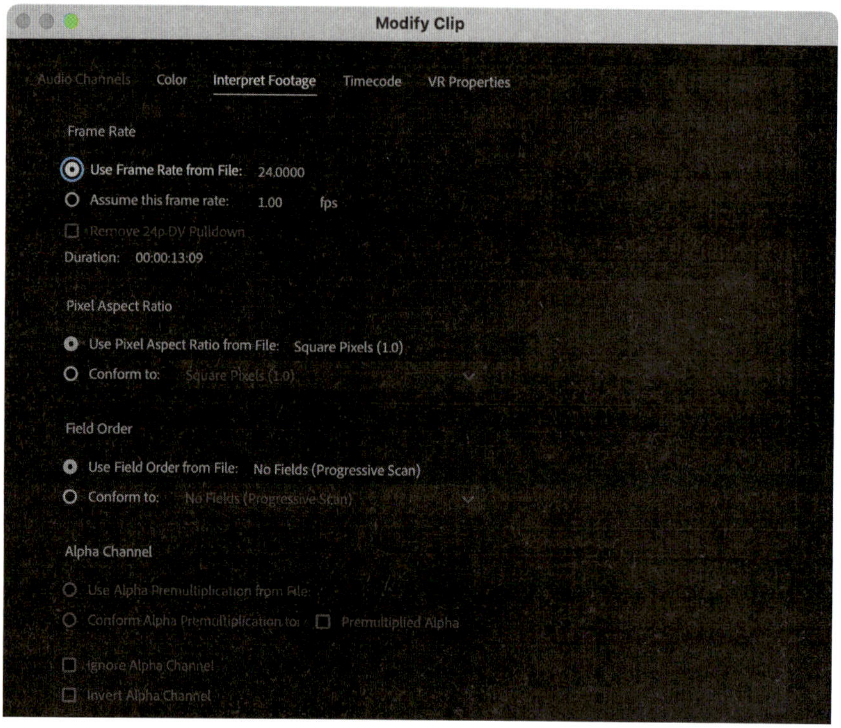

4 In the Frame Rate area, select Assume This Frame Rate and enter **96** in the fps box. This tells Premiere to play the clip at 96 frames per second (the original recording speed). Click OK.

Look back at the Timeline panel. The sequence clip has changed appearance.

You have given the clip a faster frame rate, and with the new playback speed it has a shorter duration. Rather than change the sequence clip segment duration, which might impact the timing of your edit, Premiere displays diagonal lines to indicate the portion of the clip that now has no media (because the faster playback means the clip has finished playing earlier).

5 Play the sequence again.

The clip plays at regular speed because it was originally recorded at 96 fps. It's much less smooth—not because there's anything wrong with the clip but because the original camera recording was bumpy!

> **Note:** If you're experiencing dropped frames, it might be because you are playing very high resolution, high data rate media on a drive that is not fast enough. In this case, you may need to lower the playback resolution in the Program Monitor to play clips with fast frame rates without dropping frames.

6 Drag a new instance of the Laura_01.mp4 clip from the Clips To Load bin to the beginning of the sequence, on the V2 track above the existing instance, so you can see both versions to compare them.

The new clip instance is shorter, matching the playback time at the new frame rate. The faster frame rate clip is automatically conformed to match the sequence frame rate of 24 fps, so only one frame in four is actually playing.

The duration of the clip that was already in the sequence hasn't changed (to ensure the overall timing of the sequence isn't impacted). However, the content of that original clip instance uses the new faster-playback interpretation setting, leaving an empty section of the clip segment.

Clips that have already been edited into sequences will update after making changes to the clip interpretation settings. This means it's important to re-check sequences after making changes.

Changing clip speed or duration in a sequence

Although it's more common to slow clips down, speeding up clips is a useful effect as well. The Speed/Duration command in the Timeline panel can change the playback speed for a clip in two ways. You can set a specific duration for a clip, or you can set clip playback speed as a percentage.

For example, if you set a clip to play at 50% speed, it will play at half speed; 25% would be one-quarter speed. Premiere allows you to set playback speeds up to two decimal places, so you could have 27.13% if you wanted (though only whole frames will be displayed during playback).

Let's explore this technique.

1 Open the sequence 03 Speed/Duration. Play the sequence to get a sense of the normal playback speed. It's a 20-second drone shot of the Nevada desert.

2 Right-click the clip in the sequence and choose Speed/Duration. You can also select the clip in the sequence and choose Clip > Speed/Duration, or click Adjust Speed in the Properties panel.

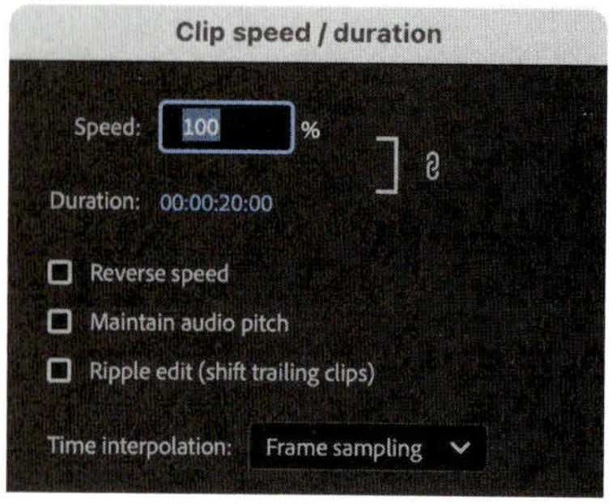

The Clip Speed/Duration dialog box gives you several options for controlling the clip playback speed.

- If you click the small chain icon, you can toggle on and off linking the sequence clip duration and clip contents' playback speed. If the chain is broken, you can change the speed or duration settings without them updating each other. When settings are linked or unlinked in this way, they are described as *ganged* or *unganged*. The result is that more or less of the clip contents will be displayed during playback within the duration of the sequence clip segment.
- By default, if there are other clips in the sequence after this one, shortening the clip will leave a gap. If you make the clip longer than the space available before the next clip, the clip will be trimmed to keep the same duration at the new playback speed. That's because the clip can't move the next clip to make room for the new duration when you change these settings. However, if you select Ripple Edit (Shift Trailing Clips), the clip will make space for itself, pushing other clips later in the sequence.
- To play a clip backward, select Reverse Speed.
- If a clip has audio, consider selecting Maintain Audio Pitch. This will keep the clip's original pitch at the new speed. With this option disabled, the pitch will naturally go up or down as the speed changes.

Tip: The Maintain Audio Pitch option is more effective for small speed changes; dramatic resampling can produce unnatural-sounding results. Consider adjusting the audio in Adobe Audition if you need to make a more significant speed change. See the *Adobe Audition CC Classroom in a Book, 2nd Edition* for audio speed change workflows and more.

Tip: You can change the speed of multiple clips at the same time. To do so, select multiple clips and choose Clip > Speed/Duration or click Adjust Speed in the Properties panel. When you change the speed of multiple clips, be sure to pay attention to the Ripple Edit (Shift Trailing Clips) option. This will automatically close or expand gaps for all the selected clips after the speed change.

3 Make sure Speed and Duration are linked with the chain icon selected. Change the speed to 200%, and click OK.

Note: Speed changes always result in a clip duration that is whole frames. The speed you set may be adjusted automatically, with the precise new speed displayed on the clip, to achieve this.

Play the clip in the Timeline panel. Notice that the clip is now 10 seconds long. That's because it's playing at 200% speed: Double the playback speed means playing for half the original time.

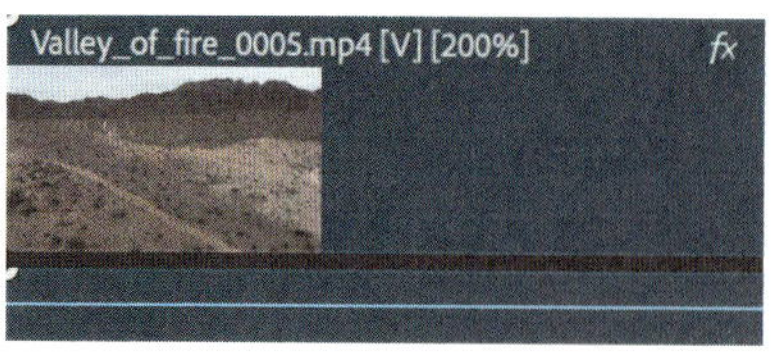

Notice the new playback speed is displayed on the sequence clip as a percentage.

4 Choose Edit > Undo, or press Command+Z (macOS) or Ctrl+Z (Windows).

5 Select the clip on the Timeline, and press Command+R (macOS) or Ctrl+R (Windows) to open the Clip Speed/Duration dialog box.

6 Click the chain icon to make sure the Speed and Duration settings are unlinked. Then, change Speed to 50%.

7 Click OK, and then play the clip. The clip plays back at 50% speed, so it should play for twice as long. But because you turned off the link between playback speed and duration, the second half has been trimmed to maintain the 20-second duration in the sequence.

Unganging the Speed and Duration options is useful when you want the visual effect of slow motion without changing the timing of your edits. For example, if you want to add a dreamlike quality to footage of waves crashing against a beach, you can reduce the speed just enough for the waves to seem dreamily slow without altering the timing of the next clip.

Note: If you set a duration that is longer than the available media, based on the playback speed percentage you set, you won't be able to click OK. The button will be dimmed.

This kind of aesthetic change often demands trial and error to achieve the result you want—a great reason to learn keyboard shortcuts for quick access to the controls you need.

Now try reversing playback.

8 Select the clip, and open the Clip Speed/Duration dialog box again.

9 Leave Speed at 50%, but this time select Reverse Speed; then click OK.

10 Play the clip. Now it plays in reverse at 50% slow motion. You'll see a negative sign next to the new speed displayed in the sequence.

Changing sequence clip speed with the Rate Stretch tool

Sometimes you'll have the perfect clip for your sequence—but it's just a little too short or a little too long. This is where the Rate Stretch tool helps.

1 Open the sequence 04 Rate Stretch.

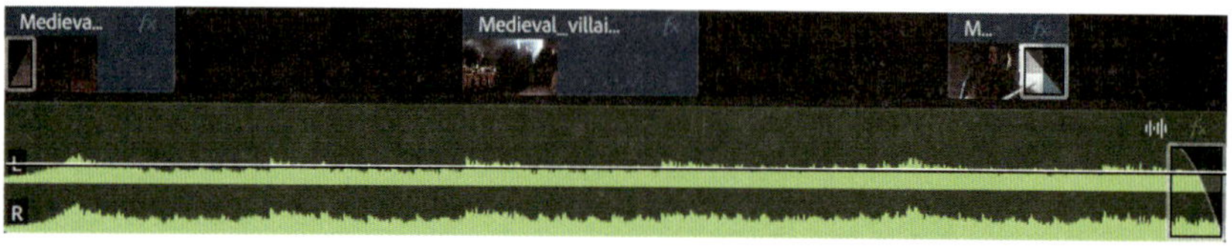

This sequence is synchronized to music. The clips contain the desired content, but the first video clip is too short. You'll need to fix the gap before the second clip begins.

You can make a guess and try to make an exact Speed/Duration adjustment, but it's easier and faster to use the Rate Stretch tool to drag the end of the clip to fill the available gap.

2 In the Tools panel, click and hold the Ripple Edit tool to select the Rate Stretch tool.

3 With this tool, drag the right edge of the first video clip until it reaches the left edge of the second video clip.

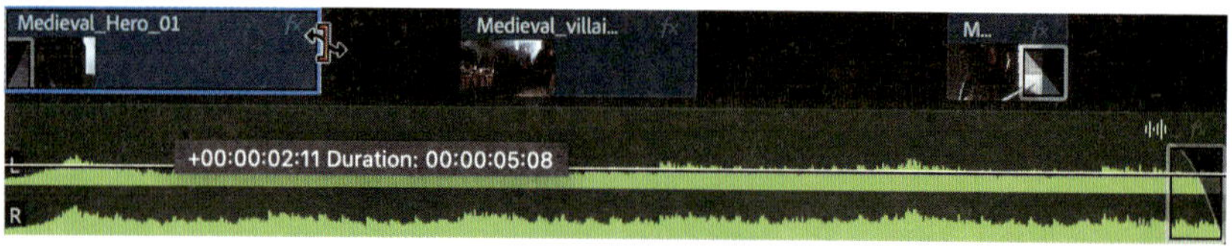

The speed of the clip changes to fill the gap. The contents haven't changed (you haven't trimmed the clip); the clip is playing more slowly.

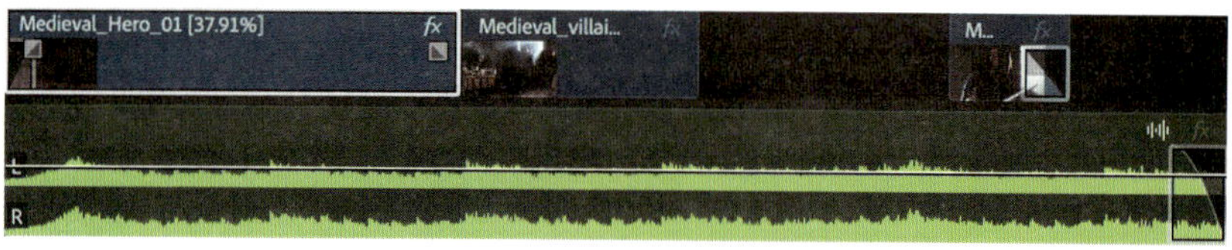

▶ **Tip:** If you change your mind about a change made with the Rate Stretch tool, you can always use it to stretch a clip back or use Undo. Alternatively, you can use the Clip Speed/Duration dialog box to enter a Speed value of 100% and restore the clip to its original speed.

4 Using the same tool, drag the right edge of the second video clip to meet the left edge of the third clip.

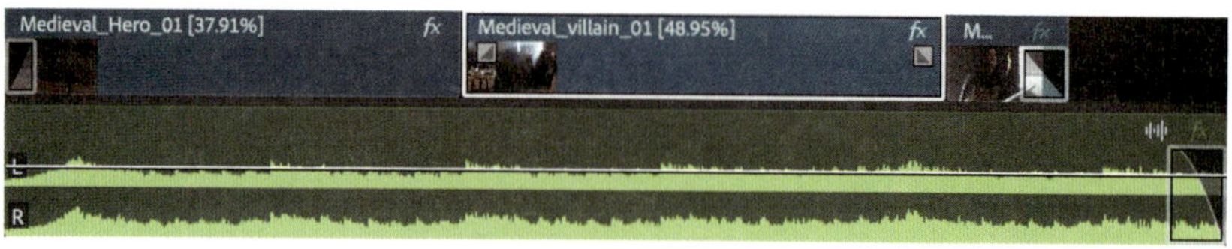

5 Check that snapping is turned on. Drag the right edge of the third clip until it snaps to the end of the audio. This clip has a Dip to Black transition effect at the end, so you'll need to drag just above the effect icon.

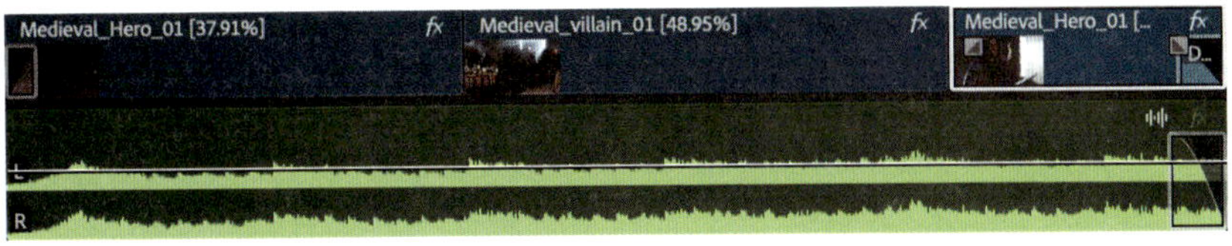

The duration of the video now matches the music. You may need to zoom in to the Timeline panel to see the new playback speeds of the clips.

6 Play the sequence to view the result. Some of the faster action is noticeably jumpy. Let's fix that.

7 Press the shortcut key V, or click the Selection tool in the Tools panel to select it.

8 With the Timeline panel active, press Command+A (macOS) or Ctrl+A (Windows) to select all the clips.

9 Right-click any clip and choose Time Interpolation > Optical Flow. This smooths playback when changing clip speed. It's a more advanced method for producing playback speed changes, and the effect needs to be rendered before you preview the result.

10 Render by pressing Return (macOS) or Enter (Windows), and play the sequence to see the result.

A great improvement!

Optical Flow is usually worth choosing when adjusting clip playback speed. You can adjust and preview the timing of playback speed changes using the default Frame Sampling renderer. Then, when the timing is right, switch to Optical Flow and preview again.

Optical Flow is also available when choosing a new playback speed using the Clip Speed/Duration dialog box.

Note: Using Optical Flow to render a new playback speed can introduce visual artifacts, particularly with footage that has motion blur as a result of a slow camera shutter speed. For example, take a look at the villain's hand at 00:00:10:18 in the current sequence (you may want to scrub through the frames or use the arrow keys to move the playhead frame by frame to see the issues). Always check your results!

Replacing clips and media

It's common to swap one sequence clip for another as you try different versions of an edit.

This might mean making a global replacement, such as replacing one version of an animated logo with a newer file. You might also want to swap out one clip in a sequence, such as an actor's performance, for another that you have available in a bin. Depending on the task at hand, you'll use different approaches.

Dragging in a replacement clip

You can drag a new shot onto a sequence clip you'd like to replace. This is called a *replace edit*. Let's try it.

1 Open the 05 Replace Clip sequence.

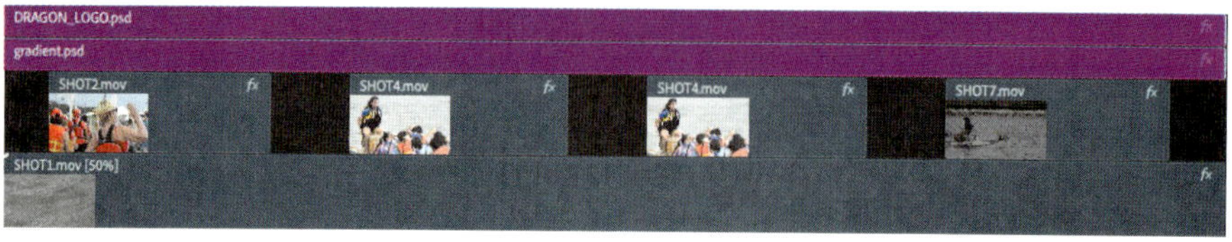

2 Play the sequence.

On the Video 2 track, the second and third clips are actually the same SHOT4 clip repeated. The clip has motion keyframes applied to make it spin onto the screen and spin off again. You'll learn how to create these kinds of animation effects in Lesson 9, "Putting Clips in Motion."

Let's replace the first instance of the clip SHOT4. This clip has the Black & White and Crop effects applied and has keyframes animating the Scale and Rotation settings for the Motion effect. You may not want to re-create these effects, as they are already set perfectly. This is an ideal scenario for replacing a sequence clip.

3 From the Clips To Load bin, drag the Boat Replacement clip straight from the Project panel over the first instance of the SHOT4 clip in the sequence, but don't release it yet. You don't need to position the pointer precisely; just make sure it's over the clip you want to replace.

Even though the new clip already has In and Out points, it's much longer than the existing clip that you intend to replace.

4 Press and hold the Option (macOS) or Alt (Windows) key. While you're holding this modifier key, the replacement clip snaps to fit the length of the clip it's replacing.

Release the clip while still holding the modifier key to replace the existing clip.

Premiere synchronizes the first frame (or In point) of the replacement clip with the first visible frame of the existing clip in the sequence. Just enough of the new clip is used to replace the existing clip in the sequence.

5 Play the sequence. All the picture-in-picture clips have the same effect applied. The new clip inherits the settings and effects from the clip it replaced. This is a quick and easy way to try different shots in a sequence.

Performing a synchronized replace edit

What if you need to synchronize a particular moment in the middle of a clip, such as a hand clap or a door closing?

For this, you can use a more advanced type of replace edit to synchronize a particular frame of the replacement clip with a particular frame of the clip it's replacing.

1 Open the sequence 06 Replace Edit.

   This is a version of the Theft Unexpected edit. All the clips in the sequence have been made black and white, with a crop applied at the top and bottom.

   Take a look at the last two clips. While the action flows from one clip to the next, there is a jump cut between the clips because the camera angle doesn't change. Next, you'll replace the shot with another angle while matching the precise timing of John sipping his tea.

2 Position the playhead in the sequence at approximately 00:00:20:00, as John lifts his teacup to his lips. The playhead will be the sync point for the edit you are about to perform.

3 From the Sources bin, open the clip Mid John in the Source Monitor.

4 In the Source Monitor, position the playhead at the same moment in the action, around 01:39:58:00 when John is about to sip his tea.

5 Back in the Timeline panel, click the last clip in the sequence to select it. (Be careful not to double-click; that would open the clip in the Source Monitor.)

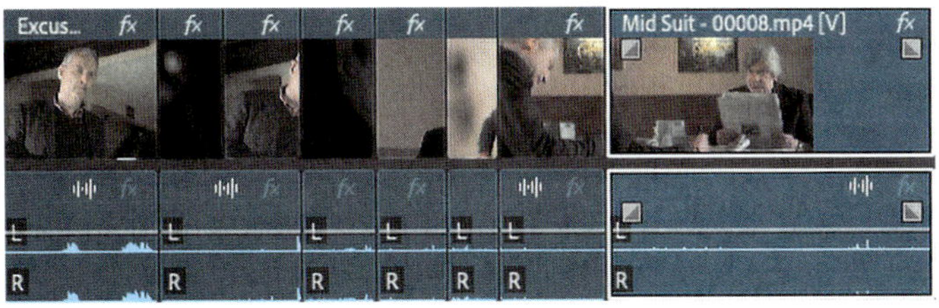

Now, with the Timeline panel active, choose Clip > Replace With Clip > From Source Monitor, Match Frame. The Mid John clip replaces the Mid Suit clip!

6 Play the newly edited sequence to check the edit.

The playhead position in the Source Monitor and Program Monitor was synchronized. While the timing at the start of the clip may need adjusting, the sequence clip duration, effects, and settings are all applied to the replacement clip. This technique can be a huge time-saver when you need to match the precise timing of action and effects that are applied to the existing sequence clip.

Using the Replace Footage feature

While a replace edit replaces the contents of a clip segment in a sequence, the Replace Footage command replaces footage in the Project panel so that the clip links to a different media file. This can be of great benefit when you need to replace a clip that occurs several times in a sequence or in multiple sequences. You might use this to update an animated logo or a piece of music, for example.

When you replace footage in the Project panel, all instances of the clip you replace are changed anywhere the clip is used.

1 Load the sequence 07 Replace Footage.

Let's replace the graphic on the Video 4 track with something more interesting.

2 In the Clips To Load bin, right-click DRAGON_LOGO.psd and choose Replace Footage.

3 Navigate to the Lessons/Assets/Graphics folder, and open the DRAGON_LOGO_FIX.psd file.

4 Play the sequence.

The clip name has been updated to match the new file, both in the Project panel and in the sequence.

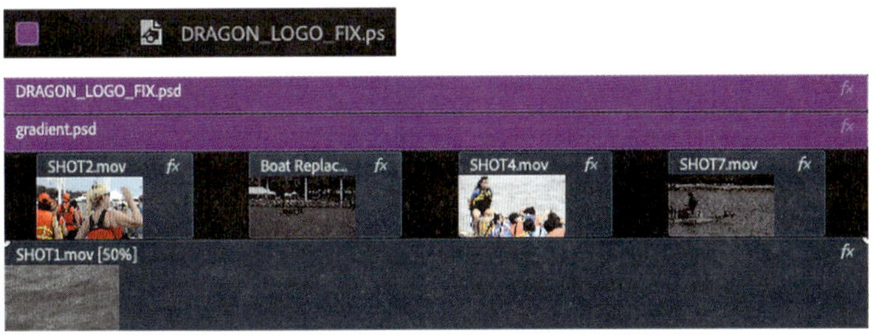

● **Note:** The Replace Footage command cannot be undone. To switch back to the original clip, choose Clip > Replace Footage again to navigate to and relink the original file, or choose File > Revert to restore the current project to the last saved version (you'll lose changes made since you last saved).

Using Text-Based Editing

Premiere can transcribe spoken word content to make it easier to navigate your footage and to produce captions and titles. You can even edit video using text-based tools.

So far, you have added clips to sequences using insert and overwrite edits. You've also moved clips within sequences and removed clips. Text-Based Editing allows you to perform these standard editing tasks for your sequences based on text alone. This process can be extraordinarily fast compared to watching content like interviews in real time to make selections and edits.

You can choose to have clips transcribed automatically when they are imported or manually using the Text panel. Let's try both.

Removing content using Text-Based Editing

Removing content with Text-Based Editing is as straightforward as editing a document in a word processing application. Begin by importing some new media and creating a sequence.

1 Make sure no existing bins are selected in the Project panel. Newly imported clips are automatically added to a selected bin, but you are going to create a new bin during import. Switch to Import mode.

2 Navigate to Lessons/Assets/Video and Audio Files/Interview and select only one clip, Coach_Interview_DCAM.

3 Under the Import settings, under the Organize Media heading, select Add To New Bin, and name the bin **Interview**.

4 Turn on Automatic Transcription. Leave the Language menu set to English; set Speaker Labeling to Yes, Separate Speakers; and set Transcription Preferences to Auto-Transcribe Only Clips In Sequence.

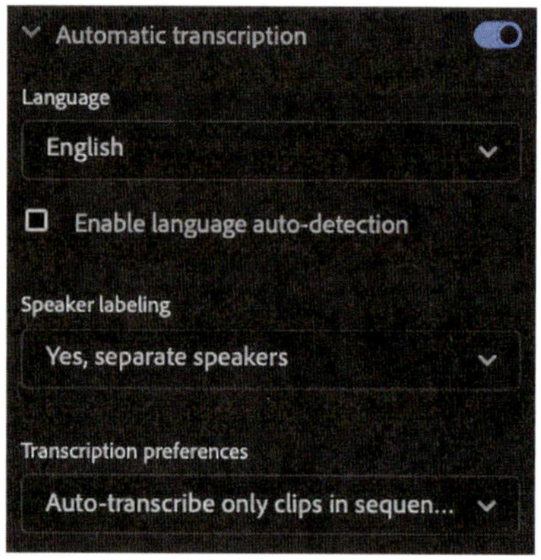

Click Import. Premiere switches back to Edit mode.

5 Open the new Interview bin, right-click the Coach_Interview_DCAM.mp4 clip, and choose New Sequence From Clip. This creates a new sequence with settings that match the format of the clip.

In the upper-right corner of the Application window, a progress indicator shows that the transcription analysis is taking place.

If you click the progress indicator, Premiere will display a list of recent processing tasks as well as the status of the current analysis.

You can access this list at any time by clicking the Open Progress Dashboard button.

6 From the Workspaces menu, choose Text-Based Editing. Then, from the same menu, choose Reset To Saved Layout.

Once transcription is complete, you can use Premiere's built-in Text-Based Editing tools to work on the sequence.

The Text-Based Editing workspace includes the Text panel, moves the Project panel to the upper-right corner, and combines the Source Monitor and Program Monitor in one frame.

Note: Automatic text transcription may contain errors or miss words entirely, particularly if the source audio is low quality or if the subject speaks in a dialect. Check and edit the transcription by double-clicking words you would like to correct.

The Text panel should already be displaying the transcription for the interview clip. If not, click to make the Timeline panel or Program Monitor active, make sure the Transcript tab is selected at the top of the Text panel, and make sure Follow Active Monitor is selected at the bottom of the Text panel.

The Text panel allows you to click a word to move the playhead to that part of your content, to search for words (and replace words in the transcript), and to perform edits.

As you are currently viewing the contents of a sequence, the editing buttons at the top of the Text panel are for lift and extract edits. If you were viewing the contents of a clip, the buttons would be for insert and overwrite edits. These buttons are the same as those found on the Source Monitor and Program Monitor.

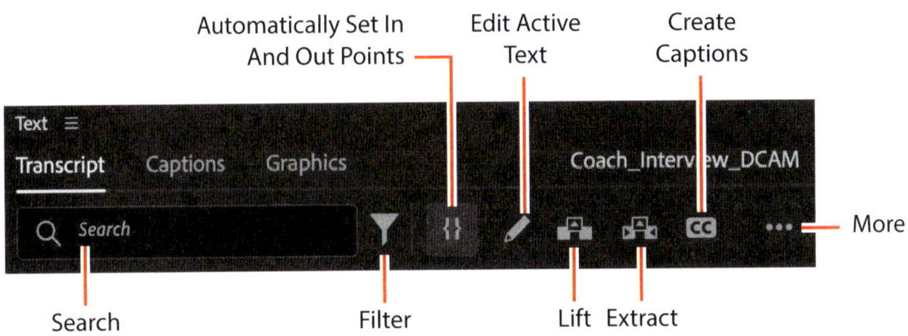

Removing content from a sequence using Text-Based Editing is straightforward. Select the text you want to remove and press Delete (macOS) or Backspace (Windows).

Tip: If you are using a non-English keyboard and discover pressing Delete (macOS) or Backspace (Windows) does not remove content selected in the Text panel, try using the shortcut for the Cut command, Command+X (macOS) or Ctrl+X (Windows).

1 Make sure the option to Automatically Set In and Out Points is selected at the top of the Text panel. With this option selected, every time you select text, In and Out points are added to the sequence, making it easy to see the part of the sequence you have selected.

   Select all of the text from the beginning up to and including the phrase *what your role is to the camera* (the first three pieces of text).

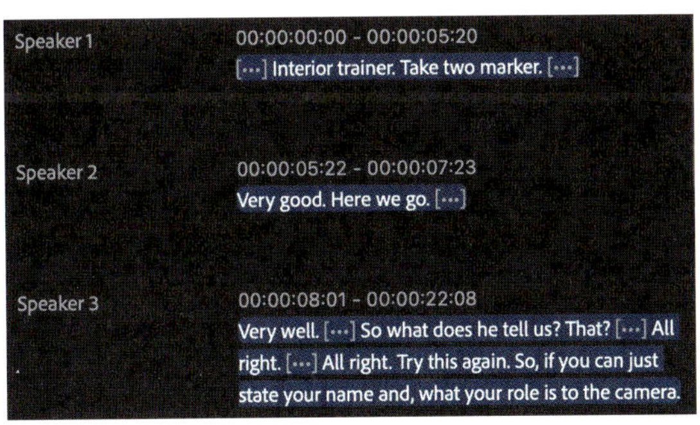

2 Press Delete/Backspace or press ' (the keyboard shortcut for Extract).

Premiere removes the first part of the interview clip from the sequence.

3 The transcription shows our subject as Speaker 2, while the interviewer is shown as Speaker 3. To remove the interviewer, you could select each part of their transcription, but there's a faster way.

Click the Filter button and choose Speakers. Note that you can also filter filler words, censored words, and pauses.

4 In the additional options that appear, click to open the menu that displays Select A Speaker and choose Speaker 3.

All of the transcription text for Speaker 3 is highlighted.

5 Click Delete, then make sure Extract is selected, and click Delete All.

All of the interviewer content is removed from the sequence.

6 There are quite a few pauses in this interview, and you can remove them all in a single step. In the Text panel, click the More menu (three dots in the upper-right corner) and choose Transcript View Options. To remove all but the shortest pauses, drag the slider to set the Minimum Pause Length to 0.5 seconds, and click Save.

7 Click the Filter button and choose Pauses. All the pauses that are longer than 0.5 seconds are highlighted, and a Delete button appears. Click Delete, then make sure Extract is selected, and click Delete All.

In just a few moments, you have removed all the content that is not the subject speaking, including the pauses.

8 You can also remove individual words or sentences. Click the Filter button and choose Text. Type the word **football** in the search box to highlight that word in the transcript. Within that section of text, select and delete the words *I played football as well. But track was my mainstay.*

You have now removed selected sentences, the interviewer, and all pauses—all by selecting and deleting text.

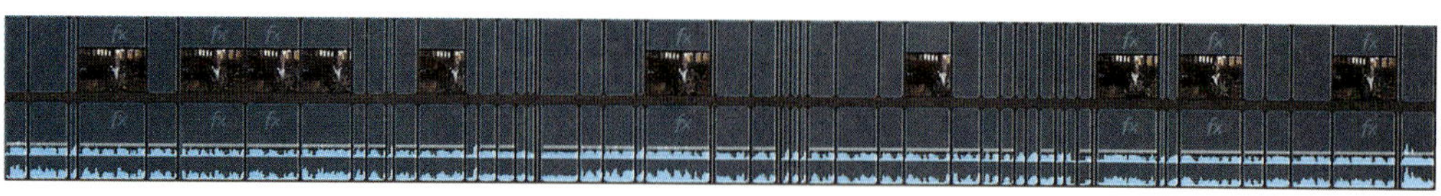

Premiere can also automatically identify and remove or hide censored words. This example media doesn't include any inappropriate language, but you can explore this feature using any words.

1 Click the Filter button, choose Censored Words, and then type **pomegranate** in the Add A Word box.

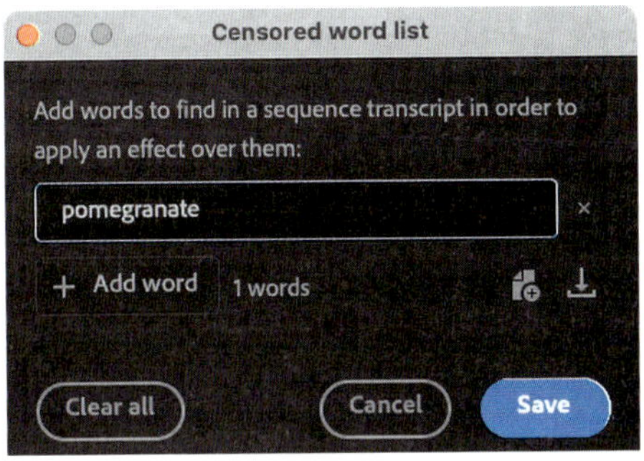

You can add multiple censored words by clicking the Add Word button. You can also import a whole batch of words by clicking the Import Word List button.

For now, click Save.

2 At the top of the Text panel, click Apply Effect; then click the menu with effect options.

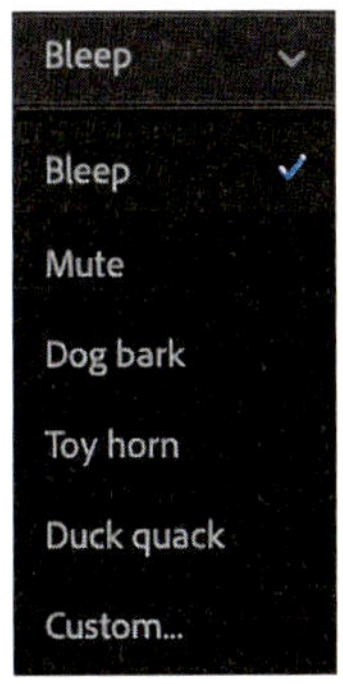

3 Choose an option, and click Apply To All.

Premiere Pro leaves the text transcription unedited but replaces the audio in your sequence with the selected effect.

Click one of the references to *pomegranate* in the Text panel to move the sequence playhead to that word; then play the sequence to hear the result.

4 Click the Filter button, and choose Text; then click the small x in the Search box to clear it if you have an entry in the box.

Now let's add some content using Text-Based Editing.

Adding content using Text-Based Editing

To add content to this sequence, you'll import a new clip and open it in the Source Monitor.

1 Scroll to the top of the Text panel and click the word *Well* that is at the beginning of the second section of the text (the line begins with Well, for Jenny in particular). This will move the sequence playhead to the beginning of the word.

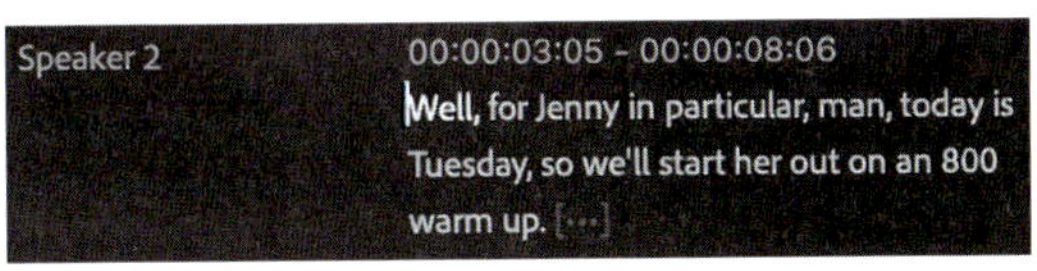

2 In the Project panel, click the Interview bin to select it. When you import a new clip, it will automatically be added to the selected bin.

3 Switch to Import mode, and select the clip Coach_Interview_ECAM. This is an alternative angle for the same interview.

4 Turn off all the Import settings, including Add To New Bin and Automatic Transcription (although you may as well leave Media Analysis on), and then click Import.

Premiere imports the new clip and adds it to the Interview bin.

5 Double-click the clip Coach_Interview_ECAM in the Interview bin to open it in the Source Monitor. In the Text panel, click the blue Transcribe button.

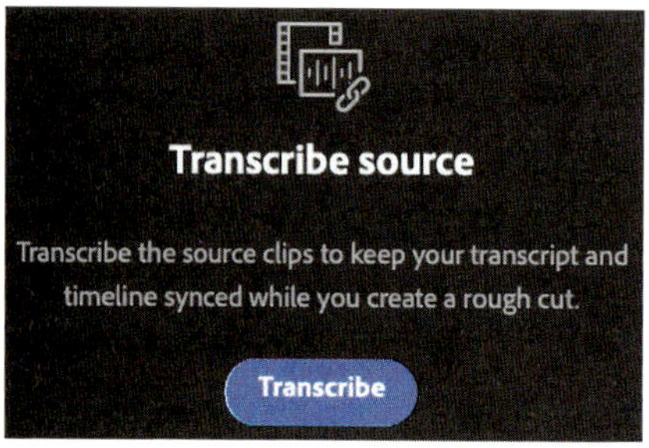

6 In the Create Transcription For Source Media dialog box, make sure the Language is set to English and that Yes, Separate Speakers is chosen from the Speaker Labeling menu. Click Transcribe, and wait a few moments for the transcription to complete.

7 In the Text panel, select the text Awesome. Well, let's start kind of broad, I guess. What's a typical training routine for a track and field athlete that you coach?

This text is in the fifth section.

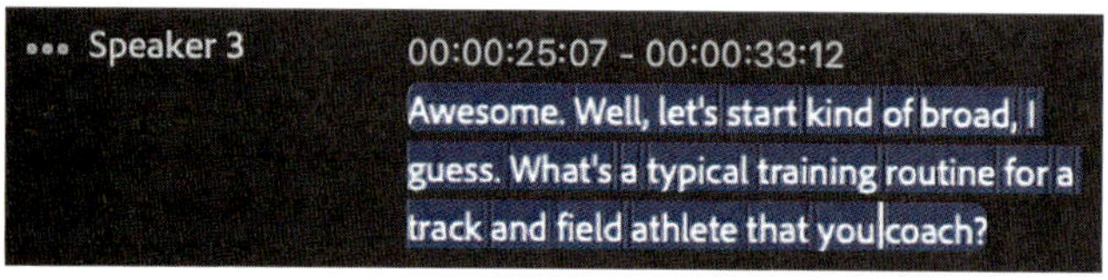

Tip: If you can't see all the buttons at the top of the Text panel, try resizing the panel.

Click the Insert button at the top of the panel, or press the , (comma) key.

The clip is added to the sequence at the location of the playhead.

8 Play the sequence to review the edits you made. There are lots of jump cuts, where the content switches from one moment to the next without changing camera angle. The timing of the edits is pretty good, though, and with some more visuals and graphics, this might work well as a social media post.

You can switch between Text-Based Editing and the other editing tools at any time. This powerful and extremely fast editing workflow is ideal for interviews, podcasts, presentations to camera—any kind of content that has a lot of speech.

Transcripts can be exported and imported, speakers can be named, and captions can be generated automatically. For more information about Text-Based Editing, see the Adobe Premiere help.

Experiment with adding and removing content using Text-Based Editing.

When you have finished practicing, use the Workspaces menu to return to the Editing workspace.

Performing regular trimming

You can adjust the part of a clip that is used in a sequence in several ways. This process is generally called *trimming*. To most of us, the word *trimming* means making something shorter. When you trim in Premiere, you can make the selected part of the original clip shorter or longer in the sequence by restoring or removing content.

Some trimming methods affect just one clip, while others can adjust the relationship between two adjacent clips, or even multiple clips.

Trimming clips

Making a single clip shorter or longer is called a *regular* trim, and it's fairly straightforward.

1 Open the sequence 08 Regular Trim.

2 Play the sequence to review the contents.

   Too little of the last shot was added to the sequence, and it needs to be extended to match the end of the music.

3 Make sure you have the Selection tool selected.

4 Position the pointer over the right edge of the last video clip in the sequence.

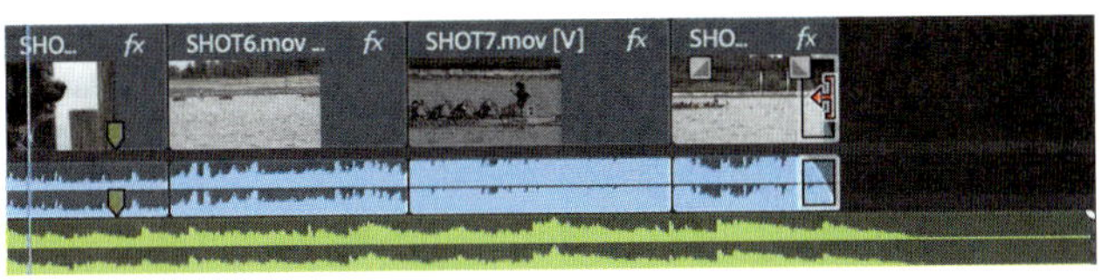

   The pointer changes into the red Trim Out pointer with a directional arrow. The arrow indicates which side of the edit you will adjust. As there is no clip next to the one you're changing, it doesn't matter which side the arrow points for this adjustment.

Tip: The keyboard shortcut for the Selection tool is V.

Precisely hovering the pointer over the end of a clip, you can change between trimming the Out point (end of a clip, to the left) and trimming the In point of the next clip (beginning of a clip, to the right). In this case, there's no next clip, of course.

This clip has a transition effect applied to the end. You may need to zoom in to make it easier to trim the clip and not adjust the transition effect.

Note: Making a clip shorter will leave a gap between it and any adjacent clips. Later in this lesson you'll learn to use the Ripple Edit tool to automatically remove gaps or push clips later in a sequence when you trim a clip (just like insert and extract edits).

5 Drag the edge to the right until it meets the end of the audio file. A tool tip shows you how much you've trimmed.

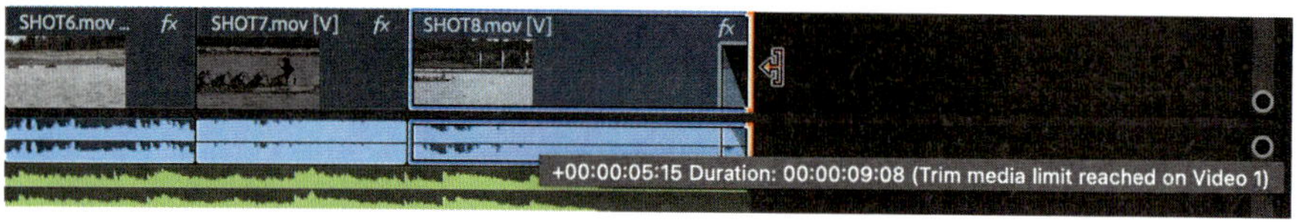

In this instance, the tool tip also shows that the trim has reached the end of the original media.

6 Release the drag to apply the trim.

Performing advanced trimming

Regular trims leave gaps in the sequence when shortening a clip or prevent you from lengthening a shot if there's an adjacent clip.

Fortunately, Premiere offers several more ways to trim. Let's check out ripple edits.

Performing ripple edits

Tip: The keyboard shortcut for the Ripple Edit tool is B.

You can avoid introducing gaps when trimming by using the Ripple Edit tool rather than the Selection tool.

You can use the Ripple Edit tool to trim a clip in the same way that you use the Selection tool. When you use the Ripple Edit tool to change the duration of a clip, the adjustment ripples through the sequence. That is, clips after the clip you have trimmed slide to the left to fill the gap, or they slide to the right to make room if the clip gets longer.

Let's try it.

1 Open the sequence 09 Ripple Edit.

2 The Ripple Edit tool is usually available in the Tools panel. Because you recently used the Rate Stretch tool, the Ripple Edit tool may be hidden. If that's the case, click and hold the Rate Stretch tool to reveal and select the Ripple Edit tool.

3 Hover the Ripple Edit tool over the inside-right edge of the seventh clip (SHOT7) until it turns into a yellow, left-facing bracket and arrow.

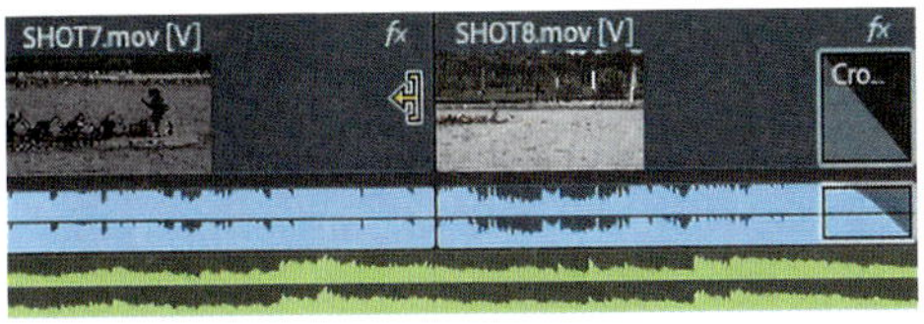

The shot is too short, so let's add some more footage from the clip handle.

4 Drag to the right until the timecode in the tool tip reads +00:00:01:10.

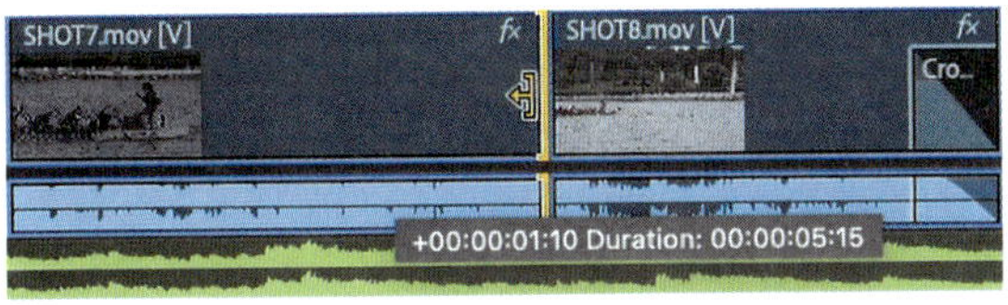

Tip: To use the Selection tool as a temporary Ripple Edit tool, hold Command (macOS) or Ctrl (Windows). Be sure to click to one side of the edit to avoid performing a rolling edit (described next).

Notice that while you're using the Ripple Edit tool, the Program Monitor displays the last frame of the clip on the left side of the edit and the first frame of the clip on the right side. The image updates dynamically while you trim.

5 Release the drag to complete the edit.

The clip you have trimmed now has a longer duration, so the clip to its right slides right (later in the sequence) to make space for it. Play that part of the sequence to see whether the timing of the edit works.

6 Make another trimming adjustment—add another +2:00 seconds to the end of the SHOT7 clip. Play through the newly trimmed edit between SHOT7 and SHOT8.

This time, trimming has exposed a slight on-camera shake that you'll work on next.

Note: Ripple edits change the timing of edits for clips later in the sequence. If you perform a ripple edit on just one track, it can leave clips on other tracks out of sync. Sync locks keep items on all tracks in sync.

Making ripple edits with keyboard shortcuts

Though the Ripple Edit tool gives fine control when trimming, there are two useful keyboard shortcuts that apply the same type of trim adjustment, based on the location of the Timeline panel playhead.

For these shortcuts to work, the correct timeline tracks must be targeted. Whichever tracks are targeted will be trimmed.

Position the Timeline panel playhead over a clip (or multiple layers of clips), and press one of the following shortcuts:

- **Q:** Ripple trims clips from their current start to the playhead position.
- **W:** Ripple trims clips from their current end to the playhead position.

This can be a fast way to trim clips, particularly in the early stages of editing, when you may simply want to "top and tail" (remove unwanted content at the start or end) your clips.

Performing rolling edits

Trimming with the Ripple Edit tool changes the overall length of the sequence. This is because one clip gets shorter or longer, and the rest of the sequence moves to close the gap (or moves out of the way).

There's another way to change the timing of an edit: a rolling edit, sometimes referred to as a *double-roller* or *dual-roller* trim.

> **Tip:** The keyboard shortcut for the Rolling Edit tool is N.

> **Tip:** You can use the Selection tool while holding the Command (macOS) or Ctrl (Windows) key as a shortcut for either the Ripple Edit tool or the Rolling Edit tool. Position the pointer just before or just after the edit to perform a ripple trim. If you place the pointer exactly on the edit, you perform a rolling trim.

When you perform a rolling edit, the overall length of the sequence does not change. Instead, a rolling edit shortens one clip and lengthens another at the same time, adjusting the clips by the same number of frames.

For example, if you use the Rolling Edit tool to extend a clip by two seconds, you will also shorten the adjacent clip by two seconds.

1. Continue working with the sequence 09 Ripple Edit.
2. In the Tools panel, click and hold the Ripple Edit tool to select the Rolling Edit tool.
3. Use the Rolling Edit tool to drag the edit point between SHOT7 and SHOT8 (the last two clips on the timeline). Use the Program Monitor split-screen display to find a better-matching edit between the two shots, dragging the edit left to remove the camera shake.

   You may need to zoom in to the Timeline panel to make more accurate adjustments.

Try rolling the edit to the left 1 second and 19 frames (–1:19). You can use the Program Monitor timecode as a reference or the tool tip that appears in the Timeline panel. If you pre-position the playhead, the edit will snap to it as you drag (if snapping is turned on).

Note: When trimming, it's possible to trim a clip to a 0 (zero) duration (removing it from the timeline altogether).

Performing slip edits

A *slip trim* changes both the In point and Out point of a single sequence clip segment at the same time, by the same amount, "rolling" the visible contents in position.

Because a slip trim changes the beginning and end by equal amounts, it doesn't change the duration of your sequence. In this way, it's similar to a rolling trim.

Slip trims change only the clip you select; adjacent clips before or after the clip you adjust are not affected. Using the Slip tool to adjust a clip is a little like moving a conveyor belt: The visible part of the original clip changes inside the timeline clip segment without changing the length of the clip or the sequence.

1 Continue working with the sequence 09 Ripple Edit.
2 Select the Slip tool.
3 Drag SHOT5 left and right to adjust both the In point and Out point for the clip.
4 Take a look at the Program Monitor while you perform the slip edit.

Tip: The keyboard shortcut for the Slip tool is Y.

The two top images in the Program Monitor are the Out point of SHOT4 and the In point of SHOT6, before and after the clip you are adjusting. They don't change. The two larger images are the In point and Out point of SHOT5, the clip you are adjusting. These edit points *do* change.

5 Try improving the timing for the shots in this sequence by slipping the clip contents.

The Slip tool is well worth taking time to get to grips with. It's usually the case that the timing for action at the beginning or the end of a clip is critical but not both, so this is sometimes the fastest tool for adjusting timing when cutting action.

Making slide edits

The Slide tool works by leaving the duration of the clip you're sliding unchanged. Instead, the Out point of the previous clip and the In point of the following clip are changed by equal amounts, in opposite directions. It's another form of dual-roller trim. In a sense, it's the opposite of a slip trim.

Tip: The keyboard shortcut for the Slide tool is U.

Because you're changing the previous and next clip durations by an equal number of frames, the length of the sequence doesn't change.

1 Continue working with the sequence 09 Ripple Edit.

2 Click and hold the Slip tool in the Tools panel to select the Slide tool.

3 Position the Slide tool over the middle of the second clip in the sequence, SHOT2.

4 Drag the clip left or right.

5 Take a look at the Program Monitor as you perform the slide edit.

The two top images are the In point and Out point of SHOT2, the clip you are dragging. They do not change because you are not changing the selected part of SHOT2. The two larger images are the Out point and In point of the previous and next clips. These edit points change as you slide the selected clip over those adjacent clips.

6 Try improving the timing for the shots in this sequence by sliding the clip contents.

When you have finished, select the Selection tool.

Trimming in the Program Monitor

If you'd like to trim with even more control, you can use the Program Monitor Trim mode. In this mode, Premiere displays both the outgoing and incoming frames of the trim you're working on and offers dedicated buttons for making precise adjustments.

When the Program Monitor is set to Trim mode, pressing the spacebar to play the sequence loops playback around the edit you have selected. This means you can continually adjust the timing of an edit and view the result immediately.

You can perform three types of trims using the Program Monitor Trim mode controls. You learned about each of these earlier in this lesson.

- **Regular trim:** This trim moves one edit point of the selected clip. This method trims only one side of the edit point. It moves the selected edit point either earlier or later in the sequence, but it doesn't shift any of the other clips.
- **Ripple trim:** Like the Regular trim, this trim moves one edit point of the selected clip either earlier or later. This method trims only one side of the edit point. Clips after the edit shift to close a gap or make room if trimming extends the clip.
- **Roll trim:** The roll trim moves the tail of one clip (the end) and the head of the adjacent clip (the beginning) in one step. It lets you adjust the timing of an edit point (provided there are handles). No gap is created, and the sequence duration doesn't change.

Accessing Trim mode in the Program Monitor

When the Program Monitor is in Trim mode, the controls change to make it easier to focus on trimming. To use Trim mode, you need to activate it by selecting an edit point between two clips. There are three ways to do this.

- Double-click an edit point (the left or right end of a clip) on the timeline with a selection tool or a trimming tool.
- With the correct Timeline panel track targeted (with a blue highlight), press Shift+T. The playhead will move to the nearest edit point.
- Drag around one or more edits using the Ripple Edit tool or Rolling Edit tool to select them.

Tip: You also can select edits and enter Trim mode by dragging a rectangle around them using the Selection tool if you hold Command (macOS) or Ctrl (Windows).

The Program Monitor Trim mode shows two video clips. The box on the left shows the outgoing clip (also called *A side*). The box on the right shows the incoming clip (also called *B side*). Below the frames are five additional buttons and two indicators.

- **A** **Out Shift Counter:** This shows how many frames the Out point for the A side has changed.
- **B** **Trim Backward Many:** This performs the selected type of trim, adjusting the A side earlier by five frames.
- **C** **Trim Backward:** This performs the selected type trim, adjusting by one frame earlier.
- **D** **Apply Default Transitions To Selection:** This applies the default transition effect to the selected edit point.
- **E** **Trim Forward:** This performs the selected type of trim, adjusting the edit one frame later.
- **F** **Trim Forward Many:** This is like the Trim Backward Many button except it adjusts the edit five frames later.
- **G** **In Shift Counter:** This shows how many frames the In point for the B side has changed.

Tip: By default, the Trim Backward Many and Trim Forward Many buttons will trim five frames. You can change this setting in the Premiere Preferences dialog box, under Trim.

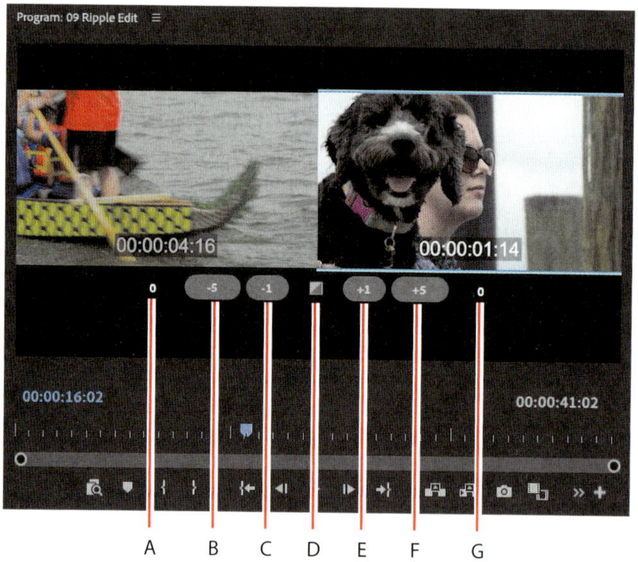

A Out Shift counter

B Trim Backward Many

C Trim Backward

D Apply Default Transitions To Selection

E Trim Forward

F Trim Forward Many

G In Shift Counter

Choosing a trimming method in the Program Monitor

You've already learned about the three types of trims (regular, roll, and ripple). Using Trim mode in the Program Monitor makes the process easier because it provides rich visual feedback. It also provides subtle control when dragging, regardless of the Timeline panel view scale: Even if the Timeline panel is zoomed a long way out, you'll still be able to make frame-accurate trim adjustments by dragging inside the Program Monitor while in Trim mode. Let's try this.

1 Open the sequence 10 Trim Mode. Play the sequence to familiarize yourself with the timing of the edits.

2 With the Selection tool (keyboard shortcut V), hold down Option (macOS) or Alt (Windows) and double-click the video edit between the first video clip and the second video clip in the sequence. Holding this modifier key overrides Linked Selection, so you can select just the video edit and leave the audio tracks untouched.

The Program Monitor switches to Trim mode.

Note: Clicking the A or B side switches which side is being trimmed. Clicking in the center switches to a rolling edit.

3 In the Program Monitor, hover the pointer over the A and B (left and right) clip images (but don't click).

As you move the pointer from left to right, you'll see the tool change from Trim Out (left side) to Roll (center) to Trim In (right).

4 Now drag in between both clips in the Program Monitor to perform a rolling edit trim.

Adjust the timing until the A-side source clip timecode overlay on the lower-left side of the Program Monitor frame reads 01:54:08:13 and the overlay on the B-side clip image reads 01:26:59:01.

5 Press the Down Arrow key three times to jump between edits until you have selected the edit between the third and fourth clips (the cut in the audio track counts as one jump because that track also has targeting turned on).

The shot before the edit plays too long and shows the actor beginning to sit down, which is repeated in the next shot.

When you drag in the Program Monitor to trim, the color of the tool indicates the type of trim you'll perform. Red indicates a regular trim, and yellow indicates a ripple trim.

You can quickly change the trim type by holding Command (macOS) or Ctrl (Windows) and clicking one of the images in the Program Monitor. After clicking, you may need to move the pointer in order for the color of the tool to update.

Tip: If the pointer does not change color when you Command-click (macOS) or Ctrl-click (Windows), you can always check the color of the clips handles in the Timeline panel to see which trim mode you have selected.

6 Command-click (macOS) or Ctrl-click (Windows) one of the images in the Program Monitor until the Trim tool pointer turns yellow. This indicates that you've selected the Ripple Trim tool.

7 Drag to the left on the outgoing clip (on the left side of the Program Monitor) to make the clip shorter.

Make sure the time display on the left reads 01:54:12:18, and stay in Trim mode in the Program Monitor.

▶ **Tip:** When you're ready to leave Trim mode, click an empty track in the Timeline panel.

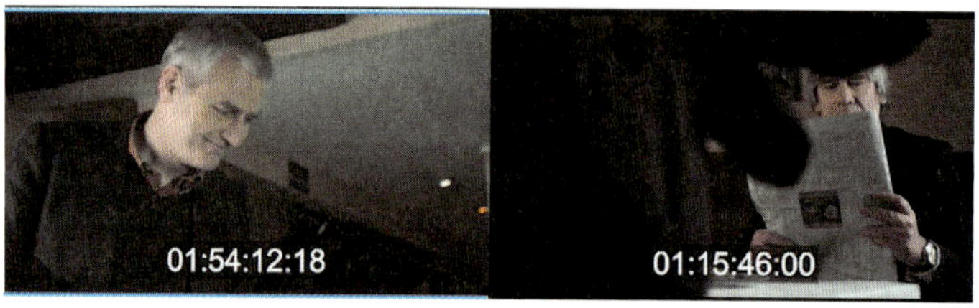

8 Play the edit by pressing the spacebar. While the Program Monitor is in Trim mode, playback loops over the edit to allow you to review it.

Modifier keys

You can use modifier keys to make precise selections before trimming.

- Hold Option (macOS) or Alt (Windows) when selecting clips to temporarily ignore Linked Selection between audio and video clip segments in a sequence. (You can also disable Linked Selection by clicking the button in the Timeline panel.)
- Hold Shift to select multiple edit points. You can trim multiple tracks or even multiple clips at the same time. Wherever you see a trim "handle," adjustments will be made when you apply a trim.
- You can combine the Shift and Option/Alt modifier keys to make advanced clip selections for trimming.
- Hold Command (macOS) or Ctrl (Windows) and drag from an empty track area across multiple edit points to select them.

Performing dynamic trimming

Much of the trimming work you perform will be to adjust the pace and rhythm of an edit. In many ways, perfecting the timing of a cut is the point at which the craft of editing becomes the art.

Because playback using the spacebar will loop in Trim mode, it's easier to get a feel for the timing of an edit. You can also trim using keyboard shortcuts or buttons while the sequence plays back in real time.

1 Continue working with the sequence 10 Trim Mode.

2 Press the Down Arrow key to move to the next video edit point, between the fourth and fifth video clips. Set the trim type to a rolling trim by clicking in the middle of the Program Monitor between the two frames.

The trim handles in the Timeline panel change to indicate a rolling edit.

3 Press the spacebar to loop playback.

You'll see a playback loop lasting a few seconds, showing the shot before the cut (*pre-roll*) and after the cut (*post-roll*). This should help you get a feel for the timing of the edit.

4 Try adjusting the trim using the methods you've learned while the playback continues to loop.

You can use the Trim Forward and Trim Backward buttons at the bottom of the Program Monitor to adjust the edit during playback.

5 Click Stop or press the spacebar to stop the playback loop. Now let's try using the keyboard for more dynamic control. The same J, K, and L keys you use to control playback can also be used to control trimming, as long as the Program Monitor is in Trim mode.

6 Press the L key to shuttle the trim to the right.

Pressing once trims in real time. You can tap the L key multiple times to trim faster.

If you are in Regular Trim mode and trimming a clip extends to the next clip, the trim will be blocked. If you are in Ripple Trim mode, clips will move to accommodate the new clip duration.

These clips are quite short, so you'll reach the end quickly. Let's refine and trim with a little more precision.

7 Press the K key to stop trimming.

8 Hold down the K key and press the J key to shuttle left in slow motion.

9 Release both keys to stop the trim.

10 Exit Trim mode by clicking an empty track in the Timeline panel.

Tip: To adjust the pre-roll and post-roll durations, open the Premiere Preferences and select the Playback category. You can set the duration in seconds.

Note: Timeline panel clip segments update after you press K to stop dynamic trimming.

Trimming with the keyboard

Here are some of the most useful keyboard shortcuts to use when trimming. If you have a color-coded keyboard, it's easier to remember which key is which.

MACOS	WINDOWS
Trim Backward: Option+Left Arrow	**Trim Backward:** Ctrl+Left Arrow
Trim Backward Many: Shift+Option+Left Arrow	**Trim Backward Many:** Shift+Ctrl+Left Arrow
Trim Forward: Option+Right Arrow	**Trim Forward:** Ctrl+Right Arrow
Trim Forward Many: Shift+Option+Right Arrow	**Trim Forward Many:** Shift+Ctrl+Right Arrow
Slide Clip Selection Left Five Frames: Shift+Option+, (comma)	**Slide Clip Selection Left Five Frames:** Shift+Alt+, (comma)
Slide Clip Selection Left One Frame: Option+, (comma)	**Slide Clip Selection Left One Frame:** Alt+, (comma)
Slide Clip Selection Right Five Frames: Shift+Option+. (period)	**Slide Clip Selection Right Five Frames:** Shift+Alt+. (period)
Slide Clip Selection Right One Frame: Option+. (period)	**Slide Clip Selection Right One Frame:** Alt+. (period)
Slip Clip Selection Left Five Frames: Shift+Command+Option+Left Arrow	**Slip Clip Selection Left Five Frames:** Shift+Ctrl+Alt+Left Arrow
Slip Clip Selection Left One Frame: Command+Option+Left Arrow	**Slip Clip Selection Left One Frame:** Ctrl+Alt+Left Arrow
Slip Clip Selection Right Five Frames: Shift+Command+Option+Right Arrow	**Slip Clip Selection Right Five Frames:** Shift+Ctrl+Alt+Right Arrow
Slip Clip Selection Right One Frame: Command+Option+Right Arrow	**Slip Clip Selection Right One Frame:** Ctrl+Alt+Right Arrow

Review questions

1 If you change the playback speed of a clip to 50% using the Clip Speed/Duration dialog box, what effect will this have on the clip duration?

2 Which tool allows you to stretch a sequence clip to change its playback speed?

3 What's the difference between a slide edit and a slip edit?

4 What is the difference between replacing a sequence clip and replacing footage?

Review answers

1 The clip will be twice as long. Reducing a clip's speed results in the clip playing for longer, unless the Speed and Duration parameters are unlinked in the Clip Speed/Duration dialog box or the clip is blocked by another clip.

2 The Rate Stretch tool allows you to adjust playback speed as if you were trimming. This is useful when you need to fill a small extra amount of time in a sequence or shorten a clip just a little.

3 You slide a clip over adjacent clips, retaining the selected clip's original In and Out points. You slip a clip under adjacent clips (or roll the contents like a conveyor belt), changing the selected clip's In and Out points.

4 Replacing a sequence clip replaces that single instance of the clip in the sequence with a new clip from the Project panel. Replacing footage replaces a clip in the Project panel with a new source clip. Any instance of the clip in any sequence in the project is replaced. In both cases, effects that were applied to the clip that is replaced are maintained.

9 PUTTING CLIPS IN MOTION

Lesson overview

In this lesson, you'll learn how to do the following:

- Adjust the Motion effect for clips.
- Change clip size and add rotation.
- Adjust the anchor point to refine rotation.
- Work with keyframe interpolation.
- Automatically reframe content for different aspect ratios.

This lesson will take about 75 minutes to complete. To get the files used in this lesson, refer to the instructions in "Accessing the lesson files and Web Edition" in the "Getting Started" section at the beginning of this book. Store the files on your computer in a convenient location.

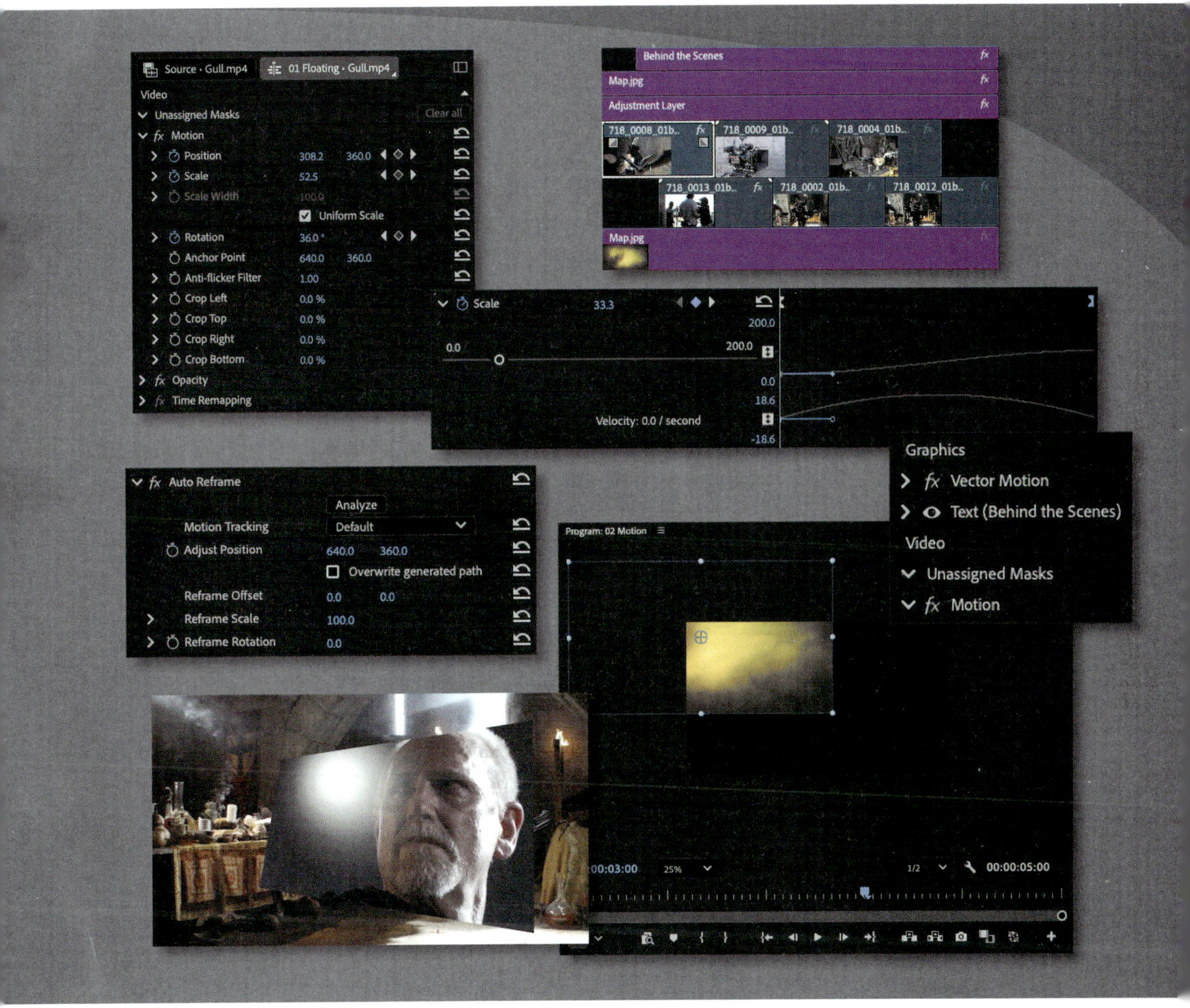

The Motion effect controls can add movement to a clip. You can animate a graphic or resize and reposition a video clip within the frame. You can animate an object's position using keyframes and enhance that animation by controlling the way those keyframes are interpreted.

Starting the lesson

Note: To ensure that the tools function and the defaults are set exactly as described in this lesson, reset the Premiere preferences by holding any modifier key (such as Shift) while launching the application, selecting Reset App Preferences, and then clicking Continue in the Reset Options dialog box.

Video projects are often motion graphics–oriented, and it's common to see multiple shots combined as complex multilayered compositions. These layers are often put into motion. Perhaps you'll see multiple video clips streaming past in floating boxes, or you'll see a video clip shrunk down and placed next to an on-camera host. You can create those effects (and many more) using the Motion effect in the Effect Controls panel, the Transform and Crop settings in the Properties panel, or a number of other clip-based effects that offer Motion settings.

The Motion effect allows you to position, rotate, or change the size of a clip within the frame. Some adjustments can be made directly in the Program Monitor. The Effect Controls panel displays controls for only one selected clip at a time. That clip could be a segment in a sequence or a clip opened in the Source Monitor.

You can animate effect settings over time using keyframes. A *keyframe* is a special kind of marker that stores settings at a particular point in time. If you use two (or more) keyframes with different settings, the settings automatically animate over time. For example, you could animate the Position setting to have a graphic move across the screen. You can apply subtle adjustments to the timing of animation using different types of keyframes.

Most settings for most visual effects can be *keyframed*—that is, animated using keyframes.

Adjusting the Motion effect

Tip: If you expand or collapse the settings for the fixed effects, the settings will remain expanded or collapsed for all clips.

Tip: Because you have been saving projects with new names while working on them, you can go back to earlier lessons and experiment again with a fresh copy of the original project file.

Tip: Click the Name heading in the Project panel to sort items in alphanumeric order.

Every visual clip segment in a Premiere sequence has certain effects applied automatically. These are referred to as *fixed effects* (also sometimes called *intrinsic effects*), and the Motion effect is one of them.

To adjust a clip's Motion effect, select the clip in a sequence and look in the Effect Controls panel. Expand the Motion effect to adjust the settings.

Most of the settings available in the Motion effect are also available in the Properties panel, including keyframing. Keyframing is a little easier and clearer to configure in the Effect Controls panel, so you'll begin there.

The Motion effect allows you to adjust the position, scale, or rotation of a clip. Let's look at the way this effect has been used to reposition a clip in a sequence.

1. Open Lesson 09.prproj in the Lessons folder.
2. Choose Window > Workspaces > Effects. Reset the workspace.
3. Save the project as **Lesson 09 Working.prproj**.
4. If it's not already open, open the sequence 01 Floating. This simple sequence has just one clip in it (Gull.mp4).

5 Make sure Fit is chosen from the Select Zoom Level menu in the Program Monitor.

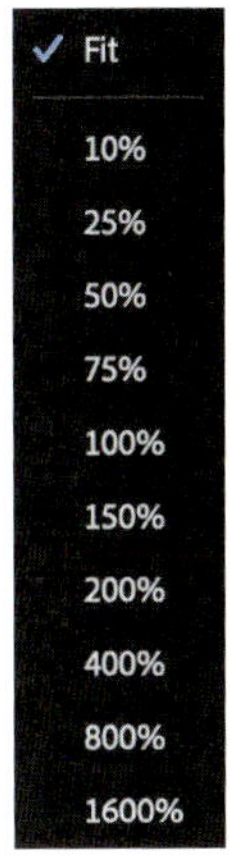

> **Tip:** You can change the zoom level in the Source Monitor and Program Monitor by hovering over the frame and scrolling. To quickly restore the Zoom Level setting to Fit, set a keyboard shortcut for View > Magnification > Fit.

It's important to see the whole composition when setting up visual effects. This menu does not change the contents of the sequence, only the way the contents are viewed. It can be helpful to zoom in or out to see fine details in an image or set up effects, but generally you will want to keep this menu set to Fit.

6 Play the sequence.

This clip's Position, Scale, and Rotation settings have been animated using keyframes added to the Motion effect. The keyframes have different settings at various points in time, so the clip animates into the frame.

Understanding Motion settings

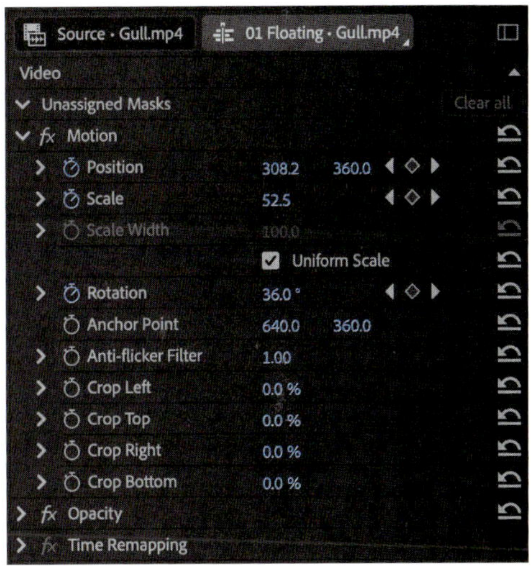

Though these controls are called Motion, there's no movement until you configure them. By default, clips are positioned in the center of the Program Monitor, at their original scale. Make sure the Effect Controls panel is visible (click the panel's name if it's hidden) and single-click the clip in the sequence now to select it. If necessary, click the chevron next to Motion in the Video Effects section of the Effect Controls panel to display the available settings.

Here are the settings:

- **Position:** This places the clip along the x-axis (horizontal) and y-axis (vertical). The position is calculated based on the location of an anchor point, which is at the center of the image by default, measured from the upper-left corner of the clip image. For example, the default position for a 1280×720 clip would be 640, 360 (halfway across, and halfway down the image). You'll learn more about anchor points later in this lesson.
- **Scale (including Scale Height, when Uniform Scale is deselected):** Clips are set to their full original size by default (100%). To shrink a clip, reduce this number. You can scale up to 10,000%—though be warned, scaling up will make images pixelated and soft.
- **Scale Width:** Deselect Uniform Scale to make Scale Width available. This lets you change the clip width and height independently.

- **Rotation:** You can rotate an image in a flat spin (as if viewing a spinning turntable or carousel from above). You can enter degrees or a number of rotations. For example, 450° is the same as 1x90 (one full 360° turn plus an additional 90°). Positive numbers result in clockwise rotation, and negative numbers result in counterclockwise rotation.

Note: The anchor point position can be animated using keyframes, just like every other Motion control.

Tip: If the Effect Controls panel is too narrow, some of the controls will overlap or be hidden. Resize the panel as necessary before working on effect settings.

- **Anchor Point:** Rotation, Position, and Scale adjustments are all based on the anchor point, which is at the center of a clip image by default. You can change this to any point, including one of the clip's corners or even a point outside the clip image.

  For example, if you set the anchor point to the corner of the clip, when you adjust the Rotation setting, the clip will rotate around that corner rather than around the center of the image. If you change the anchor point in relation to the image, you may have to reposition the clip in the frame to compensate for the adjustment.

- **Anti-flicker Filter:** This feature is useful for interlaced video clips and for images that contain high detail, such as fine lines, hard edges, or parallel lines (which can cause moiré effects). Such high-detail images sometimes flicker during motion. To add some blurring and reduce flicker, set this to 1.00.
- **Crop:** The Crop Left, Top, Right, and Bottom controls will remove pixels from the edge of the clip.

When to use the Properties panel

Many of the controls available in the Effect Controls panel are repeated in the Properties panel. In fact, if you adjust one, you'll adjust both because controls with the same name are connected.

The Properties panel has a more limited selection of controls and will not display settings for additional effects you apply to clips, like color correction adjustments or a blur.

Still, there is one feature that really makes the Properties panel stand out: You can select multiple clips and make adjustments to them all in a single step using the Properties panel.

In contrast, the Effect Controls panel will allow you to make adjustments to one selected clip at a time.

The Properties panel has a button to turn on keyframing for quick animation adjustment, while the Effect Controls panel gives full control of keyframe animation.

You'll probably find it best to learn the controls in the Effect Controls panel first, because then you'll immediately recognize the options in the Properties panel and know when to use them.

Let's look closer at the animated clip. Continue working with the sequence 01 Floating.

1 Click the clip in the Timeline panel once to make sure it is selected.

2 Make sure the Effect Controls panel is visible. It should be in the same panel group as the Source Monitor, but if you can't find it, look for it in the Window menu.

3 Still in the Effect Controls panel, if the integrated timeline is not visible, click the Show/Hide Timeline View button at the upper-right corner of the panel to open it.

The timeline in the Effect Controls panel displays keyframes.

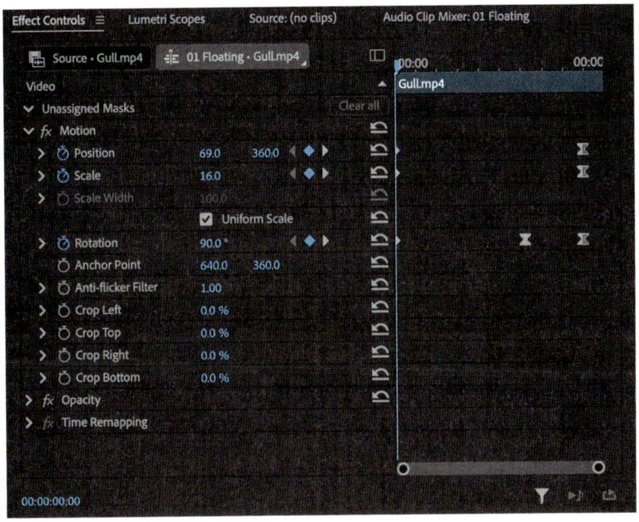

4 Each setting control has its own keyframes. Click the Go To Previous Keyframe or Go To Next Keyframe arrows to jump between existing keyframes for a particular control.

Every effect and each individual control also has its own Reset button. If you reset the whole effect, every control returns to its default state at the time where your playhead is positioned. If animation is turned on for the control, this adds a keyframe with the default setting at the current time (existing keyframes are not removed).

Tip: It can be difficult to line up the playhead with an existing keyframe. Using the Previous/Next Keyframe buttons can help you avoid adding extra unwanted keyframes.

5 Drag the playhead left and right in the Effect Controls panel timeline to see the way the position of the keyframe markers relates to the animation.

Now that you know how to view the settings for an existing animation, let's begin by resetting the clip.

Note: When the Toggle Animation button is on, clicking the Reset button will not change existing keyframes unless the playhead is currently aligned with one. Instead, a new keyframe will be added with a default setting. It's important to turn off animation before resetting the effect to avoid this.

6 Animation is turned on for any setting that has a blue Toggle Animation stopwatch button. When the stopwatch is gray, animation is turned off. Click the stopwatch for the Position property to turn off its keyframes.

   The position keyframes will be removed and the current setting will be applied to the whole clip.

7 Because the setting already has some keyframes, a warning message lets you know they will be deleted if you continue.

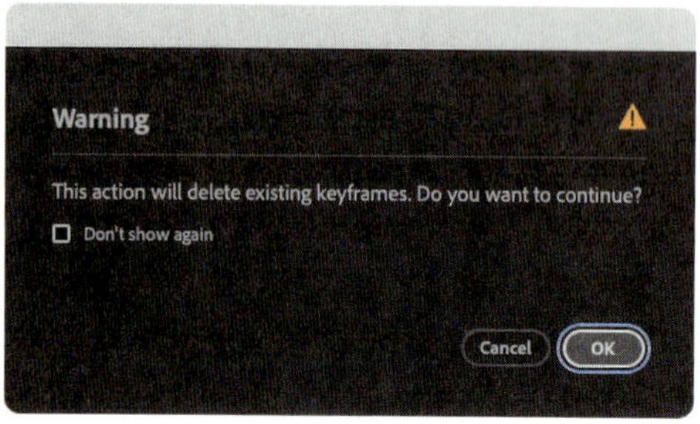

   Click OK to continue.

8 Turn off keyframes for the Scale and Rotation properties in the same way.

9 Click the Reset Effect button to the right of the Motion effect heading in the Effect Controls panel.

   Now the Motion settings are all set to their default values, and the clip no longer animates on-screen.

Exploring Motion settings

Tip: You may find it easier to work with the Motion effect in the Program Monitor if you expand the panel to fill the screen (double-click the Program Monitor panel name).

The Position, Scale, and Rotation properties are spatial. The changes you make to these settings are easy to see because the object will change in size and position. You can adjust these settings by entering numerical values, by using the scrubbable numbers (drag on the blue numbers), or by dragging the Transform controls.

1 Open the sequence 02 Motion.

2 In the Program Monitor, set the zoom level to 25% or any zoom amount that allows you to see space around the active frame.

   Setting the zoom small like this makes it easier to position items outside the sequence's frame.

   Scrub the Timeline panel playhead over the video clip so you can see the contents in the Program Monitor.

3 Click the clip in the sequence once to select it and to display its settings in the Effect Controls panel.

4 In the Effect Controls panel, click the Motion effect name to select it. This highlights the effect heading in gray.

When you select the Motion effect name, a bounding box with a crosshair and handles appears around the clip in the Program Monitor.

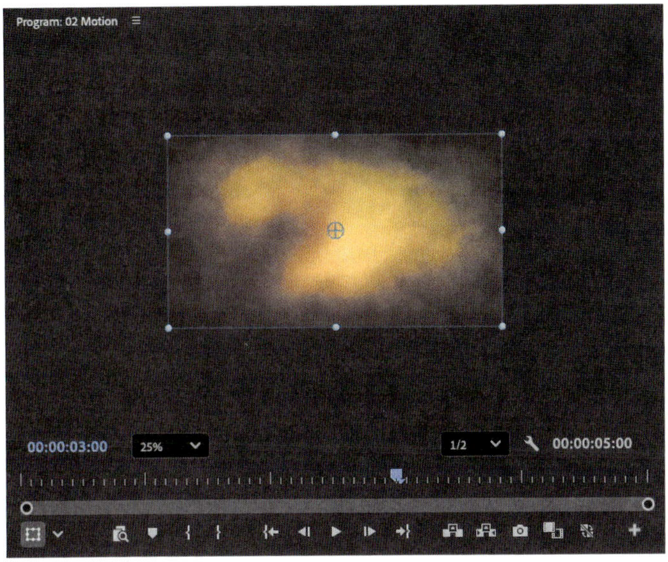

Note: Several effects, like the Motion effect, allow you to use direct manipulation in the Program Monitor when you select the effect heading.

5 Click inside the clip bounding box in the Program Monitor, avoiding the circular crosshair  in the center (that's the anchor point).

This makes the Program Monitor the active panel, which enables menu items associated with it.

6 Open the View menu and make sure that the Snap In Program Monitor option is on (checked). If it's not, choose the option now.

7 Drag the clip down and to the right so that it's partially out of the frame, with the anchor point aligned with the lower-right corner of the frame.

While dragging, the clip edges and anchor point will snap to the edges of the frame and guides will appear.

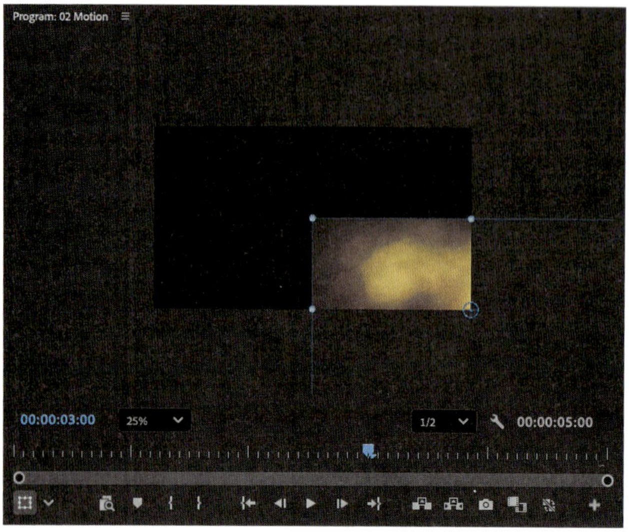

In the Effect Controls panel, the Position control values update as you move the clip.

8 Now position the clip so that it's *almost* centered in the upper-left corner of the screen but not quite—keep the clip slightly away from the center of the frame.

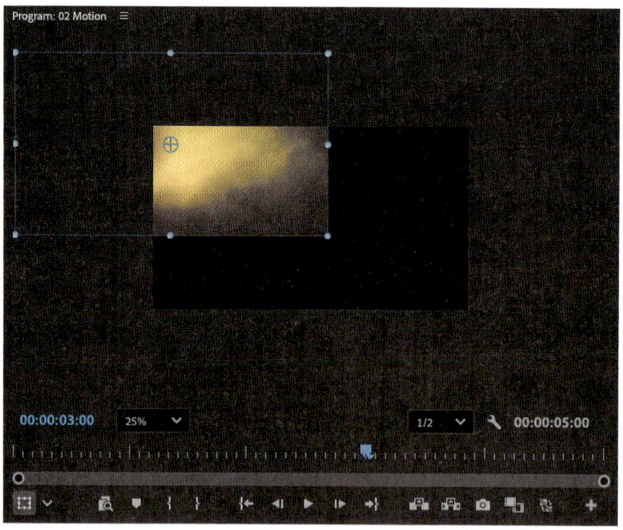

This is difficult to do! With snapping turned on in the Program Monitor, any items moved close to an edge will snap to that edge.

The anchor point is used for the Position, Rotation, and Scale settings. Be careful not to click the anchor point control when repositioning a clip in the frame or you'll move it in relation to the image.

Note: When positioning items, the upper-left corner of the frame is 0 x-axis and 0 y-axis. All x and y values to the left of the frame or above the top of the frame are negative values. All other values are positive.

Tip: You can temporarily activate or deactivate snapping in the Program Monitor by holding Command (macOS) or Ctrl (Windows).

The Position settings in the Effect Controls panel should now be close to 0, 0. You can click the numbers and type **0** into each Position field to exactly position the clip on-screen.

This is a 1280×720 sequence, so the position at the lower-right corner of the screen is 1280, 720. The middle of the screen is 640, 360.

9 In the Effect Controls panel, click the Reset button for the Motion effect to restore the clip to its default position.

10 Scrub the blue number for the Rotation value in the Effect Controls panel. As you scrub left or right, the control updates and the clip rotates.

11 Click the Reset button for the Motion effect to restore the clip to its default position.

Tip: Hold Shift while scrubbing numbers, and they'll change 10 times faster. Hold Command (macOS) or Ctrl (Windows), and they'll change 10 times slower, allowing more precise adjustment.

Changing clip position, size, and rotation

The Motion effect can combine multiple independent settings changes. In the next example, you'll build an intro segment for a behind-the-scenes featurette adjusting Motion settings for multiple clips in a sequence.

Changing position

Let's begin by using keyframes to animate the position of a layer. For this exercise, the first thing you'll do is change the clip position. The picture will begin offscreen and then move fully across the screen from left to right.

1 Open the sequence 03 Montage. Scrub through the sequence to get familiar with the content.

The sequence has several tracks, some of which have their output turned off. You'll use those tracks later.

2 Position the Timeline panel playhead at the start of the sequence.

3 Set the Program Monitor zoom level to Fit.

4 Click once to select the first video clip on track V3. You might want to make the track taller to see the thumbnails more clearly.

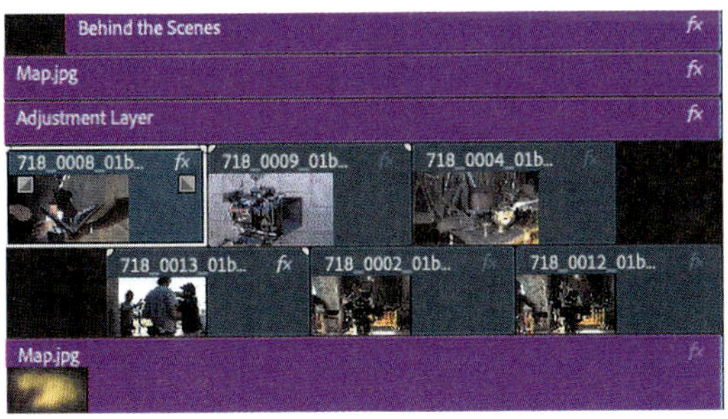

Once the clip is selected, its effect controls appear in the Effect Controls panel, with Transform and Crop controls appearing in the Properties panel.

5 In the Effect Controls panel, click the Toggle Animation stopwatch button for Position (the icon should turn blue). This turns on keyframing for that setting and automatically adds a keyframe at the current playhead position, visible in the Effect Controls panel. The keyframe icon is partially obscured because it's applied to the first frame of the clip.

   Now that animation is turned on for Position; whenever you change the setting, Premiere will automatically add a keyframe at the playhead's current position.

6 The Position control has two numbers. They are the values for the x-axis and the y-axis. Click the blue number and enter a Position setting of **–640** for the x-axis value (the first number) as a starting position.

   The clip moves offscreen to the left, revealing the contents of the V1 and V2 tracks below. Track V2 is empty at the current playhead position, so the clip Map.jpg on V1 fills the frame.

7 Drag the playhead to the last frame of the selected clip (00:00:04:23). You can do this in the Timeline panel or in the Effect Controls panel.

8 Enter **1920** for the x-axis position. The clip is now positioned off the right edge of the screen, and a second keyframe has been added to the Position setting.

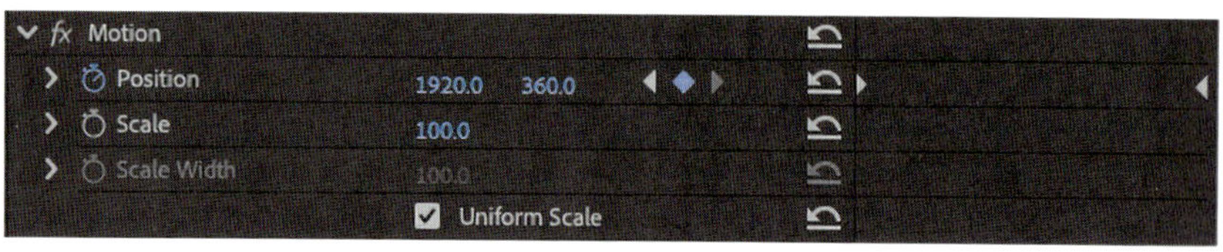

9 Play the first part of the sequence to see the clip animate from off-screen left to off-screen right. As it moves, the clip on the V2 track is revealed, but then the second clip on V3 appears suddenly. You'll animate this clip and others next.

Reusing Motion settings

Now that you've applied keyframes with new settings to a clip, you can save time by reusing those settings on other clips. Applying effects from a clip to one or more other clips is as easy as copying and pasting. In the following example, you'll apply the left-to-right floating animation you configured to other clips in the sequence.

There are several methods for reusing effects. Let's try one now.

1 In the Timeline panel, make sure the clip you just animated is still selected. It's the first clip on V3.

2 Choose Edit > Copy, or press Command+C (macOS) or Ctrl+C (Windows).

   The clip, with its effects and settings, is now temporarily stored on your computer's clipboard.

3 With the Selection tool (keyboard shortcut V), beginning on the background of the Timeline panel, drag from the right across the five other clips on the V2 and V3 tracks (you may need to zoom out a little to see all the clips). This selects the clips, but the selection should not include the first video clip.

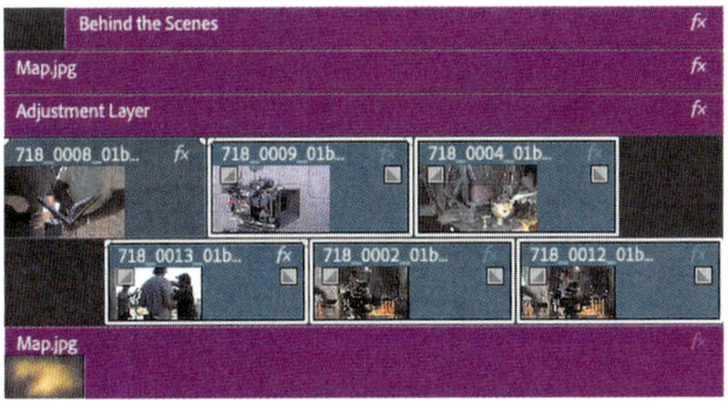

4 Choose Edit > Paste Attributes.

   The Paste Attributes dialog box opens, letting you selectively apply effects and keyframes copied from another clip.

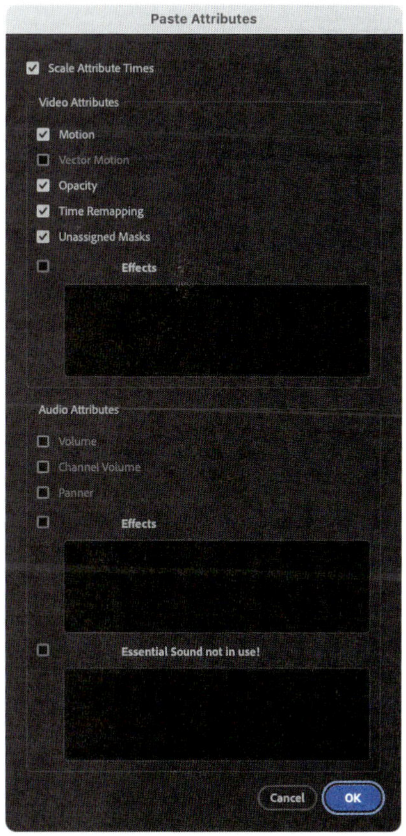

5 For the purposes of this exercise, leave the checkboxes with their default values and click OK.

   You can have only one set of fixed effects, so pasting settings from another clip will replace any existing adjustments that you may have made. You should ordinarily review the available options in the Paste Attributes dialog box carefully before clicking OK.

   Tip: As an alternative to copying a whole clip in the Timeline panel, you can always select one or more specific effect headings in the Effect Controls panel. Command-click (macOS) or Ctrl-click (Windows) to select multiple effects and choose Edit > Copy. You can then select another clip (or clips) and choose Edit > Paste to paste the selected effects, with their current settings, onto other clips.

6 Play the sequence to see the result.

Adding rotation and changing the anchor point

Moving clips around the screen can be effective, but you can really bring things to life by combining multiple animated properties. Let's start with Rotation.

The Rotation property revolves a clip around its anchor point. By default, the anchor point is in the center of the clip image. However, you can change the relationship between the anchor point and the image for more interesting animation.

Let's add some rotation to a clip.

1. In the Timeline panel, click the Toggle Track Output button for V6 to make it visible. The one clip on the track is a title graphic that reads *Behind the Scenes*.

   This clip is a title graphic created in Premiere, using vector-based design tools. This means it can be scaled to any size and will always look sharp, with smooth curves and no pixelation. Vector graphics are treated the same way as non-vector graphics; you can use the same controls, effects, and adjustments.

2. Move the playhead to the first frame of the graphic clip (00:00:01:13). Try holding the Shift key while you scrub with the Timeline panel time ruler to do this—the playhead will snap to the ends of clips.

3. Select the graphic clip in the sequence. The clip's effect controls appear in the Effect Controls panel.

   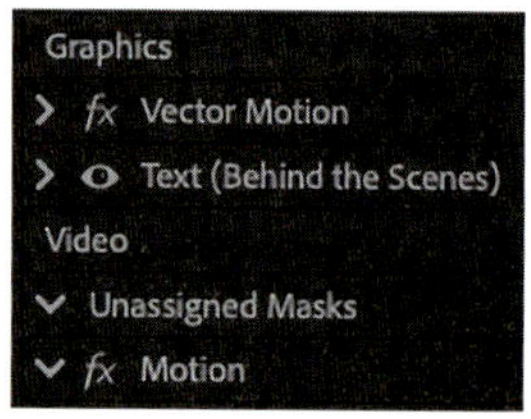

   Because this is a vector graphic, there are two types of Motion effects available:

   - **Graphics—Vector Motion:** Treats the contents of the graphic as vectors, allowing you to scale up the image and retain clean lines without pixelation.
   - **Video—Motion:** Treats the contents of the graphic as pixels. When you scale up, the pixels will increase in size, producing jagged edges and softening the image. Believe it or not, there may be a time that you want to achieve exactly this effect!

   Every graphic and text layer created in Premiere appears (with full properties) in the Effect Controls panel. This graphic has just one layer, Text (Behind the Scenes), and you can see it under the Vector Motion effect.

4. In the Effect Controls panel, select the Vector Motion effect heading (not the regular Motion effect) to display the anchor point and bounding-box controls in the Program Monitor. Notice the position of the anchor point, a small circle with a cross, in the center of the title.

   Let's adjust the Rotation property in the Effect Controls panel and see the effect it has.

5 Click the chevron to reveal the Vector Motion effect controls, and enter a value of **90.0** in the Rotation field. Press Return (macOS) or Enter (Windows).

The title rotates in the center of the screen.

6 Choose Edit > Undo.

7 Make sure the Vector Motion settings heading is still selected in the Effect Controls panel.

8 In the Program Monitor, drag the anchor point until the crosshair sits in the upper-left corner of the letter *B* in the first word.

The Position property and Anchor Point property control similar but separate settings:

- The Anchor Point settings control the position of the anchor point in relation to the original clip image.
- The Position settings in the Effect Controls panel control the location of the anchor point in relation to the sequence frame.

The clip image position within the frame follows the anchor point, so when you reposition the anchor point, the clip position will update.

Now that you have moved the anchor point in the image, both the Anchor Point and Position properties have been updated in the Effect Controls panel.

Note: The Position settings update automatically when you reposition the anchor point in the Program Monitor. If you change the Anchor Point property in the Effect Controls panel, you will need to adjust the Position property separately.

9 In the Vector Motion effect settings, click the Animation stopwatch button for Rotation to turn on animation. This adds a keyframe for the Rotation setting automatically.

10 Set the rotation to **90.0**, and press Return/Enter. This updates the keyframe you just added.

11 Move the playhead forward to 00:00:06:00, and click the reset button for the Rotation property (returning it to the default setting of 0.0). This adds another keyframe automatically.

12 Play the sequence to see your animation.

With careful positioning (or even animation) of anchor points, you can achieve advanced animation effects using the Motion or Vector Motion effects.

Just by setting different rotation values for the two keyframes you added, you animated the title.

Changing clip size

There are a few approaches you might take to changing the size of items in a sequence. By default, items added to a sequence are displayed at 100% of their original size. If a clip image size does not match the sequence frame size, it may be cropped by the edge of the sequence frame, or there may be space around it.

There are several ways to adjust clip image size in a sequence:

- In the Effect Controls panel, adjust the Scale property of the Video > Motion effect or Graphics > Vector Motion effect.
- Right-click the clip in the sequence and choose Fit To Frame. This automatically adjusts the Scale property of the Video > Motion effect to fit the clip fully in the frame. The Scale property remains fully adjustable.
- Right-click the clip in the sequence and choose Fill Frame. This automatically adjusts the Scale property of the Video > Motion effect to fit the clip in the frame so that the shortest dimension spans the frame, cropping the longer dimension if necessary.
- Right-click the clip in the sequence and choose Scale To Frame Size. This has a similar result to the Fit To Frame option, but Premiere resamples the image at the new (often lower) resolution. If you scale back up now using the Motion > Scale setting, the image might look soft, even if the original clip was very high resolution.
- You can also select Scale To Frame Size or Fit To Frame automatically by choosing Premiere > Settings > Media > Default Media Scaling (macOS) or Edit > Preferences > Media > Default Media Scaling (Windows). The setting is applied to assets as you import them (but won't change assets you have already imported).
- In the Properties panel, adjust the Scale setting or click the Fill or Fit buttons.

Let's try this.

1 Open the sequence 04 Scale.

2 Scrub through the sequence to view the clips.

The second and third clips on the V1 track are much larger than the first clip—and the sequence frame size. They are dramatically cropped by the edge of the frame.

Tip: To see the full contents of a clip, set the Source Monitor Zoom level to Fit.

3 To view the original full image frame at 100% resolution, move the Timeline playhead over the last clip in the sequence on the V1 track. Click to select the clip, and press the F key or choose Sequence > Match Frame to open the clip in the Source Monitor at its original resolution.

The Match Frame command is a useful shortcut to locate a precise frame in a source clip that you are viewing in a sequence.

4 In the Timeline panel, right-click the clip and choose Scale To Frame Size.

This conveniently scales and resamples the image to fit the sequence resolution. However, there's an issue: The clip is full DCI standard 4K, with a resolution of 4096×2160, and that is not a perfect 16:9 image. What is often referred to as 4K is actually ultra-high definition (UHD), a slightly different frame size standard with the dimensions 3840×2160 and a 16:9 aspect ratio.

This clip doesn't fit the aspect ratio of the sequence, and thin black bars are introduced at the top and bottom of the image. These bars are often called *letterboxing*. To see the bars more clearly, try choosing Transparency Grid from the Settings menu in the Program Monitor to give the image a transparent background.

This is a common outcome when working with content that has a different aspect ratio than your sequence.

5. Right-click the clip and choose Fit To Frame. This seems to achieve the same result, but now the change has been achieved by modifying the Scale setting—and you can modify it further in the Effect Controls panel.

   Choosing Fit To Frame automatically deselects Scale To Frame Size.

> **Note:** Not all settings in the Effect Controls panel indicate if they are pixels, percentages, or degrees. This can take a little getting used to, but you'll find the controls for each setting do make sense with experience.

6. With the clip selected, open the Effect Controls panel. The Scale setting has been automatically changed to 31.3% to fit the image in the sequence frame.

   You could now use the Scale control to adjust the clip's image size until it fits the sequence frame without showing letterboxing, but there's a quicker way.

7. Right-click the clip and choose Fill Frame.

   The image now fills the frame with no letterboxing. To achieve this, while keeping the original aspect ratio, Premiere crops the sides of the image by the edge of the frame.

   Choosing Fit To Frame will automatically adjust the Scale setting so that the *longest* edge of the clip fills the frame. Choosing Fill Frame adjusts the Scale setting so that the *shortest* edge fills the frame.

When clip and sequence aspect ratios don't match, you'll have to choose how to resolve the mismatch: letterboxing, *pillarboxing* (black bars at the sides), cropping, or changing the aspect ratio of the image by deselecting the Uniform Scale option in the Effect Controls panel.

Animating clip size changes

In the previous example, the clip image had a different aspect ratio compared to the sequence.

Now try another example; this time you'll animate the adjustment.

1. Position the Timeline playhead over the first frame of the second clip in the 04 Scale sequence, at 00:00:05:00.

This clip is 3840×2160-pixel UHD, which is the same image aspect ratio (shape) as the sequence, which is 1280×720 (16:9). It's also the same aspect ratio as full HD, at 1920×1080. This makes shooting UHD content convenient if you intend to mix media sources.

2 Select the clip, and look in the Effect Controls panel. The scale setting is 100%.

3 Right-click the clip in the Timeline panel and choose Fit To Frame.

In the Effect Controls panel, the Scale setting changes to 33.3% to fit the image in the sequence frame. You now know you can scale this clip between 33.3% and 100% and maintain quality (without magnifying pixels), while still filling the frame.

4 In the Effect Controls panel, turn on keyframing for the Scale control by clicking the Toggle Animation button.

5 Position the playhead over the last frame of the clip.

6 Click the Reset button for the Scale setting in the Effect Controls panel.

7 Scrub through the clip to see the result.

This creates an animated zoom effect for the clip. Because the clip never scales to more than 100%, it maintains full quality.

This clip includes motion, and it already looks like the ground is coming up to meet the camera.

8 Try reversing the timing of the keyframes, so the first keyframe sets Scale to 100% and the second keyframe sets Scale to 33.3%. To switch the settings, drag the keyframes to each other's positions in the Effect Controls panel timeline or change the settings for each keyframe in their current positions.

The result is reminiscent of the famous Dolly Zoom effect.

9 Use the Undo command to restore the timing, with the clip starting at 33.3% and animating to 100%. It's safe to experiment with effect configuration, because you can always undo to restore a recent setup.

10 Turn on Track Output for the V2 track.

This track has an adjustment layer clip on it. Adjustment layers apply effects to all footage on lower video tracks.

11 Select the Adjustment Layer clip in the Timeline panel to display its settings in the Effect Controls panel.

A Brightness & Contrast effect has been added. You'll learn more about adjustment layers in Lesson 12, "Adding Video Effects."

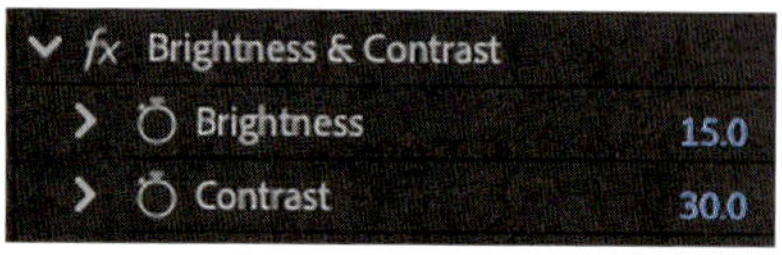

12 Play the sequence.

Filtering Effect Controls panel properties

If you have applied lots of effects to a clip and made several adjustments to specific controls, you might have a long list of headings and controls to navigate in the Effect Controls panel.

At the lower-right corner of the Effect Controls panel you can use the Filter Properties menu to reduce the number of items displayed, making it easier to navigate the controls you are using.

There are three options that you can choose:

- **Show All Properties:** This is the default option—all effects and controls are displayed.
- **Show Only Keyframed Properties:** Only properties that you have added keyframes to are displayed.
- **Show Only Edited Properties:** Only properties that you have modified from their default values are displayed.

Working with keyframe interpolation

Throughout this lesson you've been using keyframes to define your animation. The term *keyframe* originates from traditional animation, where the lead artist would draw the major poses, which were the most important (or *key*) frames, and then assistant animators would draw the individual frames illustrating each step of the animation from one key frame to the next. When animating in Premiere, you're the lead animator, and the computer does the rest of the work as it interpolates values in between the keyframes you set.

Choosing a keyframe interpolation method

One of the most useful yet least used features of keyframes is their interpolation method. This is a fancy way of describing the particular way to get from point A to point B.

Premiere has five interpolation methods. Changing the method can create a very different animation. You can access all the available interpolation methods by right-clicking a keyframe icon to see the options (some effects have both spatial and temporal options).

- **Linear:** This is the default method of keyframe interpolation. It produces a uniform rate of change between keyframes. Changes to settings begin instantly at the first keyframe and continue to the next keyframe at a constant speed. At the second keyframe, the rate of change switches instantly to the rate between it and the third keyframe, and so on. This can be effective, and even "snappy," but it can also look a little mechanical.
- **Bezier:** This gives the most control over keyframe interpolation. *Bezier* keyframes (named after the French engineer Pierre Bézier) provide manual handles you can adjust to change the shape of the value graph or motion path on either side of the keyframe. By dragging the Bezier handles that appear when the keyframe is selected, you can create smooth curved adjustments or sharp angles. For example, you could have an object move smoothly to a position on-screen and then sharply take off in another direction.

  Note: If you are familiar with Adobe Illustrator or Adobe Photoshop, you will recognize Bezier handles; they work the same way in Premiere.

- **Auto Bezier:** Auto Bezier keyframes create a smooth rate of change through the keyframe. They automatically adjust when you change settings. This is a dependable, quick-fix version of Bezier keyframes.
- **Continuous Bezier:** This option is similar to the Auto Bezier option, but it provides some manual control. The motion or value path will always have smooth transitions, but you can adjust the shape of the Bezier curve on both sides of the keyframe with a control handle.
- **Hold:** This is available only for temporal (time-based) properties. Hold-style keyframes hold their value across time, without a gradual transition. This is useful if you want to create staccato-type movements or make an object suddenly disappear. When the Hold style is used, the value of the first keyframe will hold until the next hold keyframe is encountered, and then the value will change instantly.

Temporal vs. spatial interpolation

Some properties and effects offer a choice of temporal and spatial interpolation methods for transitioning between keyframes. You'll find that all properties have temporal controls (which relate to time). Some properties also offer spatial interpolation (which refers to space or movement).

Here's what you need to know about each method:

- **Temporal interpolation:** Temporal interpolation deals with changes in time. It controls the speed at which an object moves. For example, you can add acceleration and deceleration using Bezier keyframes.
- **Spatial interpolation:** The spatial method deals with changes in an object's position. It controls the shape of the path an object takes across the screen. That path is called a *motion path*, and there are ways to display it in the Program Monitor. By making spatial interpolation adjustments, you can make an object appear to bounce around the frame with hard angular ricochets as it moves from one keyframe to the next or give it a more sloping movement with round corners.

Adding ease to motion

You can use a keyframe preset to quickly add a feeling of inertia to clip motion. For example, you can create a ramp-up effect for speed by right-clicking a keyframe and choosing Ease In or Ease Out. Ease In is used for approaching a keyframe, and Ease Out is used when leaving a keyframe.

Tip: If keyframes at the start or end of a clip are not visible in the Effect Controls panel timeline, try zooming out using the – (hyphen) key at the top right of your keyboard (if your keyboard has one). You can use the – and = (hyphen and equals) keys to zoom out and in, in the Timeline panel and Effect Controls panel (and others). If your keyboard does not have these keys, you can assign keys to the Zoom In and Zoom Out commands.

When you choose Ease In or Ease Out, a Bezier interpolation is applied to the keyframe. You'll learn more about applying interpolation methods to keyframes in Lesson 12.

Continue working with the 04 Scale sequence.

1. Select the second video clip in the sequence.
2. In the Effect Controls panel, locate the Rotation and Scale properties.
3. Place the playhead at the beginning of the clip, click the chevron next to the Scale property, and then select the Scale property heading to select the Scale keyframes and reveal the control handles and velocity graphs in the Effect Controls panel timeline.

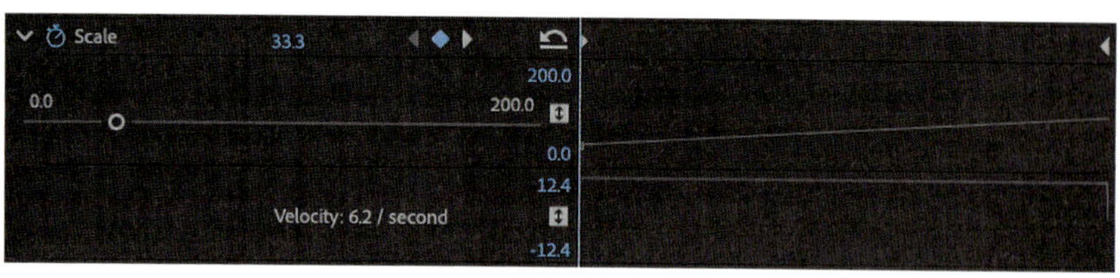

You might want to increase the height of the Effect Controls panel to make room for the extra controls.

Don't be overwhelmed by the new numbers and graphs. Once you understand just one of these controls, you'll understand them all because they use a common design.

The graph makes it easier to view the results of keyframe interpolation adjustments. For example, a straight line means a steady speed without acceleration; in other words, you're using linear keyframes.

You can make the graph taller to see it more clearly by dragging the horizontal line below the keyframes down. The line is very faint, so you'll have to look carefully to find it.

4 Click the background of the Effect Controls panel timeline to deselect the keyframes; they will change from blue (selected) to gray (unselected). Right-click the first Scale keyframe (level with the Scale heading) and choose Ease Out. The keyframe is partially obscured by the left edge of the timeline.

5 Right-click the second Scale keyframe and choose Ease In.

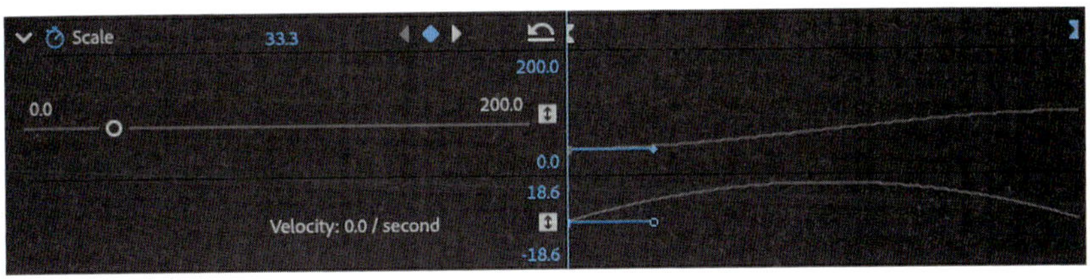

The graph now shows a curved line, which translates as a gradual acceleration and deceleration of the animation.

6 Play the sequence to see your animation.

7 Experiment by dragging the blue Bezier handles in the Effect Controls panel to see their effects on speed and ramping.

The steeper the curve you create, the more sharply the animation's movement or speed increases. After experimenting, you can choose Edit > Undo repeatedly if you don't like the changes.

Applying the Auto Reframe effect

Once upon a time…all screens were 4×3. Then they were all manner of aspect ratios until they settled eventually on 16×9 as the standard delivery aspect ratio for television shows and online video distribution platforms today. This standard is sometimes written as 1.78:1—that is, 1.78 times wider than the height.

Theatrical cinema releases tend to be wider, with the two standard aspect ratios being 1.85:1 and 2.39:1.

It's common for major film studios to produce multiple versions of a film with different aspect ratios and color standards, intended for several traditional video distribution standards. Still, these are usually close to 16×9 or 4×3.

With the development of popular social media platforms, in particular on smartphones, demand for dramatically different aspect ratios has returned.

To help you repurpose sequences, Premiere has an Auto Reframe workflow. You can largely automate the process of converting a finished sequence from one aspect ratio to another. The stand-out feature of this workflow is that Premiere analyzes the visuals in your clips and then applies and configures the Auto Reframe effect for each clip, which automatically keeps points of interest—such as faces—on-screen.

You will want to check and adjust results, but this can be a huge time-saver if you intend to deliver your content on multiple platforms. Try it now:

1 Open the sequence 05 Auto Reframe.

2 Play the sequence to familiarize yourself with the content.

The character moves around the screen quite a lot. Sequences crop the edges of clips that don't fit in the frame. If you were to nest this sequence in another sequence and manually add keyframes to reframe the content, it would take quite some time.

3 With the Timeline panel active or the sequence selected in the Project panel, choose Sequence > Auto Reframe Sequence to open the dialog box of the same name.

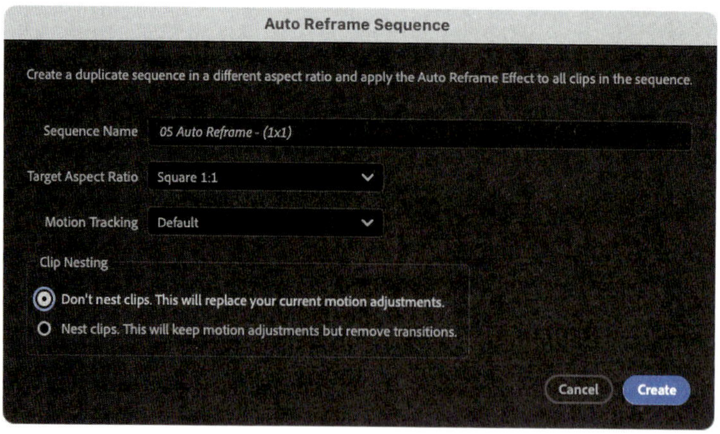

When you click Create in this dialog box, Premiere creates a new separate sequence based on the settings you choose. The original sequence will not be affected. Here are the settings:

- **Sequence Name:** Give the new sequence a name. By default, the new aspect ratio is added to the original name.
- **Target Aspect Ratio:** Specify a new aspect ratio. You can repeat this process and produce multiple sequences with different aspect ratios.
- **Motion Tracking:** Set the number of keyframes that will be used to follow the motion in the sequence. The Default setting balances speed and smooth movement. For slower, smoother movements choose Slower Motion, and for faster action choose Faster Motion.
- **Clip Nesting:** Choose whether or not to nest clips. There can be only one Motion effect on each clip, and if you have motion keyframes on your clips already, they will be replaced in the new sequence unless you choose to nest the clips. If you do nest your clips, however, you'll lose transition effects between them.

4 Leave the settings at their defaults for now, with Square 1:1 chosen from the Target Aspect Ratio menu, and click Create. Premiere performs visual analysis of the sequence.

The new sequence appears in the Project panel, inside a new bin called Auto Reframed Sequences, and it opens in the Timeline panel.

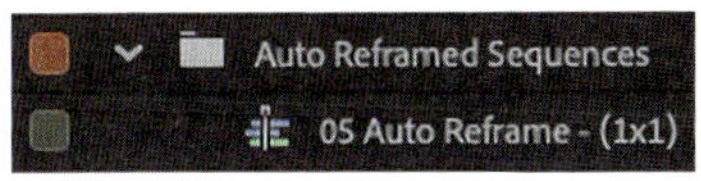

5 Play the new sequence to review the results of the reframing.

6 Select the clip in the Timeline panel, and look in the Effect Controls panel. The Motion effect is disabled, and an Auto Reframe effect is applied.

Note: Some of the results produced by Auto-Reframe are achieved by scaling clips—particularly graphics—in ways that reduce their resolution. This can result in softer-looking images when displayed at full size. To achieve the sharpest possible results, you can manually create a new sequence, copy the original sequence clips into it, and then apply the Auto Reframe effect to the individual clips (available in the Effects panel).

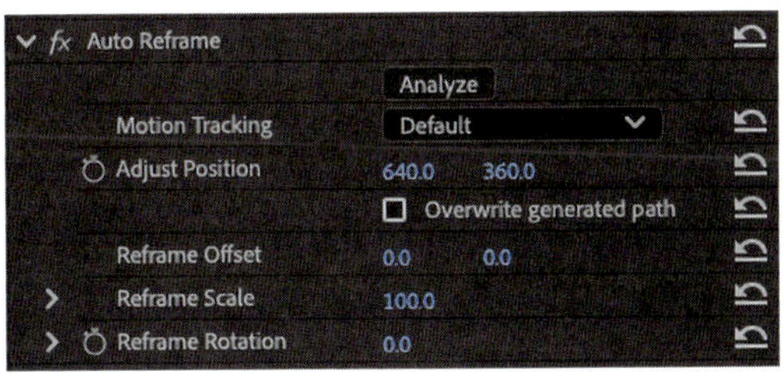

You can use the Auto Reframe effect controls to make overall adjustments to the results or select Overwrite Generated Path, and many individual Position keyframes will appear in the Effect Controls panel timeline that you can adjust one by one or delete.

Combining a drop shadow with motion effects

Premiere offers a number of effects to control motion. Although the Motion effect is the most immediately accessible, you may find yourself wanting more.

The Transform and Basic 3D effects are also useful and give more control over an object (including 3D rotation).

These effects are particularly helpful because the order in which visual effects are listed in the Effect Controls panel is the order in which they are applied, with one exception; the fixed effects (including Motion, Opacity, and Time Remapping) are always applied last.

This can lead to complications when effects that impact lighting or effects that change the shape or position of a clip are applied. In this exercise, you'll learn how to combine effects to achieve natural-looking results.

Adding a drop shadow

A drop shadow creates perspective by adding a small shadow behind an object. This is often used to help create a sense of separation between foreground and background elements. Try adding a drop shadow.

Note: The Long Shadow effect creates extruded 3D-looking shapes.

1 Open the sequence 06 Enhance.

2 Make sure the Program Monitor zoom level is set to Fit.

3 In the Effects panel, browse into Video Effects > Perspective.

4 Drag the Drop Shadow effect onto the Journey to New York Title clip on the V3 track.

5 Experiment with the Drop Shadow settings in the Effect Controls panel. You may need to scroll down to see them. When you have finished experimenting, choose the following settings:

- Darken the shadow by changing Opacity to **85%**.
- Drag the Direction value to about 320° to see the shadow's angle change.
- Set Distance to **15** so the shadow is further offset from the clip.
- Set Softness to **25** to soften the edges of the shadow. Generally, the greater the Distance setting, the more softness you should apply.

6 Play the sequence to view the result.

Adding motion with the Transform effect

An alternative to the Motion effect settings is the Transform effect, available in the Effects panel Video Effects > Transform category. These two effects offer similar controls, but the Transform effect offers three key differences.

- Changes to a clip's Anchor Point, Position, Scale, and Opacity settings are processed in the stack with other effects, unlike the Motion settings. This means effects such as drop shadows and bevels can behave differently (usually more correctly).
- There are additional Skew, Skew Axis, and Shutter Angle settings to allow a visual angular transformation to clips.
- The Transform effect can automatically simulate motion blur for more natural-looking movement.

Let's compare the two effects.

1. Open the sequence 07 Motion and Transform.
2. Scrub through the sequence to familiarize yourself with it.

   There are two sections in the sequence. Each has a picture-in-picture (PIP), rotating twice over a background clip while moving from left to right. Look carefully at the position of the shadow on each pair of clips.

   In the first example, the shadow follows the bottom edge of the PIP and appears on all four sides of the clip as it rotates, which obviously doesn't look natural because the light source producing the shadow wouldn't be moving.

   In the second example, the shadow stays on the lower right of the PIP, which is more realistic.

3 Click the first clip on the V2 track, and view the effects applied in the Effect Controls panel: the Motion effect and the Drop Shadow effect.

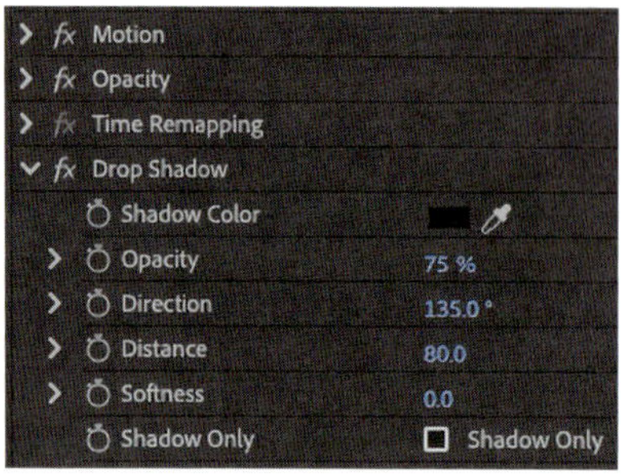

4 Now click the second clip on the V2 track. The Transform effect is producing the motion this time, with the Drop Shadow effect again producing the shadow.

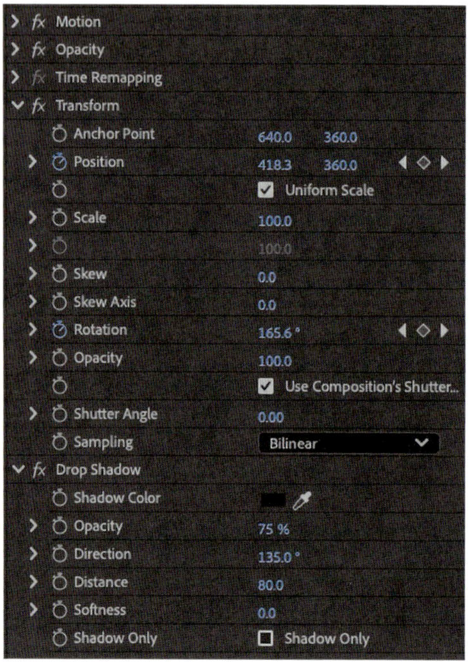

Tip: Anywhere you see a blue number in Premiere, you can usually drag across it rather than click it to change the value incrementally—this includes the timecode displays for the current playhead position.

5 Experiment with the Transform effect settings. You can click numbers to type in new values or drag across the numbers to make incremental adjustments.

The effect has many of the same options as the Motion effect, with the addition of Skew, Skew Axis, and Shutter Angle. As you can see, the Drop Shadow effect works more realistically when combined with the Transform effect than when it's used with the Motion effect alone because of the order in which the effects are applied; the Motion effect is applied after other effects.

Manipulating clips in 3D space with Basic 3D

Another option for creating movement is the Basic 3D effect, which can manipulate a clip in 3D space. It allows you to rotate the image around horizontal and vertical axes as well as move it toward or away from you. You'll also find the Show Specular Highlight option; selecting it creates the appearance of light reflecting off the rotating surface.

Let's explore the effect:

1. Open the sequence 08 Basic 3D.
2. Drag the playhead over the sequence in the Timeline panel (scrub) to view the contents.

The light that follows the motion comes from above, from behind, and from the left of the viewer. Because the light comes from above, you won't see the effect until the image is tilted backward to catch the reflection. Specular highlights of this kind can be used to enhance the realism of a 3D effect.

These are the four major properties of the Basic 3D effect:

- **Swivel:** This controls the rotation around the vertical y-axis. If you rotate past 90°, you'll see the back of the image, which is a mirror of the front.
- **Tilt:** This controls the rotation around a horizontal x-axis. If you rotate beyond 90°, again, you'll see the back of the image.
- **Distance To Image:** This moves the image along the z-axis to simulate depth. As the distance value gets larger, the image moves farther away.
- **Specular Highlight:** This adds a glint of light that reflects off the surface of the rotated image, as though an overhead light were shining on the surface. This option is either on or off.

3. Experiment with the Basic 3D options.

Review questions

1. Which fixed effect will move a clip in the frame?
2. You want a clip to appear full screen for a few seconds and then spin away. How do you make the Motion effect's Rotation feature start partway through a clip rather than at the beginning?
3. How can you start an object rotating gradually and have it stop rotating slowly?
4. If you want to add a drop shadow to a clip, why might you choose to use a different motion-related effect rather than the Motion effect?

Review answers

1. The Motion effect lets you set a new position for a clip. If keyframes are used, the effect can be animated.
2. Position the playhead where you want the rotation to begin, and click the Add/Remove Keyframe button or the stopwatch icon. Then move to where you want the spinning to end and change the Rotation parameter; another keyframe will appear.
3. Use the Ease Out and Ease In options to change the keyframe interpolation to be gradual rather than sudden.
4. The Motion effect is the last effect applied to a clip. Motion takes whatever effects you apply before it (including Drop Shadow) and spins the entire assemblage as a single unit. To create a realistic drop shadow on a spinning object, use Transform or Basic 3D and then place a Drop Shadow effect below that in the Effect Controls panel.

10 EDITING AND MIXING AUDIO

Lesson overview

In this lesson, you'll learn how to do the following:

- Work in the Audio workspace.
- Understand audio characteristics.
- Adjust clip audio volume.
- Adjust audio levels in a sequence.
- Lower music levels automatically.
- Use the Audio Clip Mixer.

This lesson will take about 100 minutes to complete. To get the files used in this lesson, refer to the instructions in "Accessing the lesson files and Web Edition" in the "Getting Started" section at the beginning of this book. Store the files on your computer in a convenient location.

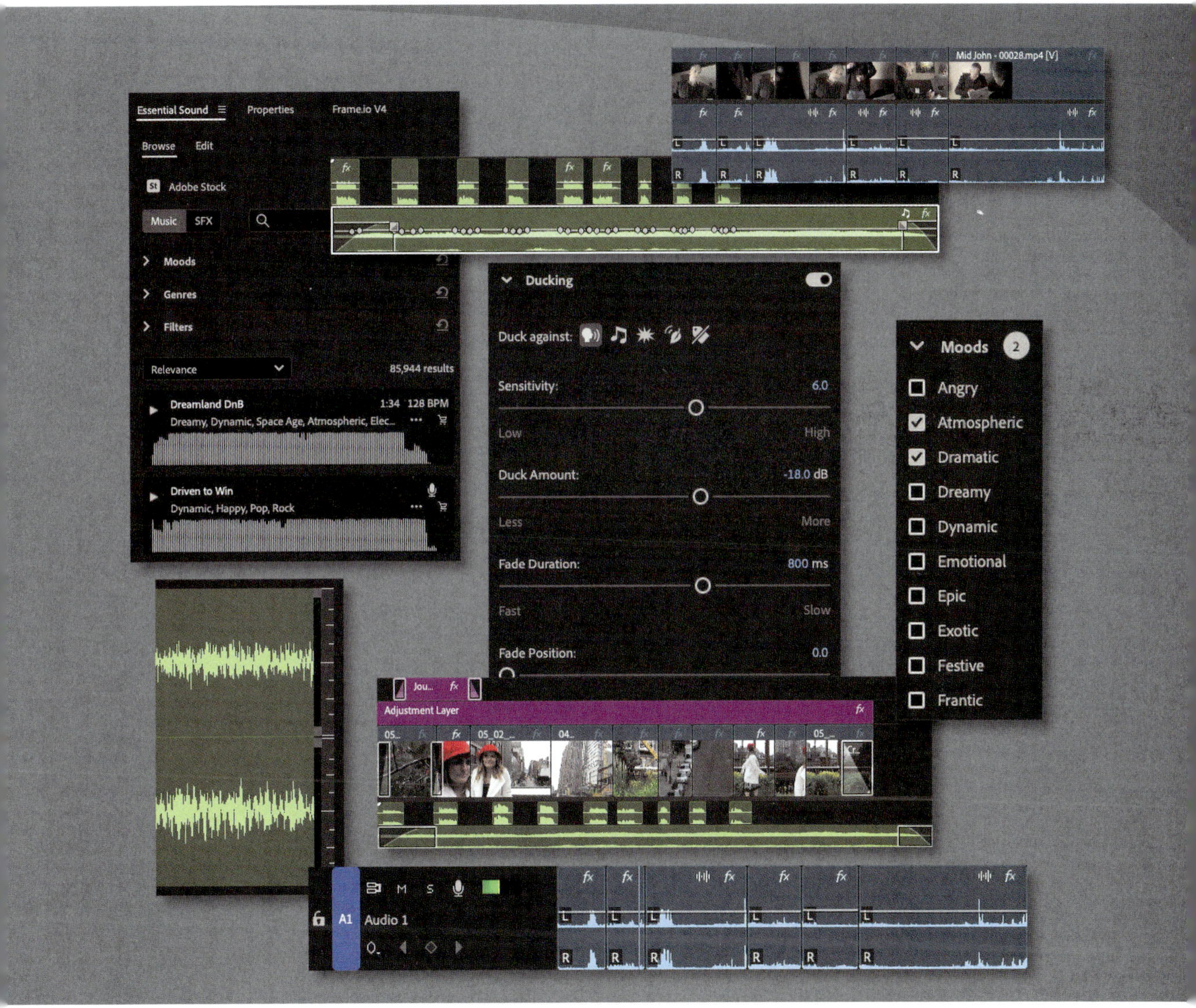

Until now, our focus has been primarily on working with visuals. No doubt about it, the pictures count, but professional editors tend to agree that sound is at least as important as the images on the screen—sometimes more important! In this lesson, you'll learn some audio-mixing fundamentals using the powerful tools provided by Adobe Premiere.

Starting the lesson

Consider the difference it makes if you turn the sound off while watching a horror movie. Without an ominous soundtrack, scenes that were scary a moment ago can seem like comedy.

Music works around many of our critical faculties and directly influences our feelings. Your body will react to sound whether you want it to or not. For example, it's normal for your heart rate to be influenced by the beat of the music you're listening to. Fast music tends to raise your heart rate, and slow music tends to lower your heart rate. Powerful stuff!

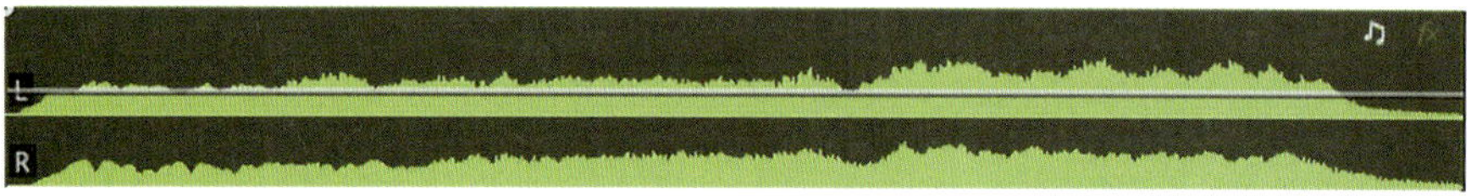

It's rare to record perfect on-camera audio that's ready for output without any adjustments, but Premiere enables you to do many things to improve your audio mix. For instance, you can:

- Make adjustments to individual audio clips or an entire audio track. Adjustments made to an audio track are applied to all clips on the track.
- Interpret recorded audio channels differently from the way they were recorded in-camera. For example, audio recorded as stereo can be interpreted as separate mono tracks.
- Clean up background sound. Whether it's system hum from your recording equipment or the sound of an air-conditioning unit, Premiere has tools for cleaning up your audio.
- Adjust the volume of specific frequencies in your clips (different tones).
- Adjust the volume level on clips in the Project panel and on clip segments in sequences. The adjustments made to clips in sequences can vary over time to create a dynamic sound mix.
- Add music, and then mix levels between music clips and dialogue clips. This can be performed automatically or manually.
- Produce a mono, stereo, or even 5.1 surround sound mix.
- Add audio spot effects, such as explosions, door slams, or atmospheric environmental sounds.
- Change the duration of a music clip to suit your sequence.

In this lesson, you'll begin by learning how to use the audio tools in Premiere, and then you'll make adjustments to clips and a sequence.

Setting up the interface to work with audio

Let's begin by switching to the Audio workspace.

1 Open Lesson 10.prproj in the Lessons folder.

2 From the Workspaces menu, choose Audio. Then return to the Workspaces menu and choose Reset To Saved Layout.

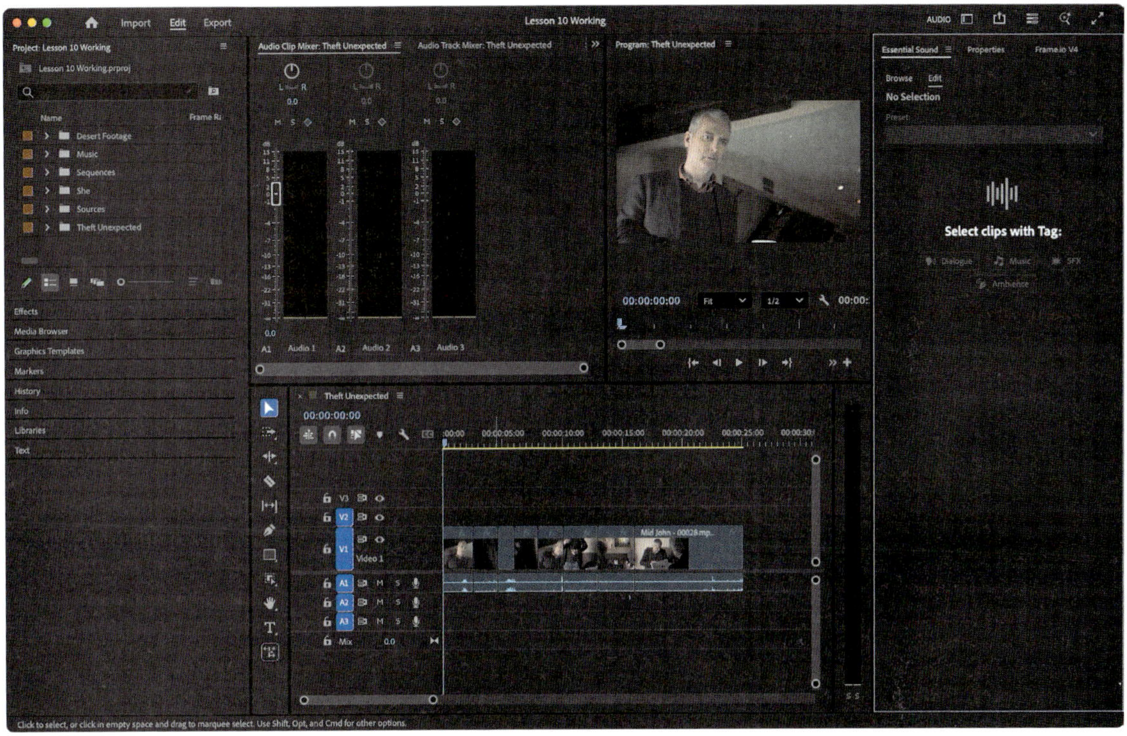

The Audio workspace uses stacked panels to maximize the number of panels that can be on-screen at a time—in this case, for the panel group that contains the Project panel.

You can turn on stacked panels for any panel group by opening the panel menu and choosing Panel Group Settings > Stacked Panel Group. The same option will turn off stacked panels.

Keep stacked panels turned on for now.

You can click the name of any stacked panel to view it. In the Project panel, you can click the chevron for any bin to display its contents. The stacked panel automatically changes height to accommodate the expanded list.

3 Save the project as **Lesson 10 Working.prproj**.

Note: To ensure that the tools function and the defaults are set exactly as described in this lesson, reset the Premiere preferences by holding any modifier key (such as Shift) while launching the application, selecting Reset App Preferences, and then clicking Continue in the Reset Options dialog box.

Working in the Audio workspace

You'll recognize most of the components of the Audio workspace from the Editing workspace you've used. One obvious difference is that the Audio Clip Mixer is displayed in place of the Source Monitor. The Source Monitor is still there; it's just hidden right now, grouped with the Audio Clip Mixer.

There are two audio mixer panels in Premiere. Let's look at the differences between the two:

- **Audio Clip Mixer:** This provides controls to adjust the audio level and *pan* or *balance* (to distribute audio between the left or right side of the sequence audio mix) of clips in sequences. As you play your sequence, you can make adjustments, and Premiere will add keyframes to clips as the playhead moves over them.

Note: Like the Effect Controls panel, the Audio Clip Mixer works on one clip at a time. Though it has fewer controls, audio adjustments can be made for multiple selected clips using the Properties panel.

- **Audio Track Mixer:** This adjusts audio level and pan on tracks rather than clips. The controls are similar, but the Audio Track Mixer offers more advanced mixing options. If the Effects And Sends section at the top of the panel has been expanded, you may need to scroll down to view the controls. See Lesson 11, "Improving Audio," for more information about audio mixing.

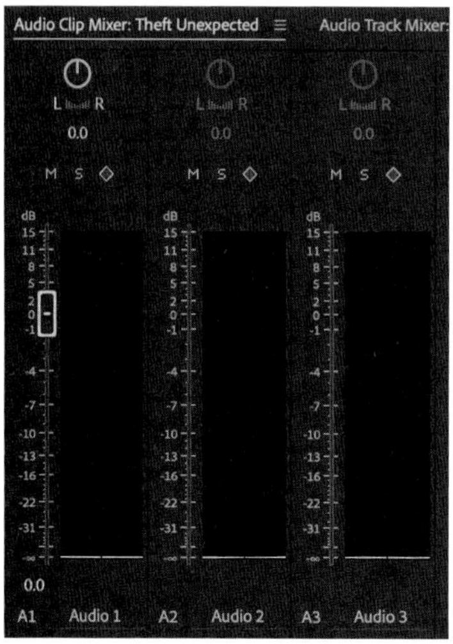

Audio Clip Mixer

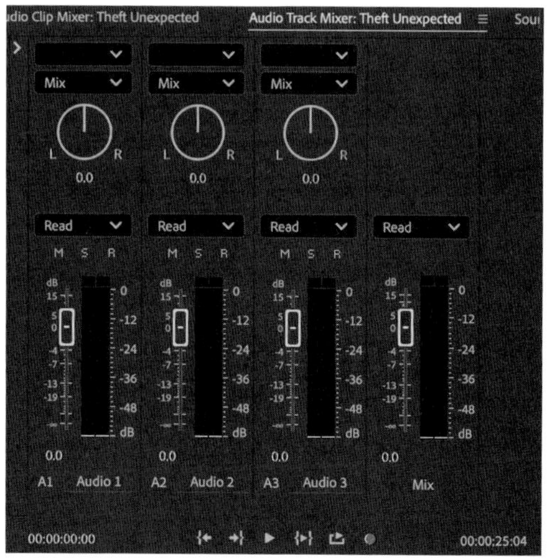

Audio Track Mixer

Clip-based and track-based audio level adjustments are combined for final output. So if you reduce a clip's audio level by –3 dB *and* reduce the track audio level by –3 dB, you'll have a total drop of –6 dB.

You can apply clip-based audio effects and modify their settings in the Effect Controls panel. In fact, adjustments made using the Audio Clip Mixer appear in the Effect Controls panel, along with any other adjustments.

Track-based audio adjustments can be modified in the Audio Track Mixer only or directly in the Timeline panel.

Premiere applies clip-based audio adjustments and effects before track-based adjustments and effects. It's important to keep this in mind, because the order in which adjustments are applied can have a big impact on results.

You can modify the Timeline panel track headers and add an audio meter for each track, along with track-based level and pan controls. This is useful when mixing audio as it helps you locate the sources of audio levels you might want to adjust.

Let's try this.

Note: You will have noticed that this project has a different bin structure and is organized in a different way. There is no one correct way to organize your project. Try a few options to find a system that works best for your editing style.

1 If it's not open already, open the Theft Unexpected sequence in the Sequences bin.

2 Open the Timeline Display Settings menu, and choose Customize Audio Header. The Button Editor appears, and the Audio 1 track expands to display the full track header.

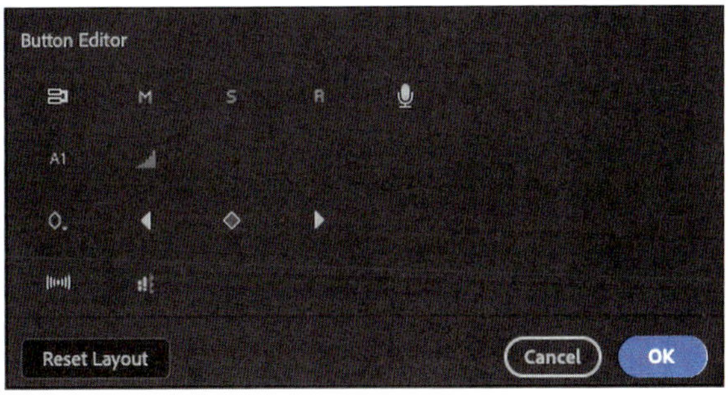

3 Drag the Track Meter icon onto a blank space on the Audio 1 track header to the side of the voice over icon, and click OK.

Notice that when you clicked OK, the Audio 1 track header returned to its previous size. Resize the Audio 1 track header vertically to see the new meter.

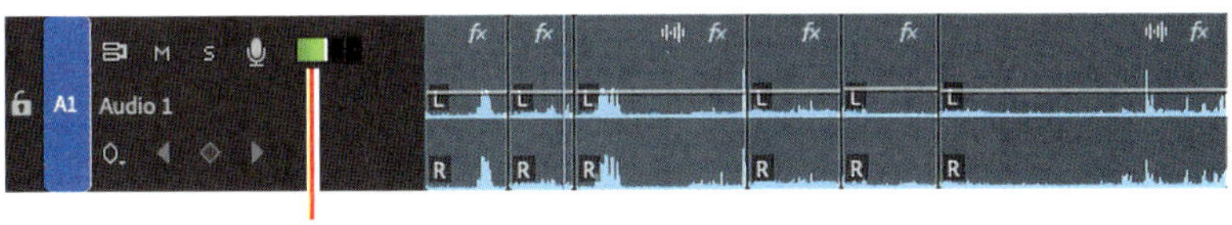

Changes made to any track header update all track headers. Now every audio track will have a small built-in audio meter—useful for working out which track is contributing most to the overall audio mix.

You can remove items from track headers by dragging them away from the header while the editor is open. You can also click the Reset Layout button in the Audio Header Button Editor to restore the default track header configuration.

Configuring the audio mix

Sequences have settings that are similar to those of media files. For example, sequences have a frame rate, frame size, and pixel aspect ratio.

The Audio Mix setting defines the number of audio channels the sequence will output. This is a little like configuring the audio channels for a media file. In fact, if you export the sequence using the option to automatically match sequence settings, the sequence audio mix setting will be the audio format for the new file.

When you create a new sequence, the Audio Mix setting is in the Tracks tab of the New Sequence dialog box, under Audio.

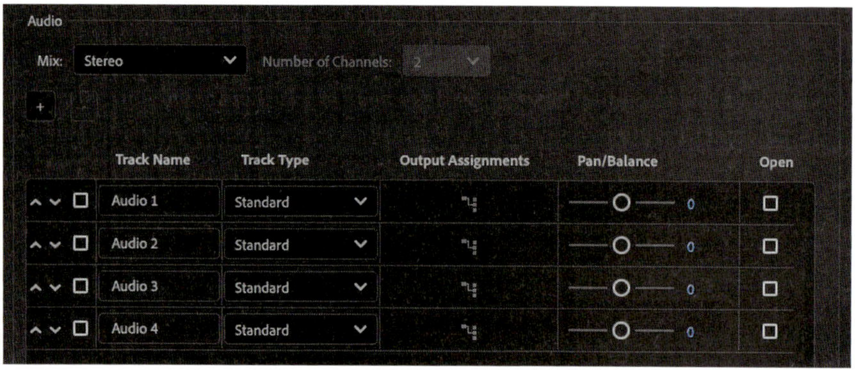

- **Stereo** has two audio channels: Left and Right. This is the most common option for delivered content.
- **5.1** has six audio channels: Middle, Front-Left, Front-Right, Rear-Left, Rear-Right, and Low Frequency Effects (LFE)—that's the sound that gets played through the subwoofer. At very low frequencies, our ears can't detect the direction sound comes from, so there's no need for two subwoofers.
- **Multichannel** has between 1 and 32 audio channels you can choose. This option is most commonly used for advanced multichannel broadcast television, documentary and feature film workflows, particularly where multilingual delivery is required.
- **Mono** has one audio channel.

You can change most sequence settings at any time, but not the Audio Mix setting. With the exception of multichannel sequences, you cannot change the number of channels that your sequence will output.

You can add or remove audio tracks at any time. If you decide to change your audio mix setting, you can copy and paste clips from a sequence with one audio mix setting to a sequence with a different setting.

What is an audio channel?

It's common to think that Left and Right audio channels are in some way intrinsically different. In fact, they are both actually mono audio channels designated as Left or Right. When recording sound, it's the standard configuration to have Audio Channel 1 as Left and Audio Channel 2 as Right.

What makes Audio Channel 1 Left is only the following:

- It's recorded from a microphone pointing left.
- It's interpreted as Left in Premiere.
- It outputs to a speaker positioned on the left.

Otherwise, it's a single, mono audio channel.

If you also perform the same recording from a microphone pointing right (but with Audio Channel 2), then you have stereo audio. They are, in fact, two separate mono audio channels.

Using the audio meters

When previewing a clip in the Source Monitor or Project panel, the audio meters display the level for each audio channel in the clip separately.

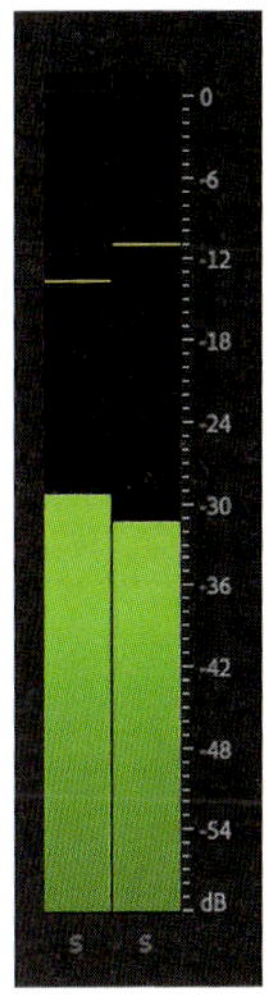

When previewing a sequence, the audio meters display the audio level for each mix channel. Regardless of the number of audio tracks in the sequence, the audio meters will give you the overall mix output volume for your sequence.

If the audio meters are not already displayed, you will find them in the Window menu.

If the audio meters are too narrow, you can resize the panel. If you make the meters wide enough, the audio level will be displayed horizontally.

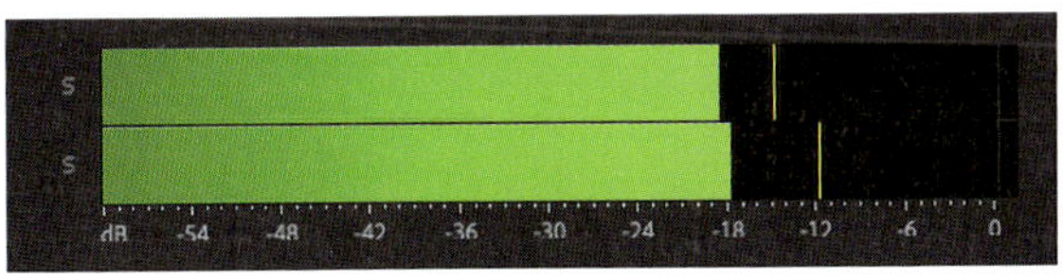

There is a Solo button S for each audio meter. This allows you to exclusively hear the selected channel (or multiple channels). If the Solo buttons are displayed as small circles, they will still work. You can drag the edge of the panel a little to make the meters wider and display larger Solo buttons if you prefer.

Note: The Solo buttons do not display when you use the mono audio mix option.

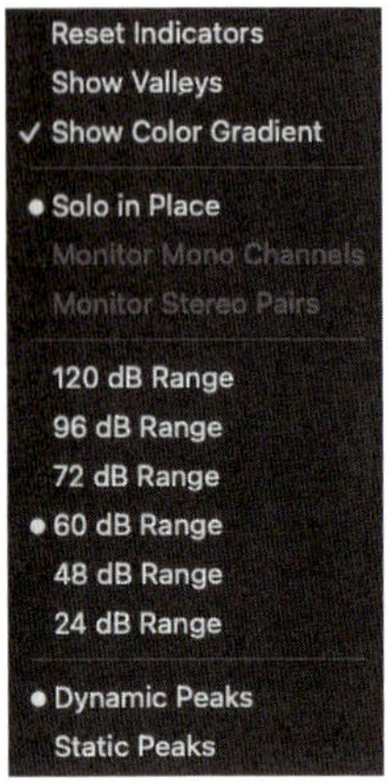

If you right-click the audio meters, you can choose a different display scale. The default is a range from 0 dB to –60 dB, which clearly shows the main information about the audio level you'll want to see.

You can also choose between static and dynamic peaks. When you get a loud "spike" in audio levels that makes you glance at the meters, the sound is usually gone by the time you look. With static peaks, the highest peak is marked and maintained in the meters so you can identify the loudest level played.

You can click the audio meters to reset the peak. With dynamic peaks, the peak level will continually update, briefly holding before disappearing; keep watching to check the levels.

About audio level

The scale on the audio meters is displayed in decibels, denoted by dB. The scale shown is a little unusual in that the highest volume is designated as 0 dB. Lower volumes become larger and larger negative numbers until they reach negative infinity.

If a recorded sound is too quiet, it might get lost in the background noise. Background noise might be environmental, such as an air-conditioning system making a hum. It also might be system noise, such as the quiet hiss you might hear from speakers when no sound is playing.

When you increase the overall volume of your audio, background noise gets louder too. This means it's often better to record audio at a higher level than you need (while avoiding such high levels that the audio distorts) and then reduce the volume later to remove (or at least reduce the impact of) the lower-level background noise.

Depending on your audio hardware, you may have a bigger or smaller signal-to-noise ratio; that's the difference between the sound you want to hear (the signal) and the sound you don't want to hear (the background noise). Signal-to-noise ratio is often described as SNR and is also measured in dB.

Viewing samples

The *audio sample rate* is the number of times per second the recorded sound source is sampled. It's common for professional camera audio to take a sample 48,000 times per second.

Let's look at an individual audio sample.

1 In the Project panel, open the Music bin, and double-click the clip Graceful Tenure - Patrick Cannell.mp3 to open it in the Source Monitor.

   Because this clip has no video, Premiere automatically displays the waveforms for the two audio channels.

At the bottom of the Source Monitor, the width of the time ruler represents the total duration of the clip.

2 Open the Source Monitor Settings menu, and choose Time Ruler Numbers. The time ruler now shows timecode indicators.

If your region uses PAL broadcast video (for example, in Europe), the number dividers will be colons. If your region uses NTSC broadcast video (for example, in North America), the number dividers will be semicolons. This means you can tell, at a glance, which broadcast video standard your system is configured for.

Try zooming in to the time ruler using the navigator just below the time ruler (drag the handles all the way together). The maximum zoom shows you an individual frame—illustrated by the width of the playhead (the shaded area to the right of the thin blue line).

Note: You may have noticed that sometimes timecode indicators separate the numbers with colons, and at other times semicolons are used. Semicolons indicate NTSC video, while colons indicate PAL video.

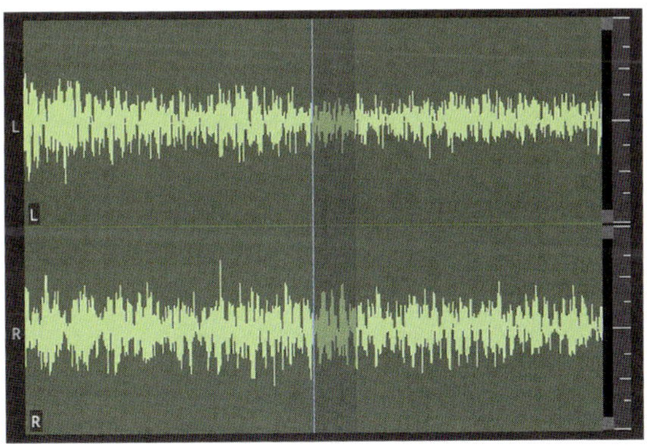

3 Open the Source Monitor Settings menu again, and choose Show Audio Time Units.

This time, you'll see individual audio samples counted on the time ruler. You can zoom in to an individual audio sample—in this case, one 48,000th of a second, the sample rate of this audio!

On the Timeline panel, you'll find the same option to Show Audio Time Units on the Timeline panel menu (rather than on the Timeline Settings menu).

4 For now, use the Source Monitor Settings menu to turn off both the Time Ruler Numbers and Show Audio Time Units options.

Showing audio waveforms

When you view a waveform in the Source Monitor, you'll see an extra vertical navigator zoom control for each channel to the right of the waveform. These controls work in a way that's similar to the navigator zoom control at the bottom of the panel. You can resize a vertical navigator by dragging the small handle at the top to view the waveforms larger or smaller, which is particularly useful when navigating quiet audio.

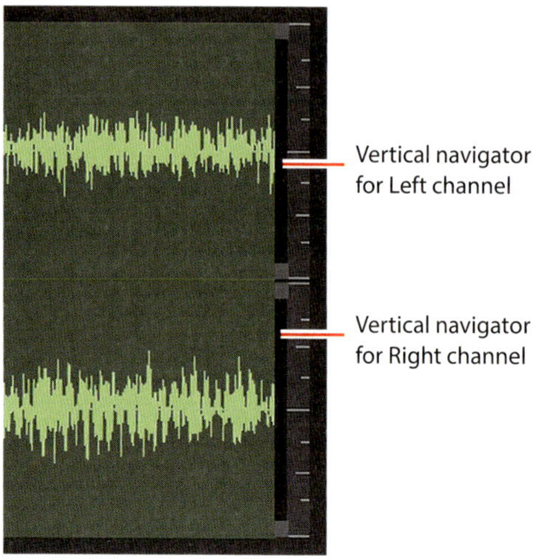

You can choose to display audio waveforms for any clip that has audio by choosing Audio Waveform from the Source Monitor Settings menu.

Note: Viewing an audio waveform is helpful if you are trying to locate specific dialogue and you are not as concerned about the video portion of the footage.

If a clip has video as well as audio, the video will be displayed in the Source Monitor by default. You can quickly switch to viewing the audio waveform by clicking the Drag Audio Only button.

Let's look at some waveforms.

1 In the Theft Unexpected bin, double-click the clip HS John to open it in the Source Monitor.

2 Open the Source Monitor Settings menu, and choose Audio Waveform.

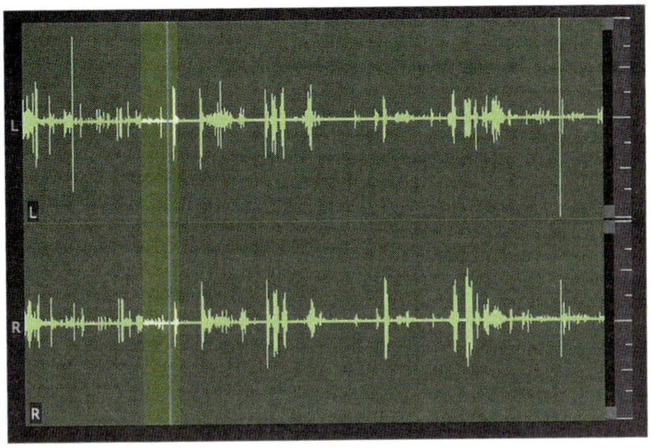

You can easily see where the dialogue begins and ends. Notice the clip's In and Out points are shown as a highlighted region on the waveform.

Notice also, you can click the waveform to move the Source Monitor playhead.

3 Switch back to viewing the composite video using the Source Monitor Settings menu.

You can also turn off and on the display of waveforms for clip segments on the Timeline.

4 The sequence Theft Unexpected should already be open in the Timeline panel. If not, open it from the Sequences bin.

5 Open the Timeline Display Settings menu, and make sure Show Audio Waveform is chosen.

6 If necessary, resize the Audio 1 track to make sure the waveform is fully visible. Notice that two audio channels are displayed in each audio clip in this sequence: The clips have stereo audio.

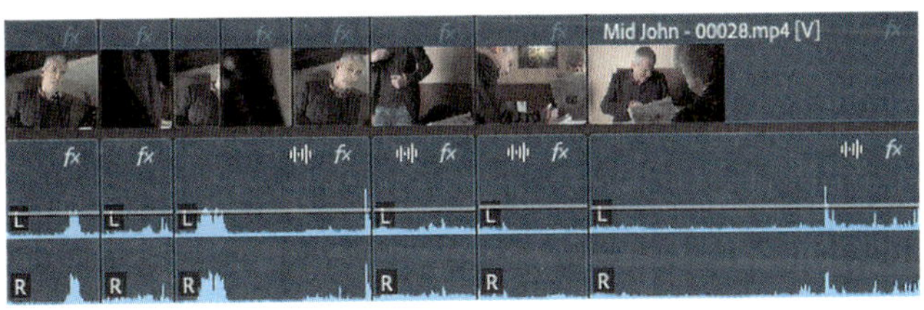

The audio waveforms on these clips look very different from the waveforms in the Source Monitor. That's because, by default, the Timeline panel displays *rectified* audio waveforms that look a little like a highly detailed bar graph. This style of waveform makes it easier to see lower-volume audio, like the dialogue in this scene.

7 Open the Timeline panel menu ☰ (not the Settings menu) and choose Rectified Audio Waveforms to deselect it.

   This switches the Timeline panel waveforms to the same type as the Source Monitor.

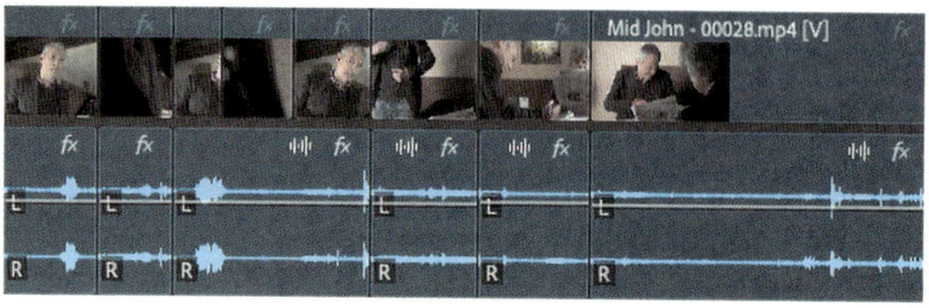

   The regular waveform display works well for louder audio, but notice the quieter parts of the speech; it's harder to follow the level changes.

8 Open the Timeline panel menu, and restore the Rectified Audio Waveforms option.

Working with standard audio tracks

In a sequence, the standard audio track type (as distinct from mono, 5.1, or adaptive tracks) can accommodate both mono audio clips and stereo audio clips. The controls in the Effect Controls panel for standard audio tracks, the Audio Clip Mixer, and the Audio Track Mixer work with both kinds of media.

If you're working with a combination of mono and stereo clips, you'll find it more convenient to use the standard track type than separate mono tracks.

Standard tracks support both mono and stereo audio, automatically displaying one or two waveforms depending on the clip audio channels.

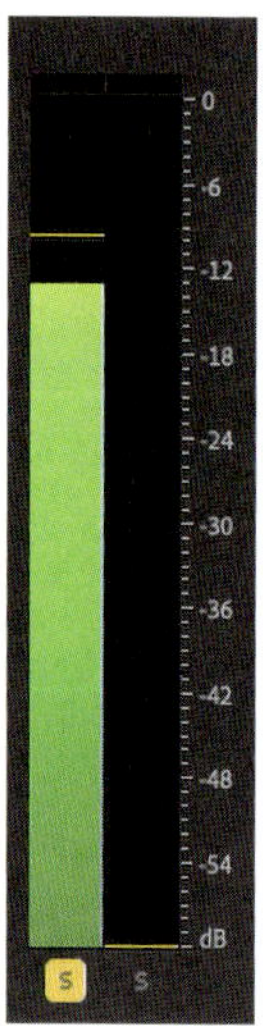

Monitoring audio

You can choose which sequence mix audio channels you hear when monitoring.

Let's try this with a sequence.

1 Open the Desert Montage sequence from the Sequences bin.

2 Play the sequence, and while you do, try clicking each of the Solo buttons at the bottom of the audio meters on the right side of the Timeline panel.

   When you select a Solo button, you'll hear only the output channel you select. You can solo multiple channels when your sequence mix includes them, to hear a specific combination—although in this example it wouldn't help much, as you have only two channels to choose between.

Soloing is useful if you're working with audio where the sound from different microphones is recorded onto different audio channels. This is common with professionally recorded location sound.

Note: The audio meters indicate levels for audio channels when playing clips in the Source Monitor or mix channels when playing sequences in the Timeline panel. To view levels for individual sequence tracks, use the Audio Clip Mixer or Audio Track Mixer.

The number of channels and associated Solo buttons you'll see when previewing a sequence depends on your current sequence Audio Mix setting.

You can also use the small track header Mute button M or Solo button S for specific audio tracks in the Timeline panel.

Examining audio characteristics

When you open a clip in the Source Monitor and view the waveform, you're seeing each channel displayed. The taller the waveform is, the louder the audio for that channel will be. In a sense, you're seeing a plot graph showing the strength of the air pressure wave over time.

Three factors affect the way audio sounds to your ears. Consider them in terms of a television speaker.

- **Frequency:** This refers to how fast the surface of the speaker moves in and out to create high and low air pressure waves. The number of times the surface of the speaker beats the air per second is described as the frequency, measured as Hertz (Hz). Human hearing ranges from approximately 20 Hz to 20,000 Hz (20 KHz). Many factors, including age, affect the frequency range you can hear. The higher the frequency, the higher the perceived pitch of the tone.
- **Amplitude:** This is how far the speaker surface moves. The bigger the movement, the louder the sound will be because it produces a higher air pressure wave, carrying more energy to your ears.
- **Phase:** This is the precise timing with which the surface of the speaker moves out and in. If two speakers push out air and pull in air in sync, they are considered "in phase." If they move out of sync, they become "out of phase," and this can produce problems with sound reproduction. One speaker can reduce the air pressure at exactly the moment the other speaker is attempting to increase it. The result is that you may not hear parts of the sound.

The movement of the surface of a speaker as it emits sound provides a simple example of the way sound is generated, but, of course, the same rules apply to all sound sources, including human voices.

What are audio characteristics?

When the surface of a speaker moves, it creates a high- and low-pressure wave that moves through the air until it arrives at your ears in much the way that surface ripples move across a pond.

As the pressure wave hits your ears, it makes tiny parts of your ear drums move, and that movement is converted into energy that is passed to your brain and interpreted as sound. This happens with extraordinary precision, and because you have two ears, your brain does an impressive job of balancing the two sets of sound information to produce an overall sense of what you can hear.

Much of the way you hear is active, not passive. That is, your brain is constantly filtering out sounds it decides are irrelevant and identifying patterns so you can focus your attention on things that matter—such as speech. For example, you have probably had the experience of being at a party where the general hubbub of conversation sounds like a wall of noise until someone across the room mentions your name. You perhaps didn't realize your brain was listening to the conversation the whole time because you were concentrating on listening to the person standing next to you.

There's a body of research on this subject that broadly falls under the title *psychoacoustics*. For these exercises, we'll be focusing on the mechanics of sound more than on the psychology, though it's a fascinating subject worthy of further study.

Recording equipment makes no such subtle discrimination, which is part of the reason why it's so important to listen to sound with headphones when you're recording on location and to take care to capture the best possible signal. It's usual practice to try to record location sound with no background sound at all. The background sound is added separately in post-production at precisely the right level to add atmosphere to the scene without drowning out the dialogue.

Adding Adobe Stock Audio

As well as importing music files to include in your sequences, you can browse and import music and sound effects (SFX) from Adobe Stock Audio using the Essential Sound panel.

Adobe Stock Audio offers an extensive catalog of royalty-free music and SFX. For more information about Adobe Stock Audio, visit *stock.adobe.com/audio*.

The Browse tab of the Essential Sound panel displays Adobe Stock Audio clips ready to search, browse, and preview.

The Search box at the top allows you to seek out clips based on their names or metadata tags. To limit music search results, you can expand and select options under the Moods, Genres, and Filters headings. For SFX, you can select options under the

Categories and Filters options. Some items are free, while others incur a fee and you can choose to view only free or premium options.

The Filters heading even allows you to specify a range of tempos or durations. There are additional partner stock audio catalogs available too.

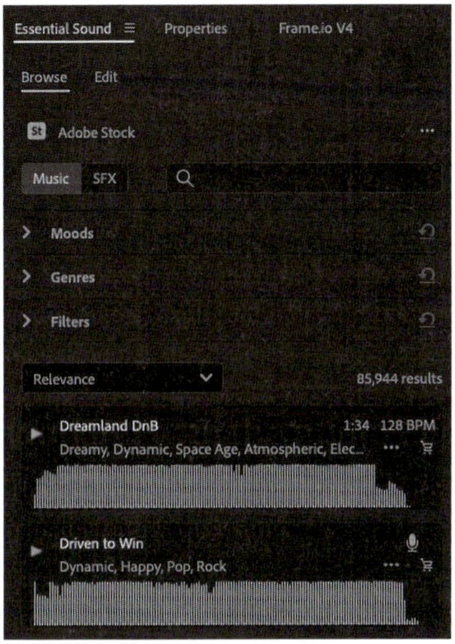

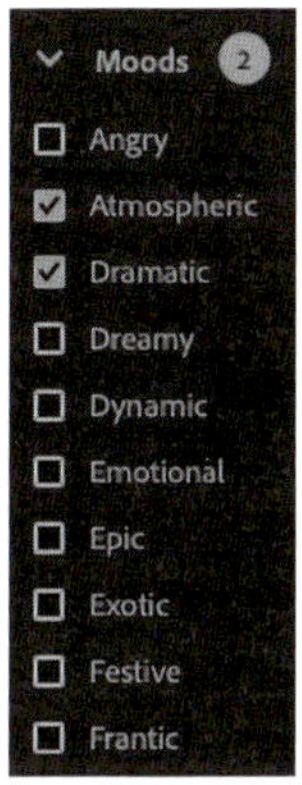

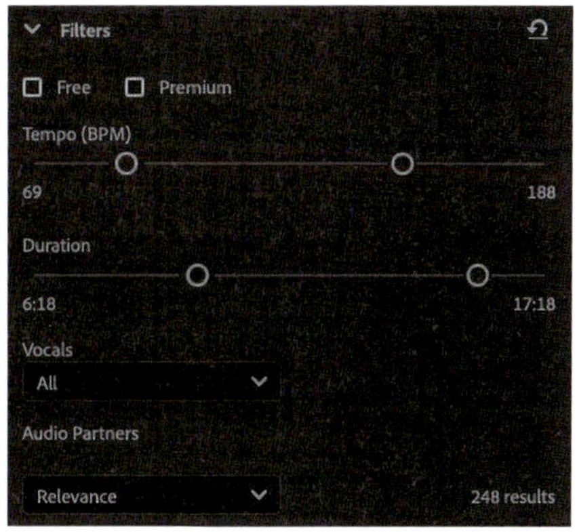

Let's add some background ambience to a sequence.

1 Make sure the Theft Unexpected sequence is open in the Timeline panel. Position the playhead at the beginning of the sequence.

2 If the Essential Sound panel is displaying the Edit settings, click Browse at the top of the panel.

3 Select SFX at the top of the Essential Sound panel.

Then make sure the Timeline Sync option is selected at the bottom.

With Timeline Sync selected, your sequence will play automatically when you play a stock audio clip in the Essential Sound panel. The audio will be combined with your existing soundtrack and visuals, so you can preview multiple options before adding one to your sequence.

4 Enter **cafe** in the search box; then click the chevron to expand the Categories and select Ambience. Click the chevron again to collapse the categories so you can see more choices listed.

Next, expand the Filters and select Free.

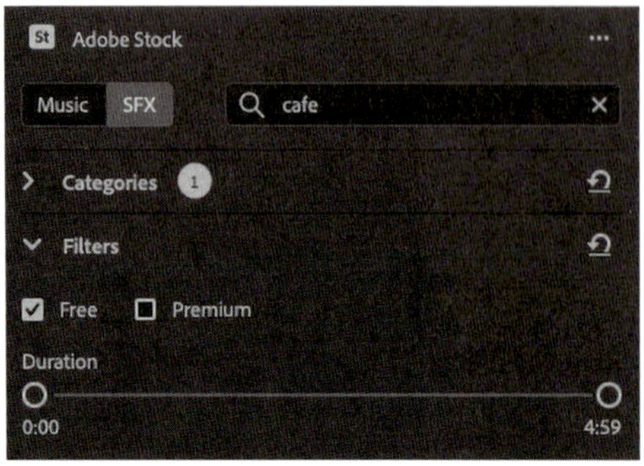

> ▶ **Tip:** You can click anywhere within a stock audio clip waveform preview to jump to another part of the audio. With Timeline Sync enabled, your playhead will also jump by just the right amount.

5 In the Essential Sound panel, click the Play button on a stock audio clip to preview it for your sequence. Then, try clicking Play for several other stock audio options.

This makes it easier to compare the timing for different stock clips.

6 Drag one of the stock audio clips from the Essential Sound panel into the sequence. Place the clip at the beginning of the Audio 2 track. The clip will need to be trimmed to shorten it, but you now have café ambience in your sequence!

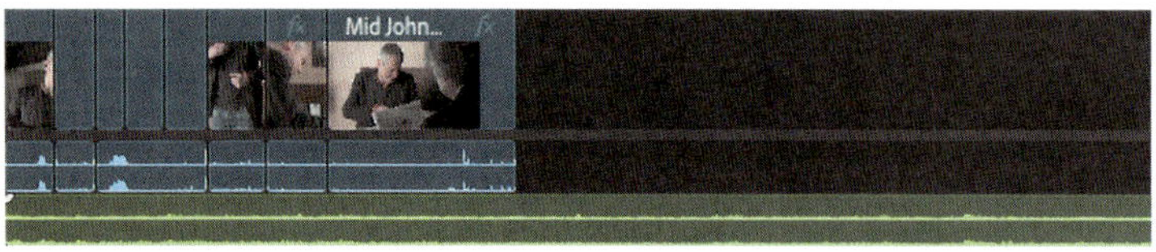

The clip automatically appears in a new Stock Audio Media bin in the Project panel. The associated audio file is added to the CC Libraries Downloads folder (the location for this is configured in the Project settings, on the Scratch Disks tab).

7 Preview your sequence. The ambience is a little loud, but you'll learn about adjusting audio volume next.

Any premium (paid) audio clips you add to sequences from the Essential Sound panel are preview quality by default. You can license full-quality versions by clicking the License button  in the Essential Sound panel or next to the clip in the Project panel.

Adjusting audio volume

There are several ways to adjust the volume of clips, and they are all nondestructive. Changes you make don't affect your original media files, so you can experiment freely and always restore the original version.

Adjusting overall clip levels

Let's try adjusting clip levels.

1 If it's not already open, open the Desert Montage sequence in the Sequences bin.

   The music already fades up and down at the beginning and end. Let's adjust the volume between those fades.

2 Use the Selection tool to drag the bottom of the A1 track header down, or hold Option (macOS) or Alt (Windows) and hover the pointer over the track header while you scroll to make the track taller. This will make it easier to apply fine adjustments to the volume.

3 The middle part of the music is a little too loud. Drag the middle part of the thin white line across the middle of the audio clip down a little. Often referred to as a *rubber band*, this control allows you to apply audio level adjustments over time.

   As you drag, a tool tip appears, displaying the amount of adjustment you are making, and the waveform updates.

4 Each time you make an adjustment of this kind, the only way to review the result is to play the audio. Try this now, and if you are not happy with the result, you can adjust the level and review the result again.

Because you're dragging the rubber band rather than an individual keyframe, you're actually adjusting the two nearest keyframes on either side of the cursor.

If the clip did not have existing keyframes, you'd be adjusting the overall level for the entire length of the clip.

Tip: There are additional keyboard shortcuts available to add and adjust keyframe settings. Assign keys to them in the Keyboard Shortcuts dialog box.

Changing clip volume with keyboard shortcuts

If the Timeline panel playhead is over a clip or if one or more clips are selected, you can also raise and lower volume incrementally using keyboard shortcuts. These are particularly convenient shortcuts for quick, precise audio level adjustments:

- Use the [key to decrease clip volume by 1 dB.
- Use the] key to increase clip volume by 1 dB.
- Use Shift+[to decrease clip volume by 6 dB.
- Use Shift+] to increase clip volume by 6 dB.

Because the adjustments are incremental, they won't change the relative volume levels for multiple selected clips.

For example, if you select two clips with volume settings of –5 dB and –10 dB respectively, pressing [will change the volume settings to –6 dB and –11 dB.

If your keyboard does not have square bracket keys, choose Premiere > Keyboard Shortcuts (macOS) or Edit > Keyboard Shortcuts (Windows) to set alternative keys.

Adjusting audio in the Effect Controls panel

Earlier, you used the Effect Controls panel to make adjustments to the scale and position of clips in a sequence. You can also use the Effect Controls panel to adjust volume.

1 Open the Excuse Me sequence from the Sequences bin.

This is a simple sequence with two clips in it (if the second clip isn't visible, scroll to the right in the Timeline panel or zoom out). In fact, it's the same clip added to the sequence twice. One version has been interpreted as stereo, and the other has been interpreted as having separate mono channels. For more on clip interpretation, see Lesson 4, "Organizing Media."

2 Click the first clip to select it, and open the Effect Controls panel.

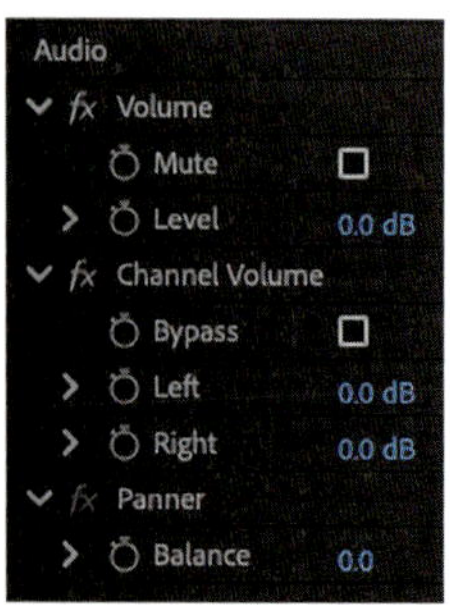

3 In the Effect Controls panel, expand the Volume, Channel Volume, and Panner controls.

Each control gives appropriate options for the type of audio you have selected.

- **Volume** adjusts the combined volume of all the audio channels in the selected clip.
- **Channel Volume** allows you to adjust the audio level for individual channels in the selected clip.
- **Panner** gives you overall stereo left/right output balance control for the selected clip.

4 Click the Timeline Display Settings menu, and make sure Show Audio Keyframes is selected.

5 Increase the height of the Audio 1 track, and use the Timeline panel zoom, so you can clearly see the clip audio waveform and the rubber band.

Note: The rubber band uses the entire height of the audio clip to adjust the volume.

6 In the Effect Controls panel, scrub left across the blue Level number that sets the volume level.

Tip: For fine control when scrubbing to adjust number values, hold Command (macOS) or Ctrl (Windows).

Set it to around –25 dB.

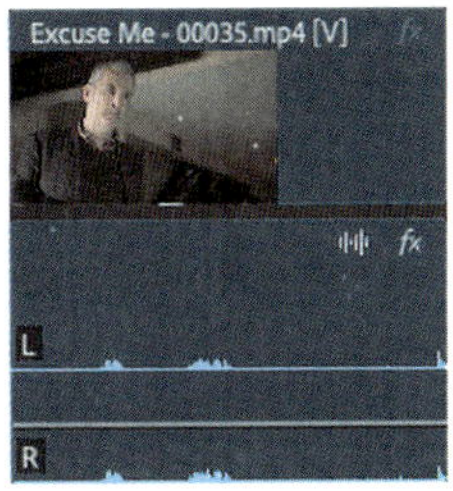

The rubber band on the clip in the Timeline panel moves down, indicating the reduced volume, and the waveform updates. The difference in the rubber band is subtle, but as you become more familiar with the Premiere interface, it'll stand out more clearly—plus the change to the waveform is clear.

7 Now select the second version of the Excuse Me clip in the sequence.

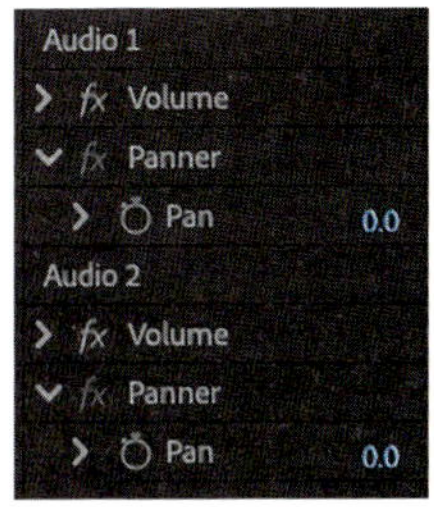

You'll notice there are similar controls available in the Effect Controls panel, but now there is no Channel Volume option. This is because each audio channel is its own clip segment, so the Volume control for each channel is already an individual one.

The Balance control has now become a Pan control. This has a similar purpose but is suited to mono audio channels, which do not need to balance with other audio channels in the same clip.

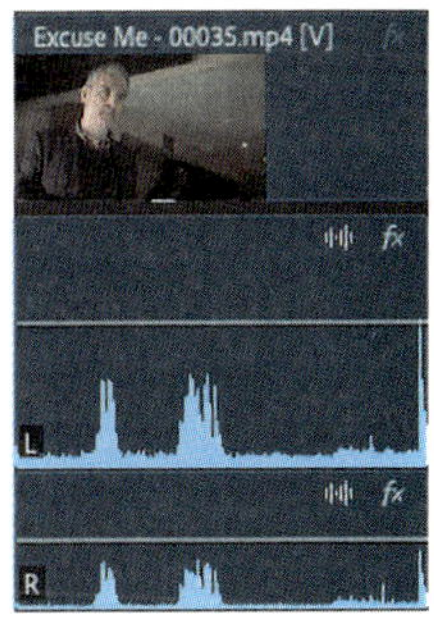

8 Experiment with adjusting the volume for these two independent clips, and listen to the results.

The difference between Pan and Balance

Mono and stereo audio clips have different panner controls to set the level for each output when producing a stereo or 5.1 surround audio sequence.

- Mono audio clips have a Pan control. In a stereo sequence, this allows you to distribute the single audio channel between the left or right side of the mix.
- Stereo audio clips have a Balance control, which adjusts the relative levels of the left and right channels in the clip.

The controls displayed vary depending on your sequence audio mix setting and the audio configuration of each clip you select.

Using the Properties panel to adjust volume

While the Effect Controls panel allows you to make adjustments to one clip at a time only, the Properties panel provides limited controls for adjusting multiple clips in a single step.

You may need to scroll down to see it, but the Properties panel includes an Audio Volume setting.

To make an adjustment, select one or more clips with the same audio channel arrangement and adjust the Volume control in the Properties panel. The Volume setting for *all* selected clips will be adjusted in the same way as if you had made the changes one by one in the Effect Controls panel.

If you check the Effect Controls for each adjusted clip, you'll find the Volume Level has been updated.

Adjusting audio gain

Most music is usually produced with the loudest possible usable signal to maximize the difference between the signal and the background noise. This is generally much too loud to use in video sequences. One way to address this issue is to adjust the clip's *audio gain.*

Audio gain adjustments are applied before any other clip volume level adjustments.

Note: The changes you make to the gain or volume of your clips will not change the original media files. You can make a change to the overall gain here, in the bin, or in the Timeline panel, in addition to any changes you make using the Effect Controls panel, and your original media files will remain unmodified.

The following method works in a similar way to the adjustment you made in the Effect Controls panel, but this time you'll adjust the clip in the Project panel, so any parts of the clip you use in any sequence will already include the adjustment.

You can apply audio gain adjustments to multiple clips in a single step, both in the Project panel and in the Timeline panel.

1 From the Music bin, double-click the clip Graceful Tenure - Patrick Cannell.mp3 to open it in the Source Monitor. You may need to adjust the zoom level on the Source Monitor to see the waveform.

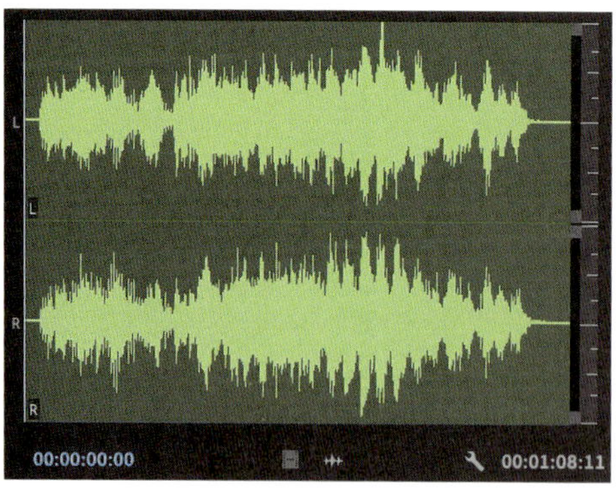

2 Right-click the clip in the Project panel and choose Audio Gain, or select the clip and press G. The Audio Gain dialog box appears.

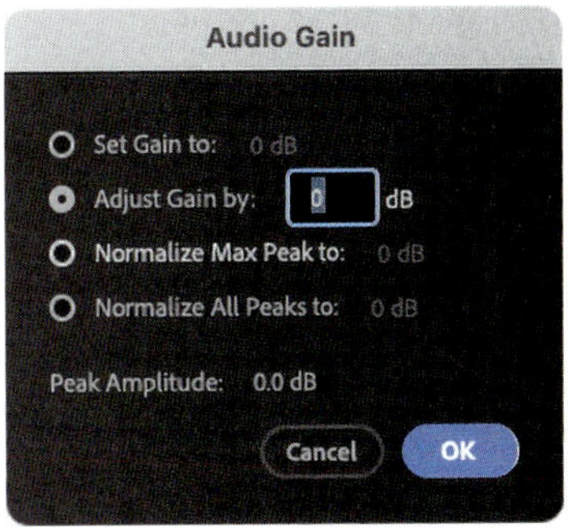

- **Set Gain To:** Use this option to specify a particular adjustment for your clip. To remove any gain adjustments, set this to 0dB.
- **Adjust Gain By:** Use this option to specify an incremental adjustment for your clip.

For example, if you set Adjust Gain By to –3 dB, this will adjust the Set Gain To setting to –3 dB when you click OK. If you open this dialog box a second time and apply another –3 dB adjustment, the Set Gain To setting will change to –6 dB, and so on.

3 Select the Set Gain To option, set the gain to **–12 dB**, and click OK. Right away, the waveform updates in the Source Monitor.

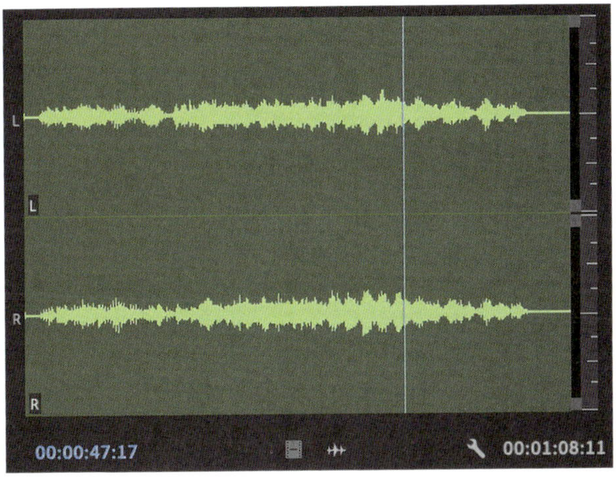

Clip instances in a sequence are separate from source clips in the Project panel. Changes like this, when you are adjusting the audio gain for clips in the bin, will not update clips already edited into a sequence, only new instances of the adjusted clips if you add them to a sequence in the future.

However, you can right-click one or more clips in a sequence and choose Audio Gain, or select clips and press G, and make the same kind of adjustment there. Doing so will adjust only the clip instance in the sequence, not the source clip in the bin.

Normalizing audio

Normalizing audio is similar to adjusting gain. In fact, the outcome of normalization is an adjustment to the clip gain. The difference is that normalization is an automatic adjustment, rather than a manual one.

When you normalize a clip, Premiere analyzes the audio to identify the single highest peak—in other words, the loudest moment in the audio. The gain for the clip is then adjusted automatically so that the highest peak matches a level you specify.

You can adjust the volume for multiple clips this way so that they match any peak volume you like.

Imagine working with multiple clips of a voice-over, recorded over several days. Perhaps because of different recording setups, different microphones, or different voices, several of the clips have significantly different volumes.

You could manually go through each clip, one by one, to make adjustments, or you could save significant time by normalizing them instead. Simply select all the clips and, in a single step, Premiere will automatically set their volumes to match.

Let's normalize some clips.

1 Open the Journey to New York sequence from the Sequences bin.

Note: You may need to adjust the track size to see the audio waveforms. Do this by dragging the divider between two track headers.

2 Play the sequence, listen, and watch the level on the audio meters.

The voice level varies quite a lot, with the first clip noticeably quieter than the third and fourth clips.

3 It's a little difficult to hear with music in the mix. To hear the voice over without the music, mute the Audio 2 track by clicking the Mute button or solo the Audio 1 track by clicking the Solo button.

4 Select all the voice-over clips in the sequence on Track A1. To do so, you can lasso them or make an item-by-item selection.

5 Right-click any of the selected clips and choose Audio Gain, or press the G key.

6 You'll normally choose a peak level for audio based on your overall intended mix. For these clips, select Normalize All Peaks To, enter **–8 dB**, and click OK.

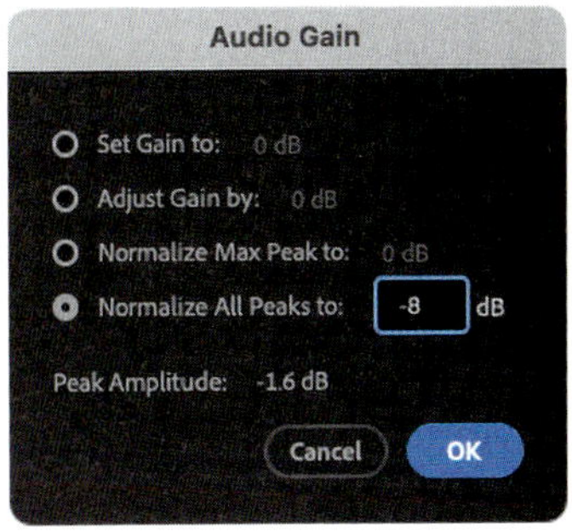

Every selected clip is adjusted so that the loudest peaks are at –8 dB, which is close to 0 dB (full volume) but allows a little headroom. Delivery standards for audio levels vary, so always check before deciding on the levels you will set in your mix.

7 Listen again to hear the result.

8 Click the Mute button on Audio 2 or the Solo button on Audio 1 to clear the setting so you can check the voice over level with the music.

9 Listen again.

Notice that the peaks of the clip waveforms now reach approximately the same level.

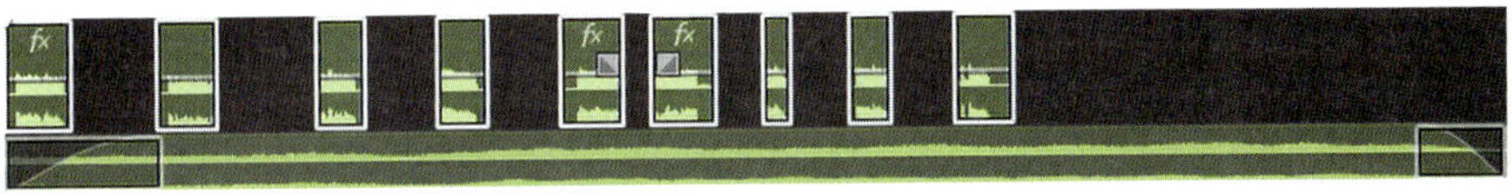

In the Audio Gain dialog box, if you choose the Normalize Max Peak To option, rather than the Normalize All Peaks To option, Premiere will make gain adjustments based on the loudest moment of all the clips combined, as if they were all one clip. The same amount of adjustment will be applied to every clip, maintaining the relative levels of all the clips.

Auto-ducking the music level

One of the most common tasks when working on an audio mix is reducing the music level during sections of speech. If there's a voice-over track, for example, you may want the music to get quieter when information is being shared and then quickly become the dominant element in the mix again. This is the way radio DJs speak over music, with the music automatically getting quieter when the DJ speaks. The technique is called *ducking*.

You can manually add audio keyframes to achieve ducking (and you'll explore this technique later in this lesson), but there's an automated way to do it too, with the Essential Sound panel.

You'll learn about the Essential Sound panel in more detail in Lesson 11. Still, this is a quick and easy workflow that saves time when creating your mix, and it's worth learning right away.

Sending audio to Adobe Audition

While Premiere has advanced tools to help you achieve most audio-editing tasks, it can't compete with Adobe Audition, which is a dedicated audio post-production application.

A component of Adobe Creative Cloud, Audition integrates neatly into your workflow when editing with Premiere. You can send a complete sequence to Adobe Audition, bringing all your clips and a video file based on your sequence, to produce an audio mix that follows along with the video. Audition can even open a Premiere PRPROJ project file natively and convert sequences into multitrack sessions for advanced audio finishing.

Unlike Premiere, Audition makes changes to audio files while working on them. For this reason, if you send a sequence to Audition, it will create copies of the audio files automatically.

If you have Audition installed, you can send a sequence to it by following these steps:

1. Open the sequence you want to send to Adobe Audition.
2. Choose Edit > Edit In Adobe Audition > Sequence.
3. Premiere will create new copies of the associated media files for you to edit in Adobe Audition, keeping your original media safe. Choose a name for the copies, and browse for a location to store them.
4. In the Video menu, you can choose Send Through Dynamic Link to view the video part of your Premiere sequence live in Audition, directly from the Premiere Timeline.
5. Choose the remaining options as you prefer, and finally click OK.

Adobe Audition has fantastic tools for working with sound. It has a special spectral display that helps you identify and remove unwanted noises, a high-performance multitrack editor, and advanced audio effects and controls.

To send your completed mix from Audition to Premiere, choose Multitrack > Export To Adobe Premiere. Choose one of the mixdown options (usually Stereo), specify a location and name for the new media file, and click Export.

You can also send an individual clip to Audition for editing, effects, and adjustment features. To send an audio clip to Audition, right-click the clip in your Premiere sequence and choose Edit Clip In Adobe Audition.

Premiere duplicates the audio clip, replaces the current clip in the sequence with the duplicate, and opens the duplicate in Audition, ready to work on it.

From now on, every time you save changes you have made to the clip in Audition, they'll automatically update in Premiere.

For more information about Adobe Audition, visit *peachpit.com/store/adobe-audition-cc-classroom-in-a-book-9780135228326* and check out *Adobe Audition CC Classroom in a Book*.

1 Continue working in the Journey to New York sequence. Make sure all the voice-over clips on the Audio 1 track are selected.

2 In the Essential Sound panel, click the Edit tab to view options that relate to the clips you have selected.

3 By tagging each clip with one of the audio types, you'll get access to tools and controls that are relevant to that type of audio.

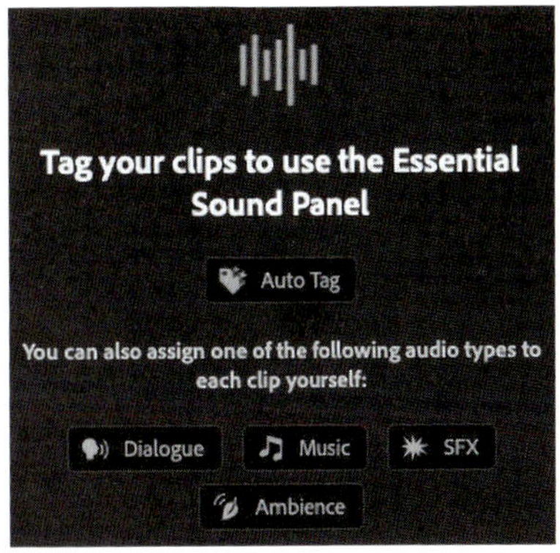

Premiere can automatically detect the audio type for clips and assign the correct tags, if you enable the Auto Tag option.

However, it may not be possible to accurately identify the audio type for short clips like these.

Click the Dialogue button to assign the dialogue audio type to the selected clips.

Assigning the Dialogue tag means Premiere now knows the audio is dialogue for the purposes of performing automatic ducking.

4 Resize the Audio 2 track so you can see the music clip's audio waveform clearly (if necessary, you can drag the divide between the video and audio tracks up or down to make more room for audio). Select the music clip, and in the Essential Sound panel select the Music audio type.

5 In the Essential Sound panel, enable Ducking, and take a look at the options.

If the settings are not showing any values, double-click each slider to restore the defaults.

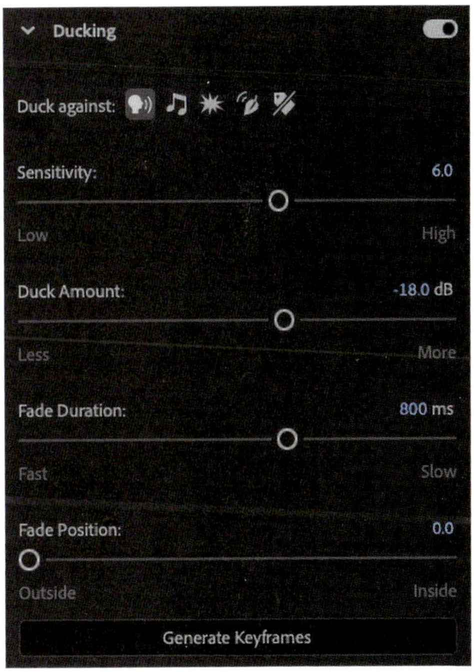

- **Duck Against:** There are multiple types of audio. You can select whether one, several, or all types of audio will trigger automatic ducking. We're ducking against dialogue, and this option is selected by default.
- **Sensitivity:** The higher the sensitivity, the lower the audio level necessary to trigger ducking.
- **Duck Amount:** This is the amount the music level will be reduced by, measured in dB.
- **Fade Duration:** The slower the fade setting, the longer it will take for the music to get quieter and then louder again.
- **Fade Position:** Adjusts the timing for the fades that are added, producing earlier or later keyframes, which may work better for different sequences.
- **Generate Keyframes:** Click this button to apply the settings and add keyframes to the music clip.

6 Choosing the right settings for audio ducking is a science and an art, and the type of audio you are working with will influence the choices you make. Experimentation is the key.

For this audio, try these settings:

- **Duck Against:** Dialogue Clips should already be selected (it's the default).
- **Sensitivity:** 6.0
- **Duck Amount:** –8.0 dB
- **Fade Duration:** 500 ms
- **Fade Position:** 5.0

7 Click Generate Keyframes.

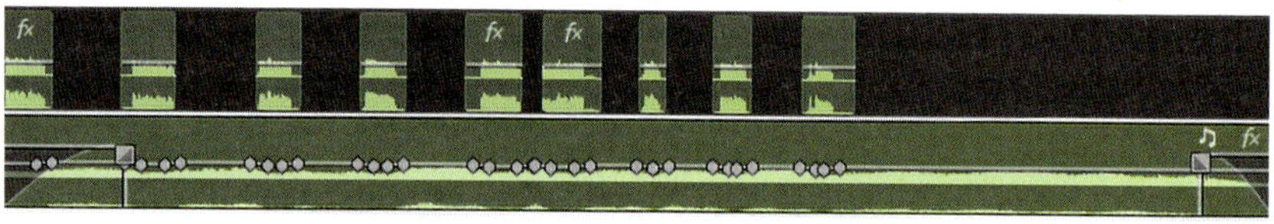

An Amplify effect is automatically applied to the music clip, and keyframes are added to it. The effect and keyframes appear in the Effect Controls panel and the Timeline panel.

8 Play the sequence to listen to the result. It's not perfect, but it's closer to a finished mix.

You can adjust the automatic ducking settings and click the Generate Keyframes button repeatedly to remove and replace existing keyframes, making it safe and easy to experiment.

You can also manually adjust the keyframes that have been added. You can remove, move, and add keyframes at any time.

Retiming music with Remix

Music can have an enormous impact on visual storytelling. Just as an action movie might feel tame without a stirring soundtrack, the most nuanced dialogue can be brought to life with exactly the right musical backdrop. In many ways, the music tells the audience how to feel, so getting it right is crucial.

You may discover exactly the piece of music you want, and even have the rights to use it in your project, only to discover it is too long or too short for your visuals. What to do?

For many years, the solution was to spend arduous hours carefully splitting and rejoining pieces of a music track in the hope of seamlessly extending or shortening it—often unsuccessfully, because it can be extremely difficult to avoid jarring joins.

Thankfully, Premiere has an extraordinary solution: Remix. This automated, intelligent technology analyzes the music and applies exactly the right edits to achieve the duration you want—in seconds.

The best way to learn about Remix is to try it.

1 Open the Drone Flight sequence in the Sequences bin.

2 From the Music bin, drag the clip Ambient Heavens - Patrick Cannell onto the beginning of the Audio 1 track.

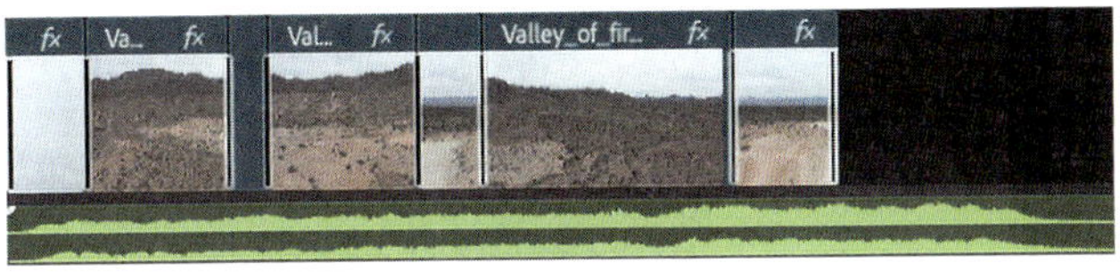

This music track is too long for the sequence. You'll use Remix to adjust the length.

3 Click and hold the Ripple Edit tool to expand the additional tool options, and select the Remix tool.

4 Check that Snapping is selected in the Timeline panel, and then use the Remix tool to trim the end of the music clip shorter until it snaps to the end of the video clips.

A progress bar shows the progress of the clip analysis, and clip duration is updated.

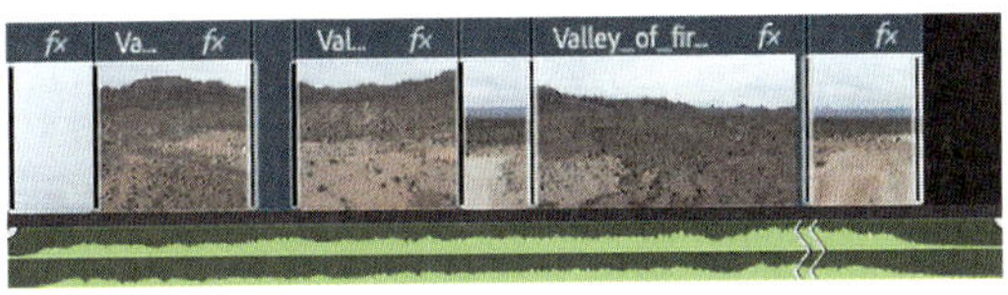

The white jagged lines indicate moments when the music clip was edited. Try playing across the edits—it's difficult to detect them. That's the magic of Remix!

Notice that the music clip does not have exactly the duration you chose. Remix makes an intelligent assessment of the clip and sets a new duration that will best allow for seamless joins.

5 Remix works for making clips longer too. Delete the Ambient Heavens - Patrick Cannell clip.

6 From the Music bin, drag the Ghost Reverie music clip onto the beginning of the Audio 1 track.

7 Use the Remix tool to trim the clip longer to match the duration of the video clips. Review the result.

If you find Remix produces a poor result, you can experiment with the detailed settings in the Duration section of the Essential Sound panel.

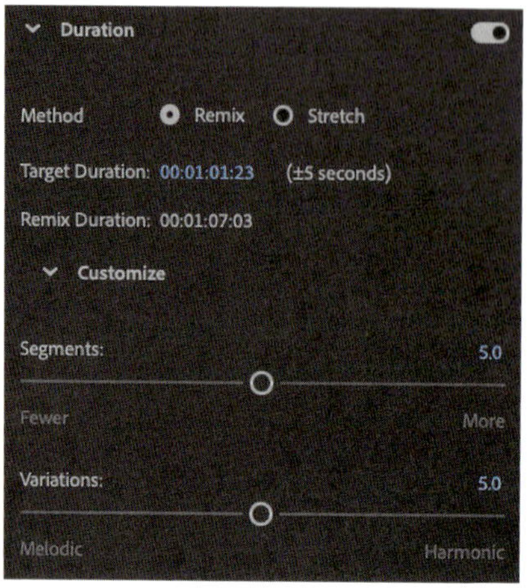

For now, choose the Selection tool, ready for the next exercise.

Creating a split edit

A *split edit* is a simple, classic editing technique that offsets the cut point for audio and video. The audio from one clip is played with the visuals from another, carrying the feeling of one scene into another.

Adding a J-cut

The *J-cut* gets its name from the shape of the edit. Picture the letter *J* over an edit. The lower part (the audio cut) is to the left of the upper part (the video cut).

1 Open the Theft Unexpected sequence in the Sequences bin.

2 Click the Solo button S for the Audio 1 track so you can hear the dialogue clearly without the background sound you added earlier.

3 Play the last cut in the sequence. The join in the audio between the last two clips is rather abrupt. You may need to turn up your speaker volume to hear the join. You'll improve things by adjusting the timing of the audio cut.

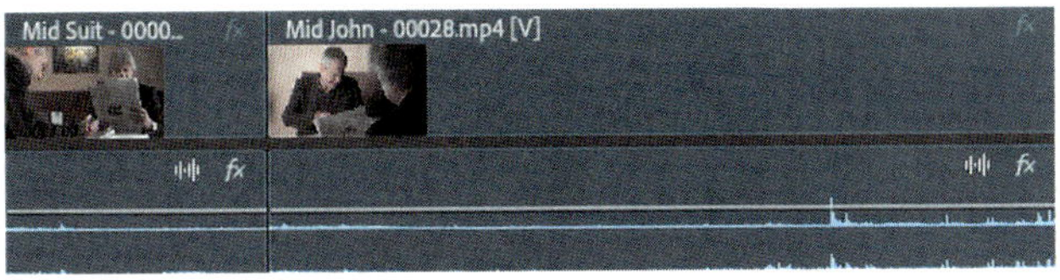

4 Select the Rolling Edit tool, accessible by clicking and holding the Remix tool icon. (If you had not earlier selected the Remix tool, you'd click and hold the Ripple Edit tool icon instead.)

5 Press and hold Option (macOS) or Alt (Windows)—this temporarily overrides linked selections—and drag the audio segment edit between the last two clips (not the video) a little to the left, in a single motion. Congratulations! You've created a J-cut!

> **Tip:** With the default Premiere preferences, you can use the Selection tool to apply a rolling edit if you hold Command (macOS) or Ctrl (Windows).

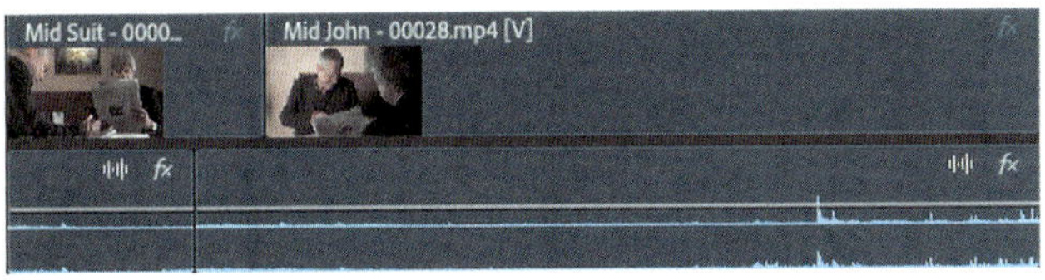

6 Play through the edit.

You might want to experiment with the timing to make the cut seem more natural, but for practical purposes the J-cut works. You could also smooth it over and improve it further with an audio crossfade later.

7 Switch back to the Selection tool (V).

> **Tip:** When you have finished working with trimming tools, it's a good idea to click the Selection tool. This prevents you from applying adjustments accidentally when you attempt to select clips in a sequence.

> **Tip:** For more information on keyboard shortcuts, see "Using and setting keyboard shortcuts" in Lesson 1, "Touring Adobe Premiere."

Adding an L-cut

An *L-cut* works in the same way as a J-cut but in reverse. Repeat the steps, but drag the audio segment edit a little to the right while holding Option (macOS) or Alt (Windows). Play through the edit to see (and hear) what you think. Naturally, you can achieve the same results by adjusting the timing of the video part of an edit.

Working with audio keyframes

As well as adjusting clip gain, you can use the rubber band to change the volume of clips in a sequence. You can also change the volume for whole tracks. These three volume adjustments combine to produce an overall output level.

If anything, using rubber bands to adjust volume is more convenient than adjusting gain because you can make incremental adjustments at any point in the sequence, with immediate visual feedback.

The result of adjusting the rubber bands on a clip is similar to adjusting the volume using the Effect Controls panel. In fact, one control automatically updates the other.

Keyframing volume changes

You can use the Selection tool to adjust existing audio keyframes added to sequence clips in the same way that you might adjust visual keyframes. If you drag a keyframe up, the audio will get louder; drag a keyframe down to make the audio quieter.

Tip: If you adjust the clip audio gain, Premiere combines that adjustment with any keyframe-based adjustments dynamically. You can change either at any time.

The Pen tool  adds keyframes to rubber bands. You can also use it to adjust existing keyframes or to lasso multiple keyframes to adjust them as a group.

You don't need to use the Pen tool, though. If you want to add a keyframe using the Selection tool, hold Command (macOS) or Ctrl (Windows) when you click the rubber band.

The result of adding and adjusting the position of keyframes up or down on audio clip segments is that the rubber band is reshaped. Just as before, the higher the rubber band, the louder the sound.

Click to view the Desert Montage sequence in the Timeline panel. Add a few keyframes to the music now, with dramatic level adjustments, and listen to the results. Go crazy with the keyframes so the adjustments are obvious, and then play the sequence to hear the results and watch the effect on the audio meters.

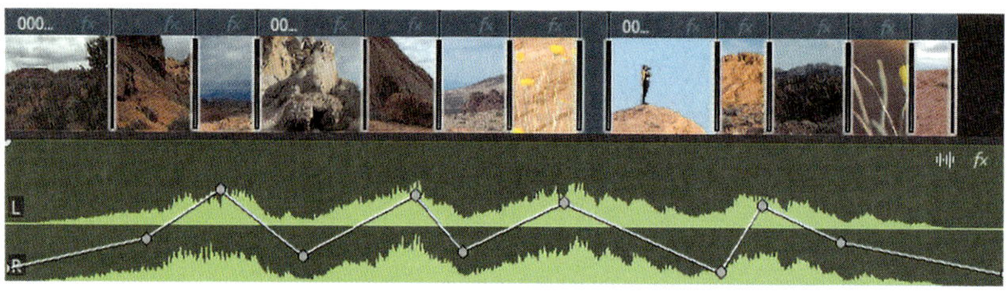

The clip waveform updates dynamically as you adjust keyframes on the rubber band, making it easier to see the level adjustment relative to the rest of the clip.

Smoothing volume between keyframes

The adjustments you just made are probably pretty overwhelming. You might want to smooth these or other adjustments.

To do so, right-click any of the keyframes. You'll see a range of standard options, including Ease In, Ease Out, Bezier, and Delete. If you use the Pen tool, you can lasso multiple keyframes and then right-click any one of them to apply a change to them all.

The best way to learn about the different kinds of keyframes is to select each kind, make some adjustments, and see or listen to the results.

Using clip vs. track keyframes

Until now, you've made all your keyframe adjustments to sequence clip segments. When working with the Audio Clip Mixer, as you will in a moment, all adjustments are made directly to clips in the current sequence.

There are similar controls for the audio tracks those clips are placed on. Track-based keyframes work in the same way as the clip-based ones. The difference is that they don't move with the clips.

This means you can set up keyframes for your audio level using track controls and then try different music clips. Each time you put new music into your sequence, you'll hear it via the adjustments you have made to your track.

As you develop your editing skills with Premiere and create more complex audio mixes, explore the flexibility offered by combining clip and track keyframe adjustments.

Working with the Audio Clip Mixer

The Audio Clip Mixer provides intuitive controls to add and adjust clip volume and pan keyframes over time.

Each sequence audio track is represented by a set of controls. Though the controls are organized by track names, the adjustments you make will be applied to clips (not tracks).

You can mute or solo a track in the Audio Clip Mixer, and you can enable an option to write keyframes to clips during playback when dragging a fader or adjusting a pan control.

What's a fader? Faders are industry-standard controls based on real-world audio-mixing decks. You move the fader up to increase the volume and move it down to decrease the volume.

Let's try this.

1 Continue working with the Desert Montage sequence.

2 Open the Audio Clip Mixer (not the Audio Track Mixer), and play the sequence from the beginning.

   Because you already added keyframes to this clip, the Audio Clip Mixer fader Audio 1 moves up and down during playback, following the adjustments you made.

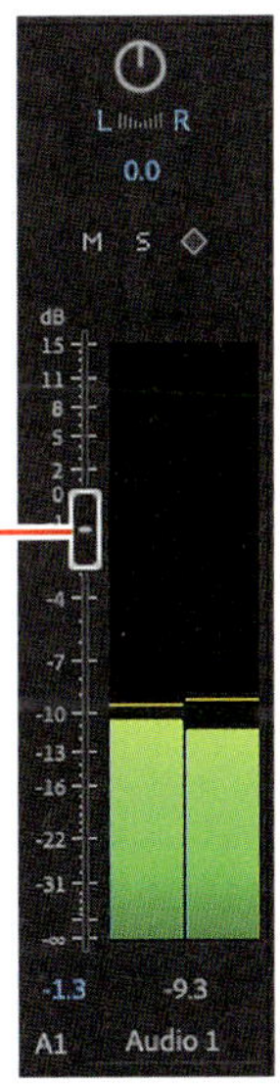

3 Position the Timeline panel playhead at the beginning of the sequence again. In the Audio Clip Mixer, select the Write Keyframes button near the top of the Audio 1 controls, next to the Mute and Solo buttons. The button is blue when active .

4 Play the sequence, and while it plays, make some really dramatic adjustments to the Audio 1 fader. Keyframes appear after you stop playback.

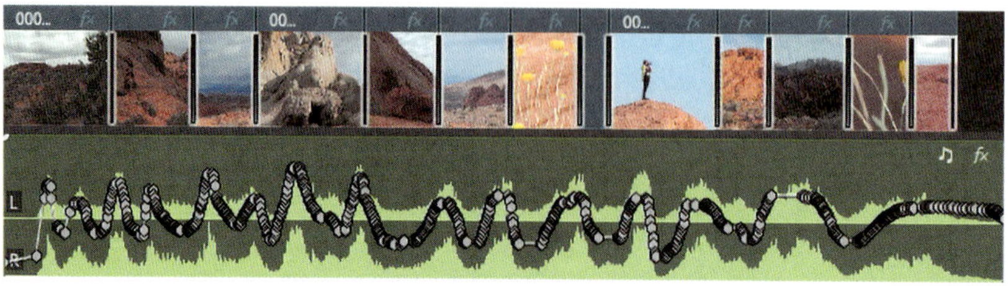

Tip: You can adjust audio pan in the same way as you would adjust volume using the Audio Clip Mixer: Enable keyframing, play your sequence, and make adjustments using the Audio Clip Mixer Pan control.

5 If you repeat the process, you'll notice that, once again, the fader follows existing keyframes until you make a manual adjustment.

When you use the fader control to add keyframes, a *lot* of keyframes are added (also, existing keyframes are replaced). By default, Premiere adds a keyframe with every adjustment. However, you can set a minimum time gap for keyframes to make them more manageable.

6 Choose Premiere > Settings > Audio (macOS) or Edit > Preferences > Audio (Windows). Select Minimum Time Interval Thinning and set a minimum time of 500 milliseconds (half a second is relatively slow, but it provides a balance between precise adjustment and keyframe overload). Click OK.

7 Set the playhead to the beginning of the sequence, and, once again, use the Audio Clip Mixer to add level keyframes using the fader control.

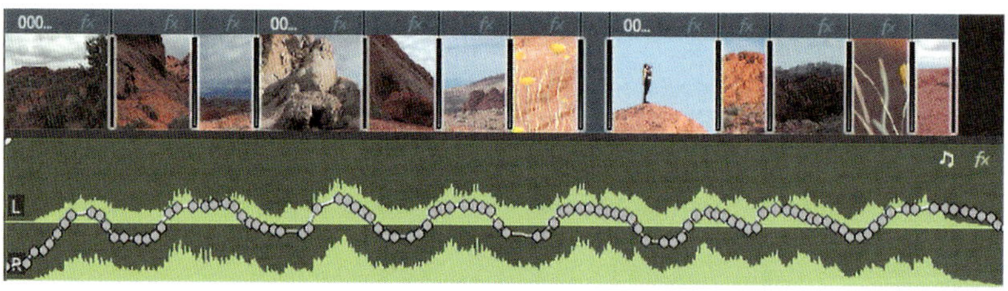

The result is a much more orderly adjustment. Even with dramatic adjustments, the smaller number of keyframes is much more manageable.

You can adjust keyframes you created this way just as you would adjust keyframes that you created using the Selection tool or the Pen tool.

The fundamental building block of animation, whether for visual effects or audio, is the keyframe. You have now explored several ways to add and adjust keyframes in Premiere. There's no right or wrong way to work with keyframes; it's entirely a matter of personal preference or the needs of a particular project.

Experiment and practice to make sure you feel truly comfortable with the concept and application of keyframes, and it will help with your developing understanding of post-production effects.

Review questions

1. How can you isolate an individual sequence mix audio channel to hear only that channel?
2. What is the difference between mono and stereo audio?
3. How can you view the waveforms for a clip that has both video and audio in the Source Monitor?
4. What is the difference between normalization and gain?
5. What is the difference between a J-cut and an L-cut?
6. Which option in the Audio Clip Mixer must be selected before you can use the fader controls to add keyframes to sequence clips during playback?

Review answers

1. Use the Solo buttons at the bottom of the audio meters to selectively hear an audio channel.
2. Stereo audio has two audio channels, and mono audio has one. It's the universal standard to record audio from a Left microphone as Channel 1 and audio from a Right microphone as Channel 2 when recording stereo sound.
3. Use the Settings menu on the Source Monitor to choose Audio Waveform. You can also click the Drag Audio Only button at the bottom of the Source Monitor. Clips in a sequence can display waveforms in the Timeline panel.
4. Normalization automatically adjusts the Gain setting for a clip based on the original peak amplitude. You use the Gain setting to make manual adjustments.
5. A J-cut means the sound for the next clip begins before the visuals (this is sometimes described as "audio leads video"). With L-cuts, the sound from the previous clip remains until after the visuals begin (sometimes described as "video leads audio").
6. Select the Write Keyframes option for each track you would like to add keyframes to.

11 IMPROVING AUDIO

Lesson overview

In this lesson, you'll learn how to do the following:

- Work with the Essential Sound panel.
- Improve the sound of speech.
- Clean up noisy audio.

This lesson will take about 75 minutes to complete. To get the files used in this lesson, refer to the instructions in "Accessing the lesson files and Web Edition" in the "Getting Started" section at the beginning of this book. Store the files on your computer in a convenient location.

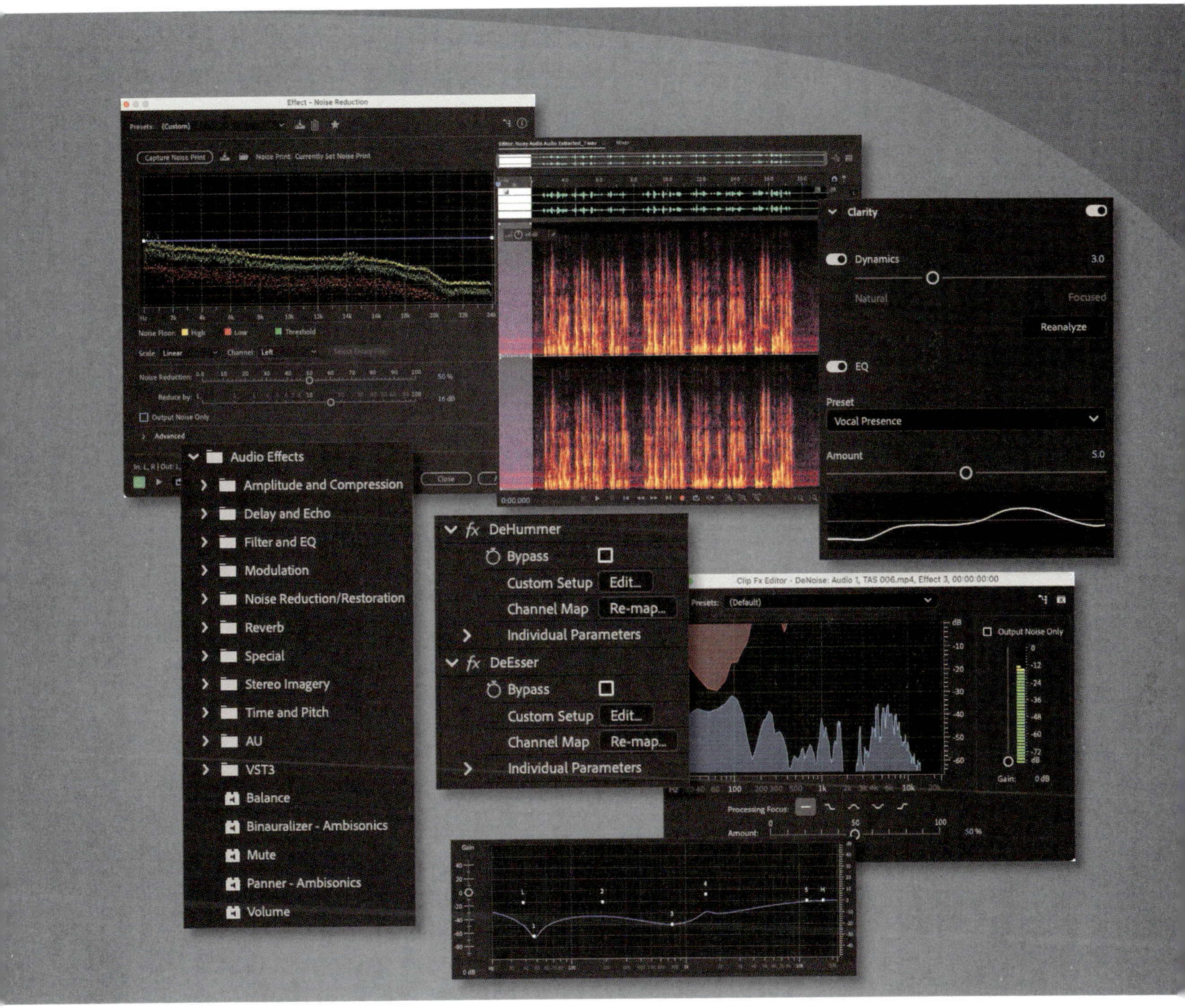

Audio effects in Premiere can dramatically change the feel of your project—and clean up audio. You can make both technical and creative adjustments to your audio. In this lesson, you'll learn some quick, easy ways to improve the quality of your sound mix.

Starting the lesson

Note: To ensure that the tools function and the defaults are set exactly as described in this lesson, reset the Premiere preferences by holding any modifier key (such as Shift) while launching the application, selecting Reset App Preferences, and then clicking Continue in the Reset Options dialog box.

You'll find many audio effects in Adobe Premiere. These effects can be used to change pitch, create an echo, add reverb, and remove tape hiss. You can set keyframes for effects and adjust their settings over time.

1 Open the project Lesson 11.prproj.
2 In the Workspaces menu, choose Audio. Then open the Workspaces menu again and choose Reset To Saved Layout.
3 Save the project as **Lesson 11 Working.prproj**.

Improving audio with the Essential Sound panel

Video production rarely produces perfect audio. You'll probably need to use audio effects in post-production to fix a few problems and improve the quality of the sound, particularly for vocals, because audiences are acutely sensitive to issues with the sound of a human voice.

Not all audio hardware plays all audio frequencies evenly. For example, listening to deep bass notes on a laptop is never the same as listening on larger speakers.

It's important to listen to your audio using high-quality headphones or studio monitor speakers to avoid compensating for a flaw in your playback hardware as you adjust the sound. Professional audio-monitoring hardware is carefully calibrated to ensure that all frequencies play evenly—a so-called "flat" response, giving you confidence that you'll produce a consistent sound for your listeners.

It can be helpful to listen to your audio on low-quality speakers too. This allows you to confirm that enough of the audio is clear and that low-frequency sound doesn't cause distortion.

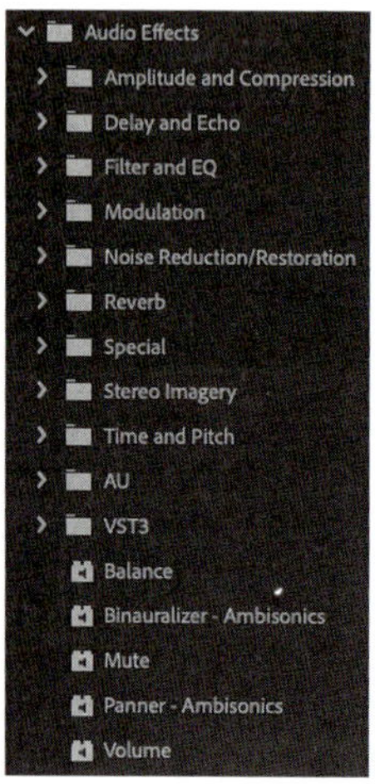

Premiere offers a variety of helpful audio effects, including the following, all of which are available in the Effects panel:

- **Parametric Equalizer:** This allows you to make subtle and precise adjustments to the audio level at particular frequencies.
- **Studio Reverb:** This can increase the "presence" in the recording using reverb. For example, it can simulate the atmosphere of a larger room.
- **Dynamics Processing:** This effect allows you to make precise dynamic adjustments to audio to compress, expand, or limit levels.
- **Bass:** This effect can adjust the low-end frequencies of a clip. It works well on narration clips, particularly for low tone voices (voices in a low frequency range).
- **Treble:** This effect adjusts the higher-range frequencies in an audio clip.

Depending upon your operating system and the third-party plug-ins you have installed (if any), you may also see AU, VST, VST3, or custom-named effect folders.

Apply effects by dragging them from the Effects panel onto clips, just as you dragged transition effects onto edits earlier. Select a clip to find its effect controls in the Effect Controls panel. There are many presets to help you get a feel for the ways you can use effects.

You can remove an effect in the Effect Controls panel by selecting it and pressing Delete (macOS) or Backspace (Windows).

You can use the 01 Effects sequence in this project to experiment with audio effects. The clips in this sequence have a range of audio to make it easy to hear the results of your adjustments.

Note: Expand your knowledge of audio effects in Premiere by experimenting. Like video effects, these effects are nondestructive, which means they do not change your original audio files. You can add any number of effects to a clip, change settings, listen, and then delete them and start again.

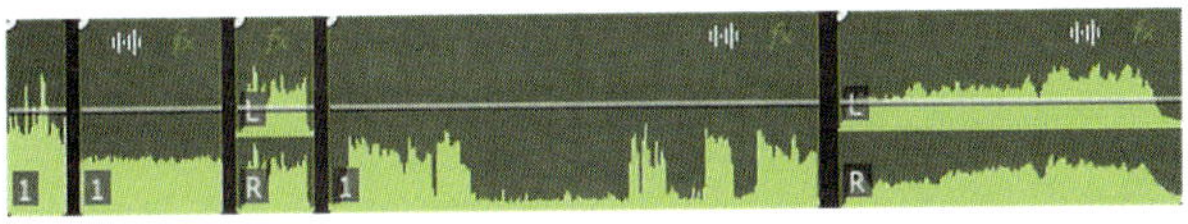

This lesson focuses on the Essential Sound panel, which offers a range of easy-to-apply professional adjustments and effects that are based on common workflows for standard media types like dialogue and music.

The Essential Sound panel contains your go-to set of options for audio cleanup and improvement.

Adjusting dialogue audio

The Essential Sound panel has a comprehensive list of features to help you work with dialogue audio. The panel is divided into sections, each with controls to adjust, clean up, and add clarity to your audio.

To use the Essential Sound panel, select one or more clips in a sequence, and select a tag that corresponds to the type of audio in the clip.

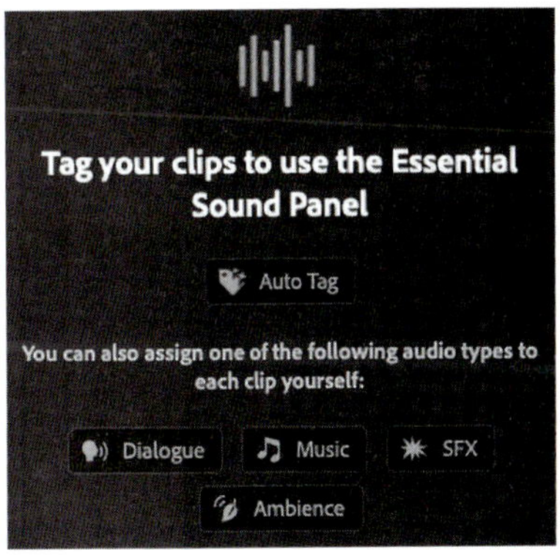

Tip: Clicking Auto Tag in the Essential Sound panel will allow Premiere to tag audio clips as audio types automatically. You'll tend to obtain more accurate results when auto tagging longer clips.

Selecting each tag displays different tools that are suitable for that type of media. There are more options for dialogue audio than any other—and for good reason! Your dialogue sound is probably the most important, and music, prepared special effects (SFX), and ambient sound files are often already mixed and ready to use.

If you select the wrong type of audio tag (or Premiere does), you can click Clear Audio Type at the top of the Essential Sound panel to remove it.

Select all the clips in the 01 Effects sequence now and click the Dialogue button in the Essential Sound panel to assign the dialogue tag.

Once a category tag is applied to a clip, a small icon representing that category of audio appears in the upper-right corner on the clip in the Timeline panel. For example, here's the icon for audio tagged as dialogue: . You can click the icon to open the Essential Sound panel directly.

Although this is a very small icon, it's instantly recognizable as the same as the one in the Essential Sound panel: .

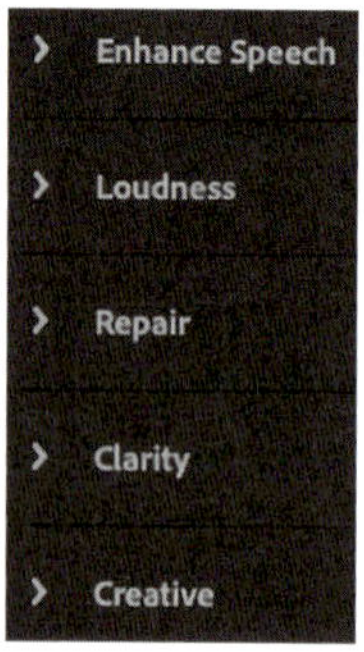

When working with clips that are tagged as dialogue, here are the sections that appear in the Essential Sound panel:

- **Enhance Speech:** Use AI to clean up noisy audio.
- **Loudness:** Automatically set volume level using the Loudness scale.
- **Repair:** Combine exactly the adjustments you need to clean up audio, reduce rumble, remove hum, and more.
- **Clarity:** Improve audio clarity, apply preset EQ adjustments, and enhance low and high tone vocals.
- **Creative:** Add subtle or more dramatic reverb to add warmth or for creative effect.

Each section and most individual controls have an on/off switch  so you can quickly compare the results of your adjustment with the unmodified original sound.

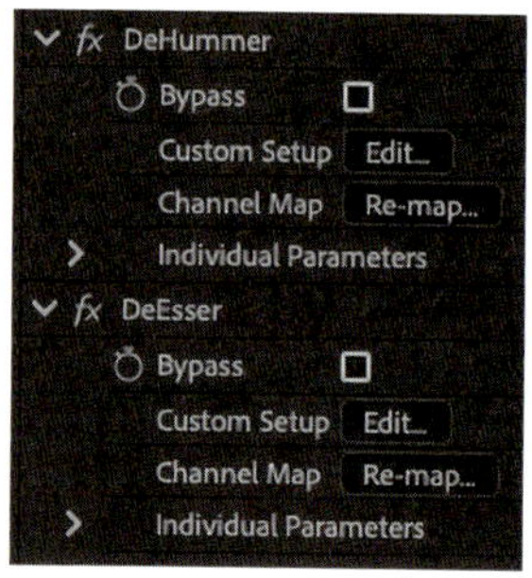

Every adjustment you apply with the Essential Sound panel actually adds one or more audio effects to your selected clips and modifies the settings for those effects. In a sense, the Essential Sound panel offers an excellent shortcut to achieving great results with simplified controls. After applying adjustments in the Essential Sound panel, you can select a clip and adjust the detailed effect settings in the Effect Controls panel.

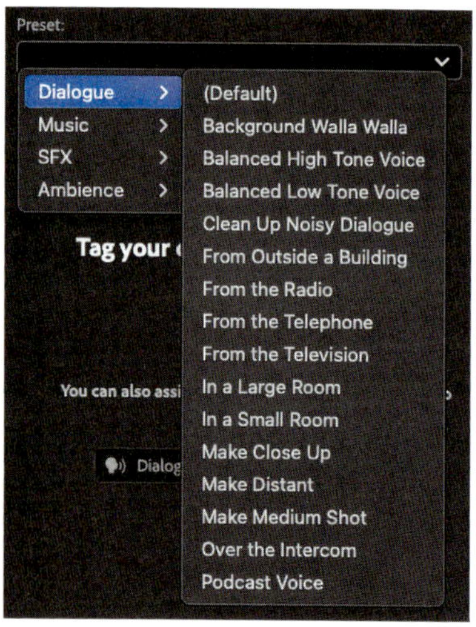

In the following exercises, you'll try several of the adjustments available in the Essential Sound panel. You can save any combination of adjustments as a preset. You access presets at the top of the Essential Sound panel. Several presets are already available.

Setting loudness

The Essential Sound panel makes it easy to set the audio level for multiple clips to an appropriate volume for broadcast television.

Let's try this.

1 Open the sequence 02 Loudness.

This is the sequence you worked with previously when learning about normalization.

2 Increase the height of the Audio 1 track, and zoom in a little so you can see the voice-over clips clearly.

3 Play the sequence to hear the different levels for the voice-over clips.

4 Select all the voice-over clips. The easiest way is to lasso across them, being careful not to select any of the other clips in the sequence.

> **Tip:** To quickly select all the clips on a single track, use the keyboard shortcut A to choose the Track Select Forward tool. Next, hold shift while you click the first clip you want to select. Afterward, remember to switch back to the Selection tool by pressing V.

5 In the Essential Sound panel, click the Dialogue button. This assigns the Dialogue audio type to these clips.

6 If necessary, click the title of the Loudness category to display the Loudness options. Clicking a category in this way is a little like clicking a chevron in the Effect Controls panel—options display or hide when you click.

7 Click Auto-Match.

Premiere analyzes each clip and automatically adjusts Audio Gain to achieve the –23 LUFS standard level for broadcast television dialogue. LUFS stands for Loudness Units relative to full scale.

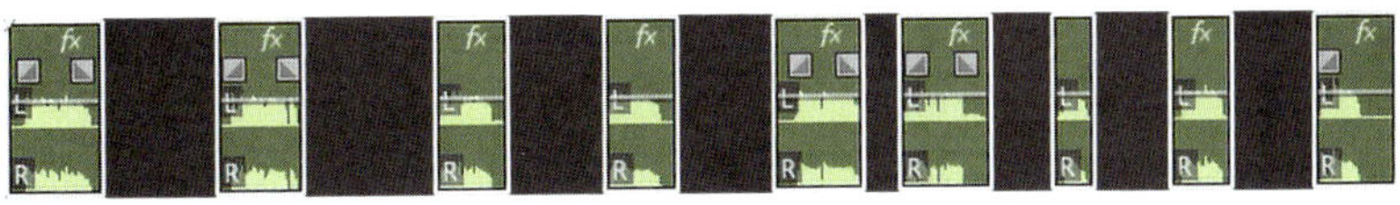

As with normalization, which also adjusts clip gain, this adjustment updates the waveforms for the clips.

If you are producing content for distribution via the internet, there's a good chance you will choose another audio level.

You can adjust the level for multiple selected clips, after using Auto-Match, using the Clip Volume control at the bottom of the Essential Sound panel.

8 Play the sequence to hear the adjustment.

About the Loudness scale

Historically, audio level was described exclusively in decibels (dB). You'll find the decibel scale a useful reference all throughout production and post-production as it is still commonly used.

Peak level (the loudest moment of a clip's audio level) is often used to set limits for audio level. Although it's a useful reference, it doesn't account for the overall power or energy in a soundtrack, and it's common to produce a mix that sets every part of the soundtrack louder than is natural, for dramatic effect. A whisper, for example, can sound as loud as a shout. As long as the peak level of the audio is within prescribed limits, it might be allowed for broadcast television.

This is why, in some parts of the world, so many television commercials sound as loud as they do—even the quiet sections of the soundtrack are loud.

Intended to resolve this issue, the widely adopted *Loudness scale* measures the total energy over time. When a Loudness limit is used, it's okay for content to have loud sections, but the total amount of energy in the soundtrack per minute can't rise above the level set.

If you are producing content for broadcast television, you will almost certainly use the Loudness scale when assessing your audio mix, and this is the scale the Essential Sound panel uses.

Repairing audio

However hard you try to capture clean audio on location, it's likely some of your footage will have unwanted background noise.

The Essential Sound panel has a number of ways to clean up dialogue clips. Take a look at the Repair category to reveal the options for repairing dialogue.

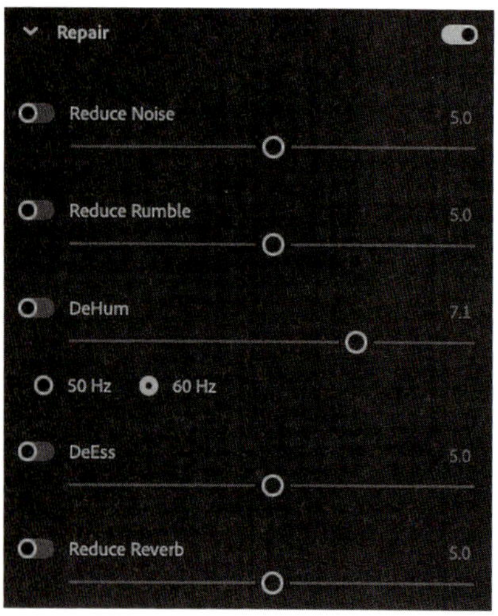

- **Reduce Noise:** Reduce the level of unwanted noises in the background, like the sound of an air-conditioning unit, rustling clothes, or background hiss.
- **Reduce Rumble:** Reduce low-frequency sounds, such as engine noise or some types of wind noise.
- **DeHum:** Reduce electrical interference hum. In North and South America, this is in the 60 Hz range, while in most of Europe, Asia, and Africa, it's in the 50 Hz range. If your microphone cable was lying next to a power cable, you may have this intrusive but easy-to-remove unwanted sound.
- **DeEss:** Reduce harsh, high-frequency *ess*-like sounds common in the sibilance part of voice recordings.

- **Reduce Reverb:** Reduce the effect of reflected sounds to make vocals clearer. When recording in an environment with a lot of reflective surfaces, some of the sound may be reflected back to the microphone as reverb.

Different clips are likely to benefit from one or more of these cleanup features, and often you will use a combination.

The default settings have high enough intensity to make it clear when a repair is turned on or off. In most cases, you will obtain the best results by starting with a setting of 0, playing the audio, and increasing the effect intensity during playback until you are happy with the result, minimizing potential distortion.

Let's try cleaning up some power hum.

1 Open the sequence 03 Noise Reduction.

2 Play the sequence to listen to the voice-over.

This is a simple sequence, with a voice-over accompanying some visuals. There's a loud electrical interference power hum in the audio. If you can't hear the hum, your speakers may not be able to reproduce audio at sufficiently low frequencies—try listening with headphones.

3 Select the voice-over clip in the sequence.

The clip has already been designated as dialogue in the Essential Sound panel, so the dialogue audio options are displayed.

4 If it's not already open, click the Repair heading in the Essential Sound panel to display the options. Select DeHum to turn it on.

5 Play the sequence to hear the difference.

The impact is significant! The electrical interference hum was loud but at a specific frequency, which makes removing it relatively straightforward.

If the amount of DeHum impacts the speech in the voice-over, try dragging the slider to adjust the amount.

Tip: You can turn the display of audio and video clip names on and off by choosing the appropriate options from the Timeline Display Settings menu.

Tip: For more challenging audio cleanup, when the repair options in Premiere don't give you a result that is clean enough, try Adobe Audition, which has advanced noise reduction features. Learn more in *Adobe Audition CC Classroom in a Book, 2nd Edition*.

This example clip has 60 Hz hum, so the default option of 60 Hz is suitable. If the default option doesn't work, try switching to 50 Hz.

After adjusting the DeHum control, check the start of the clip. You may discover a tiny amount of hum remains before the repair is applied. To remove this, add a short crossfade at the beginning of the clip.

Reducing noise and reverb

In addition to specific types of background noise like hum and rumble, Premiere offers advanced noise and reverb reduction tools. These audio cleanup effects have simple controls in the Essential Sound panel and more advanced options when accessed via the Effect Controls panel.

Reducing noise

Let's try reducing noise first.

1 Open the sequence 04 Auto Noise and Reverb. This sequence has clips suffering from background noise *and* reverberation. Play the sequence to familiarize yourself with this challenging audio—lots of unwanted background noise and reverb because it was recorded at a noisy location.

Tip: You can reset any slider in the Essential Sound panel to its default value by double-clicking the control.

The clips in this sequence have already been assigned the Dialogue audio type in the Essential Sound panel, and the Auto-Match option in the Loudness category has been applied.

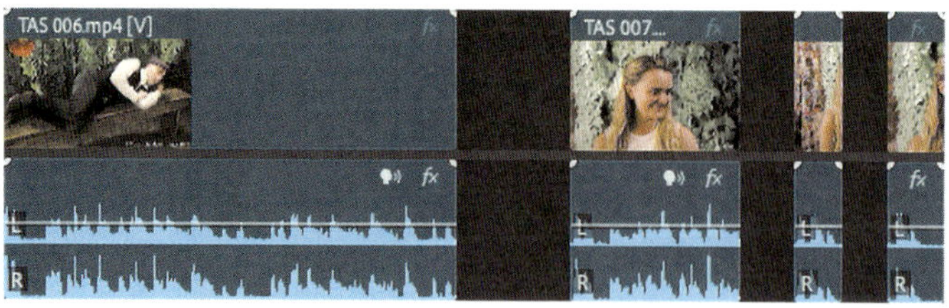

2 Select the first clip in the sequence. In the Repair section of the Essential Sound panel, select Reduce Noise. The default setting for the effect intensity is 5.0.

3 Play the clip in the sequence to hear the difference. The loud rumble that begins at about 00:00:10:00 is immediately much quieter.

4 As with many effects, trial and error will usually yield the best results. Try adjusting the effect intensity during playback. If the effect is too strong, speech might begin to sound distorted. If the effect is not strong enough, too much of the unwanted background sound might remain. When you finish experimenting, leave the setting on 5.0.

Part of the challenge in working with this audio is that some of the low-frequency background sound is close to some of the frequencies of the speech, making it harder to automatically remove. Let's use more advanced settings.

5 Make sure the first clip is still selected in the Timeline panel, and open the Effect Controls panel. Click the Edit button next to Custom Setup to access the advanced controls for the DeNoise effect, which Premiere applied to the clip when you enabled Reduce Noise in the Essential Sound panel.

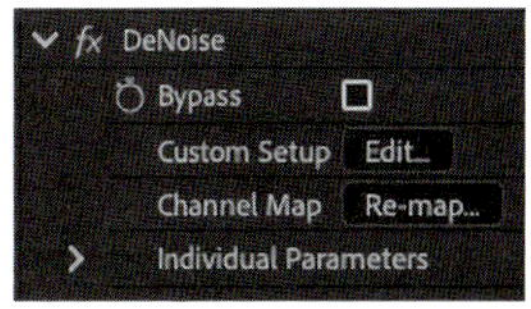

The Clip Fx Editor - DeNoise window opens. During playback, the DeNoise effect graph shows the originally detected noise (in blue at the bottom) and the cleanup adjustment applied (in red at the top). While the effect controls are open, you can still interact with the Timeline panel, placing the playhead and playing the sequence.

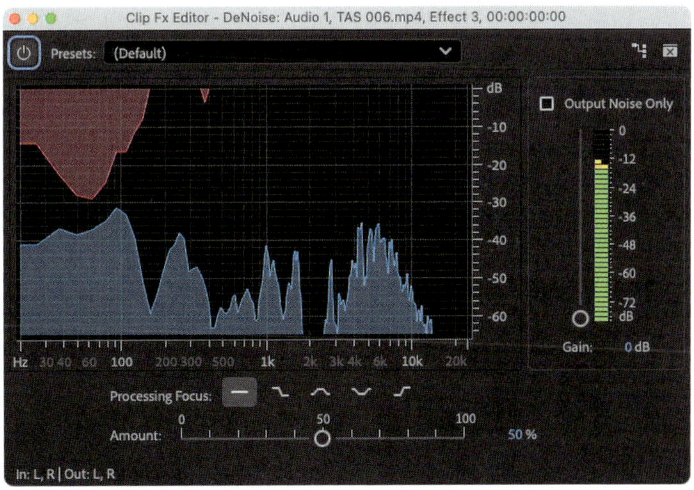

The left end of the graph shows low frequencies, and the right end shows high frequencies.

The Essential Sound panel and the Effect Controls panel

As soon as you enable Reduce Noise in the Essential Sound panel, Premiere applies a DeNoise effect to the selected sequence clip, which you'll see in the Effect Controls panel. In fact, every adjustment you make in the Essential Sound panel will result in a new effect or adjustments to existing effects accessible in the Effect Controls panel.

You can think of the Essential Sound panel as an intelligent shortcut to ideal audio effects with optimized settings that you can adjust in the Effect Controls panel. If you can't see the Effect Controls panel, you can access it via the Window menu.

6 Play the clip again and pay particular attention to the activity in the graph when there is no speech, only rumble.

It's clear that the unwanted rumble is in the low frequencies.

Take a look at the controls:

- **Presets:** You can choose Heavy or Light Noise Reduction; these two options adjust the Amount setting.
- **Amount:** Use this to adjust the intensity of the effect.
- **Output Noise Only:** Enable this option to hear only the noise that is being removed. This is helpful when assessing whether you're removing too much of the desired audio.
- **Gain:** When reducing noise, you'll naturally be reducing the overall level of the audio. You can adjust the overall gain here to compensate. By looking at the level meter before and after applying the effect, you can see how much gain to apply to keep the overall audio at the original level.

The Processing Focus control is a little less self-explanatory but is a powerful feature that you can't access in the Essential Sound panel.

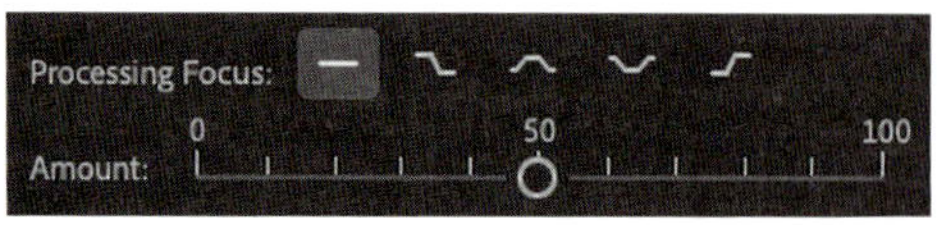

By default, Premiere applies the DeNoise effect to the full frequency range of a clip—that means it applies equally to low, medium, and high tone sounds. Using the Processing Focus control, you can selectively apply the effect to particular frequencies. If you hover your pointer over an option, a tool tip describes it, but you'll probably be able to guess which is which from the shape of the button icons.

7 Click to select the Focus On Lower Frequencies option, and play the clip again. This sounds good, but let's push the effect a little harder.

8 Drag the Amount slider up to around 80%, and play the clip again. Next, try setting the slider to 100%, and play the clip.

With the focus on the lower frequencies, even setting the effect to full allows the speech to be audible, and the rumble is almost gone. Even with this more advanced control, you will need to experiment to get the ideal result.

9 For now, set the amount to 80%, and close the Clip Fx Editor - DeNoise window.

Note: When you modify effect settings, related options in the Essential Sound panel are marked with a warning triangle as a reminder that you customized the settings. You may need to close the effect editor before a triangle will be displayed.

Reducing reverb

The Reduce Reverb option works in a similar way to the Reduce Noise option.

Let's try it.

1 Listen to the second clip in the sequence. The audio has strong reverb caused by the hard surfaces at the recording location bouncing audio back to the microphone.

The background noise is less of a challenge in this clip, but the reverb is quite intense.

2 Select the clip, and select Reduce Reverb under the Repair heading in the Essential Sound panel.

The difference is dramatic! Just as you finessed the Reduce Noise setting, you should experiment with the Reduce Reverb setting to get the optimum balance between the effect being applied with enough intensity and the speech sounding natural.

When you selected Reduce Reverb, Premiere applied a DeReverb effect to the clip. You can access the effect controls in the Effect Controls panel.

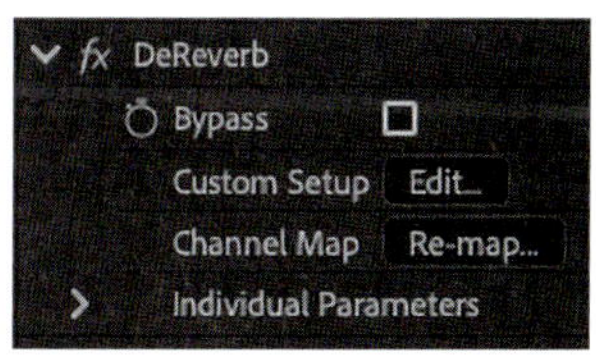

3 Click the Edit button for the effect in the Effect Controls panel, and play a little of the second clip in the Timeline panel to update the graph in the Clip Fx Editor - DeReverb window.

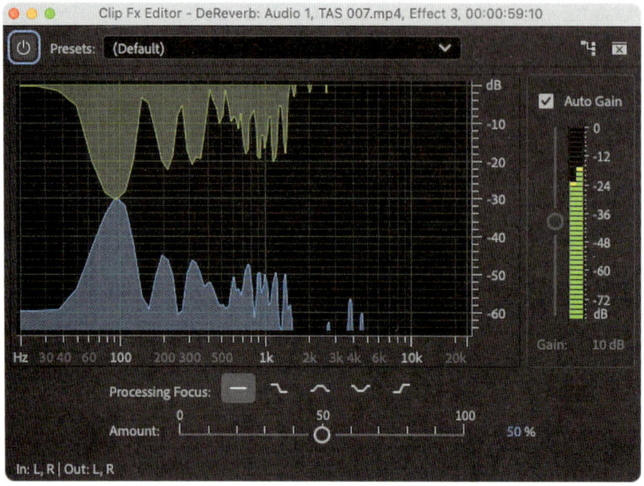

Although the colors are a little different, the DeReverb settings are otherwise almost identical to the DeNoise settings. However, you'll notice the Auto Gain option in the upper-right corner.

When reducing reverb, a reduced overall level is inevitable. Auto Gain automatically compensates, making this effect even easier to set up.

4 Deselect Auto Gain. The Gain slider becomes available, and you can make manual adjustments.

5 Select Auto Gain, and play the clip to compare the result. Notice the Gain slider updates as soon as you select Auto Gain.

6 There are two more clips in this sequence for you to experiment with. Try combining the Reduce Noise and Reduce Reverb options for these clips, with lower values for subtler results.

7 Close the DeReverb settings window.

Enhancing speech

The Enhance Speech section of the Essential Sound panel has just two controls: an Enhance button and a Mix Amount slider, which allows you to blend the enhanced audio with the original audio to achieve a mix that works best for your media.

This remarkable audio cleanup feature uses Adobe AI technology to generate new, original audio that is separate from but inspired by the audio in your clip. The result is intended to be the audio you *would have wanted* to record.

There are no other controls, and the process is fully automated. The audio processing is also performed on your computer, so there is no need for an internet connection to upload or download the audio for processing on a server.

To try this feature with the first clip in the current sequence, first turn off Reduce Noise in the Repair section of the Essential Sound panel. Next, click Enhance in the Enhance Speech section and wait for the processing to complete.

Tip: For more advanced enhancement, try the free online version of Enhance Speech at *https://podcast.adobe.com/en/enhance*.

To compare the results with the original clip audio, experiment with the Mix Amount slider. For this audio, you will likely get the best results with a low mix amount.

Improving clarity

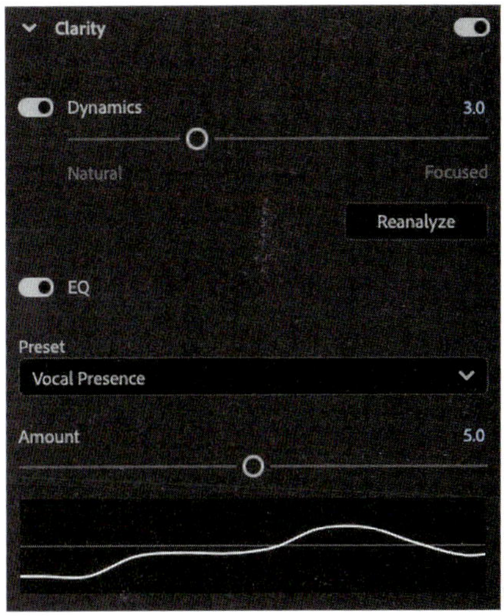

The Clarity category in the Essential Sound panel gives you three quick and easy ways to improve the quality of spoken audio:

- **Dynamics:** Increases or decreases the dynamic range of the audio—that is, the range of volume between the quietest and loudest parts of the recording.
- **EQ:** Applies amplitude (volume) adjustments at specific frequencies. A list of presets makes selecting useful settings easy.
- **Vocal Enhancer:** Improves clarity at specific frequencies, depending on your selection of a high-tone or low-tone voice.

Experiment with all three controls, as you'll find different dialogue recordings will benefit from different combinations of settings.

Let's try these settings.

1 Open the sequence 05 Clarity.

   This sequence has the same content as the 03 Noise Reduction sequence, but there are two versions of the voice-over. The first version is cleaner than the second.

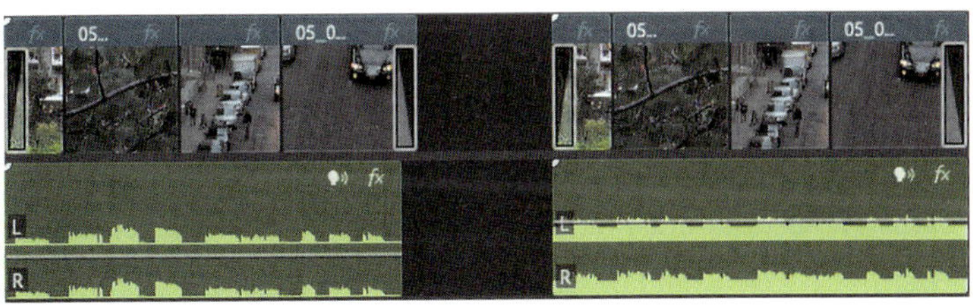

2 Listen to the first voice-over clip.

3 Select the first voice-over clip, and in the Essential Sound panel, scroll down to the Clarity options. You may need to click the Clarity heading to expand the options.

4 Select Dynamics, and experiment with different levels of adjustment. You can play the sequence while making adjustments in the Essential Sound panel, and the effect will be applied "live." Deselect Dynamics when you have tried a few settings.

5 Select EQ and experiment with the Preset options. Some presets, like Old Radio, produce dramatic results!

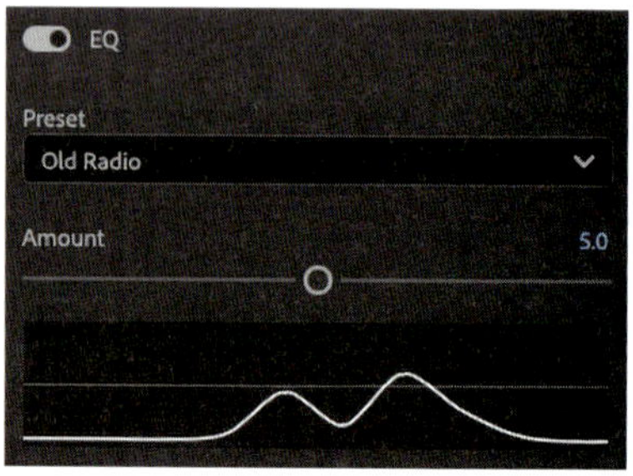

When you apply an EQ preset, a diagram illustrating the adjustment appears. This diagram is based on a Parametric Equalizer effect (see "Using the Parametric Equalizer effect" later in this lesson for more on this effect). You can adjust the Amount slider to add more or less of the effect.

6 Play the second voice-over clip.

7 Select the second voice-over clip, and in the Clarity section of the Essential Sound panel, select Vocal Enhancer and make sure High Tone is selected.

8 Play the second voice-over clip. Try selecting and deselecting Vocal Enhancer during playback.

The difference is subtle. In fact, you may need headphones or good-quality studio monitors to clearly detect the improvement. This option clarifies speech to make it more apprehensible, and in some cases, this means reducing the power in the lower frequencies.

Making creative adjustments

This section houses just one adjustment: Reverb. The effect can be similar to recording in a large room with lots of reflective surfaces, or it can be subtler.

Experiment with this effect on the first voice-over clip in the 05 Clarity sequence.

Just a small amount of reverb can "thicken" a voice to give it more presence.

Adjusting volume

In addition to adjusting the gain for clips in the Project panel, setting the volume level for clips in a sequence, and applying an automated Loudness adjustment, you can also set clip volume using the option at the bottom of the Essential Sound panel.

It's curious that this additional option exists—especially considering the number of ways you can already adjust the volume of your clips.

But there's something special about this volume control: No matter how much you change the volume of your clips using this control, the level will not distort (unless you combine it with other adjustments). That is, the clips won't *override* (become so loud that the loudest parts of the audio cannot be played).

Try this now.

1 Open the sequence 06 Level.

This sequence contains just one clip—a reasonably loud version of the voice-over clip you have heard already.

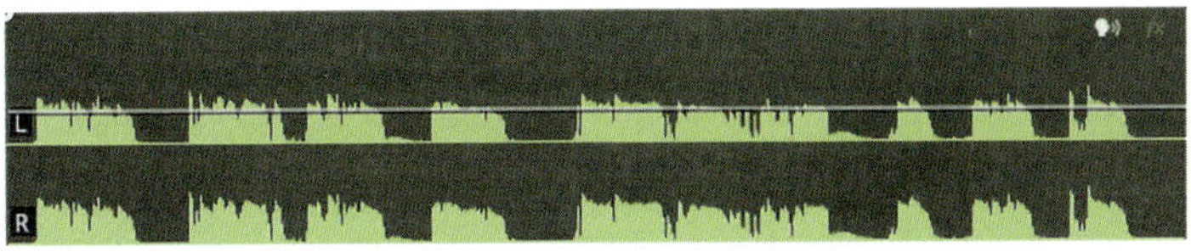

2 Select the clip and play the sequence. While the sequence plays, use the Clip Volume Level adjustment to increase and decrease the playback level.

3 Try increasing the level to the maximum, +15 dB.

No matter how much you adjust the audio level, it won't override. Even if you combine a clip gain increase with a clip volume increase (using the rubber band) and then apply this adjustment, the clip will not override.

4 Reset the Clip Volume Level adjustment by double-clicking the slider.

Note: It's a good idea to reset controls in the Essential Sound panel to their default values before making adjustments. You can do this quickly by double-clicking a control.

Using additional audio effects

As mentioned at the beginning of this lesson, there are many audio effects available in the Effects panel.

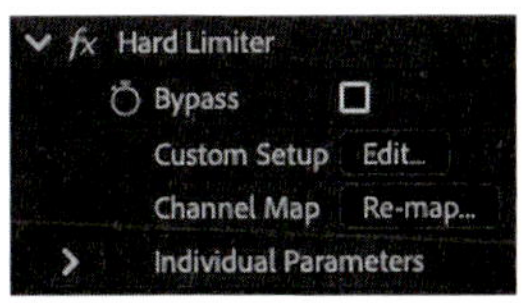

The adjustments you have made with the Essential Sound panel have resulted in regular audio effects being added to clips automatically as you worked.

Setting up effects in this way is quicker because all of the Essential Sound panel adjustments work like presets—as soon as you have set things the way you want them in the Essential Sound panel, the effects are set up appropriately in the Effect Controls panel.

Take a look now at the Effect Controls panel, with the clip you worked on in the 06 Level sequence selected.

When you made a Clip Volume Level adjustment in the Essential Sound panel, Premiere applied a Hard Limiter effect to the clip, with detailed settings to match the adjustment you applied. To see the settings in the Effect Controls panel, click the chevron next to the Individual Parameters heading.

Click the Edit button for the Hard Limiter effect in the Effect Controls panel to open the Clip Fx Editor, and you'll discover all of the settings for this advanced effect are available in case you'd like to change them. If you make changes to Clip Volume in the Essential Sound panel, you can even watch the controls update dynamically in the Effect Controls panel.

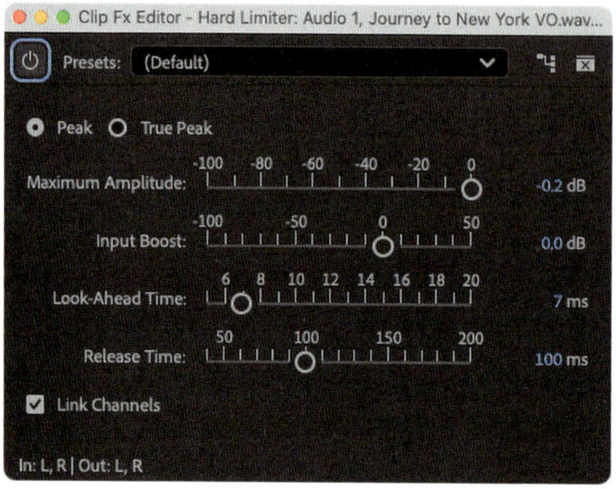

In most cases, the settings applied by the Essential Sound panel will be suitable, but the option to make further subtle changes will always be available.

Close the Hard Limiter Clip Fx Editor now.

Using Essential Sound panel presets

If you expect to use a combination of Essential Sound panel settings often, consider creating a preset. To create a preset, select an audio type, apply some settings, and click the Save Settings As A Preset button  at the top of the Essential Sound panel. Once it's created, you can apply a preset without first assigning the audio type.

Essential Sound panel presets are not fixed—you can apply a preset, make changes to the settings, and even create a new preset based on the adjustments you have made.

Using the Parametric Equalizer effect

The Parametric Equalizer effect offers a nuanced and intuitive interface for precise audio level adjustment at specific frequencies.

It includes a graphic interface you can use to drag level adjustment controls that are linked together to achieve nuanced, natural-sounding audio.

Let's try this effect.

1 Open the sequence 07 Full Parametric EQ. This sequence has one musical clip and one voice-over clip.

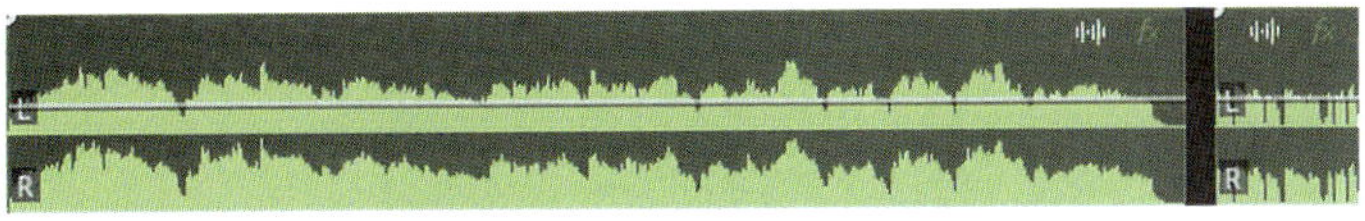

2 Locate the Parametric Equalizer effect in the Effects panel (try using the Search box at the top of the window), and drag the effect onto the first clip.

3 Make sure the clip is selected, and in the Effect Controls panel, click the Edit button to access the Clip Fx Editor for the Parametric Equalizer effect.

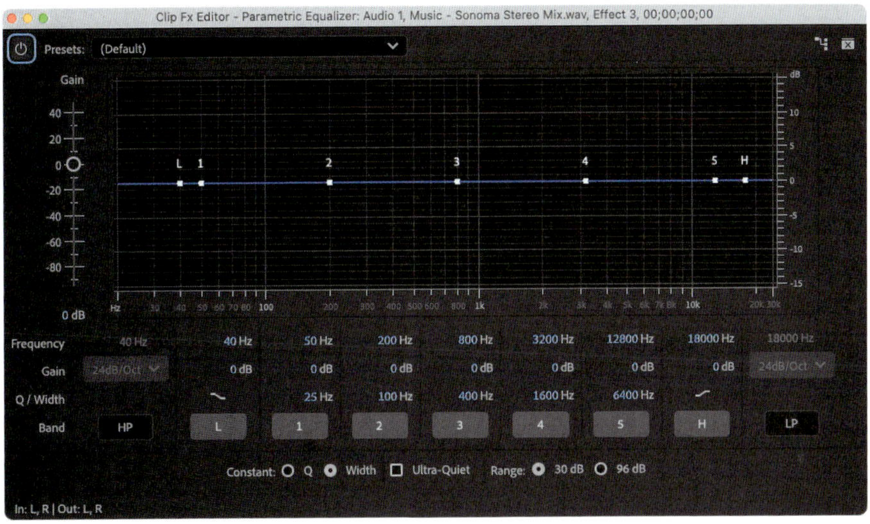

The horizontal axis of the graphic control area indicates frequency, while the vertical axis shows amplitude. The blue line across the middle of the graph represents any adjustments you have made.

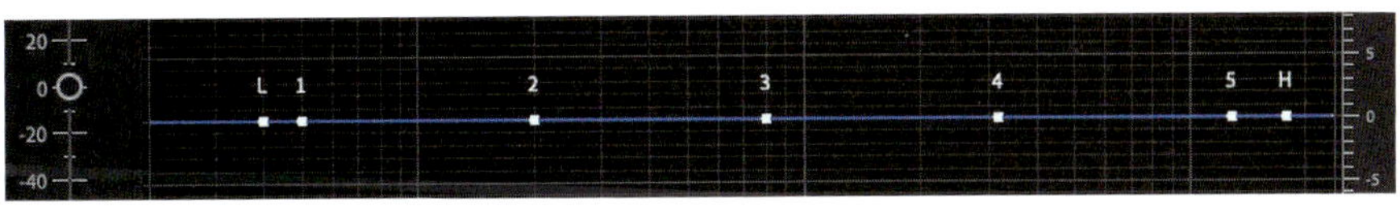

Wherever the blue line is higher or lower in the display, adjustments are made to the audio level at those frequencies. You can reshape the line by dragging any of the five main control points directly, as well as the Low Pass (labeled *L*) and High Pass (labeled *H*) controls at the ends.

On the left is an overall Gain level adjustment, which offers a quick fix if the changes you make result in audio that is too loud or too quiet overall.

4 Play the clip to get familiar with its sound. The graphic control area displays the level throughout the frequency range, just as the DeHum and DeReverb effects did.

At the bottom of the dialog box, there's a Range option. By default, with 30 dB selected as the Range, the Parametric Equalizer effect graph allows adjustments up to +/–15 dB.

Change Range to 96 dB now, so you can make adjustments up to +/–48 dB.

5 Drag Control Point 1 on the blue line quite a long way down in the graph to reduce the audio level at low frequencies. Listen to the music again.

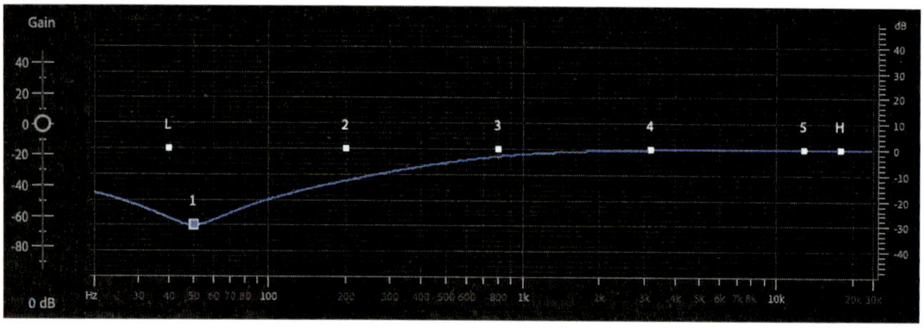

Changes you make to a specific frequency reshape the blue line, impacting surrounding frequencies and resulting in a more natural sound.

The control points you drag have a range of influence that is defined by their Q setting.

Adjustments made to the blue line update the detailed controls below. These two areas of the dialog box are connected—adjust one and the other updates automatically.

The control point numbers are at the bottom of each column of settings, and they double up as an enable/disable toggle for the control point.

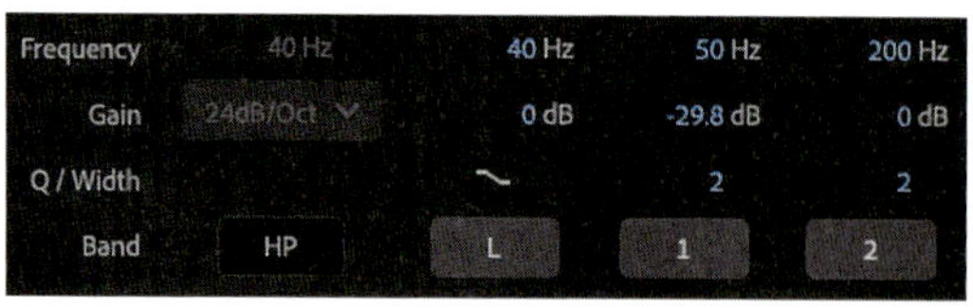

In the example, Control Point 1 was set to 50 Hz (which is very low frequency), with a gain adjustment of –29.8 dB (which is a big gain reduction) and a Q of 2 (which is quite a wide curve for the blue line).

6 Change the Q factor for Control Point 1 from 2 to 7. You can click the 2 and type in a new setting directly.

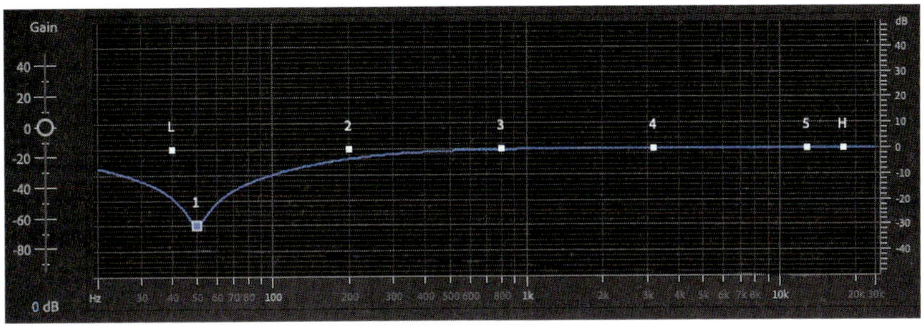

The line has a much sharper curve, so the adjustment you are making now applies to fewer frequencies.

7 Play the sequence to hear the changes.

Let's refine the vocals.

8 Vocals are mostly in the range of 100–4000 Hz, with most of the power in the 300–500 Hz range. Control Point 3 is close to 800 Hz by default, which is in the most prominent portion of the vocal range. Drag Control Point 3 down to about –20 dB, and set the Q factor to **1** for a very broad adjustment. You can also click the blue numbers to add these settings.

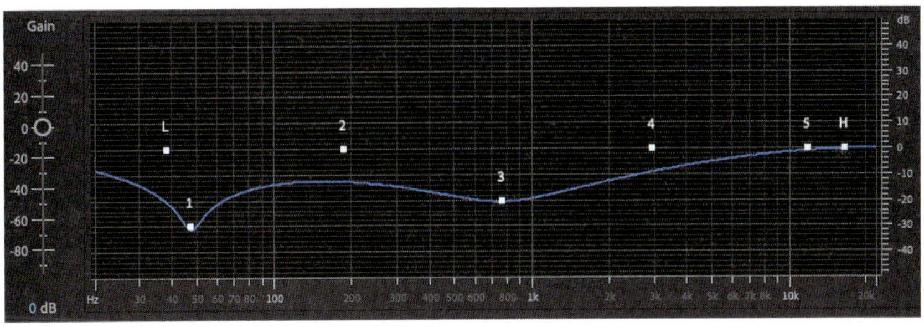

9 Play the sequence to hear the changes. The vocals are much quieter.

10 Drag Control Point 4 to around 1500 Hz, with a gain of +6.0 dB. Adjust the Q factor to **3** for more precise adjustment on the EQ adjustment.

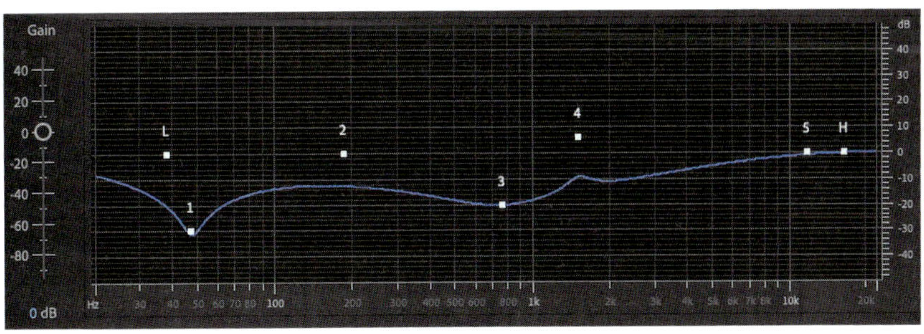

Tip: Another way to use the Parametric Equalizer effect is to target a specific frequency and either boost it or cut it. You can use this effect to cut a particular frequency, like a high-frequency noise or a low hum.

Note: Avoid setting the volume too high (the Audio Meters will show some red, and the peak monitors will light up). This can lead to distortion.

11 Play the sequence to hear the changes.

12 Drag the High Pass control (the H control) down, setting its gain to around –8.0 dB to make the highest frequencies quieter.

> **Tip:** If your audio meters are not displayed, you can access them by choosing Window > Audio Meters.

13 Use the Gain control to adjust the overall level. You may need to see your audio meters to find out whether your mix is right.

14 Close the Clip Fx Editor for the Parametric Equalizer.

15 Play the sequence to hear the changes.

These are dramatic changes intended to illustrate a technique. Of course, you'll usually make subtler adjustments.

One of the most common uses for the Parametric Equalizer effect is for improving the quality of vocals. The second clip in the sequence is a voice-over clip. Use this to experiment with the Parametric Equalizer effect. The quality of the audio is already acceptable, but you should be able to add nuance and power to the speech with subtle adjustments using this effect.

Audio adjustments and effects can be modified during playback. You might want to enable looping playback in the Program Monitor rather than clicking repeatedly to play a clip or sequence.

You can enable looping playback by choosing Loop from the Program Monitor Settings menu.

There are also useful additional buttons available in the Program Monitor Button Editor.

- **Loop**: This toggles looped playback on and off. If you have set In and Out points, playback will loop between them.
- **Play Video In To Out**: If you have set In and Out points, the sequence will play between them and stop.

Audio Plug-in Manager

It's easy to install third-party plug-ins. Choose Premiere > Settings > Audio (macOS) or Edit > Preferences > Audio (Windows). Then click Manage Audio Plug-ins.

1 If you would like to add a directory that contains AU (macOS only) or VST plug-ins, click the Add button.

2 If needed, click the Scan For Plug-Ins button to find all available plug-ins.

3 Click the Enable All button to activate all of the plug-ins, or select individual plug-ins to activate them alone.

4 Click OK to apply your changes.

Using the Notch effect

The Notch effect removes frequencies near a specified value. The effect targets a frequency range and eliminates those sounds. The effect works well for removing radio interference hum and other electrical interference.

1 Open the sequence 08 Notch Filter.

2 Play the sequence, and listen for the electrical hum. You can hear fluorescent light bulbs buzzing.

3 In the Effects panel, locate the Notch Filter effect (not the Simple Notch Filter effect) and apply it to the clip in the sequence. When you do, the clip is automatically selected, so the effect controls will appear in the Effect Controls panel.

4 In the Effect Controls panel, click the Edit button for the Notch Filter effect to open the Clip Fx Editor.

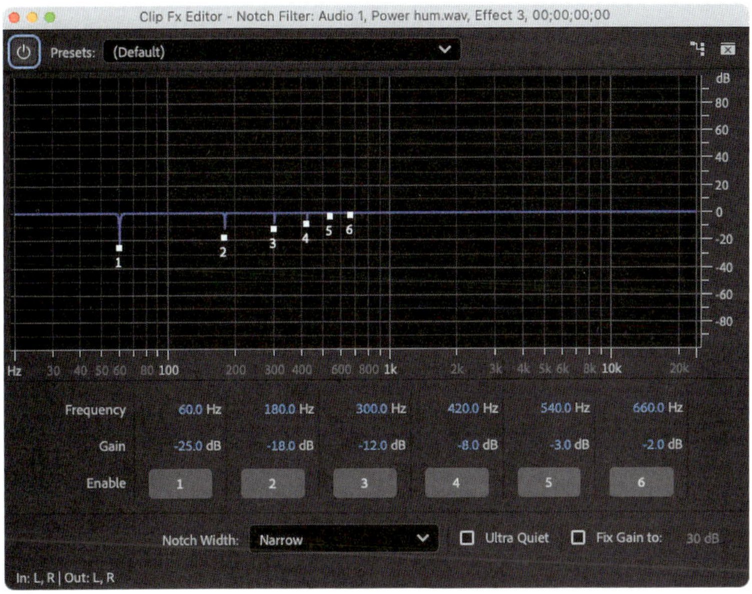

The Notch Filter effect looks a lot like the Parametric Equalizer effect and functions in a similar way. However, you will notice there's no Q control, which sets the sharpness of the curves. By default each adjustment is extremely acute, and a Notch Width menu allows you to adjust the curves.

5 While playing the sequence, experiment with presets and listen to the results.

The presets usually apply multiple adjustments. This is because signal interference is often found in multiple harmonic frequencies.

6 Choose 60 Hz And Octaves from the Presets menu, and then listen to the sequence again to find out whether it's improved.

7 Often, when working with the Notch Filter effect, you'll listen, adjust, and listen again until you get the settings you need.

This audio has hum at 60 Hz, 120 Hz, and 240 Hz. These and more have been targeted by the preset you chose. Click the Enable buttons for Control Points 3, 4, 5, and 6 to turn them off.

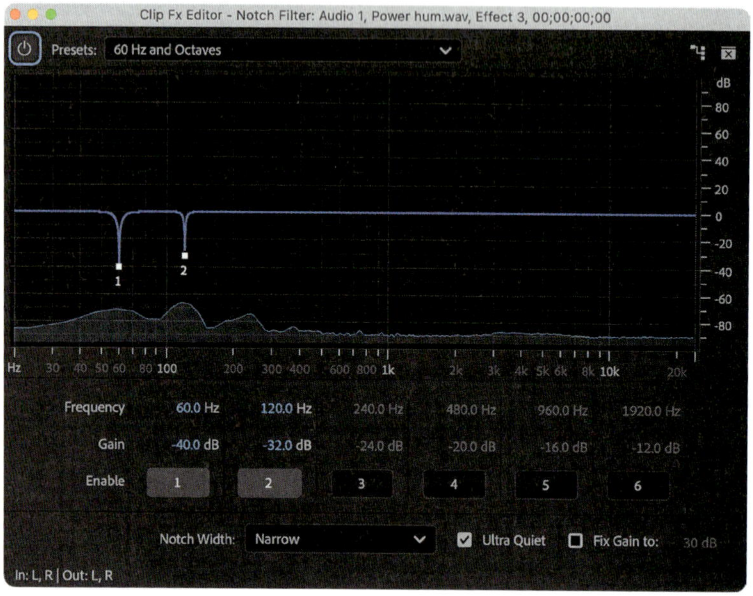

Now play the sequence again to review the effect. Even though the interference was at precise frequencies, it made hearing the vocals difficult. Now it's removed, and everything sounds clearer.

8 Close the Clip Fx Editor.

When you used the Essential Sound panel to apply DeHum, a similar effect was applied to the clip—the DeHummer.

The Notch Filter effect has slightly more advanced controls, so if you don't get the result you need using the Essential Sound panel, try this next.

Close this project by choosing File > Close Project. If you are asked if you would like to save, do so.

Review questions

1. How would you use the Essential Sound panel to set an industry-standard audio level for broadcast television dialogue clips?
2. What's a quick, easy way to remove electrical interference hum from clips?
3. Where can you find the more detailed controls for the options you set using the Essential Sound panel?
4. What does the blue line indicate in the Clip Fx Editor for the Parametric Equalizer effect?

Review answers

1. Select the clips you want to adjust. In the Essential Sound panel, choose Dialogue as the audio type. Then, in the Loudness section, click Auto-Match.
2. Use DeHum in the Essential Sound panel to remove electrical interference hum. Try the 60 Hz or 50 Hz option, depending on the origin of your source footage.
3. Adjustments you make using the Essential Sound panel are applied as effects to clips. You can find the detailed controls by selecting a clip and looking in the Effect Controls panel.
4. The blue line indicates audio level adjustments at different frequencies. Check the frequency range along the bottom of the graphic control area to see which frequencies will be adjusted.

12 ADDING VIDEO EFFECTS

Lesson overview

In this lesson, you'll learn how to do the following:

- Work with fixed effects.
- Browse effects with the Effects panel.
- Apply and remove effects.
- Mask and track video effects.
- Use keyframing effects.
- Use effect presets.
- Explore frequently used effects.
- Render effects.

This lesson will take about 120 minutes to complete. To get the files used in this lesson, refer to the instructions in "Accessing the lesson files and Web Edition" in the "Getting Started" section at the beginning of this book. Store the files on your computer in a convenient location.

Adobe Premiere features 90 video effects. In this lesson, you'll learn the main skills you need to work with all kinds of effects, as well as some of the more advanced workflows. Most effects come with an array of controls, almost all of which you can change over time using keyframes.

Starting the lesson

Note: To ensure that the tools function and the defaults are set exactly as described in this lesson, reset the Premiere preferences by holding any modifier key (such as Shift) while launching the application, selecting Reset App Preferences, and then clicking Continue in the Reset Options dialog box.

You might use video effects for many reasons. They can solve problems with image quality, such as underexposure or a color balance offset. They can create complex composite video effects using techniques such as chromakey. They can also help solve a number of production problems, such as camera shake or a poorly lit subject.

1 Open Lesson 12.prproj.
2 Switch to the Effects workspace by choosing Effects from the Workspaces menu.
3 Reset the workspace by returning to the Workspaces menu and choosing Reset To Saved Layout.
4 Save the project as **Lesson 12 Working.prproj**.

Effects can also serve stylistic purposes. You can distort footage or alter its color, and you can animate the size and position of a clip within the frame. The exciting challenge is in knowing when to use an effect and when to keep it simple.

Standard effects can be constrained within elliptical or polygon masks, and these masks can automatically track your footage. For example, you might blur someone's face to hide their identity and have the blur follow them as they move through the shot. You can use the same feature to relight a scene in post-production.

Working with video effects

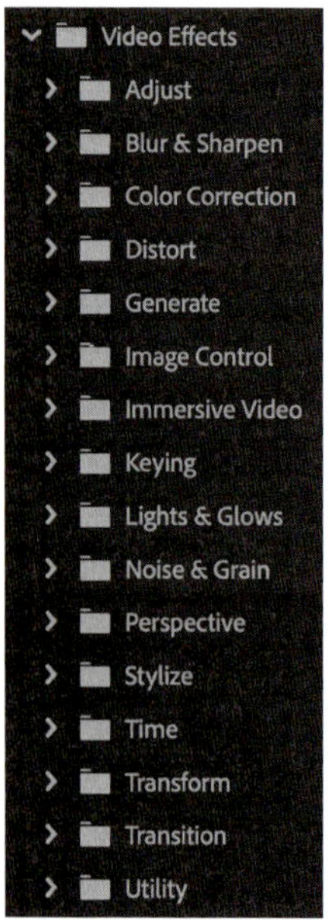

You already know how to apply effects and change their settings. You can drag a video effect onto a clip, as you have already done with audio effects, or you can select the clip (or multiple clips) and double-click the effect in the Effects panel. You can combine as many effects as you want on a single clip, which can produce surprising results. You can use an adjustment layer to add effects to a collection of clips.

When it comes to deciding which video effects to use, the number of choices in Premiere can be a little overwhelming. Plus, *many* additional effects are available from third-party manufacturers for sale or free of charge.

Although the range of effects and their controls can be complex, the techniques you'll use to apply, adjust, and remove effects are straightforward and consistent.

Modifying fixed effects

When you add a clip to a sequence, it will automatically have a few effects applied. These effects are called *fixed* effects, or *intrinsic* effects, and you can think of them as controls for the usual geometric, opacity, speed, and audio properties that every clip should have.

Although fixed effects are applied automatically, they don't change the appearance of clips until you modify their settings. The effects include:

- **Motion:** The Motion effect allows you to animate, rotate, scale, and crop a clip. You can also use the Anti-flicker Filter control to decrease shimmering edges for an animated object. This comes in handy when you scale down a high-resolution or interlaced source and Premiere must resample the image.
- **Opacity:** The Opacity effect lets you control how opaque or transparent a clip is. You can also access special blend modes to create visual effects from multiple layers of graphics or video. You'll explore this more in Lesson 14, "Exploring Compositing Techniques."
- **Time Remapping:** This effect lets you slow down, speed up, or reverse playback, and it even lets you freeze a frame. Think of it as a more advanced version of the Clip Speed/Duration options in the Timeline panel. In fact, the two controls are linked.
- **Audio Effects:** If a clip has audio, Premiere displays its Volume, Channel Volume, and Panner controls. You learned about these in Lesson 10, "Editing and Mixing Audio."

You can modify all fixed effects using the Effect Controls panel. Some controls are also available in the Properties panel.

Though the Effect Controls panel gives more advanced controls, you can work on only one clip at a time. The controls in the Properties panel allow you to make adjustments to multiple selected clips in a single step.

Adjustments made in either panel will update both.

1 If it's not already in the Timeline panel, open the sequence 01 Fixed Effects. Scrub through the sequence to familiarize yourself with the content.

2 Click the first clip in the sequence to select it. In the Effect Controls panel, review the fixed effects applied to this clip.

3 Click the chevrons > next to headings or individual controls to display their properties.

> **Tip:** To expand or collapse all headings in the Effect Controls panel or the Project panel, hold Option (macOS) or Alt (Windows) when you click a chevron.

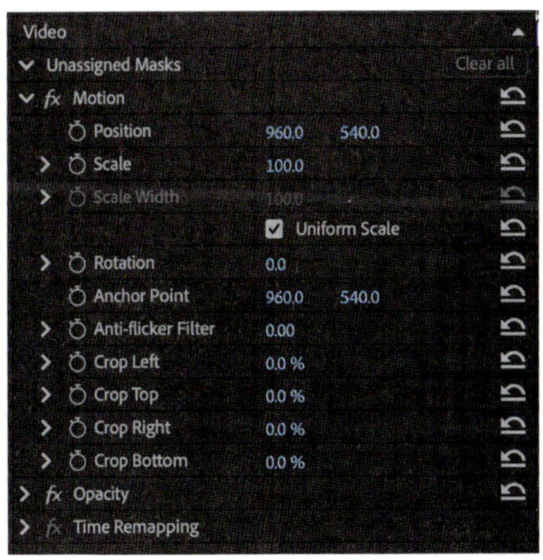

4 Click to select the second clip in the sequence, and look at the Effect Controls panel.

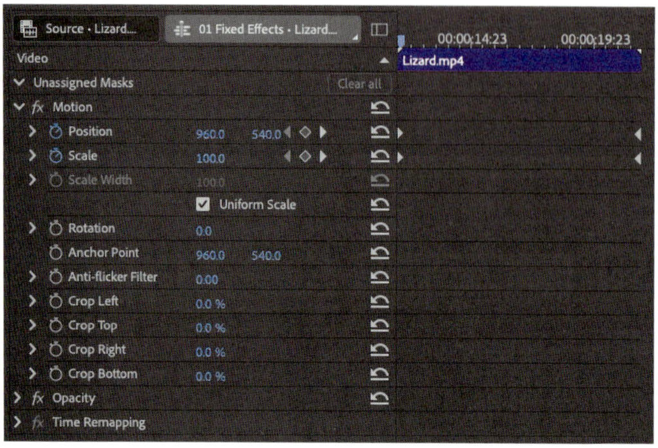

These Position and Scale controls under the Motion effect heading have keyframes, so the settings can change over time. In this case, a slow Scale and Position animation was applied to the clip to create a digital zoom that didn't exist before and to recompose the shot.

When people fix attention on an object, they tend to experience subtle tunnel vision. A slow zoom-in effect can feel the same way for your audience, enhancing the viewer's focus and adding tension in a dramatic moment.

5 Play the current sequence to compare the two clips and view the animation.

Navigating the Effects panel

Tip: The keyboard shortcut to display the Effects panel is Shift+7.

In addition to the fixed video effects, Premiere has standard effects that change a clip's appearance. Because there are so many to choose from, effects are organized into categories, such as Distort, Keying, and Time, so you can more easily navigate them. If you install third-party effects, you will have even more categories.

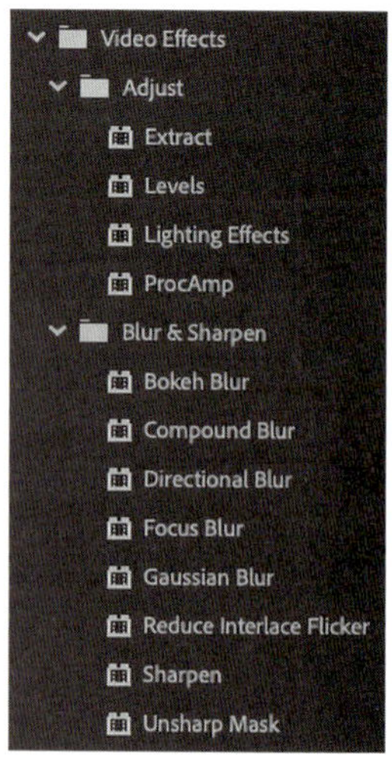

Each category has its own bin in the Effects panel. Like the Project panel, the Effects panel includes the option to create new bins to store copies of effects to make it easier to locate them.

1 Open the Effects panel, and expand the Video Effects category.

2 Click the New Custom Bin button at the bottom of the panel.

Tip: With so many video effect categories, it's sometimes tricky to locate the effect you want. If you know part or all of an effect's name, start typing it in the search box at the top of the Effects panel. Premiere will display all effects and transitions that contain that letter combination, narrowing the search as you type.

A new custom bin appears in the Effects panel at the bottom of the list (you may need to scroll down to see it). Let's rename it.

3 Click once to select the bin, and click once more, directly on the bin's name (Custom Bin 01), to select that.

4 Change its name to **Favorite Effects**.

Note: When you add an effect to a custom bin in the Effects panel, the original effect remains in its original folder. You can use custom bins to create your own additional effect categories.

5 Expand a few video effects categories and drag several effects into your new Favorite Effects bin to copy them. You may need to resize the panel to make it easier to drag effects. Choose any effects that sound interesting to you. You can add or remove effects from a custom bin whenever you like. You can also click the Delete Custom Items button to remove copied effects.

Effect types

If you are working on a smaller computer monitor, some additional useful icons may be hidden in the Effects panel.

If necessary, resize the Effects panel until you can see all of the Effect Type buttons next to the search box.

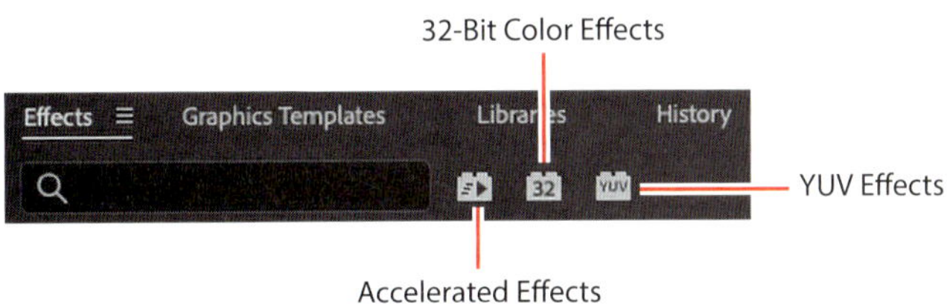

If you widen the Effects panel a little more, you'll notice icons next to many of the effect names (you may need to resize the Effects panel to see the icons). Understanding these icons should influence your choices when working with effects.

Only some effects have all three icons. Click the effect type buttons at the top of the Effects panel to display only effects with those features.

Accelerated effects

The Accelerated Effects icon indicates that the effect can be accelerated by your graphics processing unit (GPU). The GPU (often called the video card or graphics card) can greatly enhance the performance of Premiere. The range of cards supported by the Mercury Playback Engine is broad, and with the right card installed, these effects offer accelerated or even real-time performance and need rendering only on final export (which is also hardware accelerated).

32-bit color (high-bit-depth) effects

Effects with the 32-Bit Color icon can be processed in 32 bits per channel (sometimes called high-bit-depth or float processing).

The more bits, the better, so for maximum quality, use 32-bit color effects.

Understanding bit depth

Bit depth is the number of steps from one end of a scale to another. A good example is the brightness of a pixel. How many steps should there be between 0% brightness and 100% brightness?

Many video cameras record 8-bit video by default. Without getting into how it's calculated, 8-bit video gives 256 steps per color channel from one end of the scale to the other.

For every 1 bit you add, the number of steps doubles. So 10-bit video (a popular option) has 1,024 steps.

Because these scales begin at 0 (not 1), they are really:

8-bit: 0–255

10-bit: 0–1,023

32-bit processing allows more than 4 billion possible steps—that's a lot of doubling! When rendering effects in 32-bit color, the result is as good as lossless—no quality is lost when calculating the effect.

YUV effects

Effects with the YUV icon will process color in YUV (processed in Premiere as Luminance, Color-Blue, Color-Red channels).

Note: To learn more about YUV effects, be sure to read the article at *www.provideocoalition.com/what_is_yuv*.

YUV effects break down the video into a Y (or luminance) channel and two channels for color information, which is how most video footage is structured natively. Because the brightness of the image is separate from the colors, it's easy to adjust contrast and exposure without shifting the colors.

Effects without the YUV icon are processed in the computer's native RGB space, which might make adjusting exposure and color less accurate.

Applying effects

Once you have applied a video effect, the effect settings are accessible in the Effect Controls panel. You can add keyframes to nearly every control to apply changes over time (just look for controls with a stopwatch icon). In addition, you can use Bezier curve handles on those keyframes to adjust the velocity and acceleration of those changes.

1 Open the sequence 02 Browse, and scrub through the content to review it.

2 Type **white** into the Effects panel search box to narrow the results. Locate the Black & White video effect.

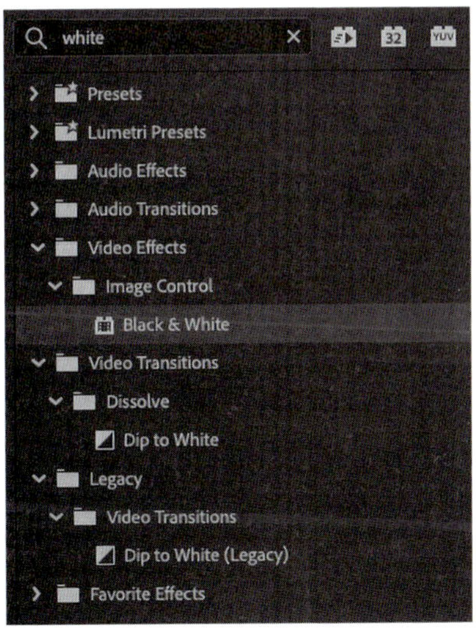

3 Drag the Black & White video effect onto the Run Past clip in the Timeline panel.

Tip: If you type the word *black* instead of *white* into the Effects panel search box, you'll see a fantastic list of Lumetri presets for Blackmagic Cameras. Typing the word *white* instead displays a shorter list of effects to scroll through. You can use any part of the name of an effect to filter for it, even just a few letters.

This effect immediately converts your full-color footage to black and white, or, more accurately, grayscale.

4 Click the small FX icon that lit up on the clip in the Timeline panel after you applied the effect.

This selects the clip and opens the Effect Controls panel.

5 Turn the Black & White effect off and on by clicking the FX button next to the effect name in the Effect Controls panel. Be sure the sequence playhead is over the clip to view the result.

Toggling an effect on and off is a good way to see how it works with other effects.

6 Make sure the clip is selected in the Timeline panel. In the Effect Controls panel, click the Black & White effect heading to select it, and press Delete (macOS) or Backspace/Delete (Windows). This removes the effect.

Note: If you have a clip selected, you can apply effects by double-clicking them in the Effects panel or by dragging them into the Effect Controls panel directly.

Tip: The upper limit for a slider may be smaller than the number you can enter by typing.

Note: You won't always use video effects to achieve dramatic results for visual impact. Sometimes effects are intended to look natural.

7 Type **direction** into the Effects panel search box to locate the Directional Blur video effect.

8 In the Effects panel, double-click the Directional Blur effect in the Blur & Sharpen category to apply it to the selected clip.

9 In the Effect Controls panel, expand the Directional Blur effect's controls if they are not already expanded.

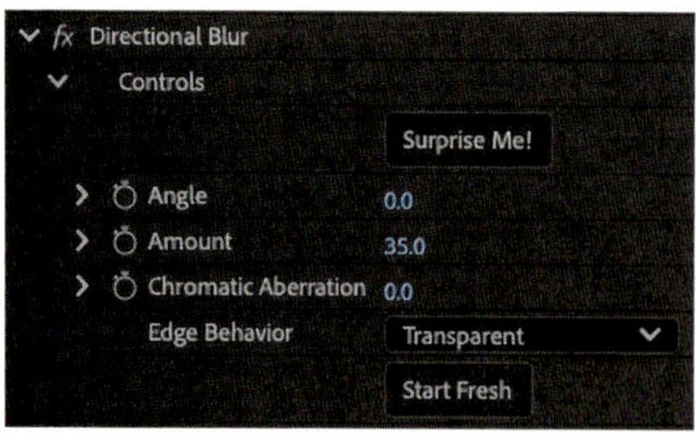

10 Set Angle to **75.0** degrees and Amount to **45**.

It's an interesting result, but now it's impossible to tell what's going on in the image, and there's a dark frame around the edge. Let's tone down the intensity and adjust the frame.

11 Click the chevron to expand the Amount control, and move the slider to reduce the strength of the effect.

As you change the setting, the result is displayed in the Program Monitor.

The shot is looking better, but we still have the dark frame. What's actually happening here is that the edge of the image is fading to transparent, revealing the background of the timeline, which is black.

12 In the Program Monitor (using the Settings menu), choose Transparency Grid to see the transparency more clearly.

13 In the Effect Controls panel, if they aren't already expanded, expand the Directional Blur effect controls and set Edge Behavior to Mirrored.

This gives the image a clean edge. The Mirrored option reflects the pixels inside the edge of the frame, while the Repeat Edge option expands the blur effect from the pixels at the edge of the frame.

There is no right or wrong option, just personal creative preference. Use the Program Monitor settings menu to deselect Transparency Grid.

In the Effect Controls panel, at the top of the Directional Blur effect controls, you can click the Surprise Me! Button to apply random settings for the effect. If you need inspiration, this is a good place to begin.

The Start Fresh button at the bottom of the effect controls resets the controls to a neutral state. This is slightly different from the Reset Effect button, which applies default settings.

Many of the effects available in Premiere, including transition effects, include these two useful buttons.

14 Click the panel menu for the Effect Controls panel, and choose Remove Effects. The Remove Attributes dialog box opens.

15 The Remove Attributes dialog box lets you select which effects to remove and deselect which effects you want to keep. By default, everything is selected. You want to remove them all, so click OK. This is an easy way to start fresh.

Tip: You can also access the Remove Attributes dialog box by right-clicking one or more selected clips in the Timeline panel and choosing Remove Attributes from the contextual menu or by selecting one or more clips and choosing Edit > Remove Attributes.

Premiere processes effects in a particular order, which can lead to unwanted scaling or resizing. You can't reorder the fixed effects (like Motion), but you can bypass them and use other, similar effects. For example, you can use the Transform effect to achieve similar results to the Motion effect, or you can use the Alpha Adjust effect instead of the Opacity effect. These effects are not identical, but they're a close match, they behave similarly, and they can be placed in any order you choose.

Other ways to apply effects

There are multiple ways to reuse an effect you have already configured:

- You can select an effect name from the Effect Controls panel, choose Edit > Copy, select a destination clip (or several clips) in the Timeline panel, and choose Edit > Paste.
- You can copy all the effects from one clip so you can paste them onto another clip: Select a clip and choose Edit > Copy; then select the destination clip (or clips) and choose Edit > Paste Attributes.
- You can create an effect preset to store an effect (or multiple effects) with preselected settings for reuse later. You'll learn about this advanced technique later in this lesson.

Using adjustment layers

Adjustment layers offer a convenient way to apply effects to multiple clips. The concept is straightforward: Create an adjustment layer clip that can hold effects, and position it above other clips on the timeline, on a higher video track. Everything beneath the adjustment layer clip is viewed through it, receiving any effects it contains.

You can easily adjust the duration and opacity of an adjustment layer clip, as you would adjust any graphics clip, making it easy to control which other clips on lower tracks are seen through it. An adjustment layer makes it faster to work with effects because you can change the settings on the layer (a single item) to influence the appearance of several other clips.

Let's add an adjustment layer to a sequence.

1 Open the sequence 03 Multiple Effects.

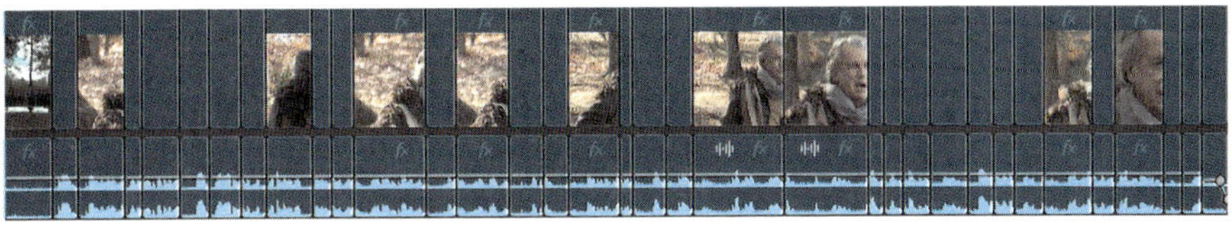

2 At the bottom right of the Project panel, click the New Item button, and choose Adjustment Layer. You may need to resize the Project panel to see the New Item button.

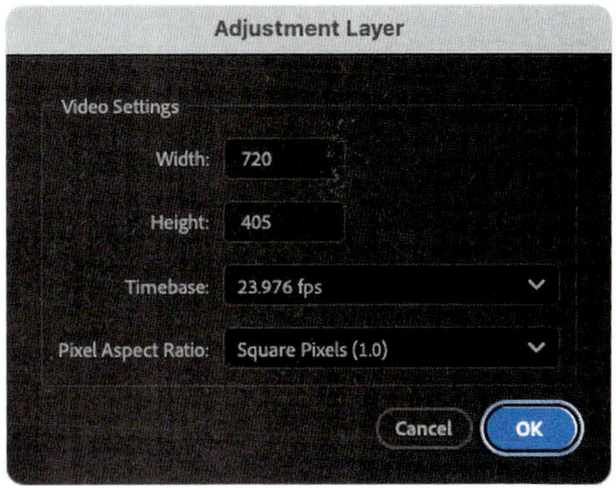

The Adjustment Layer dialog box appears, allowing you to specify settings for the new item you're creating. The settings in the dialog box will reflect the settings in the current sequence.

3 Click OK. Premiere adds a new adjustment layer to the Project panel.

4 Drag the adjustment layer from the Project panel to the beginning of the Video 2 track in the Timeline panel.

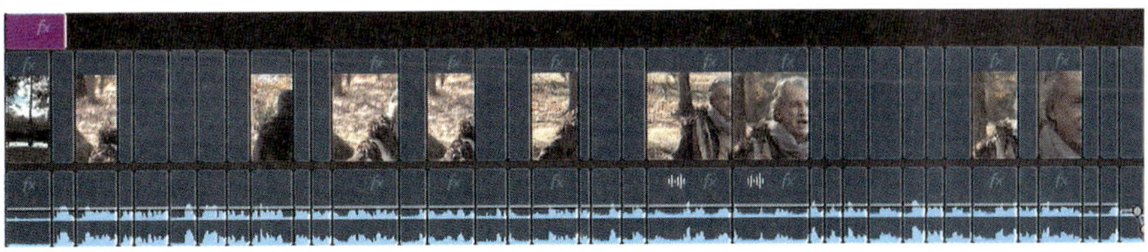

5 Click the right edge of the adjustment layer clip in the Timeline panel to select just the Out point. A red trim handle icon appears on the end of the clip.

Next, position the playhead at the end of the sequence, just after the last clip. You can achieve this quickly by pressing the End key.

Tip: If you are using a Mac keyboard without an End key, you can use Fn+Right Arrow.

Press E to perform an extend edit. This extends the selected trim handle to the location of the playhead. Press the Esc key or click an empty space in the Timeline panel to deselect the end of the adjustment layer.

Now that the adjustment layer is in place, let's apply an effect to it. Once the effect is set up, you can change the adjustment layer's opacity to alter the intensity of the effect.

6 In the Effects panel, search for and locate the Volumetric Rays effect.

7 Drag the effect onto the adjustment layer clip in the sequence.

8 Move the playhead to 27:00 to have a good close-up shot to use when designing the effect. Audiences pay particular attention to the eyes of your subjects, so it can be helpful to use a close-up as a reference when applying effects.

The effect is dramatic! Still, for this fantasy genre footage perhaps it adds a dreamlike quality.

9 Make sure the adjustment layer is selected in the Timeline panel, and then, in the Effect Controls panel, review the available controls for the effect.

It's quite a list of options! Sometimes the best way to familiarize yourself with an effect is to experiment with the controls. For now, leave everything set to default values.

Perhaps the effect is too strong. Let's blend the adjustment layer with the clips beneath it using a blend mode to create a film look.

Blend modes let you mix two layers together based on their brightness and color values. You'll learn more about them in Lesson 14.

10 With the adjustment layer still selected in the sequence, click the chevron next to the Opacity control in the Effect Controls panel to view the settings (you may need to scroll up to view the Opacity control).

11 Choose Soft Light from the Blend Mode menu to create a gentle blend with the footage.

12 Set Opacity to **75%** to reduce the effect. Because you are adjusting the opacity for the adjustment layer clip, reducing the opacity reduces the impact of the effect.

Your eyes will quickly adjust to the new appearance of the clip. So, to compare the before and after states, turn on and off the Track Output for the Video 2 track in the Timeline panel using the Toggle Track Output button.

Adjustment layers are a great way to apply a look to a whole scene. Once you have adjusted the colors for individual clips so they match, you can give the overall scene a particular look with an adjustment layer. The same is true of your entire sequence: You can place an adjustment layer above the clips and below graphics to give all clips the same look.

Sending a clip to Adobe After Effects

If you're working with a computer that also has Adobe After Effects installed, you can easily send clips back and forth between Premiere and After Effects. Thanks to the close relationship between the two applications, you can seamlessly integrate them more easily than with any other editing platform. This is a useful way to significantly extend the effects capabilities of your editing workflow.

You don't need to learn to use After Effects to get the most out of Premiere. Still, many editors find working with both applications expands their creative toolset in exciting ways. The process you use to share clips is called *Dynamic Link*. With Dynamic Link you can seamlessly exchange clips with no unnecessary rendering. When a clip is sent from Premiere to After Effects, it is put into a new *composition* (After Effects compositions are similar to sequences in Premiere). The new composition has settings that match the original Premiere sequence, with a composition name based on the Premiere project name, followed by the words *Linked Comp* (because it's a linked composition). If you'd like to try this, follow the steps in this sidebar.

For After Effects to complete installation, it needs to be started at least once. You'll also need to restart Premiere after installing After Effects so that the installation is recognized. If restarting Premiere after installing After Effects does not enable Premiere to detect the After Effects installation, try restarting your computer. Do this before you perform the following workflow.

continues on next page

1 Open the sequence AE Dynamic Link, and scrub through the sequence to familiarize yourself with the content.

This sequence has several drone shots of the Valley of Fire State Park in Nevada, with an opening title placed above the second clip. The title would benefit from the advanced text animation features offered by After Effects.

2 Right-click the Nevada Desert graphic clip on the Video 2 track in the sequence and choose Replace With After Effects Composition.

3 If it's not running already, After Effects launches. If the After Effects Save As dialog box appears, enter a name and location for the After Effects project. Name the project **Lesson 12-01.aep**, and save it to a new folder inside the Lessons folder.

4 If it is not already selected, click the Default workspace name at the top right of the After Effects interface. Then click the panel menu next to the Default workspace name and choose Reset To Saved Layout.

Clips become layers in After Effects compositions to make it easier to work with advanced controls in the Timeline panel.

There are lots of ways to apply effects with After Effects. To keep things simple, let's work with animation presets (these are similar to effect presets in Premiere). For more on effects workflows, see *Adobe After Effects Classroom in a Book 2026 Release*.

5 The composition should be open in the Timeline panel already. If not, look for it in the After Effects Project panel, and double-click to load it. It should be called Lesson 12 Working Linked Comp 01 (the number may be higher if you have tried this workflow before). There's just one layer, called Nevada Desert. The layer contains the text that you'll work on next.

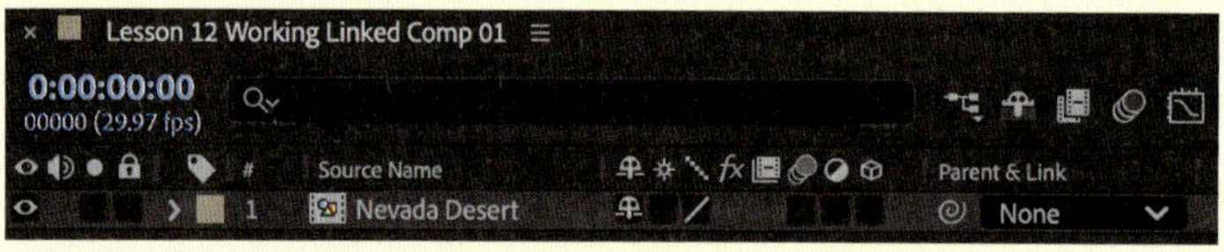

6 Double-click the Nevada Desert layer, under the Source Name heading, to open it in a new Timeline panel.

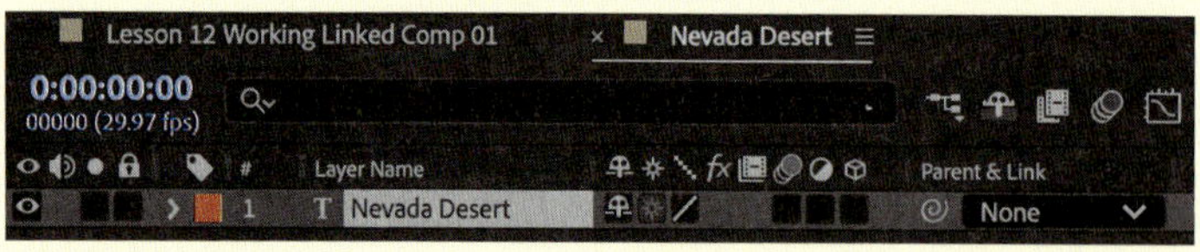

7 Locate the Effects & Presets panel (you can find this in the Window menu if it's not onscreen already). Click the chevron to expand the *Animation Presets category. If the category is not displayed, check that it is selected in the Effects & Presets panel menu.

Animation presets in After Effects use standard built-in effects to achieve impressive results. They are an excellent shortcut to producing a professional finish for your work.

8. Expand the Text category and then the Animate In group. You may need to resize the panel a little to read the full preset names.

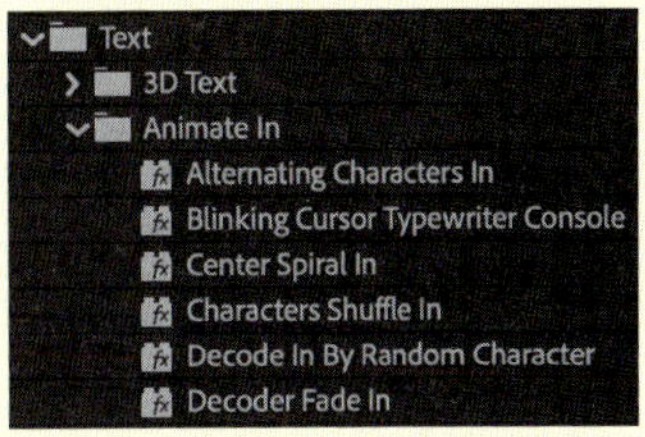

9. Make sure the playhead is at the beginning of the composition (it should be already). Drag the Decoder Fade In preset onto the Nevada Desert layer in the Timeline panel.
10. Press the spacebar to play the animation—a cool animated effect as the text appears.

    The green line at the top of the Timeline panel indicates After Effects created a temporary preview. Only playback of the highlighted section of the timeline is likely to be smooth.
11. This looks great, but it's hard to know what the effect looks like against the desert background. Switch back to Premiere to check.

    In Premiere, the title has been replaced with the dynamically linked After Effects composition you just created. The new animation plays right away in Premiere. Any changes made in After Effects appear automatically in Premiere.

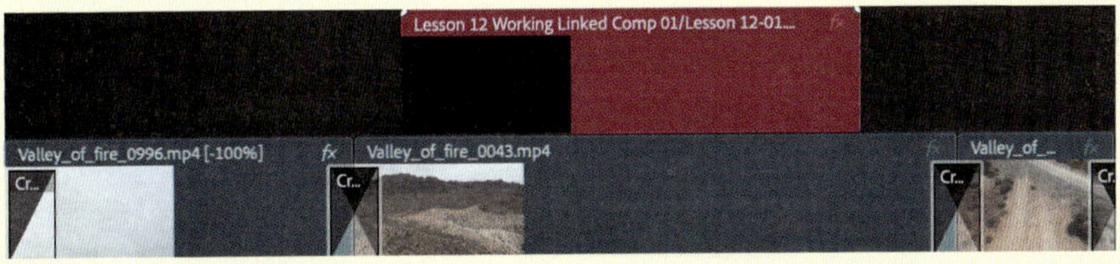

12. Switch back to After Effects, and choose File > Save. Then quit After Effects.

    The frames are processed in the background and handed off from After Effects to Premiere. As Premiere has the After Effects playback engine built in, the result continues to display properly.
13. Preview your sequence in Premiere. To improve preview playback performance, you can select the clip in the Timeline panel and choose Sequence > Render Selection.

You're not limited to sending single clips from Premiere into new After Effects projects. If an After Effects project is already open when you send a clip, the clip will be added as a new composition to the existing project, rather than needing a new project. You can also:

- Select multiple clips to send to After Effects in a single step, making it easier to check compositions and set up more complex animated compositions.
- Drag a sequence from the Premiere Pro Project panel into the After Effects Project panel to use as a dynamically linked asset in After Effects.
- Drag a composition from the After Effects Project panel into the Premiere Pro Project panel to use as a dynamically linked asset in Premiere Pro.

Applying source clip effects

You can also apply video effects to clips in the Project panel. You use the same effects and work with them in the same way. Clips in the Project panel are called *source clips* (to distinguish them from *sequence clip instances*), and effects applied to them are called *source clip effects*. With source clip effects, any instance of a clip, or part of a clip, you add to a sequence will inherit the effects you have applied. You can even apply source clip effects *after* adding clips to sequences, and the sequences will update—a powerful way to make adjustments to multiple parts of the same source clip in a sequence, in a single step.

For example, you could add a color adjustment to a clip in the Project panel so that it matches other camera angles in a scene. Each time you use that clip or part of that clip in a sequence, the adjustment will already be applied. Even if you don't make the adjustment until after the scene is edited, you can use a source clip effect to quickly match the colors.

Let's add a source clip effect now.

1 Open the sequence 04 Source Clip Effects.

   This has one clip, Laura_02, edited five times into the same sequence. The copies of the clip are separated by a number of other, similar shots.

2 Position the Timeline panel playhead somewhere over the first instance of the Laura_02 clip. You want to open this sequence clip's original source clip in the Source Monitor so you can apply an effect to it. It won't work to double-click the clip in the sequence because it will open the instance you clicked instead of the original.

   Select the clip and press the F key. This is the shortcut for Match Frame, which opens the original source clip in the Source Monitor at the frame that is displayed in the Program Monitor.

   This is a useful shortcut to remember, as you will often want to check source clips when reviewing sequences, either to see a version of a clip without effects applied or to check for alternative content.

   You now have the same clip open in the Source Monitor (the source clip) and displayed in the Program Monitor (the sequence segment), so you can see how the changes affect the sequence as you apply them.

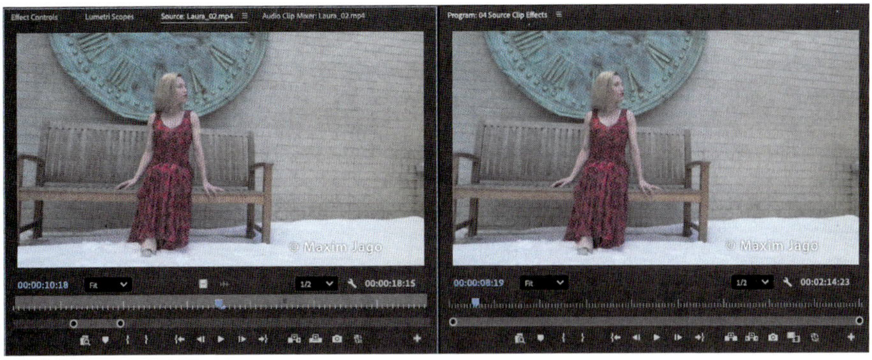

3 In the Effects panel, type **100** in the search box to quickly locate the Lumetri Look effect preset named Cinespace 100.

4 Drag the Cinespace 100 effect into the Source Monitor.

This applies the effect to the source clip.

5 Click the Source Monitor to make sure it's the active panel, and then open the Effect Controls panel to see the effect options.

Tip: You can also apply an effect to a source clip by dragging the effect onto the clip directly in the Project panel or by selecting a clip in a sequence and clicking the source clip name at the top left of the Effect Controls panel and then dragging the effect into that panel.

Note: Selection is important in Premiere. Clicking to activate the Source Monitor before going to the Effect Controls panel is necessary to see the correct options.

Because you applied the effect to the clip in the Source Monitor and then selected the Source Monitor to make it active, the Effect Controls panel shows the effect applied to the source clip, rather than the instance in the sequence.

This is a Lumetri Color effect, and you will be learning a lot more about these effects in Lesson 13, "Applying Color Correction and Grading."

6 Because the effect has been applied to the source clip, every instance of the clip in the sequence shows the results. Play the sequence to see that the effect is applied to every copy of the Laura_02 clip. You can tell a source clip effect is applied to a clip because the FX badge is not only highlighted (to indicate an effect has been applied) but is also underlined fx. The underline indicates a source clip effect.

The result of the effect is displayed in the Source Monitor *and* the Program Monitor because sequence clips inherit their source clip effects dynamically.

From now on, anytime you use this source clip, or part of it, in a sequence, Premiere will include the effect.

Because the source clip has the effect applied, even though the timeline instances of the clip (the sequence clips) show the result of the effect, none of them shows that an effect has been applied in the Effect Controls panel.

7 Single-click any of the sequence instances of the Laura_02 clip on the timeline to select it, and look in the Effect Controls panel—no Lumetri Color effect, just the usual fixed effects (which are applicable only to sequence clips, not clips in the Project panel).

At the top of the Effect Controls panel there are two tabs. The tab on the left shows the name of the source clip, Source • Laura_02.mp4.

The tab on the right shows the name of the sequence followed by the name of the sequence clip, 04 Source Clip Effects • Laura_02.mp4.

Because you selected the clip in the sequence, the tab on the right is highlighted, showing that you're working on that instance of the clip.

There's no Lumetri Color effect displayed because you haven't applied the effect to the Timeline panel's instance of the clip.

8 In the Effect Controls panel, click the tab at the top that shows the source clip name. Now you'll see the source clip effect options.

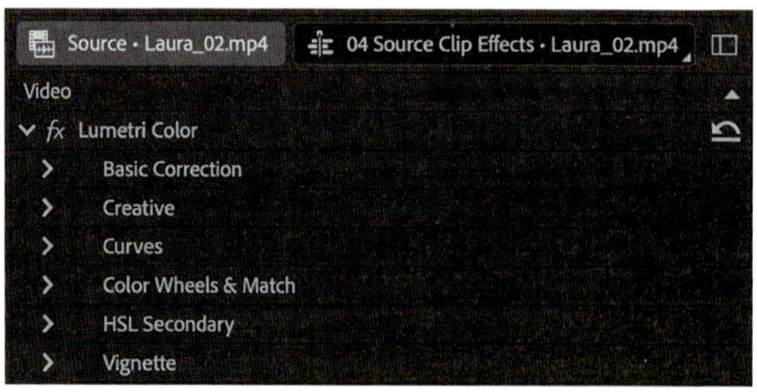

9 Experiment with the controls for the Lumetri Color effect, and then play the sequence. You'll see the changes are applied to every instance of the clip.

Source clip effects provide a powerful way to manage effects in Premiere. You may need to experiment a little to make the most of them. You use the same video effects as you would use on the timeline, so the techniques you're learning in this book will work the same way, but the planning is a little different.

Masking and tracking video effects

All standard video effects can be constrained within elliptical, polygonal, or custom masks, which you can manually animate using keyframes.

Put simply, a *mask* is an area in the frame within which a video effect can be applied, leaving the rest of the frame unchanged. For instance, you could apply a mosaic effect to hide someone's face, but there are many creative uses for masks beyond this classic function.

Masks can track the contents of your shots to animate their position, following the action with the constrained special effect. For example, you might use a mask to blur the number plate on a vehicle and have the mask follow the position of the plate on-screen as the vehicle moves.

In this exercise, you will use a mask and mask tracking to change the lighting in a shot.

Note: This example uses a vivid adjustment to illustrate a technique. You will usually make subtler adjustments.

Continue working with the 04 Source Clip Effects sequence.

1 Position the playhead over the first frame of the second clip in the sequence, Evening Smile.

It looks good, but it would benefit from a stronger light on the subject to help separate the foreground from the background.

2 Search the Effects panel for the Brightness & Contrast effect.

3 Apply this effect to the clip.

4 In the Effect Controls panel, scroll down to the Brightness & Contrast controls.

Choose the following settings:

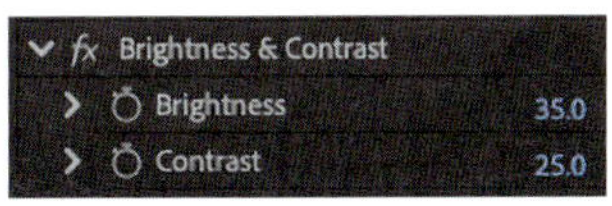

- Brightness: **35**
- Contrast: **25**

You can set these levels by clicking the blue numbers and typing the new setting, by scrubbing the blue numbers, or by expanding the controls and using the sliders.

This effect changes the entire picture. You're going to constrain the effect to just one area of the shot.

To do so, you'll create a mask that will define the limited area of the effect. First you'll create a mask manually; then in the next section you'll learn an automated method.

5 In the Tools panel, click and hold the Object Mask tool to access and select the Ellipse Mask tool.

6 Now drag in the Program Monitor to draw an ellipse that covers the subject's face. Don't worry about precision as the position can easily be adjusted.

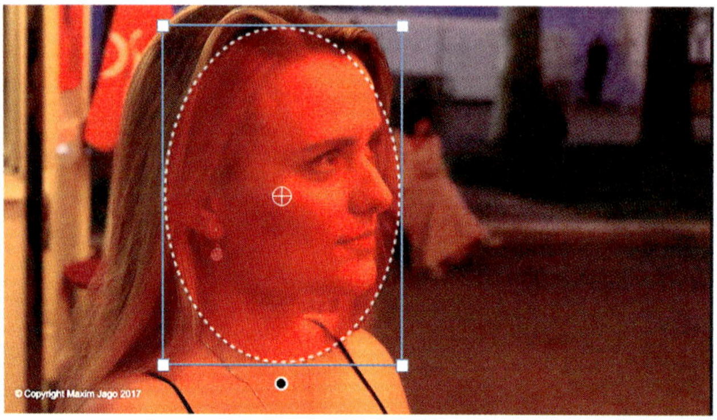

When you release the drag:

- The mask and its resizing and repositioning controls appear in the Program Monitor.
- Settings for the mask appear in the Effect Controls panel under the Unassigned Masks heading.
- While the mask is selected, which it is automatically when you first create it, additional controls appear in the Program Monitor.

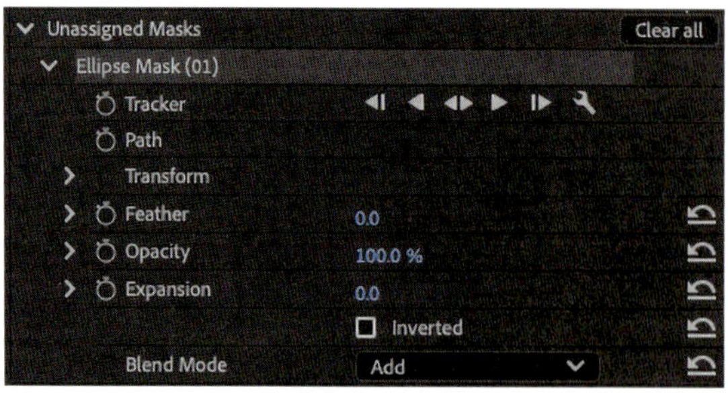

You can use the Mask Overlay menu to choose a color for the tint that appears, and you can switch between applying mask settings to the whole clip or just to the one frame you are currently viewing.

7 Set the Mask Overlay to None, so it's easier to see the results of the effect, and leave adjustments set for the whole clip.

8 Take a moment to adjust the position and shape of the mask so that it covers the subject's face, most of their hair, and a little room in front of their face.

If you deselect the mask, the controls will disappear in the Program Monitor. To bring them back, select the name of the mask in the Effect Controls panel. In this case, select Ellipse Mask (01) to display the controls again. Double-click the mask in the Program Monitor to display the bounding box.

Tip: You can add multiple masks to a clip and apply them to the same effect or separate effects. If you select a mask in the Effect Controls panel, you can modify the shape in the Program Monitor.

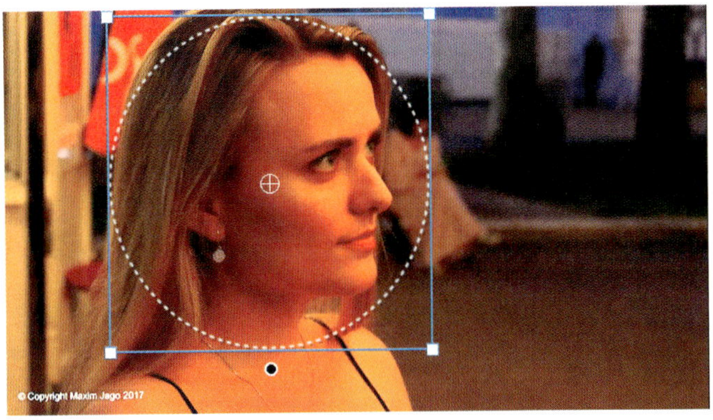

9 In the Effect Controls panel, apply the mask to the Brightness & Contrast effect by dragging it down from the Unassigned Masks heading onto the effect. You may need to resize the panel to do this.

10 Feathering softens the edge of the mask. In the Effect Controls panel, set Mask Feather to **240**.

You have brightened the area around the subject's face, with a natural return to regular lighting in the rest of the picture. Now you just need the mask to follow the moving video.

In the Effect Controls panel, just under the Ellipse Mask heading, there are several mask-tracking controls.

11 Click the Track Selected Mask Forward button. Premiere quickly tracks the contents of the clip to reposition and resize the mask to continue covering the subject's face as it moves in the frame.

   The movement is quite subtle, so it's easy for Premiere to follow the action.

12 Scrub the Effect Controls panel playhead to see the movement of the mask.

13 Deselect the mask by clicking away from the mask name in the Effect Controls panel or by clicking an empty track in the Timeline panel. The mask handles in the Program Monitor will be removed.

Premiere can also track both backward *and* forward at the same time. You can select an item partway through a clip and then click Track Selected Mask Forward And Backward in the Effect Controls panel to track in both directions, creating a natural path for the mask to follow.

The effect is subtle, and your eyes may adjust quickly to the new image. To compare it with the original look, in the Effect Controls panel click the Brightness & Contrast FX button a few times to turn the effect off and on. Even this small change dramatically changes the result.

Using the Object Mask tool

The Object Mask tool automatically creates precise masks that match complex shapes. This makes it ideal for changing the appearance of a specific object in the frame. Because automated tracking also tracks changes to shapes, you'll find this an excellent tool for picking out subjects and adjusting their appearance. Try this with a new shot.

Continue working with the 04 Source Clip Effects sequence.

1 Position the Timeline playhead over the first frame of the fourth clip in the sequence, and make sure the clip is selected.

Like the Effect Controls panel, the Object Mask tool needs to know which clip you will be working on.

2 In the Tools panel, click and hold the Ellipse Mask tool to reveal and select the Object Mask tool.

With this tool, when you hover over objects in the Program Monitor they are highlighted automatically.

3 Hover over the subject, and when it highlights, click with the Object Mask tool. A notification may appear to let you know that the mask data you are creating will be stored in a folder next to your project file. Click OK.

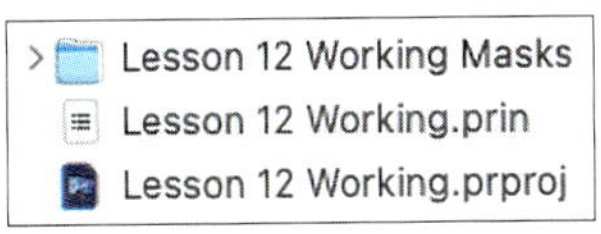

A dotted line indicates the edge of the mask you created, and an object mask appears in the Effect Controls panel under the Unassigned Masks heading.

4 In the Effects panel, search for the Gaussian Blur effect and drag that effect onto the clip in the Timeline panel.

Unassigned masks are automatically assigned to the next effect you apply, so the object mask now appears under the Gaussian Blur effect heading in the Effect Controls panel. If the mask is not assigned automatically, you can drag it onto the Gaussian Blur effect name in the Effect Controls panel to assign it.

Note: If an effect already applied to a clip is selected in the Effect Controls panel when a new mask is created, the mask is automatically assigned to the selected effect (rather than being added to the Unassigned Masks list).

5 In the Effect Controls panel, click the Track Selected Mask Forward button ▶ to animate the mask.

It will take a little longer to complete the analysis, because there is a lot more detail to track.

6 Deselect the mask in the Effect Controls panel, and play the clip to review the result.

7 This shot would look a lot more interesting if we could see the subject! In the Effect Controls panel, check the Inverted box in the Object Mask settings to reverse the application of the mask. Then set Feather to **20** to smooth out the edge a little.

You can apply masks to most video effects. Take a little time to explore the creative results you can achieve.

Keyframing effects

When you add keyframes to an effect, you're setting particular values for controls at precise moments in time. Each keyframe will store a setting for one control. If, for example, you were intending to keyframe Position, Scale, and Rotation, you would need three separate keyframes.

Set keyframes at precise moments where you need a particular setting, and let Premiere work out how to animate the controls between them.

Adding keyframes

You can change almost all parameters for all video effects over time using keyframes. For example, you can have a clip gradually become out of focus, change color, or lengthen its shadow.

1 Open the sequence 05 Keyframes.

2 View the sequence to get familiar with the footage, and then position the Timeline playhead over the first frame of the clip.

3 In the Effects panel, locate the Light Leaks effect and apply it to the clip in the sequence. This is not a subtle effect, but it will illustrate Motion keyframes well.

4 In the Effect Controls panel, set the Feather control for the Light Leaks effect to **120**.

Increasing the feathering expands the clear region in the middle of the frame.

5 Select the Light Leaks effect heading. With the effect selected, the Program Monitor displays a small control handle. Use the handle to reposition the center of the effect to match the following figure so that the center is in front of the face of the subject on the left.

6 Make sure the Effect Controls panel timeline is visible. If it isn't, click the Show/Hide Timeline View button next to the clip name at the top right of the panel to toggle the display.

7 Click the stopwatch icons to turn animation on for the Position property. Clicking the stopwatch icon enables keyframing and adds a keyframe at the current location with the current settings.

8 Move the playhead to the last frame of the clip.

To do this, you can drag the playhead directly in the Effect Controls panel.

9 Use the control handle in the Program Monitor or adjust the Position property in the Effect Controls panel to reposition the center of the effect over the face of the subject on the right.

Because you have enabled animation for the Position property, a keyframe is added automatically when you make the adjustment.

10 Deselect the Light Leaks effect to hide the controls in the Program Monitor, and play the sequence to watch the effect animate over time.

Adding keyframe interpolation and velocity

Keyframe interpolation changes the behavior of an effect setting as it moves between keyframes with different settings. The default behavior you've seen so far is linear; in other words, it produces a constant change between keyframes. What generally works better is something that mirrors your real-world experience or exaggerates it, such as gradual acceleration or deceleration.

Premiere offers a way to control those changes: keyframe interpolation and the Velocity graph. Keyframe interpolation is easy and simplified, whereas adjusting the Velocity graph can be complex but more precise.

Velocity graphs appear in the timeline on the right side of the Effect Controls panel, along with the keyframes, when you expand a property by clicking its chevron.

1 Open the sequence 06 Interpolation. This has the same content as the sequence you have been working on with the Light Leaks effect already applied and animated.

2 Position the playhead at the beginning of the sequence, and select the clip.

3 In the Effect Controls panel timeline, right-click the first keyframe for the Light Leaks Position property. Choose Temporal Interpolation > Ease Out to create a gentle transition into the move from the keyframe.

Note: When working with position-related parameters, the context menu for a keyframe will offer two types of interpolation: spatial (related to location) and temporal (related to time). You can make spatial adjustments in the Program Monitor as well as in the Effect Controls panel if you select the effect in the Effect Controls panel. You can make temporal adjustments on the clip in the Timeline and Effect Controls panels. These motion-related topics were covered in Lesson 9, "Putting Clips in Motion."

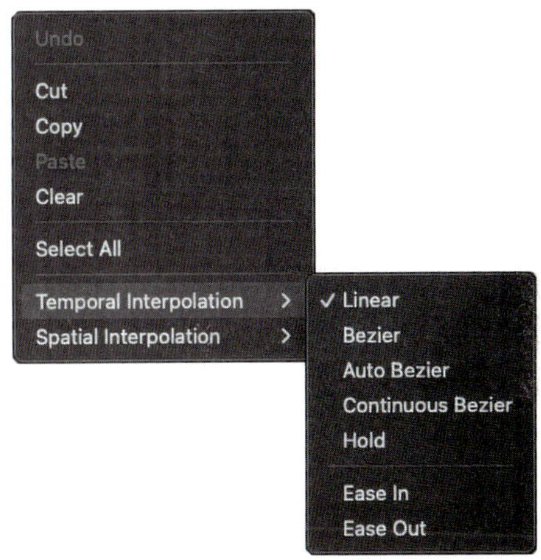

4 Right-click the second keyframe for the Position property and choose Temporal Interpolation > Ease In. This creates a gentle transition into the stationary position of the last keyframe.

Tip: Be sure to use the Next Keyframe and Previous Keyframe buttons to move between keyframes efficiently. This will keep you from adding unwanted keyframes.

5 Play back the animation to watch the changes you've made. The difference is subtle, but now the motion of the clear section in the middle of the effect is smoother.

When you animate position, a clip anchor point or effect center (in this example, the Position control) follows a path across the frame. This path is called the *motion path*.

6 In the Effect Controls panel, select the Light Leaks effect name. Scrub through the clip to see the animation with the effect motion path displayed.

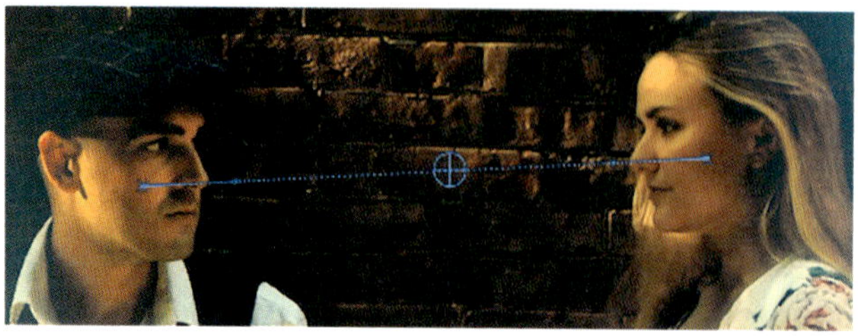

Let's refine the keyframes with the Velocity graph.

7 Hover the pointer over the Effect Controls panel, and then press ` (accent grave) to maximize the panel (or double-click the panel name, if your keyboard doesn't have that key). This will give you a clearer view of the keyframe controls.

8 If necessary, click the chevron next to the Position control to show the velocity graph.

The Velocity graph shows the velocity between keyframes. Any sudden drops or jumps represent sudden changes in velocity. The farther the point or line is from the baseline, the greater the velocity.

9 Select a keyframe, and then adjust its extended handle to change the steepness of the velocity curve. If you can't see all the keyframes, try pressing the – (minus) key while the Effect Controls panel is active to zoom out in the Effect Controls panel timeline.

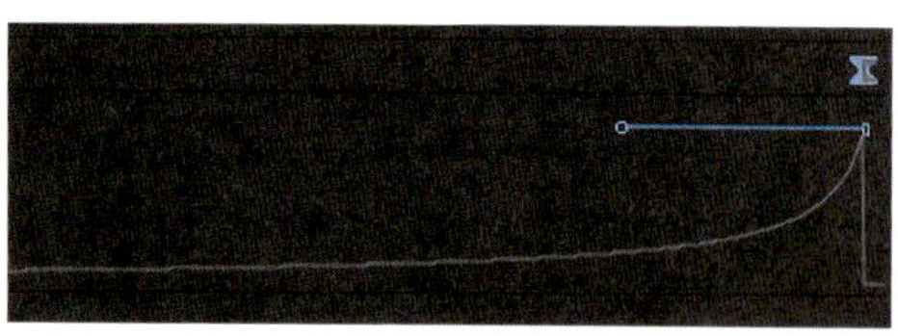

10 Press the ` (accent grave) key, or double-click the panel name, to restore the Effect Controls panel, and play back your sequence to see the impact of your changes. Experiment some more to get familiar with keyframes and interpolation.

Understanding interpolation methods

Here's a rundown of the keyframe interpolation methods available in Premiere:

- **Linear:** This is the default behavior and creates a uniform rate of change between keyframes.
- **Bezier:** This lets you manually adjust the shape of the graph on either side of a keyframe. Beziers allow for sudden or smooth acceleration into or out of a keyframe.
- **Continuous Bezier:** This method creates a smooth rate of change through a keyframe. Unlike with regular Bezier keyframes, if you adjust one handle of a Continuous Bezier keyframe, the handle on the other side moves equally to maintain a smooth transition through the keyframe.
- **Auto Bezier:** This method creates a smooth rate of change through a keyframe even if you change the keyframe value. If you choose to manually adjust the keyframe's handles, it changes to a Continuous Bezier point, retaining the smooth transition through the keyframe. The Auto Bezier option can occasionally produce unwanted motion, so try one of the other options first.
- **Hold:** This method holds a setting until the next keyframe. The graph following a keyframe with the Hold interpolation applied appears as a horizontal straight line.
- **Ease In:** This method slows down the value changes entering a keyframe and converts it to a Bezier keyframe.
- **Ease Out:** This method gradually accelerates the value changes leaving a keyframe and converts it to a Bezier keyframe.

Perhaps the change to the velocity of the keyframes for the position isn't enough to make the movement appear perfectly smooth. Try dragging the first keyframe later and the last keyframe earlier to allow time before and after the movement, and adjust the velocity keyframes to suit.

Using effect presets

Once you have configured an effect perfectly, you may want to use it again with exactly those settings. Perhaps you have set up a transition effect that you'll use throughout your sequence or there's a color adjustment that you intend to apply to multiple clips in a scene.

You can copy and paste effects between clips within a single project, but if you want to reuse customized effects between different projects, it's easy to create a preset.

Saving effect presets

You can easily create a new effect preset, and a single preset can contain more than one effect—and can even include keyframes for animation. You can also import and export presets to share them between editing systems.

1 Open the sequence 07 Creating Presets.

This sequence has two clips, each with an adjustment layer on the V2 track and a title on the V3 track.

2 Play the sequence to watch the opening animation.

3 Select the first instance of the "Laura in the snow" title clip on the V3 track and look in the Effect Controls panel. A Fast Blur effect has been applied to the title, and there are keyframes animating several controls.

4 In the Effect Controls panel, click the Vector Motion effect heading to select it. Next, hold Command (macOS) or Ctrl (Windows) while you click the effect headings for the Fast Blur effect and then the Opacity effect. Now all three effects are selected.

5 Right-click any of the selected effects and choose Save Preset.

6 In the Save Preset dialog box, name the effect **Title Animation**. Click in the Description box, and type **Title blurs into view**.

When you apply an animated preset to a clip with a different duration, Premiere needs to know how to distribute the keyframes.

There are three options.

- **Scale:** Redistributes the original preset keyframes to the duration of the new clip proportionally.
- **Anchor To In Point:** Preserves the position of the first keyframe as well as the relationship of other keyframes in a clip relative to its In point.
- **Anchor To Out Point:** Preserves the position of the last keyframe as well as the relationship of other keyframes in a clip relative to its Out point.

7 For this preset, select Anchor To In Point so the timing matches at the start of each clip the preset is applied to.

8 Click OK to store the effects and keyframes as a new preset.

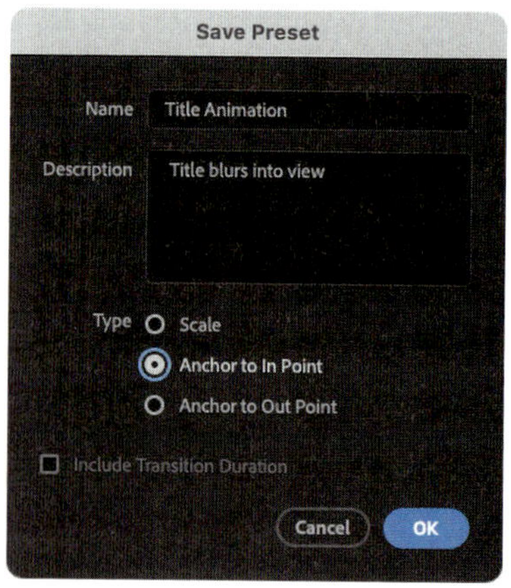

9 In the Effects panel, locate the Presets category and your newly created Title Animation preset. Hover the pointer over the preset to see the description you added appear as a tool tip.

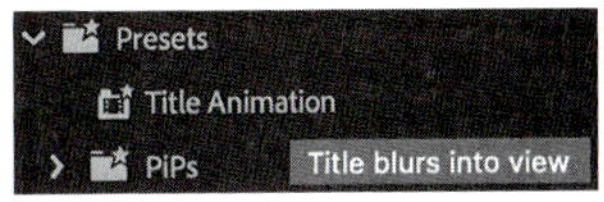

10 Drag the new Title Animation preset from the Effects panel onto the second instance of the "Laura in the snow" title clip on the V3 track in the Timeline.

11 Watch the sequence play back to see the newly applied title animation.

▶ **Tip:** Effect presets can be exported and imported so they can be shared. You'll find the Import and Export options in the Effects panel menu. You can select and export an individual preset or a whole custom bin containing multiple presets. You'll find a number of free presets at *premierepro.net/presets*.

12 Select the second title clip on the V3 track and look in the Effect Controls panel. All three effects included in the preset have been added to the clip. The name of the preset is included in parentheses after each effect name, so you know the way the effect has been configured. You can still edit the effect controls, but it's a useful way to check which preset you used in the first place.

You can change the configuration of a preset by right-clicking it in the Effects panel and choosing Preset Properties or by double-clicking it. Double-clicking an effect (rather than a preset) will apply the effect to a selected clip.

Exploring useful effects

Although it's beyond the scope of this book to explore all the effects available, these are useful in many editing situations. You'll learn about color adjustments in the next lesson.

Applying image stabilization and rolling shutter reduction

The Warp Stabilizer effect can remove jitter caused by camera movement (which is common with lightweight cameras). The effect is useful because it can remove or reduce camera shake.

The result is achieved by zooming into the image by just enough to automatically animate the clip position within the frame to compensate for unwanted camera movement.

Let's explore the effect.

1 Open the sequence 08 Warp Stabilizer.

2 Play the first clip in the sequence to see the wobbly shot.

3 In the Effects panel, locate the Warp Stabilizer effect and apply it to the shot.

As Premiere analyzes the clip, a banner briefly appears across the footage to let you know you'll need to wait before working with the effect. The Effect Controls panel also displays a detailed progress indicator. The analysis takes place in the background, so you can carry on working while waiting for it to complete.

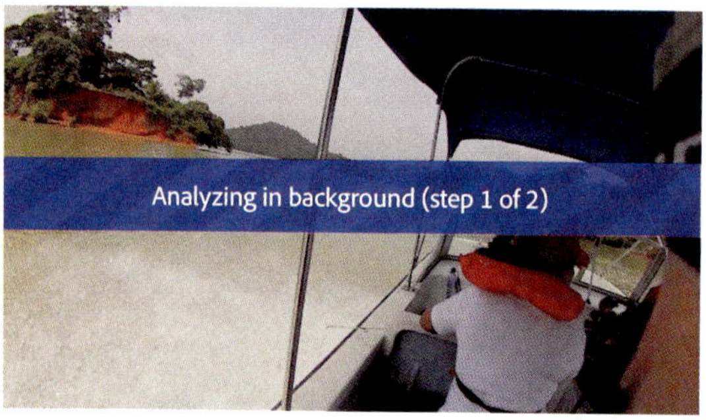

4 Once the analysis has completed, you can adjust settings in the Effect Controls panel to improve results by choosing options that better suit the shot.

- **Result:** In the Stabilization > Result menu, you can choose Smooth Motion to retain the general camera movement (albeit stabilized), or you can choose No Motion to attempt to remove all camera movement. For this exercise, choose Smooth Motion.
- **Smoothness:** This option specifies how much of the original camera movement should be retained for Smooth Motion. Use a higher value to smooth out the shot the most. Experiment with this shot until you're happy with its stability.
- **Method:** There are four methods available. The two most powerful, because they warp and process the image more heavily, are Perspective and Subspace Warp. If either method creates too much distortion as the effect compensates for camera movement, try switching to Position, Scale, Rotation, or just Position. More of the image will probably be cropped using these alternative methods, but it may be worth it when working with very shaky footage.

5 Play the clip—the impact is dramatic.

Tip: If you notice that some of the details in the shot appear to wobble, you may be able to improve the overall effect. In the Advanced section, select Detailed Analysis. This makes the Analysis phase do extra work to find elements to track. You can also use the Enhanced Reduction option from the Rolling Shutter Ripple option in the Advanced category. These options are slower to render but often do produce better results.

6 Play the second clip in the sequence to review it. This shot should be static, but it's handheld, so there's a little movement. Apply the Warp Stabilizer effect to this clip. Choose No Motion from the Warp Stabilizer > Stabilization > Result menu.

The Warp Stabilizer effect is amazingly effective at locking these kinds of shots into position.

Because the results are achieved by moving the image to compensate for camera wobble, the copyright notice that is burned into this footage now appears to move. This is a good reason to avoid using footage with burned-in graphics or text.

The Warp Stabilizer effect adds quite a lot of data to the Premiere project file. If you plan to stabilize lots of clips, consider performing the stabilization in a separate project and exporting new media files for use in your main project. Large project files take longer to open and to save.

Using an adjustment layer to display clip names

If you intend to send a review copy of a sequence to a client or colleague, you can apply the Metadata & Timecode Burn-in effect to an adjustment layer and have it generate visible clip names for the entire sequence.

This is helpful because it allows others to give feedback based on a particular clip. You can control the clip name format position, size, and opacity.

You can enable a similar timecode overlay when exporting media, but this clip effect has more options.

> **Tip:** If you work with multiple sequences with different format settings in a single project, it's worth naming adjustment layers to make it easier to identify their resolution. You can rename adjustment layers in the Project panel just as you would any other item.

1 Open the sequence 09 Clip Names.

2 At the lower right of the Project panel, click the New Item menu (you may need to resize the Project panel to see it), and choose Adjustment Layer from the menu. Click OK in the Adjustment Layer dialog box.

A new adjustment layer is added to the Project panel, with settings that match your current sequence.

● **Note:** Adjustment layers have a frame size. When you create a new adjustment layer, the default frame size will match the sequence currently displayed in the Timeline panel.

3 In the Project panel, you will now have two adjustment layers. Rename the new layer **Metadata Adjustment Layer** to make it easier to stay organized.

4 Drag the new adjustment layer to the beginning of track V2 in the current sequence.

5 Position the Timeline playhead at the end of the sequence. Click once to select the right edge of the new adjustment layer clip, and press E. Then press Esc to deselect the edit.

6 You can add most video effects to an adjustment layer. Let's try an example effect.

In the Effects panel, locate the Horizontal Flip effect. Drag it onto the adjustment layer to apply it. This switches the video horizontally, giving the effect of changing the direction of movement.

There are no controls for the Horizontal Flip effect. You can still use masks to constrain the effect, which produces interesting results where there is movement in the shot.

This effect works well with this kind of content but may not work if there is visible text or a recognizable logo in the picture.

Let's add the Metadata & Timecode Burn-in effect.

7 In the Effects panel, search for the Metadata & Timecode Burn-in effect.

8 Apply the Metadata & Timecode Burn-in effect to the adjustment layer clip.

By default, the effect shows the timecode of the clip you applied it to, which in this case is the Adjustment Layer—not very useful!

▶ **Tip:** You can click the Metadata & Timecode Burn-in effect heading in the Effect Controls panel and then drag the anchor point for the name displayed in the Program Monitor to reposition it.

9 In the Effect Controls panel, in the Metadata & Timecode Burn-in effect controls, use the Metadata menu to choose Sequence Clip Name, and use the Source Track menu to choose Video 1. Now the clip names from the V1 track are displayed.

10 Clear the Effects panel search box by clicking the X.

Rendering all sequences

If you have several sequences with effects you want to render, you can render them all as a batch, without opening each sequence to render it individually.

Select the sequences you would like to render in the Project panel, and choose Sequence > Render Effects In To Out.

All effects that need to render in the selected sequences will be rendered.

Using the Render And Replace command

If you are working on a low-powered system and your media is high resolution, you may find media tends to drop frames routinely when previewing. You may also see dropped frames when working with dynamically linked After Effects compositions or complex third-party video effects that don't support GPU acceleration.

If all your media is high resolution, you may decide to use the proxy workflow, which allows you to switch between full-resolution and lower-resolution media file playback.

However, if just one or two clips are difficult to play back, you also have the option to render just those clips as new media files and replace the original items in a sequence quickly and easily.

To replace a sequence clip segment with a version that's easier to play back, right-click the clip and choose Render And Replace.

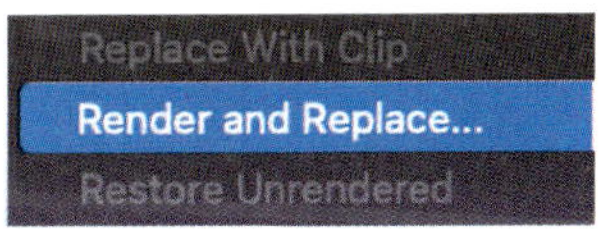

The Render And Replace dialog box allows you to choose the settings for the new media file that will be created. Here are the main settings:

- **Source:** Choose whether the new media file that will be created will match the frame rate and frame size of the sequence, the original media, or a preset.

Tip: Another benefit of using the Render And Replace command is that clips do not need to be re-rendered if you move them to a different part of your sequence or combine them with other clips in a layered composition. This can be a huge time-saver.

- **Format:** Specify your preferred file type. Different formats give access to different codecs.
- **Preset:** Choose a preset here. You can use a custom preset created with Adobe Media Encoder or one of the several built-in options.

If you enable Include Video Effects for an option, Premiere will incorporate the effects into the new file, which means you will no longer be able to adjust those effects' settings in the Effect Controls panel.

Once you have chosen a preset and a location for the new file, click OK and the sequence clip is replaced.

A rendered and replaced clip is no longer directly linked to the original media—it's linked to a new media file. This means, for example, changes that you make to a dynamically linked After Effects composition will not update in Premiere. To restore the link to the original item, right-click the clip and choose Restore Unrendered.

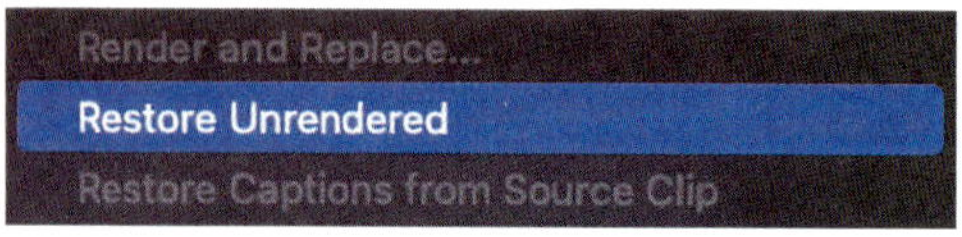

If you had chosen the option to include video effects, they would be restored along with the original file and fully editable again.

Review questions

1 What are two ways to apply an effect to a clip?

2 List three ways to add a keyframe.

3 Dragging an effect onto a clip turns on its parameters in the Effect Controls panel, but you don't see the effect in the Program Monitor. Why not?

4 Describe how you can apply one effect to a range of clips.

5 Describe how to save multiple effects to a custom preset.

Review answers

1 Drag the effect to the clip, or select the clip and double-click the effect in the Effects panel.

2 Move the playhead in the Effect Controls panel to where you want a keyframe and activate keyframing by clicking the stopwatch icon to turn animation on; move the playhead and click the Add/Remove Keyframe button; and with keyframing activated, move the playhead to a position and change a parameter. You could also set up and use a custom keyboard shortcut.

3 You need to move the Timeline panel playhead to the selected clip to see it in the Program Monitor. Selecting a clip does not move the playhead to that clip. Also, many effects do not produce visible changes until you adjust the controls.

4 You can add an adjustment layer above the clips you want to affect. You can then apply an effect to the adjustment layer that will modify all the clips below the layer. You can also select the clips you would like to apply the effect to and then drag the effect onto the group or double-click the effect in the Effects panel.

5 With the Effect Controls panel active, you can choose Edit > Select All. You can also hold Command (macOS) or Ctrl (Windows) while you select multiple effect headings in the Effect Controls panel. Once the effects are selected, right-click the selection and choose Save Preset. You can also choose Save Preset in the panel menu.

13 APPLYING COLOR CORRECTION AND GRADING

Lesson overview

In this lesson, you'll learn how to do the following:

- Work in the Color workspace.
- Use the Lumetri Color panel.
- Use vectorscopes and waveforms.
- Compare and match clip colors.
- Use color correction–related effects.
- Fix exposure and white balance problems.
- Work with special color effects.
- Create a look.

This lesson will take about 150 minutes to complete. To get the files used in this lesson, refer to the instructions in "Accessing the lesson files and Web Edition" in the "Getting Started" section at the beginning of this book. Store the files on your computer in a convenient location.

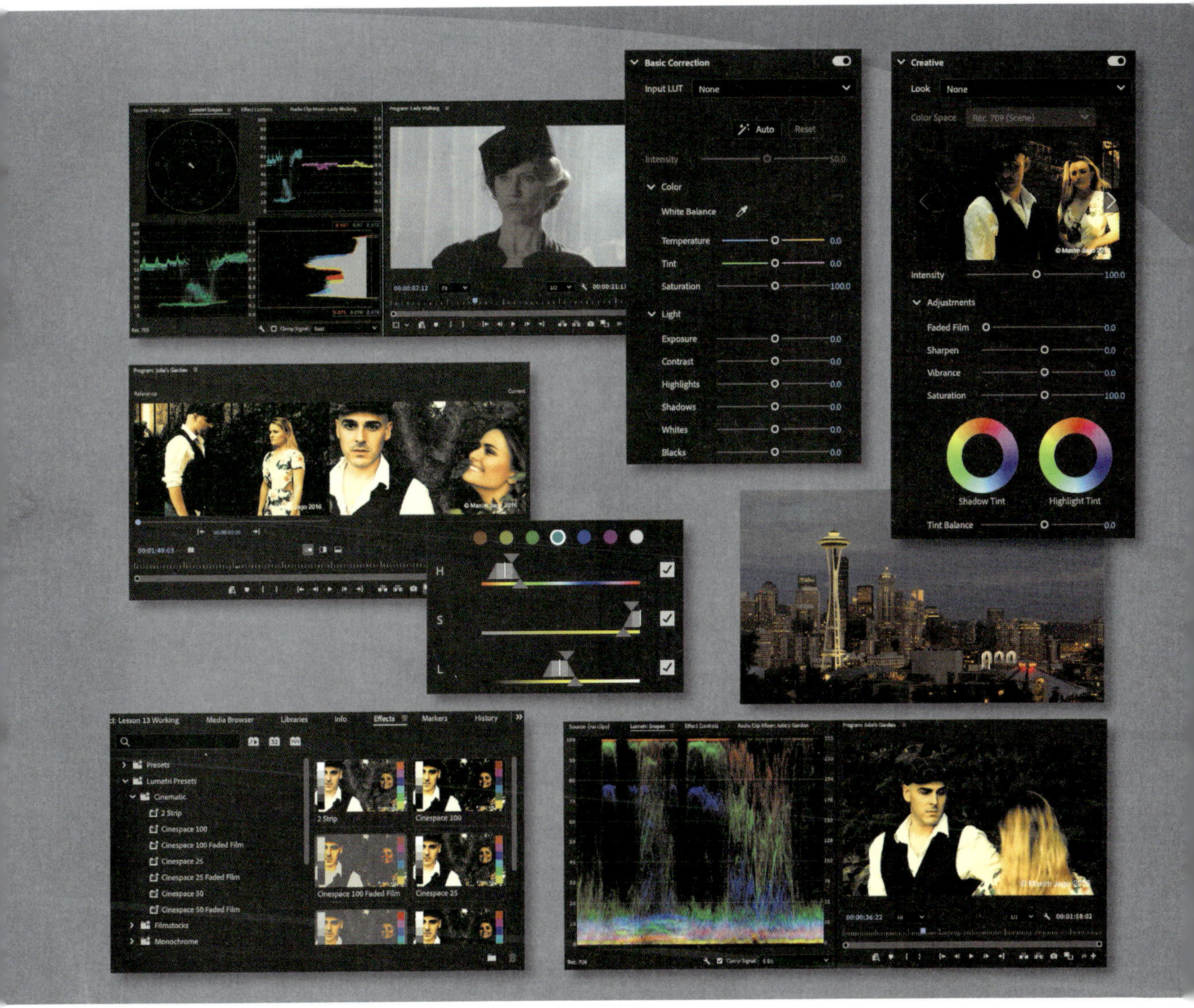

Editing your clips together is just the first part of the creative process. Now it's time to work with color. In this lesson, you'll learn some key techniques for improving the look of your clips to give them a distinctive atmosphere.

Starting the lesson

Note: To ensure that the tools function and the defaults are set exactly as described in this lesson, reset the Premiere preferences by holding any modifier key (such as Shift) while launching the application, selecting Reset App Preferences, and then clicking Continue in the Reset Options dialog box.

So far, you've organized your clips, built sequences, and applied special effects. All of these skills come together when working with color correction.

Consider the way your eyes register color and light, the way cameras record it, and the way your computer screen, a television screen, a video projector, a phone, a tablet, or a cinema screen displays it. There are a great many factors when considering the final look of your production.

Premiere has multiple color correction tools and makes it easy to create your own presets. In this lesson, you'll begin by learning some fundamental color correction skills and then explore some of the most popular color correction special effects, before using them to deal with common color correction challenges.

1 Open Lesson 13.prproj in the Lessons folder.
2 Choose Color from the Workspaces menu to switch to the Color workspace.
3 Open the Workspaces menu again, and choose Reset To Saved Layout.

   This changes the workspace to a preset that was created to make it easier to work with color correction effects and, in particular, the Lumetri Color panel and Lumetri Scopes panel.

4 Save the project as **Lesson 13 Working.prproj**.

Understanding display color management

Computer monitors generally use a different system for displaying color than do TV screens and cinema projectors (see the sidebar "About 8-bit video" for more on this).

If you're producing video for online distribution, you can be reasonably confident your audience will be viewing on an RGB laptop or phone screen similar to yours and you can be confident the colors and brightness levels of your images will be comparable. If you're delivering video for TV or the cinema screen, you'll need a way to view video that matches the type of screen it's intended for.

Professional colorists have multiple display systems to check their work on. If they're working on a film intended for theaters, they'll use the same kind of projector a theater would use—projecting the image onto a screen for review purposes.

Some computer monitors offer excellent color reproduction—better than television screens. Premiere can adjust the way video is displayed in the Source Monitor and Program Monitor to match the colors a television screen would display.

Premiere automatically detects if you have the right kind of monitor. To enable this feature, choose Premiere > Settings > Color (macOS) or Edit > Preferences > Color (Windows), and select Display Color Management (Requires GPU Acceleration).

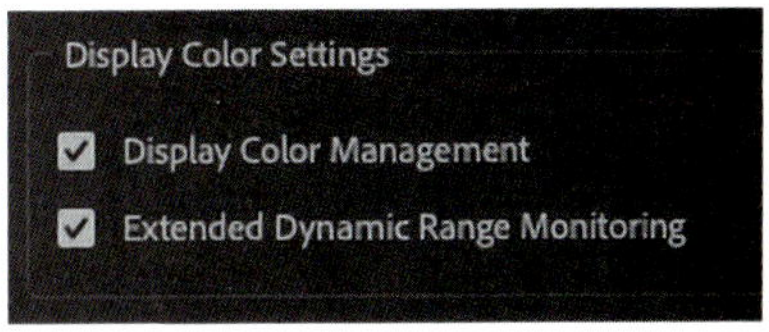

If you are delivering high dynamic range (HDR) media and have a monitor that can display in HDR, you can also enable the Extended Dynamic Range Monitoring option to display the full contrast range.

These options are also available in the Lumetri Color panel under the Settings tab, which you'll learn about in this lesson.

About 8-bit video

8-bit video works on a scale from 0 to 255 for each of the three color channels. That means, for RGB color, each pixel has red, green, and blue (RGB) values somewhere on that scale, which combine to produce a particular color. You can think of 0 as 0% and 255 as 100%. A pixel that has a red value of 127 is equivalent to having a red value of 50%.

Broadcast video uses a similar but different range, with a color system called YUV.

Although YUV color uses the three color channels differently, it still uses 8 bits per channel. However, if you were to compare the YUV scale with the 0 to 255 RGB scale, you'd find that the 8-bit YUV scale ranges from 16 to 235.

TVs usually use YUV color, not RGB. However, your computer screen is RGB. If you are producing video for broadcast television, you may encounter issues because you are looking at your video footage on a different kind of screen than the kind it will ultimately be viewed on. There is only one sure way of overcoming the uncertainty this creates: Connect a TV or calibrated broadcast monitor to your editing system and view your footage on that screen.

The difference is a little like comparing a photograph you view on-screen in Photoshop with a printed version. The printer and your computer screen use different color systems, and it's an imperfect translation from one to the other.

Sometimes you will view footage with visible detail in the brightest and darkest pixels on an RGB screen (like your computer display) that disappears when viewed on a TV screen. You'll need to make adjustments to the color to bring those details into the TV screen color range.

Some TVs give you the option to display color as RGB, using a range of names such as Game Mode or Photo Color Space. If your screen is set up this way, you may see the full 0 to 255 RGB range, and the only way to know is to check the settings—confusing!

With some computer screens, Premiere can adjust the way video colors are displayed to more accurately mimic other screens (see "Understanding display color management," later in this lesson).

Choosing preview gamma

Gamma, in simple terms, sets the midpoint for the brightness of pixels. Changing the gamma will make midtones look brighter or darker.

It would be helpful if there were just one universal standard for video gamma, but there are three to choose between. Projects have a gamma setting to ensure that clips are displayed correctly.

There is a gamma setting for video media that you export and a setting for viewing video media in Premiere. You will usually want these two gamma settings to match so you can make color adjustments accurately.

The export presets include a gamma setting that is usually suitable for the media you're exporting, so you most likely will need to choose only the project Viewer Gamma, while keeping in mind the media you plan to export.

You can set the Viewer Gamma in the Color tab of the Project settings or in the Project section of the Lumetri Color panel settings tab.

Viewer Gamma options are described as a number that sets the relationship between the original video (the input) and the way it is displayed (the output). Don't worry if this sounds complicated—you can choose a gamma setting based on your intended video delivery.

Here are the three options:

- **2.4 (Broadcast):** This is the standard gamma for Rec 709 (HD) video intended for broadcast television.
- **2.2 (Web):** This gives slightly lighter midtones than gamma 2.4 and is the standard gamma for web content.
- **1.96 (QuickTime):** This is the standard gamma setting for video intended for display in Apple QuickTime. It produces brighter midtones than gamma 2.4 or 2.2.

As you can tell from the numbers, the differences are quite small.

Premiere defaults to Gamma 2.4 (Broadcast), which is ideal for video intended for broadcast TV. If you are creating videos for social media or other forms of online distribution, choose Gamma 2.2.

Matching the Viewer Gamma with the export video gamma will mean your midtones will match in Premiere and in your exported video. Naturally this is important when you're making adjustments to color!

Following the color adjustment workflow

Now that you've switched to the Color workspace, it's a good time to switch to a different kind of thinking too. With your clips in place, it's time to look at them less in terms of the action, events, and continuity of movement, and more in terms of whether they fit together aesthetically and have the right look.

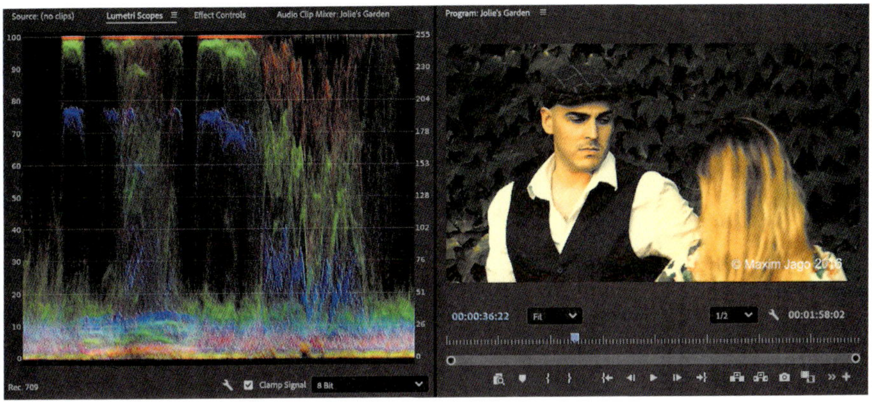

You'll use the same tools to achieve both of these goals, but it's common to approach them in this order, separately. If two clips from the same scene don't have matching colors, it creates a jarring continuity problem that will distract the audience. This might be your goal, but most of the time you will want your audience to focus on the story.

Color correction and color grading

You might have heard of both color correction and color grading. There is often confusion about the difference. In fact, both types of color work use the same tools, but there's a difference of approach.

Color correction is usually aimed at standardizing the shots to make sure they fit together and to improve the appearance in general—to give brighter highlights and stronger shadows or to correct a color bias captured in-camera. This is more craft than art.

Color grading is aimed at achieving a look that conveys the atmosphere of the story more completely.

This is more art than craft. There is, of course, a debate about where one ends and the other begins, and you will sometimes alternate between the two approaches.

Exploring the Color workspace

The Color workspace includes the Lumetri Color panel in the same panel group as the Properties panel. This has a number of sections offering color adjustment controls and places the Lumetri Scopes panel in the same group as the Source Monitor. The Lumetri Scopes panel contains a set of image analysis tools.

The remaining screen area is devoted to the Program Monitor, Timeline panel, Project panel, Tools panel, and Audio Meters. The Timeline panel is shortened to accommodate the Lumetri Color panel.

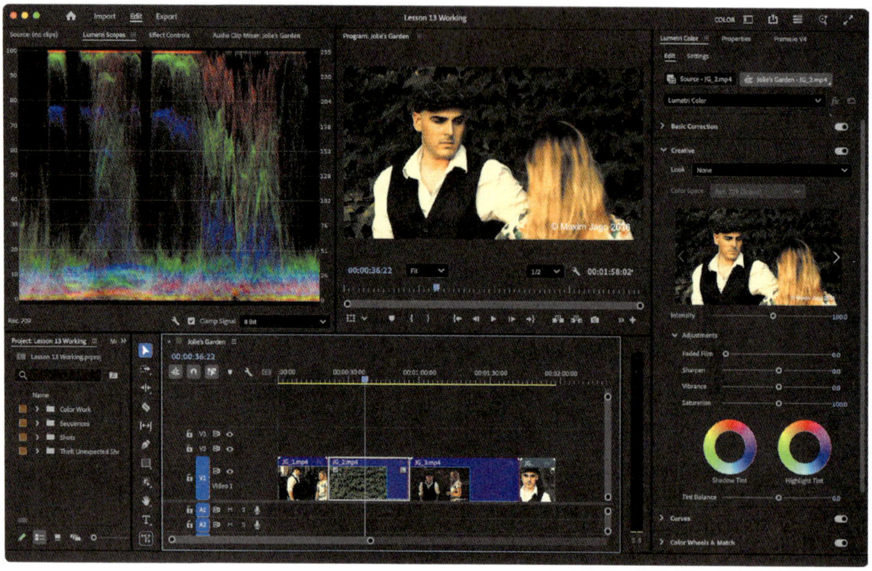

The Lumetri Scopes panel contains a set of image analysis tools, called *scopes*. Presets allow you to view various combinations of scopes. For example, to view several scopes together, right-click in the middle of the Lumetri Scopes panel or click the Settings menu and choose Presets > Vectorscope YUV/Parade RGB/Waveform YC. You'll learn more about these important tools later in this lesson.

You can open and close any panel at any time, but this workspace focuses on finishing work, rather than organizing or editing your project.

Tip: If more than one track-targeted track has a clip under the playhead, the clip on the highest targeted track is selected.

Automatically selecting clips

Sequence clips on tracks that have track targeting turned on can be selected automatically as you scrub the playhead over them.

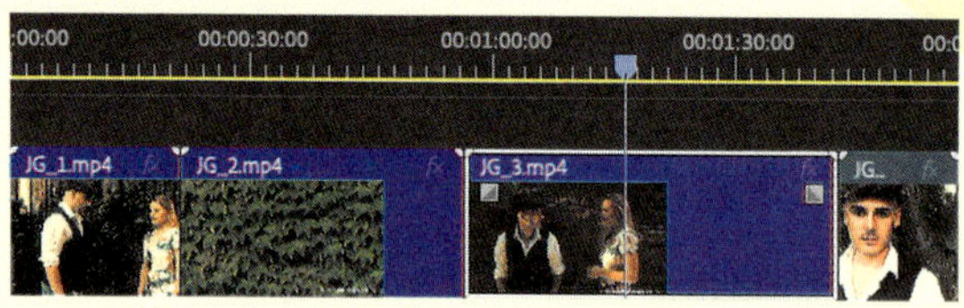

This feature is helpful because adjustments made with the Lumetri Color panel, like other effects, are always applied to the selected clip. You can apply an adjustment and quickly move the Timeline panel playhead over the next clip to automatically select it, and then you can work on it.

You can turn automatic clip selection on or off by choosing Sequence > Selection Follows Playhead.

Automatic clip selection selects only clips on targeted tracks. If there are multiple clips overlapping on different tracks, the clip on the highest targeted track will be selected. You can turn off track targeting for any tracks you would like to be ignored by automatic clip selection.

Introducing the Lumetri Color panel

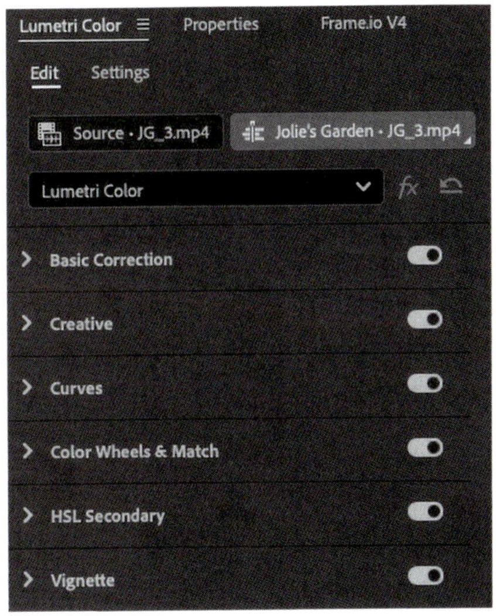

The Lumetri Color panel offers several ways to adjust the colors of clips. The panel has an Edit tab with six sections, each with different types of controls, and a Settings tab that gives quick access to all color settings for clips, sequences, and your project.

Some sections in the Edit tab offer standard controls that you are likely to use for particular purposes like adjusting brightness or adding a vignette. Other sections offer controls that you might use as a matter of preference. After experimenting, you'll discover your preferred controls for making creative color adjustments.

You can use any or all of the sections to achieve the result you want. You can expand or collapse a section by clicking its heading. Let's take a look at each section.

Note: You can use the control at the right side of the title of each section to enable and disable it, making it easy to toggle the result on and off. This lets you check the effect against the original image.

Basic Correction

The Basic Correction section provides you with simple controls to apply quick fixes to your clips.

At the top of the section, the Input LUT menu allows you to apply a preset adjustment to your media in the form of an Input LUT (Lookup Table), which makes standard adjustments to media that might otherwise look quite flat.

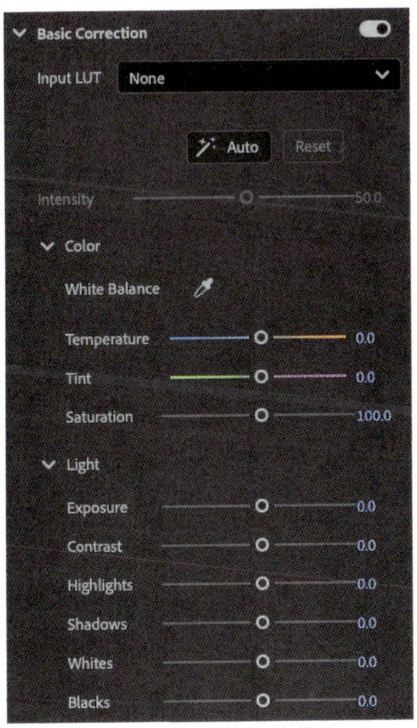

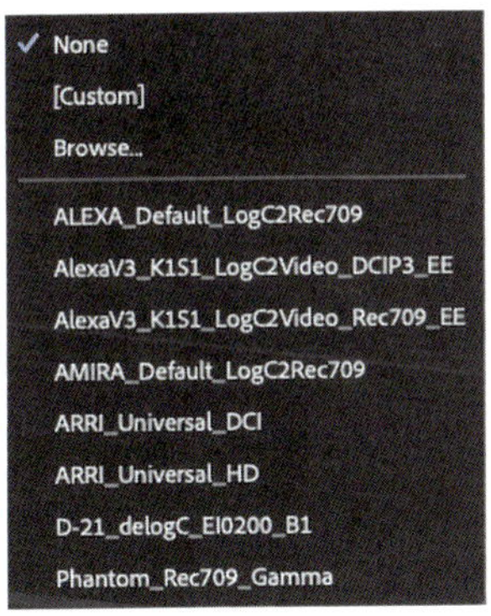

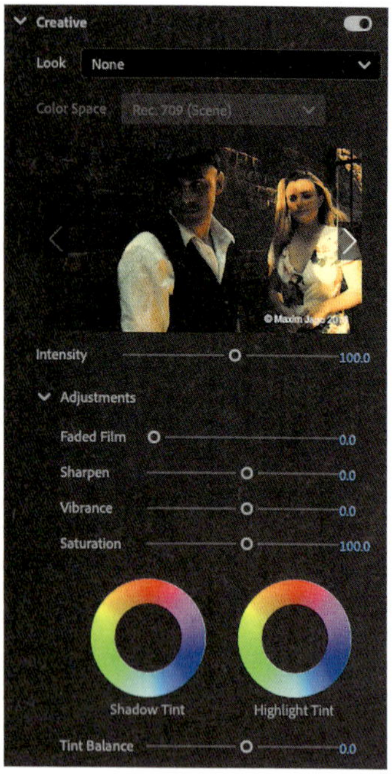

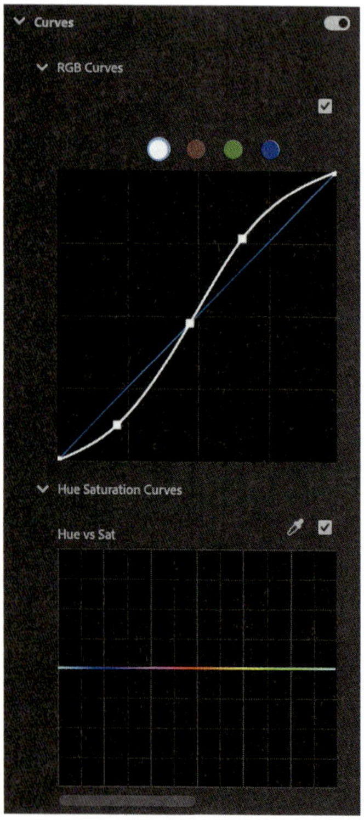

A LUT is actually a file, a little like an effect preset, intended to adjust the appearance of clips. LUTs can be imported and exported for advanced collaborative color grading workflows.

If you're familiar with Adobe Lightroom, you'll recognize the controls in the Basic Correction section. You can work your way down the list making adjustments to improve the look of your footage, or you can click the Auto button to let Premiere work out some settings for you.

Creative

As the name suggests, the Creative section allows you to go a little further into developing a look for your media.

A number of creative Looks are included, with a preview based on your current clip. Click the arrows on the preview to review different Looks, and then click the image to apply a Look to the clip.

You can make subtle adjustments to the color intensity, and there are color wheels configured to adjust the color for the shadow (darker) pixels or highlight (lighter) pixels in the image.

Curves

With curves you can make precise adjustments to visuals. They make it easier to achieve natural-looking results with just a few clicks.

These are some of the more advanced controls, providing nuanced adjustments to the luminance of the clip, and to the red, green, and blue pixels.

Adjustments are made in a similar way to those you applied to the Parametric Equalizer effect graph or the audio rubber bands on clips. The position of the line in the graph indicates the adjustment.

In addition to traditional RGB curves, the Curves section contains multiple controls for hue, saturation, and luma curves. Each of these gives precise control over a specific adjustment.

For example, the first control, Hue Vs Sat, allows you to add (by clicking) and position (by dragging) control points to increase or decrease color saturation for specific hues.

The next, Hue Vs Hue, allows you to change one hue into another. For an exploration of these controls, check out *blog.frame.io/2017/11/06/advanced-curves-techniques*.

Tip: You can reset most controls in the Lumetri Color panel by double-clicking the control.

Color Wheels & Match

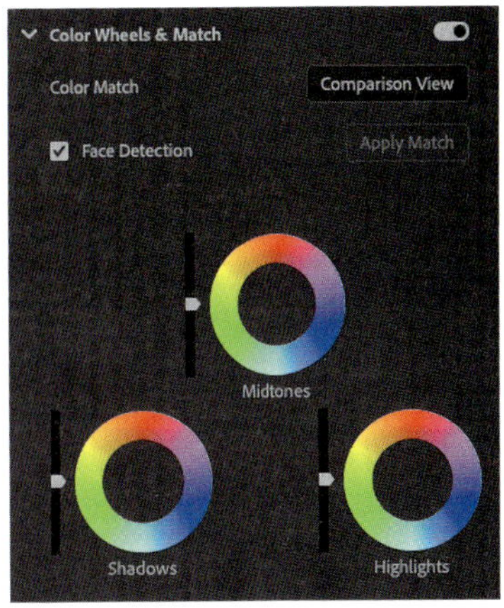

The Color Wheels & Match section provides precise control over the shadow, midtone, and highlight regions in the image. Drag from the center of a wheel toward the edge to apply an adjustment.

Each color wheel has a luminance control slider on the left, which allows you to make adjustments to the brightness for each of the three types of pixels.

There's also a button that opens the Program Monitor Comparison view and another button to automatically color match clips.

HSL Secondary

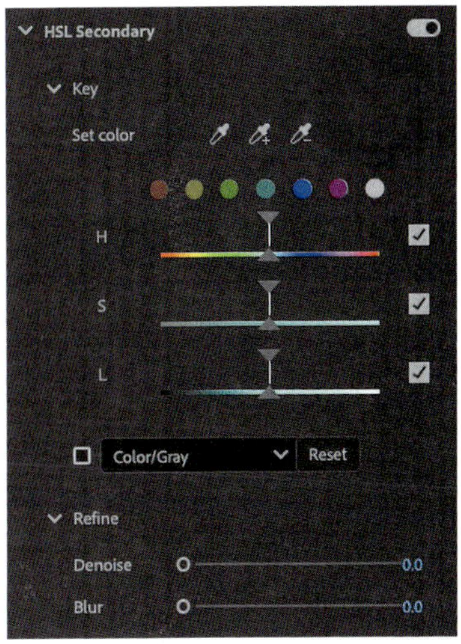

The HSL Secondary settings enable you to make color adjustments to precisely selected areas of an image, defined by selecting Hue, Saturation, and Luminance ranges.

Using this section of the Lumetri Color panel, you could selectively make a blue sky even bluer or make a field of grass a deeper green, without affecting other areas of the picture.

The Hue Saturation Curves controls (in the Curves section of the Lumetri Color panel) can provide similar results, and you are likely to choose one method or the other based on personal preference.

Vignette

It's surprising how much difference a simple vignette effect can make to a picture.

A classic vignette is caused by camera lenses darkening the edge of the frame. Modern lenses produce a subtler effect than older lenses.

Instead, a vignette is commonly used to bring attention to the center of an image, and it can be highly effective, even when the adjustment is subtle.

Working with the Lumetri Color effect

There is an effect available in the Effects panel called Lumetri Color, which provides all the same controls and options available in the Lumetri Color panel. Like any other effect, its controls are displayed in the Effect Controls panel.

It's not necessary to apply the Lumetri Color effect to a clip because the first time you make an adjustment to a clip using the Lumetri Color panel, the effect is applied. If there is a Lumetri Color effect already applied to the clip, the settings for that existing effect are updated as you make adjustments.

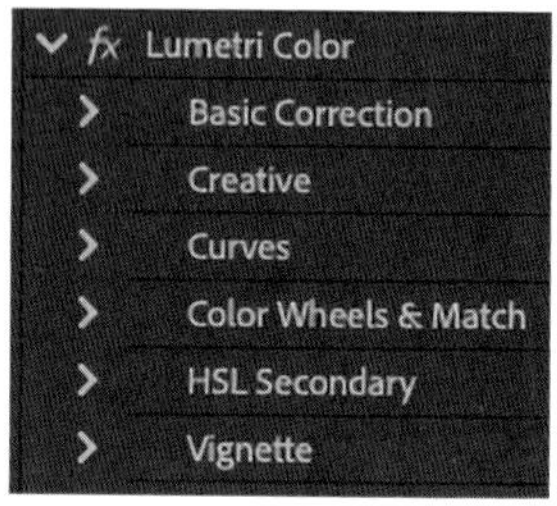

The controls in the Lumetri Color panel *actually* adjust the Lumetri Color effect settings in the Effect Controls panel. As with any other video effect, you can create presets, copy and paste Lumetri Color effects from one clip to another, and change the settings in the Effect Controls panel. Changing a setting in either panel updates both.

You can apply more than one Lumetri Color effect to the same clip, each making different types of adjustments to produce a combined result. This can make it easier to stay organized when working on complex projects. For example, you might use one Lumetri Color effect to match the colors between clips and another to add a particular color tint. Keeping the effects separate makes it easier to apply precise adjustments later.

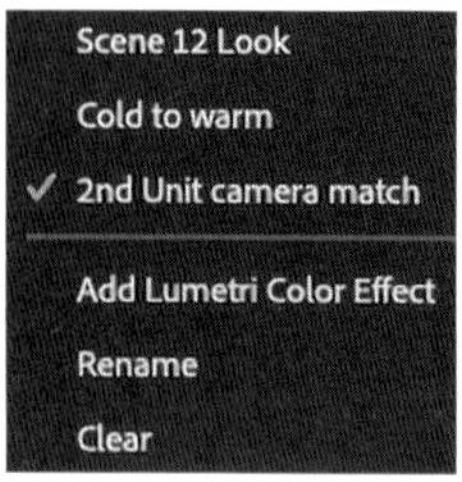

At the top of the Lumetri Color panel, you can choose which Lumetri Color effect you're currently working on. You can also add a new Lumetri Color effect.

The same menu allows you to rename the current Lumetri Color effect to make it easier to navigate your effects. You can also rename effects in the Effect Controls panel by right-clicking the effect name and choosing Rename.

The Settings tab

The Lumetri Color panel Settings tab includes several important settings that impact the way color is interpreted and displayed.

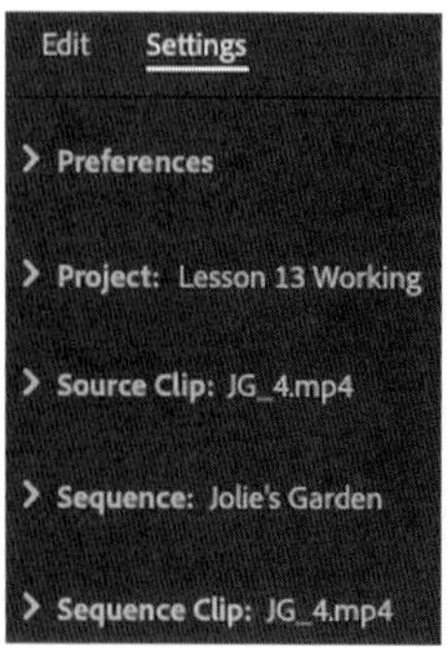

Many of these settings are repeated in other menus, but it's convenient to have them all in one place as part of the Lumetri Color panel. Here you'll find settings for your general user preferences, your project, the source clip for a currently selected clip, the currently active sequence, and the currently selected sequence clip. For example, the Display Color Management and Extended Dynamic Range Monitoring options you explored earlier are also available here. Changing any of these settings in one place changes them everywhere.

By default, clips that have no defined color space are interpreted as having Rec.709 color (the industry standard for HD video), and Premiere automatically adjusts clip tones to display them correctly in newly created sequences (this is described as *tone mapping*). Sequences created using previous versions of Premiere may not have

Input Tone Mapping selected, but you can change this by selecting Input Tone Mapping in the Advanced section under the Sequence heading on the Settings tab.

In most cases, the default settings on this tab will work well for broadcast TV. If you are creating content for the web, click the chevron to expand the Project section and use the Viewer Gamma menu to choose 2.2 (Web). With this setting, the Source Monitor and Program Monitor will display video correctly for web delivery.

If you are working with high dynamic range (HDR) video shot on a phone, you will probably get acceptable results by setting the sequence color setup to the Direct Rec. 709 (SDR) preset, which will configure several settings. Next, under the Project heading, select Color Manager Auto Detected Log And Raw Media.

For now, switch back to the Edit tab.

Working with video shot on a phone

You may be working with HDR video shot on a phone and intending to deliver video for the web using Rec. 709 color (the most common choice).

To automate adjusting the video colors, make sure your sequence is selected in the Project panel or open in the Timeline panel (with that panel active), and make these selections in the Settings tab of the Lumetri Color panel:

- Under Project > Viewer Gamma, select 2.2 (Web).
- Under Sequence > Color Setup, select Direct Rec. 709 (SDR). This preset will configure other related settings automatically.

The Lumetri Color panel in action

Because adjustments made using the Lumetri Color panel are added collectively as a regular Premiere effect, you can also enable and disable the effect in the Effect Controls panel or create an effect preset.

Let's start with some prebuilt Looks.

1 If it's not already open, open the sequence Jolie's Garden in the Sequences bin. This simple sequence has a series of clips that have a good range of color and contrast.

2 Make sure Selection Follows Playhead is chosen from the Sequence menu.

3 Position the playhead over the first clip in the sequence. The clip should highlight automatically in the Timeline panel.

4 Click the Creative section heading in the Lumetri Color panel to reveal its controls.

5 Browse through several prebuilt Looks by clicking the arrows on the right and left sides of the preview display. When you see a Look you like, click the preview image to apply it.

6 Try adjusting the Intensity slider to vary the amount of adjustment.

This is a good time to experiment with the other controls in the Lumetri Color panel. Some controls will make sense immediately, while others will take time to master. Use the clips in this sequence as a testing ground to learn about the Lumetri Color panel through experimentation; drag all the controls from one extreme to the other to see the result. You'll learn about many of these controls in detail later in this lesson.

Understanding Lumetri Scopes essentials

You might have wondered why the Premiere interface is dark gray. There's a good reason: Human vision is subjective. In fact, it's also highly relative.

If you see two colors next to each other, the way you see one is changed by the presence of the other. To prevent the Premiere interface from influencing the way you perceive colors in your projects, Adobe has made the interface almost entirely gray. If you've ever seen a professional color-grading suite, where artists provide the finishing touches to films and television programs, you've probably noticed that most of the room is gray. Colorists sometimes also have a large gray piece of card, or a section of a wall, that they can look at for a few moments to "reset" their vision before checking a shot.

The combination of your subjective vision and the variations in the way computer monitors and television monitors display color and brightness means we need a way to objectively measure color and brightness.

Video scopes provide exactly that. And they're used throughout the media industry; learn them once, and you'll be able to use them everywhere!

1 Open the sequence Lady Walking.

2 Position the Timeline playhead so that it's over the clip in the sequence. There's quite a lot of smoke, so choose a frame where you can see the subject's face clearly.

3 The Lumetri Scopes panel should be sharing the panel group with the Source Monitor. Click to select the panel and make it active, or choose it from the Window menu.

4 Open the Lumetri Scopes panel Settings menu, and choose Presets > Premiere 4 Scope YUV (float, no clamp).

> **Tip:** You can also access the Lumetri Scopes Settings menu by right-clicking anywhere in the panel.

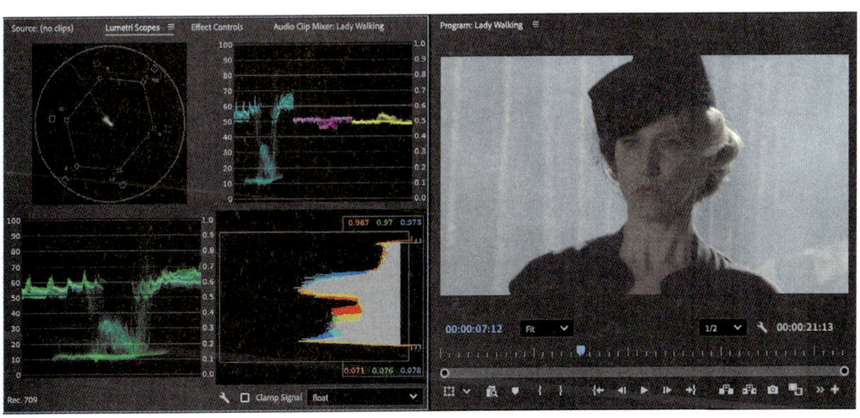

You should see the lady walking in the street in the Program Monitor, along with the synchronized display in the Lumetri Scopes panel. For an exploration of the Lumetri Scopes panel, see *blog.frame.io/2017/09/27/introduction-to-video-scopes*.

Working with the Lumetri Scopes panel

The Lumetri Scopes panel displays an array of industry-standard meters to get an objective view of your media.

The full complement of displays can be a little overwhelming at first, plus you'll have smaller graphs because they are all sharing one panel. You can turn individual items off and on by opening the Settings menu and choosing items on the list.

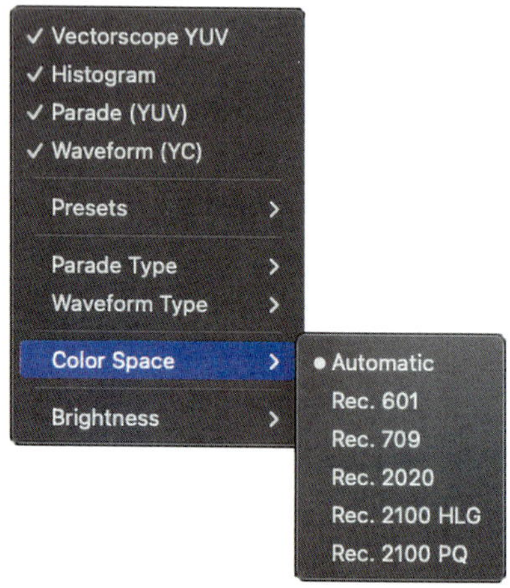

In the Settings menu (which you can also access by right-clicking in the panel), you can specify which professional color space you are working to. If you're producing content for broadcast television, you will almost certainly be working to one of these standards. For now, make sure Automatic is chosen.

At the bottom right of the Lumetri Scopes panel, you can choose to display the scopes in 8 Bit, 10 Bit, Float (which is 32-bit, floating-point color), or HDR.

The option you choose does not change the clip or the way effects are rendered, but it does change the way the scopes display the information.

The HDR option refers to High Dynamic Range, which has a much bigger range between the darkest and brightest parts of the picture than SDR (Standard Dynamic Range). Though HDR is beyond the scope of these lessons, it's an important technology that is increasingly supported by cameras and displays.

The Clamp Signal option (the checkbox to the left of the scopes bit depth menu) constrains the scopes to standard legal levels for broadcast television. Again, this doesn't impact the image or the result of your effects—it's a matter of personal preference if you would like to limit the range of the scopes in this way to see the scales more clearly.

Let's simplify the view and take a look at two of the main components in the Lumetri Scopes panel.

Begin by using the Lumetri Scopes Settings menu to choose Presets > Waveform RGB.

Waveform

If you're new to waveforms, they can look a little strange, but they're actually a relatively simple graph. They show you the brightness and color intensity of your images.

Every pixel in the current frame is displayed in the waveform. The brighter the pixel, the higher it appears on the graph. The pixels have their correct horizontal position (that is, a pixel halfway across the screen will be displayed halfway across the waveform), but the vertical position is not based on the pixel's position in the image.

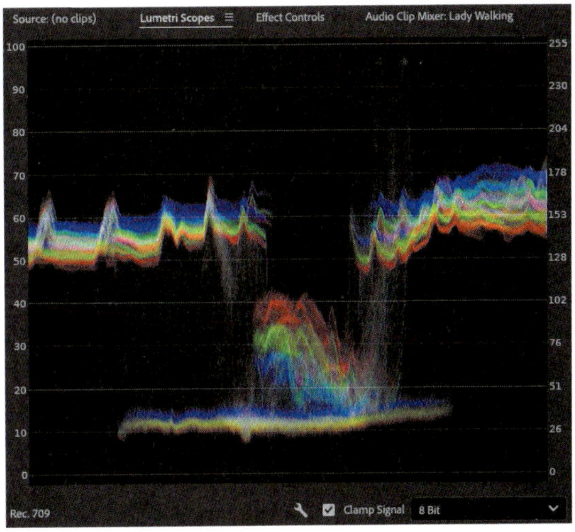

Instead, the vertical position indicates brightness or color intensity; the brightness and color intensity waveforms are displayed together in this version of the waveform, using different colors.

With the Lumetri Scopes panel bit depth set to float:

- 0 or 0.0, at the bottom of the scale, represents no luminance at all and/or no color intensity.
- 100 or 1.0, at the top of the scale, represents a pixel that is fully bright. On the 8-bit RGB scale, this value would be 255 (if you set the Scope to 8 Bit, you can see this scale on the right side of the waveform display).

This all might sound rather technical, but in practice it's straightforward. There's a visible baseline that represents "no brightness" and a top level that represents "fully bright." The numbers on the edge of the graph might change depending on your settings, but the use is essentially always the same.

You can view the waveform in several ways. To access a type, open the Lumetri Scopes Settings menu and choose Waveform Type, followed by one of these options:

- **RGB:** Shows the values of Red, Green, and Blue pixels separately.
- **Luma:** Shows the brightness (luminance) value of pixels against a scale of –20 to 120, called IRE (Institute of Radio Engineers). This allows for precise analysis of bright spots and contrast ratio.
- **YC:** Shows the image luminance (brightness) in green and the chrominance (color intensity) in blue.
- **YC No Chroma:** Shows the luminance only, with no chrominance.

Why *YC*?

The letter *C*, for chrominance (color), makes simple sense, but the letter *Y*, for luminance, takes a little explaining. It comes from a way of measuring color information that uses x-, y-, and z-axes, where *Y* represents the luminance. The idea was originally to create a simple system for recording color, and the use of *Y* to represent brightness, or luminance, stuck.

Let's try this display a little.

1 Continue using the Lady Walking sequence. Set the Timeline playhead to 00:00:07:00 so you can see the subject against the smoky background.

2 Set the waveform display to YC No Chroma. This is a brightness-only waveform.

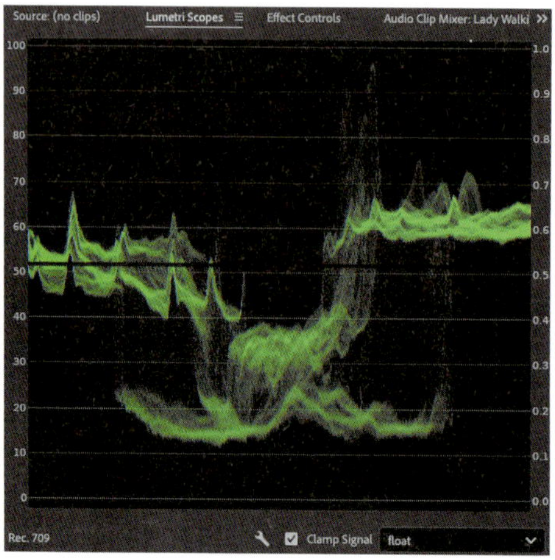

The smoky parts of the image have little contrast and are displayed as a relatively flat line in the waveform display. The lady's head and shoulders are darker than the smoky background. They're around the middle of the image, and they are clearly visible in the middle area of the waveform display.

3 Expand the Light settings in the Basic Correction section of the Lumetri Color panel.

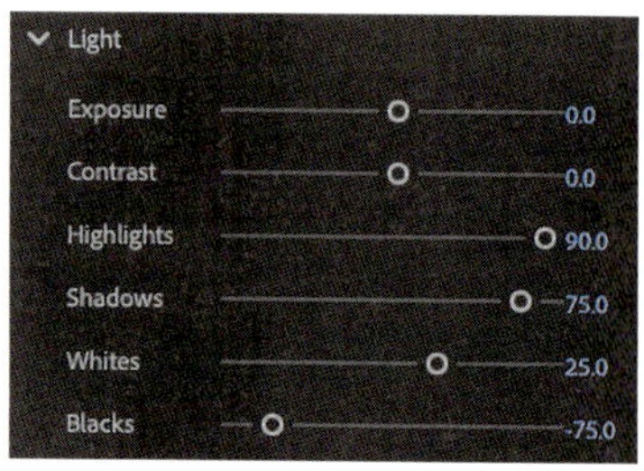

4 Experiment with the Exposure, Contrast, Highlights, Shadows, Whites, and Blacks controls. As you adjust the controls, watch the waveform display to see the result.

If you make an adjustment to the image and then wait a few seconds, your eyes will adjust to the new appearance, and it will seem normal. Make another adjustment, and a few seconds later the new appearance seems normal too. Which is correct?

Ultimately, the answer is based on perceived quality. If you like what you see, it's right. However, the waveform display will give you objective information about how dark or bright pixels are or how much color is in the shot, which is useful when attempting to meet delivery standards.

If you scrub through the sequence or play the sequence, you'll see the waveform display update live.

The waveform display is useful for showing how much contrast you have in your images (the difference between the bright and dark areas of the image) and for checking whether you are working on video that has "legal" levels (that is, the minimum and maximum brightness or color saturation permitted by a broadcaster). Broadcasters adopt their own standards for legal levels, so you will need to find out for each case where your work will be broadcast.

You can see right away that you do not have great contrast in this shot. There are some strong shadows but few *highlights* in the upper part of the waveform display. Anytime you see perfectly flat horizontal lines in the waveform display, it means there's no visible detail. In the following example, the shadows have been darkened so much, they're flattened at the bottom of the waveform.

The flattening in the Lumetri Scopes panel may not be visible until you select Clamp Signal to limit the waveform display to the visible part of the output.

The result is not necessarily bad and might be exactly the look you are seeking—it's certainly dramatic! It's just important to know when adjustments are so extreme that detail is being lost.

Tip: It can sometimes seem as if the waveform display is showing an image. Remember, the vertical position of the pixels in your images is not indicated in a waveform display.

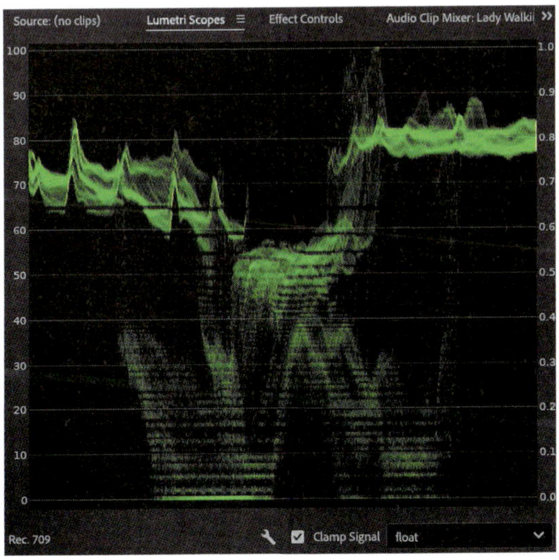

Reset the Lumetri Color panel by clicking the Reset Effect button at the upper-right corner of the panel.

YUV vectorscope

Whereas the Luma waveform shows luminance in terms of the vertical position of pixels displayed, with brighter pixels displayed at the top and darker pixels displayed at the bottom, the vectorscope shows only color.

1 Open the sequence Skyline.

2 Open the Lumetri Scopes Settings menu, and choose Vectorscope YUV; then open the Settings menu again, and choose Waveform (YC No Chroma) to deselect it.

Pixels in the image are displayed in the vectorscope. If a pixel appears in the center of the circle, it has no color saturation. The closer to the edge of the circle, the more color a pixel has.

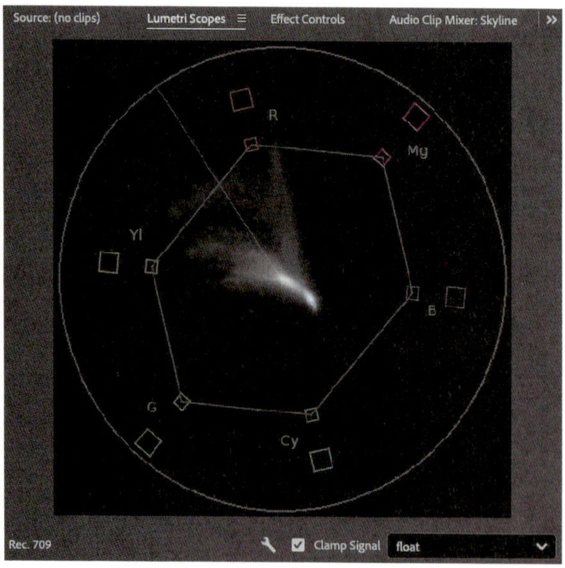

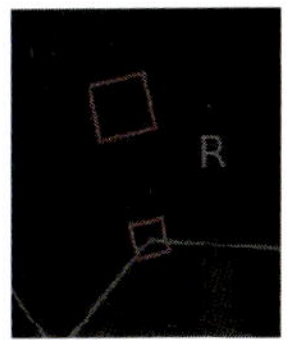

If you look closely at the vectorscope, you'll see a series of targets indicating primary colors.

- R = Red
- G = Green
- B = Blue

There are two boxes for each target. The smaller, inner box is at 75% saturation, the YUV color limit, while the larger, outer box is at 100% saturation, the RGB color limit. RGB color extends to a greater level of saturation than YUV. The thin line connecting the inner boxes shows the YUV color gamut (the range of YUV colors).

For broadcast television, you'll want to keep colors inside the YUV color gamut. For web delivery, you can use the full RGB color gamut.

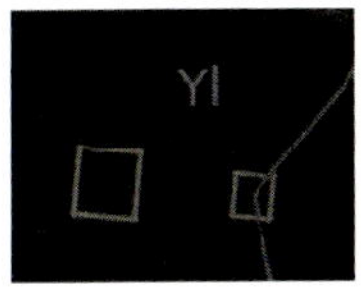

You'll also see a series of targets indicating secondary colors.

- Yl = Yellow
- Cy = Cyan
- Mg = Magenta

The closer a pixel is to one of these targets, the more of that color it has. Unlike in the waveform display, which indicates the horizontal position of each pixel, no position information is indicated in the vectorscope.

About primary and secondary colors

Computer screens and televisions use additive color, which means the colors are created by generating light in different colors and combining them to produce a precise mix.

When you draw with color on paper, it is usually white paper, which reflects a full spectrum of colors. You subtract from the white of the paper by adding pigment with your paint, pencils, pastels, or markers. Because the pigment absorbs light in a portion of the spectrum and prevents those parts of the light from being reflected, this is called *subtractive color*.

Red, green, and blue are the primary colors used by video displays. Television screens and your computer monitor combine these three colors in varying relative amounts to produce the colors you see. You produce white by combining equal amounts of red, green, and blue.

There's a beautiful symmetry to the way a standard color wheel works, and a color wheel is essentially what the vectorscope displays.

Any two primary colors will combine to produce a secondary color. The secondary colors for additive color (yellow, cyan, and magenta) appear opposite the remaining primary color on a color wheel.

For example, red and green (two of the primary colors) combine to produce yellow, which is the opposite of blue (the third primary color).

The secondary colors used in additive color are equivalent to the primary colors used in subtractive color. It's an elegant symmetry!

It's clear enough to see what's happening in this shot of Seattle. There's a lot of blue, and there are a few spots of red and yellow. The small amount of red is indicated by the streak of peaks reaching out toward the R marking in the vectorscope.

The vectorscope is helpful because it gives you objective information about the colors in your sequence. If there's a color cast, perhaps because the camera was not calibrated properly, it's often obvious in the vectorscope display. You can use one of the Lumetri Color panel controls to reduce the amount of the unwanted color or add more of the opposite color.

Some of the controls for color correction adjustments have the same color wheel design as the vectorscope, making it easy to see what you need to do.

Tip: You can jump to 00:00:01:00 by clicking the timecode in the Source Monitor, Program Monitor, or Timeline panel; or you can type **1.** (that's 1 followed by a period), and then press Return (macOS) or Enter (Windows). Each period (.) adds one pair of zeros.

Let's make an adjustment and observe the result in the vectorscope display.

1 Continue working with the Skyline sequence. Position the Timeline playhead at 00:00:01:00, where the colors are more vivid than at the end of the clip.

2 In the Lumetri Color panel, expand the Basic Correction section.

3 While watching the result in the vectorscope display, drag the Temperature slider from one extreme to the other. Try making an extreme blue adjustment.

The pixels displayed in the vectorscope move away from the orange area of the display toward the blue.

4 The adjustment enhances the existing blue tint. Now try an extreme orange adjustment.

Shifting the color temperature toward orange compensates for the original tint and makes the shot look more natural.

5 Double-click the Temperature slider to reset it.

6 In the Lumetri Color panel, drag the Tint slider from one extreme to the other.

The pixels displayed in the vectorscope move between the green and magenta areas of the display.

7 Double-click the Tint slider to reset it.

By making adjustments while checking the vectorscope, you can get an objective indication of the change you're making.

RGB parade

Open the Lumetri Scopes Settings menu and choose Presets > Parade RGB.

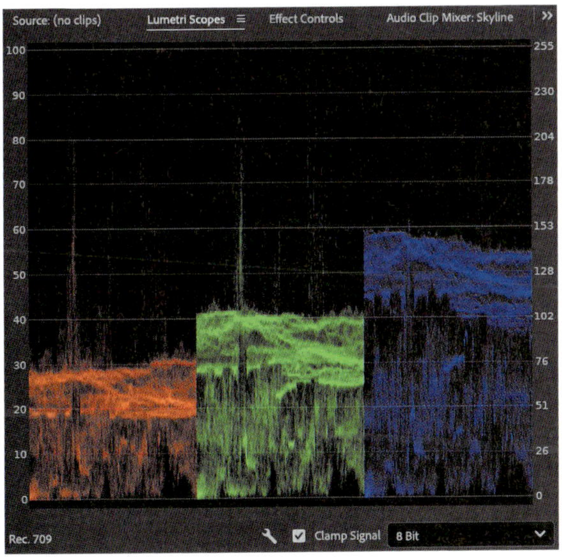

The RGB parade provides another form of waveform-style display. The difference is that the red, green, and blue levels are displayed separately. To fit all three colors in, each display is squeezed horizontally to one-third of the total width.

You can choose which kind of parade you see by clicking the Lumetri Scopes Settings menu or by right-clicking in the Lumetri Scopes panel and choosing Parade Type.

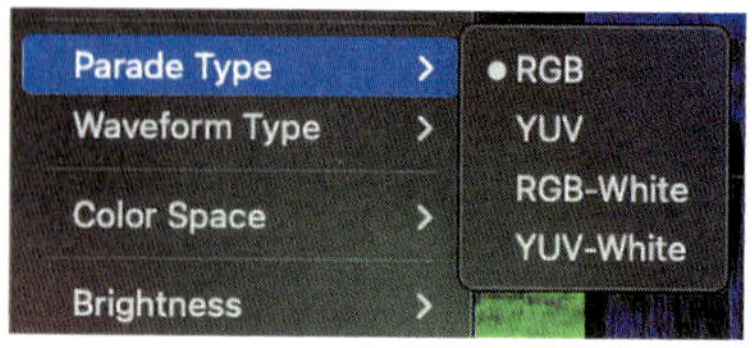

The three parts of the parade have similar patterns in them, particularly where there are white or gray pixels, because these parts will have equal amounts of red, green, and blue. The RGB parade is one of the most frequently used tools in color correction because it clearly shows the relationship between the primary color channels.

To see the dramatic impact color adjustments can have on the parade, go to the Basic Correction section of the Lumetri Color panel and try adjusting the White Balance using the Temperature and Tint controls. Be sure to reset them when you finish by double-clicking each control.

Using Comparison view

Let's take a moment to consider two important stages in the process when adjusting colors.

- **Color correction:** Correcting for color cast or brightness issues and matching shots in the sequence to ensure they look like part of content that was shot at the same time in the same location or that they match an in-house standard for final delivery.
- **Color grading:** Establishing a creative look for shots on a shot-by-shot, scene-by-scene, or sequence-wide basis.

When color correcting, it's helpful to compare one shot with another to achieve a match. This is especially helpful when the two shots come from different scenes, meaning some color variation is expected even if the overall tone should be similar.

You can drag your current sequence from the Project panel into the Source Monitor to use that monitor as a reference for side-by-side comparison, but there's an easier way: You can set the Program Monitor to Comparison view.

Let's explore the controls:

1 Open the Jolie's Garden sequence, and position the Timeline playhead over the last clip in the sequence.

2 Click the Comparison View button in the Program Monitor.

Let's take a look at the new controls.

- **Reference frame:** The frame in the current sequence you are using as a reference or for color matching.
- **Reference position:** The timecode for the reference frame.
- **Reference Playhead:** Indicates the reference frame position within the current sequence. You can drag this to change the reference frame.
- **Playhead position:** The timecode for the current frame.
- **Shot Or Frame Comparison:** Toggle between using another frame as a reference and using the current state of the current frame. The latter option is useful when working on effects, as it allows a constant before-and-after view when working with effects so your eyes can't adjust to the finished version.
- **Side By Side:** View the two images separately, side by side.
- **Vertical Split:** View the two images as a single vertically split screen, with a divider you can drag to reposition.
- **Horizontal Split:** The same as the Vertical Split option but now with a horizontal divider.
- **Swap Sides:** Switch the sides displayed of the reference and current frame images.
- **Current frame:** The frame you're working on now.

Note: The Comparison View button may not be visible on smaller displays. In the Program Monitor, click the double arrow in the lower-right corner and choose Comparison View from the menu. You can also choose Comparison View from the Program Monitor Settings menu.

Tip: Whenever the Program Monitor is not already set to Comparison view, you can click the Lumetri Color panel's Comparison View button in the Color Wheels & Match section, just under the heading. It has the same function as the button in the Program Monitor.

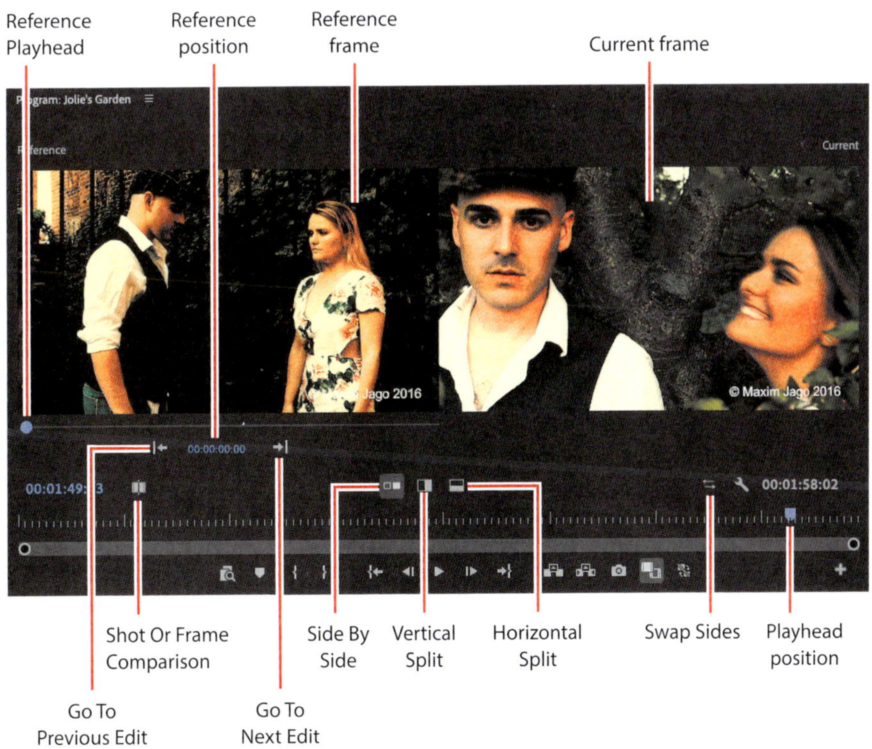

3 Make sure the last clip in the sequence is selected, and in the Lumetri Color panel, open the Color Wheels & Match section.

4 Try changing the reference frame in one of these ways:

- Drag the small circular playhead under the reference frame to a new position.
- Click the reference position timecode, and enter a new time or scrub the timecode to choose another time.
- Click the Go To Previous Edit or Go To Next Edit button on either side of the reference position timecode to jump between clips.

5 Try the split view options, and drag the divider between the two sides of the split.

At first, Comparison view might seem to have lots of new buttons to remember. They all work together, however, giving you precise control over the two clips you are comparing and how they are displayed.

Viewing two parts of your sequence using Comparison view is helpful, and it's the starting point for an automated color adjustment available in the Lumetri Color panel.

Now that you're familiar with Comparison view, it's time to work on these clips and match their colors.

Matching colors

One of the most powerful and time-saving features of the Lumetri Color panel is the option to automatically match colors between two clips.

To use this feature, you'll switch to Comparison view in the Program Monitor, choose a reference frame and a current frame, and click the Apply Match button in the Color Wheels & Match section of the Lumetri Color panel.

The result will not always be perfect, and you may need to experiment with different reference and current frame selections to get a closer match. However, the result *is* often close enough for you to make final adjustments that are guided by the initial automated adjustment. If Premiere gets the color 80% right, it's a huge time-saver.

Let's try this with our current sequence.

1 Continuing from the previous exercise, set the reference frame to 00:00:01:00.

2 Position the Timeline panel playhead on the first frame of the last clip in the sequence (which should automatically select the clip), and set the comparison view to Side By Side.

3 These are clips from different scenes in the same film. They don't need to have exactly the same colors, but it would be helpful if the skin tones matched better. Make sure the Face Detection option is selected in the Lumetri Color panel. This way, Premiere will automatically detect faces and prioritize matching those tones.

4 Click the Apply Match button in the Lumetri Color panel, and Premiere applies a color adjustment to the selected clip.

5 The difference is clear. However, within a few moments, your eyes are likely to adjust to the new appearance of the current frame. To help see the change more clearly, toggle Color Wheels & Match off and on repeatedly.

6 Click the Comparison View button under the Color Wheels & Match heading to return to the regular playback view in the Program Monitor.

7 Make sure the Program Monitor Zoom Level menu is set to Fit.

The automated color matching offered by the Lumetri Color panel is not likely to produce an identical color match, partly because the perception of color is so subjective and contextual. However, all of the adjustments that were applied are editable, so you can finesse the result until it's perfect.

Exploring the color-adjustment effects

As well as adjusting color using the Lumetri Color panel, there are a number of regular color adjustment effects worth familiarizing yourself with. Just as with the other effects, you can use keyframes to modify the settings over time. In fact, the same is true of the Lumetri Color effect, if you adjust the controls in the Effect Controls panel.

Tip: You can always find an effect using the search box at the top of the Effects panel. A good way to learn how to use an effect is to apply it to a clip that has a good range of colors, highlights, and shadows and then adjust all the settings to see the result.

As you build familiarity with Premiere, you may find yourself uncertain about which effect is best for a particular purpose; this is normal! There are often several ways of achieving the same outcome in Premiere, and sometimes the choice comes down to which interface you prefer.

Using the Video Limiter effect

In addition to creative effects, the color correction repertoire available in Premiere includes effects used for professional video production.

When you prepare video for broadcast TV or cinema distribution, keep in mind that the video must not exceed specific limits for maximum luminance, minimum luminance, and color saturation. Although it's possible to confine your video levels to the limits permitted using manual controls, it's easy to miss parts of your sequence that need adjustment.

Tip: While in the Color workspace, the Effects panel may not be easy to locate. You can always access any panel by choosing it from the Window menu.

In the Effects panel, the Video Limiter effect, found in Video Effects > Color Correction, automatically limits the levels of clips to ensure they meet the standards you set.

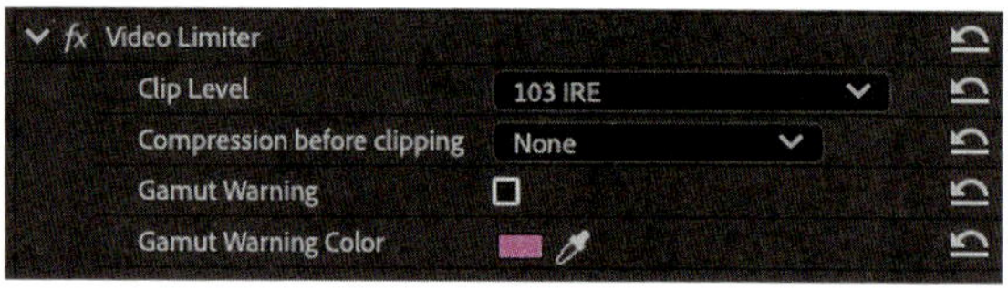

Check the limits approved by your broadcaster or distributor before adjusting the Clip Level setting. This is the level above which the broadcaster will enforce prescribed limits and cut off luminance and/or saturation.

Tip: It's common to apply the Video Limiter effect to the whole sequence by using it on an adjustment layer or by enabling it as an export setting (see Lesson 16, "Exporting Frames, Clips, and Sequences").

Next, it's simply a question of choosing the Compression Before Clipping amount. You can have Premiere apply a gradual compression of the higher levels to produce a more natural-looking result before the absolute cut-off level set in the Clip Level menu.

The compression can be set to begin 3%, 5%, 10%, or 20% before the cutoff level.

If you turn on the Gamut warning, pixels that would have gone above the Clip Level setting or would be affected by the compression setting are highlighted in the Gamut Warning color. This is useful when reviewing your sequence, but be sure to deselect the Gamut Warning option before exporting your sequence, as the color highlight will be included in the exported file!

Using Lumetri Color presets in the Effects panel

In addition to the controls available in the Lumetri Color panel, there are a number of Lumetri Color presets available in the Effects panel. These are a fantastic way to get started with advanced color adjustments, and as they are presets, you can modify the settings to achieve exactly the finish you want. If you resize the Effects panel to make it wider, you can reveal previews of the presets.

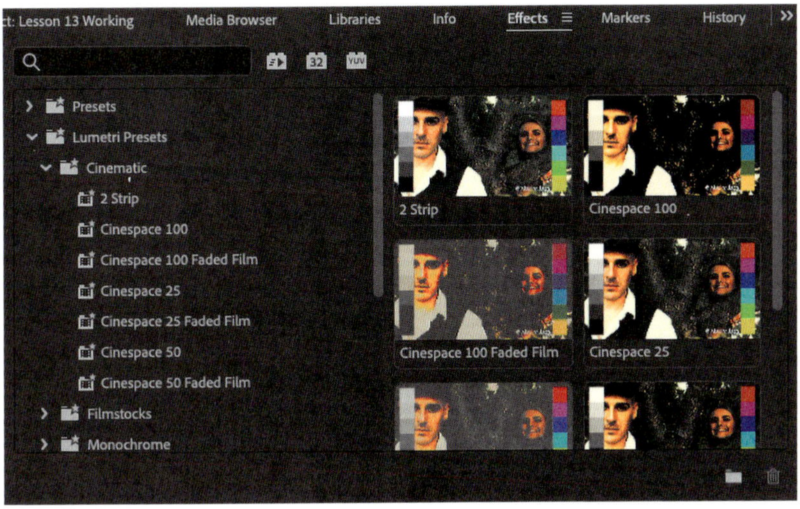

You apply a Lumetri Color preset effect in the same way that you would apply any other effect available in the Effects panel.

Lumetri Color presets are Lumetri Color effects with an input LUT applied in the Basic Correction settings or a Look applied in the Creative settings.

You can switch or remove these in the Effect Controls panel or in the Lumetri Color panel.

Fixing exposure problems

Let's look at some clips that have exposure issues and use some of the Lumetri Color panel controls to address them.

1 Make sure you are in the Color workspace, and reset it to the saved layout if necessary.

2 Open the sequence Color Work.

3 In the Lumetri Scopes panel, right-click or open the Settings menu to choose Presets > Waveform RGB.

4 Again, in the Lumetri Scopes panel, right-click or open the Settings menu to choose Waveform Type > YC No Chroma. This changes the display to a waveform that uses the standard broadcast television range, which is a useful reference for most video projects.

5 Position the Timeline playhead over the first clip in the sequence. It's the shot of the lady walking. You're going to add some contrast.

This composition is smoky; 100 IRE (at the top of the scale on the left on the waveform) means fully exposed, and 0 IRE (at the bottom of the scale on the left) means not exposed at all. No part of this image comes close to these upper or lower limits. Your eye quickly adjusts to the image, and it'll soon appear fine, but it's relatively low contrast and the waveform shows it. Let's see whether you can bring it to life a little.

6 In the Lumetri Color panel, click the Basic Correction heading to display that section.

7 Use the Exposure and Contrast controls to make adjustments to the shot while checking the waveform display to make sure the image doesn't become too dark or too light.

You'll get the best perceived results if you have a frame from later in the clip on the screen. Around 00:00:07:19 there's a section of sharp focus.

▶ **Tip:** You can create a keyboard shortcut to temporarily turn off all instances of the Lumetri Color effect. Use the Keyboard Shortcuts dialog box to assign a keyboard shortcut to the Bypass Lumetri Color Effects command. For information on assigning keyboard shortcuts, see Lesson 1, "Touring Adobe Premiere."

Try an Exposure setting of **0.6** and a Contrast setting of **60**.

8 Your eyes are likely to adjust quickly to the new image. Click the control to toggle the Basic Correction section off and on to compare the image before and after.

The subtle adjustment you made adds depth to the image, increasing color saturation and giving it stronger highlights and shadows. As you toggle the effect off and on, you'll see the waveform changing in the Lumetri Scopes panel, with the distance between the brighter and darker pixels expanding or contracting. The image still doesn't have bright highlights, but that's fine because the colors, particularly in the fog, are mainly midtones.

Fixing underexposed images

Now let's work with an underexposed image.

1 Switch to the Effects workspace, and reset the layout if necessary.

2 Position the Timeline playhead over the second clip in the Color Work sequence. When you first look at this clip, it might look fine. The highlights don't look strong, but there's a reasonable amount of detail throughout the image. The face, especially, is sharp and detailed.

> **Tip:** The Lumetri Scopes panel isn't limited to the Color workspace. You can always open it from the Window menu.

3 Open the Lumetri Scopes panel so you can view a waveform representation of this clip. At the bottom of the waveform there are quite a few dark pixels, with some touching the 0 IRE line.

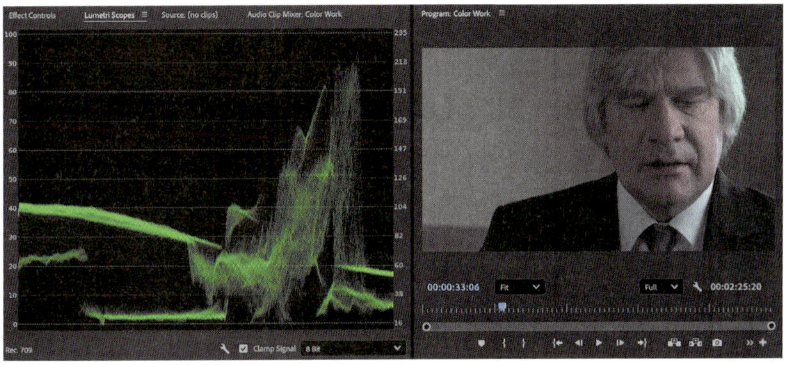

For this clip, it looks like the missing detail is in the shoulder of the suit, on the left. The problem with such dark pixels is that increasing the brightness will simply change the strong shadows into gray, and no detail is likely to emerge.

4 In the Effects panel, locate the Brightness & Contrast effect. Apply the effect to the clip.

5 Drag the Lumetri Scopes panel to the right and down to move it into a new panel group on the left of the Program Monitor.

This way, you can view the Effect Controls panel and Lumetri Scopes panel together with the Program Monitor.

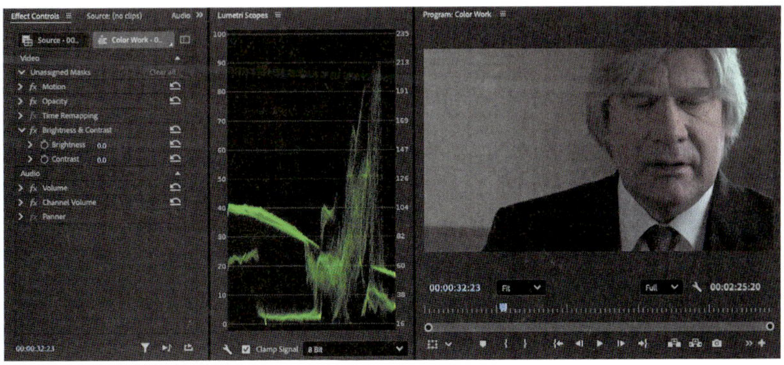

6 Use the Brightness control in the Effect Controls panel to increase the brightness. Rather than clicking the blue number and typing a new number, drag to the right on the number so you can see the change happening incrementally.

As you drag, notice that the whole waveform moves up. This is fine for bringing out the highlights in the image, but the shadows remain a flat line. You're changing the black shadows to gray. If you drag the Brightness control all the way to 100, clipping the highlights a little, you'll see just how flat the image still is.

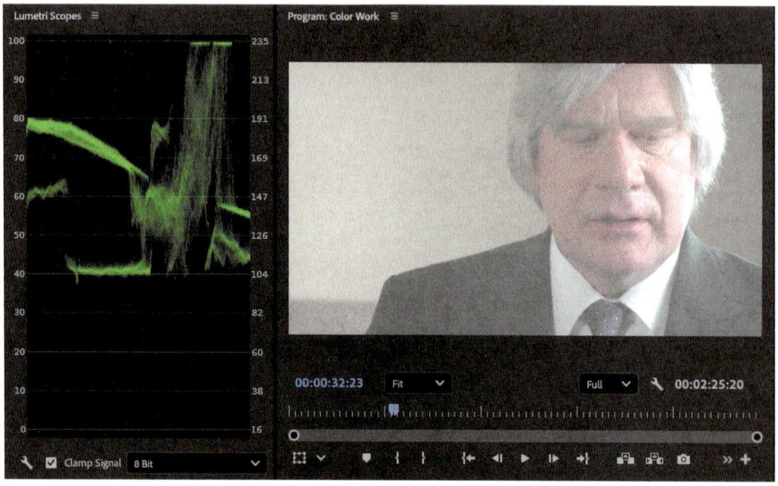

7 Remove the Brightness & Contrast effect.

8 Switch back to the Color workspace. Try making an adjustment using the RGB Curves control in the Curves section of the Lumetri Color panel. Here's an example of an RGB Curves adjustment that would improve the image.

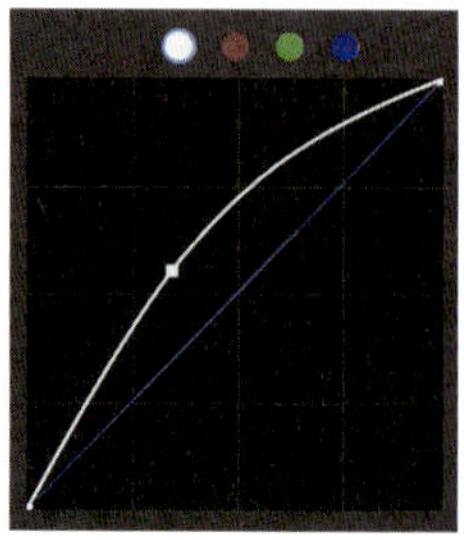

9 Experiment with the third clip in the sequence. This clip demonstrates that there are limits to what can be "fixed in post!"

That doesn't mean it's unusable, but you'd probably have to apply some significant artistic effects to create a look that seemed intentional.

10 Try the fourth clip in the sequence. This drone shot of a desert was underexposed. Drag the lowest RGB Curves control point to the right until the darkest pixels displayed in the Lumetri Scopes panel waveform touch the bottom of the range. This darkens the shadows.

11 Next, drag the top RGB Curves control point to the left, until the lightest pixels touch the top of the waveform range. This brightens the highlights.

The effect of both darkening the shadows and brightening the highlights increases the contrast overall.

12 Finally, click in the middle of the curve to add a control point to the RGB Curves control and drag up and left until you are satisfied with the result—a dramatic improvement!

Fixing overexposed images

The next clip you'll work with is overexposed.

1 Move the Timeline playhead to the fifth clip in the sequence. A lot of the pixels are burned out. Just as with the flat shadows in the second clip in the sequence, there's no detail in burned-out highlights. This means that lowering the brightness will simply make the character's skin and hair gray; no detail will emerge.

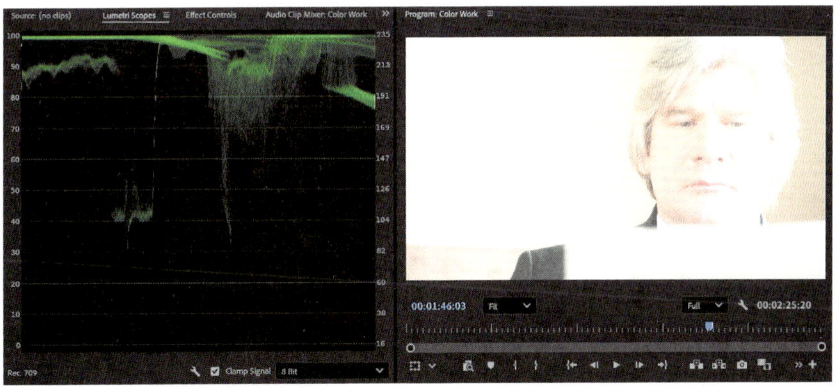

2 Notice that the shadows in this shot don't reach the bottom of the Waveform Monitor. The lack of properly dark shadows has a flattening effect on the image.

3 Try using the Lumetri Color panel to improve the contrast range. You might produce acceptable results, although the clip will definitely end up looking processed.

This footage is 8 bit, so there is less detail available to reveal when making adjustments to the image. If it had been shot in 10 bit or even 16 bit, it might have been possible to achieve an acceptable result.

When is color correction right?

Making adjustments to images is highly subjective. Though there are precise limits for image formats and broadcast technologies, whether an image should be light, dark, blue-tinted, or green is ultimately a subjective choice. The reference tools that Premiere provides, such as the Lumetri Scopes panel, are a helpful guide, but only you can decide when the picture looks right.

If you're producing video for display on TVs, it's vital that you have a television screen connected to your Premiere editing system to view your content. Television screens usually display color differently from computer monitors, and consumer screens sometimes have special color modes that change the appearance of video. For professional broadcast television, editors usually have a carefully calibrated preview monitor connected to their editing system. The Display Color Management option helps to show the colors as they might be displayed on a TV, but nothing compares to a calibrated monitor.

The same rule applies if you are producing content for digital cinema projection, Ultra High Definition TV, or High Dynamic Range TV. The only way to know exactly how the picture will look is to view it using the destination medium. Thankfully, the same principle means if your ultimate destination is a computer screen, perhaps as web video or part of a software interface, you are already looking at the perfect test monitor.

Correcting color offset

Your eyes adjust to compensate for changes in the color of light around you automatically. It's an extraordinary ability that allows you to see white as white, even if objectively it's orange, for example, because it's lit by tungsten light.

Cameras can automatically adjust their white balance to compensate for different lighting in the way that your eyes do. With the right calibration, white objects look white, whether you are recording indoors (under oranger tungsten light) or outdoors (in bluer daylight).

Sometimes automatic settings are hit or miss, so professional shooters often prefer to adjust white balance manually. If the white balance is set wrong, you can end up with some interesting results. The most common reason for a white balance problem in a clip is that the camera was not calibrated properly.

Balancing with the Lumetri color wheels

Let's try using the Lumetri Color panel color wheels to adjust the last shot in the sequence.

1. Make sure you are still viewing the Color workspace, and reset it if necessary.
2. Position the Timeline playhead over the last clip in the Color Work sequence.
3. In the Lumetri Color panel, expand the Basic Correction section and click the Auto button to automatically adjust the levels.

Premiere automatically adjusts the Color and Light controls to compensate for both the luminance levels and color balance in the shot. The result is an improvement, but there's still a strong blue color cast.

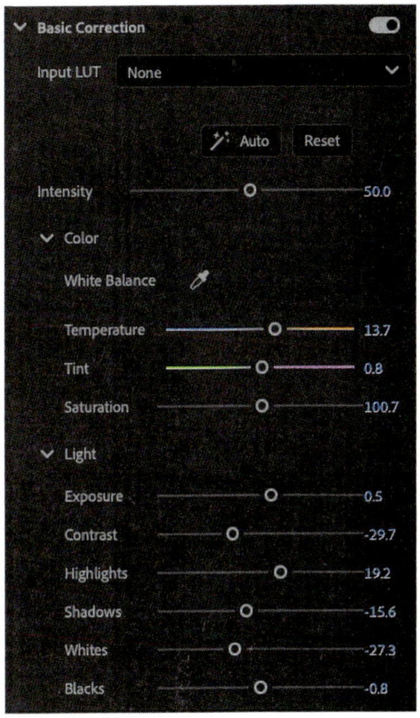

Applying an automatic adjustment in this way will usually produce results that are close to ideal, but because the shot includes mixed light sources (interior and exterior), Premiere can't know which color temperature is correct.

4 If the Lumetri Scopes panel isn't at the front of its panel group, click its tab to bring it forward.

5 Right-click the middle of the Lumetri Scopes panel and choose Presets > Vectorscope YUV.

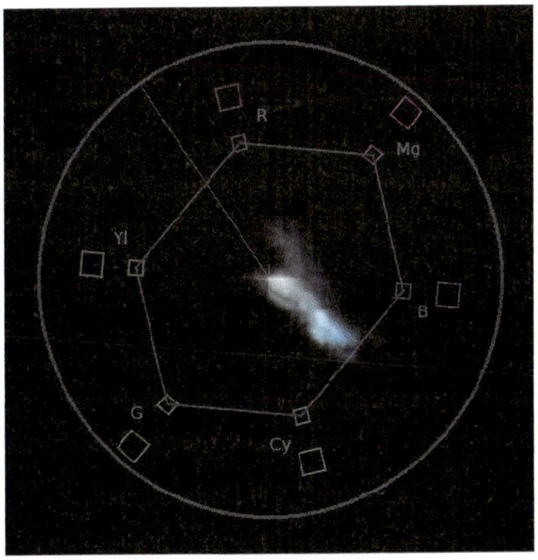

It's clear there's a strong bias toward the blue. Though the scene has mixed lighting, the bluer daylight coming from the window dominates warmer tungsten light coming from the interior of the room.

6 In the Basic Correction section of the Lumetri Color panel, use the Temperature slider to push the colors toward the orange. You'll need to push the adjustment all the way to 100 to see a reasonable result because the color shift is so strong.

The result is an improvement, but perhaps it could be better.

The darker pixels in this shot are generally lit by the interior, warmer room light, while the lighter pixels are generally lit by the bluer daylight. This means different color wheels will interact with different areas of the picture in convincing and natural ways.

7 Expand the Color Wheels & Match section of the Lumetri Color panel. To emphasize the different light sources, try using the Shadows color wheel to pull the color toward the orange, use the Midtones color wheel to pull the

color toward the red, and adjust the Highlights color wheel to pull the color toward cyan.

8 You've adjusted the color wheels to warm up the shadows and midtones and cool down the highlights. Experiment with the midtones to obtain the most natural result possible. Use the images as a guide.

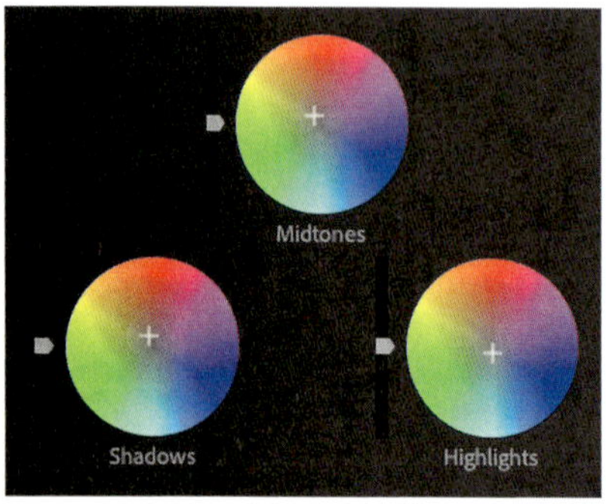

Experiment with the other controls in the Lumetri Color panel to see whether you can improve the result further.

For more precise control of the image, you can add two Lumetri effects and mask them using the controls in the Effect Controls panel. With one effect constrained to the left side of the image and another constrained to the right, you will be able to make adjustments to suit the interior and exterior lighting in more natural ways.

Making a secondary color adjustment

The Lumetri Color panel allows you to make adjustments that are limited to a particular range of hues, a level of color saturation, or a level of brightness.

This is useful if you want to bring out the blue in a subject's eyes or give a flower a color boost. Let's try it.

1 Open the sequence Yellow Flower, and position the Timeline playhead over the first clip. This sequence has two shots, each with clearly defined areas of color.

2 Expand the HSL Secondary section of the Lumetri Color panel.

3 Click the first Set Color eyedropper to select it, and then click the yellow petals of the flower to pick that color.

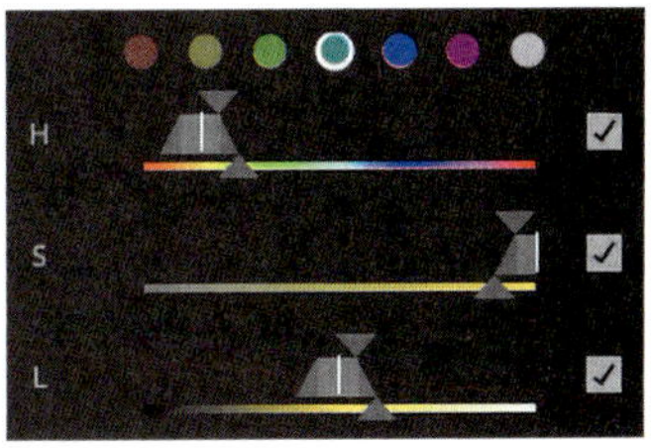

If you hold Command (macOS) or Ctrl (Windows) while clicking, the sample that is captured is based on a 5×5-pixel average.

The Hue, Saturation, and Luminance selection controls update based on the area of the petal you clicked.

> **Note:** If you're using macOS, you may see an alert asking you to give Premiere permission to record your computer screen. To do so, click Open System Settings and use an administrator password to unlock Security & Privacy preferences. You'll have to quit Premiere and restart it to confirm the change.

4 Drag the H, S, and L (Hue, Saturation, Luminance) color range selection controls to expand the selection. Your initial selection probably selected only a few pixels, as there is quite a lot of variation in the yellow petals.

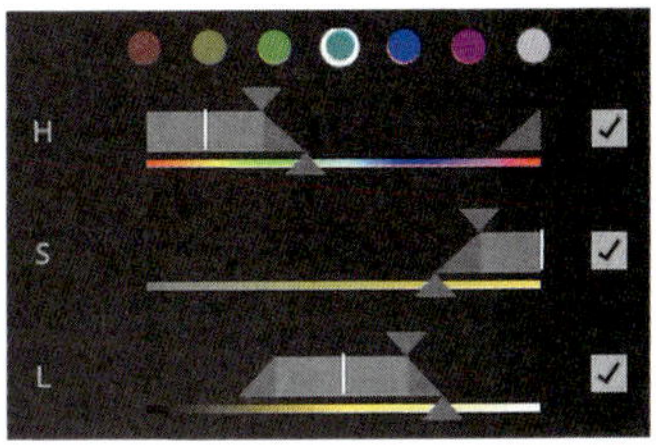

For each control, the upper triangle represents the hard-stop range of the selection, which is mirrored on either side of the vertical white line. The lower triangle extends the selection with a softening that reduces hard edges.

As you drag the controls, the image hides unselected pixels with gray. When you release, the image returns.

5 Experiment with the Denoise and Blur options in the Refine category. These help to smooth the selection range, rather than adjusting the image contents.

6 Once you're satisfied you have selected all the pixels in the petals of the flower, adjust the Temperature and Tint controls under the Correction heading.

The adjustments you make will be limited to the pixels you selected.

7 Now that you have mastered these controls, experiment with the second clip in the sequence. Select the pixels in the blue sky, and then increase the color saturation and add a blue tint to the selection.

Making precise adjustments with curves

The Hue Saturation Curves controls in the Curves section of the Lumetri Color panel offer precise control when adjusting hue and luminance.

Though there are several different controls, they all work essentially the same way. Each control focuses on a different type of precise selection. Adjustments are applied to pixels that have been selected by reshaping the curve—if this feels a little like adjusting the Parametric Equalizer audio effect, you're right!

The result is similar to the HSL Secondary adjustment you just made but with simplified, faster controls.

Curves start as a straight line but become curved when you add control points to them by clicking. The position of the control points can be set by dragging, and this determines the type of adjustment applied.

The first part of the name of a curve indicates its horizontal axis, while the second part of the name indicates the vertical axis.

Let's take a look at each one.

- **Hue Vs Sat:** Select pixels with a particular hue, and change their level of saturation.
- **Hue Vs Hue:** Select pixels with a particular hue, and change that hue.
- **Hue Vs Luma:** Select pixels with a particular hue, and change their brightness (luma).
- **Luma Vs Sat:** Select pixels with a particular brightness (luma), and change their color saturation.
- **Sat Vs Sat:** Select pixels with a particular level of color saturation, and change their level of color saturation. This is particularly useful for reducing the impact of highly color-saturated parts of an image while leaving the rest of the image untouched.

As with so many effects, the quickest way to learn what the controls can do is to try them with extreme adjustments and then experiment to achieve subtler results.

Let's try these controls on some clips.

1. Open the sequence The Ancestor Simulation. Play the sequence to familiarize yourself with the shots. These images have muted colors with some specific regions with distinguishable colors, such as the flowers on the table.
2. Expand the Curves section of the Lumetri Color panel, position the Timeline playhead over the second clip (at 00:00:06:00), and make sure the clip is selected.

At the top right of each Hue Saturation Curves control, there's an eyedropper . When you use the eyedropper to click the image, Premiere adds three control points to the curve control: One matches the part of the image you clicked, and the other two (one on either side) separate the adjustment you'll make from the rest of the curve.

3 Click the eyedropper for the Hue Vs Sat curve to select it, and then click the petals of the reddish flower closest to the camera on the table to sample the color.

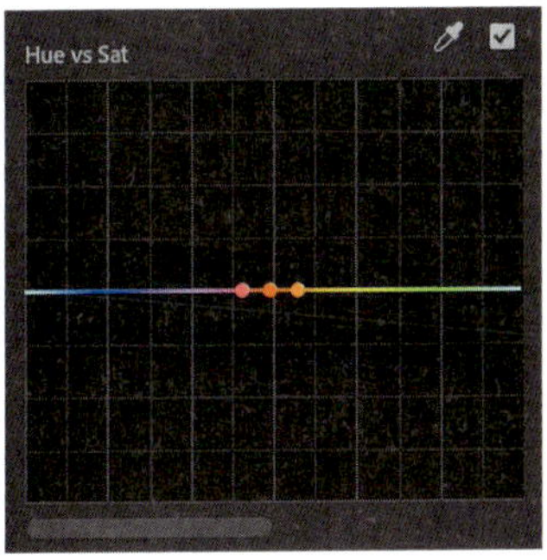

4 If the selection is right at the edges of the hue graph, drag the scroll bar at the bottom of the curve control to access the control points more easily.

5 Drag the middle control point up to dramatically increase the saturation for the flower.

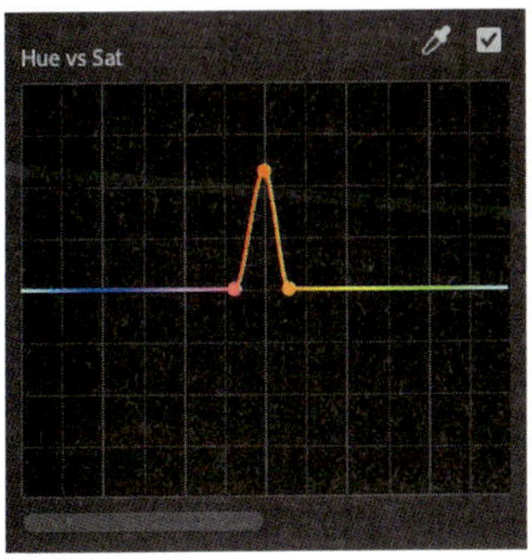

The shape of the curve produces a smoothing effect for the selection. Even so, you may want to reduce the intensity of the adjustment for a more natural result.

Note: The example video clips are low resolution and are compressed to keep file sizes small. The result is softer edges in images than you can expect when working with your original media files.

6 Place the Timeline playhead at the beginning of the sequence, on the first frame. Use the eyedropper for the Sat Vs Sat curve to select the pale beige color of the sofa. This selects pixels that have little color saturation. Drag the left control point up, quite high in the graph, to bring some life to the sofa and similar pale areas of the image.

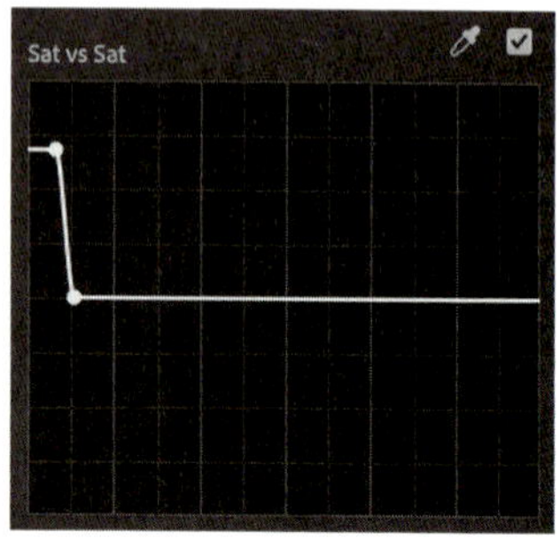

Because you exclusively selected pixels that originally had little color saturation, other areas of the image, with more saturation, are unaffected. The result is a natural-looking adjustment.

7 Experiment with the other clips in this sequence. For example, for the sixth clip, showing the castle with trees, try using the Hue Vs Sat curve to increase the saturation of the green in the trees and then use the Hue Vs Luma curve to darken the leaves. This adds more visual interest and contrast without making an adjustment to the whole clip.

Creating a distinctive look

Once you've spent a little time with the color correction effects available in Premiere, you should have a feel for the kinds of changes you can make and the impact those changes have on the overall look and feel of your footage.

You can use effect presets to create a distinctive look for your clips. You can also apply an effect to an adjustment layer to give your sequence, or part of a sequence, an overall look.

Let's try using an adjustment layer to apply a color adjustment to a scene.

1 Open the Theft Unexpected sequence.

2 Click into the Project panel to make it active, and choose File > New > Adjustment Layer. The settings automatically match the current sequence, so click OK.

3 Drag the new adjustment layer to the beginning of the Video 2 track in the sequence. If snapping is enabled in the Timeline panel, the clip should snap to the beginning of the sequence. If snapping is disabled, you can enable it while still dragging the clip by pressing S.

Note: If you use adjustment layers in this way on a sequence that has graphics, such as titles, you may want to ensure that the adjustment layer is on a track between the titles and the video. Otherwise, you will adjust the appearance of your titles too.

The default duration for adjustment layers is the same as the duration of still images. It's too short for this sequence.

4 Trim the adjustment layer until it stretches from the beginning to the end of the sequence.

5 In the Effects panel, browse to Lumetri Presets > SpeedLooks > Universal. Drag one of these SpeedLooks onto the adjustment layer. The example uses the SL Gold Heat (Universal) preset.

The Look will apply to every clip in the sequence, and you can modify it using the controls in the Effect Controls panel or in the Lumetri Color panel.

You can apply any standard visual effect this way and use multiple adjustment layers to apply different looks to different scenes.

The Lumetri Color panel controls will adjust whichever Lumetri Color effect is selected at the top of the panel.

This is just a brief introduction to color adjustment, and there's an enormous amount more to explore. It's worth investing the time to familiarize yourself with the advanced controls in the Lumetri Color panel. There are a great many visual effects that can add nuance or a striking look to your footage. Experimentation and practice are key to developing your understanding in this important and creative aspect of post-production.

For an exploration of the Lumetri Color panel controls, check out *blog.frame.io/2024/08/25/complete-2024-premiere-pro-color-correction-guide.*

Tip: SpeedLooks available in the Effects panel are applied as regular effects, so it's easy to combine them—just apply another.

Review questions

1 How do you change the display in the Lumetri Scopes panel?

2 How do you access the Lumetri Scopes panel when not viewing the Color workspace?

3 Why should you use the vectorscope rather than depending on your eyes?

4 How can you apply a Look to a whole sequence?

5 Why might you need to limit your luminance or color levels?

Review answers

1. Right-click in the panel, or open the Settings menu, and choose the display type you would like.
2. You can choose the Lumetri Scopes panel from the Window menu.
3. Color perception is subjective and relative. Depending on the colors you have just seen and the colors surrounding an image, you will perceive image colors differently. The vectorscope display gives you an objective reference.
4. You can use effect presets in the Effects panel to apply the same color correction adjustments to multiple clips, or you can add an adjustment layer and apply the effects to that. Any clips on lower video tracks covered by the adjustment layer will be affected.
5. If your sequence is intended for broadcast television or professional online distribution, you'll need to ensure you meet the stringent requirements for maximum and minimum levels. The broadcasters you work with will be able to tell you their required levels.

14 EXPLORING COMPOSITING TECHNIQUES

Lesson overview

In this lesson, you'll learn how to do the following:

- Use the alpha channel.
- Use compositing techniques.
- Work with opacity.
- Work with a greenscreen.
- Use mattes.
- Remove backgrounds with the Object Mask tool.
- Use the Track Matte Key effect to combine layers.

This lesson will take about 60 minutes to complete. To get the files used in this lesson, refer to the instructions in "Accessing the lesson files and Web Edition" in the "Getting Started" section at the beginning of this book. Store the files on your computer in a convenient location.

Anything that combines two images is compositing, including blending, layering, keying, masking, and cropping. Premiere has powerful tools that enable you to combine layers of video, photos, graphics, and titles in your sequences. In this lesson, you'll learn about the technologies that make compositing work, as well as ways to prepare for and perform compositing.

Starting the lesson

Until now, you have been mainly working with single, whole-frame visuals. You have created edits in which you have transitioned between one image and another or edited clips onto upper video tracks to have them appear in front of clips on lower video tracks.

In this lesson, you'll learn about ways to combine those layers of video. You'll still use clips on upper and lower video tracks, but now they will become foreground and background elements in one combined composition.

Note: To ensure that the tools function and the defaults are set exactly as described in this lesson, reset the Premiere preferences by holding any modifier key (such as Shift) while launching the application, selecting Reset App Preferences, and then clicking Continue in the Reset Options dialog box.

You might combine layers by cropping part of the foreground image, masking, or *keying*—setting pixels with a specific color to become transparent—but whatever the method, the way you edit clips onto a sequence is the same as ever.

Let's begin by learning about the important concept of *alpha*, which explains the way pixels are displayed, and then try several compositing techniques.

1. Open Lesson 14.prproj in the Lessons folder.
2. Use the Workspaces menu to switch to the Effects workspace.
3. Reset the workspace by opening the Workspaces menu and choosing Reset To Saved Layout.
4. Save the project as **Lesson 14 Working.prproj**.

What is an alpha channel?

Cameras record the red, green, and blue parts of the light spectrum as separate color *channels*. Because each channel has a single color, the channels are commonly described as *monochrome*.

Adobe Premiere uses these three monochromatic (single-color) channels to produce the corresponding primary color channels. They are combined using what's called *additive color* to create a complete RGB image. Your eyes perceive the three channels combined as full-color video.

This approach of combining multiple monochromatic colors to produce a full color range is a little like combining two mono audio channels to produce a stereo mix.

Finally, there is a fourth monochromatic channel: *alpha*. The fourth channel defines no colors at all. Instead, it defines *opacity*—how visible each pixel is. The opacity of pixels is independent of their colors because the alpha channel is separate from the color channels. This fourth channel has several different names, including *visibility*, *transparency*, *mixer*, and *opacity*. The name is not particularly important as long as you can find the setting.

Just as you might use color correction to adjust the amount of red in a clip, you can use Opacity controls to adjust the amount of alpha. By default, the alpha channel, or opacity, of clips is 100%, or fully visible. On the 8-bit video scale of 0 to 255, this means it will be at 255. Not all media will include an alpha channel. Video cameras do not record an alpha channel, for example. In fact, most codecs (methods for storing image and sound information) cannot store an alpha channel.

Animation clips, titles, or graphics will often include alpha channels to define which parts of an image are opaque or transparent.

You can set the Source Monitor and Program Monitor to display a checkerboard background instead of black, just as in Adobe Photoshop, to make it easier to identify transparent pixels. Let's compare views:

Note: PNG and TIFF files support an alpha channel in addition to the color channels, unlike BMP or JPEG files. This makes them good choices when creating images with transparent regions.

1 From the Graphics bin, open the clip Theft_Unexpected.png in the Source Monitor (be sure to open the PNG clip).

2 Open the Source Monitor Settings menu, and make sure Transparency Grid is *not* selected.

It looks as if the graphic has a black background, but those black pixels are actually the background of the Source Monitor. If you were to export this as a media file with a codec that does not support an alpha channel, the new file would indeed have a black background.

3 Open the Source Monitor Settings menu again and choose Transparency Grid to turn it on.

Now you can clearly see which pixels are transparent. However, for some kinds of media, the transparency grid is an imperfect solution, and this is a good example. It's a little difficult to see the edges of the text against the grid.

4 Open the Source Monitor Settings menu, and choose Transparency Grid again to turn it off.

Tip: If there are any specialist words in this lesson that you are not familiar with, check out "Understanding essential terminology," later in the lesson.

Media files that are created using a codec that does not support an alpha channel will always have a black background rather than transparent areas.

The Source Monitor and Program Monitor can also display the alpha channel as a grayscale image. To enable or disable this view, choose RGBA Channels > Alpha from the Source Monitor or Program Monitor Settings menu.

Making compositing part of your project

Using compositing effects and controls can take your post-production work to a whole new level. Once you begin working with the compositing effects available in Premiere, you'll find yourself discovering new ways of filming and new ways of structuring your edit to make it easier to blend images together.

A combination of pre-production planning, filming techniques, and precise effects setup will produce the most powerful results when compositing. You can combine still images of environments with complex, interesting patterns to produce extraordinary textured moods. Or you can cut out parts of an image that don't fit and replace them with something else.

Compositing is one of the most creative, flexible, and fun parts of nonlinear editing with Premiere.

Shooting videos with compositing in mind

Much of the most effective compositing work begins in pre-production, when you are planning your shoot. Right at the start, you can think about how to help Premiere identify the parts of the image you'd like to be transparent, and there are a number of ways to do this. Consider *chroma keying*, for example, a standard special effect used by major feature film productions to allow action to take place in environments that would otherwise be too dangerous or physically impossible—like the inside of a volcano!

The actors are actually standing in front of a screen that is solid green. The green color is used to identify which pixels should be transparent. The video image of the actors is used as the foreground of a composition, with some visible pixels (the actors) and some transparent pixels (the green background).

Next, it's just a question of putting the foreground video image in front of another background image. In an epic action feature film, it's the prebuilt set, a real-world location, or a composite created by visual effects artists; it could be anything.

The result is a combined composition.

Planning ahead makes a big difference to the quality of your compositing. For the greenscreen effect to work well, the background needs to be a consistent color. It also needs to be a color that does not appear anywhere on your subject. Green-colored jewelry, for example, might turn transparent when a chroma key effect is applied.

Note: Sometimes chroma key effects are achieved using a blue background. Many of the reasons in favor of using green also apply to blue; it was a more popular background color in the past. Developments in camera technology allowed green backgrounds to produce better results, which is why green has become the standard.

When shooting greenscreen footage, the way you film can make a big difference to the finished result. Try to match the lighting for your subject to the replacement background you intend to use, in particular when considering the direction of shadows.

Note: Heavily compressed media files will generally not give the same high-quality result as a raw or lightly compressed file (such as ProRes 4:4:4:4) captured using a high-end camera.

Capture the greenscreen background with soft, evenly distributed light, and try to avoid *spill*, where light reflected from the greenscreen in the background bounces onto your subject. If this happens, you'll be in danger of *keying out*, or making transparent, parts of your subject because they will be in the same green color that you are removing.

Preprocessing footage

In a perfect world, every greenscreen clip would have a flawless green background and nice, clean edges on your foreground elements. In reality, there are lots of reasons why you might face less-than-perfect material.

There are often problems caused by poor lighting when the video is created. However, there's a further problem caused by the way many video cameras store image information.

Because our eyes do not register color as accurately as they do brightness information, it's common for cameras to reduce the amount of color information stored. This saves storage space and is rarely immediately visible.

The approach varies from system to system. Sometimes color information is stored for every other pixel; other times it might be recorded for every other pixel on every second line. This type of file-size reduction is usually a good idea because otherwise the storage required would be *huge*. However, it can make keying more difficult because there isn't as much color detail.

If you find that your footage is not keying well, try the following:

- Consider applying a light blur effect before keying a foreground clip or try increasing the Ultra Key > Matte Cleanup > Soften setting. This blends pixel detail, softening the edges and often giving a smoother-looking result. If the amount of blur is light, it should not dramatically reduce the quality of your image. You can apply a blur effect to the clip, adjust the settings, and then apply a chroma key effect on top of the blur.
- Consider color correcting your shot before you key it. If your shot lacks good contrast between your foreground and background, you can sometimes help the key by adjusting the picture first using the Lumetri Color panel.

Understanding essential terminology

In this lesson, you'll encounter some terms that might be new to you. Let's run through the important ones.

- **Alpha/alpha channel:** The fourth channel of information for each pixel. An alpha channel defines transparency for a pixel. It's a separate channel, and it can be created and adjusted entirely independently of the content of the image. Whether or not your original media file includes an alpha channel, you can work with it in sequences in Premiere.
- **Matte:** An image, shape, or video clip used to identify a region of your image that should be transparent or semitransparent. Premiere allows multiple types of mattes, and you'll work with them in this lesson. You can use an image, another video clip, or a visual effect like a chroma key to generate a matte dynamically based on pixel colors.

When you made a secondary color adjustment in Lesson 13, "Applying Color Correction and Grading," Premiere dynamically generated a matte that was applied only to the color adjustment based on the selection you made.

This limited the pixels that were changed by the color adjustment. In contrast, a chroma key effect applies its matte to the alpha channel, selectively making pixels transparent.

- **Opacity:** The overall alpha channel value for clips in a sequence in Premiere. The higher the value, the more opaque the clip is—the inverse of transparency. You can adjust the opacity for a clip over time using keyframes, just as you adjusted audio level in a previous lesson.
- **Blend mode:** A technology originally seen in Adobe Photoshop. Rather than simply placing foreground images in front of background images, you can select one of several blend modes that cause the foreground to interact with the background in various ways. You might, for example, choose to view only pixels that are brighter than the background or to apply only the color information from the foreground clip to the background. You used a blend mode in Lesson 12, "Adding Video Effects." Experimentation is a good way to learn about the many blend modes available. You'll find them on the Effect Controls panel, under the Opacity effect.

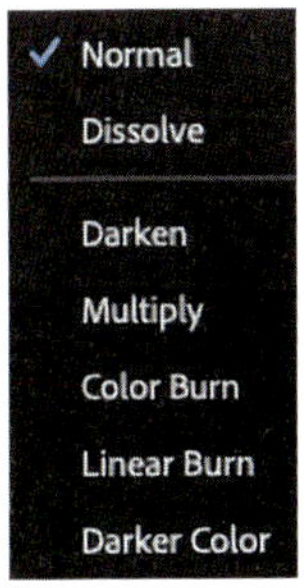

- **Key/keying:** The process of selectively making pixels transparent based on their color or brightness. Chroma key effects use color as a reference to generate transparency (that is, to modify the alpha channel). Luma key effects use brightness.
- **Greenscreening or bluescreening:** The process of filming a subject in front of a screen that is solid green or blue and then using a special effect to selectively turn green pixels transparent. The clip is then combined with a background image. Greenscreening is a type of chroma key effect.

Working with the Opacity effect

You can adjust the overall opacity of a clip using keyframes in the Timeline panel or in the Effect Controls panel.

1. If it's not already open in the Timeline panel, open the sequence Desert Jacket. This sequence has a foreground image of a man putting on a jacket, with a background image of a desert. The composition was created using the Ultra Key effect. You'll learn how to use this effect later in this lesson.
2. Increase the height of the Video 2 track so the thumbnail is easily visible. You can do this by dragging the dividing line in the track header (at the far left of the Timeline panel) between Video 2 and Video 3. You can also hover the pointer over the Video 2 track header, hold Option (macOS) or Alt (Windows), and scroll with your mouse wheel or two fingers using a trackpad.

3 Open the Timeline panel Display Settings menu , and make sure Show Video Keyframes is selected.

Now you can use the rubber band (the thin horizontal black-and-white line on clips) to adjust the settings and keyframe effects. There is only ever one rubber band per clip, and it allows the adjustment of one control at a time.

By default, the rubber band on visual clips controls the Opacity setting. The default for audio clips is the Volume setting.

The small FX badge in the upper-right corner of a clip changes from gray to white if an effect is applied to a clip or if an intrinsic effect is adjusted. The FX badge for the foreground clip in this sequence is white because the Ultra Key chroma key effect has been applied.

If you want to specify that a rubber band adjusts an effect parameter other than opacity, right-click the FX badge and choose an effect and parameter from the menu.

4 Using the Selection tool, try dragging the rubber band on the Video 2 clip up and down. Set it close to 50%.

When you use the Selection tool in this way, the entire rubber band is moved without additional keyframes being added.

You can make more precise adjustments by holding Command (macOS) or Ctrl (Windows) after you have begun dragging. Be careful not to press the modifier key before clicking or you'll add a keyframe instead.

Keyframing opacity

Keyframing opacity in the Timeline panel is similar to keyframing volume. You use the same tools and keyboard shortcuts, and the results are likely to be exactly as you expect: The higher the rubber band, the more visible a clip will be.

1 Open the Theft Unexpected sequence in the Sequences bin. Scrub through the sequence to familiarize yourself with the content.

   This sequence has a title in the foreground, on the V2 track. It's common to fade titles up and down at different times and with different durations. You can do so using a transition effect, just as you would add a transition to a video clip; or, for more control, you can use keyframes to adjust the opacity.

2 Make sure track Video 2 is expanded so you can see the rubber band for the foreground title, Theft_Unexpected.png. Zoom in enough to be able to make precise adjustments to the title graphic's rubber band.

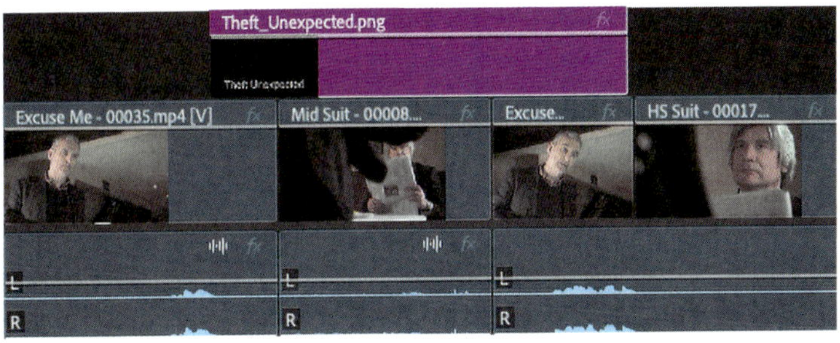

3 Command-click (macOS) or Ctrl-click (Windows) the rubber band for the title graphic four times to add four keyframes—two near the beginning and two near the end. Don't worry about the precise positions of the new keyframes; you'll adjust them in a moment.

4 Adjust the keyframes so the title fades up and down, just as you would with audio keyframes.

5 Play through the graphic clip in the sequence, and watch the results of your keyframing.

You can also use the Effect Controls panel to add keyframes to the opacity for a clip. If you select the title clip in the Timeline panel, you'll see that the keyframes you just added are also displayed in the Effect Controls panel.

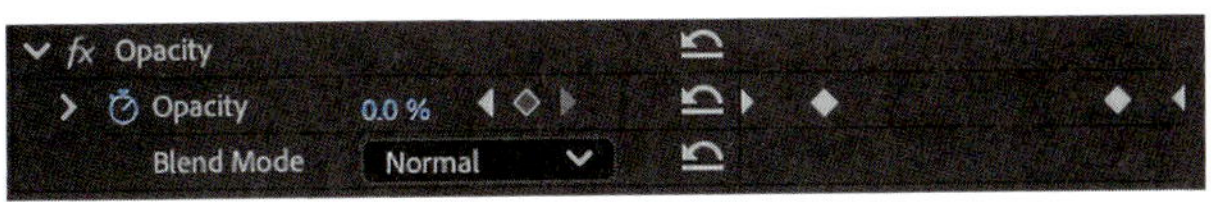

Tip: It's sometimes easier to add the keyframe markers to set the timing first and then drag them vertically to adjust them.

Tip: Once you've added a keyframe by Command-clicking (macOS) or Ctrl-clicking (Windows), you can release the key and start dragging to set the keyframe position.

Note: You could use fade handles to add a simple fade up and down for a clip, but keyframes give more precise control and visual feedback in the Timeline panel.

Combining tracks using a blend mode

Blend modes are special ways for foreground pixels (in clips on upper tracks) to combine with background pixels (in clips below them). Each blend mode applies a different calculation to combine the foreground red, green, blue, and alpha (RGBA) values with those of the background. Each pixel is calculated in combination with the pixel directly behind it.

The default blend mode is called Normal. In this mode, the foreground image has a uniform alpha channel value across the entire image. The more opacity the foreground image has, the more strongly you will see those pixels in front of the pixels in the background.

The best way to find out how blend modes work is to try them.

1 Replace the current title in the Theft Unexpected sequence with the more complex title Theft_Unexpected_Layered.psd in the Graphics bin.

   You can replace the existing title by dragging the new item onto it while holding Option (macOS) or Alt (Windows). Notice that replacing a clip this way retains the sequence clip keyframes you added.

2 Select the new title in the sequence, and take a look at the Effect Controls panel.

3 In the Effect Controls panel, expand the Opacity controls, and browse through the Blend Mode menu options.

4 Right now, the blend mode is set to Normal. Try a few different options to see the results. Each blend mode calculates the relationship between the foreground layer pixels and the background pixels differently. For a description of the blend modes, see *helpx.adobe.com/premiere/desktop/add-video-effects/create-masks-and-composites/blend-mode-options.html.*

   To quickly browse through the modes, hover the pointer over the Blend Mode menu, without clicking to open it, and scroll with your mouse wheel or trackpad.

Try the Lighten blend mode, for instance. In this mode, a pixel is visible only if it is lighter than the pixel behind it.

5 Choose the Normal blend mode when you have finished experimenting.

Adjusting alpha channel transparencies

Many types of media will already have an alpha channel. A title graphic is an obvious example: Where text exists, pixels generally have 100% opacity, and where there is no text, pixels usually have 0% opacity. Elements such as drop shadows around text typically have a value somewhere in between. Keeping some transparency in a drop shadow helps it look a little more realistic.

Premiere sees pixels with higher values in the alpha channel as being more visible. This is the most common way to interpret alpha channels, but occasionally you might come across media that is configured in the opposite way. You will immediately recognize the problem because you'll see a cutout in an otherwise black image. This is easy to address because, just as Premiere can interpret the audio channels on a clip, it's also possible to choose a different interpretation of an alpha channel.

You can see the results using a title in the Theft Unexpected sequence.

1 Locate Theft_Unexpected_Layered.psd in the Project panel.

2 Right-click the clip and choose Modify > Interpret Footage. In the lower half of the Modify Clip dialog box, you'll find the Alpha Channel interpretation options.

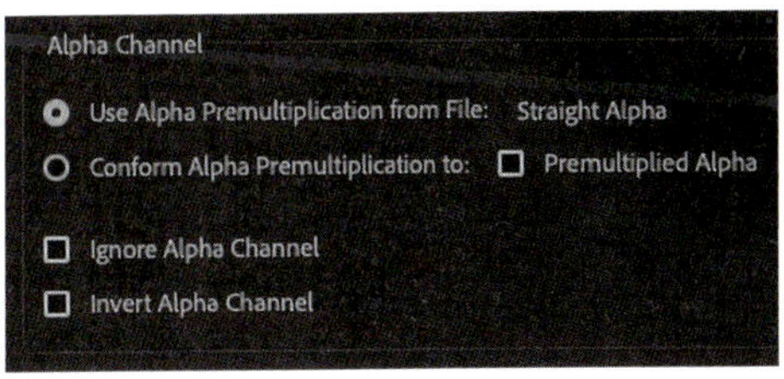

- **Alpha Premultiplication options:** Relates to the way semitransparent areas are interpreted. If you find that soft semitransparent image areas are blocky or poorly rendered, try selecting Premultiplied Alpha and compare the results.

- **Ignore Alpha Channel:** Treats all pixels as having 100% alpha, with no transparency. This can be useful if you don't intend to use a background clip in your sequence and would prefer black pixels.
- **Invert Alpha Channel:** Reverses the alpha channel. This means that pixels that were fully opaque will become fully transparent, and pixels that were transparent will become opaque.

Note: Blend modes still apply when changing the interpretation of the alpha channel. For example, if you invert the alpha channel and use a blend mode like Lighten, the black background won't be visible.

3 Try selecting Ignore Alpha Channel, and click OK; then open the Modify Clip dialog box again, deselect Ignore Alpha Channel, and then select Invert Alpha Channel. Compare the results in the Program Monitor.

4 When you have finished experimenting, make sure the Alpha Channel option is set to Use Alpha Premultiplication From File and Invert Alpha Channel is deselected. You can use Undo to restore the clip interpretation.

Color keying a greenscreen shot

When you change the opacity level of a clip using the rubber band or the Effect Controls panel, you adjust the alpha for every pixel in the image by the same amount. There are also ways to selectively adjust the alpha for pixels, based on their position on the screen, their brightness, or their color.

Chroma key effects adjust the opacity for specific pixels, selected based on their luminance, hue, and saturation level.

The principle is straightforward: Select a color or range of colors, and the more similar a pixel is to the selection, the more transparent it becomes. That is, the more closely a pixel matches the selection, the more its alpha channel value is lowered, until it becomes fully transparent.

Let's create a chroma key composition.

1 If necessary, resize the Project panel to display the New Item button. Drag the clip Timekeeping.mp4 from the Greenscreen bin onto the New Item button in the Project panel. This creates a sequence with settings that match the media. The clip will be added to the Video 1 track.

2 In the sequence, drag the Timekeeping.mp4 clip up to Video 2—this will be the foreground. You may need to resize the Video 2 track to see the thumbnail for the clip. You can do this quickly by double-clicking the blank part of the Video 2 track header.

3 Drag the clip Seattle_Skyline_Still.tga from the Shots bin to track Video 1, under the Timekeeping.mp4 clip on the Timeline panel.

Because this is a single-frame graphic, its default duration is too short.

4 Trim the Seattle_Skyline_Still.tga clip so that it's long enough to be a background for the full duration of the foreground clip on Video 2.

A quick way to extend the background clip is to position the playhead at the end of the Timekeeping.mp4 clip, select the Out point of the Seattle_Skyline_Still.tga clip (the right edge of the clip in the sequence), and press E (the keyboard shortcut for Extend).

5 In the Project panel, your sequence is still named after the Timekeeping.mp4 clip, and it's stored in the same Greenscreen bin. Rename the sequence **Seattle Skyline**, and drag it into the Sequences bin.

This kind of on-the-fly organization is worth the extra effort, as it helps you stay in control of your project.

You now have foreground and background clips. All that remains is to make the green pixels transparent.

Note: To create a new sequence with matching settings, you can also right-click a clip in the Project panel and choose New Sequence From Clip. Both options work with multiple selected clips too. If you select clips with multiple formats, the first item selected will be used to configure the new sequence.

Using the Ultra Key effect

Premiere includes a powerful, fast, and intuitive chroma key effect called Ultra Key. To apply a key, you'll choose a color that should be transparent and then adjust settings to improve the color selection.

The Ultra Key effect generates a matte (defining which pixels should be transparent) dynamically based on the color selection. The matte is adjustable using the detailed settings in the Effect Controls panel. Let's try using the Ultra Key effect on the Timekeeping clip.

Tip: Avoid using too much in-camera sharpening when filming greenscreen footage, as it can make it difficult to get a clean edge when configuring a chroma key effect.

1 Apply the Ultra Key effect to the Timekeeping.mp4 clip in the new Seattle Skyline sequence. You can find the effect by typing **Ultra** in the Effects panel search box.

2 Position the Timeline panel playhead over the Timekeeping clip to display the contents in the Program Monitor. In the Effect Controls panel, click the Key Color eyedropper (not the color swatch) to select it.

3 Holding the Command key (macOS) or Ctrl key (Windows), use the eyedropper to click a green area in the Program Monitor. This clip has a consistent green background, so it's not too important where you click. With other footage, you may need to experiment to find the best spot.

Note: If you're using macOS, you may see an alert asking you to give Premiere permission to record your computer screen. To do so, click Open System Settings and use an administrator password to unlock Privacy & Security settings; then open the Screen & System Audio Recording settings. You'll see applications with access. Make sure Premiere is enabled. You may have to quit Premiere and restart it to confirm the change.

If you hold Command (macOS) or Ctrl (Windows) when you click with the eyedropper, Premiere takes the average of a 5×5-pixel sample, rather than a single-pixel selection. This often captures a better color for keying.

The Ultra Key effect identifies all pixels that have the green you selected and sets their alpha to 0%.

4 In the Effect Controls panel, under the Ultra Key effect, choose Alpha Channel from the Output menu. In this mode, the Ultra Key effect displays the alpha channel that has been generated as a grayscale image, where dark pixels will be transparent and light pixels will be opaque.

It's a pretty good key, but there are a few areas of gray where the pixels will be partially transparent, which you don't want. Where there's naturally semitransparent detail, like hair or the soft edges of clothing, there should be some gray, and the right and left sides of the image don't have any green, so none of those pixels can be keyed. We'll fix that later. Still, the main areas of the alpha channel should be solid black or white.

5 In the Effect Controls panel, under the Ultra Key effect, choose Aggressive from the Setting menu. This cleans up the selection a little. Scrub through the shot to see whether it has clean black areas and white areas. If you see gray pixels in this view, the result will be partially transparent parts in the picture. This might be desirable if the image area should be partially transparent. Expect to switch back and forth between viewing the composite image and the alpha channel often when setting up the Ultra Key effect.

6 Choose Composite from the Ultra Key effect Output menu to see the result.

The Aggressive setting works better for this clip.

Tip: You may notice the image looks cleaner when paused than during playback. If so, this may be because you have the Program Monitor playback resolution set to 1/2 (which is the default). Try setting it to full quality. You may also want to try turning on High Quality Playback in the Program Monitor Settings menu.

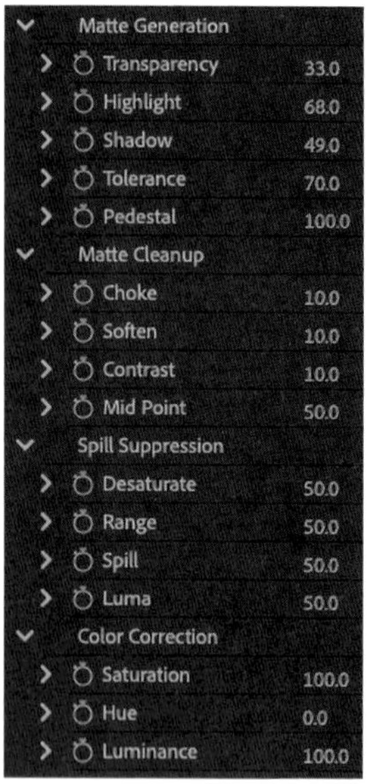

The Default, Relaxed, and Aggressive settings actually modify the Matte Generation, Matte Cleanup, and Spill Suppression settings. You can also modify these manually to get a better key with more challenging footage.

Here's an overview of those settings:

Matte Generation: Once you've chosen your key color, the controls in the Matte Generation category change the way it's interpreted. Even with challenging footage, you'll often get positive results by adjusting these settings.

In the example you are working on, there are issues with the original media, particularly around the edge of the subject. These are more visible during fast motion, such as when the jacket is moving quickly. Try matching the settings in the figure shown here.

When adjusting settings, try dragging each control to its extremes first, and then find the middle ground to discover the best configuration possible. You will often find you will need to re-adjust a parameter as you finesse the settings.

Matte Cleanup: Once your matte is defined, you can use these controls to adjust it:

- **Choke** shrinks the matte, which is helpful if your key selection misses some edges. Be careful not to choke the matte too much because you'll begin to lose edge detail in the foreground image, often applying a *digital haircut* in the vernacular of the visual-effects industry.
- **Soften** applies a blur to the matte, which often improves the apparent "blending" of the foreground and background images for a more convincing composite.
- **Contrast** increases the contrast of the alpha channel, making that black-and-white image a stronger black-and-white version and more clearly defining the key. You will often get cleaner keys by increasing the contrast, at the risk of producing unwanted hard edges.
- **Mid Point** is the level from which contrast is adjusted—a kind of anchor point for contrast. Adjust contrast around a different level for more subtle control.

Note: In this example, you're using footage with a green background. If you have footage with a blue background, the workflow is the same.

Spill Suppression: Spill Suppression compensates for color that bounces from the green background onto the subject. When this happens, the reflected green color does not affect the subject's own colors enough to cause them to be keyed out (made transparent). However, it does not look good when the edges of your subject are green!

Spill Suppression automatically compensates by adding color to the foreground element edges that are positioned opposite, on a color wheel, to the key color. For example, Spill Suppression adds magenta when you're greenscreen keying and yellow when you're bluescreen keying. This neutralizes the color "spill" in the same way that you'd fix a color cast.

Color Correction: The built-in Color Correction controls give you a quick and easy way to adjust the appearance of your foreground video to help it blend in with your background more naturally. For more comprehensive color adjustment controls, use the Lumetri Color panel.

These color adjustment controls are often enough to make a more natural match. The adjustments are applied after the key, so you won't cause problems for the key by adjusting the colors with these controls. You can use any color adjustment tools in Premiere, including the Lumetri Color panel.

Partially masking clips

The Ultra Key effect generates a matte dynamically, based on the colors in your shot. You can also create your own custom-shaped matte or use another clip as the basis for a matte.

Earlier, you used a mask to constrain an effect to a region in the image. The Opacity setting can be combined with a mask in the same way, allowing you to specify with great precision image regions that should be transparent.

Let's create a matte to remove the unwanted edges from the Timekeeping.mp4 clip.

Note: A rough mask of this kind, used to remove unwanted image elements, is often referred to as a *garbage matte*.

1 Return to the Seattle Skyline sequence.

   As you discovered earlier, the foreground clip has an actor standing in front of a greenscreen, but the screen does not reach the edge of the picture. It's common to shoot greenscreen footage this way, particularly when filming on location, where full studio facilities may not be available.

2 Turn off the Ultra Key effect, without removing it, by clicking the Toggle Effect button in the Effect Controls panel. This allows you to clearly see the green areas of the picture again.

3 Set the Program Monitor zoom to 25% so you can see around the frame.

4 Make sure the Timekeeping clip is selected in the Timeline panel. Click and hold the Object Mask tool to select the Rectangle Mask tool. Use the tool to draw a rectangle over the frame in the Program Monitor. Don't worry about precision, just make sure you exclude the sides.

   This creates a new unassigned mask that appears in the Effect Controls panel.

5 In the Effect Controls panel, drag the Rectangle Mask you just created onto the Opacity effect.

The mask is applied to the Opacity effect, making pixels outside of the mask transparent.

6 Scrub through the clip. If the edge of your mask overlaps the action, resize it in the Program Monitor.

As long as you have the mask selected in the Effect Controls panel, you can click directly in the Program Monitor to reposition the corner control points for the mask. Don't worry about precisely matching the edges of the frame. Instead, focus on selecting the areas in the picture the subject moves into.

7 Set the Program Monitor zoom option to Fit.

8 Toggle the Ultra Key effect back on in the Effect Controls panel, and deselect the clip to hide the visible mask handles.

Tip: If you deselect the mask, the control points displayed in the Program Monitor will disappear. Select the mask in the Effect Controls panel to reactivate them.

This is challenging footage to key because the original camera recording includes adjustments to the edges of the subject, and it uses a color compression system that reduces color fidelity. With patience and precise adjustments, you can still achieve a reasonable result.

Removing backgrounds with the Object Mask tool

In Chapter 12, "Adding Video Effects," you used the Object Mask tool to select a subject and then apply a video effect that was constrained to the mask. You can use the same tool combined with the Opacity effect to remove backgrounds when working with layered compositions.

While the Ultra Key effect identifies which pixels to make transparent based on their hue, the Object Mask tool intelligently identifies the edges of a shape you select.

Let's try this.

1 Open the bin Object Mask. This sequence has a shot from the Theft Unexpected on the V2 track, with the Seattle Skyline Still on the V1 track.

2 Select the Excuse Me clip on the Video 2 track. In the Effect Controls panel, select the Opacity control under the Opacity heading. Preselecting the Opacity effect will mean the mask you create will automatically be applied to the clip Opacity.

3 Position the Timeline playhead on first frame of the sequence, and select the Excuse Me clip.

4 Select the Object Mask tool, and click the clip's subject.

If you see a notification about the storage of object mask data, click OK. The mask is applied to the Opacity effect, making unselected pixels transparent.

5 In the Effect Controls panel, click the Track Selected Mask Forward button to animate the mask, following the subject in the frame.

6 Deselect the mask in the Effect Controls panel, and preview the sequence to see the result.

It's a clean result—even more impressive because this is not greenscreen footage. Because the lighting is different for the two clips, color adjustment would help blend the layers and make the composition appear more natural.

Separating part of an image in this way is usually called *rotoscoping*, which historically involved lots of work manually drawing masks for each frame. Results may vary with the Object Mask tool, but it will always speed up the process.

Using the Track Matte Key effect

Adding any kind of mask to the Opacity effect in the Effect Controls panel sets a user-defined region that should be visible or transparent. Premiere can also use another sequence clip, positioned above the clip to be affected, to generate a custom matte, achieving a similar result.

The Track Matte Key effect uses the luminance information or existing alpha channel information from clips placed on one track to define a transparency matte for a clip on another track. With a little planning and preparation, this simple effect can produce powerful results because you can use any clips as a reference and even apply effects to them, changing the resulting matte.

Let's use the Track Matte Key effect to add a layered title to the Seattle Skyline sequence.

1 Open the Seattle Skyline sequence. Trim the Seattle_Skyline_Still.tga clip longer so you can use it as the background for another foreground clip. Trim it to a duration of around 50 seconds.

2 Edit the clip Laura_06.mp4, from the Shots bin, onto the Video 2 track, lined up with the end of the background clip.

3 Drag the graphic clip SEATTLE from the Graphics bin onto the Timeline V3 track, directly above the Laura_06.mp4 clip. This clip has an alpha channel that defines the non-text portion of the image as transparent, allowing you to see the background.

4 Trim the SEATTLE graphic clip to match the duration of the Laura_06.mp4 clip.

5 Find the Track Matte Key effect in the Effects panel, and apply it to the Laura_06.mp4 clip on the Video 2 track. The effect is applied to the clip you want to change (not the clip or clips you are using as a reference for the effect).

6 Make sure the Laura_06.mp4 clip is selected. In the Effect Controls panel, choose Video 3 from the Matte menu in the Track Matte Key controls. Any clips on the chosen track will be used as the reference for the newly generated matte.

> **Tip:** In this example, you're using a still image as a reference for the Track Matte Key effect. You can use any type of visual clip, though, including video clips.

7 Scrub through the sequence to see the result. The white text in the title clip on Video 3 is no longer visible. Instead, it's being used as a guide to define the visible and transparent regions of the clip on V3.

By default, the Track Matte Key effect uses the alpha channel from clips on the selected track to generate a key. If your reference clips don't use an alpha channel, change the Composite Using menu to Matte Luma, so the Track Matte Key effect uses the brightness of the reference clips instead.

The Track Matte Key effect is an unusual effect because most other effects exclusively change the clip they are applied to. The Track Matte Key effect changes both the clip it's applied to *and* the clip used as a reference, which is made transparent for the duration of the effect.

The colors in the Laura_06.mp4 clip work well against the blue in the background clip, but they could be more vivid. You might want to experiment with color correction tools to make the red stronger and brighter so it's a more compelling composition.

You could animate the SEATTLE title too, having it move on-screen or gradually increase in size.

You could also add a blur effect to the Laura_06.mp4 clip before adding the Track Matte Key effect and change the playback speed to create a softer, slower-moving texture.

Review questions

1 What is the difference between the RGB channels and the alpha channel?

2 How do you apply a blend mode to a clip?

3 How do you keyframe clip opacity?

4 How do you change the way a media file's alpha channel is interpreted?

5 What does it mean to key a clip?

6 Are there any limits to the kinds of clips you can use as a reference for the Track Matte Key effect?

Review answers

1 RGB channels contain color information; the alpha channel describes opacity.

2 Choose a blend mode from the Blend Mode menu in the Opacity category in the Effect Controls panel.

3 You adjust clip opacity in the same way you adjust clip volume, in the Timeline panel or in the Effect Controls panel. To make an adjustment in the Timeline panel, make sure you're viewing the Opacity rubber band for the clip you want to adjust and then drag with the Selection tool. If you hold Command (macOS) or Ctrl (Windows) while clicking, you'll add keyframes. You can also work with keyframes in more advanced ways using the Pen tool.

4 Right-click the file in the Project panel and choose Modify > Interpret Footage.

5 A key is usually a special effect where the color or brightness of pixels is used to define which part of the image should be transparent and which part should be visible.

6 You can use just about anything visual to create your key with the Track Matte Key effect, as long as it is positioned on a track above the clip you apply the effect to. You can apply special effects to the reference clip, and the results of those effects will be reflected in the matte. You can even use multiple clips because the setting is based on the whole track, rather than a particular clip.

15 CREATING NEW GRAPHICS

Lesson overview

In this lesson, you'll learn how to do the following:

- Use the Properties panel.
- Work with video typography.
- Create graphics.
- Work with shapes and logos.
- Make text roll and crawl.
- Work with Motion Graphics templates (MOGRTs).
- Create captions.

This lesson will take about 90 minutes to complete. To get the files used in this lesson, refer to the instructions in "Accessing the lesson files and Web Edition" in the "Getting Started" section at the beginning of this book. Store the files on your computer in a convenient location.

Although video and audio clips are the primary ingredients in a sequence, you will also often choose to incorporate text and graphics into your project. Adobe Premiere includes powerful title and graphic-creation tools you can work with right in the Program Monitor, or you can browse editable templates in the Properties panel.

Starting the lesson

Text can help to convey information quickly to your audience. For example, you can identify a speaker in your video by superimposing their name and title during the interview (often called a *lower third*). You can also use text to identify sections of a longer video (often called *bumpers*) or to acknowledge the cast and crew (with *credits*).

Note: To ensure that the tools function and the defaults are set exactly as described in this lesson, reset the Premiere preferences by holding any modifier key (such as Shift) while launching the application, selecting Reset App Preferences, and then clicking Continue in the Reset Options dialog box.

Text can be clearer than a narrator's voice and allows for additional information to be presented in the middle of dialogue. Text can also reinforce key information.

In the Program Monitor, the Properties panel, and the Text panel, you'll find a range of text-editing and shape-creation tools that you can use to design graphics. You can use the fonts loaded on your computer (and those available via Adobe Fonts as part of your Creative Cloud membership).

You can also control opacity and color and insert graphic elements or logos.

Let's try a few graphic and titling techniques.

1. Open Lesson 15.prproj in the Lessons folder.
2. Switch to the Captions and Graphics workspace by choosing Captions And Graphics from the Workspaces menu or by choosing Window > Workspaces > Captions And Graphics.
3. Reset the workspace by opening the Workspaces menu and choosing Reset To Saved Layout, or by choosing Window > Workspaces > Reset To Saved Layout.
4. Save the project as **Lesson 15 Working.prproj**.

The Captions and Graphics workspace repositions and resizes the Properties panel, which you will use to configure and design captions and graphics. The Graphics Templates panel shares the same panel group, offering a wide range of free and paid pre-built static and animated graphics templates that you can add to sequences.

The templates available are updated from time to time so you may discover new options are available when you review them.

The Source Monitor is now hidden and shares a panel group with the Text panel, which is brought to the front of the group. The Tools panel is now next to the Program Monitor to give quick access to text and shape tools.

Here are some important panels when working with captions and graphics:

- **Graphics Templates:** Browse and manage pre-built or user-created, editable graphics templates you can add to a sequence.
- **Properties:** Configure and adjust captions and graphics.
- **Text:** Transcribe audio, and generate and edit captions.
- **Tools:** Select tools to create or adjust shapes and add type.

Configuring graphics

In addition to starting with an editable built-in template, you can use the Type tool, Pen tool, Rectangle tool, Ellipse tool, or Polygon tool to create new graphics by clicking in the Program Monitor with no clips selected (if a graphic clip is selected, you'll add to that clip).

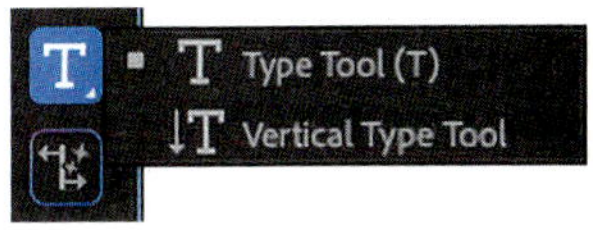

If you click and hold the Type tool, you'll reveal the Vertical Type tool, which allows you to type text in a column, instead of a row.

You can also use the Pen tool directly in the Program Monitor to create custom shapes to use as graphic elements in titles.

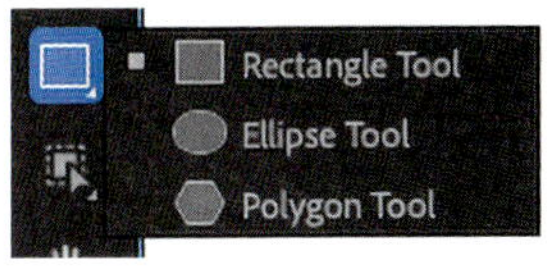

You can click and hold the Rectangle tool to reveal the Ellipse tool and the Polygon tool.

You can select, reposition, and resize graphic and text elements using the Selection tool.

You perform all of this creative work directly in the Program Monitor. As soon as you click to add text or a shape, Premiere creates a new clip in the Timeline panel. You apply adjustments in the Properties panel.

Let's start with some preformatted text and modify it. This is a good way to get an overview of the powerful features of the Properties panel. Later in this lesson, you'll build a new title.

1 If it's not open already, open the sequence 01 Clouds.

2 Position the playhead over the Cloudscape title on the V2 track and select it.

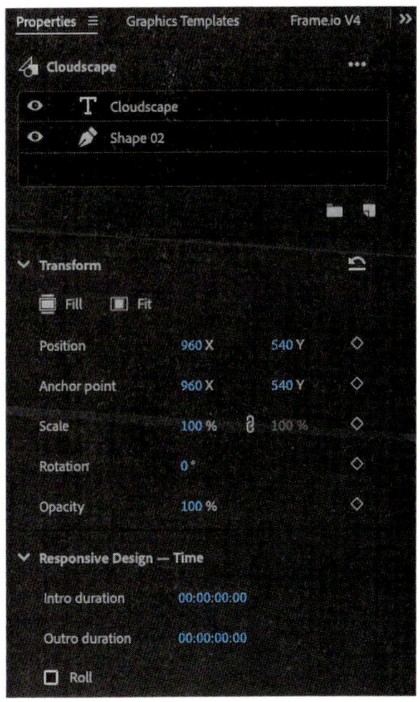

3 The Properties panel shows options for whichever clip is selected in the Timeline panel.

As with the Lumetri Color panel, changes made in the Properties panel actually appear as effects in the Effect Controls panel, with the full range of settings available, including the options to create effect presets and to animate graphic elements with keyframes.

Graphics and titles use a vector-based version of the Motion effect, which works the same way as the video version you are familiar with but which maintains the clean edges of fonts and shapes.

Notice there are two items listed at the top of the Properties panel: Cloudscape and Shape 02.

If you are familiar with Adobe Photoshop, you'll recognize these as layers. Every item in a graphic is displayed as a *layer* in the Properties panel, a little like tracks in the Premiere Timeline panel.

The layers at the top are in front of the layers at the bottom, and you can drag items up and down the list.

You'll also see an eye button for making layers visible or invisible.

Provided no layers are selected in the Properties panel and no graphic or text items are selected in the Program Monitor, below these layers you'll see the transform controls for the entire graphic and the Responsive Design controls. These allow you to specify a time duration at the start and end of the graphic clip that will not be adjusted if you change the duration of the clip in the sequence. This protects the timing of animation keyframes at the start and end of the graphic.

4 Click to select the Shape 02 layer at the top of the Properties panel. This is the red band that goes across the screen.

Now the Properties panel displays alignment, transform, and appearance controls for the shape.

In the Appearance section, you can set colors for shape fill, stroke (a colored line on the edges of a shape or text), background (directly behind the text), and shadow (see "Styling text" later in this lesson for more information about these settings).

Perhaps these color swatches are already familiar to you. They work in an intuitive way.

To the right of the Align And Transform controls, you'll find buttons to enable keyframe animation . Clicking one of these will enable animation for the property in the Effect Controls panel.

Many of the options will be familiar to you from the Motion effect in the Effect Controls panel.

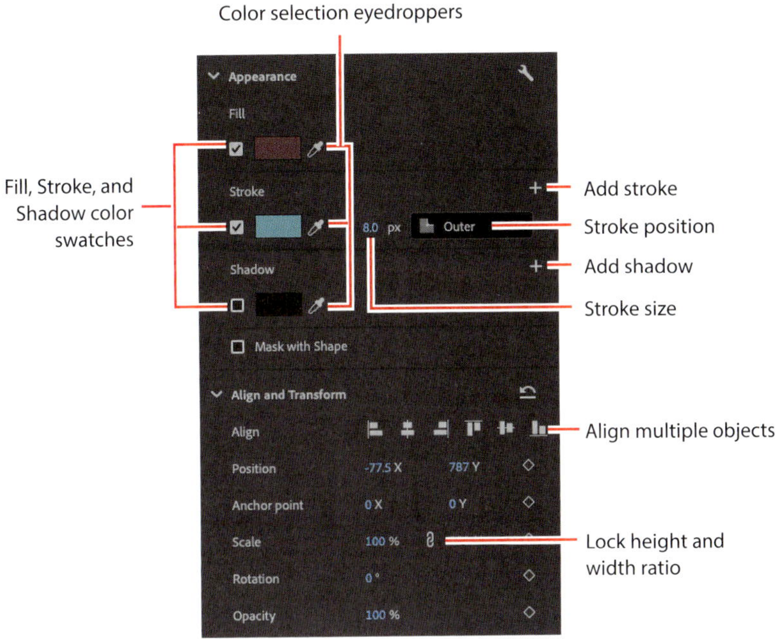

5 Click the Fill color swatch.

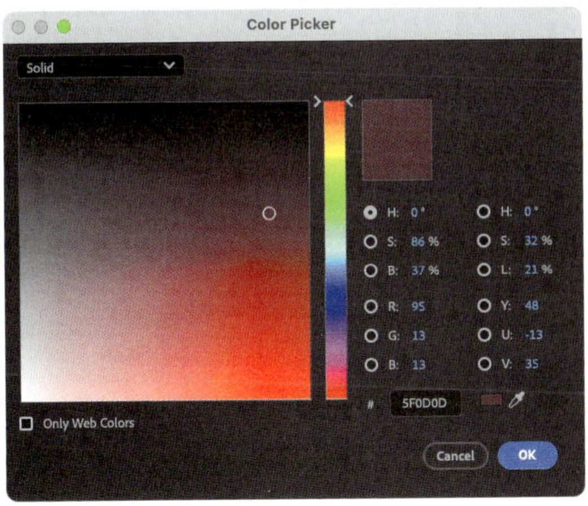

A Color Picker appears that allows you to choose a precise color. There are a number of color models to choose from, or you can move your pointer over a sample of the color you want and click to select it directly.

6 Click Cancel, and then click the eyedropper for the fill color.

The eyedropper allows you to pick a color from anywhere in the image. In fact, you can pick colors from anywhere on your computer screen! This is particularly useful if you have a range of colors you always want to use. For example, you may need to be certain that you match a logo or branding color.

▶ **Tip:** With all the clicking and testing, it's easy to accidentally deselect layers. If there's no bounding box with handles around the text or shape, select it using the Selection tool.

● **Note:** You may have to expand the window or scroll to see all the Properties panel options.

▶ **Tip:** If you're unsure about the purpose of a control, hover the pointer over an icon and a tool tip will tell you the name.

7 In the Program Monitor, use the eyedropper to click the thin blue band of sky between the clouds. The shape fill changes color to match the sky.

8 Make sure you have selected the Selection tool in the Tools panel and that the Shape 02 layer is still selected in the Properties panel.

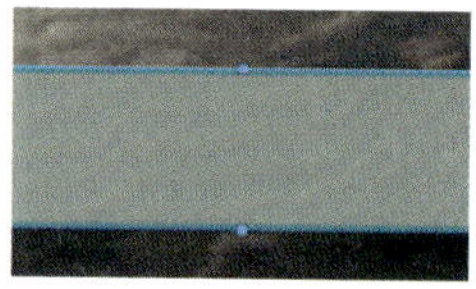

Notice the tiny control handles visible on the midpoint of the shape in the Program Monitor. You can use the Selection tool to change the shape directly.

If you use the Zoom level menu to reduce the size of the image (perhaps to 50% or less), you will be able to see all of the control handles for the shape. The shape stretches beyond the sides of the frame so that the stroke is not visible at the ends of the rectangle.

For now, you're going to use the Selection tool to select another layer in the title.

To select a layer in the Program Monitor, you may need to first deselect the layer that's already selected. You can do this by clicking the background of the Program Monitor or by deselecting the title clip in the Timeline panel.

9 Use the Selection tool to click the word *Cloudscape* in the Program Monitor.

The familiar Align And Transform and Appearance controls are displayed in the Properties panel, but now there are additional controls for the text.

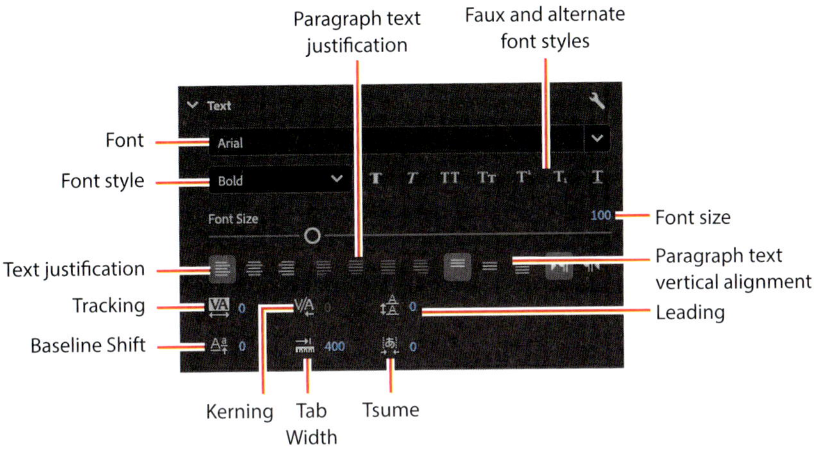

Note: When working with Chinese, Japanese, and Korean fonts, Tsume adjusts the spacing around characters without adjusting the vertical or horizontal scaling of the characters.

10 Try a few fonts and font styles to experiment with the controls. Anywhere you see blue numbers, you can scrub to change the value. You can also click a blue number to select it and use the Up Arrow and Down Arrow keys to change a setting incrementally. If you hold Shift while using the arrow keys, you'll change the settings by 10 at a time.

This is a quick way to find out what a control is for—make an extreme adjustment to view the result; then undo.

The specific fonts loaded on each system will vary, and your Adobe Creative Cloud membership includes access to many more fonts than you will have available to begin with.

Note: Premiere saves your titles in the project file. They do not show up as separate files on your hard drive.

To add fonts, click the Add Adobe Fonts button that appears while browsing fonts (or choose Graphics And Titles > Add Fonts From Adobe Fonts). This will open the Adobe Fonts website in your default internet browser, where you will find thousands of fonts to use.

Learning video typography essentials

When you design text for video, it's helpful to follow typography conventions. If text is composited over a moving video background with multiple colors, it can take some adjustment to create a clear design.

Find a balance between legibility, style, and making sure enough information is on the screen. The more text there is, the harder it is to read, particularly if the words are moving.

Choosing a font

▶ **Tip:** If you'd like to learn more about typography, consider the book *The Complete Manual of Typography: A Guide to Setting Perfect Type, 2nd Edition* (Adobe Press, 2011), by Jim Felici.

Your computer has many fonts installed, which can make choosing a good option for video work time-consuming. To simplify the selection process, try using a triage approach and consider these factors:

- **Readability:** Is the font easy to read at the size you're using? Are all the characters readable? If you look at it quickly and then close your eyes, what do you remember about the text?
- **Style:** Using adjectives only, how would you describe the font you've chosen? Does the font convey the right emotion? Type is a little like a wardrobe or a haircut; picking the right font is essential to the overall success of the design.
- **Flexibility:** Does the font mix well with others? Does it come in various weights (such as bold, italic, and semibold) that make it easier to convey significance? Can you create a hierarchy of information that conveys different kinds of information, such as a name and title for a speaker's lower-third name graphic?
- **Language compatibility:** Does the font include all the characters required for the language you are using? Some fonts have limited character sets.

The answers to these guiding principles should help steer you toward better-designed titles. You may need to experiment to find the best font. Fortunately, you can easily modify an existing title or duplicate it and change the copy for a side-by-side comparison.

When creating text for use in a video, you will often find yourself placing it over a background that has many colors present. This will make it difficult to achieve proper contrast (which is essential to preserving legibility). To help in this case, you may need to add a stroke or shadow to get a contrasting edge. For more information about adding a stroke or shadow, see "Styling text" later in this lesson.

Choosing a color

Note: The Adobe Color service helps you choose harmonious and appealing color combinations for your design projects. For more information, visit *color.adobe.com*. Check out the Contrast Checker, available in the Accessibility Tools section, to see the contrast ratio between selected colors.

Although you can create a near-infinite number of color combinations, choosing the right colors to use in a design can be surprisingly tricky. This is because only a few colors work well for text while remaining clear for the viewer. This task becomes even more difficult if you're editing your video for broadcast television or if your design must match the style and branding of a show, product, or company. The text may also need to work when placed over a busy moving background.

While it may feel a little conservative, the most common choices for text in video are black and white. If colors are used, they tend to be very light or very dark shades or have a thick, strongly colored stroke.

The color you choose must provide suitable contrast with its background, which means you'll be making constant assessments about ideal colors, which often include factors such as branding requirements or a consistent color palette for your sequence.

Consider a positive example with clear light text over a dark background.

And now here's a less positive example. The text is similar in color and tone to parts of the sky.

Adjusting the kerning

It's common to adjust the spacing between the letters in a title to improve the appearance of text and help match it to the design of the background. This process is called *kerning*. Taking the time to manually adjust text becomes more important the larger the font gets (because it makes improper kerning more visible). The goal is to improve the appearance and readability of your text while creating visual flow.

Note: It's common to begin kerning by adjusting the spacing between an initial capital letter and the succeeding lowercase letters, particularly in the case of a letter with very little "base," such as *T*, which creates the illusion of excessive space along the baseline.

You can learn a lot about kerning by studying professionally designed materials such as posters and magazines. Kerning is applied letter by letter, allowing for creative use of spacing.

Try kerning an existing title.

1 In the sequence 01 Clouds sequence, locate the title clip White Cloudscape in the Assets bin. Edit the clip into the sequence after the first title on the Video 2 track and make sure the timeline playhead is positioned over the clip.

Make sure the title is positioned over the background video clip so you can use it as a reference for positioning.

2 Select the Type tool (the keyboard shortcut is T). In the Program Monitor, click to place the insertion point between the *D* and the *S* of the word *CLOUDSCAPE.*

3 In the Properties panel, in the Text section, set Kerning to **400**. This increases the spacing between the *D* and the *S.*

The Kerning option is available only when you select a single letter or place the text cursor between two letters.

Note: After using a different tool, it's a good idea to return to the Selection tool to avoid accidentally adding new text or making unwanted changes to your sequence.

4 Repeat this process for the other letters to the right, adjusting kerning between each pair of letters.

5 Click the Align Center Horizontally button in the Align And Transform section of the Properties panel to reposition the text. Then deselect the text by clicking an empty track in the Timeline panel.

6 Select the Selection tool.

Setting the tracking

Another important text property is *tracking* (which is similar to kerning). This is the overall control of spacing between multiple selected letters. You can use tracking to globally condense or expand selected text.

Here are some common scenarios:

- **Tighter tracking:** If a line of text is too long (such as a lengthy title for a speaker's lower third), you might tighten the tracking slightly. This keeps the font size the same but fits more text into the available space.
- **Looser tracking:** When using all uppercase letters or a more complex font, it can help readability to spread out the letters. It's used often for large titles or when text is used as a design or motion-graphics element.

You can adjust tracking for a selected layer (or item or selected text in the Program Monitor) in the Text section of the Properties panel. Let's try it.

1 Drag the clip Cloudscape Tracking from the Assets bin onto the clip White Cloudscape in the 01 Clouds sequence to overwrite one clip with the other.

   If Snap is turned on in the Timeline panel, the new clip will snap to the beginning of the existing title in the sequence. They have the same duration, so the new clip will perfectly replace the old one.

2 Make sure the clip is selected, and use the Selection tool to select the text in the Program Monitor.

3 In the Properties panel, experiment with the tracking control. As you increase the tracking, the letters expand to the right, away from the anchor point.

4 Set the tracking to **530**.

5 In the Text section of the Properties panel, click the Center Align Text button  to center the text in its bounding box.

   This moves the text object too far to the left.

6 Click the Align Center Horizontally button  in the Align And Transform section of the Properties panel to align the text object with the center of the frame. You may need to scroll down in the Properties panel to see the Align buttons.

7 Now that the text is centered, try adjusting the tracking to **700**. Notice that the text stays centered.

   Tracking adjustments tend to look neater and more intentional than individual kerning adjustments.

8 Restore the tracking to **530** to continue working on this design.

Adjusting the leading

Kerning and tracking control the horizontal space between characters. *Leading* (pronounced "led-ing") controls the vertical space between lines of text. The name comes from a time when strips of lead were used on a printing press to create space between lines of text.

You adjust the leading in the Text section of the Properties panel. Let's add another line of text.

1 Continue to work with the Cloudscape Tracking clip in the 01 Clouds sequence.

2 With the Cloudscape Tracking clip selected in the Timeline panel, use the Selection tool to double-click the CLOUDSCAPE text in the Program Monitor or the CLOUDSCAPE layer at the top of the Properties panel.

   This highlights the text, ready for editing, and changes the Selection tool to the Type tool.

3 Press the Right Arrow key to move the cursor to the end of the text.

4 Press Return (macOS) or Enter (Windows) to enter a second line of text. Type (in all capital letters) **A NEW LAND**.

5 Triple-click the new second line of text to select the whole line. Give the new text a font size of **48**, set the tracking to **1000**, and set the leading to **40**. You may need to resize the Properties panel to see the font size setting fully.

6 Click an empty track in the Timeline panel to deselect the graphic.

   Increasing the leading helps to separate the second line of text, but it's still a little difficult to read because of the background image.

7 Using the Selection tool, select the text in the Program Monitor. This is a quick way to access a specific element in a graphic.

   At the top of the Properties panel, the text layer CLOUDSCAPEA NEW LAND is selected (the text in the layer is condensed into a single layer name).

   Increase the leading to **140**. This adds space between lines and improves readability.

8 Click an empty track in the Timeline panel to deselect the clip.

In most cases, you'll find the default setting works well for leading. Adjusting leading can have a big impact on your title. Don't set the leading too tight; otherwise, descenders from the top line (such as the downward lines on *j*, *p*, *q*, and *g*) will cross ascenders from the lower line (like the upward lines or diacritical marks on É, Ä, *b*, *d*, *k*, and *l*). This collision is likely to make the text more difficult to read, particularly against a moving background.

Setting the alignment

Although you may be used to seeing text left-justified for things like a newspaper, there are no hard-and-fast rules for aligning text for video. Generally, text used for a lower-third title is left-aligned or right-aligned.

You'll often center text used in a rolling title sequence or segment bumper. In the Properties panel, there are buttons for aligning and justifying your text. The alignment buttons align selected text to the left, center, or right relative to the text bounding box.

You can create a text box by dragging with the Type tool in the Program Monitor, rather than clicking.

With text inside a box, use the justification buttons to make the text fill the width of its bounding box.

With text inside a box, you can also use the vertical alignment buttons to make the text align with the top, middle, or bottom edge of the box.

It's safe to experiment and use the Undo option if necessary, so don't worry about memorizing which alignment option is which.

You may find the position of text in the frame changes when you choose a new alignment setting. If so, manually reposition the text, or click the Align Center Vertically button or Align Center Horizontally button to bring the text back into the middle of the frame.

Setting the safe title margin

When creating titles, you may want to view guides to help you position text and graphic elements.

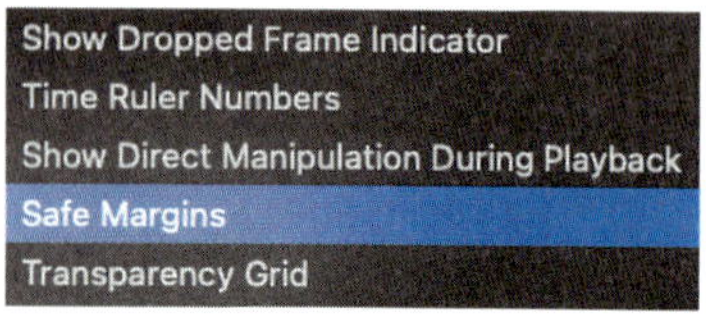

You can enable or disable these by opening the Settings menu  in the Program Monitor and choosing Safe Margins.

By default, the outer guide leaves a 10% margin on each edge of the screen. The area inside this box is considered the *action-safe area*. Things that fall outside this box may get cut off when the video signal is viewed on a television monitor. Be sure to place all critical elements that are meant to be seen (like a logo) inside this region.

By default, the inner guide leaves a 20% margin on each edge of the screen. The area inside this box is called the *title-safe area*. Just as this book has margins to keep the text from getting too close to the edge, it's a good idea to keep text inside the innermost safe margin. This will make it easier for your audience to read the information.

If text is outside the title-safe area, there's a chance some letters may be missed on a miscalibrated screen.

Screen technology has improved over time, and it's now common to set the action-safe area to 3% from the edge, and the title-safe area to 5% from the edge.

You can change these settings by opening the Settings menu in the Source Monitor or Program Monitor and choosing Overlay Settings > Settings.

To hide the safe margins, choose the option again from the Program Monitor Settings menu.

Creating new titles

When you create a title, you'll need to make some choices about how the text is displayed. There are two approaches to creating text, each offering both horizontal and vertical text direction options.

- **Point text:** This approach builds a text bounding box as you type. The text runs on one line until you press Return/Enter. Changing the shape and size of the box changes the Scale property in the Properties panel (and the Effect Controls panel).
- **Paragraph (Area) text:** You set the size and shape of a text box before entering text inside it. Changing the box size later displays more or less text but does not change the size of the text.

When using the Type tool in the Program Monitor, you choose which sort of text you are adding when you first click.

- Click and type to add point text.
- Drag to create a (resizable) text box and then type to add paragraph text inside the box.

Most of the options in the Properties panel apply to both types of text.

Tip: To change point text to paragraph text or paragraph text to point text, select the text object or layer and click Text Properties in the Properties panel. Choose the new type from the Text Layer Type menu.

Adding point text

Now that you have been introduced to some of the main factors when modifying and designing a graphic, let's create a new one.

You'll create a new title to help promote a tourist destination.

1 Open the sequence 02 Cliff.

2 Position the Timeline playhead at the beginning of the sequence, and select the Type tool.

3 Click in the Program Monitor, and type **The Dead Sea**.

Premiere adds a new graphic clip to the sequence in the Timeline panel on the next available video track. In this case, it's Video 2.

The settings you last used are applied to new titles when you create them.

4 Try changing the background video frame by dragging the Timeline playhead. Choose the background frame carefully when designing a title. Because video moves, you may find a title works at the start of a clip but not at the end.

5 Select the Selection tool by clicking it in the Tools panel. You won't be able to use a keyboard shortcut for the Selection tool because you're typing into a text bounding box. Handles appear on the text bounding box.

Choose the following settings in the Properties panel:

Font: Arial Bold
Font size: 83
Tracking: 0
Kerning: 0
Leading: 0
Fill color: White

In the Appearance options, enable Fill only (deselect Stroke, Background, and Shadow). Try to match the example given here.

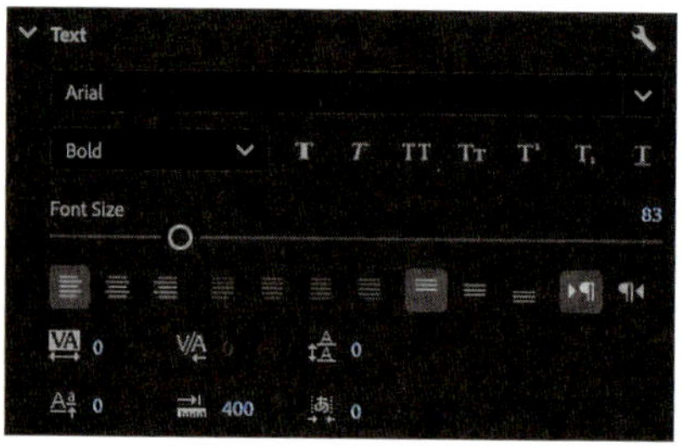

6 Try using the Selection tool to drag the corners and edges of the text bounding box. Notice that the Font Size, Width, and Height settings do not change. Instead, the Scale setting in the Align And Transform section is adjusted.

By default, the height and width maintain the same relative scale. You can adjust the height and width separately by clicking Set Scale Lock.

Set Scale back to 100%, and make sure Set Scale Lock is selected.

7 Hover the pointer just outside a corner of the text box until a curved pointer appears. This allows you to rotate the text box. Drag to rotate the bounding box off its horizontal orientation.

The anchor point is the point around which objects will rotate and the single point that's referenced by position controls. When you adjust position settings, the position applies specifically to the anchor point, which itself has a position on the object. For many items it's the exact center of the object (which makes sense, particularly when rotating).

This is not the case with text objects. The default location of the anchor point for this left-aligned text is the lower-left corner of the text (not the box around the text). When you rotate the text, it doesn't pivot around the center but instead around that corner.

8 With the Selection tool still active, click the blue number for the Rotation setting in the Properties panel, type **45**, and press Return/Enter to manually set the angle to 45 degrees.

9 Click anywhere in the bounding box and drag the text and its bounding box toward the upper-right corner of the frame.

10 Disable the Video 1 track output by clicking the Toggle Track Output button in the Timeline panel.

11 Open the Program Monitor Settings menu, and choose Transparency Grid to enable it.

Now you can see the graphic against a transparency checkerboard, but it's almost impossible to read!

12 Make sure the text object is selected, go to the Appearance section of the Properties panel, and select the Stroke option to add an outline to the letters. Set the color to black, and set Stroke Width to **5.0** px.

Tip: You can quickly open the Text panel by clicking the More menu (the three dots) in the upper-right corner of the Properties panel and choosing Open Text Panel.

Now it's easy to see the text, and you can be confident it will remain readable against a range of background colors. For more information about adding a stroke or a shadow to text, see "Styling text" later in this lesson.

The Text panel offers direct access to the contents of graphics added to a sequence.

1 Open the Text panel. If it's not open already, you will find it in the Window menu.

2 Click the Graphics tab.

The thumbnail of only one graphic is displayed because all of the text you have added is part of one graphic clip.

3 Double-click the text to the right of the thumbnail to edit it. Try this now, and watch the text update directly in the Program Monitor.

4 Use Undo to restore the original version of the text.

Adding paragraph text

Although point text is flexible, you'll have more control over your layout using paragraph text. This option will automatically wrap the text onto the next line when it reaches the edge of the paragraph text box.

Note: If a title clip is selected, clicking to add new text or a shape will add to the existing clip. If no graphic clip is selected in the Timeline panel, a new clip will be created on the next available track above.

Continue working with the same graphic clip selected in the 02 Cliff sequence.

1 Select the Type tool, and make sure the graphic clip is selected in the Timeline panel.

2 Drag inside the Program Monitor to create a text box that fills the lower-left corner, leaving space between the box and the edges of the frame.

3 Start entering names of participants who will be attending the tour. Use the names shown here or add your own. Press Return/Enter after each name for a new line.

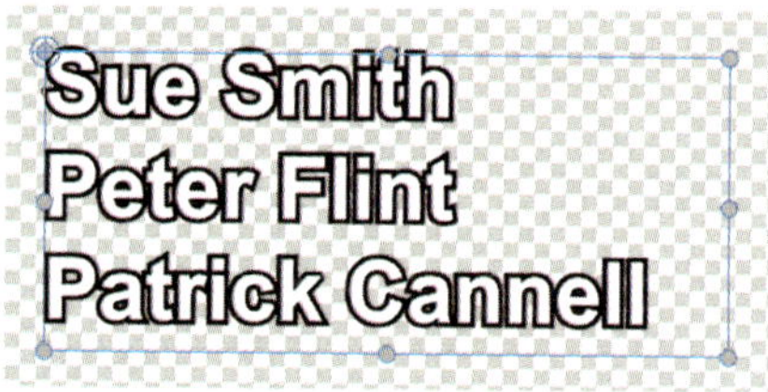

Tip: A good way to avoid spelling mistakes is to copy and paste text from an approved script or email that has already been reviewed by your client or producer.

Type at least one name with enough characters to go beyond the right edge of the text box. Unlike point text, paragraph (area) text remains within the confines of the bounding box you defined, and it wraps at the edges of the box onto the next line. If you add so much text that some won't fit in the text box, the extra letters won't be visible.

4 Use the Selection tool to change the size and shape of the bounding box to fit around the text a little better.

When you resize a text box, the text stays the same size, adjusting its position in the text box.

5 In the Properties panel, the Stroke Position menu sets whether a stroke is on the outside, centered, or on the inner edge. Change this to Center to give a sharper edge to the new paragraph text and make sure the stroke width is still set to 5.0 px.

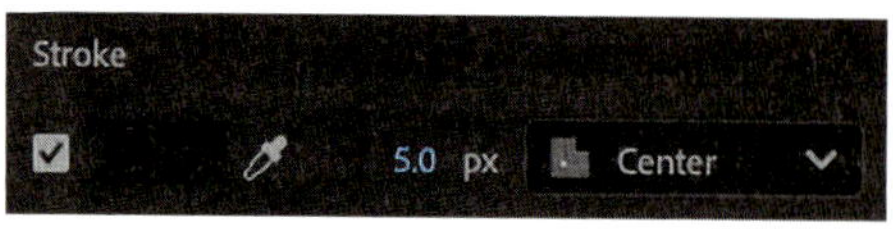

Each item has its own layer in the graphic, so there are now two layers displayed in the Properties panel. When selected, each item has its own controls.

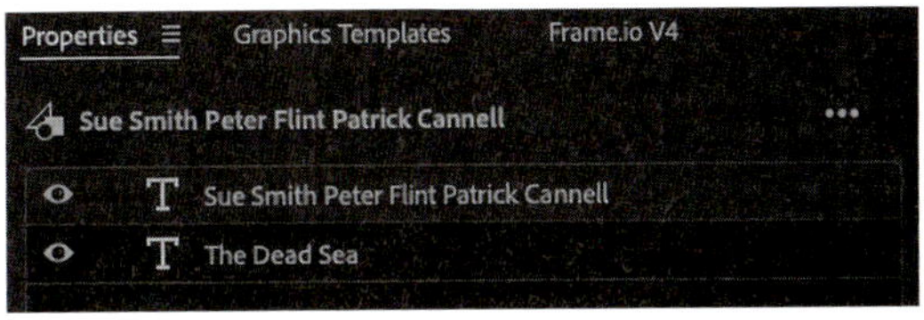

Styling text

In addition to offering settings for fonts, position, and opacity, the Properties panel also enables you to apply a stroke and shadow to text or shapes in a graphic.

When you'd like to reuse a particular group of text settings—for example, to ensure all the lower-thirds in your video match—you don't have to manually re-enter the settings each time. Instead, you can save them as a *text style* (think of it as a preset look for text). You can then use the text style to apply all the settings at once.

After we refine the appearance of the graphics in the sequence a bit more, we'll save each appearance as a text style.

Changing a title's appearance

The Appearance section of the Properties panel offers three main features for improving the readability of text.

- **Stroke:** An edge added to text. It helps to keep text legible over moving video or a complex background.
- **Background:** A solid color that appears behind the letters, creating a controllable backdrop for the text.
- **Shadow:** A common addition to video text because it makes the text easier to read without being intrusive. Be sure to adjust the Blur of the shadow. Also, be sure to keep the angle of shadows identical for all titles in a project for consistency.

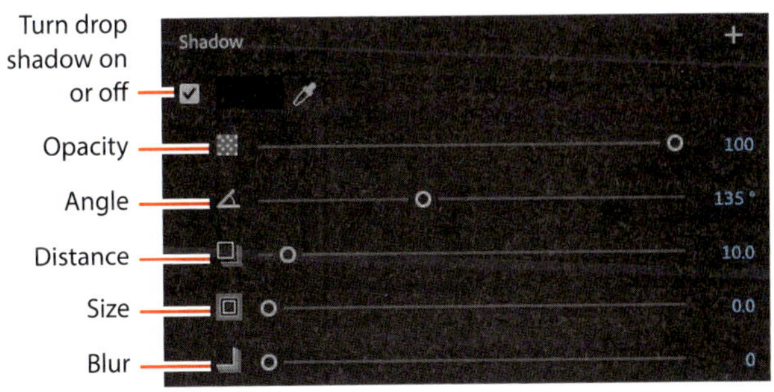

Just as with the text fill, you can assign any color to strokes, backgrounds, and shadows.

1 Turn on the track output for Video 1.

2. Experiment with the options in the Properties panel to make the text more readable and add more color to the composition.
3. To set the color for the text in the upper right, select the text box in the Program Monitor or select the text layer in the Properties panel and use the Fill color eyedropper to select the orange rocks.
4. To set the color for the text in the lower left, select the text box in the Program Monitor or select the text layer in the Properties panel and use the Fill color eyedropper to select a pale blue from the sky around the clouds.

   The colors in the rocks and clouds vary, so you may want to use the eyedropper to select an approximate color and then click the Fill color swatch to manually adjust the selection. Alternatively, keep clicking with the eyedropper until you find a color in the image you like.

   Try to match the appearance of the title in this example.

Saving styles

If you create a text style you like, you can store it and reuse it in the project. A style describes the color, font, and appearance for text. You can use a style to change the appearance of a text object with a single click; all the properties of the text update to match the preset.

Let's create a style from the text you modified in the previous exercise.

1. Continuing to work on the same title, use the Selection tool to select the paragraph text in the lower-left corner.
2. In the Properties panel, in the Linked Style section near the bottom, click the Add Style menu + and choose Create Style.

   The New Text Style dialog box opens.

   Tip: You can copy styles from one open project to another. Plus, you can right-click a style in the Project panel and choose Export Text Styles to save it as a PRTEXTSTYLE file that can be imported into other projects. You can also save a style to your local styles library, accessible in the Style Browser. Click Open Style Browser in the Properties panel to choose a style.

3 Enter the name **Blue Bold Text**, make sure Save To Project is selected, and click OK.

The new style is added to the Style menu in the Properties panel and appears in the Project panel.

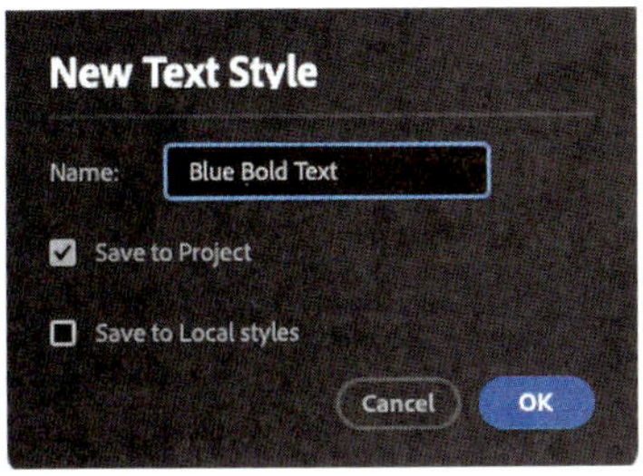

4 Select the other text in the upper-right corner and use the Style menu to apply the Blue Bold Text style.

Any styles that are in the Project panel will appear on the list of available styles in the Properties panel. To remove a style, delete it from the Project panel. To save a style for use in other projects, select Save To Local Styles when creating it.

Saving Source Graphics

So far, you have worked with a title that was already created in a sequence, edited one from the Project panel, and created a new one.

In most cases, Premiere requires that items included in sequences also exist in the Project panel. Graphics created in Premiere are an exception to this rule.

Earlier, you edited the Cloudscape Tracking title into the 01 Clouds current sequence. Open that sequence now, and from the Project panel, edit a second instance of the same title into the timeline on the Video 2 track. You may need to move the other version of the title out of the way to make space for the second copy.

Compare the two instances of the Cloudscape Tracking clip. The changes you made to the title in the sequence, including adding text, have also been applied to the source clip in the Project panel. That's because the title is a *Source Graphic*.

Note: Titles have a default duration set in the user preferences, just like other single-frame media.

You can convert any graphic to a Source Graphic by selecting it in the Timeline panel and choosing Graphics And Titles > Upgrade To Source Graphic.

A new graphic clip is added to the Project panel that you can share between multiple sequences or multiple projects.

Note: Newly created titles use text in the title as a name for the clip. When you upgrade a title to a Source Graphic, the name Graphic is used. You can change this in the Project panel.

Any graphic clips made from that Source Graphic, including the one you upgraded it from, are duplicates of each other. Any changes made to the text, style, or contents in any instance of a Source Graphic are reflected in all other instances of the same Source Graphic.

Source Graphics are useful when you expect to use the same graphic elements multiple times in a project. You might work on a multipart episodic show with standard opening titles, for example, or a documentary with the same lower-third design used to introduce every subject.

Being able to make adjustments to one item that updates everywhere can be a great time-saver.

Working with shapes and logos

Tip: If you have disabled canvas guides in the Photoshop View options, you can enable them by choosing View > Show > Canvas Guides.

When creating title graphics, you'll likely need more than just words to build a complete graphic. Premiere also offers the ability to create vector shapes as graphic elements. Many of the settings you adjusted when working with text also apply to shapes. You can also import completed graphics (like a logo) as a layer in a new graphic clip.

Creating shapes

If you've created shapes in graphics-editing software such as Photoshop or Adobe Illustrator, you'll find creating geometric objects in Premiere similar.

Note: Until you quit Premiere and start it again, new shapes will have the same appearance you last selected for a shape in the Properties panel. You can easily change the settings. New titles will have the same appearance you last selected for a title.

You can use the Pen tool to click multiple points in the Program Monitor to create a unique shape.

You can also use the Rectangle tool, Ellipse tool, or Polygon tool. Access the Ellipse tool and Polygon tool in the Rectangle tool submenu. Using any of those tools, drag in the Program Monitor to create a new shape.

Try creating some shapes and adjusting their settings:

1 Open the sequence 03 Shapes.

2 Select the Pen tool, and click multiple points in the Program Monitor to create a shape. Each time you click, the tool adds a new control point. Create something small and unique in the lower-left corner of the frame.

Complete the shape by clicking the first control point, and switch to the Selection tool.

3 Try changing the fill color, adding a stroke, and changing the stroke color.

4 Create a new shape with the Pen tool, in the lower-right corner. This time, instead of just clicking, drag each time you click.

Dragging when you click creates control points with Bezier handles; these are the same handles you experimented with when setting up keyframes. These handles give you precise control over the shape you have created, allowing you to design more organic-looking shapes.

5 Select the Rectangle tool.

6 Drag to create rectangles in the Program Monitor. After you begin dragging, hold the Shift key to create squares.

7 Now click and hold the Rectangle tool in the Tools panel to select the Ellipse tool. Try drawing ellipses. The Shift key allows you to create perfect circles.

8 Click and hold the Ellipse tool in the Tools panel to select the Polygon tool. Try drawing a polygon, and then select the Selection tool.

With a polygon selected, you can use the Corner Radius and Number Of Sides settings in the Align And Transform section of the Properties panel to change its appearance.

The Corner Radius setting can be changed for any polygon or rectangle. Using the Selection tool, drag the small circles inside a shape to adjust the corner radius directly in the Program Monitor. Hold Option (macOS) or Alt (Windows) to adjust individual corners.

These kinds of random shapes may not win design awards, but they are the basic building blocks of some of the most common multilayer graphics.

You can use the Pen tool to adjust any selected shape. You can even click to add control points for more complex shapes. Try changing the selected shape using the Pen tool now.

9 If you want a clean slate, press Command+A (macOS) or Ctrl+A (Windows), and then press Fn+Delete (macOS) or Delete (Windows)—this is the Forward Delete key. You can also select layers in the Properties panel and delete them. For now, keep some shapes onscreen to work with later.

10 Experiment with the different shape options. Try overlapping them and using different colors, with different levels of opacity.

The layer positions of objects in the Properties panel set which objects appear in front, just as tracks do in the Timeline panel. You can drag objects to different positions on the list.

Adding a graphic

You can add image files to your graphic clips using common file formats, including vectors (AI, EPS) and still images (PSD, PNG, JPEG).

Let's try this with an existing graphic.

1 Open the sequence 04 Logo.

This is a simple sequence with space in the graphic for a logo.

2 Using the Selection tool, select the "Add a logo" title clip in the Timeline panel.

3 In the Properties panel, just below the layers area in the Edit tab, open the New Layer menu and choose From File, or choose Graphics and Titles > New Layer > From File.

4 Browse to the file logo.ai in the Lessons/Assets/Graphics folder, and click Import (macOS) or Open (Windows).

5 With the Selection tool, drag the logo to position it where you want it in the title. Then adjust the size, opacity, rotation, or scale of the logo.

Note: When resizing imported items in a graphic clip, scaling over 100% of the original item's image size will lead to a loss of perceived quality because the result is displayed as pixels rather than as a vector image.

Masking with a layer

There's one further option in the Properties panel that deserves an explanation: Mask With Text.

This is best understood by trying it.

1 Open the sequence 05 Mask. This simple sequence has a slow-moving background clip and a graphic with one layer that is an imported image of some ivy. The background clip has a color adjustment and a blur to help separate it from the color and texture of the foreground clip.

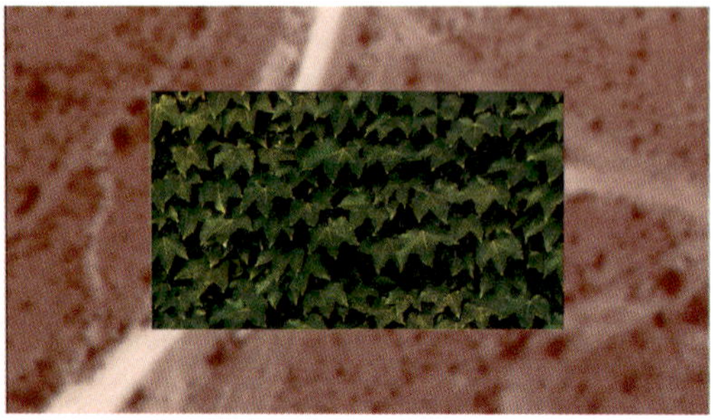

2 Position the Timeline playhead at the beginning of the sequence. Select the Graphic clip, and select the Type tool. Click in the Program Monitor, and type the word **IVY**, in all capital letters.

3 Switch to the Selection tool. Use the options in the Properties panel to expand the *IVY* text to fill the ivy clip area as closely as possible. Reposition the text with the Selection tool as needed to match this example.

Don't worry about the fill color or the stroke color—these will be ignored in the next step. If your text has a shadow or a stroke, deselect them in the Properties panel.

4 With the text item selected, scroll down to the Appearance section of the Properties panel and select Mask With Text.

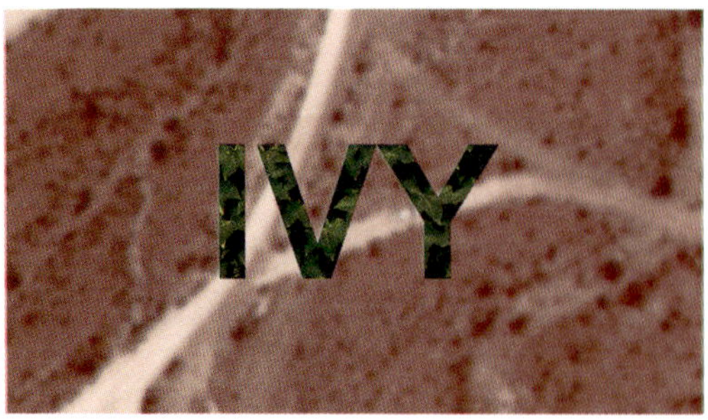

The Mask With Text option masks any layer inside a graphic, using the selected layer as the mask. This is similar to the masking you performed earlier using the Track Matte Key effect. The difference is that the effect is limited to the contents of the current graphic.

Using rulers and guides

There are several ways to arrange and align items in the Program Monitor. By default, you'll be able to move items freely in view, but, as with the snapping option in the Timeline panel, there are also ways to snap items into position in the Program Monitor.

1 Open the 03 Shapes sequence you worked on earlier.

2 With the Selection tool, try moving the shapes around. They'll move freely and overlap based on their stacking order in the Properties panel.

3 With the Program Monitor active, choose View > Snap In Program Monitor if it isn't already selected. Now as you drag items, lines appear showing alignment with other items or the center or edge of the Program Monitor. Any item you drag will also snap into alignment.

Tip: If you find the Snap In Program Monitor option is unavailable, check that you have the right panel active. The option is also available in the Program Monitor Settings menu.

In this complex graphic, snapping can be a little overwhelming, as there are just so many items.

4 Create a new graphic, with one shape, toward the end of the sequence, where the frame is clear again. Try dragging the graphic around the frame, and take note of the satisfying certainty when the shape snaps into position.

5 Make sure the Program Monitor is the active panel (indicated by a blue outline), and choose View > Show Rulers. Rulers are not interactive, but they give you a reference for the next step.

6 Click the ruler at the top of the Program Monitor and drag down. This creates a guide that you can snap items to. As you drag, the pixel position is shown as a tool tip. You can drag multiple guides from either ruler.

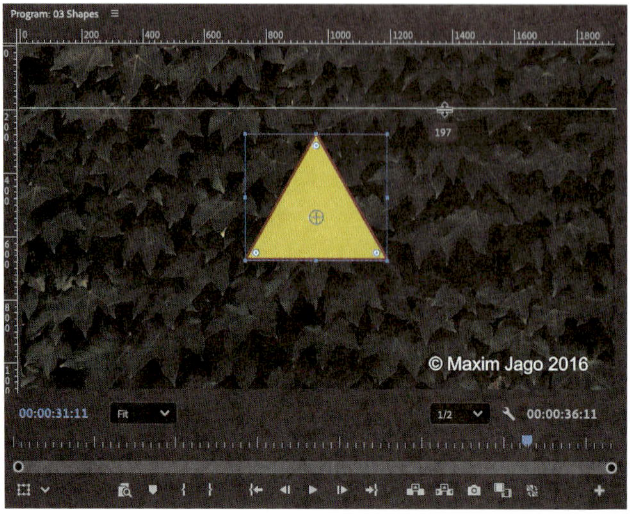

> **Note:** If you want to use specific guides as a long-term reference, you can lock them in position. Choose View > Lock Guides. Choose the option again to unlock the guides.

You can also right-click a guide and choose Edit Guide to assign a new color and specify a precise position.

You can show or hide rulers and guides by choosing them from the View menu. Guides are persistent. If you hide them and then show them again, they will be exactly where you left them.

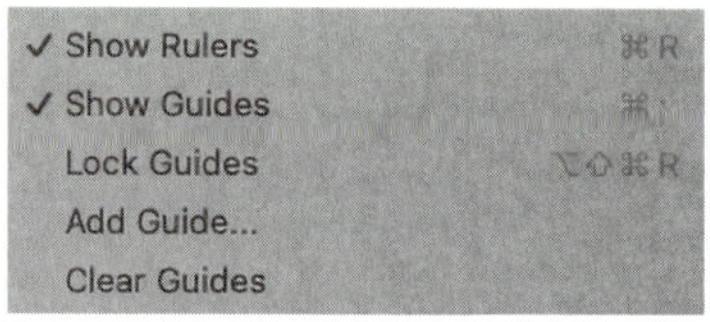

You can also use the View menu to clear any guides you have added.

In the Program Monitor, you can use the Button Editor to add buttons that let you select and deselect these options.

Making a title roll

You can make rolling text for opening and closing credits. In fact, you can apply a roll to any graphic, not just to text.

1. Open the 04 Logo sequence. Use the Program Monitor Settings menu to make sure the Transparency Grid is not active.
2. Position the Timeline panel playhead at the end of the sequence, just after the clip on the Video 1 track.
3. Using the Type tool, click in the Program Monitor to add point text.
4. Type several lines of text that you would like to use as a credit roll, pressing Return/Enter after each line.

   For the purposes of this exercise, don't worry about the precise words.

It can be difficult to add many lines of text without constantly repositioning it. It's often easier to have the text ready in a document so you can copy and paste it into Premiere.

5 When you have typed a few lines, use the Properties panel to format your text as desired.

6 Deselect the text layer (by clicking the background of the Program Monitor with the Selection tool) while making sure the new clip is still is selected in the Timeline panel.

The Edit tab of the Properties panel will now show properties for the whole graphic, not just the text item you were typing.

7 In the Properties panel, select Roll to roll the title.

When you set a title to Roll, a scroll bar appears in the Program Monitor. Now, when you play through the clip, it will roll on and off the screen.

With the scroll bar in place, it's much easier to add more lines of text and navigate through a long title.

You have the following options:

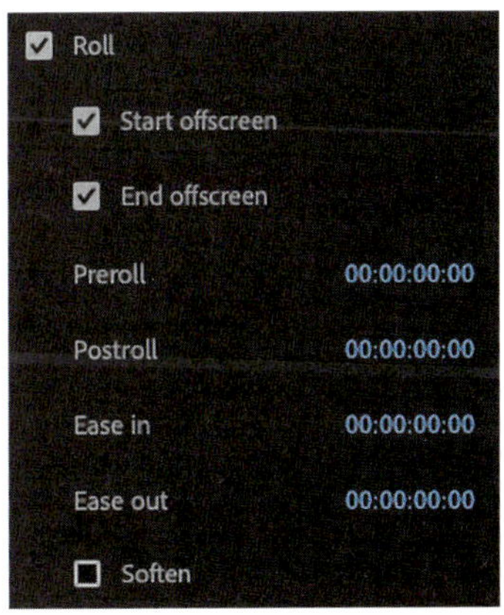

- **Start Offscreen:** This sets whether the credit begins offscreen and rolls in or whether it begins where you positioned it in the Program Monitor. Combined with a Cross Dissolve effect, you could have your title fade up onscreen and roll off.
- **End Offscreen:** This indicates whether the credits roll completely off the screen or end on the screen. Combined with a Cross Dissolve effect, you could have your title roll on-screen and fade out.
- **Preroll:** This sets the amount of time to delay before the rolling motion begins.
- **Postroll:** This specifies the amount of time to play after the roll ends.
- **Ease In:** This specifies the number of frames at the beginning to gradually increase the speed of the roll from zero to full speed.

Note: The Responsive Design options that were touched on earlier are for motion graphics with a precisely timed intro and outro. Use these time controls to prevent clip duration changes from retiming start and end animations.

- **Ease Out:** This specifies the number of frames to slow down the speed of the roll at the end.
- **Soften:** This softens the edges of your rolling text.

If your credits begin or end offscreen, the Preroll, Postroll, and Ease options won't have much impact because the contents will be out of the frame.

When you trim a title to set the length, this sets the playback speed of a rolling title. A shorter title will roll faster than a long one because, one way or another, all of the contents of the title will be displayed in the duration you set for the clip.

8 Play through your rolling title.

Working with Motion Graphics templates

The Graphics Templates panel includes many built-in template graphics you can add to your sequences. They are all customizable. Many of the presets include motion, so they are referred to as Motion Graphics templates (often abbreviated to MOGRTs).

You can add a Motion Graphics template to a sequence by dragging it onto a video track.

Motion Graphics templates can be created in Premiere or Adobe After Effects, and there are differences in the templates each application creates.

Tip: For an in-depth exploration of Motion Graphics template creation in After Effects, check out *blog.frame.io/2024/08/12/mogrt-guide-after-effects-2024-motion-graphics-workflow*.

- Motion Graphics templates created in Premiere produce graphics that are completely editable.
- Motion Graphics templates created in After Effects can include more advanced design and complex animation. They also have restricted controls, set by the original designer to give flexibility while retaining the original core design.

Drag a template directly into any sequence to add it. Some templates may have a yellow font warning symbol to let you know the template uses a font not currently installed on your system.

If you use a template that includes fonts available on Adobe Fonts and you are online, Premiere automatically downloads and installs the missing fonts. If in doubt, you can right-click a template in the Properties panel and choose Sync Missing Fonts.

If it's not possible to install a missing font automatically, you'll see a warning message advising you that the missing font can't be downloaded. The Resolve Fonts dialog box will appear, letting you know which fonts are missing.

The easiest way to resolve a missing font is to go online and add the template again. If that's not possible, you can choose another font in the Properties panel. You can also set a default replacement font in the Premiere user preferences, in the Graphics section.

Experimenting with Motion Graphics templates is a great way to learn about what's possible when designing animated graphics. Add any template to a sequence and then explore the settings that have been used in the Properties panel.

Creating a custom Motion Graphics template

You can add your own custom graphics to the Graphics Templates panel. Simply select a graphic clip in a sequence, and choose Graphics And Titles > Export As Motion Graphics Template.

Choose a name for the new template graphic, and choose a location from the Destination menu. You can add keywords to make the template easier to locate when searching by entering each keyword and pressing Return/Enter.

Tip: You can quickly add multiple keywords, separating them with a comma (,) before pressing Return/Enter.

When you're happy with the settings, click OK. The new Motion Graphics template will automatically be added to the Graphics Templates panel.

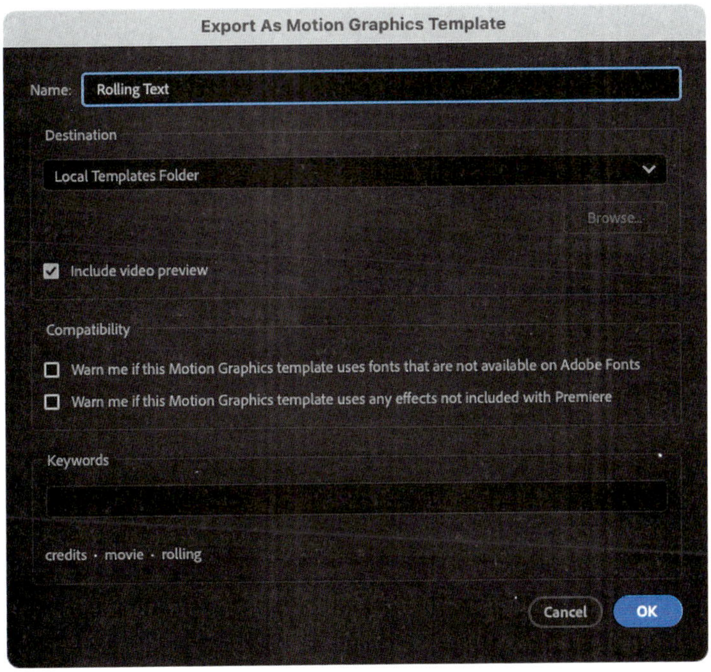

You can import an existing Motion Graphics template file on any computer by choosing Graphics And Titles > Install Motion Graphics Template or by clicking the button in the upper-right corner of the Graphics Templates panel.

This makes it easy to share your custom template titles or store them in a collection for future use.

Adding captions

Video content can be enjoyed by more people when it is accessible. It's a requirement for most broadcast television stations to add closed-captioning information that can be decoded by television sets. Visible captions are inserted into a video file and travel through supported formats to specific playback devices.

Over 80% of social media videos are watched with the sound off, so it's important to include captions for your audience to follow the story.

There are two types of captions: closed and open.

Closed captions are embedded in the video stream and can be displayed or hidden by the player. *Open* captions are always on-screen—and are described as "burned in."

The colorful onscreen captions that often accompany social media content are examples of open captions.

Premiere allows you to work with either kind of caption in the same way. In fact, you can even convert one kind of caption to another (though there are some limitations set by caption delivery standards).

Closed-captions have a more limited range of colors and design features than open captions. This is because closed captions are actually generated and displayed by the viewer's TV, set-top box, or online viewing software, so display options are universal and fixed.

Using caption files

Adding closed-captioning information is relatively easy. You can work with a captions file or generate new captions in Premiere.

Here's how to add captions to a sequence using an existing file.

1 Keeping the current project open, choose File > Open Project. Browse to the Lessons folder, and open Lesson 15_02.prproj.

2 Click the Lesson 15_02 Project panel to make it active, and save the project as **15_02 Working.prproj**.

3 If it's not displayed in the Timeline panel already, open the sequence Coach Interview.

4 In the Text panel, click the Captions tab and then click Import Captions From File. Navigate to the Lessons/Assets/Video and Audio Files/Interview folder. Import the file Coach Interview.srt. The DFXP, MCC, SCC, SRT, STL, and XML formats are all supported.

Premiere adds the caption file to the bin as if it were a video clip, with a frame rate and duration.

5 The New Caption Track dialog box appears.

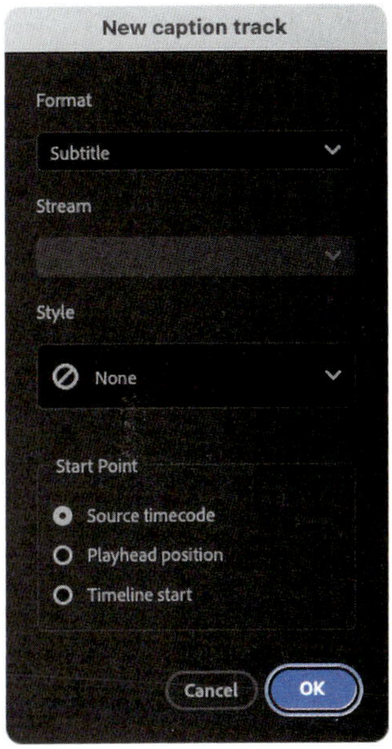

There are different caption formats for different television systems:

- **Australian OP-47** is the Australian closed-captioning standard, used by Australian broadcast television networks.
- **CEA-608** (also known as Line 21) was the most commonly used standard for analog broadcast in the US and Canada.
- **CEA-708** is for digital broadcast in the US and Canada.
- **EBU Subtitle** is an older but popular subtitle type with broad compatibility.
- **Subtitle** is a newer subtitle type.
- **Teletext** is sometimes used in countries that adhere to the PAL video standard.

Within each type there are multiple possible streams. For example, one stream might be English language, while another might be French. The settings displayed are correct, so click OK.

A new caption track is added to the sequence, with each part of the captions displayed as separate clips.

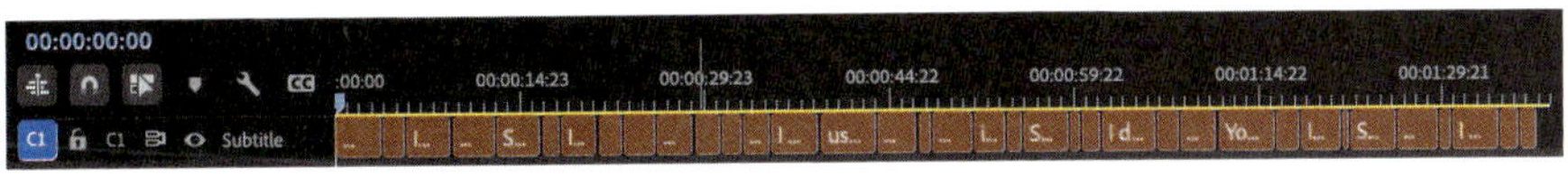

6 You can add multiple caption tracks to a sequence. You can enable output for one caption track at a time by clicking the Toggle Active Caption Tracks button .

Try toggling the caption output off and on now.

7 Play the sequence to see the captions.

You can trim caption clips to adjust their timing like any other kind of sequence clips.

After selecting one or more caption clips in a sequence, you can adjust their appearance by changing settings in the Properties panel.

You can also edit caption text directly in the Program Monitor by double-clicking it.

Premiere can translate captions into multiple languages, making it easier to provide accessibility internationally.

To translate existing captions, click the More menu (three dots) at the top of the Captions section in the Text panel and choose Translate Captions.

In the Translate Captions dialog box, specify the source language and target language, as well as your format and style preferences, and then click Translate.

A new caption track is added to the sequence in the language you chose.

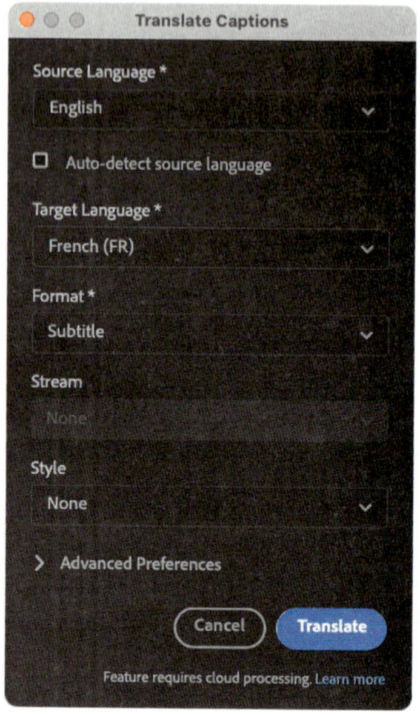

Creating new captions

You can create your own captions automatically within Premiere. There's even an option to automatically transcribe clips when you add them to a sequence.

You can click to transcribe the current sequence, but to automatically transcribe all clips when they are added to a sequence, choose Premiere > Settings > Media Analysis & Transcription (macOS) or Edit > Preferences > Media Analysis & Transcription (Windows), and select Automatically Transcribe Clips.

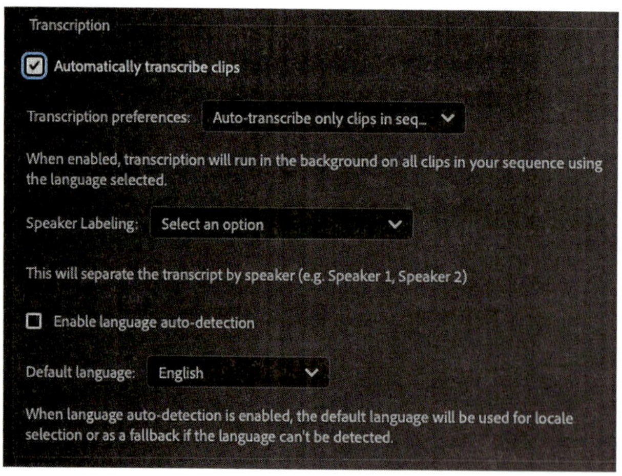

To automatically transcribe all clips when they are imported, choose Auto-Transcribe All Imported Clips from the Transcription Preferences menu. You can also instruct Premiere to label speakers automatically and to detect the speaker's language automatically. Having set your preferences, click OK to close the Preferences dialog box. For now, click Cancel to leave the setting unchanged.

Let's transcribe a sequence:

1 Open the Transcribe sequence.

2 Open the Text panel, and set it to the Transcript tab. If the Text panel isn't open already, you'll find it in the Window menu.

You may see a notification in the Text panel inviting you to automatically transcribe clips. For the purposes of this exercise, ignore the message.

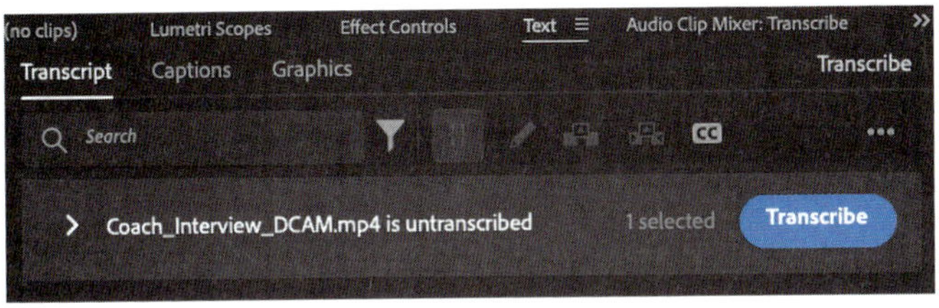

3 Click the blue Transcribe button. Premiere transcribes the audio in the sequence.

The accuracy of the transcription depends in part on the quality of the original audio recording. If you find a word that should be replaced, double-click it in the Text panel and retype it.

Note: By default, Premiere will transcribe the first audio channel for clips with multiple channels. If you are working with multi-channel audio clips, it may be helpful to check and configure the channels before transcribing. Select the clips; then right-click the selection and choose Modify > Audio Channels to access the settings, or press Shift+G.

4 Click the Create Captions button CC at the top of the Text panel. You may need to resize the panel to see the button.

The Create Captions dialog box opens.

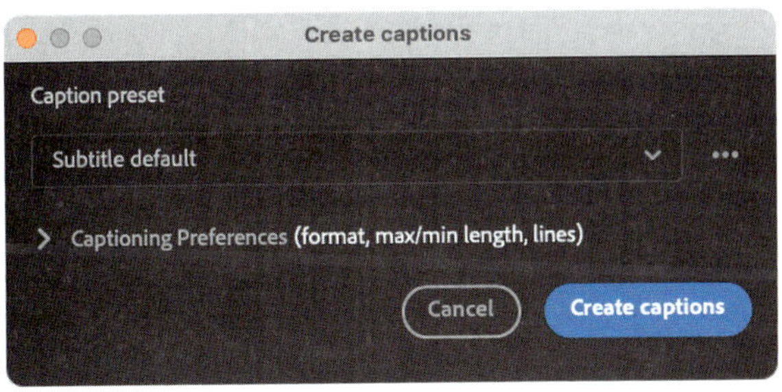

There are several options available to configure the way captions will be displayed. Initially, the Subtitle Default preset option is selected. If you click the triangle to expand the Captioning Preferences, all of the detailed options become available. If you know the settings you need for your project, you can select them here.

Keeping the default settings, click Create Captions.

A new caption track is added to the sequence, much like the one you created when importing a caption file.

5 Play the sequence. The captions will update in the Text panel as the sequence plays.

Tip: Double-click a caption clip to quickly display the Properties panel.

You can use the Properties panel to change the appearance of captions. You can select more than one caption clip and changes made in the Properties panel will apply to all selected items.

After making changes, you can click the Redefine Style button to apply the changes to all captions in the track.

You can also click the Add Style button to create multiple styles to apply to whole caption tracks. Styles applied to tracks work in the same way as the linked styles you worked with earlier.

Upgrading captions to graphics

The appearance options for captions are limited to ensure compatibility with players. If you'd like to get a little more creative with your captions, you can convert them to graphics.

To upgrade, select one or more caption clips and choose Graphics And Titles > Upgrade Caption To Graphic.

The selected captions will be removed from the caption track and added as graphics to an empty video track.

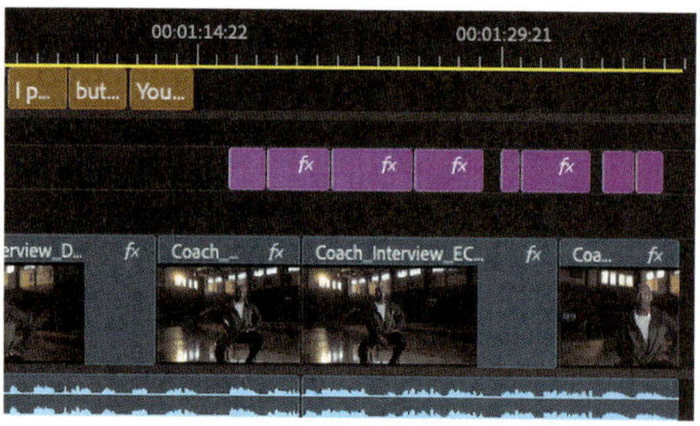

Now you'll have the full range of design features available in the Properties panel.

Closing multiple projects

You currently have two projects open at the same time. To close them both in a single step, choose File > Close All Projects. If you are invited to save a project, do so.

Review questions

1 What are the differences between point text and paragraph (or area) text?

2 Why display the title-safe zone?

3 How do you use the Rectangle tool to make a perfect square?

4 How do you apply a stroke or drop shadow?

5 What is the difference between kerning and tracking?

Review answers

1 You create point text by clicking in the Program Monitor with the Type tool. Its text box expands as you type. When you drag in the Program Monitor with the Type tool, you define a bounding box for paragraph text, and the characters remain within its confines. Changing the box's shape displays more or fewer characters.

2 Some TV sets cut off the edges of the picture. The amount lost varies from set to set. Keeping your text within the title-safe area ensures that viewers will see all your title. This is less of a problem with newer flat-screen TVs and isn't important for online video, but it's still a good idea to use the title-safe zone to frame your titles.

3 To create a perfect square, hold down the Shift key after you begin dragging as you draw using the Rectangle tool. You can create a perfect circle with the Ellipse tool in the same way.

4 To apply a stroke or drop shadow, select the text or object to edit, and enable the Stroke or Shadow options in the Properties panel.

5 Kerning adjusts the spacing between two characters. Tracking adjusts the spacing between multiple selected characters.

16 EXPORTING FRAMES, CLIPS, AND SEQUENCES

Lesson overview

In this lesson, you'll learn how to do the following:

- Make quick exports.
- Configure your exported video for a specific audience and medium.
- Export single frames.
- Create movie, image sequence, and audio files.
- Use Adobe Media Encoder.
- Upload to social media and Adobe Stock.
- Share projects with editors using other editing apps.

This lesson will take about 60 minutes to complete. To get the files used in this lesson, refer to the instructions in "Accessing the lesson files and Web Edition" in the "Getting Started" section at the beginning of this book. Store the files on your computer in a convenient location.

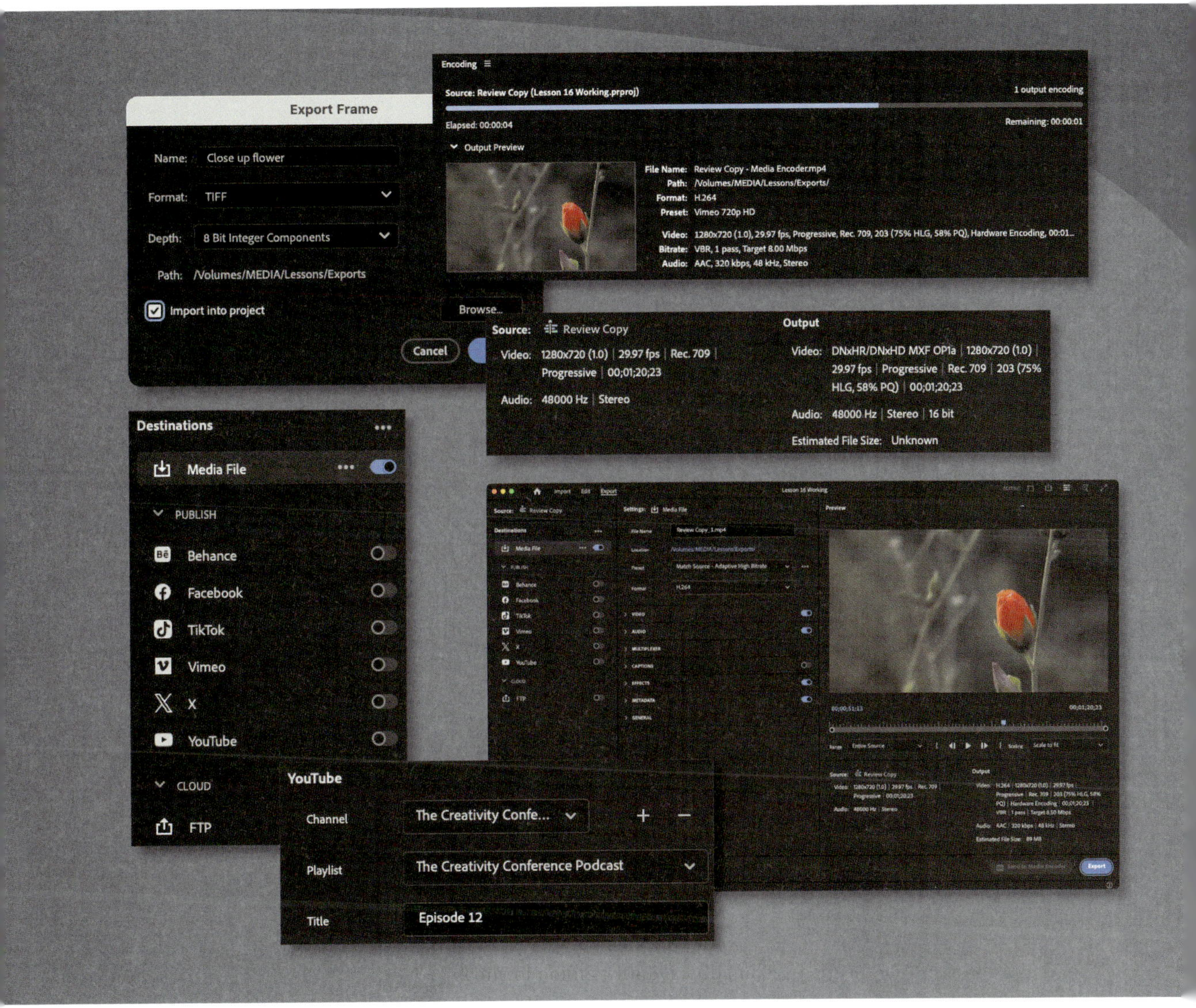

One of the best things about editing video is the feeling you have when you can finally share it with your audience. Adobe Premiere offers a wide range of export options. You can export to multiple high-level output formats using simplified Quick Export presets, using fully detailed settings, direct to social media, or even in batches via Adobe Media Encoder.

Starting the lesson

Note: To ensure that the tools function and the defaults are set exactly as described in this lesson, reset the Premiere preferences by holding any modifier key (such as Shift) while launching the application, selecting Reset App Preferences, and then clicking Continue in the Reset Options dialog box.

The most common form of media distribution is via digital files. Whether your completed project will be put out on social media or shown on a television, big screen, computer, or phone, you will usually deliver a file that has the particular specifications required for that medium.

To create a file, you can export directly from Premiere or use Adobe Media Encoder. Adobe Media Encoder is a stand-alone application (included with your Creative Cloud membership and installed alongside Premiere automatically) that handles file exports in batches, so you can export in several formats simultaneously and process in the background while you work in other applications, including Premiere and Adobe After Effects.

Making quick exports

Premiere offers a Quick Export option that's perfect when you want to expend the minimum number of clicks to export a media file with settings that are appropriate for your current sequence or clip. You can produce several file types by choosing the appropriate preset.

Let's give Quick Export a try.

1 Open Lesson 16.prproj from the Lessons folder.

2 Switch to the Editing workspace, and reset the workspace to the saved layout.

3 Save the project as **Lesson 16 Working.prproj**.

4 If it's not already open, open the sequence Review Copy.

5 Click the Quick Export icon in the upper-right corner of the Premiere window to open the Quick Export dialog box.

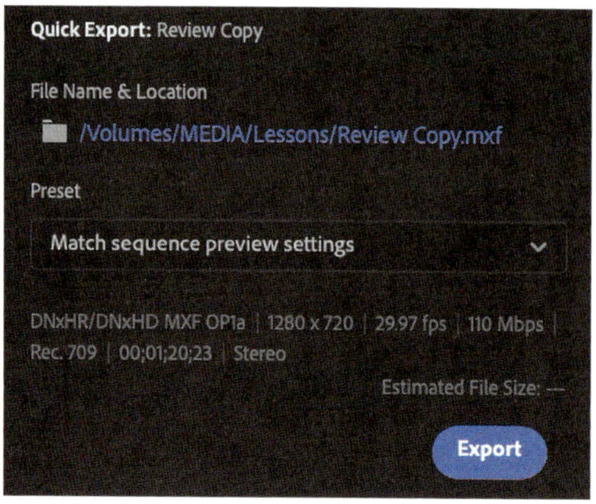

6 Use the Preset menu to choose Match Source – Adaptive High Bitrate. These settings automatically match the frame size and frame rate of your sequence (or clip if you had selected one to export) and are encoded using the popular H.264 codec, which is perfect for uploading to social media or to streaming services.

There are also high-quality 4K (Ultra High Definition), HD (High Definition), and SD (Standard Definition) presets available that will conform your export to a particular delivery standard.

A summary displays the settings you have chosen.

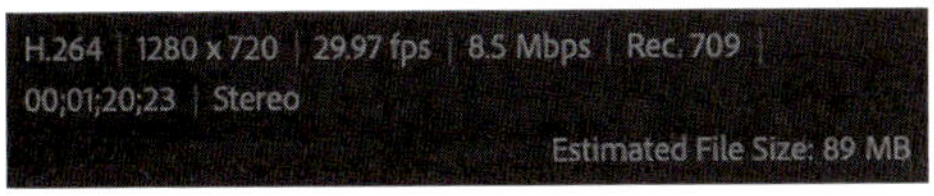

Note: Click the Preset menu and choose More Presets to see a full list of available presets.

7 The blue text showing the output name is actually a button that opens a Save As dialog box. You'll find the same type of text-as-a-button in Adobe Media Encoder. Click the blue File Name & Location text button now. Create a folder named **Exports** in the Lessons folder. Browse into the new folder, name the file **Review Copy.mp4**, and click Save.

8 Click Export to create your new media file.

When encoding is completed successfully, a notification will appear in the lower-right corner of the Premiere interface.

Understanding the full media export options

Whether you've completed a project or you just want to share an in-progress version for review, you have several export options.

- You can export to an appropriate file type, format, and codec for your chosen delivery medium.
- You can export a single frame or a series of frames.
- You can choose audio-only, video-only, or full audio/video output.
- Captions can be included, embedded in the output file, or stored in a separate file.
- Exported media can be reimported into the project automatically for easy reuse.

Note: Whatever is selected when you export is what Premiere will use as the new media file source. This can consist of clips, sequences, or parts of clips or sequences.

Beyond choosing an export format (frame size, frame rate, and so on), there are several other important options when exporting a file:

- You can choose to create files in a similar format and at the same visual quality and data rate as your original media, or you can compress them to a smaller size to make distribution easier.

- You can transcode your media from one codec to another to make it easier to exchange with creative collaborators.
- You can set the frame size, frame rate, data rate, or audio and video codec and configuration if an existing preset doesn't fit your needs.
- You can apply a color lookup table (LUT) to assign a Look. You can also apply a video limiter, HDR-to-SDR conversion, and audio normalization.
- You can burn in timecode, name, or image overlays.
- You can upload an exported file directly to social media accounts or an FTP server.
- You can choose to exclude, embed, or burn in captions.

Exporting single frames

Even while a project is in progress, you may want to export a still frame to send to a team member or client for review. You might also want to export an image to use as the thumbnail of your video file when you post it to social media.

When you export a frame from the Source Monitor, Premiere creates a still image that matches the resolution of the source media file.

When you export a frame from the Program Monitor, Premiere creates a still image that matches the resolution of the sequence.

Let's give it a try.

1 Continue working with the sequence Review Copy. Position the Timeline playhead on a frame you want to export.

2 In the Program Monitor, click the Export Frame button on the lower right. If you can't see the button, resize the Program Monitor.

Note: If resizing the panel doesn't bring the button to light, it's possible that you removed it if you customized the Program Monitor buttons. You can select the Program Monitor or the Timeline panel and press Shift+E (macOS) or Shift+Ctrl+E (Windows) to export a frame.

3 In the Export Frame dialog box, enter a filename.

4 Choose a still-image format from the Format menu.

- **JPEG**, **PNG**, and **BMP** (Windows only) are universally readable. JPEG and PNG files are commonly used in website design.
- **TIFF**, **TGA**, and **PNG** are suitable for print and animation workflows.
- **DPX** is often used for digital cinema or color-grading workflows (fine color finishing).
- **OpenEXR** is used to store high dynamic range picture information.

5 Click the Browse button to choose the Exports folder you created earlier.

6 Select Import Into Project to add the new still image into your current project, and click OK.

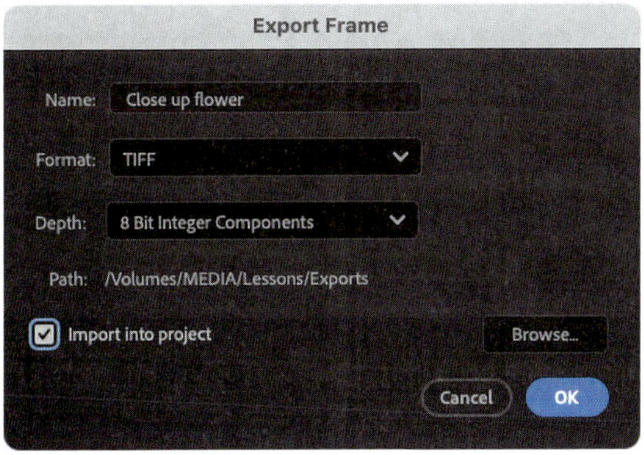

The new still image is created, and a clip linked to it is added to the Project panel.

Note: If your video format uses non-square pixels, the resulting image file will appear to have a different aspect ratio. This is because still image formats have square pixels. Using Adobe Photoshop, you can resize the image horizontally and restore the original aspect ratio.

Note: In Windows, you can export to the BMP, DPX, GIF, JPEG, OpenEXR, PNG, TGA, and TIFF formats. In macOS, you can export to the DPX, JPEG, OpenEXR, PNG, TGA, and TIFF formats.

Note: If you export a TIFF file from Premiere, the file will have a three-letter .tif file extension, rather than .tiff. Both are valid and work interchangeably.

Exporting a full-quality media file

It can be useful to produce a pristine digital copy of your edited project that can be archived for future use. This is a self-contained, fully rendered output file from your sequence at the highest resolution and best quality possible. You can use a file of this kind as a source media file to produce other compressed output formats without opening the original project in Premiere.

Though basing other copies on this source file technically means losing a tiny amount of quality (one digital generation), the loss is so minimal relative to the convenience and time-savings that many editors find it a worthwhile exchange.

In the next exercise, you'll learn about the various settings you can configure when exporting to a new media file. Premiere can also automatically post to social media accounts and an FTP (File Transfer Protocol) server (see "Uploading to social media," later in the lesson).

Once you have configured your output options, you'll be able to quickly export new files in just a couple of clicks.

Matching sequence settings

Ideally, the frame size, frame rate, and codec of a full-quality media file will match the sequence it's based on. It can seem like a lot of settings to think about when creating a new exported media file. Thankfully, Premiere makes matching your sequence or original clip settings easy.

1 Continue working with the Review Copy sequence.

2 With the sequence selected in the Project panel or open in the Timeline panel, with that panel active (with a blue outline), click Export in the upper-left corner of the Application window, or choose File > Export > Media. You can also press Command+M (macOS) or Ctrl+M (Windows).

   Premiere switches to Export mode.

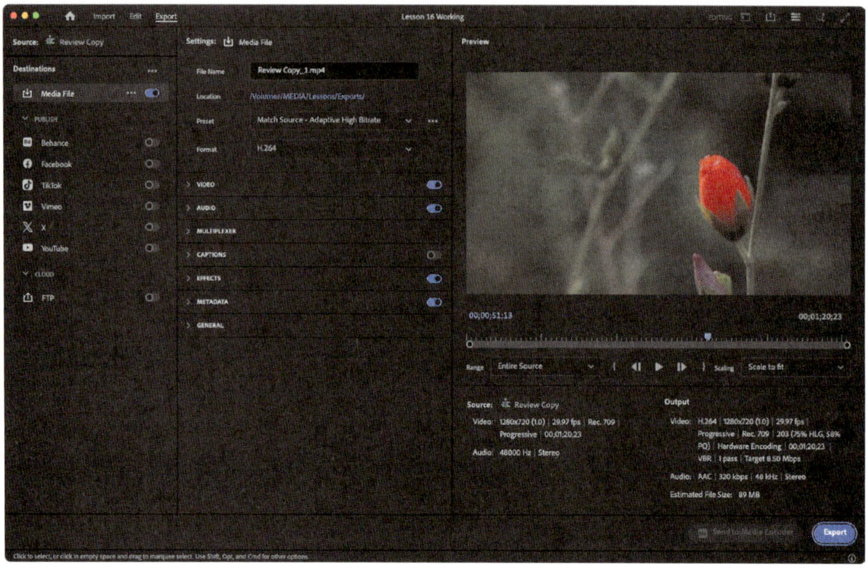

Note: In some cases, the Match Sequence Preview Settings option cannot produce an exact match of the original camera media. For example, XDCAM EX will write to an MPEG2 file. In most cases, the file written will have an identical format.

3 You'll learn more about this mode later. For now, scroll down in the Preset menu if necessary and choose Match Sequence Preview Settings.

4 In the File Name box, enter **Review Copy - Match Previews**. (Don't worry about the file extension; Premiere adds it automatically.)

5 If necessary, click the blue Location text. Browse to and choose the Exports folder you created earlier.

6 Review the Output information to check that the output format matches the sequence settings. In this case, you should be using DNxHD media at 29.97 fps. The Summary information is a quick, easy reference that helps you avoid minor errors that can have big consequences. If the Source and Output settings match, it minimizes conversion, which helps maintain the quality of the final output.

Note: The number in parentheses after the frame size in the export summary is the pixel aspect ratio.

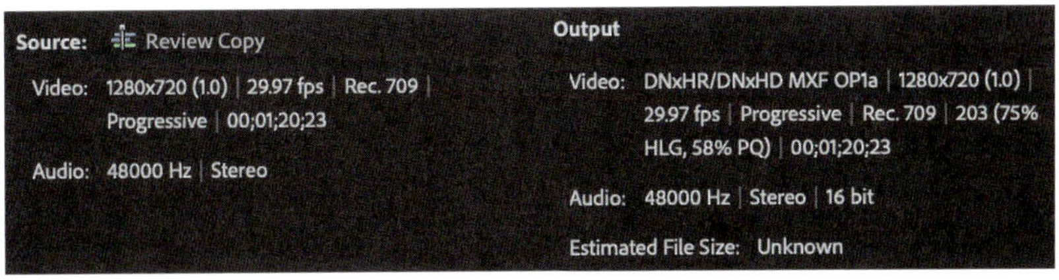

When exporting a sequence, the sequence itself is the source in the Export dialog box—not the clips inside the sequence, because these will have already been conformed to the sequence settings.

7 Click the Export button to create a media file based on the sequence.

When the export is complete, Premiere returns to Edit mode. You can switch between Import, Edit, and Export mode at any time.

Choosing the source range

You don't have to export a whole sequence. In fact, you'll commonly export only a selected part of your sequence for review.

Click to make the Timeline panel active; then click Export in the upper-left corner to switch to Export mode.

On the right side, above the output summary, you'll see a preview, with controls for making a partial selection for export.

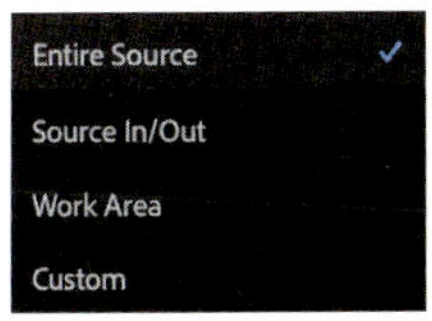

If your source sequence or clip has In and Out points already, they are automatically used to define the partial output. They are also displayed on the preview time ruler. You can override existing In and Out points by choosing Entire Source from the Range menu.

You can set new In and Out points by positioning the preview playhead and clicking the Set In Point and Set Out Point buttons or pressing I and O.

If you set new In and Out points, the Source Range menu updates to show Custom.

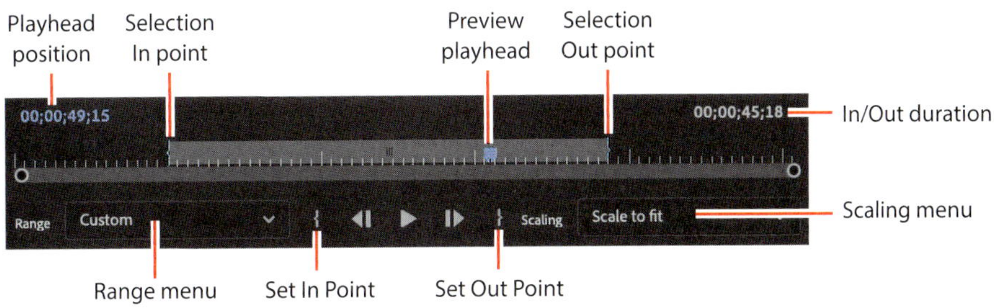

Configuring mismatched exported aspect ratios

Occasionally, you might need to export to an image format with a different aspect ratio than your sequence (or source clip). For example, you might export a 2.39:1 cinemascope aspect ratio sequence to a 16:9 widescreen aspect ratio video file.

As another example, you might export a widescreen sequence to square video for social media delivery. In both cases, you might decide to crop, stretch, or scale the frame to fit the new aspect ratio. There are both creative and technical reasons for choosing any of these options, and it's easy to choose between them.

The Scaling menu lets you choose the way a mismatch between the source aspect ratio and the output settings is handled.

- **Scale To Fit:** The original aspect ratio will be maintained, and the frame will be scaled to ensure the whole image can be seen within the new aspect ratio. This results in black areas at the top and bottom (letterboxing) or sides (pillarboxing), where there are gaps.
- **Scale To Fill:** The image will be scaled to ensure the frame is filled with no gaps. This results in cropping.
- **Stretch To Fill:** The image is stretched, changing its aspect ratio, so that it fits the new aspect ratio with no gaps and no cropping.

When you export a file with black bars at the top and bottom or sides, those bars become part of the file. These black pixels are sometimes desirable as it helps to ensure the image will be displayed with the correct aspect ratio within the delivered video.

Choosing another codec

When you export to a new media file, there are many settings available to define the output format and codec, audio encoding, metadata, effects, and more. The number of options can be overwhelming at first. The good news is that you will usually be able to choose settings based on a file delivery specification that is given to you.

Tip: Even if your original media is 8 bit, it is likely you will have been editing using higher-quality effects. The subtle results of color grading and adding graphics can be better preserved in a 10-bit file than in an 8-bit file.

In most cases, you will probably choose a preset and make just one or two adjustments (if any) to that preset before you click Export.

One of the most important choices you'll make is the output file's codec. Some camera capture formats (such as the H.264 MP4 files commonly produced by phones) are already heavily compressed, to save storage space. Using a higher-quality codec can help to preserve quality.

Choose your preset and format, decide whether you'd like to export audio, video, or both by turning those options on  or off, and then modify settings to suit. You can access groups of export settings by clicking a group heading.

1 With the Timeline panel active, press Command+M (macOS) or Ctrl+M (Windows) to switch to Export mode (if you're not already still in Export mode.)

2 Next to the Preset menu, click the three dots for more options and choose More Presets.

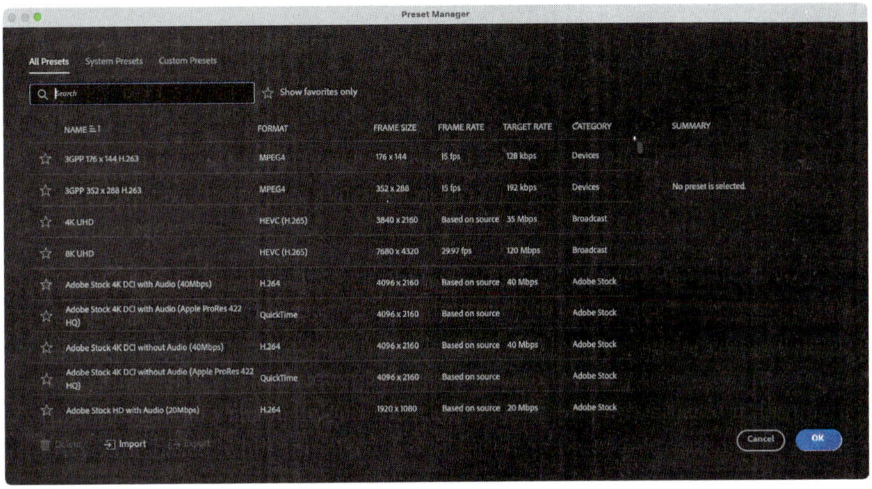

The Preset Manager offers many different presets you can use as a starting point for your configured export. To apply a preset, select it and click OK. For now, click Cancel.

3 Open the Format menu, and choose QuickTime.

A quick glance at the export summary on the right will tell you this format leads to an Apple QuickTime file with ProRes 422 HQ compression. This is a popular option for professional media delivery.

4 Enter the filename, **Review Copy QT**, and make sure the Location is set to your Exports folder.

Below the Format menu, you'll find a series of sections containing important additional options. Click a section name to view it.

Here's an overview:

- **Video:** The Video section allows you to set the video codec, frame size, frame rate, field order, and profile. The settings available are based on the preset you chose.
- **Audio:** The Audio section allows you to adjust the bit rate of the audio and, for some formats, the codec.

Note: ProRes is a professional codec that is supported natively by Adobe Creative Cloud applications. Like all codecs, it will play back only in media applications that support it.

Note: The settings displayed in each section change depending on the format you choose.

- **Captions:** If your sequence has captions, you can specify whether they are ignored, burned in (added to the visuals permanently), or exported as a separate file (referred to as a *sidecar file*).
- **Effects:** You can add a number of useful effects and overlays as you output your media (see these options in the section "Applying effects during export").
- **Metadata:** Specify the way metadata associated with your sequence or source clip will be handled, as well as the start timecode for the new media file.
- **General:** Choose whether you would like the new media file to be imported into your project and whether you would like to use sequence previews or proxy files as the source.

5 Click the Video section to open it. In the Video Codec menu, browse the available codecs.

   When you have finished browsing, choose Apple ProRes 422 HQ. This produces a high-quality file that many editors choose for final delivery.

   Click the More button to access the detailed video compression controls. Choose Rec. 709 in the Export Color Space menu. This is a standard dynamic range color space that matches the current sequence.

Note: If you're working with a professional format (such as MXF OP1a, DNxHD MXF OP1a, or QuickTime), you can export up to 32 channels of audio. To do so, the original sequence must be configured to use a multichannel mix track with the corresponding number of tracks.

6 Click to expand the Audio section. In the Basic Audio Settings area, make sure 48000 Hz is chosen from the Sample Rate menu and 16 bit is chosen from the Sample Size menu. Click More, and in the Audio Channel Configuration area, make sure Stereo is chosen from the Output Channels menu.

   These audio options are common standards for professional media delivery.

7 Click Export at the lower-right corner to export the sequence and transcode it to a new media file.

The most popular delivery format and codec is MPEG4 (.mp4), using the H.264 codec. These media files are smaller than Apple ProRes 422 HQ files, so they are faster to upload to websites, and they produce acceptable quality for most online viewing purposes. You'll find built-in presets for YouTube and Vimeo in the Preset Manager.

Applying effects during export

At the time of export, you can apply visual effects, add information overlays, and make automated adjustments to the output file.

Here's an overview of the options in the Effects section. To browse these, switch to Export mode and expand the Effects section.

- **Tone Mapping:** If you are working on a High Dynamic Range (HDR) sequence but exporting a Standard Dynamic Range (SDR) media file, use this option and select a Tone Mapping Method to automatically adjust the tones to fit the lower range.

- **Lumetri Look/LUT:** Choose from a list of built-in Lumetri Looks or browse to your own, allowing you to quickly apply a nuanced adjustment to the appearance of your output file. This is most commonly used when viewing recordings at the end of each day of production (the dailies).
- **SDR Conform:** If your sequence uses high dynamic range and you are delivering a standard dynamic range media file, you can make manual adjustments to the brightness and contrast using this effect.
- **Image Overlay:** Add a graphic, such as a company logo or network "bug," and position it on-screen. The graphic will be incorporated into the image (burned in).
- **Text Overlay:** Add a text overlay to the image. This is particularly useful as a watermark to protect your content or as a way to identify different versions.
- **Timecode Overlay:** Display timecode for your finished video file, making it easy for viewers without specialized editing software to note reference times for commenting purposes.
- **Time Tuner:** Specify a new duration or playback speed, up to +/–10%. This is achieved by applying subtle adjustments to periods of low action where the soundtrack is silent. Results vary depending on the media you are working with, so test different speeds to compare the end results. A continuous music soundtrack will interfere with the Time Tuner.
- **Video Limiter:** Although it's usually best to get your video levels right in the sequence, you can apply a limiter here too, to ensure your resulting file meets the required levels for broadcast television.
- **Loudness Normalization:** Use the Loudness scale to normalize audio levels in your output file. As with video levels, it's best to get this right in the sequence, but it can be reassuring to know your levels will be limited during export.

Working with Adobe Media Encoder

Adobe Media Encoder is a stand-alone application that you can run independently or launch from Premiere. One advantage of using Media Encoder is that you can send an encoding job directly from Premiere and then continue working on your edit as the encoding is processed. If your client asks to see your work before you finish editing, Media Encoder can produce the file in the background without interrupting your flow.

By default, Media Encoder pauses encoding when you play video in Premiere to maximize playback performance. You can change this in the Premiere Playback preferences.

Configuring the export

To export from Premiere to Adobe Media Encoder, you'll need to queue the export. The first step is to use Export mode to make choices about the file you're going to export. Beyond choosing the export format, there are some useful additional settings to learn.

Switch to Export mode to review these settings.

Queuing the export

When you're ready to create your media file, you have a few more options to consider. These are some of the more advanced options available in Export mode. You may not decide to use any of these when exporting a particular sequence, or they may be central to your workflow. Either way, it's worth taking a moment to consider them before proceeding.

These are available whether you are exporting directly from Premiere or queuing the export in Adobe Media Encoder.

- **Video** > **More** > **Render At Maximum Depth:** When you choose this option, video will be rendered at the maximum bit depth supported by the output settings you have configured. This will usually result in the best possible quality output at the expense of some additional processing time.
- **Video** > **More** > **Use Maximum Render Quality:** If your sequence includes transformations like Scale, Position, or Rotation adjustments, or if you have used effects like the Warp Stabilizer, consider choosing this option to produce the highest-quality output possible. It requires more RAM, though, and can take longer to encode.
- **Video** > **More** > **Render Alpha Channel Only:** Some post-production workflows require a separate grayscale file representing the alpha channel (the channel that defines opacity). This option produces that file, rather than a full-color version.
- **Video** > **More** > **Time Interpolation:** If your exported file will have a different frame rate than your sequence or source clip, this menu lets you specify the way the frame-rate change is rendered. The options are the same as those that apply when changing clip playback speed in a sequence.
- **Metadata** > **Set Start Timecode:** This allows you to specify a start timecode other than 00:00:00:00 for the newly created file. This is useful if you are working in a broadcast environment where a specific timecode start may be a delivery requirement.
- **General** > **Import Into Project:** This option automatically imports the newly created media file into your current project so you can review it or use it as new source footage.

- **General > Use Previews:** When you render effects, preview files are produced that look like your original footage combined with the effects. If you choose this option, the preview files will be used as the source for the new export. This can save a significant amount of time that would otherwise be spent rendering the effects again. The result might be lower quality, depending on the format of the sequence preview files (see Lesson 2, "Setting Up a Project").

  If you have configured your sequence previews to be very high quality and have rendered all effects already, this option can save an enormous amount of time when exporting—possibly 10x faster or more. If you have enough storage space, a good example of this workflow would be setting your previews to ProRes 422 HQ and then delivering a ProRes 422 HQ media file.

- **General > Use Proxies:** If you have created and/or attached proxies to your media to speed up previews, Premiere will normally use the original media files for the purposes of exporting. If you choose Use Proxies from the menu, the proxies will be used instead. This can speed up exporting in a similar way to the Use Preview option—though be warned that proxy video files are usually low quality to keep file sizes small.

Finally, there are these options to consider when exporting any kind of media file:

- **Send To Media Encoder:** Click Send To Media Encoder to send the file to Adobe Media Encoder, which will open automatically, allowing you to continue working in Premiere while the export takes place.

- **Export:** Click Export to export directly from the Export Settings dialog box rather than sending the file to the Adobe Media Encoder queue. This is a simpler workflow and usually a faster export, but you won't be able to edit in Premiere until the export is complete.

Let's try sending an export to Media Encoder:

1. For this example, open the Preset menu and choose More Presets. (You could also click the three dots next to the Preset menu and choose More Presets.) Type **Vimeo** in the Search box; then select the Vimeo 720p HD preset and click OK.

   These settings match the frame size and frame rate of the sequence.

2. Click the File Name box and give the file a new name, **Review Copy – Media Encoder**. The location should already be set to your Exports folder. If not, set it now.

3. Check the summary information text to verify your choices.

4 Click Send To Media Encoder to send the file to Adobe Media Encoder. Media Encoder should start automatically, with your media encoding tasks ready to go.

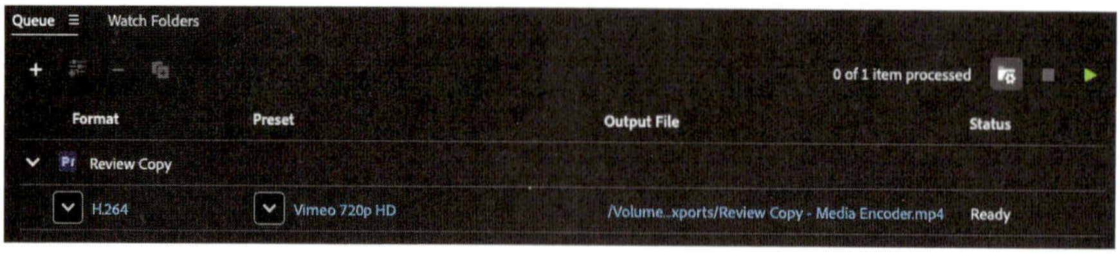

5 Media Encoder will not begin encoding automatically. To begin encoding, click Start Queue in the upper-right corner or press Return/Enter.

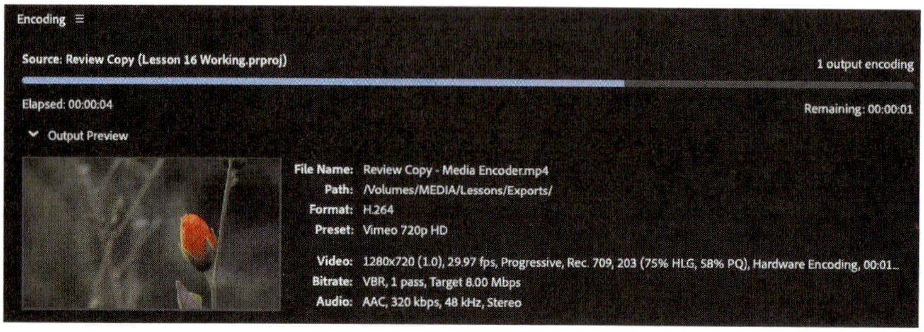

6 To add another item to the queue, choose more export settings in Premiere and click Send To Media Encoder. Adobe Media Encoder will encode items in the order that they are added to the queue.

Exploring additional options in Adobe Media Encoder

Adobe Media Encoder brings a number of additional benefits. Although it involves a few extra steps beyond simply clicking the Export button in the Export Settings dialog box of Premiere, the extra options are often worthwhile.

Note: Adobe Media Encoder does not have to be used from Premiere. You can launch Adobe Media Encoder on its own and browse inside Premiere projects to choose items to transcode.

Here are some useful features:

- **Add files for encoding:** You can add files to Adobe Media Encoder by choosing File > Add Source. You can even drag files in from the Finder (macOS) or Windows Explorer (Windows). There's a Media Browser too, which you can use to locate items just as you would in Premiere.
- **Import Premiere sequences directly:** You can choose File > Add Premiere Sequence to select a Premiere project file and choose sequences to encode without ever launching Premiere.
- **Render After Effects compositions directly:** You can import and encode compositions from Adobe After Effects by choosing File > Add After Effects Composition. Once again, you don't need to open Adobe After Effects.

- **Use a watch folder:** If you'd like to automate some encoding tasks, you can create watch folders by choosing File > Add Encoding Watch Folder and then assigning a preset to that watch folder. Watch folders exist in the Finder (macOS) or Windows Explorer (Windows) like any other folder. Provided Adobe Media Encoder is running, media files placed into the folder can be automatically encoded to the format specified in the preset.
- **Modify a queue:** You can add, duplicate, or remove any encoding tasks using buttons at the top of the list.

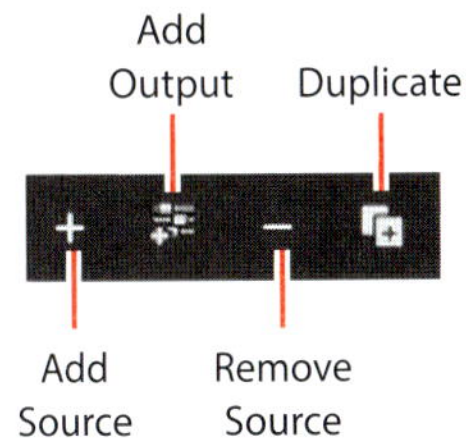

- **Modify settings:** Once the encoding tasks are loaded into the queue, changing settings is easy; click the item's Format or Preset entry (in blue text), and the Export Settings dialog box appears.

When encoding has completed, you can quit Media Encoder.

Uploading to social media

Back in Premiere, when encoding is complete, the next step is often to publish the video. In Export mode, you can pre-configure publishing settings to automatically upload your video when encoding is complete.

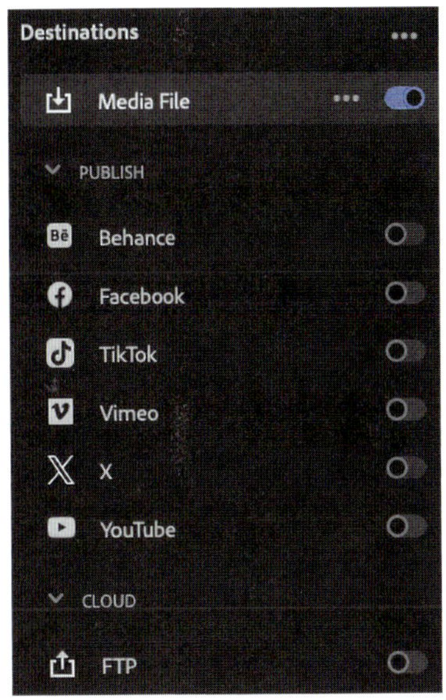

You will have noticed there are several Destination options displayed on the left side of the Export mode interface.

By default, the only enabled option is Media File, and these are the settings displayed in the middle of the interface. There are several other options that you can enable or disable at any time.

After selecting and activating a social media destination to display its settings, click Sign In beside the Publish heading in Settings to log in to your account. You can configure media encoding and metadata settings, and Premiere will upload the file automatically when it is created.

Tip: Adobe Media Encoder has similar options for uploading to social media accounts, with a different interface. Access these settings by editing the encoding format or preset from inside Media Encoder.

The settings you choose are stored for future exports. This powerful feature is particularly useful: It allows you to preconfigure your social media upload settings and apply those settings to multiple future media uploads simply by activating an option.

If you click the three dots ••• at the top of the list of output options, you'll find the option to add a media file destination. You can add multiple destinations, and each can have its own encoding settings.

All the activated output options are produced when you click Export. This means, in a single step, you can produce a full-quality exported media file, create a low-resolution small-file-size version for quick sharing and reviews, and upload to multiple social media accounts.

1 Click Edit to return to the Edit mode.

2 Make sure the Timeline panel is active, click Export at the top left of the interface.

3 Select and activate one of the social media output options to view its settings.

4 Click Sign In beside the Publish heading in Settings and to choose particular ways to deliver the file. For example, the YouTube output options allow you to specify a particular channel and/or playlist.

The menus populate automatically based on the account you have logged in to.

5 When you are ready, click Edit to return to the Edit mode.

Each platform has its own delivery standards, though in many cases you can choose a high-quality source file and let the platform do the work of producing more highly compressed alternative versions from that file. Adobe Stock, for example, supports a range of video formats and codecs. If you produce a high-quality UHD (3840×2160) file, the server can handle the rest.

Exchanging projects with other editing applications

Collaboration is an essential part of post-production. Premiere can both read and write project files and footage files that are compatible with many of the top editing and color-grading tools on the market. This makes it easier to share creative work, even if you and your collaborators are using different editing systems.

Premiere supports EDLs (Edit Decision Lists), OMF (Open Media Framework), AAF (Advanced Authoring Format), ALE (Avid Log Exchange), and XML (Extended Markup Language) import and export.

If you're collaborating with an Avid Media Composer editor, you can use AAF as an intermediary, allowing the exchange of clip information, edited sequences, and some effects.

If you're collaborating with an Apple Final Cut Pro editor, you can use XML as an intermediary similarly.

It's straightforward to export an AAF or XML file from Premiere; select a sequence you want to export, and either choose File > Export > AAF or choose File > Export > Final Cut Pro XML.

For information about best practices and workflows for Long Form and Episodic post production, see *helpx.adobe.com/premiere/desktop/get-started/preferences-and-settings/best-practices.html.*

Now that you have explored the export options, make sure you are in Edit mode, choose File > Close Project, and click Yes if you are invited to save.

Final practice

Congratulations! You have now learned how to import media; organize projects; create sequences; add, modify, and remove effects; mix audio; work with graphics and titles; and output to share your work with the world.

Now that you have completed this book, you may want to practice. To make this easier, the media files for a few productions have been combined in a single project file so you can explore the techniques you have learned.

These media files can be used only for personal practice and are not licensed for any form of distribution, including YouTube or any other online distribution, so please *do not upload* any of the clips or the results of any editing work you do with them. They are not for sharing with the public; they are just for you to practice with privately.

Trying out other workspaces

Throughout these lessons, you have worked in just a few of the available workspaces. Now that you have tried out several tools and explored many of the available panels, you may want to try out other workspaces.

All the available workspaces are listed in the Workspaces menu .

Consider starting with the Essentials workspace, which includes several panels you may find useful for different aspects of post-production.

Using practice media

The Final Practice.prproj project file, in the Lessons folder, contains bins with several types of clips for a few productions that you can use to practice the editing techniques you have learned in this book:

- **Andrea Sweeney NYC:** This is a short road-movie diary piece. Use the voice-over as a guide to practice combining 4K and HD footage in a single timeline.

Experiment with panning and scanning in the 4K footage if you choose to use HD sequence settings.

- **Bike Race Multi-Camera:** This is simple multicamera footage. Experiment with live editing on a multicamera project. To learn about working with multi-camera media in Premiere, see *helpx.adobe.com/premiere/desktop/edit-projects/set-up-multi-camera-sequences-for-editing/create-a-multi-camera-source-sequence.html*.
- **Boston Snow:** This is a mixture of shots of Boston Common filmed in three resolutions. Use this media to experiment with Scale To Frame Size, Fit To Frame, Fill Frame, and keyframe controls to scale shots. Try using the Warp Stabilizer effect to lock one of the high-resolution clips and then scale up the clip and create a pan from one side to the other.
- **City Views:** This is a series of shots from the air and on land. Use these to experiment with image stabilization, color adjustment, and visual effects.
- **Desert:** Use the diverse colors to try color correction tools and combine the footage with music to produce a montage.
- **Interview:** This footage is useful for experimenting with the transcription and captioning tools. There are two camera angles for the same interview. You'll find an SRT file in the original media folder in case you want to practice importing captions.
- **Jolie's Garden:** This consists of atmospheric tableaux shot at 96 fps, set to play back at 24 fps, and filmed for a new feature film social media marketing campaign. Use these clips to experiment with the Lumetri Color panel Looks and speed change effects.
- **Laura in the Snow:** This is media for a commercial shot at 96 fps, set to play back at 24 fps. Use this footage to practice color correction and grading adjustments. Experiment with ramping slow motion and masking both the video and the effects you apply.
- **Music:** Use these music clips to practice creating an audio mix and editing visuals to music.
- **She:** This is a series of stylized, mostly slow-motion clips that will be useful for experimenting with speed changes and visual effects.
- **TAS:** This is footage from a short film, *The Ancestor Simulation*. Use this footage to try color grading and, as the footage is in two aspect ratios, mixing and matching the shots.
- **Theft Unexpected:** This is footage from an award-winning short film directed and edited by the author. Use this footage to experiment with trimming, and practice adjusting timing in simple dialogue to achieve different comic and dramatic results, changing the actors' performances.

- **Valley of Fire:** Try color adjustments to bring variation and visual interest, use speed changes to transform the experience of flying across a desert, and keyframe the rotating view to compensate for the movement and produce a static shot.

One of the best ways you can learn to edit with Premiere is to create new projects of your own and explore new techniques. Nonlinear editing means ongoing learning to continually improve your skills and expand your creativity.

Review questions

1 What's an easy way to export digital video if you want to create a self-contained file that can be played by most devices?

2 What social media–ready export options are available in Adobe Media Encoder?

3 What encoding format should you use when exporting a high-quality source file?

4 Must you wait for Adobe Media Encoder to finish processing its queue before working on a new Premiere project?

Review answers

1 Click the Quick Export button in the upper-right corner of the Premiere interface, set a location, choose a preset, and click Export. The Match Source – Adaptive High Bitrate preset will usually produce a high-quality media file.

2 There are built-in preset options for Vimeo, YouTube, X, and Facebook. While these options are optimized for social media, you will often get the best results by choosing the Match Source – Adaptive High Bitrate preset. Social media platforms re-compress media automatically. Uploading a high-quality file will usually produce the best results.

3 Use a format that supports high-quality codecs. A popular choice is QuickTime, which supports the ProRes codec. You could also choose DNxHR/DNxHD. It's important to check the required media specifications before exporting.

4 No. Adobe Media Encoder is a stand-alone application. You can work in other applications or even start a new Premiere project while the render queue is processed.

GLOSSARY

Throughout this book, specialized terms will be used that relate to video and audio technology and to nonlinear post-production in particular. If you are learning to edit for the first time, several of these may be new or perplexing to you. This glossary is designed to help. Return to it when you need an explanation or a reminder as you explore the lessons in this book.

- **Alpha channel:** A nonvisible channel that defines the opacity of a pixel. This fourth channel is stored in a similar way to the three visible color channels (see *RGB color*) and can be adjusted in a multitude of ways using manual adjustments or visual effects. When you create a greenscreen effect, for example, Premiere adjusts the alpha channel level for your selected pixels to allow a background to be visible.
- **Aspect ratio:** This describes the shape of an image, expressed as the ratio of Width:Height. 1:1 is square. 16:9 is standard widescreen. Regardless of the size of the screen or the resolution of an image, the frame will have a particular aspect ratio. Sequences have an aspect ratio, and so do pixels. Most pixels are square, but there are some video formats that use non-square pixels.
- **Bin:** Bins look and work very much like folders in the Finder (macOS) or Explorer (Windows). However, they exist only in the Premiere project file you are working on.
- **Bit depth:** The number of possible steps from completely dark to fully bright (for example, from no blue at all to fully blue) is set by the bit depth for your media. The number used to describe bit depth is literally the number of bits (0s and 1s) that are being used to record the information.

  Bit depth produces scales that are multiples of 2, doubling with each added bit.

  8-bit video allows 256 steps from completely dark to fully bright. 10-bit video is 2 bits more than 8 bit, or 1,024 steps (256 doubled twice). 16-bit video allows a staggering 65,536 steps.

  These scales always need to begin at 0, so the actual ranges are 0–255, 0–1,023, and 0–65,535.

  Increased bit depth makes it easier to maintain high-quality visuals when adjusting levels using color correction techniques and avoid posterizing the image, which produces visible bands of color.
- **Clip:** This is a link (think of an alias or shortcut) to a media file (which might be video, a graphic, audio, or any other kind of media). Clips look and behave as if they were the media file they link to, and they display information that relates to the media file, such as image size and frame rate (fps).

- **Codec:** This is short for *coder/decoder*. This is a way of storing digital information (like video and audio) that often allows the data to be stored in a more compact form than the original. Like shorthand writing, this takes less space but requires more effort to write and, later, to read.
- **Color space:** This describes a range of possible colors with numerical values attached to them. There are multiple popular color spaces, each developed for a particular purpose. For example, Rec. 709 is the color space for HDTV, while Rec. 2020 was developed for UHDTV. ACEScct has a wide color gamut, useful for working with RAW media and when converting color spaces. Video is recorded using a color space, and sequences have a color space setting. Sometimes conversion is necessary to maintain perceived colors and brightness when adding a clip to a sequence.
- **Compression:** This word has two different meanings: First, it's a reduction in the size of video and audio files brought about by storing the information using a codec (coder/decoder). Second, it's a reduction in the difference between the loudest and quietest parts of sound. This allows the overall sound level to seem louder.
- **Cut:** In a sequence, a cut is the moment one clip ends and another begins. The term comes from celluloid film editing, where the film is literally cut. A cut is technically a form of *transition* and is the most common kind.
- **Effect:** This is a process that modifies the appearance of images or the quality of sound. Video and audio effects are used to change the shape of an image, to make visuals brighter or darker, to animate the position of images on the screen, to make audio louder or quieter, or to apply any number of other adjustments.
- **Export:** After your clips are combined in a *sequence* in Premiere, you must then *export* that sequence to share the creative work with the world in the form of a new media file. When you export, you choose the format, codec, and settings for the file that will be created.
- **Footage:** Originally this was a film term used to indicate recording duration because film is measured in feet. This now refers to any original video material and is usually described in hours and minutes—rather than the file size.
- **Format:** Sometimes this word is used to refer to a media file type (AVI, MOV, MP4, etc.), but it actually refers to the specific frame size (image size), frame shape, pixel shape, and frame rate (measured in frames per second).
- **Frame:** This means one whole still image. Video is made up of a series of frames that play fast enough to appear to be a continuous moving image. The number of frames playing per second is called the *frame rate*, measured in frames per second (fps).

- **Generative AI/Gen AI:** A broad term that describes a range of technologies that generate new media. For example, in Premiere, you can extend the duration of clips by generating new content using the Generative Extend tool.
- **High Dynamic Range (HDR):** The brightness of a screen can be measured in several ways; a unit commonly used for this purpose is the *nit*. Historically, the average home TV screen might have had a maximum brightness of around 200 nits, while a cinema screen might reach only 100 nits.

  In basic terms, this can be considered to be a measure of the total range between the darkest level that will still show detail and the brightest level. The range between the two is called the *dynamic range*. A range of around 0–200 nits is considered to be *standard dynamic range*, or *SDR*.

  As it became possible to produce much brighter screens, a new term was defined: *high dynamic range*, or *HDR*. This describes a range of technologies for cameras, editing systems, delivery standards, and screens that can display up to 10,000 nits.

  To give a sense of the difference, most home TV sets that are described as HDR have a dynamic range of around 1,000 nits. This means you can see detail in the shadows of a scene at night and make out the color and image details of fireworks in the sky.
- **Import:** To bring a media file into a Premiere project, you *import* it. No data is really moved into the project file. Instead, Premiere creates links (called *clips*) that contain information about the media, and it's those links that you combine when editing.
- **Keyframe:** A keyframe marks the point in time where you specify the value of a property, such as spatial position, opacity, or audio volume. To create a change in a property over time, you set at least two keyframes: one keyframe for the value at the beginning of the change and another keyframe for the value at the end of the change. Premiere automatically changes the values over time between the keyframes—a process called *interpolation*.
- **Look Up Table (LUT):** This is a file that stores color adjustments. You can apply LUTs in several ways in Premiere, including by using the Source Clip Input LUT menu in the Settings tab of the Lumetri Color panel. LUTs are a convenient way to store information about color adjustments that you intend to reuse or share.
- **Media:** This is your original and newly created content. This could be video files, graphics, photos, animation, music, voice-over, or audio special effects (like a sword clash or explosion).
- **Metadata:** Metadata is information about information. There are many forms of metadata, but they always include information about something. For example, metadata associated with a video file might include the camera system used to record it, the name of the camera operator, or the log color space used.

- **Pixel:** This is a single dot, or point, of light. Pixels have color values that are often (but not always) measured as a combination of red, green, and blue colors.
- **Project:** This is the container for all of your clips and sequences. A project is stored as a file that contains your creative work.
- **Proxy file:** A media file that is used, usually temporarily as a low-resolution, small file size replacement for a full-quality media file. The small file size and low resolution makes proxy files easier to play (improving playback performance) and to transport (useful when collaborating with other editors remotely). Proxy files are often used when the original source media is such high resolution and at such a high file size that it's difficult for the editing system to play smoothly.
- **RGB color:** There are three color channels that combine to produce a full-color video image. While there are several arrangements of colors that can be used, the most commonly known combination is Red, Green, and Blue. When combined, these three monochromatic channels can produce the full range (or *gamut*) required to produce color images.
- **Sequence:** This is a series of clips, combined in a particular order, often in multiple layers. Most of the creative work you will perform in Premiere will be on clips in sequences.
- **Timecode:** This is a system for measuring time in recorded media. Its units are hours, minutes, seconds, and frames (the number of frames per second will vary depending on the media). Professional video recording systems always record timecode information.

  American broadcast television uses a system that drops frames from the timecode to compensate for the slightly slower playback during broadcast. This is called *drop frame timecode* and is displayed in Premiere with semicolons as dividers. If you are delivering content for broadcast television, you will use a US frame rate, such as 29.97 fps, in preference to a non–drop frame timecode frame rate, such as 30 fps.

  Drop frame timecode looks like this: 00;15;07;19.

  Non–drop frame timecode looks like this: 00:15:07:19.

  The difference is subtle but important.
- **Timeline:** Premiere has a Timeline panel, in which you will view and edit sequences. Editors often use the words *timeline* and *sequence* interchangeably. For example, "On the timeline" and "in the sequence" have the same meaning. "A timeline" also means "a sequence." In this book, we generally use the terms *Timeline panel* or *sequence* for clarity.

- **Tone mapping:** A (usually automated) system for converting color and luminance values between one color system and another. In Premiere, tone mapping is used to convert high dynamic range and/or log footage to standard dynamic range.
- **Transition:** This is the change that occurs when one clip ends and another begins. The most common type of transition between two clips is a *cut*. However, there are many transition effects available to add visual interest or enhance storytelling. A dip to black, for example, usually tells the viewer some time has passed. Transitions are part of a film language that audiences have a nuanced understanding of.
- **Vector-based graphics:** Images are usually made up of lots of dots, called *pixels*. The more pixels you have (the more visual resolution), the clearer the image usually appears. Pixel-based visuals are described as *raster*, or *bitmap*, images.

  When you increase the size of a rasterized image by scaling it up, the dots get bigger, which can produce softening or even jagged edges on organic shapes and curves.

  Vector graphics are not made up of pixels. Instead, they use a mathematical method to describe the image. You can display vector graphics at any resolution (any size), and they will always be perfectly sharp because they are drawn newly every time. This way, for example, a circle is a circle at any resolution (it won't turn into a blocky shape if you scale it up in size). Graphics created in Premiere are vector-based, while imported vector-based graphics are treated as pixels.
- **VR video:** A 360° video camera system produces a sphere of video that can be viewed from the inside. With a virtual reality headset, viewers can turn to look in any direction—in 360 degrees. Though this type of video is technically *not* true virtual reality, the need for a VR headset to enjoy it means that many filmmakers refer to it simply as VR video.

  Premiere has a viewing mode and dedicated visual effects for VR. In addition, you can edit via a VR headset to review content more easily and quickly.

INDEX

D

N

O

P

Q

R

U

V